THE COLUMBIA HISTORY OF LATINOS IN THE UNITED STATES SINCE 1960

THE COLUMBIA HISTORY OF LATINOS IN THE UNITED STATES SINCE 1960

EDITED BY DAVID G. GUTIÉRREZ

COLUMBIA
UNIVERSITY
PRESS
NEW YORK

Columbia University Press
Publishers Since 1893
New York Chichester, West Sussex

Library of Congress Cataloging-in-Publication Data
The Columbia history of Latinos in the United States since 1960 / edited by David G. Gutiérrez.
p. cm.
Includes bibliographical references and index.
ISBN 978–0–231–11808–8 (cloth : alk. paper) — ISBN 978–0–231–11809–5 (pbk. : alk. paper)
1. Hispanic Americans—History—20th century. 2. Hispanic Americans—History—21st century. 3. Hispanic Americans—Social conditions. 4. United States—Ethnic relations. I. Title: History of Latinos in the United States since 1960. II. Gutiérrez, David (David Gregory)
E184.S75C644 2004
973'.0468—dc22

2004041310

Columbia University Press books are printed
on permanent and durable acid-free paper.
Printed in the United States of America
c 10 9 8 7 6 5 4
p 10 9 8 7 6
Designed by Lisa Hamm

CONTENTS

ACKNOWLEDGMENTS

AS IS true with most anthologies, this collection of essays took more time to bring to press than I am sure any of its contributors had thought possible when they signed on to the project. I thank them all not only for their excellent contributions to the work but also for the patience, forbearance, and good will they showed the editor. James Warren at Columbia University Press was equally patient and encouraging, and I thank him for staying the course long enough to see the book come into being. I would also like to thank all the authors, as well as Roberto Alvarez, Bill Deverell, Jorge Mariscal, James Warren, and Michael Haskell for their excellent advice and editorial input, and Tony Grafton, Marc Rodríguez, Jennifer Houle, and the Shelby Cullom Davis Center for Historical Studies at Princeton for providing the financial support and rich intellectual environment that allowed me to complete work on the volume in the 2002–3 academic year.

To the friends and colleagues who graciously invited me to take parts of this show on the road to share and debate some of the major ideas that inform the volume, I offer thanks. Tomás Almaguer at the University of Michigan; Steve Aron at UCLA, Roy Ritchie at the Huntington Library; Dean Frantisek Deak at the University of California, San Diego; Bill Deverell at the Division of Humanities and Social Sciences and the students in my immigration and ethnicity seminar at the California Institute of Technology; Susan Johnson, Camille Guerin-Gonzales, and Patricia Nelson Limerick at the University of Colorado, Boulder; Matt García and Peggy Pascoe at the University of Oregon; the site committee of the National Association for Chicano and Chicana Studies (NACCS)—especially Greg Rodríguez and Raquel Rubio-Goldsmith—at the University of Arizona; Elliott Barkan and the Immigration and Ethnic History Society; Guadalupe San Miguel Jr., Joe Glatthaar, John Mason Hart, Luis

Alvarez, and Raúl Ramos at the University of Houston; Becky Horn at the University of Utah; Christina Jiménez at the University of Colorado, Colorado Springs; and Ramón A. Gutiérrez and the Department of Ethnic Studies at the University of California, San Diego all provided the collegial space to air and debate many of the issues that are discussed in these pages. And finally, to my nuclear and extended families—Mary Lillis Allen, Luis Alvarez, Steve and Lori Buchsbaum, Al and Susan Camarillo, Mort and Maureen Darrow, Bill, Jennifer, and Helen Deverell, Susie Golden, Luis and Rebecca Murillo, Bill Perry, Pamela Radcliff, Raúl Ramos and Liz Chiao, and, as always, my *compañero* on the beaches and in the trenches, Stuart Swanson, my heartfelt gratitude for your warm hospitality, good criticism, and spiritual support over a particularly rough stretch. I owe each of you one, at least.

PREFACE

AT THE end of the last century and in the first months of the new millennium, newspapers and news magazines in cities across the United States began reporting a remarkable phenomenon. "Nevada Jumps 66.3% in 10 Years: A Tripling of the Number of Latinos Led the Increase" read one headline. "Hispanics Drive State Growth" read another. "Census Reflects Large Gains for Latinos," "Latinos Add State House Seats Nationwide," proclaimed others. "Hispanics Reshape Culture of the South" and "North Carolina's Trade in Foreign Farm Workers Draws Scrutiny" read two others. "Mexicans Change Face of U.S. Demographics" and "Racial, Ethnic Diversity Puts New Face on Middle America" proclaimed two more. And more recently, in a news release that was as stunning as it was understated, the Census Bureau quietly announced that as of July 2001, the United State's population of Hispanic origin or descent had surpassed the African American population as the nation's largest aggregate "minority group."[1] Of course, one could cite literally hundreds more such headlines and taglines in the American mass media of the past five or six years, and, slowly but surely, it seems that the message has started to sink in. Print and broadcast media outlets may have been slow to pick up on a trend that has been building in momentum for many years, but it is clear that Americans are finally awakening to a demographic revolution that has transformed—and continues to change—U.S. society in ways that will powerfully influence the economic, political, and cultural life of the United States for the foreseeable future.

The Columbia History of Latinos in the United States Since 1960 is among the first major attempts to offer a comprehensive historical overview of the astonishing "Latinization" of the United States that has occurred over the past four decades.[2] Bringing together the views of some of the foremost scholarly interpreters of the recent history of Latinos in the United States, this collection was designed from the outset to be a collaborative, interdisciplinary effort to ponder, analyze, and provide context for these dramatic historical developments. More specifically, our intent was to provide a broad overview of this era of explosive demographic and cultural change by developing essays that explore the recent histories of all the major national and regional Latino subpopulations and reflect on what these historical trends might mean for the future of both the United States and the other increasingly interconnected nations of the Western Hemisphere. Indeed, as the essays that follow amply demonstrate, while at one point it may have been considered feasible to explore the histories of national populations in isolation from one another, all of the contributors to this volume highlight the deep transnational ties and interconnections that bind different peoples across national and regional lines. Thus, each of the chapters on Latino national subpopulations explores the ambiguous and shifting boundaries that so loosely define them both in the United States and in their countries of origin. In addition, the volume includes five important thematic chapters addressing political and cultural themes that transcend national and intercultural boundaries while simultaneously revealing some of the more salient sources of internal division among persons of Latin American descent or heritage. These chapters include explorations of Latino religion and religiosity; gender and changing gender systems; politics, political mobilization, and political organization; language, expressive culture, and cultural change; and Latinos and the law.

Contributors were selected from a broad spectrum of scholarly fields and intellectual perspectives, and represent broad expertise drawn both from traditional, established fields of academic inquiry like history, sociology, law, and political science, as well as emergent, more explicitly politically contentious interdisciplinary areas of study such as gender studies, religious studies, cultural studies, ethnic studies, and comparative Latin American and Latino studies. Contributors were given wide latitude regarding the conceptual, methodological, and interpretive approaches they brought to their individual assignments. Indeed, my hope as compiler and editor was to bring together the work of scholars in different fields and in different stages of their careers in an effort to create a kind of dynamic tension between and among a variety of different perspectives and points of view and thus to reflect to the extent possible some of the tensions that so obviously characterize the social, cultural, and political life of Latinos in the United States today. In keeping with this approach, authors were asked to develop in basic outline the broad contours of the history of their topical areas of study but also to depart from historical convention where appropriate by engaging in informed speculation both about contemporary trends and likely trajectories for the future. Finally, all of the contributors to the *Columbia History of Latinos in the United States Since 1960* were also strongly encouraged to frame their analyses and write in a style that would be engaging and accessible to both specialists and a broader reading audience. By giving all the authors or groups of authors free rein in framing their studies while also encouraging them to refrain from using the technical academic jargon typical of their respective disciplines, we hoped to produce a volume that provides cutting-edge interpretations of the broad contours of the recent history of Latinos in the United States and one that also provides readers with insight into the major areas of contention and debate in Latino scholarship in the early twenty-first century.

Thus, as should be clear, the tasks faced by the individual authors in conceptualizing and executing their individual assignments were not as neat and straightforward as they might at first glance appear. On the most fundamental level, each contributor needed to address the challenge of analyzing populations that have been, and continue to be, in the midst of tremendous social flux and transformation. For example, while each author was charged with the task of recounting the recent histories of populations that currently constitute the pan-Latino population of the United States, we all were cognizant of the many ways the extreme geographic mobility of these groups—both within the boundaries of the United States and across international frontiers—raises conceptual and analytical challenges of a kind usually not faced by scholars studying more sedentary populations. Hundreds of thousands of Latinos continue to move between the United States and Latin America and otherwise maintain strong organic ties to their communities, and this combination of physical mobility and deep ties to places elsewhere in the Western Hemisphere represent unique and fundamental components of Latinos' social reality. Consequently, as all of the chapters that follow demonstrate in some detail, it is impossible to situate Latinos' experience within the historical tradition of a single nation-state, whether that nation-state is their country of origin or the United States of America. Of course, the persistence of transnational ties has always been a fact of Latinos' lives in the United States (and, to a greater or lesser degree, of other migrant populations), but the dynamism of Latinos' more recent history requires that interpreters employ regional and multinational perspectives in attempting to analyze these restless and constantly shifting populations-in-motion. Similarly, while each author was charged with developing an analysis temporally focused on the last four decades of the last century, each was forced to grapple in his or her own way with the long reach of American economic, political, and military imperialism in Latin America over a much longer stretch of time. Thus, although each contributor employed different points of analytical departure and emphasis, the historical legacies and contemporary specter of the United States' ongoing colonial relationship with Latin America can be seen in each chapter.

On a related plane, it is equally important to emphasize from the outset the extent to which the history of racism in the United States and the troubled history of United States–Latin American relations has colored and continues to influence scholarship on the subject under discussion. Each of us has been trained to aspire to professional standards of scholarly objectivity, but we all also recognize that the fields of Latin American and U.S.–Latino studies have always been arenas of intense intellectual and ideological contestation and debate around these and other areas of social hierarchy and social conflict. The essays that follow clearly reveal both the tensions inherent in these areas of inquiry and the lack of consensus over conceptualization, theoretical framing, methodologies, and ultimate lines of interpretation that currently exists in the evolving field of Latino studies (an issue discussed in greater detail in the introduction that follows). Again, however, by juxtaposing our different frames of reference and lines of argumentation against one another, we hope both to help sharpen the ongoing academic debate about the recent history of Latinos in the United States and to provoke critical thinking and discussion about this rich and complex history among both academic and more general readers.

Most of the themes discussed in this preface are touched upon in chapter 1, which is my contribution to this collection. As both the largest Latino subpopulation and the group with the longest continuous contact with American society, ethnic Mexicans have in many ways epitomized the Latino experience along the historical axes of both imperialism and neoliberalism. The first Mexican Americans were incorporated by imperial conquest—initially during the Anglo-American infiltration of Texas and other Mexican territories in the 1820s and 1830s and then as spoils of war during the Texas Revolution of 1836 and the 1846 to 1848 War of the North American Invasion (as it is known in Mexico to this day). Since the late nineteenth century, and increasingly over the course of the last century, Mexican American history has been characterized by three major factors that have increasingly come to characterize other Latino populations in the United States: the steady penetration of U.S. economic interests into a neighboring Latin American nation; the growth of a multinational resident ethnic population within the boundaries of the United States caused both by natural increase and the extensive and ongoing incorporation of foreign workers into the domestic economy; and the experience of racialization and discrimination in the United States by both native- and foreign-born components of that population. The abiding paradox of this troubled history is that although American economic and governing elites historically strove to maintain social, cultural, and economic distance between the ethnic Mexican minority (whether citizen, denizen, or alien) and the white Americans they considered to be their primary social constituents, U.S. policies and practices over the course of nearly two centuries—and especially in the period since 1960—have encouraged the rapid growth of all subpopulations of ethnic Mexicans and the increasing de facto integration of the social, cultural, and economic systems of the United States and Mexico along a 2,000-mile border.

In their contribution, sociologists Kelvin Santiago-Valles and Gladys Jiménez-Muñoz argue along similar lines but focus more directly on the baldly colonial nature of the historical relationship between the United States and Puerto Rico. Indeed, in their incisive and highly critical chapter, Santiago-Valles and Jiménez-Muñoz argue that the current colonial relationship between the United States and Puerto Rico should not be viewed as some kind of anomaly but rather should be seen as the predictable result of a self-conscious hemispheric and global policy to which the government of the United States has adhered for nearly 200 years. They develop their argument further, however, by pointing out the complicated ways that American imperialism historically has entailed more than the economic subordination and racialization of subject peoples, although these have clearly been crucial components of that relationship. From their point of view, the process of colonization, in both its classic forms and in its current neoliberal manifestation, has always also fundamentally involved the conceptual reduction and feminization of Puerto Ricans (and, by extension, of other Latin Americans and U.S. Latinos). When viewed from this perspective, the persistence of drastic inequality both between Puerto Ricans and other American residents of the United States and between the United States and the rest of Latin America is neither an accident of history nor a "natural" anomaly of uneven development but a symptom of the ongoing elaboration of an international division of labor largely shaped and driven by U.S. interests. Skillfully weaving together close analysis of social, economic, and cultural factors that have contributed to these historical patterns on the island, in Puerto Rican communities on the mainland, and in Latin America generally, the authors offer a provocative and ultimately compelling synthetic interpretation of some of the most persistent and vexing issues in hemispheric social science research.

In some ways, the historian María Cristina García's analysis of the recent history of ethnic Cubans explores the obverse effects of the United States' larger historical relationship with Latin America. Although García points out that turn-of-the-century Cuban migration to the United States and elsewhere was driven by the same economic and political forces that characterized the United States' relationship to other nations in Latin America (particularly Mexico and the Central American countries), Cuba was not annexed in the same direct manner in which Puerto Rico was seized after the Spanish-American War. Nevertheless, as García demonstrates, the United States assumed "informal" control of Cuban affairs after the war and maintained that control for most of the next half century—thus helping to establish the troubled relationship that has existed between the two nations ever since. The constant meddling in the internal affairs of the Cuban government, the establishment of a permanent U.S. naval base at Guantánamo Bay, and a long history of direct U.S. military interventions on the island since 1898 provide an indication of just how firmly the United States either kept Cuba under its sway or otherwise closely monitored its internal affairs.

After Fidel Castro's takeover 1959, this situation changed abruptly. As García notes, whether Castro initially intended to strike an antagonistic posture with the United States remains an open question to this day, but as he consolidated power on the island, thousands of anti-Castro Cubans either chose or were forced to depart Cuba for the United States. Thus began a very different kind of migration cycle. García carefully demonstrates how the predicament of the Cuban expatriates meshed well with the intensifying anticommunist American foreign policy of the time and thus paved the way for the very different treatment Cubans received as political refugees. Still, García documents the difficulties of settlement and adjustment faced both by the initial groups of emigrants and those who came later. Although the special welcome extended to the first waves of Cubans in the form of relaxed immigration regulations, job-training programs, and financial and educational assistance is well chronicled here, García skillfully illustrates just how heterogeneous the total influx has been, and just how complicated the circumstances surrounding Cuban emigration and settlement—particularly for those who entered during and after the infamous Mariel influxes of the 1980s. Despite the recent sensation caused by the Elián González controversy, García is among a growing number of scholars who emphasize the increasing class, cultural, "racial," and political diversity of the ethnic Cuban population and who anticipate potentially surprising and unexpected developments in both Cuban American politics and the Cuban–American relationship in the twenty-first century.

Sociologist Norma Chinchilla and political scientist Nora Hamilton offer a sweeping chapter on the growth of the multinational Central American population that echoes many of the themes explored in the previous chapters. Like the Cuban case, the mass movement of Central Americans to the United States since the 1970s and 1980s originated in the regional geopolitical turmoil that tore hundreds of thousands of people from their local communities and, eventually, from their homelands. Again, like the other contributors, Chinchilla and Hamilton carefully trace the different ways the penetration into the region of U.S. economic and military interests in the late nineteenth century gradually pulled developing Central American nations into the North American economic and political orbit. In a story that was repeated in nations around the Gulf of Mexico and the Caribbean basin, the authors map the processes that led North American corporate interests to invest in a variety of enterprises ranging from cattle and oil to plantation export crops like coffee, bananas, and cotton. Of course, U.S. strategic interests in securing an interoceanic canal early in the twentieth century added to the United States' growing sense of proprietorship in the region.

In any case, the reorientation of the Central American regional economy toward export markets started a chain reaction of widespread social instability, displacement of rural and urban workers, and eventual population movement. As more and more arable land fell under the control of local oligarchies (often representing a small, interlocking set of prominent families), the stage was set first for a massive wave of rural-to-urban internal migration and then, gradually, for increased rates of transnational migration. As with Mexico, the sporadic eruption of indigenous uprisings over the course of the twentieth century added to the flows of both economic migrants and political refugees. Up until the late 1960s, migration from Central America to the United States was moderate, but with the eruption of new waves of violence in the face of unrelenting displacement and repression—often aided and abetted by the actions of the U.S. government—the rate of migration northward exploded in the late 1970s and 1980s. As Chinchilla and Hamilton demonstrate, the bulk of the largest émigré populations from Honduras, Guatemala, El Salvador, and Nicaragua originated during this long period of regional instability and violence.

Given the broad diversity and recentness of the Central American migration, Chinchilla and Hamilton's analysis raises some provocative questions about the future trajectory of this rapidly expanding pan-Latino population. While many, if not most, of the Central American migrants who originally entered the United States in the 1980s and early 1990s may well have planned on returning to their nations of origin, the persistence of economic and political instability in Central America and the broadening social networks the migrants have established in the North have created yet another constellation of vibrant Latino subcultures in the United States. Thus, while Central Americans maintain strong and abiding transnational ties to their homelands—and through their remittances continue to contribute huge amounts of foreign capital to the economy of the region—their future increasingly appears to be tied to that of the United States. That their patterns of settlement have often increased tensions with already-established Latino populations adds another dimension of uncertainty. Thus, as with other Latino populations comprising significant numbers of low-skilled and indigenous workers, whether the future involves a process of gradual socioeconomic integration and upward mobility or, conversely, will reveal yet another example of the "segmented assimilation" of Central Americans into a growing pan-American underclass remains very much an open question.

Sociologist Peggy Levitt's discussion of the recent history of Dominicans in the United States adds other intriguing dimensions to the complex history of Latino migrants and settlers. As the opening paragraphs of her essay illustrate so dramatically, the deep transnational ties that have bound migrants from the island to receiving communities in the United States are fundamental components of life at both ends of the international circuit of migration. Indeed, due to the extension by the Dominican government of dual citizenship to its expatriate population, the republic's second-largest concentration of voters now resides in New York City, and its last president, Leonel Fernández, spent most of his life in New York before winning the presidency in 1996. Levitt's essay—and the larger body of research from which it builds—demonstrates that while Dominican migration is a relatively recent phenomenon, the historical combination of the island's development under a series of autocratic governments, the concentration of land ownership into the hands of a tiny local elite, and the domination of the republic's economic affairs by the United States all deeply influenced subsequent patterns of both permanent immigration and circular migration from the island to the United States.

Levitt's work stands as a strong case study of how the forces of globalization and chronically uneven regional economic development in the hemisphere have simultaneously stimulated the mass migration of underemployed workers to places where they hope to find work while also fostering the maintenance of strong transnational ties among migrants. Indeed, as is the case for ethnic Mexicans, Puerto Ricans, and perhaps some other Latino subpopulations, many Dominicans have come to see circular migration as a rational life strategy that fosters the development of organically linked Dominican communities in both nations. Building on her previous work and the work of other migration scholars, Levitt argues that as complex migrant networks linking the Dominican Republic to the United States have thickened over time, the continual circulation of people, goods, communication networks, and remittances have helped to join the two countries into a single transnational "social field." Levitt is careful to point out that the existence of such common social fields does not imply that the Dominican Republic and the United States are somehow fading away as distinct national entities. Nor does she diminish the important development of what are now thriving and growing permanent Dominican American communities in the northeastern United States and elsewhere. However, by carefully exploring the many ways that the activities of Dominicans' everyday lives now transcend national borders (whether those activities include travel, the sending of remittances, the maintenance of intimate and engaged family ties, or voting in American, Dominican, or both nation's elections), Levitt's analysis provide insight into the ways the forces of the global market continue to undermine discrete, bounded nation-states while greatly strengthening the many economic, social, cultural, and political ties that bind human beings across currently constituted national borders. As she notes in the essay's conclusion, "these widespread, enduring ties also challenge conventional understandings of the determinants of inequality, civic engagement, and community development." The dramatic example of Dominican Americans voting and standing for elective office in Dominican elections may well represent an extreme case of transnationalism at work, but the current situation may well also represent a harbinger of trends that will become much more commonplace in the Western Hemisphere and elsewhere in the world in the near future.

Marilyn Espitia's chapter on the migration, settlement, and growth of South American peoples adds more layers of complexity and ambiguity to the recent history of Latino peoples in the United States. Although South Americans have been emigrating in small numbers to the United States since the days of the California Gold Rush, it is only recently that their numbers have begun to rise to significant levels. As Espitia notes, while the dynamics of South American migration, settlement, and adjustment are similar to those of other Latin American and U.S. Latino groups, clear differences exist as well. The most obvious and significant of these are the higher aggregate socioeconomic characteristics of the population of South American origin. Of course, broad status variations exist in the growing multinational South American population in the United States, but, generally speaking, most South American immigrants enter the country with higher levels of education, job skills, and class standing than virtually all other Latin American subpopulations. (As a result, South Americans also tend to enter the United States through officially sanctioned immigration channels and appear to have much lower rates of undocumented migration than do the other populations, especially Mexicans and Central Americans). Espitia argues that these distinct characteristics may well have important effects on the manner in which Latinos of South American origin or heritage eventually come to identify and situate themselves vis-à-vis other residents of the United States. Whether they eventually choose to meld into mainstream structures of society or, as Espitia suggests, explore a new, cosmopolitan sense of *latinidad* is one of the most intriguing questions in contemporary Latino studies research.

Like Espitia's contribution, sociologist Pierrette Hondagneu-Sotelo's chapter, the first of this volume's thematic essays, broadens the framework of analysis away from a single nationality or geographic group by exploring the theme of changing gender relationships among Latinos in the U.S. context. Like all other authors in the volume, Hondagneu-Sotelo argues that the construction and ongoing transformation of gendered relationships among Latinos cannot be considered in isolation. From her point of view, to even begin to comprehend the ways gendered systems change over time requires discussion not only of the dynamics of gender construction in the United States and in the "sending" nations of Latin America but also awareness of the many profound ways that global economic change and the emergence of international political movements—especially the rise of feminist critical thought since the 1960s—have together influenced socially constructed definitions of what is considered "feminine" and what is considered "masculine" in modern life. Given the way gender systems and gender roles have shifted and evolved over the past half century, the author cautions readers not to assume that sharp dichotomies necessarily exist between "traditional" relationships in sending regions of Latin America and a more "modern" situation in the United States. Arguing instead that gender roles and sexual orientations are subject to constant contestation and negotiation between and among men and women, Hondagneu-Sotelo attempts to situate her analysis in the broadest possible historical and regional context. Still, building on her own extensive previous research in the area of migration and gender, Hondagneu-Sotelo suggests that the process of transnational migration itself often helps reconfigure gender relationships in significant ways, as women and men are often forced by circumstances beyond their control to adjust and adapt to rapidly changing social environments. From her standpoint, gauging "progress" in gender relationships is, therefore, an extremely complicated process involving assessment of a broad range of variables and gender, family, and sexual stereotypes (like the persistence of *machismo* and *marianismo*) in cultural settings in both Latin American nations and in the United States. In the end, however, Hondagneu-Sotelo cautiously suggests that gender roles in various Latino subpopulations in the United States have gradually become more flexible—and perhaps even more egalitarian—over time.

This sense of guarded optimism is also present in Anthony Stevens-Arroyo's far-ranging essay on the recent history of Latino religion and religiosity in the United States. Like Hondagneu-Sotelo, Stevens-Arroyo, a professor of religious studies, grounds his analysis of changing patterns of Latino religious orientation and practice in social, cultural, and political trends that transcend national boundaries. Indeed, much like the other contributors, Stevens-Arroyo argues that it is impossible to separate Latino religious history and the deep religious beliefs held by so many Latinos from the political and intercultural currents that have otherwise shaped their lives so deeply since the 1960s. In this piece, Stevens-Arroyo argues that when combined with the politicization that occurred in the 1960s among Mexican Americans (primarily in the Southwest) and Puerto Ricans (primarily in the Northeast), the steady demographic growth of the pan-Latino population laid the foundations for a massive "resurgence" in Latino religiosity (importantly, he notes, among both Catholics and Protestants). He carefully traces the ways the religiously inspired *cursillo* movement inflected the campaigns of César Chávez and the United Farm Workers Union in the West and converged with Puerto Rican activism in the East to compel deep change in both the American Catholic Church and in many Protestant sects. The author argues that church institutions, officials, and laypeople have served as vital intermediaries (for both social integration and resistance) between established Latino communities and newcomers from Latin America. Indeed, Stevens-Arroyo's analysis of the origins and evolution of the Latino religious resurgence since the 1960s in some ways provides a powerful counterpoint to more pessimistic analyses in this volume by demonstrating the complicated ways that successful faith-based grassroots efforts have continued among Latinos even in the face of their systemic marginalization and outright repression. With the explosive growth of the Latino population since 1980, it seems certain that grassroots, ecumenical, faith-based political mobilizations based in religious practices ranging from traditional Catholicism to indigenous and Afro-Caribbean spiritualism will continue to play important roles for U.S. Latinos and that they may well also provide the basis for building a stronger pan-ethnic solidarity among the various populations in the new century.

Frances R. Aparicio follows a similar tack in her exploration of the intricately complicated terrain of Latino cultural production and expression in the United States. As with the book's other contributors, Aparicio, director of the Latino and Latin American Studies program at the University of Illinois, Chicago, foregrounds the colonial context in which Latino cultural expression in the United States has unfolded. Within this colonial context, she argues, one must pay special attention to the role expressive culture plays as both entertainment and as a site in which identity is played out, empowered, and reformed—sometimes in opposition to dominant norms and practices and sometimes in conjunction with them. Thus, in this subtle and penetrating analysis, Aparicio explores the ways different forms of Latino cultural expression serve to mediate between conflicting social formations and traditions while also sometimes being appropriated, co-opted, and absorbed by U.S. corporate interests. And here Aparicio exposes the crux of the matter. Building on insights raised by other Latino cultural critics and developed in her own previously published work and ongoing research, Aparicio carefully explicates the manner in which Latinos are locked in a continuous struggle to express themselves in their own idioms, forge new identities, and maintain a distinctive sense of Latino or Latin American aesthetics in the face of the inexorable homogenizing pressures of the U.S. consumerist juggernaut. The cultural tensions, modes of resistance, and syncretism that are expressed in Latino letters, music, art, and performance thus speak to the very essence of the Latino experience in the United States. As Aparicio notes, these different modes of "Latino expressive cultures . . . exhibited the effects of the push and pull of the forces of mainstreaming, integration, and institutionalization, on the one hand, and new and continuous oppositional forces, on the other, that explored new forms of identity and urged resistance to assimilation."

Many of these same tensions and ambivalence resonate throughout legal scholar Kevin Johnson's essay on Latinos and U.S. law. In the increasingly ambiguous and potentially dangerous current political and legal environment of the United States, the tortured historical relationship of Latinos to the U.S. system of law and jurisprudence has once again come into sharp relief. In this piece, Johnson explores the uneven history of Latinos' interactions with three crucial and overlapping areas of American law: immigration and nationality law; civil-rights litigation and jurisprudence; and the long and contentious legal struggle to gain access to public education. While Johnson, a professor of law and associate dean at the University of California, Davis, School of Law, acknowledges that the U.S. legal system has often proved a powerful ally in Latinos' efforts in these areas, he emphasizes the manner in which nearly two centuries of discrimination continue to shape and color the Latino experience even after the civil-rights revolution of the 1950s and 1960s. Drawing on close readings of relevant case law and legal histories, Johnson plots the checkered history of Latinos' intimate involvement with U.S. immigration law and policy in the last half of the twentieth century. Johnson's analysis in this area is consistent with that of other immigration scholars in pointing out that while the United States has asserted its sovereign right to protect its borders, government agencies have long either looked the other way or actually cooperated with U.S. businesses as they actively recruited and employed huge numbers of both officially sanctioned and unauthorized immigrant workers. Johnson explores the many implications of this profound contradiction in the areas of employment and naturalization and the potential social and political integration of Latinos into American society. In the arena of civil rights in the U.S. legal context, Johnson traces recent gains and setbacks in areas including search and seizure (an area that often involves "racial profiling" by law enforcement authorities), political asylum, and the increasingly contentious issue of language usage and rights, and he speculates on the extent to which the recent growth of the Latino population may help break the traditional formula that has long equated "civil rights" with white–black relations in the United States. In the final section of the chapter, Johnson explores the recent history of the Latino struggle to gain access to all levels of public education, beginning with a brief review of the mixed legacies of the famous 1954 *Brown v. Board of Education* decision and ending with an analysis of the political challenges of bilingual education, the alarming resegregation of Latino students in the public schools since the 1980s, and the future of "affirmative action" in education and the workplace. With the recent Supreme Court rulings on the legality of such approaches (in the crucial "reverse discrimination" cases brought against the University of Michigan), this and the other general areas of Latino concern will remain especially sensitive for the foreseeable future.

Political scientist Louis DeSipio concludes the volume with some important and insightful reflections both on the recent political history of Latinos in the United States and on what the future might hold for Latinos in American politics. From the outset, DeSipio brings sharp focus to the issue of what the Chicano political scientist Rodolfo de la Garza in another context has called "*el cuento de los números*" (roughly, "the myth of the numbers"—or the myth that increasing population numbers automatically equal rising political power). Analyzing both population and voting data since the 1960 national elections, DeSipio argues that although the Latino population obviously has grown tremendously over that period, its political influence has not kept pace. More importantly, DeSipio goes further and questions whether dramatic population increases will necessarily translate into increasing political clout in the near future. Carefully building his case from both historical and contemporary sources, DeSipio argues that the same structural forces that limit participation in traditional American politics generally may well be even more influential in the Latino example. It has long been recognized that age, socioeconomic status, education levels, language proficiency, and other basic social-structural characteristics strongly influence political participation (or nonparticipation) in American politics. As is noted in more detail in the introduction, with an extremely youthful demographic structure, comparably low aggregate levels of education and job skills, and a disproportionate share of the nation's poor, the Latino population meets all the predictors for comparably low levels of political engagement and activity. Add to this the glaring fact that at least 40 percent of the Latino population are noncitizens—and thus ineligible to vote—and the full dimensions of the obstacles Latinos face in achieving their full political potential become clear. Indeed, DeSipio goes so far as to note that in the cold calculus of winner-take-all American electoral politics, the apex of Latino political participation and efficacy may well have already occurred, during the Nixon–Kennedy campaign of 1960. His disquieting assertions, contrary to common sense, that Latinos simply do not matter in most elections, provides much food for sober thought and reflection.

This is not to say that there have not been recent signs of more positive movement. As DeSipio notes, with the extension of provisions of the Voting Rights Act to Latinos in 1975 (the act had been designed primarily to empower African Americans when first passed in 1965), Latinos have gradually seen increased representation in all levels of government. The recent debate held in New Mexico between Democratic Party presidential candidates provides further evidence of this. Moreover, population growth and increasing political sophistication have resulted in the emergence of powerful lobbies and political-education groups, such as the Southwest Voter Registration Project and the National Council of La Raza, and the establishment of important national civil-rights advocates in the Mexican American Legal Defense and Education Fund (MALDEF) and other similar organizations—and these trends probably will continue in the future. DeSipio also notes that at a less visible and yet in some ways more interesting level, the involvement of Latinos in faith-based organizations, the sporadic mobilizations of resident aliens (as occurred during the debate over California's Proposition 187), and the recent spike in the unionization of certain sectors of the Latino workforce (for example, among laborers, dry wallers and other construction workers, hospital employees, janitors and other service workers, and a small minority of farm workers) at the very least provide intriguing glimpses of avenues for potential social and political empowerment in the future. In addition, on another level, the increasing level of remittances from Latin American expatriates, increasing numbers of dual nationals among Latino residents, and other strong forms of continuing connection between emigrants and their places of origin may be signs of the emergence of new, if still inchoate forms of political orientation, mobilization, and action among Latinos.[3] Still, for the foreseeable future, as DeSipio and virtually all of the contributors to this volume have to some degree argued, the peculiar structural features of American politics ensures that Latinos will remain much less influential in U.S. political life than their aggregate numbers would seem to suggest. Whether Latinos' collective actions in the United States translates into a new era of empowerment, integration, and participation—or results in a process of deepening social and political destabilization in both the United States and Latin America—will surely be one of the single most critical social and political questions of the twenty-first century.

NOTES

1. See U.S. Census Bureau, "Census Bureau Releases Population Estimates by Age, Sex, Race, and Hispanic Origin," *United States Department of Commerce News*, 21 January 2003.
2. In this preface and my other contributions to this volume, the term "Latino" (and, in a few cases, "pan-Latino") are rather arbitrarily used to describe all inhabitants of the United States (of both genders) with at least one parent of Latin American heritage or descent, regardless of formal citizenship or nationality status. For reasons discussed in more detail in the introduction, one should not assume, however, that a consensus exists about the conceptualization and definition of the "Latino" population. Similarly, although I am fully aware of pitfalls of sexism and "heterocentrism" in academic discourse, in the interest of keeping the text clear of the constant use of wordy or awkward constructions such as "Latina/os," "Latinos and Latinas," "Latino/a men and women," and the most recent neologism, Latin@, I have chosen to use the masculine form of the noun, except when specifically referring to women of Latin American origin or descent. In those cases, the feminine Spanish term, "Latina," is used. Each of the other authors in the volume was asked to choose a consistent form for their treatment of ethnic, national, and gendered labels. As I hope this preface makes clear, the umbrella term "Latino," like all markers of ethnicity, nationality, citizenship, and/or gender, has become increasingly freighted and unwieldy in a period of accelerating economic globalization, transnational migration, and an ongoing academic debate over gendered language in all contexts. For similar reasons, the term "Hispanic" is almost completely absent from this volume. This problematic term was appropriated for use by the federal government in the 1970s as an easy way to impose an orderly, bounded category onto a population that otherwise was profoundly diverse—and whose putative members do not necessarily think of themselves in the same corporate terms. The term has gained some popularity among people interested in accepting the U.S. government's logic, but few individuals of Latin American origin or heritage use the term as a primary self-referent, whereas most recognize "Latino" as a loose and general marker for what is perceived as the larger linguistic/historical/cultural community of greater Latin America. It is imperative to note, however, that most Latinos continue to identify first with national origin (however distant that origin might be) and then with pan-ethnic designations such as "Latino" or "Hispanic." In addition, as discussed below, it is also important to note that significant numbers of immigrants originating in Latin American nations tend to self-identify as members of indigenous groups and thus have problematic relationships with dominant populations in their regions of origin. For illuminating discussions of the social complexities and political implications of the ongoing debate over nomenclature, ascription, and self-identity, see articles on the topic in the special issue, "The Politics of Ethnic Construction: Hispanic, Chicano, Latino . . . ?" in *Latin American Perspectives* 19, no. 4 (Fall 1992); Sharon M. Lee, "Racial Classifications in the U.S. Census, 1890–1990," *Ethnic and Racial Studies* 16, no. 1 (January 1993): 75–94; Suzanne Oboler, *Ethnic Labels, Latino Lives: Identity and the Politics of (Re)presentation in the United States* (Minneapolis: University of Minnesota Press,

1995); and Clara E. Rodríguez, *Changing Race: Latinos, the Census, and the History of Ethnicity in the United States* (New York: New York University Press, 2000). For a broader, comparative discussion of these issues, see Melissa Nobles, *Shades of Citizenship: Race and the Census in Modern Politics* (Stanford: Stanford University Press, 2000).

3. For an intriguing glimpse into the prospects for and limitations in pan-Latino transnational organizing and mobilization, see *Cross-Border Dialogues: U.S.-Mexico Social Movement Networking*, ed. David Brooks and Jonathan Fox (La Jolla, Calif.: Center for U.S.–Mexican Studies, University of California, San Diego, 2002).

THE COLUMBIA HISTORY OF LATINOS IN THE UNITED STATES SINCE 1960

INTRODUCTION

DEMOGRAPHY AND THE SHIFTING BOUNDARIES OF "COMMUNITY": REFLECTIONS ON "U.S. LATINOS" AND THE EVOLUTION OF LATINO STUDIES

DAVID G. GUTIÉRREZ

IN 1960, at the beginning of the period under examination in this volume, few observers of American society—including Americans of Latin descent themselves—thought of Latinos as part of a discernable "minority" population. Of course, people in the Southwest were aware of the regional presence of a significant ethnic Mexican minority, and residents of the Northeast recognized how much the Puerto Rican population had grown in the years since World War II. But beyond the fact that Puerto Ricans and Mexicans came from "mixed-race" backgrounds, spoke Spanish, tended to be Roman Catholic, and seemed to share certain aesthetic affinities, there was little awareness of larger connections that transcended the different national-historical and regional backgrounds of these populations. For their part, most Americans of Latino descent tended also to focus on the regional- or national-origins dimensions of their individual and collective senses of identity, orientation, and affiliation. Little empirical research was done on the question of the cultural identity and national orientations of various Latino populations, but what there was seemed to indicate that, like other immigrant and/or ethnic groups in U.S. society, the largest of these groups—Mexican Americans and Puerto Ricans—thought of themselves broadly as either "hyphenated Americans"; as expatriate members of the countries or regions of origin; or, for a smaller number, as members of an indigenous minority (such as the descendants of Spanish settlers in California, Colorado, New Mexico, and Texas). Few apparently viewed themselves as members of a larger historically or culturally related pan-ethnic or multinational entity.[1]

The demographic revolution of the last four decades of the twentieth century has very much changed the dynamics of identity and social orientation among various Latino subpopulations. Not only have the resident ethnic Mexican and Puerto Rican populations exploded over that period, but their numbers have been greatly augmented by the addition of millions of other people of Latin American origin or descent. As these populations have expanded and become more geographically dispersed, Latinos of all national origins, heritages, and class backgrounds now reside and intermingle in a broad range of different urban and rural settings in communities across the United States. Indeed, the pan-Latino population has grown so quickly and in so many different regions of the country that the full effects of these striking new trends have yet to be completely understood. In some cases, rapid Latino population growth and dispersal has resulted in increased levels of conflict between Latinos and non-Latinos (again, in both urban and rural locales)—and in a palpable increase in intraethnic friction and competition. The latter points of contention are often rooted in class differences but can be predicated on linguistic, national, and perceived "racial" and cultural differences. It is important to note that in other cases, however, the expansion of pan-Latino communities has prepared the ground for very different kinds of social interactions. For example, in the increasingly ethnically complex, cosmopolitan social settings of places like New York City, Chicago, Houston, Los Angeles, and San Francisco, the intermeshing of different Latino subpopulations has laid the foundations for the emergence and ongoing evolution of a strong sense of *latinidad*—a collective sense of cultural affinity and identity deeply rooted in what many Latinos perceive to be a shared historical, spiritual, aesthetic, and linguistic heritage, and a growing sense of cultural affinity and solidarity in the social context of the United States.[2]

In discussing some of the major dimensions of the dialectical tension between the psychology of conflict and the dynamics of community formation, which has long represented one of the central, unresolved paradoxes of Latino life in the United States, I hope with this introduction to explore the nature and implications of that paradox, introduce the main themes of the volume, and, in the process, provide some of the larger historical contexts in which to frame the chapters that follow.

THE CHANGING DEMOGRAPHIC STRUCTURE OF THE PAN-LATINO POPULATION

To a large degree, all the essays in this volume are ultimately reflections on the significance of demographic change in recent U.S. and Latin American history.[3] Indeed, as data from the 2000 U.S. census has slowly been released and analyzed over the past few years, even professional demographers have expressed surprise about the breadth and depth of the transformation of the American population that occurred in the decade of the 1990s. The census revealed that more immigrants entered the United States between 1990 and 2000 than in any other ten-year period of American history—including more famous epochs of transnational migration such as the Irish famine immigration, the great influx of German immigrants in the 1840s and 1850s, and the mass migrations from Asia, Mexico, Europe, and Russia that occurred between the 1880s and the 1920s. The motivations underlying such massive transnational movements of humanity have not changed much over time. Drawn by the perception of political stability and economic opportunity in the United States and propelled from their countries of origin by massive population growth, political turmoil, war, chronic poverty, and, more recently, by the ravages of the international drug trade, new immigrants entered the country by the millions. All told, more than 8.6 million new immigrants entered the United States between 1990 and 1999, joining an already immense population of the foreign-born. By 2001, the Census Bureau estimates that there were more than 30 million foreign-born people living within the boundaries of the United States. When immigrants' U.S.-born children are counted in the mix of new Americans, the numbers are even more stunning. Demographers estimate that the combined population of first- and second-generation residents reached nearly 56 million people by 2001—or one of five inhabitants of the United States.[4]

Of course, while the demographic explosion in the foreign-born and their children has been particularly dramatic, these figures are but the most recent manifestations of much longer social and demographic trends. The sources of these dramatic, long-term shifts in population are complex, but much of the ongoing demographic transformation of American society can be traced to the explosive population growth in Latin America since 1960. Up until about 1950, the populations of Latin America and the United States were roughly comparable, but since then the Latin American population growth rate has far outstripped that of Anglo North America. For example, between 1960 and 2000, the population of Latin America jumped from a little more than 218 million to more than 520 million. By contrast, the populations of the United States and Canada together grew from about 199 million to just under 307 million over the same period. Even with a steadily declining birth rate in Latin America, demographers predict that these hemispheric population patterns will hold well into the future. According to estimates generated in a recent United Nations study, Latin America's population is expected to reach 802 million by 2050.[5]

On the U.S. side of the equation, shifting demographic balances over the last four decades are also attributable in part to fundamental changes in

American immigration laws and policies resulting from the passage of the landmark Hart-Celler Immigration and Nationality Act Amendments of 1965. The Hart-Celler Act greatly liberalized U.S. immigration policy by abolishing the harshly discriminatory national-origins quota system that had been the foundation of U.S. immigration law since the 1920s. Under the old system, which was developed in the 1920s to grapple with what was widely perceived at the time to be an alarming increase in the immigration of "racially inferior" populations to the United States, potential immigrants from Western European nations were given de facto priority, while immigration from much of the rest of the world was severely limited by the imposition of tiny quotas on "undesirable" nations, in some cases amounting to no more than 100 peeople per country.[6] By removing national-origins limitations, lifting more specific, long-standing bars against potential immigrants from Asian nations, prioritizing occupational criteria, and reinforcing the general principle of family reunification as the bedrock objective of U.S. immigration policy, the INA Amendments of 1965 cleared the way for a dramatic shift in the composition of immigrant populations coming to the United States.

The results of the policy can be seen by the clear change in the composition of immigrant flows over the last four decades of the twentieth century. Whereas in 1960 75 percent of all immigrants to the United States came from Europe and only about 14 percent from Asia and Latin America, by the end of the century that ratio had been inverted. In 2000, only 15 percent of the foreign-born population of the United States originated in the nations of Europe—the vast majority, upward of 77 percent, originated in the nations of Latin America and Asia.

The most striking immediate effect of the dismantling of the discriminatory national-origins quota system in 1965 was the steady proportional increase in migration to the United States from Asia. After years in which Asians had been systematically excluded from immigration to the United States because they were deemed racially "ineligible to citizenship," people of Asian and Asian American origin or descent now represent the fastest growing segment of the overall American population. In conjunction with this trend, however, immigration from Latin America has almost kept pace with the pan-Asian influx over the same period. Passage of the Hart-Celler Act initially dampened Latin American immigration for a short time in the late 1960s (because formal numerical ceilings on migration from the Western Hemisphere were imposed for the first time as part of the reform package), but this proved to be but a short deviation from longer-term historical trends. The huge and growing demand for labor in the United States during the war in Vietnam, aggressive U.S. economic policy and practices abroad, and the persistence of political and economic instability in Latin America, which many analysts have argued was exacerbated by U.S. foreign policy and economic practices, eventually combined to stimulate significant immigration flows. With the intensified restructuring of the global economy that commenced during and after the Arab oil embargo of the early 1970s, the impetus for mass migration increased even more.

Again, aggregate migration statistics provide a rough indication of the direction of these general trends. In 1960, there were fewer than one million foreign-born Latin Americans in the United States. In the decade of the 1960s, however, more than a million additional Latin American immigrants entered the country through legal, officially documented channels. In the 1970s, another 1.4 million came. In the 1980s, with Mexico in economic turmoil, civil wars raging in Central America, and many other Latin American nations torn by social, economic, and political strife, the number of officially authorized immigrants jumped to 2.8 million. Between 1990 and 2000, the trend turned upward even more dramatically, and at least 4.6 million Latin American immigrants legally entered the United States. It is critical to note, however, that throughout this period, the officially authorized and acknowledged immigrant flow was always augmented by, and at times almost certainly exceeded, by the constant circulation into and out of U.S. territory of millions of unauthorized, "illegal" migrants—some of whom were temporary sojourners, but many eventually became permanent residents.[7] Although it is impossible to tell exactly how many undocumented migrants settled permanently in the United States (current estimates put the total at nearly 8 million), clandestine immigration has long been a major source of the growth of the permanent U.S. Latino population.

As it has grown over the years, the foreign-born Latin American population in the United States has also become increasingly diverse (for reasons discussed in greater detail below, migration from Puerto Rico must be considered as a separate case). Whereas most immigrants from Latin America historically originated in Mexico, over time, influxes from Central America, the Spanish-speaking Caribbean, and, most recently, from the South American continent have all added increasing numbers to the mix. In 2000, Mexico continued to have the largest emigrant component of all Latin American groups in the United States, with an estimated foreign-born population of at least 8.8 million. The multinational Central American population, with an estimated 1.948 million people, represents the second largest group of foreign-born residents. Because a significant number of Central Americans clandestinely entered the United States under duress and outside of official channels, it is difficult to generate precise enumerations of the different nationality groups, but the Census Bureau estimates that approximately 765,000 originated in El Salvador, 372,000 in Guatemala, 250,000 in Honduras, and 245,000 in Nicaragua. The 1990s also saw a significant increase in the number of immigrants coming from the Spanish-speaking nations of South America. In 2000, out of a combined population of approximately 1.876 million people (counting Portuguese-speaking Brazilians), the largest numbers of South American immigrants originated in Columbia (435,000), followed by Peru (328,000), Ecuador (281,000), Venezuela (126,000), Argentina (89,000), and Chile (83,000). Of the Spanish-speaking regions of the Caribbean, Cuba (with 952,000) and the Dominican Republic (with 692,000) had the largest foreign-born U.S. populations.[8]

Of course, these new Latin American immigrants have joined a large population of Latino origin or descent already living in the United States. This native-born population has a complex history as well. As noted previously, a small number of Americans of Latin American heritage trace their ancestors to the Spanish colonial era (ca. 1598–1821) and the early Mexican Republic (1821–1848) in the territory that now encompasses the states of Texas, New Mexico, Utah, Colorado, Nevada, Arizona, California, and parts of other states. When these territories were annexed by the United States as the spoils of the U.S.–Mexican War in 1848, the Spanish-speaking residents who came with the conquered lands (numbering somewhere between 75,000 and 100,000) became the first generation of Mexican Americans and thus the foundation of the current pan-Latino population.[9] However, a far larger proportion of the pre-1960 pan-Latino population traces its origins to a series of migrations that occurred at different times over the course of the twentieth century and originated either in Mexico or Puerto Rico. In the Mexican case, the mass movement of migrants into the United States was stimulated by the deepening poverty of the Mexican countryside (which was exacerbated by the increasing domination and resulting reorientation of the Mexican economy by the United States and major European nations) and the concomitant increase in the demand for labor in the American Southwest in the last quarter of the nineteenth century. The eruption of the Mexican Revolution in 1909 and 1910 helped to push hundreds of thousands more Mexicans into the United States. The vast economic disparities between the two nations guaranteed a steady northward influx of laboring migrants over the course of the twentieth century. Indeed, with millions of Mexicans displaced from their lands and wages in the United States ranging anywhere from ten to fifteen times higher than those available in Mexico in the first half of the century—with the exception of the Depression decade of the 1930s, when Mexican migration slowed to a trickle—the mass movement of people north from Mexico that began in the late nineteenth century has continued largely unabated ever since. Largely as a result, the combined population of Mexican Americans and Mexican immigrants in the United States reached approximately 3.5 million by 1960.[10]

For reasons discussed in more detail below, the growth of the Puerto Rican population on the U.S. mainland has even more complicated origins. The acquisition of Puerto Rico after the defeat of Spain in the Spanish–American War of 1898 raised many of the same questions that emerged after the Mexican –American War in the Southwest, but, as in the earlier case, Puerto Rico also became a permanent possession of the United States. After some years of intense political debate, Congress granted Puerto Ricans U.S. citizenship in 1917. Puerto Ricans began migrating to the U.S. in significant numbers soon thereafter, and the movement from the island to the mainland intensified in the years following World War II.[11]

The cumulative effects of the combination of American economic imperialism in Latin America and subsequent migrations from the region can be seen in the exponential growth of the combined Latino population in the last half of the twentieth century. Between 1960 and 1970, the combined pan-Latino population (of all nationalities) grew modestly from just under 7 million, or about 3.9 percent of the U.S. population, to more than 9 million, or about 4.5 percent of the total. By 1980, however, driven by a combination of higher rates of officially sanctioned and unsanctioned migration, high rates of natural increase in the resident population, and significant improvements in population enumeration techniques, the Latino population jumped to at least 14.6 million people. By 1990 the number had grown to 22.35 million. According to the latest estimates, there are now close to 38 million Latinos in the United States, who represent almost 13 percent of the U.S. population. As noted above, in January 2003, the U.S. Census Bureau announced that sometime in 2001, according to its best estimates, the combined Latino population had finally surpassed people of African American descent as the largest aggregate "minority" population in the United States.[12]

Population growth of this magnitude has also significantly affected the spatial distribution of Latinos in the country. Since the nineteenth and early twentieth centuries, most Latinos were located in population clusters in the border states, southern Florida, and the New York and Chicago metropolitan areas. In recent years, however, the population has dispersed to the extent that Latinos can now be found in significant numbers in virtually every state of the union, including Alaska and Hawaii. Ethnic Mexicans, with a combined U.S.-native and foreign-born population of nearly 21 million, or about 58.5 percent of the total, continue to represent the largest subpopulation of U.S. Latinos, though their numbers have gradually dropped a bit in relation to other groups. Reflecting a more general trend among Latinos, in the 1990s significant numbers of ethnic Mexicans began to move away from their traditional concentrations along the U.S.–Mexican border and the western states to new areas—especially the Midwest and Deep South.[13] For example, there are now more than a half million ethnic Mexicans in metropolitan Chicago and more than one million in the state of Illinois. The most remarkable example of the internal migration of ethnic Mexicans, however, has occurred in the American South. Indeed, the highest rate of Mexican population growth between 1990 and 2000 (augmented by smaller numbers of other Latinos) occurred in the American South, where their numbers in many states tripled or even quadrupled.[14]

With a population of at least 3.4 million in 2000 (somewhere between 9 and 10 percent of the total), Puerto Ricans have the second largest Latino subpopulation on the U.S. mainland. Puerto Ricans remain concentrated in New York and in the urban areas of the greater Northeast, but there are now also significant population clusters in Florida, Illinois, and California.[15] The multinational Central American population constitutes the next largest group of Latinos. Like Mexicans, most Central Americans (whose combined numbers represent about 5 percent of the total) live in the West, especially in southern California, but there are also significant population clusters of different nationality groups in Washington, D.C., Miami, New York, the San Francisco Bay area, and Houston, Texas. Following Central Americans, Cubans and Cuban Americans represent the next largest Latino subpopulation. Numbering approximately 952,000 foreign-born and another 360,000 Cuban Americans, their combined population accounts for about 4 percent of the U.S. Latino population. Southern Florida, where the first waves of anti-Castro refugees settled in the early 1960s, still contains 70 percent of the ethnic Cuban population. Dominicans constitute the next-largest Latino subpopulation. The nearly 765,000 Dominicans of native and foreign birth are even more geographically concentrated than Cubans, with the overwhelming majority living in New York, New Jersey, and other northeastern states. Finally, Spanish-speaking U.S. residents of South American origin or heritage, who had an estimated combined population of at least 1.3 million in 2000, tend to be much more dispersed than other Latino groups, although significant concentrations of different nationality groups can be found in traditional areas of pan-Latino concentration such as New York City, Chicago, southern Florida, and California.[16]

These numbers are obviously significant by themselves, but it is also important to note that because of their youth and comparatively high rates of natural increase, the huge number of Latinos currently present in the United States will continue to shape U.S. population growth even if immigration rates decline in the future. In aggregate, the current Latino population is generally much younger than the native U.S. population and as a result has a much higher proportion of individuals in their childbearing years. In 2000, for example, the estimated median age of Latinos was only 25.9 years (24.2 for Mexicans, 27.3 for Puerto Ricans, 29.2 for Central Americans, and 29.5 for Dominicans), compared to a U.S. national median age of more than 35 years.[17] The dramatic effects of this age disparity can already be seen. Although Latinos currently constitute only about 13 percent of the U.S. population, in 2001 they already accounted for almost 20 percent of all U.S. births. Another way to look at the engine of demographic growth and change is to examine the structure of American families. According to a recent U.S. Census Bureau study, two-thirds of all Latino families with at least one foreign-born member reported having children in their households, compared to only 48 percent for families whose members were all U.S.-born.

As a result of these built-in multiplier effects at the national level, even the most cautious demographic forecasters see the pan-Latino population growing to at least one-quarter of the total population of the United States by the middle of the twenty-first century. In states with the largest concentrations of immigrant populations—California (with 26 percent of its total population), New York (19.8 percent), Florida (18.4 percent), and Texas (12.2 percent)—demographic projections are even more dramatic. In California, the state with the largest number of immigrants, the dramatically growing demographic weight of Latino children is seen with each passing year. In a state whose economy produces one-seventh of the total economic output of the United States and that also has the highest numbers of Latinos (rapidly approaching one-third of the state's total population), Latino children of all nationalities already constitute more than half of the school-age population—and this percentage will continue to rise sharply for the foreseeable future. Another recent report revealed that as of 4 July 2001, more than half of all newborns in California were Latino. And overall in 1999, the proportion of what the Census Bureau terms the "non-Hispanic white" population of California dropped below 50 percent for the first time since the era of the Gold Rush. If current demographic trends hold, it is conservatively estimated that fully half of the Golden State's population will be of Latino origin or descent by the year 2040.[18]

DEBATES OVER CONCEPTUALIZATION AND INTERPRETATION

While it is clear to most informed observers that a demographic transformation of this magnitude has to be considered one of the great social developments in both modern U.S. history and the broader history of the Western Hemisphere, scholars, social critics, policy makers, and ordinary people are deeply divided in their views about the ultimate significance of these trends. Indeed, depending on which end of the spectrum of interpretation one hears, these demographic developments are seen either as the latest chapter in a long and essentially benign history of immigration to the United States, and thus not really a matter of concern over the long term, or, conversely, as a chilling manifestation of a radical shift in international relations that portends even greater demographic and negative economic change—and profound social instability—for the foreseeable future. The radical difference between these points of view speaks both to the complexity and peculiarity of the long, uneasy relationship between the United States and Latin America and to the difficulties scholars face in interpreting the historical trajectory and broad social implications of that complex and uneven relationship. Thus, while it might seem that the dramatic growth of the pan-Latino population of the United States between 1960 and the beginning of the twenty-first century provides a completely compelling rationale for a book of this type, it is critical to note that enough disagreement exists about the putative subject of "Latino studies" to compel careful explication of the evolution of the debate about how best to conceptualize and characterize the recent history of U.S. residents of Latin American origin or descent.[19]

Much of the current debate over how best to analyze this diverse population derives from the complex colonial and postcolonial history of Spanish-speaking people in the Western Hemisphere. On the one hand, Latinos in the United States obviously are bound by a number of powerful historical and cultural ties. For example, Latinos share a Spanish-language heritage (despite the fact that many indigenous peoples in Latin America speak Spanish as a second language and a significant minority of U.S.-born Latinos do not speak Spanish at all[20]); a complicated and controversial legacy of both genetic and cultural creolization and *mestizaje* (a melding over the 500 years since initial contact of European, African, and indigenous gene pools and cultural traits and practices); a Christian tradition (largely Roman Catholic, but increasingly sectarian Protestant)[21]; and a common, if uneven history of national liberation from Spanish imperialism. Both native- and foreign-born Latinos also share a critical legacy in contending with the effects of a long history of U.S. imperialism in the hemisphere—and the integrally related experience of varying degrees of discrimination in the United States.

The importance of these last two factors should not be underestimated. Dating almost from the creation of the United States, the general attitude of government officials and much of the American public toward Latin America has been, at best, one of ignorance and, at worst, one of disdain, if not outright animus. Born out of a long historical tradition of white supremacy in the United States and the huge economic disparities that have always distinguished the "Colossus of the North" from the nations of Latin America, over time this rather casual and informal sense of American disregard and disrespect toward Latin America gradually ossified into a much harder system of invidious stereotypes about individual Latin American nations and their institutions and about Latin American people and their cultures more generally. With Americans accustomed to deeply engrained ideologies of white supremacy, a highly developed sense of their own nation's cultural and economic superiority, and an almost evangelical sense of mission toward other nations of the world, it had become second nature by the middle of the nineteenth century for both individuals of influence and much of the general public to attribute Latin American poverty, political instability, and general economic and infrastructural underdevelopment to what was widely perceived and argued to be the fundamental racial and cultural inferiority of Latin Americans themselves. It was no coincidence that such attitudes also tended to mesh well with American desires to dominate the economic and political affairs of the Western Hemisphere. By the turn of the century, the North American nation's increasing economic and political domination of the hemisphere was widely viewed as a foregone conclusion and, indeed, as a "natural" outgrowth of the superiority of the American "race"—and of American institutions, the American way of doing things, the American way of life.[22]

Such attitudes were manifest both in the patterns of American investment and business practices and in the closely related history of U.S. military interventions in the region during the nineteenth century. For example, although the United States' military conquest of Mexico's northern territories in 1848 was justified at the time (and has largely been explained away today) by boosters of the ideology of the United States' "Manifest Destiny," most historians now view the war with Mexico as part of the same imperial impulse that undergirded the nation's deep involvement with the institution of slavery and the systematic despoliation of indigenous peoples that occurred incident to "westward expansion."[23]

The history of the United States' relationship with Puerto Rico is perhaps even more telling in this regard. While the Spanish–American War of 1898 has been the subject of a long tradition of critical historical analysis that dates to the era of the war itself, there is an equally long tradition of explaining and justifying the imperial adventure that resulted in the permanent or expediently temporary annexation of Puerto Rico, the Philippines, Guam, and Cuba as part of the burden a reluctant United States had to bear as an emerging world power.

Faced suddenly with an overseas empire that stretched over several thousand miles, the United States government confronted monumental questions involving, among other things, budgetary considerations and constraints, the issue of its own extraterritorial constitutional authority, and most of all, the best means to administer far-flung colonies whose populations differed fundamentally from the United States in language, culture, and political traditions. In the case of Puerto Rico, at least, the territorial issues at hand were fairly straightforward. The island of Puerto Rico was ceded to the United

States after Spain's defeat in 1898 (along with the Philippines, Guam, and the Northern Marianas). After intensive debate between imperialist and anti-imperialist interests in the Congress, American leaders decided that maintaining permanent sovereignty over the fractious Philippines was untenable, but they made it clear that Puerto Rico would remain in the American political, economic, and military orbit. But the questions surrounding the eventual disposition of the *inhabitants* of Spain's former territories were much more complicated. This was particularly the case with Puerto Rico.

During the debate that unfolded in the years immediately following annexation, the U.S. Supreme Court weighed in on these questions in a famous series of decisions that collectively became known as the "Insular Cases." To the present day, legal scholars continue to analyze the ultimate constitutional, political-philosophical, and moral implications of these complex, even arcane, decisions, but with regard to Puerto Rico, the Court was fairly clear. The Court ruled that since Puerto Rico had been acquired by the United States as what the justices deemed an "unincorporated territory" of the United States, the inhabitants of Puerto Rico had *not* gained full protection of the Constitution (even though they had become American "nationals" once the island was annexed) and were entitled only to those rights explicitly granted them by the U.S. Congress.[24]

Although the executive branch and most members of Congress apparently believed that the permanent annexation of the territories implied that their inhabitants would eventually become American citizens, the Court's decision in the Insular Cases established once again that the formal legal status of U.S. citizenship did not necessarily mean the same thing for everyone. Citing the "plenary power" granted Congress by the Constitution (in general, the power the Constitution bestows on Congress to regulate commerce and establish the "rules of membership" both within the borders of the United States and in any territories subsequently acquired by the nation), the Court ruled that Congress had virtually unlimited authority to determine what the content and quality of citizenship status would entail.[25] Thus, even though Congress eventually decided to grant Puerto Ricans U.S. citizenship in 1917, it was clear from the outset that virtually no one in Congress envisioned granting the mixed-race, Spanish-speaking Puerto Rican population rights equal to those enjoyed by white Americans. In fact, as one of the leaders of the debate in the Senate put it at the time, most members of Congress intended to grant Puerto Ricans "only those rights the American people want[ed] them to have."[26] In other words, the congressional leaders who pushed through the citizenship legislation apparently envisioned that the citizenship extended to Puerto Ricans would have the same second-class quality and content that had been bestowed on Mexican Americans in the aftermath of the Mexican War nearly seventy years before. One of the foremost scholars of the convoluted history of Puerto Rican citizenship puts the issue clearly:

> By bestowing citizenship upon the inhabitants of the island, Congress proclaimed the future of Puerto Rico to be something other than national independence and thereby sought to resolve the question of how the United States would deal with this part of its empire. Accordingly, the citizenship granted was not complete . . . The very word "citizenship" suggested equality of rights and privileges and full membership in the American political community, thereby obscuring the colonial relationship between a great metropolitan state and a poor overseas dependency. But the creation of a second-class citizenship for a community of persons that was given no expectation of equality under the American system had the effect of perpetuating the colonial status of Puerto Rico.[27]

Thus, while the Congressional leaders who granted U.S. citizenship to Puerto Ricans recognized the strategic importance of the island and desired to effect control over its material resources, they were intent on establishing dominion over the island without having to deal with the daily administrative details over what was widely perceived as yet another potentially troublesome "race problem." After more than a century of American domination of Puerto Rican affairs, the ambiguous current "commonwealth" status of Puerto Rico demonstrates that the colonial relationship established at the turn of the twentieth century continues to a significant extent to the present day. Obviously not an independent nation, but neither a state of the federal union, Puerto Rico remains in a kind of juridical limbo.[28]

But just as the annexation of what is now the American Southwest in the 1840s almost immediately exposed the exquisite contradictions and profound inequities inherent in the extension of formal citizenship to a large number of nonwhite people in the nineteenth century, the inherent contradictions of the United States' actions in Puerto Rico quickly became apparent in the early years of the twentieth. Indeed, one of the lasting ironies of the government's action at the time was that even though congressional leaders obviously expected to be able to control Puerto Rico as an insulated colonial possession, another Supreme Court ruling soon revealed the Pandora's box that Congress had opened by extending what it had thought to be an inferior brand of citizenship to the island's inhabitants. Nearly a decade after the last of the Insular Cases, the Court ruled in the case *Balzac v. Porto Rico* (1922) that while it was true that Puerto Ricans on the island did not have the same constitutional standing as "ordinary" U.S. citizens (based again on the logic that Congress had ultimate authority to decide what specific rights people in unincorporated territories were to enjoy), the Congress's conferral of citizenship on Puerto Ricans automatically also allowed them the unfettered right to migrate to the continental United States. More importantly, the Court ruled further in *Balzac* that, *once there*, Puerto Ricans were eligible "to enjoy every right of any other citizen of the United States, civil, social, and political."[29] Thus once again, as in the Mexican American case, despite the best efforts of political leaders to impose strict controls on the subordinate populations acquired through conquest, the labyrinthine logic of American law inadvertently opened up to those populations both the right of unrestricted movement within U.S. territory and potential avenues of resistance and redress as U.S. citizens.

Puerto Ricans soon took advantage of this ironic oversight by exercising one of the most basic rights of American citizenship—that of free movement within the territorial boundaries of the United States and its possessions. Consequently, beginning soon after the 1922 ruling, but especially after the Great Depression, increasing numbers of Puerto Ricans began moving to the continent. Slowly growing from just 11,811 in 1920, the number of Puerto Ricans on the U.S. mainland jumped to almost 70,000 in 1940 and to 226,000 just ten years later.[30] By the 1960s, spurred by the massive social dislocations caused by the economic restructuring of Puerto Rico under the U.S. government's "Operation Bootstrap" (a massive social welfare program designed to stimulate economic development and blunt the effects of Cuban-style socialism in the Caribbean), huge numbers were moving in both directions between the island and the mainland. Indeed, as Kelvin Santiago-Valles and Gladys Jiménez-Muñoz note in their contribution to this volume, circular migration between the island and the mainland during this juncture eventually became such a central part of Puerto Rican life that by 2000, the number of Puerto Ricans living in each locale was comparable, with about 3.4 million residing on the continent and 3.9 million living on the island.[31]

THE "BIG STICK": THE IMPACT OF U.S. FOREIGN POLICY AFTER 1898

The Puerto Rican case is perhaps the most dramatic example of the gulf between intentions and outcomes in U.S.–Latin American affairs, but American business practices and U.S. leaders' consistently heavy-handed applications in Latin America of the Monroe Doctrine (and Theodore Roosevelt's famous "corollary" to it) have had similarly mixed, and often unintended historical results. As it was applied over the course of the twentieth century, the political logic of the Roosevelt Corollary—especially his assertion that the United States had the inherent right "to the exercise of an international police power" in the Western Hemisphere—was similar to U.S. actions vis-à-vis Puerto Rico.[32] Based on an abiding faith that as the dominant political, military, and economic power in the hemisphere, the United States had the right not only to bar interference by other world powers but to unilaterally meddle in the internal affairs of virtually any nation in the Western Hemisphere, the Roosevelt Corollary to the Monroe Doctrine has been the bedrock of U.S. policy toward Latin America for more than a century. Indeed, in the view of one prominent historian of U.S.–Latin American affairs, the policies followed by Roosevelt and subsequent American administrations in the Western Hemisphere have long served as the basic general template of U.S. foreign relations and "exemplified [many of the] central themes of post-1890 U.S. foreign policy—a willingness to use force to obtain order, an emphasis on a special U.S. responsibility to guarantee stability in Latin America and Asia, and a belief that Anglo-Saxon values and successes gave Americans a right to conduct such foreign policy."[33]

Following what has long since become an all too familiar logic, and despite the many dissenting voices raised over time both in Latin America and within the United States, the regional political manipulation and direct U.S. military intervention behind the eventual annexation of the Panama Canal Zone, at least two major American military incursions into Mexico during the Mexican Revolution, and a long series of other military interventions in Cuba, the Dominican Republic, Haiti, Honduras, El Salvador, Nicaragua, and elsewhere have been similarly explained away as the unfortunate necessity of a great and benevolent power finding it reluctantly necessary to impose order and the rule of law over people who obviously were unable to do this for themselves and, worse, who were seen as standing in the way of the inevitable march of world civilization. More recent interventions in Latin America, ranging from the CIA-orchestrated Guatemalan coup of 1954 under Eisenhower, the Bay of Pigs debacle in 1961 under Kennedy, the landing of U.S. Marines in the Dominican Republic in 1965 under Johnson, the violent overthrow of Salvador Allende's government in a coup in 1973 under Nixon and Henry Kissinger, and the sordid string of overt and covert U.S. interventions in Central America during the Reagan administration, have been couched in official circles in much the same way, with the additional rationale, of course, that the U.S. was now also combating the spread of communism in the Western Hemisphere. As will be discussed below, since the 1970s and 1980s the United States' neoliberal economic policies and other dimensions of "globalization" have been explained (or explained away) in similar terms.[34]

The combined effects of nearly two centuries of such policies and practices have been felt with brutal force by ordinary Latin American people, but the most insidious long-term legacy of this imperial tradition may well be the extent to which the constant exertion of U.S. power in Latin America has influenced perception (and thus subsequent analysis) by perpetuating the negative stereotypes of Latin Americans and, by extension, of U.S. Latinos. Just as earlier examples of the systematic conceptual reduction of different indigenous groups to a generic category—first "Indians" and then the similar rendering of individual enslaved African peoples to the category "Negro" (or worse)—had the long-term effect on popular thought of both stripping people of color of their individuality, cultural distinctiveness, and internal differences *and* largely erasing them from the American polity, American imperial practices in the Western Hemisphere have had a similar effect in obliterating Latin Americans' national and cultural differences and transforming them into an internally indistinguishable, racialized population that is, by definition, inferior to the people of the United States (or more accurately, the "white" population of the United States).[35]

But just as American society's attempts to deal with the legacies of slavery and the decimation of indigenous peoples created deep contradictions and festering long-term tensions in American social and political life, the incorporation of large numbers of Latinos into the United States established similarly ambiguous and socially destabilizing legacies. As has already been seen, the clearest example of this was the bestowal of U.S. citizenship on ethnic Mexicans and, later, Puerto Ricans. In a society in which for much of its history the rights of full citizenship were reserved only to those deemed members of the "white race," the granting of U.S. citizenship in 1848 and again in 1917 to people who clearly were *not* white muddled the categorical definitions and labels that were critical in determining the shape and reproduction of the American social hierarchy.[36] Over the long run, the presence of Mexican American citizens, and later, the extension of citizenship to Puerto Ricans, helped to confound the extant American racial hierarchy by providing glaring exceptions to a system of formal membership that had long been based on deeply held notions of white superiority. Bestowal of formal national citizenship clearly did not—nor does it now—guarantee equal rights or equal opportunity in a social system that is otherwise predicated on the autonomous workings of global capitalism, but despite the best efforts of legislators to maintain the racial hierarchy of the United States, the mere presence of Latinos as permanent members of American society simply deepened the contradictions of their status in the United States, and provided subsequent grounds for the intensification of political activism among them.

Since the 1960s, the tensions and contradictions created by these circumstances have played out in new ways in different arenas. On the one hand, the federal government and local authorities have been compelled to contend with the increasing political agitation by various groups of Latinos—especially Mexican Americans, Puerto Ricans, and Cubans—to have their particular political concerns and needs as American citizens addressed. In this manner, these groups—and, lately, Latino groups of more recent origin in the United States—have had real incentive to organize themselves as "ethnic Americans" of Latin American descent (or, as the government has labeled them, as "Hispanics").[37] Thus, in the 1960s and 1970s the passage of voting-rights legislation, the establishment of bilingual/bicultural educational programs and the institution of other curriculum reforms in public education, demands for the extension of affirmative action programs in the workplace and in higher education, and the founding of centers for Chicano, Puerto Rican, Cuban, and pan-Latino studies in certain locales in the United States all speak to the growing numbers and increasing political influence of U.S. citizens of Latino descent. Similarly, the creation of increasingly powerful ethnic lobby and advocacy groups such as the League of United Latin American Citizens (LULAC), the National Council of La Raza, the Congressional Hispanic Caucus, the National Association of Latino Elected and Appointed Officials (NALEO), the Mexican American Legal Defense and Education Fund (MALDEF), and the Puerto Rican Defense and Education Fund are also powerful manifestations of the ongoing corporate organization and political mobilization of different groups of Latinos. These trends also reveal the complicated ways in which the lure of American consumerism and the power of traditional structures of American race relations have combined to encourage members of otherwise disparate groups to conceive of themselves, organize, and make claims against the state as aggrieved "minorities" within the U.S. polity.[38]

THE DIVERSITY OF LATINO POPULATIONS

On the other hand, however, it is critical to remember that despite all their common cultural bonds, the similarities of their experience of American imperialism and capitalism abroad, and their common, intrinsically linked experiences of systematic discrimination once within the boundaries of the United States, the pan-Latino population has never been politically or socially monolithic—indeed, the population is today more diverse than at any point in modern history. This internal heterogeneity, which can be seen across a broad range of variables, thus must also be taken into account in any attempt to conceptualize and analyze the collective histories and contemporary experiences of the rapidly growing pan-Latino population of the United States. It also raises profound questions both about the likelihood that Latinos are necessarily destined to coalesce into a self-conscious, pan-ethnic political force that cuts across class lines—and about their future relationships with communities and countries of origin in Latin America.[39]

Latino heterogeneity has played out in a variety of ways in recent history. For example, simply assessing the different dates of entry into the United States of the various Latino subpopulations often reveals much about their current cultural preferences and practices, class standing, median age and fertility rates, levels of education and language proficiency, political orientations and general sense of position within American society, and a broad range of other factors. As mentioned above, the vast majority of Latinos—especially Mexicans, but smaller numbers of other groups as well—trace their families' histories to one of many economically motivated migrations that have occurred over the past hundred years, and their varied political and cultural orientations and attitudes reflect that long and complicated history. Another significant, although much smaller group traces its forebears' presence in territory that is now the United States to the Spanish colonial era of the seventeenth and eighteenth centuries and the California Gold Rush of the 1840s and 1850s. More recently, an even less remarked immigrant group comprises the increasing number of "mixed-heritage" and indigenous peoples from Mexico and Central America—such as the Garifuna, various groups of Afro-Latinos, and a huge array of native peoples ranging from different groups of Mayan peoples to Zapotecs, Mixtecs, Purépechas, Tarahumaras, Yaquis, Miskitos, and many other *indígenas* who have migrated from Mexico and Central America. While members of all these groups are technically "Latino" by dint of their nationalities (that is, as formal citizens of Mexico, Guatemala, Honduras, El Salvador, and so on), they often speak Spanish as a second language (if at all) and can be as profoundly alienated from the dominant societies of their home countries as they are from that of the United States. The same can be said of the smaller numbers of different Quechua- and Aymara-speaking peoples who have recently migrated to the United States from Andean South America.[40]

Once established in the United States, the tremendously diverse origins, social histories, and primary cultural orientations of all these groups have created tensions and fissures between and among the various Latino subpopulations that often override their many commonalities and affinities. That Latin Americans can be of any nationality, ethnicity, or class standing and that they range phenotypically from "white," "black," "brown," "Asian," "Indian," and any combination of these adds both to the confusion and potential sources of tension in the pan-Latino population in the U.S. context. At the same time, however, the constant social admixtures over the years of immigrant Latinos with one another, of native-born Americans of Latino descent with each other and with newer immigrants, and, of course, of Latinos with "non-Latinos" often create rich ground for comity, exchange, and partnering—especially in the bustling, pan-Latino communities of places like New York City, Washington, D.C., Miami, Chicago, Houston, Los Angeles, and San Francisco. Commenting on the many layers and complexities that both natives and immigrants face as they mingle and build evolving communities in the United States, one observer has recently noted that in such contexts,

> similarities and differences meet, and the result is an unusually complex common sense, in which people are forced to move from one [identity] classification system and one sense of narrative plot to another, sometimes on a daily basis. Not only do people move from one system or set to another, but the proliferation of classification systems and narrative plots within which a single person can be placed means that people constantly mix different systems and plots to make sense of the perceived "other."[41]

Indeed, the ways in which different groups of U.S.-native and immigrant Latinos react—and are allowed to react—to the traditional processes of racialization and what might be termed "minoritization" in the American political context constitute one of the great unanswered questions raised by the explosive growth of the pan-Latino population. In other words, how their own senses of personal and collective identity and "race" interact with the powerful socializing forces of life in the United States will undoubtedly be a source of tension between Latinos and non-Latinos (as has already been seen in cities where large Latino and African American populations come into contact)—and among Latinos themselves. The constant dynamic tension between peoples who share such deep cultural affinities and otherwise have so much else in common adds yet another dimension to an ever more complicated social, cultural, and political matrix. For the foreseeable future, making sense of this complexity will be one of the major challenges facing scholars of Latinos—and socially and politically aware people both in the United States and Latin America.[42]

Of course, on yet another level, analysis and interpretation of this great Latino drama of displacement, physical mobility, settlement, and continuous demographic combination and recombination has been deeply colored and further complicated by the ideological and conceptual legacies of the larger history of immigration to the United States—and of the powerful tropes of "assimilation" and the great American "melting pot" that have been central components of American national mythology since the days of Tocqueville and Crevecoeur. Most scholars of immigration and ethnicity have largely rejected the once-dominant paradigm of "straight-line assimilation"—the idea that immigrants and their children slowly but surely "lose" their original cultures and replace them with "American" (read "United Statesian") values and orientations on their way to the socioeconomic and national political "mainstream." But to the present day, the powerfully homogenizing notion of assimilation obviously maintains a central place in both official discourse and popular thinking about immigration to the United States. In many ways, the continuing power of such notions is understandable. Part an ideological prescription about what *should* happen to immigrants and part a quasi-empirical, modernist description about what historically *has* happened to immigrants, this centerpiece of American national mythology has become, in the apt words of one scholar, "an enduring talisman of the American dream."[43] Given the centrality in the popular imagination and official discourse of the United States as an egalitarian "nation of immigrants," such deeply rooted assumptions about the appropriate mechanisms involved in the social, economic, and political incorporation of immigrants and "ethnics" speak not only to the presumed social trajectory of immigrants and their children but, on a much more profound level, to fundamental beliefs about the very nature and character of U.S. society.

But once again, the rapid growth of the increasingly heterogeneous pan-Latino population of all national, ethnic, class, and phenotypical combinations over the past forty years—some circulating through U.S. territory and some settling permanently—has threatened what one social critic has called the "American gospel" about what has happened historically and what is likely to happen to immigrant and ethnic populations in the future.[44] The debates currently simmering in American politics over volatile issues ranging from affirmative action, to bilingual education, reparations for slavery, and the very definition of both "race" and "culture" in contemporary American life are all emblematic of these fears and tensions.[45] Needless to say, the events of September 11, 2001, have heightened these fears for many people. The contemporary salience of the analytical and ideological tensions created by the uncertainty about whether the pan-Latino population will meld into American society in the manner most Americans like to think previous generations of immigrants did, or whether, because of their large numbers, their proximity to their countries of origin, and the degree of their cultural differences, they are destined to change American society in unfamiliar and potentially irrevocable ways, will be one of the central political and social questions of the twenty-first century.

As the different perspectives informing the essays in this volume indicate, the history of Latinos over the past forty years has probably done more to sharpen these questions than to answer them. On the one hand, as mentioned previously, some argue that Latinos are on a social trajectory that is, in the main, similar to previous immigrant and ethnic groups. From this standpoint, it is only a matter of time before members of the current Latino population and their U.S.-born children become part of the "mainstream" of American life. To support this thesis, proponents point to clear signs that a small but significant segment of the Latino population has entered the American middle class, a trend that some observers argue represents an indication of ongoing Latino integration into the American bourgeoisie, if not full-blown sociocultural assimilation into society as "Americans." Some socioeconomic and popular cultural trends seem to support this view, if only tentatively. For example, despite the economic recession of the first years of the new millennium, it *is* apparent that dimensions of American life for some segments of the Latino population appear to have changed dramatically for the better. Latino entrepreneurship is booming. Advertisers are increasingly committed to tapping into a rapidly expanding Latino consumer market segment that is currently estimated to be well in excess of $500 billion per year. Spanish-language media networks are also expanding, and a variety of Latino artists, writers, entertainers, and athletes ranging from Sandra Cisneros, Richard Rodríguez, Oscar Hijuelos, and Victor Villaseñor in literature; John Leguízamo, Carlos Santana, Los Lobos, Jennifer López, Ricky Martin, Christina Aguilera, Shakira, and the late Selena in the entertainment industry; to Oscar de la Hoya, Sammy Sosa, and Alex Rodríguez in professional sports, have obviously garnered the attention of and "crossed over" to a broad and growing audience that includes Latinos and increasing numbers of "non-Latinos" as well.[46]

More general socioeconomic data indicate that at least some ordinary Latinos are also reaping the material benefits of these trends. For example, according to U.S. Census data, median Latino household income reached $31,663 in 1999, the highest level ever recorded.[47] Depending on the income and occupational definitions used, other studies have suggested that anywhere between 23 and 30 percent of the Latino population has attained what the government defines as middle-class status, with 14 percent holding managerial or professional jobs, which, if true, represents a huge leap from the 1960s.[48] Nationwide, the 2000 census also reported that Latino home ownership rates rose from about 41 percent in 1990 to 46 percent in 2000.[49] Some go further to suggest that Latinos' racial self-identification provides another bit of evidence indicating a general trend toward "assimilation." For example, when queried about their "race" in the 2000 census, almost 48 percent of Latinos surveyed identified themselves as "white." While it is difficult to cull from such raw census data precisely what respondents meant by this response, and whether they correlate their racial self-image with a sense of increasing integration into American society, the response does raise questions about the extent to which at least some Latinos consider themselves a "racial minority" in the traditional American sense of the term.[50] This issue is, of course, complicated further as increasing numbers of the Latin American educated, technically trained elite (primarily from South American nations, but with smaller numbers from other countries as well) come to the United States to work and live. How such individuals—and their U.S.-born children—choose to sustain a relationship with their countries of origin (if they do at all) and situate themselves vis-à-vis U.S. Latinos and other social segments of the receiving society remain some of the more intriguing unanswered questions in Latino research.[51]

On the other hand, however, many scholars and social critics have argued that to focus primarily on elite migrants and the upwardly mobile segments of the resident pan-Latino population and to infer from the experience of this small group that Latinos are on a collective trajectory toward "assimilation" is to ignore the fact that the vast majority of both native-born and immigrant Latinos continue to toil in the bottom rungs of what has steadily become a more internationally integrated, but increasingly segmented and starkly polarized economy. And, as Arlene Dávila has pointed out in a series of important recent studies, the ongoing commodification and "multicultural encompassment" of Latinos as part of the American consumer marketing juggernaut has added even more layers of mystification to the true socioeconomic straits and prospects of most Latinos in the United States.[52] Adherents of this critical point of view tend to advance a much different kind of argument, insisting instead that globalization has blurred the distinction between the "domestic" and "international" economies to the detriment of working populations on both sides of the frontier dividing the "developed" world from the "developing" world. Indeed, some have gone so far as to argue that the integration of labor markets across national borders, the related trend toward the "outsourcing" of manufacturing and assembly processes to workers in "Third World" nations, and the general expansion of the so-called informal or gray economy (that is, licit and illicit economic activities that occur outside regulation of the state) have had the long-term effect of moving the border between the United States and Latin America northward, as millions of Spanish-speaking workers *on both sides of the border* toil for poverty-level wages in a radically restructured global economy.[53]

The blurring of the distinctions between "citizen" and "alien" caused by the emergence and elaboration of the new international division of labor that has crystallized in recent years can readily be seen on another plane in the rapid expansion of so-called "mixed status" families in the United States. Indeed, for many years now it has not been at all uncommon to find officially unsanctioned "illegal" immigrants, legally sanctioned "permanent resident aliens," individuals on tourist or student visas, and U.S. citizens (either native-born or naturalized) all living in the same neighborhoods and, in some cases, under the same roof, and this trend obviously intensified during the 1990s. Given the jumbling together of people of all these statuses caused by the massive movement and settlement of populations within and across national borders, this development is not all that surprising. As in previous periods of mass global migration, as large numbers of immigrants settled in communities in the United States and elsewhere in the world, they naturally formed bonds of friendship and sociability, established business and romantic partnerships, and eventually produced offspring. Although not readily visible, this ongoing social process of partnering between "aliens" and "natives" inevitably complicated population demographics and contributed to an even greater jumbling and erosion of a system of categories that otherwise has long been based on the fundamental legal and political distinction between "citizens" (that is, individuals considered to be legally vested members of the American polity) and those who, by dint of their birth and noncitizen status, are considered "outsiders"—no matter how long they have lived in the United States. In the post–September 11 political environment of the nation, the tensions associated with such arrangements have almost certainly increased and, depending on how the U.S. government eventually decides to deal with the presence of large numbers of noncitizens in American territory, may well develop into something of political crisis in the not so distant future.[54]

The growing significance of the implosion of the underdeveloped world into the developed world can be seen in other ways as well. For example, the rate of Latino poverty is double that of the general population and has persisted at roughly that same level for more than a quarter century.[55] Latinos in aggregate experienced some slight socioeconomic gains in the boom years of the early 1990s, but in 2000 nearly one-quarter of all Latino heads-of-household earned income that placed their families below the U.S. poverty line (defined by the federal government as $17,463 per year for a family of four).[56] Children are particularly hard hit by the stubborn persistence of poverty in Latino communities. In 1993, more than 53 percent of all Puerto Rican children and 40 percent of children of Mexican origin or descent lived in poverty, and the poverty rate may actually have worsened since then.[57]

The negative cascading effects of such material circumstances are manifest in a number of related areas of Latino life. For example, life under such materially and socially impoverished circumstances has obviously exerted negative pressure on the educational opportunities and potential academic achievement of Latino students. High school dropout rates for both Latino immigrants and U.S.-born Latino students are a national disgrace, approaching 50 percent in many areas. In 2000, 43 percent of all Latinos had not graduated high school and less than 11 percent of all Latinos had graduated college (compared to 85 and 26 percent, respectively, of the non-Hispanic white population).[58] As a result of low levels of education, marketable job skills, and other forms of "social capital," Latinos unsurprisingly remain tremendously overrepresented in low-skilled occupations in what increasingly has become a restructured "hourglass" economy. For example, in 1990, when Latinos represented about 9 percent of the U.S. labor force, Latinos made up 13 percent of all service workers, more than 14 percent of the unskilled and semiskilled operator, fabricator, and laborer category, more than one-fifth of all busboys, and fully 40 percent of all farm workers. The Latino occupational distribution is strongly gendered as well: in 1990, nearly 27 percent of all sewing machine operators and one-quarter of all domestic workers were Latina.[59]

More critically, evidence indicates that low levels of educational attainment, placement in dead-end occupations, and the general poverty associated with life in the growing Latino underclass is not only persisting in the immigrant population but is being inherited by the second, third, and even fourth generations of Latino Americans. That such circumstances do not simply reflect the skewing effects of large numbers of recent immigrants, observers (including Santiago-Valles and Jiménez-Muñoz, in this volume) note that the socioeconomic profile of Puerto Ricans, who, as discussed above, have been U.S. citizens for nearly a century, is even worse than the general Latino population—whether they are long-term mainland residents or recently arrived from the island.

The stubborn persistence of poverty and the disturbing indications that impoverished conditions are being handed down from one generation to the next have thus caused at least some analysts to argue for a significant reconsideration of the applicability of the traditional American immigration paradigm to the Latino population. Although scholars continue to disagree about the specific lines of causation, a growing body of research indicates that while assimilation has been occurring for immigrants and their children, the process of assimilation is now very different from the mechanisms of adaptation that Americans traditionally have associated with the term. According to the theory of "segmented assimilation" developed over the past decade or so by Princeton sociologist Alejandro Portes and his colleagues, recent working-class immigrants—particularly those of color—confront a changing, segmented American economy (that itself has been shaped by the restructuring of the global economy) in which the overwhelming majority enters the lowest strata and tends to stay there over time. According to this theory of social inequality, because recent working-class immigrants enter an evolving economic structure that has been harshly polarized between low-skilled, low-status, low-paid occupations at the bottom, and very high-skilled, high-status, and comparatively high-paid technical and professional occupations in the upper rungs, the disadvantages immigrants bring with them tend to be reproduced in daily life. Since so many are trapped in blighted urban neighborhoods, immigrants and their children subsequently become enmeshed in a cycle of poverty that tends to reinforce itself over time and thus negatively influences the life chances of even the U.S.-born. Needless to say, habituation to this kind of dead-end social position has obvious negative effects on social attitudes and on the propensity of Latinos to participate and the character of their participation in the legal system, electoral politics, and other institutions of American life.[60] As one scholar describes this process of "dissonant acculturation":

> When [immigrants] enter the bottom of the ethnic hierarchy of drastic social inequality, the forces of assimilation come mainly from the [existing] underprivileged segments of this structure, and this is likely to result in distinct disadvantages, viewed as maladjustment by both mainstream society and the ethnic community. Such contextual differences mean that the paths to social mobility may lead to upward as well as downward outcomes. In the case of those that start from the very bottom, of course, the outcome is not so much assimilating downward as staying where they are.[61]

Many observers have responded to such arguments by insisting that if Latin American and other immigration were more strictly controlled and the economies of "sending nations" improved, then many of these negative structural features would dissipate over time. Clearly, there is something to this argument, since demographic and social capital factors such as nativity, language proficiency, education and job-skill levels, citizenship status, and length of residence in the United States all obviously influence individuals' opportunities in an economy that is increasingly polarized between high-skilled occupations requiring extensive education and low-skilled jobs requiring little or no formal training. According to 2000 census estimates, a huge proportion of the Latino population (40 percent) is foreign-born and of very recent residence in the United States: at least 43 percent of the total foreign-born Latino population entered the country in the 1990s and another 29.7 percent entered in the 1980s. Of this large group of recent immigrants, only 23.9 percent of those who entered between 1980 and 1989 and 6.7 percent of those who entered between 1990 and 2000 had become naturalized citizens of the United States.[62] Largely because of this skewed demographic structure (and because of the comparative youth of Latinos), it is estimated that fully 60 percent of the entire resident Latino population is not eligible to vote in U.S. elections.[63]

But again, analysis focusing primarily or exclusively on immigrants as individuals has a strong tendency to "blame the victim" rather than casting light on the increasingly complex structural relationship between transnational migration and the ongoing reconfiguration of the hemispheric and global economies under neoliberal principles, thus distorting what is actually a much larger and more complicated set of issues.[64] For example, while it has been tempting to many recent analysts to attribute the current structural position of working-class Latinos to the downward pressure immigrants exert on aggregate socioeconomic conditions in the United States, it is important to consider immigrants and the entire process of transnational migration in the appropriate regional and global contexts. Since World War II, and especially since the early 1970s, transnational migration has occurred in an increasingly enmeshed hemispheric and global context in which markets, capital investment, technology, production processes and facilities, communication and transportation systems, and labor sources have become functionally integrated under "free market" principles established by global capitalists, often directed by American corporate interests in partnership with the U.S. government. Such globalizing practices have had decidedly mixed results for the developing nations of Latin America and the Caribbean. They have been implemented and are currently pursued in the name of international economic development, which in theory should help to suppress the outflow of immigrants. But in reality, the long-term effect of neoliberal policies and practices since the 1970s in developing nations such as those in Latin America has been to reconfigure their economies in a manner that tends to stimulate both migrations *within* nations (usually from rural to urban areas) and, eventually, *across* international boundaries. As César Gaviria, the secretary-general of the Organization of American States, recently put it after meeting with U.S. Secretary of State Colin Powell, "Clearly, we live in a time when not only has our economic growth been seriously hampered, but also more and more questions are raised about how our governments should act to overcome such obstacles. It has surely been a mistake to have believed that development is determined solely by economic factors."[65]

The result of the convergence of these powerful forces has been to set millions of people in motion over the past forty years. Moreover, by encouraging and sometimes absolutely compelling people to move in order to survive, neoliberal economic policies and practices have laid the foundations for the establishment and maintenance of even more deeply rooted transnational circuits and networks that tie communities in the United States to communities hundreds and even thousands of miles away in Mexico, the Caribbean, and Central and South America. Over time, these ties of mutual dependence have become self-sustaining.

When the volume of remittances sent back to countries of origin by Latino expatriates in the United States is considered, the growing importance of these self-sustaining ties is illustrated in sharp relief. Overall, Latino migrants sent more than $23 billion in remittances to Latin America and the Caribbean in 2000. By way of comparison, this amount dwarfed the $772 million in foreign aid that the State Department's USAID programs granted the region. Remittances also exceeded by far the combined amount of loans extended by the

Inter-American Development Bank (about $7 billion) and the $5 billion in loans extended by the World Bank. The impact on individual countries of this immense transfer of funds by immigrants to their communities of origin is dramatic. In 2001, for example, Mexican expatriates sent an estimated $9 billion in remittances to their communities of origin in Mexico. If anything, the level of remittances sent back to other Latin American nations from expatriates abroad is even more arresting. When broken down by nationality groups, remittances to communities of origin from Latin Americans abroad were equivalent to 14.4 percent of the gross domestic product (GDP) of Nicaragua, 13 percent of El Salvador's, and at least 10 percent of the GDPs of Ecuador and the Dominican Republic. According to a recent study on remittances conducted by the Inter-American Development Bank, remittances to communities of origin from Latin American expatriates worldwide are expected to reach a stunning $70 billion by 2012.[66]

Yet another sign of the intermeshed patterns of hemispheric convergence and the growing disjuncture between older views of the distinction between national citizenship and alienation and new transnational realities is the strong recent trend toward the extension of dual nationality to many Latin American expatriates by the governments of sending nations.[67] The United States government has officially discouraged these developments, but to date, Columbia, Costa Rica, the Dominican Republic, Ecuador, El Salvador, Mexico, Panama, Peru, and Uruguay have all extended some form of dual nationality to their expatriates, and other nations around the world are considering similar moves. In fact, as Peggy Levitt points out in her contribution to this volume, in addition to the more limited rights other nations have extended their nationals abroad, the Dominican Republic now extends to its expatriates both the right to vote and to stand for election to political office in absentia. Most nations have yet to take the radical step of extending the full panoply of political rights to expatriates living abroad, but the trend is clear. Cognizant of the billions of dollars of remittances that expatriates send to their countries of origin each year—and of the socially stabilizing effects of these continuous inflows of cash—Latin American governments have in many cases been compelled to adjust their notions of nationhood, sovereignty, polity, and community in the face of globalizing trends that are transforming national and international politics around the world.[68]

SOME CONCLUDING THOUGHTS

Until fairly recently, the many ironies of the United States' hell-bent pursuit of neoliberal trade and economic policies have been lost on all but the most astute social analysts. But in the aftermath of the events of September 11, a growing number of scholars, social critics, grassroots political activists, and nongovernmental organizations have begun to point out the increasing tensions and contradictions associated with globalization. The effects on both the domestic economies and the societies of sending nations are readily apparent. As mentioned previously, although neoliberal policies seemed to work for a time in stimulating economic growth in large Latin American countries, the historical unevenness of economic development and the current chaotic economic conditions in countries including Mexico, Columbia, Venezuela, Brazil, and Argentina have all caused serious reconsideration about the wisdom of such policies. It has become apparent to a growing number of scholars and social critics around the world that such policies and practices have not only contributed to an accelerating internationalization of the labor force within U.S. borders but, by encouraging the continuing influx of undereducated, low-skilled, and comparatively impoverished workers, have also contributed to the polarization of income and wealth that has been an increasingly troubling feature of the class structures of both Latin America and the United States since the 1970s. In short, such critics argue that we may be witnessing a systemic institutionalization of hemispheric inequality that absolutely dwarfs anything that has come before.[69]

But the ultimate irony of these intertwined trends may well be that by helping to transform the fundamental demographic and social structures of nations over the length and breadth of the Western Hemisphere (and beyond), these economic patterns have also had the effect of eroding traditional notions of sovereignty in both the nations of Latin America and the United States and of undermining the concept of national citizenship more generally. In other words, by tolerating economic policies and practices that have intensified the process of globalization and the subsequent displacement and emiseration of growing numbers of people, the ruling elites of the United States and their "junior partners" in Latin America have contributed to an erosion of the institution of national citizenship. The great irony here is that by making a vast and growing pool of both sanctioned and unsanctioned noncitizen workers a permanent feature of the labor force based in U.S. territory, and simultaneously contributing to the constant expansion of a denationalized labor sector that is constantly in motion, following "outsourced" production facilities wherever they may alight in the global marketplace, governing national elites may well have prepared the ground for the eventual undermining of the basis of their own authority and legitimacy.

Although the persistence of such complex, constantly shifting circumstances make it impossible to predict with any precision the social, cultural, and political trajectories that will emanate from the volatile combination of continuing demographic flux and massive economic restructuring in the

Western Hemisphere, these ongoing developments raise profound questions about the current and future relationship between free-trade globalization and the prospects for democracy and ordinary people's well-being in this vast region. Whether the tremendous social tensions created by these powerful ongoing processes will result in a continuation of the United States' ability to impose its will on the hemisphere's people, socioeconomic structures, and politics—and to the continued material and cultural impoverishment of millions of people on *both* sides of the border—or will eventually lead to an era of increasing protest, resistance, empowerment, and democratization fomented by groups and individuals no longer willing to tolerate political marginalization, economic exploitation, and elite-imposed cultural regimentation will surely be one of the most impelling social issues of the new century.

NOTES

1. In the late 1950s and early 1960s, very little empirical social science research had been generated on the social, political and cultural orientations of the United States' major Latino subpopulations, and what was produced tended to situate Latinos in both the ethnic-minority "culture of poverty" literature and the traditional narrative of American immigration history. For some representative examples of the dominant themes of the times, see, for example, John H. Burma, *Spanish-Speaking Groups in the United States* (Durham, N.C.: Duke University Press, 1954); Oscar Lewis, *La Vida: A Puerto Rican Family in the Culture of Poverty—San Juan and New York* (New York: Random House, 1965); Nathan Glazer and Daniel Patrick Moynihan, *Beyond the Melting Pot: The Negroes, Puerto Ricans, Jews, Italians, and Irish of New York City* (Cambridge, Mass.: MIT Press, 1963); and (in a more balanced analysis) Leo Grebler, Joan W. Moore, and Ralph C. Guzmán, *The Mexican American People: The Nation's Second Largest Minority* (New York: Free Press, 1970).
2. For recent discussion of evidence pointing to the expansion of a sense of *latinidad* in the United States' burgeoning pan-Latino population, see, for example, Gloria Anzaldúa, *Borderlands/La Frontera: The New Mestiza* (San Francisco: Spinsters/Aunt Lute Press, 1987); Ilan Stavans, *The Latino Condition: Reflections on Culture and Identity in America* (New York: HarperCollins, 1995); Frances R. Aparicio and Susana Chávez-Silverman, eds., *Tropicalizations: Transcultural Representations of Latinidad* (Hanover: N.H.: University Press of New England, 1997); and Juan Flores, *From Bomba to Hip-Hop: Puerto Rican Culture and Latino Identity* (New York: Columbia University Press, 2000).
3. For the purposes of this book, "Latin America" refers to the predominantly Spanish-speaking nations of the Western Hemisphere, including the Spanish-speaking Caribbean. Although some scholars question whether places like Belize, Guyana, Suriname, and Brazil should be considered part of Latin America, these places are not included in this discussion because of their different (English,

French, Dutch, and Portuguese) linguistic and colonial heritages. Since 1960, fully 52 percent of all immigrants who have come to the United States are of Latin American origin, with 29 percent of all immigrants over that period coming from Mexico alone. See Peter H. Hong and Patrick J. McDonnell, "Proportion of Immigrants in U.S. Population Has Doubled since 1970," *Los Angeles Times*, 7 February 2002; and Reed Ueda, *Postwar Immigrant America: A Social History* (Boston: Bedford/St. Martins, 1994), 163, table A7.

4. For discussion of the growing estimates of the foreign-born population of the United States, see Cindy Rodríguez, "Latino Influx Boosts Number of U.S. Immigrants to All-Time High," *Boston Globe*, 12 September 2000; Alejandro Portes and Rubén G. Rumbaut, *Legacies: The Story of the Immigrant Second Generation* (Berkeley and New York: University of California Press and the Russell Sage Foundation, 2001), xvii; Robin Fields, " '90s Saw a Tide of New People," *Los Angeles Times*, 6 March 2001; and Dianne A. Schmidley, U.S. Census Bureau, Current Population Reports, Series P23–206, *Profile of the Foreign-Born Population of the United States: 2000* (Washington, D.C.: U.S. Government Printing Office, 2001).
5. See Jorge A. Brea, "Population Dynamics in Latin America," *Population Bulletin* 58, no. 1 (March 2003): 7, 10.
6. For general discussions of the evolution and troubled history of the national-origins quota system, see John Higham, *Strangers in the Land: Patterns of American Nativism, 1860–1925* (New Brunswick, N.J.: Rutgers University Press, 1955); Roger Daniels and Otis L. Graham, *Debating American Immigration, 1882–Present* (Landham, Md.: Rowman & Littlefield, 2001); and Mae Ngai, *Illegal Aliens and Alien Citizens: Immigration Restriction, Race, and Nation, 1924–1965* (Princeton, N.J.: Princeton University Press, in press).
7. See Betsy Guzmán and Eileen Díaz McConnell, "The Hispanic Population: 1990–2000 Growth and Change," *Population Research and Policy Review* 21 (April 2002): 109–26; and U.S. Immigration and Naturalization Service, *Statistical Yearbook of the Immigration and Naturalization Service, 2000* (Washington, D.C.: U.S. Government Printing Office, 2002), 14, table 3. The terminology used to describe unauthorized migration into the United States has always been an area of intense contention and debate. For those of a legalistic bent, anyone entering U.S. territory outside of officially authorized channels has broken U.S. law and is, therefore, ipso facto an "illegal alien." However, many scholars and social critics have argued that since American employers have actively recruited and employed noncitizen workers—and have often themselves broken extant U.S. laws in the process—the issue of immigrant "criminality" should at the very least be placed in this context. Most of the essays in this volume explore this issue in one form or another. For more detailed discussion of the historical evolution and contemporary implications of such debates, consult citations in note 6, above.
8. U.S. Census Bureau, "Profile of the Foreign-Born Population in the United States, 2000," *Current Population Survey* (March 2000): table 3-4, "Country or Area of Birth of the Foreign-Born Population from Latin America and North America: 2000."
9. For analysis of the period of the change of sovereignty in the territory that is now the American Southwest from the Republic of Mexico to the United States, see Al-

bert M. Camarillo, *Chicanos in a Changing Society: From Mexican Pueblos to American Barrios in Santa Barbara and Southern California, 1848–1930* (Cambridge, Mass.: Harvard University Press, 1979); David J. Weber, *The Mexican Frontier, 1821–1846: The American Southwest Under Mexico* (Albuquerque: University of New Mexico Press, 1982); Arnoldo De León, *The Tejano Community, 1836–1900* (Albuquerque: University of New Mexico Press, 1982); David Montejano, *Anglos and Mexicans in the Making of Texas, 1836–1986* (Austin: University of Texas Press, 1987); Ramón A. Gutiérrez, *When Jesus Came, the Corn Mothers Went Away: Marriage, Sexuality, and Power in Colonial New Mexico, 1500–1846* (Stanford, Calif.: Stanford University Press, 1992); and Tomás Almaguer, *Racial Fault Lines: The Historical Origins of White Supremacy in California* (Berkeley: University of California Press, 1994). For a larger synthetic discussion of the Spanish colonial enterprise in North America, see David J. Weber, *The Spanish Frontier in North America* (New Haven, Conn.: Yale University Press, 1992).

10. For good overviews of the initial period of mass labor migration from Mexico, see Carey McWilliams, *North from Mexico: The Spanish-Speaking People of the United States* (Philadelphia: J.P. Lippincott, 1949); Mark Reisler, *By the Sweat of Their Brow: Mexican Immigrant Labor in the United States, 1900–1940* (Westport, Conn.: Greenwood Press, 1976); and Lawrence J. Cardoso, *Mexican Emigration to the United States, 1897–1931: Socio-Economic Patterns* (Tucson: University of Arizona Press, 1980).

11. For overview discussions of Puerto Rico's troubled historical relationship with the United States, see, for example, Raymond Carr, *Puerto Rico: A Colonial Experiment* (New York: Vintage, 1984); *Divided Borders: Essays on Puerto Rican Identity*, ed. Juan Flores (Houston: Arte Público Press, 1993); Kelvin Santiago-Valles, *"Subject People" and Colonial Discourses: Economic Transformation and Social Disorder in Puerto Rico, 1898–1947* (Albany: State University of New York Press, 1994); and Frances Negrón-Muntaner and Ramón Grosfoguel, eds., *Puerto Rico Jam: Rethinking Colonialism and Nationalism* (Minneapolis: University of Minnesota Press, 1997).

12. As virtually all the chapters of this volume make abundantly clear, the government's habit of imposing "minority" labels on populations that are, in fact, loose aggregations of disparate peoples tends to obscure the inherent complexity of demographic processes. More importantly, such practices have a strong tendency to simplify and obfuscate the even more complex social dynamics occurring as a matter of course in an increasingly polyglot, multinational society. For further discussion of the conceptual and political problems with this tendency, see the text below. For contextual discussions of the raw population data that has recently garnered so much publicity, see U.S. Census Bureau, "Resident Population Estimates of the United States by Race and Hispanic or Latino Origin: July 1, 2001, and April 1, 2000," *United States Commerce Department News*, 21 January 2003; and Lynette Clemetson, "Hispanic Population Is Rising Swiftly, Census Bureau Says," *New York Times*, 19 June 2003. Although census enumeration techniques have improved over the past several years, most demographers believe that official counts always miss a significant number of people who are in the United States without official authorization. For discussions of political and methodological issues and recent best estimates, see Frank Bean and Marta Tienda, *The Hispanic Population of the United States* (New York: Russell Sage Foundation), 56–59; Harvey M. Choldin, "Statistics

and Politics: The 'Hispanic Issue' in the 1980 Census," *Demography* 23, no. 3 (August 1986): 403–18; and Mary M. Kent, Kelvin M. Pollard, John Haaga, and Mark Mather, "First Glimpses from the 2000 Census," *Population Bulletin* 56, no. 2 (June 2001): 14.

13. See, for example, *Latino Workers in the Contemporary South*, ed. Arthur D. Murphy, Colleen Blanchard, and Jennifer A. Hill (Athens: University of Georgia Press, 2001); Micki Neal and Stephanie A. Bohon, "The Dixie Diaspora: Attitudes Toward Immigrants in Georgia," *Sociological Spectrum* 23 (2002): 181–212; Raymond A. Mohl, "The *Nuevo* New South: Hispanic Migration to Alabama," *Migration World* 30, no. 3 (2002): 14–18; and Leon Fink, *The Maya of Morganton: Work and Community in the Nuevo New South* (Chapel Hill: University of North Carolina Press, 2003). For a good recent journalistic account of these trends, see Ken Ellingwood, "With Immigrant Boom, South Makes Translation: Police Are Learning Spanish to Accommodate the Growing Population from Mexico and Central America," *Los Angeles Times*, 27 May 2003.

14. For more detailed discussion, see David G. Gutiérrez, "Globalization, Labor Migration, and the Demographic Revolution: Ethnic Mexicans in the Late Twentieth Century," chapter 1, this volume. See also Patrick J. McDonnell, "Mexicans Change the Face of U.S. Demographics," *Los Angeles Times*, 10 May 2001.

15. For complex reasons discussed below, because the island of Puerto Rico is an American possession and all Puerto Ricans are Americans citizens, they technically do not have a "foreign-born" component. Nevertheless, with a population of 3.9 million, the island of Puerto Rico continues to serve as an important source of migration (as opposed to immigration) to the United States.

16. See U.S. Census Bureau, "Profile of the Foreign-Born Population in the United States, 2000"; Melissa Therrien and Roberto R. Ramírez, *The Hispanic Population of the United States: March 2000*, Current Population Reports, P20–535 (Washington, D.C.: U.S. Census Bureau, March 2000); Population Reference Bureau, *2001 World Population Data Sheet* (Washington, D.C.: Population Reference Bureau, 2001); and Leonel Sánchez, "Latino Population Young and Growing," *San Diego Union-Tribune*, 1 April 2001. For discussions of the ongoing diversification of Latino populations in major urban areas, see, for example, Alejandro Portes and Alex Stepic, *City on the Edge: The Transformation of Miami* (Berkeley: University of California Press, 1993); Roger Waldinger and Mehdi Bozorgmehr, eds., *Ethnic Los Angeles* (New York: Russell Sage Foundation, 1996); Gabriel Haslip-Viera and Sherrie L. Baver, eds., *Latinos in New York: Communities in Transition* (South Bend, Ind.: University of Notre Dame Press, 1996); Michael Jones-Correa, *Between Two Nations: The Political Predicament of Latinos in New York* City (Ithaca, N.Y.: Cornell University Press, 1998); and Augustín Laó and Arlene Dávila, eds. *Mambo Montage: The Latinization of New York* (New York: Columbia University Press, 2001).

17. See McDonnell, "Mexicans Change Face of U.S. Demographics."

18. Currently, California's non-Hispanic white population is about 47 percent of the state's total. See Schmidley, *Profile of the Foreign-Born Population*, 2; Dean E. Murphy, "New Californian Identity Predicted by Researchers," *New York Times*, 17 February 2003; Melissa Healy and Robert Rosenblatt, "State Leads as Home to Immigrants," *Los Angeles Times*, 5 October 2000; Leonel Sánchez, "State Sees New Latino

Revolution Take Hold as Population Booms, *San Diego Union-Tribune*, 7 January 2001; and Maria L. LaGanga and Shawn Hubler, "California Grows to 33.9 Million, Reflecting Increased Diversity," *Los Angeles Times*, 30 March 2001. The relative youth of the Latino population will play out in other ways as well. Indeed, because of the gap in age and fertility rates separating Latinos from the non-Latino population, the dependency ratio—the ratio of nonworking people (people younger than fifteen and or older than sixty-five) to working-age people (ages fifteen to sixty-four)—will continue to rise. As a consequence, even if immigration were to stop today—an unlikely event in any case—the comparatively youthful Latino workforce already in the United States inevitably will support a steadily rising proportion of the aging general American population (especially baby boomers) over time. For intriguing discussions of the potential long-term social consequences and potentially far-reaching political implications of such demographic trends, see David E. Hayes-Bautista, Werner O. Schink, and Jorge Chapa, *The Burden of Support: Young Latinos in an Aging Society* (Stanford, Calif: Stanford University Press, 1988); and William A. V. Clark, *The California Cauldron: Immigration and the Fortunes of Local Communities* (New York: Guilford Press, 1998). Although these studies deal primarily with California, their conclusions are certainly relevant for other areas of high immigration.

19. Indeed, the demographic revolution has stimulated a far-reaching reassessment among scholars of the relationship between U.S. Latino studies, Latin American studies, and "area studies" and the entire enterprise of the production of knowledge in the humanities and social sciences in this era of intense globalization. For some recent ruminations on the state of the debate over the conceptualization and conduct of Latino-studies research in this larger context, see, for example, Antonia Castañeda, "Women of Color and the Rewriting of Western History: The Discourse, Politics, and Decolonization of History," *Pacific Historical Review* 61, no. 4 (1992): 501–33; Frank Bonilla, Edwin Meléndez, Rebecca Morales, and María de los Angeles Torres, eds. *Borderless Borders: U.S. Latinos, Latin Americans, and the Paradox of Interdependence* (Philadelphia: Temple University Press, 1998); V. Bulmer Thomas and J. Dunkerly, eds. *The United States and Latin America: The New Agenda* (Cambridge, Mass.: Harvard University Press, 1999); Adriana Estill, "Mapping the Minefield: The State of Chicano and U.S. Latino Literature and Cultural Studies," *Latin American Research Review* 35, no. 3 (2000): 241–50; Juan Flores, *From Bomba to Hip-Hop*; Refugio I. Rochín and Dennis N. Valdes, eds., *Voices of a New Chicana/o History* (Lansing: Michigan State University Press, 2000); Juan Poblete, ed., *Critical Latin American and Latino Studies* (Minneapolis: University of Minnesota Press, 2003); Pablo Vila, ed., *Ethnography at the Border* (Minneapolis: University of Minnesota Press, 2003); Gilbert G. González and Raul A. Fernández, *A Century of Chicano History: Empire, Nations, and Migration* (New York: Routledge, 2003); and José F. Aranda, *When We Arrive: A New Literary History of Mexican America* (Tucson: University of Arizona Press, 2003).

20. Language issues are particularly difficult to track given the inherently dynamic and uneven nature of the process of language acquisition and language loss. However, recent estimates indicate that about one-quarter of the Latino population is functionally monolingual in Spanish; about half functionally bilingual in English and

Spanish; and the remaining quarter is functionally monolingual in English. See Calvin Veltman, "The Status of the Spanish Language in the United States at the Beginning of the Twenty-first Century," *International Migration Review* 24, no. 1 (Spring 1990): 108–23; Alejandro Portes and Richard Schauffler, "Language and the Second Generation: Bilingualism Yesterday and Today," *International Migration Review* 28, no. 4 (1998): 640–61; Alejandro Portes and Lingxin Hao, "E Pluribus Unum: Bilingualism and Loss of Language in the Second Generation," *Sociology of Education* 71 (October 1998): 269–94; Howard LaFranchi, "Will Bilingual Trend Make U.S. 'Habla Español'?" *Christian Science Monitor*, 30 June 1999; and Mireya Navarro, "Is Spanish the Measure of 'Hispanic?'" *New York Times*, 8 June 2003.

21. While it is true that an overwhelming proportion of Latinos and Latin Americans at least nominally come from a Christian tradition, this heterogeneous population also has a tremendously complicated religious heritage. For recent discussions of this complexity, see Carol Ann Drogus, "Religious Pluralism and Social Change: Coming to Terms with Complexity and Convergence," *Latin American Research Review* 35, no. 1 (2000): 261–70; David Lehman, "Religion in Contemporary Latin American Social Science," *Bulletin of Latin American Research* 21, no. 2 (April 2002): 290–307; and Anthony M. Stevens-Arroyo, chapter 8, this volume.

22. For an exhaustively researched and convincingly argued analysis of the evolution of negative American political and social thought about Latin America and her people over time, see Lars Schoultz, *Beneath the United States: A History of U.S. Policy Toward Latin America* (Cambridge, Mass.: Harvard University Press, 1998).

23. For discussion of some of the major effects of the rhetoric of Manifest Destiny on popular ideology and perceptions of Latin America and Latin Americans in the United States, see, for example, Ramón E. Ruiz, *The Mexican War: Was It Manifest Destiny?* (Hinsdale, Ill.: Dryden Press, 1963); Reginald Horsman, *Race and Manifest Destiny: The Origins of American Racial Anglo-Saxonism* (Cambridge, Mass.: Harvard University Press, 1981); Thomas R. Hietala, *Manifest Design: Anxious Aggrandizement in Late Jacksonian America* (New York: Cornell University Press, 1985); David G. Gutiérrez, "Significant To Whom? Mexican Americans and the History of the West," *Western Historical Quarterly* 24, no. 4 (November 1993): 519–39; David G. Gutiérrez, "Myth and Myopia: Hispanics and the History of the West," in *The West: An Illustrated History*, ed. Geoffrey Ward (Boston: Little Brown, 1996), 166–71; Sam W. Haynes and Christopher Morris, eds., *Manifest Destiny and Empire: American Antebellum Expansionism* (College Station, Tex.: Texas A&M University Press, 1997); and Joseph A. Rodríguez and Vicki L. Ruiz, "At Loose Ends: Twentieth-Century Latinos in Current U.S. History Textbooks," *Journal of American History* 86, no. 4 (2000): 1689–99.

24. The technical points of the Insular Cases remain the subject of intense legal debate even today, but the Court essentially ruled that it was the *mode* of incorporation that made the difference in the Puerto Rican case. The Court reasoned that the people who came with the Mexican territories acquired by the United States at the end of the Mexican War were explicitly granted elective U.S. citizenship under the terms of the Treaty of Guadalupe Hidalgo (an international treaty ratified by the U.S. Senate) and therefore gained the full protection of the Constitution (at least in theory). But the Court ruled that since no such provisions were made for the people

of Puerto Rico under the terms of the treaty that officially ended hostilities between the United States and Spain in 1898, Congress had final discretion in determining Puerto Ricans' political and juridical status. Thus, as the Supreme Court subsequently ruled, the territories acquired after 1898 were considered "subject to the jurisdiction of the United States, [but] not *of* the United States." See *Downes v. Bidwell*, 182 U.S. 244 (1901), 278, cited in T. Alexander Aleinikoff, *Semblances of Sovereignty: The Constitution, the State, and American Citizenship* (Cambridge, Mass.: Harvard University Press, 2002):, 23.

25. For an enlightening critical discussion of the convoluted history and legal application of Congress's "plenary power," see Aleinikoff, *Semblances of Sovereignty.*
26. See José A. Cabranes, *Citizenship and the American Empire: Notes on the Legislative History of the United States Citizenship of Puerto Ricans* (New Haven, Conn.: Yale University Press, 1979), 6.
27. Cabranes, *Citizenship and the American Empire*, 6–7. See also, Aleinikoff, *Semblances of Sovereignty*, 21–26, 74–94.
28. For incisive recent discussions of Puerto Rico's anomalous relationship to the United States see, Christina D. Burnett and Burke Marshall, eds. *Foreign in a Domestic Sense: Puerto Rico, American Expansion, and the Constitution* (Durham, N.C.: Duke University Press, 2001); E. R. Ramos, *The Legal Construction of Identity: The Judicial and Social Legacy of American Colonialism in Puerto Rico* (Washington, D.C.: American Psychological Association, 2001); and Ramón Grosfoguel, *Colonial Subjects: Puerto Ricans in a Global Perspective* (Berkeley: University of California Press, 2003).
29. See *Balzac v. Porto Rico* [sic], 258 U.S. 298, 308, cited in Cabranes, *Citizenship and the American Empire*, 51.
30. For reasons discussed above, Puerto Ricans today are not counted as "foreign-born," but (in the tortured bureaucratic logic of American-style colonialism) as "natives born in outlying areas." For the growth of the mainland population of Puerto Rican nativity, see Campbell J. Gibson and Emily Lennon, "Historical Census Statistics on the Foreign-Born Population of the United States, 1850–1990," in *Population Division Working Paper No. 29* (Washington, D.C.: U.S. Census Bureau, 1999), table 1, "Nativity of the Population and Place of Birth of the Native Population: 1850–1990."
31. Circular migration between the island and the mainland has become such a central feature of Puerto Rican cultural life that Puerto Rican transmigrants have colloquially dubbed the circuit "*el vaivén*" (roughly, the coming-and-going or fluctuation between places). For insightful recent discussions of the long-term implications of the deeply ambivalent historical relationship between the United States and Puerto Rico, see Jorge Duany, "Nation on the Move: The Construction of Cultural Identities in Puerto Rico and the Diaspora," *American Ethnologist* 21, no. 1 (February 2000): 5–30; Luis Rafael Sánchez, "The Flying Bus," in *Images and Identities: The Puerto Ricans in Two World Contexts*, ed. Asela Rodríguez de Laguna (New Brunswick, N.J.: Transaction Books, 1987), 17–25; Justine Daniel, "Migration and the Reconstruction of Identity: The Puerto Rican Example," in *The Politics of Identity: Migrants and Minorities in Multicultural States*, ed. Robert Hudson and Fred Reno (New York: St. Martin's Press, 2000), 3–23; Virginia Sánchez-Korrol, "Puerto Rican Migration up in the Air: Air Migration, Its Cultural Representations, and

Me 'Cruzando el Charco,'" in *Puerto Rican Jam: Rethinking Colonialism and Nationalism*, ed. Frances Negrón-Muntaner and Ramón Grosfoguel (Minneapolis: University of Minnesota Press, 1997), 189–208; and Kelvin Santiago-Valles and Gladys Jiménez-Muñoz, chapter 2, this volume.

32. For a brief, but informative discussion of the assertion of the "international police power" in the context of U.S. foreign affairs more generally, see Alexander DeConde, *Ethnicity, Race, and American Foreign Policy: A History* (Boston: Northeastern University Press, 1992): 76–77.
33. See Walter LaFeber, *The American Age: U.S. Foreign Policy at Home and Abroad, 1750 to the Present*, 2nd ed. (New York: Norton, 1994), 235.
34. Of the immense body of scholarship in English discussing the implications of a long history of U.S. political and economic imperialism in Latin America, see for example, Schoultz, *Beneath the United States;* DeConde, *Ethnicity, Race, and American Foreign Policy*; Walter LaFeber, *Inevitable Revolutions: The United States in Central America* (New York, Norton, 1984); James D. Cockcroft, *Latin America: History, Politics, and U.S. Policy*, 2nd ed. (Chicago: Nelson-Hall, 1996); William M. LeoGrande, *Our Own Backyard: The United States in Central America, 1977–1992* (Chapel Hill: University of North Carolina Press, 1998); and John Mason Hart's magisterial *Empire and Revolution: The Americans in Mexico Since the Civil War* (Berkeley: University of California Press, 2002).
35. Again, there is an extensive body of published work that analyses these intertwined processes. For some of the best-known examples, see Schoultz, *Beneath the United States;* George M. Frederickson, *The Black Image in the White Mind: The Debate on Afro-American Character and Destiny, 1817–1914* (New York: Harper & Row, 1971); Robert F. Berkhofer Jr., *The White Man's Indian: Images of the American Indian from Columbus to the Present* (New York: Knopf, 1978); Philip J. Deloria, *Playing Indian* (New Haven, Conn.: Yale University Press, 1998); and Walter D. Mignolo, *Local Histories/Global Designs: Coloniality, Subaltern Knowledges, and Border Thinking* (Princeton, N.J.: Princeton University Press, 2000).
36. Since the framing of the U.S. Constitution in the 1780s, citizenship generally has been narrowly restricted to people deemed "white." Obviously, African Americans did not become citizens of the United States until passage of the civil rights acts and ratification of the Fourteenth Amendment after the Civil War. Even then, African Americans needed to engage in a protracted struggle over the next century to win even a modicum of civil rights. The legal-juridical plight of other peoples of color was similar. Most Native Americans did not become citizens of the United States until 1924; most Asian immigrants were entirely barred from citizenship from 1793 until 1952; and the general system of racial exclusion in matters of immigration and naturalization was not lifted completely until passage of the Hart-Celler Act in 1965. The more general issue of birthright citizenship was not settled definitively until 1940 and remains a point of significant social, legal, and political contention and debate. Still, throughout this period, defining who was "white" and who was not for the purposes of defining citizenship and access to civil rights was always fraught with ambiguity and contradiction, as the tortured history of Mexican American and Puerto Rican citizenship amply demonstrates. For general discussions of the convoluted history of racialized American citizenship, see Aleinikoff, *Semblances of*

Sovereignty; James H. Kettner, *The Development of American Citizenship, 1608–1870* (Chapel Hill: University of North Carolina Press, 1978); Phillip E. Lothyan, "A Question of Citizenship," *Prologue* (Fall 1989): 267–73; Peggy Pascoe, "Miscegenation Law, Court Cases, and Ideologies of 'Race' in Twentieth-Century America," *Journal of American History* 83, no. 1 (June 1996): 44–69; Ian Haney-López, *White By Law: The Legal Construction of Race* (New York: New York University Press, 1996); Rogers Smith, *Civic Ideals: Conflicting Visions of U.S. Citizenship in U.S. History* (New Haven, Conn.: Yale University Press, 1997); and Mae M. Ngai, *Illegal Aliens and Alien Citizens: Immigration Restriction, Race, and Nation, 1924–1965* (Princeton: Princeton University Press, in press).

37. For an excellent analysis of how this process is currently playing out among Central American migrants and their children, see Nora Stoltz Chinchilla and Nora Hamilton, chapter 4, this volume.
38. For an insightful recent discussion of these processes, see Jorge Klor de Alva, "The Invention of Ethnic Origins and the Negotiation of Latino Identity," in *Challenging Fronteras: Structuring Latina and Latino Lives in the United States*, ed. Mary Romero, Pierrette Hondagneu-Sotelo, and Vilma Ortíz, (London: Routledge, 1997): 55–80.
39. For provocative discussion of some of these issues, see, for example, Marta E. Giménez, "Latino/Hispanic—Who Needs a Name? The Case Against a Standard Terminology," *International Journal of Health Services* 19, no. 3 (1989): 557–71; Felix Padilla, "Latin America: The Historical Basis of Latino Unity," *Latino Studies Journal* 1, no. 1 (1990): 7–27; the special issue on the dynamics of Latino identity formation of *Latin American Perspectives* 19, no. 4 (1992); Rodolfo O. De La Garza and Louis DeSipio, "Interests, Not Passions: Mexican American Attitudes Toward Mexico, Immigration from Mexico, and Other Issues Shaping U.S.-Mexico Relations," *International Migration Review* 32 (Summer 1998): 401–22; Michael Jones-Correa, *Between Two Nations: The Political Predicament of Latinos in New York City* (Ithaca, N.Y.: Cornell University Press, 1998); and Oscar Casares, "Crossing the Border Without Losing the Past," *New York Times*, 16 September 2003.
40. For discussion of the many intriguing questions raised by the recent migration to the United States of indigenous peoples from Latin America, see, for example, Carole Nagengast and Michael Kearney, "Mixtec Ethnicity: Social Identity, Political Consciousness, and Political Activism," *Latin American Research Review* 25, no. 2 (1990): 61–91; Michael Kearney, "Borders and Boundaries of State and Self at the End of Empire," *Journal of Historical Sociology* 4, no. 1 (March 1991): 52–74; Jacqueline M. Hagan, *Deciding to Be Legal: A Maya Community in Houston* (Philadelphia: Temple University Press, 1994); Gaspar Rivera-Salgado, "Mixtec Activism in Oaxácalifornia: Transborder Political Strategies," *American Behavioral Scientist* 42, no. 9 (June/July 1999): 1439–58; Felipe H. López and Pamela Munro, "Zapotec Immigration: The San Lucas Quiavin Experience," *Aztlán* 24, no. 1 (1999): 129–49; Jeffrey H. Cohen, "Transnational Migration in Rural Oaxáca, Mexico: Dependency, Development, and Household," *American Anthropologist* 103, no. 4 (2001): 954–67; Stephen Lynn, "Globalization, the State, and the Creation of Flexible Indigenous Workers: Mixtec Farm Workers in Oregon," *Urban Anthropology* 3, nos. 2–3 (2001): 189–214; Nora Hamilton and Norma Stoltz Chinchilla, *Seeking Community in a*

Global City: Guatemalans and Salvadorans in Los Angeles (Philadelphia: Temple University Press, 2001); and James F. Smith, "Mexico's Forgotten Find Cause for New Hope," *Los Angeles Times*, 23 February 2001. For a broader comparative discussion of the emergence of contemporary indigenous-rights movements around the world, see Ronald Niezen, *The Origins of Indigenism: Human Rights and the Politics of Identity* (Berkeley: University of California Press, 2003).

41. See Pablo Vila, "The Polysemy of the Label 'Mexican' on the Border," in *Ethnography at the Border*, ed. Pablo Vila (Minneapolis: University of Minnesota Press, 2003): 106–7.
42. For provocative discussions of this challenge, see Suzanne Oboler, *Ethnic Labels, Latino Lives: Identity and the Politics of (Re)Presentation in the United States* (Minneapolis: University of Minnesota Press, 1995); Hortensia Amaro and Ruth E. Zambrana, "Criollo, Mestizo, Mulato, LatiNegro, Idígena, White, or Black? The US Hispanic/Latino Population and Responses in the 2000 Census," *American Journal of Public Health* 90, no. 1 (November 2000): 1724–8; the essays in Poblete, ed., *Critical Latin American and Latino Studies*, 76–102; and Marilyn Espitia, chapter 6, this volume.
43. Howard M. Sachar, *A History of the Jews in America* (New York: Alfred A. Knopf, 1992), 115.
44. See John O'Kane, "Class, Liberal Pluralism, and Counterhegemony," *Cultural Studies* 15, no. 2 (2001): 295–325. Although addressing a broader set of issues, the article is particularly germane to the discussion of working-class Latinos and other workers in the United States' so-called new economy.
45. Indeed, for all the many things revealed about contemporary American "race relations" during the political firestorm unleashed by former Senate Majority Leader Trent Lott's comments on the occasion of Senator Strom Thurmond's one hundredth birthday in December 2002, it is remarkable how much the fierce subsequent national debate about "race" in the United States continued to revolve around a discussion of traditional white–black relations while virtually ignoring the social implications of the presence of 38 million Latinos. For recent reflections on similar issues from a very different point of view, see Hugh Davis Graham, *Collision Course: The Strange Convergence of Affirmative Action and Immigration Policy in America* (New York: Oxford University Press, 2002).
46. *Hispanic Business*, a major monthly, has closely monitored these trends over the past two decades. For positive discussions of Latinos' economic trajectory, see, for example, Tim Dougherty, "Star Power: A New Generation of Hispanic Pop Musicians is Dominating the Mainstream" *Hispanic Business* (April 2000): 32, 34; Tim Dougherty, "Media Markets Report: Breakout Year," *Hispanic Business*, (December 2000): 46, 47; Robert R. Brischetto, "The Hispanic Middle Class Comes of Age," *Hispanic Business* (December 2001): 21–32. See also Rubén Navarette Jr., "Latino Immigrants Have Done Just Fine in Pursuing Dreams," *Los Angeles Times*, 28 May 2003. However, for contrasting—and decidedly more skeptical—readings of the phenomenon of "crossing over," the commodification of culture, and the general dynamics of recent Latino cultural trends, see Arlene Dávila, *Latinos, Inc.: The Marketing and Making of a People* (Berkeley and Los Angeles: University of California Press, 2001); and Frances R. Aparicio, chapter 9, this volume.

47. U.S. Census Bureau, *Statistical Abstract of the United States: 2001*, 40, table 37; and Karen Robinson-Jacobs, "Brokers Investing Effort to Lure Minority Clients," *Los Angeles Times*, 6 August 2001.
48. See Robinson-Jacobs, "Brokers Investing"; and Barry R. Chiswick and Michael E. Hurst, "Hispanics and the Labor Market," in *Hispanics in the United States: An Agenda for the Twenty-first Century*, ed. Pastora San Juan Cafferty and David W. Engstrom (New Brunswick, N.J.: Transaction Publishers, 2000), 175–94.
49. Although the Latino home ownership rate obviously was significantly lower than the rate for what the Census Bureau terms "non-Hispanic whites" (which was about 74 percent in 2000), some observers see these trends as yet more evidence of the gradual assimilation of Latinos into the "American mainstream." See Diane Wedner, "Education, Employment Help More Latinos Become Homeowners," *Los Angeles Times*, 27 August 2001.
50. See Eric Schmitt, "American Standards of Living Up in the 1990s," *San Diego Union-Tribune*, 6 August 2001; and Guzmán and McConnell, "The Hispanic Population," 117–22. For a fascinating, important, and significantly different reading of the shifting meanings of "race" among Latinos in the United States, see Clara E. Rodríguez, *Changing Race: Latinos, the Census, and the History of Ethnicity in the United States* (New York: New York University Press, 2000), especially 129–52.
51. For some glimpses at various dimensions of this complicated question, see Oboler, *Ethnic Labels, Latino Lives*; Alejandro Portes, "Determinants of the Brain Drain," *International Migration Review* 10, no. 4 (winter 1976): 489–508; Edwin Meléndez, "Puerto Rican Migration and Occupational Selectivity, 1982–1991," *International Migration Review* 28, no. 1 (spring 1994): 49–67; Christopher Mitchell, "International Migration as an Issue on Today's Inter-American Agenda," *Journal of Interamerican Studies and World Affairs* 36, no. 3 (autumn 1994): 93–110; and E. Luttwack, *Turbo-Capitalism: Winners and Losers in the Global Economy* (New York: Weidenfeld and Nicolson, 1999).
52. See Arlene Dávila, "Latinizing Culture: Art, Museums, and the Politics of U.S. Multicultural Encompassment," *Cultural Anthropology* 14, no. 2 (1999): 180–202; Dávila, *Latinos, Inc.*; and John Beverley, "Multiculturalism and Hegemony," in Poblete, ed., *Critical Latin American and Latino Studies*, 223–37.
53. For incisive articles that review recent scholarship along this vein, see Michael Kearney, "The Local and the Global: The Anthropology of Globalization and Transnationalism," *Annual Review of Anthropology* 24 (1995): 547–65; Saskia Sassen, *Globalization and Its Discontents* (New York: New Press, 1998); and Peggy Levitt, "Transnational Migration: Taking Stock and Future Directions," *Global Networks* 1, no. 3 (July 2001): 195–216. It is estimated that by 1990 nearly a third of all workers in Latin America were employed in the informal sector. For discussion of the explosive expansion of the informal economy in Latin America, see Alejandro Portes, "Competing Perspectives on the Latin American Informal Sector," *Population and Development Review* 19, no. 1 (1993): 33–60.
54. For a provocative discussion of some of the complex social and political implications of the rapid growth of "mixed status" households, see Michael Fix and Wendy Zimmerman, "All Under One Roof: Mixed Status Families in an Era of Reform," *International Migration Review* 35, no. 2 (summer 2001): 397–419. The diplomatic

impasse between the governments of the United States and the Republic of Mexico regarding the status of the huge number of Mexican citizens currently residing in the United States provides a stark example of the way the events of September 11 have complicated this situation. With nearly nine million Mexican expatriates currently within the national jurisdiction of the United States, their status as noncitizens presents both governments with what may eventually become an explosive political issue. This is, of course, to say nothing about the millions of other noncitizens currently within the national boundaries of the United States. On the increasing social and political tensions this has created since 2001, see Eric Lichtblau, "U.S. Report Faults the Roundup of Illegal Immigrants After 9/11," *New York Times*, 3 June 2003.

55. See Jonathan Peterson, "Poverty Rate Falls to 11.3%, but Trouble Looms," *Los Angeles Times*, 26 September 2001.
56. Stuart Silverstein and Lee Romney, "Middle-Class Families Put in Economic Bind," *Los Angeles Times*, 6 August 2001. Since nearly 31 percent of all Latino families consist of five or more members, the poverty statistics are even more distressing. See Therrien and Ramírez, *The Hispanic Population of the United States*, 3.
57. Melissa Roderick, "Hispanics and Education," in *Hispanics in the United States: An Agenda for the Twenty-first Century*, ed. Pastora San Juan Cafferty and David. W. Engstrom (New Brunswick, N.J.: Transaction Publishers, 2000), 140.
58. Again, however, the internal diversity of the Latino population can be seen in the fact that unlike the vast majority of Latinos, 80 percent of all immigrants from South American nations have at least high school educations. For discussions of these complex trends, see Heather Knight, "Graduation Rates Rise for Blacks, Whites, Not Latinos," *Los Angeles Times*, 1 August 1997; Gary Orfield and John T. Yun, *Resegregation in American Schools* (Cambridge, Mass.: The Civil Rights Project, Harvard University, 1999); Teresa A. Sullivan, "A Demographic Portrait," in *Hispanics in the United States: An Agenda for the Twenty-First Century*, ed. Pastora San Juan Cafferty and David W. Engstrom (New Brunswick, N.J.: Transaction Publishers, 2000), 15; Mireya Navarro, "For Hispanics, Language and Culture Barriers Can Further Complicate College," *New York Times*, 10 February 2003; U.S. Census Bureau, *Statistical Abstract: 2001*, 139, table 215; and Marilyn Espitia, chapter 6, this volume.
59. See U.S. Census Bureau, *Statistical Abstract: 2001*, 18. See also Grace Chang, *Disposable Domestics: Immigrant Women Workers in the Global Economy* (Boston: South End Press, 1990); Mary Romero, *Maid in the U.S.A.* (New York: Routledge, 1992); and Pierrette Hondagneu-Sotelo, *Doméstica: Immigrant Workers Cleaning and Caring in the Shadow of Affluence* (Berkeley: University of California Press, 2001). Of course, untold thousands more toil in similar occupations in the informal economy, outside the purview of government officials and statisticians.
60. See, for example, Wendy K. Tam Cho, "Naturalization, Socialization, Participation: Immigrants and (Non-)Voting," *Journal of Politics* 61, no. 4 (November 1999): 1140–55. See also the detailed analysis on this issue and related questions by Kevin Johnson and Louis DeSipio, chapters 10 and 11, respectively, this volume.
61. Min Zhou, "Segmented Assimilation: Issues, Controversies, and Recent Research on the New Second Generation," *International Migration Review* (1997): 999. See

also Rubén Rumbaut, "The Crucible Within: Ethnic Identity, Self-Esteem, and Segmented Assimilation Among Children of Immigrants," *International Migration Review* 18 (winter 1994): 748–94; and Marcelo M. Suárez-Orozco and Carola E. Suárez-Orozco, *Transformations: Immigration, Family Life, and Achievement Motivation Among Latino Adolescents* (Stanford, Calif.: Stanford University Press, 1995).

62. See Zhou, "Segmented Assimilation," 999.
63. See Pew Hispanic Center and Henry J. Kaiser Family Foundation, *Fact Sheet*, "The Latino Population and the Latino Electorate: The Numbers Differ," October 2002.
64. For some of the most egregious recent examples of this, see Richard D. Lamm and Gary Imhoff, *The Immigration Time Bomb: The Fragmenting of America* (New York: Truman Talley Books, 1985); Peter Brimelow, *Alien Nation: Common Sense About America's Immigration Disaster* (New York: Harper Perennial, 1996); Georgie Anne Geyer, *Americans No More* (New York: Atlantic Monthly Press, 1996); and Patrick J. Buchanan, *The Death of the West: How Dying Populations and Immigrant Invasions Imperil Our Country and Civilization* (New York: St. Martin's Press, 2002). In fairness, it should be noted that Buchanan himself has long been a fierce critic of the spread of unfettered neoliberal economic policies and practices.
65. See Larry Rohter, "Latin Lands Don't Share Powell's Priorities," *New York Times*, 10 June 2003. The recent deterioration of Mexico's *maquiladora* industries—which had grown dramatically in the first years of NAFTA but have lost at least 250,000 jobs over the past two years—provides further evidence of the structural shifts that continue to unfold. See Gutiérrez, chapter 1, and Santiago-Valles and Jiménez-Muñoz, chapter 2, this volume; and Juan Forero, "As China Gallops, Mexico Sees Factory Jobs Slip Away," *New York Times*, 3 September 2003. That the issue continues to smolder was made crystal clear during the sudden collapse of recent meetings of the World Trade Organization in Cancún, Mexico, after protestors insisted on being heard. See Kevin Sullivan, "Rich-Poor Rift Triggers Collapse of Trade Talks," *Washington Post*, 15 September 2003; and Juan Forero, "Brazil Pushes for South American Trade Pact," *New York Times*, 17 September 2003. For brief explications of a larger line of argument about the damaging effects of completely unfettered global markets, see, for example, Saskia Sassen, "U.S. Immigration Policy Toward Mexico in a Global Economy," *Journal of International Affairs*, 43, no. 2 (winter 1990): 369–83; Nestor Rodríguez, "The Battle for the Border: Notes on Autonomous Migration, Transnational Communities, and the State," *Social Justice* 23, no. 3 (fall 1996): 21–37; Gustavo Esteva and Madhu Suri Prakash, *Grassroots Post-Modernism: Remaking the Soil of Cultures* (London: Zed Books, 1998); W. I. Robinson, "(Mal)Development in Central America: Globalization and Social Change," *Development and Change* 29, no. 3 (July 1998): 467–97; Karen Brodkin, "Global Capitalism: What's Race Got to Do with It?" *American Ethnologist* 27, no. 2 (May 2000): 237–56; and Alejandro Portes and Kelly Hoffman, "Latin American Class Structures: Their Composition and Change During the Neoliberal Era," *Latin American Research Review* 38, no. 1 (February 2003): 41–81.
66. See B. Lindsay Lowell, Rodolfo O. de la Garza, and Mike Hogg, "Remittances, U.S. Latino Communities, and Development in Latin American Countries," *Migration World* 28, no. 5 (2000): 13–17; Tessie Borden, "Migrants' Cash Builds Dreams in Mexico," *The Arizona Republic*, 21 June 2001; Mary Beth Sheridan, "Work Permit

Draws Flood of Salvadorans," *The Washington Post*, 21 June 2001; Chris Kraul, "Mexican Immigrants Sending More Money Home," *Los Angeles Times*, 24 September 2001; Peter Gammeltoft, "Remittances and Other Financial Flows to Developing Countries," *International Migration* 40, no. 5, Special Issue 2, (2002): 181–211; and "Emigrants' Remittances Still Going Strong," *Latin American Weekly Report*—02-05 (29 January 2002): 56–57, cited in Alejandro Portes and Kelly Hoffman, "Latin American Class Structures," 74.

67. The distinction between "dual *nationality*" and "dual *citizenship*" should be noted: dual nationality usually implies the possession by emigrants of a smaller bundle of rights in their countries of origin than the status of dual citizenship—which usually implies full standing in the society of a sending nation, including both the right to vote and to stand in elections. While a growing number of nations are granting dual nationality to expatriates, to date few nations have extended the full rights of national citizenship to emigrants abroad.

68. See Michael Jones-Correa, "Under Two Flags: Dual Nationality in Latin America and Its Consequences for the United States," *International Migration Review* 34, no. 4 (winter 2001): 997–1030. For another recent example, see the discussion of the growing importance of dual nationality in India in Amy Waldman, "India Harvests Fruits of a Diaspora," *New York Times*, 12 January 2003. For a broader, comparative discussion of this global trend, see Linda G. Basch, Nina Glick Schiller, Cristina Szanton Blanc, *Nations Unbound: Transnational Projects, Postcolonial Predicaments, and Deterritorialized Nation-States* (Langhorne, Penn.: Gordon & Breach, 1994).

69. A study by the Congressional Budget Office found that in the period between 1977 and 1995, average after-tax income for workers in the United States fell for the bottom two-fifths of the population (which, of course, included huge numbers of immigrants), was stagnant for the middle fifth, and rose for the upper 40 percent. However, for the top 1 percent of the population after-tax income rose 87 percent. See Isaac Shapiro and John Springer, "The Not-Rich Are Getting Not Richer," *Los Angeles Times*, 9 October 2000; and O'Kane, "Class, Liberal Pluralism and Counterhegemony." For broader discussions of the relationship of these trends to globalization and transnational migration, see Portes and Hoffman, "Latin American Class Structures"; Stephen Castles and Alastair Davidson, *Citizenship and Migration: Globalization and the Politics of Belonging* (New York: Routledge, 2000); and Bill Jordan and Franck Duvell, *Migration: The Boundaries of Equality and Justice* (Cambridge: Polity Press, 2003).

ONE

GLOBALIZATION, LABOR MIGRATION, AND THE DEMOGRAPHIC REVOLUTION: ETHNIC MEXICANS IN THE LATE TWENTIETH CENTURY

DAVID G. GUTIÉRREZ

IN SEPTEMBER 1999, in the small town of Dalton, Georgia, local citizens were treated to an unusual sight as hundreds, and eventually more than two thousand, Latinos lined the city's streets for a parade commemorating *el dieciseis de septiembre*—Mexican Independence Day. Like most other towns in the deep South, Dalton had until recently a population demarcated by the old racial divide between blacks and whites. On this day in September, however, with street merchants peddling tacos, *pan dulce* (sweet bread), *raspadas* (snow cones), and other Mexican delicacies, and other vendors hawking miniature Mexican flags, T-shirts, and bumper stickers proclaiming love for Zacatecas, Jalisco, and Guanajuato, the celebration provided dramatic proof of just how much Latin American immigration has transformed American society over the past twenty years. The Mexican presence in Dalton also presents powerful evidence of the extent to which the ethnic Mexican and Latino populations[1] have dispersed from their traditional concentrations along the United States–Mexico border to new places of settlement in every state in the union—including Hawaii and Alaska.[2] Although the case of Dalton, Georgia, and other locales in the American South represent some of the more dramatic and interesting recent developments in a Mexican and greater Latino diaspora that has been intensifying since the 1960s, the drama being played out here—and in hundreds of other towns and cities across the United States—is part of a sweeping social trend that is clearly one of the most important in recent continental history. This essay is an attempt to contextualize and analyze the major features of the development of the ethnic Mexican population—the largest of the Latino subpopulations in the United States—

as it has contributed to an ongoing social and cultural revolution that shows every sign of defining the future of American society well into the twenty-first century and beyond.

LEGACIES OF CONQUEST

This essay is primarily concerned with the period since 1960, but it is important to address, at least in passing, the larger context of the historical presence of ethnic Mexicans in the United States. This history extends back for more than four centuries, beginning with the Spanish settlements in St. Augustine, Florida, and Santa Fe, New Mexico, in the late sixteenth century. Between this initial period of settlement and the late eighteenth century, small groups of Spanish-speaking colonists established footholds in a series of outposts extending in a wide arc from Mexico City to Florida in the northeast; north to the Gulf Coast of Texas; northwest to Paso del Norte (present-day El Paso), the upper Rio Grande Valley of New Mexico, and the Gila River valley of Arizona; and, in the far northwest, to the coastal plain of California from San Diego to Sonoma. These northern territories, which became part of the Mexican Republic after Mexico gained independence from Spain in 1821, included all or part of the present states of California, Arizona, Nevada, Utah, Wyoming, Colorado, New Mexico, Kansas, and Texas. Mexico lost Texas in 1836 after the Texas Revolution, and the rest of the northern territories were annexed by the United States in the aftermath of the United States–Mexican War of 1846–1848, part of the United States' long campaign of westward imperial expansion. Included in this territorial annexation was a *mestizo* (mixed-race) Spanish-speaking population of approximately 75,000–100,000, concentrated in four major fingers of settlement: southern Texas along the lower Rio Grande and the San Antonio area; the upper Rio Grande Valley of New Mexico; southern Arizona around present-day Tucson; and coastal California. The population living in these areas represented the first group of Mexican Americans.

Although a significant portion of the contemporary Mexican American population can trace its roots to this first group, the overwhelming majority of persons of Mexican descent or heritage now living in the United States trace their roots to people who entered the United States from Mexico in one of several waves of migration over the course of the twentieth century. Most of the Mexican migrants who entered the United States in the first decades of the century came seeking economic opportunity. This first large group of labor migrants was recruited by employers after earlier groups of immigrant workers like the Chinese, Japanese, and Sikhs were barred entry to the United States by a series of restrictive immigration laws passed between the 1880s and the early 1900s. Beginning in the 1890s, regional employers, who sought to replace the unskilled or semiskilled Asian laborers that were so vital to regional economic development, began to employ increasing numbers of Mexican migrant workers in a broad range of jobs in agriculture and food processing, and in the mining, transportation, and construction industries.

Labor recruitment of this type contributed to a rapid increase in the population of ethnic Mexicans in the United States between 1900 and 1929, especially after the eruption of the Mexican Revolution in 1910. Although the bulk of this population tended to stay concentrated in the border states (especially Texas and California), the demand for labor in the agricultural, transportation, construction, and meat-packing industries and in heavy industries like steel and auto manufacturing also contributed to the establishment of new pockets of urban settlement in places like the agricultural areas of the Great Plains and Midwest and in industrial cities like Chicago, Detroit, and Gary, Indiana.[3] Shifting racial categorizations and census techniques make it impossible to know the precise dimensions of population growth during this period, but demographic historians believe that the total ethnic Mexican population grew from somewhere between 350,000 and 500,000 in 1900 to between 1 and 1.5 million in 1929.[4]

The onset of the Great Depression briefly reversed this upward demographic trend. As millions of American workers lost their jobs after 1929, local, state, and federal government officials began a concerted set of campaigns to "encourage," or compel, hundreds of thousands of Mexican nationals (along with an unknown but surely significant number of their U.S.-born children) to return to Mexico. Concerned with the well-being of its citizens and embarrassed by the pervasive negative stereotyping of Mexicans in the United States, the government of Mexico often cooperated in these repatriation efforts. Again, repatriation statistics are sketchy, but these mass campaigns led to a reverse migration into Mexico of at least 350,000 people—and probably many more—between 1929 and 1937. This reversal of the migrant flow proved to be short-lived, however, reflecting just how dependent the U.S. economy had become on Mexican workers. Indeed, once the United States mobilized for world war in the early 1940s, the demand for labor very quickly helped to reestablish the Mexican migration trends first seen thirty years earlier. However, whereas much of the first period of Mexican migration could be attributed to the more or less informal workings of the regional labor market (that is, largely outside the formal regulation of the government), in this new phase of mass migration after 1942, much of the labor migration from Mexico occurred by official contract under the auspices of a series of bilateral agreements that collectively became known as the Bracero Program (in Spanish, a *bracero* is one who works with one's arms, or *brazos*).

The Bracero Program was originally designed to meet the increased wartime demand for agricultural and railroad workers, but after the war the program was extended several times in different versions. Over the next quarter-century, this "temporary" foreign labor importation program was responsible for recruiting more than 5 million workers to the United States. The terms of the various labor agreements prohibited contract workers from settling permanently in the United States unless they first returned to Mexico and went through ordinary immigration application procedures, but the constant circulation of this volume of workers inevitably led to a steady increase of the number of Mexicans who settled in the United States. The Bracero Program also stimulated a dramatic parallel increase in the circulation of similar numbers of undocumented workers who were drawn into the U.S. labor market outside of the official labor-recruitment channels. As braceros became familiar with life in the United States, they encouraged friends and relatives to try their luck in the north, again, often outside of the formal labor-recruitment mechanisms. Of course, U.S. employers who sought to avoid both the red tape and the contract guarantees of the program welcomed the renewed flow of unsanctioned Mexican workers. Thus, after the war, a number of interlocking factors contributed to a continuing increase in the ethnic Mexican population. The volatile combination of the constant circulation of a large number of temporary, legally sanctioned workers, a similar transnational circulation of even larger numbers of unsanctioned, "illegal" laborers, and the smaller, but still significant entry of thousands of Mexican immigrants through regular immigration channels all led to the steady growth of the ethnic Mexican population. Combined with a high birth rate in the resident population, these factors contributed to a population increase of at least 73 percent between 1940 and 1950, and another 54 percent increase between 1950 and 1960.[5] By 1960, the ethnic Mexican population of the United States had reached approximately 3.5 million.[6]

THE AMBIGUOUS LEGACY OF THE 1960S

Although Mexicans had begun to disperse to different areas of the United States by this time, the majority of Mexican Americans and Mexican immigrants—upwards of 80 percent—remained concentrated in their traditional cultural redoubt in the region along the United States–Mexico border: Arizona, California, Colorado, New Mexico, and Texas. Enclaves previously established in the Midwest, especially those in the Chicago metropolitan area, also experienced significant growth. The demographic structure of the population also changed as the immigrant-to-native ratio, which some demographers estimate to have been at least two- or even three-to-one in 1929, gradually declined. By 1960, nearly 85 percent of Mexican Americans were American citizens by birth. Despite this structural shift toward the native-born, however, it is important to note that a great many Mexican Americans maintained strong ties to friends and relatives in Mexico—ties that by this time often extended over many generations.[7] In addition, the presence in the United States in 1960 of at least half a million Mexican nationals, an even larger number of U.S.-born children with at least one immigrant parent, and an unknown but always significant number of undocumented people, make population demographics much more complicated than they appear. Thus, while the majority of all ethnic Mexicans in the country in 1960 may well have been born and raised in the United States, a large percentage (45.2) either had at least one immigrant parent (29.8) or had been born in Mexico (15.4).[8]

The general socioeconomic profile of Mexican Americans and Mexican immigrants in the early 1960s mirrored these complex demographics. In many ways, the poverty that had characterized the population at the turn of the century continued to beleaguer both Mexican immigrants and U.S.-born Mexican Americans. This persistent poverty stemmed from a combination of factors. The constant entry of immigrants with low levels of formal education and similarly low job skills obviously contributed to the depressed socioeconomic conditions, but deeply rooted historical patterns of discrimination against ethnic Mexicans (regardless of citizenship status) also strongly influenced the situation.

Ethnic Mexicans' structural position in American society starkly illustrated the complex ways in which historical patterns of discrimination interacted with the continual circulation of poor migrants and immigrants into the United States to keep both groups down. In 1960, ethnic Mexicans in aggregate lagged behind non-Hispanic whites in educational attainment by at least 5 years (7.1 years versus 12.1 years), and the gap was much worse in rural areas and among recently arrived immigrants. In turn, wage and occupational data reflected these low levels of education. Ethnic Mexicans of both nationalities, like other American minority populations, had partly closed the earnings gap separating them from non-Hispanic whites in the postwar economic boom between 1945 and 1960, but the average annual earnings of ethnic Mexican families remained nearly $4,000 lower than that of non-Hispanic whites ($7,120 versus $10,750) as late as 1969. The occupational structure of the Mexican and Mexican American work force reveals why this was so. By 1960, a small number of ethnic Mexicans (again, particularly U.S.-born males) had experienced some upward movement within the U.S. occupational hierarchy, but nearly a third of all male workers continued to toil either as unskilled laborers or as farm workers. Another 24 percent worked in semiskilled occupations, and less than 10 percent held professional or managerial positions. The female workforce showed a similar clustering at the bottom. In 1960, fully 26 percent of ethnic Mexican women employees worked in the service sector (primarily in domestic occupations); another 25 percent worked as semiskilled operatives.[9]

The general socioeconomic profile of the ethnic Mexican population, for both nationalities and both genders, remained grim, but because aspiring middle-class Mexican Americans played key roles in various kinds of political mobilizations in the postwar United States, it is also important to note that there were signs that at least a small segment of the population had begun to make some halting socioeconomic strides in this period. A number of factors helped loosen the opportunity structure for ethnic Mexicans, women, and other minority groups in the years after 1945. Active service and civilian employment in the U.S. military, new opportunities for employment in civil service and other government jobs, and especially veterans' access to the educational, job-training, and mortgage benefits that came with the newly passed G.I. Bill opened new windows of economic opportunity for some Mexican Americans. As a consequence, by the late 1960s, a small but steadily increasing number of Mexican Americans and an even smaller number of Mexican immigrants began to gain entry into professional and managerial positions. Whereas less than one percent of ethnic Mexicans had been employed in the professions in 1930, the proportion of the labor force employed in professional occupations crept up to 2.2 percent in 1950, 4.1 percent in 1960, and 6.4 percent in 1970. The proportion of workers employed as managers increased at a comparable rate. The 1930 census indicated that just 2.8 percent of ethnic Mexicans were employed as managers, but the number in this important niche inched up to 4.4 percent in 1950, 4.6 percent in 1960, and an estimated 6.4 percent in 1970.[10]

SOCIAL AND CULTURAL CHANGE

The social and cultural life of ethnic Mexicans during this period mirrored both the tenuousness of their material circumstances in American society and the strong ties that continued to bind the resident population to communities throughout Mexico. As was true historically of other minority populations with significant immigrant and first-generation components, most ethnic Mexicans, particularly those in the working classes, lived in dynamic tension within the complex class and cultural milieu they encountered in the United States. Nevertheless, in other important ways, their concentration in segregated urban barrios and isolated rural hamlets helped to create and maintain vibrant regional variations of Mexican culture. Proximity to Mexico along the

2,100-mile border and the constant circulation of thousands of Mexican workers into and out of U.S. territory constantly reinvigorated the cultural mix. In this continually shifting cultural matrix, ethnic Mexicans of both nationalities maintained some Mexican cultural traditions and practices, adopted American ones, and constantly combined and melded these and others into a broad range of local amalgams. Indeed, it was impossible for any ethnic Mexican who traveled in the United States not to recognize the strong cultural and historical affinities that bound them to their far-flung compatriots in different locales. At the same time, however, it was equally impossible to ignore the subtle and not-so-subtle intraethnic differences that made local customs, religious practices, cuisines, musical tastes, and language patterns among Mexican immigrants and Mexican Americans in San Antonio distinct, say, from those in Chicago or Detroit or Albuquerque or Los Angeles.

For example, local preferences for *música norteña* (the popular folk music of northern Mexico) versus Texas swing or rock and roll, American football or baseball versus international *fútbol* (soccer), or local tastes for *tortillas de maíz* (corn) versus *tortillas de harina* (wheat flour) on the daily menu, all depended on the complex ways that specific local conditions interacted with migration patterns to create unique cultural amalgams. The kinds of cultural choices people made and the regional cultural combinations that resulted depended on how a wide variety of variables, including population densities, education levels, language proficiencies and preferences, region of origin, and time of residence in the United States, all came together in local communities. Whether these processes of cultural change and differentiation within the United States were perceived as positive or negative depended on how personal experience influenced an individual's point of view. For some, the erosion of what individuals of both nationalities regarded as "authentic" Mexican tradition in the daily encounter with American consumerism was viewed with dismay. For others, such changes were viewed as an important and necessary part of their "Americanization" and thus played a role in setting them apart from people they considered to be culturally old-fashioned and provincial.

Of course, this kind of in-group tension and friction has long been familiar to Mexican people of virtually all backgrounds (and other immigrants generally) and dates to even before the period of the first major population movements from Mexico to the United States. Indeed, in the 1910s and 1920s, some of the earliest observers of the ethnic Mexican population noted the tensions created by cultural change and exchange in the social context of the United States.[11] In the early 1960s, propinquity to Mexico and the large-scale circulation of both permanent and temporary migrants into and out of the United States guaranteed that this kind of tension would continue to play itself out in ethnic Mexican enclaves across the country.

Perhaps the most persistent and compelling examples of this tension involved the inevitable conflicts that emerged between immigrant parents and their children, whether those children were born in Mexico or in the United States. Largely because the opportunity structure had begun to loosen in the early 1960s, Mexican American children generally had access to significantly more schooling than their parents and grandparents had. This inevitably increased the social distance between immigrants and their children. In addition, socialization and acculturation in American public schools and the constant exposure to the cornucopia of creature comforts advertised or displayed in print media, radio broadcasts, and especially film and television deeply influenced the desires and aspirations felt most forcefully by the young. Thus, as much as some ethnic Mexican parents may have wanted to insulate their children from what they considered to be the threatening elements of consumerism, the siren call of American fashion, fads, and fantasy played a central role in the inevitable "Americanization" of both their children *and* themselves.[12]

The constant struggle between older and newer cultural practices and older and newer forms of sociability played themselves out in countless ways in everyday life, but they were probably most apparent in gender relations as men and women, husbands and wives, and children and parents engaged in a daily tug-of-war over appropriate gender roles and behaviors. Whereas some ethnic Mexican men tried mightily to preserve and reproduce the strict control over "their" women that they remembered (or imagined they remembered) from some idyllic past either in the Mexican countryside or earlier in the United States, the process of migration and subsequent life in the States inevitably transformed gender dynamics in unpredictable ways. This was particularly true when women entered the paid labor force. As more and more native and immigrant women entered the paid workforce, their increasing influence over family purse strings and ongoing negotiations with men over the appropriate division of labor at home contributed to the erosion of patriarchic norms in many ethnic Mexican families. As sociologist Pierrette Hondagneu-Sotelo has noted in her published work and in her contribution to this volume, "while it is too hasty to proclaim that gender egalitarianism prevails in interpersonal relations among [ethnic] Mexican[s], there is a significant trend in that direction. . . . With the diminution of patriarchal gender relations, women gain power and autonomy, and men lose some of their authority and privilege."[13]

But the breakdown of more traditional lines of authority did not come without cost. While countless ethnic Mexican parents tried to shield their children from what they considered to be the looser social and cultural mores in their daily lives in the United States, Mexican American and Mexican immigrant children inevitably absorbed new behaviors along with fads, fashions, and fantasies. Among these changing norms were freer association between boys and girls (up to and including sexual experimentation) and different kinds of leisure, entertainment, and amusements, which by the late 1960s increasingly involved the quintessential American world of sex, drugs, and rock and roll. Most Mexican American children probably went through the powerful transition of adolescence without deep scars, but, like immigrant and ethnic children before them, significant numbers spun out into the demimonde of drug abuse, gang association, crime, and social alienation.[14] Like American parents of all ethnic and class backgrounds, Mexican and Mexican American parents in the 1960s struggled to adjust to the profound social forces that were inexorably transforming their children.

THE SHIFTING TERRAIN OF POLITICS

Perhaps the most dramatic of these powerful forces of social change was the rapid shift in politics that occurred during the 1960s. Before the mid-1960s, the political orientation and activities of the ethnic Mexican population strongly reflected the tensions and ambivalences associated with racially subordinate populations with a significant immigrant component, particularly in the working-class majority. Historically, political involvement (or lack thereof) among ethnic Mexican workers varied greatly depending on the same kind of variables that shaped their cultural lives. Obviously, nationality, citizenship, and the fact that so many ethnic Mexicans were essentially economic refugees played central roles in shaping political activity. Proximity to Mexico and the belief of many Mexicans that they would some day return to *la patria* created a situation in which very few immigrants sought to become naturalized U.S. citizens. Lack of citizenship automatically disqualified hundreds of thousands of resident nationals from participation in American electoral politics.[15] This is not to argue that immigrants were apolitical, but, as Louis DeSipio and Kevin Johnson argue in their chapters in this volume, lack of U.S. citizenship constrained the kind of "mainstream" political activities in which they could engage. In addition, in both the Mexican American population and among Mexican immigrants who sought to participate, socioeconomic factors constrained potential political participation. For example, whether one read and spoke English, where one lived and for how long, and how well educated an individual was, all had significant effects on political behavior, and historically these factors contributed to what were generally very low levels of "formal" political activity (that is, within the realm of traditional American electoral politics) among ethnic Mexicans. Consequently, until the late 1960s, when resident Mexican nationals did take political action, their activism often as not involved basic bread-and-butter job-place issues in struggles over wages, hours, and working conditions.[16]

Among Mexican Americans of longer residence in the United States, political activity was a bit more varied. Mexican American citizens faced many, if not all, of the same deeply rooted patterns of prejudice and discrimination confronted by more recent arrivals from Mexico, but their status as American citizens at least potentially opened up more avenues for political mobilization and redress. This was particularly true in the years after World War II. As formerly rigid social and economic barriers began to break down as a result of the combination of the continuing demand for labor, accelerating urbanization (more than 80 percent of all Mexican Americans lived in urban areas by 1960), and the return stateside of thousands of battle-hardened veterans, Mexican Americans began to assert themselves in the political arena with new force. In the late 1940s and 1950s, this trend was manifest in the establishment of several important Mexican American civil-rights and advocacy organizations such as the American G.I. Forum in Texas (1948), and the Community Service Organization (CSO) and the Mexican American Political Association (MAPA) in California (founded in 1947 and 1959, respectively). The leadership of this new type of organization generally came from the ranks of an aspiring middle class and reflected a centrist, and sometimes even conservative, brand of activism, but most members of such groups were also deeply committed to pursuing political strategies designed to empower all ethnic Mexicans. By the late 1950s, Mexican American activists had honed their political skills by lobbying for legislation, encouraging Mexican nationals to learn English and become naturalized citizens, organizing and registering voters, and, ultimately, by mobilizing for greater participation in electoral politics.

By the early 1960s, these efforts had begun to pay important dividends. Combined with the continuing activities of older groups such as the League of United Latin American Citizens (LULAC), the civil-rights campaigns of the newly established organizations led to a series of key local victories in the national effort to desegregate public facilities like theaters, restaurants, swimming pools and other recreational facilities, and, especially, schools.[17] Similar limited victories were won in the areas of police brutality and harassment, jury selection, voter registration, and the "redlining" practices of real estate agents, mortgage brokers, and insurance companies. And finally, the establishment of "Viva Kennedy" clubs within the Democratic Party during John Kennedy's run for the presidency, and the election to national office of the first handful of Mexican American candidates, such as Senator Joseph Montoya of New Mexico, Congressmen Edward R. Roybal of California, and Henry B. González and Kika de la Garza of Texas, signified the extent to which ethnic Mexicans were beginning to make themselves heard as actors in American electoral politics. By the end of the decade, with the support of philanthropic organizations such as the Rockefeller and Ford Foundations, political activists established what today are probably the most important Mexican American civil-rights organizations, the Southwest Voter Registration and Education Project (SVREP), a critical regional political education and voter registration campaign, and the Mexican American Legal Defense and Education Fund (MALDEF), a vital litigation and advocacy group molded on earlier African American civil-rights organizations such as the National Association for the Advancement of Colored Peoples (NAACP).

But as was true with the African American struggle for civil rights during this period, such limited successes had the paradoxical effect of stimulating the desire for even more fundamental change among different sectors of the nation's ethnic Mexican population—particularly among the young. This desire manifested itself in different ways in different parts of the country. In virtually all cases, however, the movement toward more direct and immediate political action drew on a deepening sense of ethnic solidarity that grew out of a general frustration with both the pace and the direction of social change. As frustration grew by mid-decade, local protests began to erupt in widely scattered locales throughout the Southwest and, to a more limited extent, in Midwestern communities like Chicago, Detroit, and Madison, Wisconsin.[18] Over time, these scattered local protests would coalesce into a more cohesive national campaign that became known as the Chicano Movement.

Some of the first political flashpoints of the 1960s occurred in the area of rural northern New Mexico and southern Colorado and centered on the issue of land and land tenure. In these areas, local Mexican Americans (who tended to term themselves *Hispanos* to signify their long presence in the region and to distance themselves from Mexican immigrants) began to organize in 1966 around claims that the federal government and private parties had illegally appropriated their ancestors' lands in contravention of the 1848 Treaty of Guadalupe Hidalgo. These irredentist activists were led by a passionate and emotive former Pentecostal preacher, Reies López Tijerina, who argued that much of the public land that had been engrossed by private owners and the federal government in the region since the nineteenth century should be returned in common to the members of local communities who held Spanish- and Mexican-era land grants. The movement was quashed and Tijerina eventually imprisoned by local authorities (for acts of violence occurring during the political protests of 1966–1969), but the drama of the land-grants movement served as a catalyst for the subsequent emergence of other kinds of militant action among Mexican Americans elsewhere in the Southwest.[19]

For example, in Texas, where the second largest concentration (after California's) of ethnic Mexicans resided, local activists began stepping up organization at about the same time, despite Mexicans' facing there what was undoubtedly the most deeply entrenched prejudice and discrimination in the country. Anglos and Mexicans had lived in close proximity in Texas longer than in any other region, but local Anglo residents had used violence or the threat of violence to control the Mexican population ever since the Texas Rebellion of 1836. Thus, more than elsewhere in the Southwest, ethnic Mexicans in Texas always had to be careful about the way they articulated political concerns. Nevertheless, as Mexican Americans began organizing in the Southwest in the early 1960s, *tejanos* (Texas Mexicans) were often in the vanguard of political agitation. One of the earliest examples of the growing militancy of Mexican Americans occurred in 1963 in the south Texas town of Crystal City, where tejano union activists forged an electoral upset that resulted in the unprecedented election of an all–Mexican American city council. Ethnic Mexicans had long constituted a majority in Crystal City and the larger region of southern Texas (making up more than 73 percent of the region's population in 1970), but the local Anglo minority used poll taxes, gerrymandering, and outright intimidation to keep Mexican Americans locked out of elective office. The victory at "Cristál" (as the town was known by local tejanos) not only came as a shock to the local ruling elite, but it instantly helped galvanize Mexican Americans in other areas to begin to organize and claim their rights. Building on the dramatic success at Cristál, student activists established a number of new militant organizations such as the Mexican American Youth Organization (MAYO) that pressed an aggressive civil-rights campaign against segregation, police brutality, and inferior education. As will be discussed below, these efforts eventually resulted in the creation of La Raza Unida Party—a Chicano third-party alternative to the extant American two-party system.[20]

In California, where the largest numbers of Mexican American and Mexican immigrants lived, the existence of distinct populations in urban locales and in the state's vast rural hinterlands made ethnic politics even more complicated. Indeed, the establishment in the state in the 1940s and 1950s of new advocacy groups such as the CSO and MAPA in some ways symbolized both the tensions inherent in the rural/urban split and the increasing intersection of the political concerns of urban and rural ethnic Mexicans. That ferment came to a head as a result of César Chávez's efforts to organize California farm workers in the early sixties. Chávez, who was born in Arizona but spent most of his early life as a farm worker in California, was recruited into a CSO chapter in San José in 1952. After several years as a CSO organizer, Chávez tried to convince the CSO board of directors to commit funds for a major new effort to organize farm workers into a strong union. When his efforts were rebuffed, Chávez resigned from the CSO in 1961 to devote his time to labor organizing. A year later, Chávez and his chief lieutenants, Dolores Huerta and Gilbert

Padilla, founded the United Farm Workers Union—the UFW—and initiated a critical new phase in Mexican American social and political history.

Chávez's original plan was simply to employ CSO community-organization techniques to slowly build a membership base. But when Filipino farm workers led by Larry Itliong unexpectedly went on strike in September 1965, Chávez reluctantly decided to join the effort. In the process, Chávez began his almost legendary crusade against the forces of corporate agriculture in California. Facing overwhelming odds, Chávez and his organizers built a campaign that eventually captured the nation's imagination. The UFW skillfully employed a strategy that combined traditional union organization tactics with an innovative and brilliant public-relations campaign. By combining philosophical elements of his Catholic faith with the nonviolent political philosophy and tactics of the American transcendentalists, Mohandas Gandhi, and the Reverend Martin Luther King Jr., Chávez was able to mobilize support in the farm worker community. Over time, the UFW also built support not only among urban ethnic Mexicans, but also among politically progressive white Americans who otherwise would have had little or no contact with the impoverished and exploited farm workers. Chávez used a similar combination of tactics when he called for a national boycott of grapes in 1968. The boycott helped to broaden the UFW's base of support by allowing people around the country to participate in the struggle, even if only indirectly.

Given the long history of the brutal exploitation of farm workers of all racial and ethnic backgrounds in the American West, Chávez's successes in building the union and in publicizing the plight of Mexican Americans more generally were spectacular. Although even at its peak in the mid-1970s the union represented only a small fraction of farm laborers, the victories the UFW achieved in the fields, packing sheds, and, eventually, in pathbreaking pro-worker legislation in California made Chávez the most famous Mexican American in the United States. More importantly, Chávez's national visibility helped galvanize the ethnic Mexican population. For perhaps the first time in their long history, ethnic Mexicans had a positive, successful national role model to look up to, and this served as a powerful inducement for Mexican Americans and Mexican immigrants in all walks of life to reassess their own position in American society. When combined with the intensification of the African American civil-rights campaign symbolized by the emergence of the "black power" movement at about the same time, Chávez's efforts, though obviously very different in tone, succeeded in fostering a new sense of ethnic pride and purpose among ethnic Mexicans of both nationalities. Consequently, by the end of the 1960s many Mexican Americans and some Mexican immigrants—particularly the young—began to fight aggressively for a more equitable position in American society.

Examples of this new political and social aggressiveness began to be seen in widely scattered locales across the country. In California, direct, voluntary participation in the UFW campaign by college students, clergy, and ordinary people helped stimulate a new level of political consciousness and commitment. Indeed, as later events would demonstrate, direct participation in UFW activities during the 1960s and 1970s often served as a crucial training ground for a new generation of Mexican American political leaders, who began to assume power in more "mainstream" political pursuits in the 1980s and 1990s. Indirect influences, however, were probably more important over the long run. Once it was demonstrated that unconventional political tactics (i.e., political action outside the electoral system) seemed to be effective, many ethnic Mexicans began articulating their grievances with new force.

One of the most dramatic manifestations of this shift occurred in the spring of 1968 when students in East Los Angeles–area high schools walked out of their classes en masse. For months, tensions had been building in the schools as students stepped up demands for a variety of reforms, including more access to college preparatory classes; the addition of bilingual, bicultural, and Mexican American history classes; the hiring of more Mexican American teachers, administrators, and counselors; and the serving of Mexican food in school cafeterias. When these demands were ignored or dismissed, more than 10,000 students walked out in protest. The famous Los Angeles "Blowouts," which soon spread to other high schools in the Southwest, represented an important turning point. For the first time, Mexican American students—who increasingly called themselves "Chicanos" as a sign of their newfound ethnic pride, independence, and militancy—emulated some of the tactics of mass civil disobedience that African American students had earlier employed in the South with such success. In the process, the students announced a new stage of Mexican American political activism.[21]

The political situation elsewhere in the country played out along similar lines. In Denver, for example, Rodolfo "Corky" Gonzales, a former local Democratic Party operative, reacted to his growing frustration with the pace of social change by abandoning the party and establishing a new organization he called the Crusade for Justice. The organization was originally designed to serve the needs of ethnic Mexicans in the greater Denver area, but when the group called for a national meeting of student activists, the Crusade and its leader suddenly became central players in the budding national movement. Convened in Denver in the spring of 1969, the First National Chicano Youth Liberation Conference marked the largest national gathering of Chicano activists to that point in time. Participants from the Southwest, the Midwest, and beyond attended workshops and cultural performances, compared notes on their experiences, and, most importantly, explored and shared a newfound sense of cultural pride and political potential. Of course, the regional, class, and gender differences that otherwise divided the Mexican American population inevitably caused some tensions at the gathering, but, overall, participants were energized by a newfound spirit of unity and common purpose.

This sense of solidarity was galvanized even more when the young Chicano poet Alurista, with contributions from other conference participants, marked the moment by composing a political manifesto he called "El Plan Espiritual de Aztlán" (The spiritual plan of Aztlán). The Plan of Aztlán symbolized the slow crystallization of political thought that synthesized trends of the previous few years. Alurista's evocative statement of Aztlán, a mythical Chicano homeland roughly equivalent to what was by then the American Southwest, drew its power from a variety of sources: his interpretation of Aztec myth, the rhetoric of the land-grants movement in New Mexico, the recent intensification of political activism in urban barrios, and especially from the separatist, quasi-nationalistic rhetoric of the militant Black Power Movement. Declaring that the time had come for a proud *mestizo* people to claim its rightful heritage as natives of the Southwest—and to the more extended "bronze continent" of North America—the Plan of Aztlán echoed the Black Panthers' contemporary call for "self-determination," "self-defense," and "community control" of local institutions. But most of all, the Plan of Aztlán called for Mexican Americans to adopt an aggressive new form of cultural identity as "Chicanos"—that is, as persons of Mexican descent in the United States who consider themselves culturally and politically distinct both from white Americans and from *mexicanos del otro lado*—Mexicans from "the other side" of the border.

Alurista took some rather glaring liberties with his readings of Mexican national history and the regional history of Spanish-speaking people in the Southwest, his emphasis on Chicano indigenousness, and his appropriation of potent Mexican cultural symbols, but his stirring poetic manifesto struck a chord with young Chicano activists, who returned to their homes intent on implementing the Plan's political and cultural vision. This was particularly true in the areas of electoral reform and political organization. For example, in May 1969, just two months after the Denver conference, Chicano activists met in Santa Barbara, California, to expand the Plan's principles into the area of education reform. Out of this meeting came "The Plan of Santa Barbara"—simultaneously a prototype plan for the establishment of Chicano studies programs in colleges and universities and a call for the consolidation of the many student groups that had been established across the country into a single umbrella organization dubbed *El Movimiento Estudiantil Chicano de Aztlán* (MEChA, or the Chicano Student Movement of Aztlán). MEChA remains the dominant Chicano student organization on campuses to the present day.[22]

Another important offshoot of the National Youth Liberation Conference was the establishment in various locales of local chapters of an experimental new Chicano political party—El Partido de la Raza Unida, or as it was popularly known, La Raza Unida Party (LRUP). Born in the flush of enthusiasm out of Denver, the establishment of LRUP was intended to break the stranglehold that the traditional two-party system had imposed on Chicanos and other oppressed peoples in the United States. Once again, the formation of the party reflected the ambivalence of the political philosophies that characterized this period of mobilization. The rhetoric of the LRUP was often militant and even revolutionary, but the very fact that the party was organized with the intent of running Chicano candidates and educating other people about "Chicano issues" in the context of American electoral politics provides insight into the fractured nature of the enterprise.

The first chapter of LRUP was founded in Texas in May 1969 under the leadership of José Angél Gutiérrez. A year later, a branch of the party was established in Colorado under the leadership of Corky Gonzales, and, soon thereafter, several chapters of LRUP were established in different communities in both northern and southern California. Again, although LRUP developed as an offshoot of the call for unity and action that had emerged at the National Youth Liberation Conference, each chapter of the party strongly reflected the particular exigencies that characterized each locale. In Texas, for example, strong concentrations of Mexican Americans (especially in the border counties of southern Texas) allowed LRUP to leap immediately into local electoral politics and score a limited number of victories at the level of school boards and city councils in a number of places, notably Crystal City, Robstown, Eagle Pass, and San Marcos. In California, however, where the Mexican American population tended to be much more geographically dispersed, LRUP had a more difficult time establishing a foothold. Between 1971 and 1974, LRUP candidates in California were able to influence several local elections, but the party could never mount an effective campaign in a statewide race because it failed to collect a sufficient number of voter signatures to qualify. By the end of 1974, the party was in decline everywhere, and by the end of the decade LRUP had effectively ceased to exist as a serious political alternative in the Mexican American community.[23]

The brief rise and rapid descent of La Raza Unida Party provides an accurate reflection of the quick florescence and decline of the militant phase of the Chicano movement in the 1960s and 1970s. Born in a period of intense social and cultural ferment, the various elements that constituted the diverse movement clearly contributed to a number of positive and lasting changes in the status of ethnic Mexicans in the United States. At the most basic level, the activities of Cesar Chávez, the UFW, and the ancillary political movements that erupted across the country after the grape boycott, placed Mexican Americans and Mexican immigrants on the national political map for the first time. Chicano activists never came close to exerting the same kind of moral pull on the public's consciousness that their counterparts in the black-liberation and antiwar movements were able to achieve, but the movement probably did help to increase general awareness about the "nation's second largest minority" and to intensify federal, state, and local governmental efforts on its behalf.[24] The establishment of Chicano studies programs and the validation of Mexican American history as an area of academic inquiry—both directly attributable to movement agitation—were also powerful monuments to the courageous efforts of ethnic Mexican men and women to change people's lives for the better. The argument can also be made that by providing a "radical" threat to the power structures of the status quo, Chicano movement activists almost certainly opened up more opportunities for "moderate" Mexican American politicians than would have existed without the mobilizations of the period.[25]

Still, in hindsight the trajectory of Chicano political activism in this period probably did more to expose the broad demographic heterogeneity, increasing class stratification, and deep ideological divisions within the ethnic Mexican population than it did to stimulate an enduring spirit of common cause among them. Most Mexican Americans and long-term resident Mexican immigrants no doubt identified with and supported the efforts of student groups and organizations like the UFW—although the union's long-held anti-immigrant stance clearly gave some Chicanos and *mexicanos* cause for deep concern throughout the 1960s and 1970s. But even at the height of the movement in the early 1970s, much of the ethnic Mexican population of both nationalities continued to be more concerned either with individual advancement or with the prosaic issues of daily economic survival, and thus they remained only dimly aware of broader political activities occurring outside of their state or their local community. More importantly, despite their enthusiasm, most Chicano-movement activists tended to underestimate the moderate and even conservative political orientation of many of their intended constituents. While in hindsight it is difficult to dispute that militant activists accelerated the pace of social change in some areas of American politics (especially in dismantling systems of de jure segregation and opening up the educational system to curricular reform and greater access for Mexican American students), the fact remains that even at its peak, the rhetoric of militant *Chicanismo*, and even self-identification as "Chicano," appealed only to a fraction of the ethnic Mexican population.

Another crucial flaw in the logic of militant Chicanismo had to do with the deeply contradictory implications of the movement's stated objectives, particularly with regard to educational reform. Efforts in this area were obviously necessary, but very few activists seemed willing to recognize the instrumental nature of their demands for educational access and reform. While the rhetoric of separatism and self-determination seemed to imply a radical, even revolutionary break with the dominant institutions and structures of American society, most of the demands of even the most radical activists centered not on the complete overthrow of the system, but rather on gaining increasing access to its benefits. To be sure, some activists—particularly those affiliated with various left-wing organizations such as the Socialist Workers Party and the *Centro de Acción Social Autonoma* (CASA)—attempted to redress this flawed logic by advocating a more class-centered analysis of the "Chicano condition" and by actively seeking to build working coalitions with Latinos and other "third world" peoples, but few recognized the difficulty of maintaining political energy in a situation in which some activists were seeking an ethnically separatist solution while others were hustling to gain access to better education, training, and well-paying jobs in the American economy. In short, despite the radical rhetoric of militants within various wings of the movement, very few seemed aware that mobilization around questions of education and jobs was similar in kind to the earlier bourgeois activism that was the raison d'être of the conservative groups like LULAC and the G.I. Forum. This kind of ideological split continues to characterize politics in the ethnic Mexican population to the present day.[26]

On a different but related plane, even fewer political activists in the 1960s and 1970s acknowledged the profound implications of gender in their emerging ideologies and daily activities. Until the mid-1970s, when women activists forcefully began raising the issue, few activists had the ability to recognize how deeply influenced they were by the predominant norms of patriarchy within the confines of traditional Mexican cultural practices. Indeed, as with their counterparts elsewhere in the national civil-rights and antiwar movements, most male Chicano activists tended to think of themselves as the primary actors in and leaders of the movement while relegating women to subordinate roles—even when women were deeply involved in every aspect of community and organizational activities. To make matters worse, when Chicana activists—like their black, white, and Asian counterparts in the other social movements—tried to raise the issue of gender inequality within the Chicano movement, they were derided as irrelevant, castigated for undermining political unity, or simply dismissed and ridiculed for mimicking white feminists. Many men in the movement strongly believed that women's primary responsibilities lay in supporting the men and in reproducing Chicano/Mexican culture as sexual partners, mothers, and the primary caregivers and teachers of children. Needless to say, women activists like Elizabeth "Betita" Martínez, María Varela, Enriqueta Longauex y Vásquez, Marta Cotera, and others—

strong willed, articulate, and independent individuals who all had extensive prior grassroots organizing experience in groups such as the Student Nonviolent Coordinating Committee, Students for a Democratic Society, and other frontline groups—flatly refused to tolerate such attitudes and behavior. By the early 1970s, women were not only demanding equality within movement organizations (as well as their fair share of leadership positions), but, more importantly, had begun to develop a critique of the male-dominated movement that would resonate for years after most Chicano groups had dissolved.[27]

MIGRATION AND DEMOGRAPHIC CHANGE SINCE THE 1970S

In the final analysis, however, Chicano activists' general failure to recognize the central social, cultural, and political significance of mass migration from Mexico caused by ongoing global economic restructuring probably was the most serious flaw in a politics based on notions of ethnocultural difference. As mentioned earlier, despite the cultural, linguistic, and historical affinities that have always bound ethnic Mexicans across borders, relations between Mexican Americans, Mexican immigrants in the United States, and Mexicans in Mexico have always been deeply complicated by the subtle differences that members of all these groups perceive in one another. When ethnic Mexicans' relationships with other Latinos are considered, the issues become even more complicated. These issues were largely subsumed in the United States during the Chicano political mobilizations of the 1960s and 1970s, but such tensions were apparent even then. For example, Chicano activists' largely unexamined chauvinistic presumption that Mexicans in the United States would somehow eventually "become" Chicanos—or that they might want to in the first place—was often viewed as an insult by both working-class and elite *mexicanos.* In fact, from the point of view of many Mexicans, militant Chicanos were little more than deracinated poseurs who had already become so Americanized that the claim they were making to Mexican cultural "authenticity" was absurd on its face. At best, Mexican immigrants viewed with bemusement Chicano militants' widespread adoption and use of Mexican national and cultural iconography. At worst, such performances of "culture" were viewed as an affront.[28] Thus, although many Chicano militants claimed to speak for a larger ethnic Mexican (and sometimes even a larger Latino) population, national sentiments cut many different ways, with some *mexicanos* identifying with Chicanos, others fiercely maintaining a strong sense of *mexicanidad* (individual and collective identity as Mexicans), others aspiring to become "American," and many others simply trying to survive and prosper in what was often a harsh environment.[29]

This type of intraethnic tension has undoubtedly become more salient following a tenfold increase in the number of Mexican immigrants between 1970, when there were 760,000 Mexican-born residents of the United States, and 2000, when that number had exploded to almost 8.8 million.[30] Overall, the combined ethnic Mexican population of both nationalities in the United States had been growing steadily from both migration and natural increase since the 1940s, but the rate of increase began to spike sharply in the late 1970s and has continued on a steep upward curve ever since. The U.S. Census estimated that the resident population grew at least 60 percent between 1970 and 1980—from approximately 5.4 million to 8.8 million. By 1990, the population had grown to nearly 14.5 million people.[31]

Population movement and expansion of this magnitude has grown out of a number of complex intersecting trends in Mexico in the United States, but the massive economic restructuring on both sides of the border occurring in the 1970s and beyond provided the main catalyst behind the tremendous migrations that began at this time. In the United States, economic restructuring and the beginnings of a major reorganization of the social relations of production played central roles as catalysts to hemispheric mass migration and demographic flux. Corporate agriculture, construction, garment and carpet manufacturing, and other industries that traditionally relied on Mexican labor continued to draw huge numbers of both migrants and permanent immigrants from Mexico in the 1970s and 1980s, but the rapid reconfiguration of the American economy from one based on manufacturing, heavy industry, and Cold War defense spending to one skewed more toward high technology on the upper end, and services, manual labor, and labor-intensive manufacturing in the lower strata, stimulated a massive new demand for low-skilled foreign labor. At the same time, as competition in the international marketplace intensified after the oil embargo of the early 1970s, multinational firms redoubled their efforts to lower labor costs by moving their production facilities to developing nations, like Mexico, with lower wages and taxes, fewer unions, and more lenient environmental and occupational safety requirements. In both cases, economic restructuring of this kind had the effect of stimulating even greater rates of migration as people around the world scrambled to find work.

On the Mexican side of the equation, the foundations of the massive migration of the last third of the twentieth century were laid not by an extended period of depression but, ironically, by tremendous economic growth in the postwar era. Driven by more efficient exploitation of the country's huge oil reserves; massive investment in national public-works projects like roads, hydroelectric power, public transit, communications systems, and irrigated agriculture; and by infrastructural advances in public education, rural electrification, and health care, Mexico's economy grew at a rate comparable to that of the

United States between the 1940s and early 1970s. But the paradox of the extended period of explosive economic growth known as the "Mexican Miracle" was that while the standard of life improved for virtually all strata of Mexican society, the Mexican model of development—a volatile blend of import substitution, political patronage and cronyism, and widespread government corruption—never came close to creating the number of jobs necessary to meet the needs of a population that grew from just 19 million in 1940 to more than 48 million in 1970. The result was an increasingly unstable and economically polarized situation in Mexico in which the already wide gap between the rich and the poor steadily increased. Under these circumstances, the choice faced by millions of the jobless, whether to stay in Mexico or try one's luck in the United States, increasingly became viewed as a matter of sheer survival.[32]

In the early 1980s, that sense of desperation rose even higher for millions of Mexicans. A combination of a severe contraction in the international oil market, a crushing—and increasing—national debt, protracted deficit spending by the federal government, and the general inability of the Mexican economy to absorb the hundreds of thousands of new workers who entered the workforce each year led to the eruption of an economic crisis of historic proportions. By 1982 it was conservatively estimated that 25 percent of Mexican workers were jobless and fully half the workforce was chronically underemployed. At the same time, a series of currency devaluations in 1976, 1982, and again in 1987 severely eroded the buying power of Mexican consumers and investors. As a result, the inflation rate increased precipitously, rising from an annual rate of 60 percent in the mid-1970s, to 64 percent in 1985, 106 percent in 1986, and 159 percent in 1987.[33] As yet another gauge of the deepening misery of ordinary Mexicans during the 1980s, infant mortality rose, and average daily caloric intake per capita dropped for the first time since the Great Depression.[34]

The combination of the Mexican economic crisis of the 1980s and the skyrocketing demand for cheap labor created by economic restructuring in the United States laid the foundations for one of the largest and most sustained human migrations in history. It would be a mistake, however, to view these developments simply in terms of the classic "push-pull" model of immigration. There were obviously many factors pushing and tugging on potential immigrants in the 1980s, but one needs to keep in mind the extent to which the circulation of workers traversing an ever expanding international labor market had already become a *self-sustaining and integrated* element of U.S.-Mexican relations even before the bracero era of the 1940s and 1950s. The intensification of labor migration flows since the early 1980s should be seen as but the latest phase of the historical circulation of labor that, on one level, was occurring between two distinct and sovereign nations, but on another, perhaps even more important level, was unfolding in an increasingly integrated transnational labor market.[35] The structural changes of the early 1980s stimulated a dramatic increase in immigration to the United States, but by that time migration had already become part of a well-established social process and survival strategy for hundreds of thousands of individuals. Over many generations, families in Mexico developed strong bonds of mutual dependence with communities in the United States. In fact, by utilizing lines of communication and social networks that had been laid over many years between sending communities in Mexico and receiving communities in the United States, the migrants of the 1980s and beyond were simply following well-worn paths and utilizing well-established social networks to cross the border, find work and housing, and eventually support both themselves in the United States and their dependents in Mexico. In addition, just as previous generations of both permanent immigrants and circulating migrants had sent millions of dollars of vital remittances to family, friends, and business associates in their hometowns in Mexico, the new migrants either sent or carried remittances and goods back to their home communities in even greater volume—and thus closed the circle that has historically tied hundreds of locales in Mexico to their counterparts in the United States.[36]

All of this occurred even after Mexico implemented and expanded programs like the Border Industrialization Program (BIP), which were designed to spur the kind of domestic economic development that would forestall such massive social dislocations. The BIP, which soon became known popularly as the *maquiladora* program, was established in 1965 in the aftermath of the defunct Bracero Program to encourage economic growth and employment in the immediate U.S.-Mexico border region by permitting the establishment of various kinds of assembly plants built and operated by foreign firms. Mexico hoped to attract investment and increase employment opportunities by allowing foreign-owned companies to take advantage of lower wages as well as relaxed labor, safety, and environmental standards. Firms from the United States, Japan, Korea, Germany, and elsewhere jumped at the chance, attracted by the possibility of exporting part of their production processes "offshore" to this lower-cost environment. Growing from just a few plants employing several hundred workers in the 1960s, the program exploded thereafter. By the early 1970s, the maquiladora industry had become one of Mexico's most dynamic economic sectors. Manufacturing everything from processed food, shoes, clothing, and furniture to auto parts, prefabricated metal and plastic products, machine tools, and electronic components, the maquiladoras have played an increasingly important role in the economies of Mexico, the United States, and the other postindustrial nations involved. Operating with 219 plants employing just 3,000 workers in 1970, by the mid-1980s the program had grown to 680 factories employing more than 184,000 workers. By the mid-1990s the program had grown to 2,200 firms employing more than 700,000 workers.[37] While there have been some signs that the post–September 11, 2001, global economic slowdown has undercut maquiladora production for the first time since the program was established, the general trend since the adoption of the North American Free Trade Agreement (NAFTA) in 1994 has been the steady expansion of this sector. By 2000, maquiladora production had grown to $83 billion per year, accounting for nearly half of Mexico's exports.[38]

The maquiladora program has been lauded by the Mexican government as a model of economic development, but as Gladys Jiménez-Muñoz and Kelvin Santiago-Valles point out in their analysis of similar programs in the Caribbean in their contribution to this volume, the expansion of maquiladora industries in Mexico and elsewhere in Latin America in the 1980s and 1990s tended to obscure the extent to which this kind of reorganization of production reflected much larger and more pernicious international trends. On the most basic level, the expansion of the maquiladora sector was a manifestation of U.S. companies' more generalized practice of reducing their reliance on comparatively expensive domestic U.S. citizen labor by exporting production processes to developing nations like Mexico.[39] But the rise of maquiladora industries in Mexico and the expansion of similar offshore plants elsewhere in the developing world also indicated a general—and much more radical—rearranging of the international division of labor, characterized by a dramatic increase in the number of women hired to work in these plants. Part of a larger historical trend that had been developing from the end of World War II, the reorganization of production processes to exploit the cheapest labor drew unprecedented numbers of young, single women into the new assembly plants. To be sure, employers also experimented with using young men in some of these jobs, but the clear trend has been the widespread use of young women in the maquiladora labor force. Since the late 1980s, the proportion of female workers in the plants has fluctuated between two-thirds to three-quarters of the work force.

Scholars remain divided about the direct long-term demographic implications of this kind of transnational reorganization of production, but most agree that by attracting workers to the border region from the Mexican interior, the proliferation of maquiladora industries has not only added to the skyrocketing population of Mexico's northern tier of states, but has also contributed to the uprooting of women and men from traditional occupations and attachments to the land, and thus the process, at least potentially, pushes them into the internal and transnational migrant stream.[40] Whether there is a direct causal relationship or not, the fact remains that as female employment in the maquiladoras increased steadily in the 1980s and 1990s, the number of women and children who emigrated to the United States also exploded, increasing to five times the number who crossed the border in the 1970s[41]

DEMOGRAPHIC TRENDS SINCE THE 1980S

The combination of these almost tectonic forces intensified after the 1980s and began a fundamental transformation of the social geography on both sides of the international frontier. It is obvious that when even the lowest wages in the United States are six to seven times what can be earned in comparable occupations in Mexico, migration—often through illegal, unsanctioned channels—continues to be seen as the only means of survival for millions of Mexicans. Again, however, to fully understand the dynamics of regional transnational migration and demographic change over the past two decades, it is necessary to consider these developments as part of an increasingly integrated international system of labor exploitation that encompasses both sides of the border. One of the most critical dimensions of the use of this transnational labor pool is the continuing growth and internal movement of the population of Mexico, which by June 2000 had reached nearly 100 million. The population growth rate of 1.44 percent per year has dropped precipitously from the explosive 3.4 percent growth rate of the 1960s, but even then, the Mexican economy has been unable to absorb the working-age Mexicans who enter the workforce each year. This is especially salient when one considers that fully 36 percent of the Mexican population was under age 15 in 2000, which means that this cohort is entering both the workforce and reproductive age.[42]

Steady population growth, the expansion of the working-age population, increasing poverty in Mexico, the expansion of employment opportunities in the Mexican North, and the constant circulation of hundreds of thousands of other Mexicans into and out of the constantly expanding *zona fronteriza* (border zone) linking the two nations have combined to reconfigure regional demographics. These developments have had the clear effect of creating a huge migrant staging area in northern Mexico while gradually also helping to "Mexicanize" huge expanses of U.S. national territory on the other side of the border.

These trends are readily apparent in the dynamic binational zone along the 2,100-mile U.S.-Mexico border, which is now home to a surging population of 12.3 million people—6.5 million on the U.S. side and 5.8 million in northern Mexico. Between 1970 and 1990, the population of Mexico's northern tier of states (Baja California Norte, Sonora, Chihuahua, Coahuila, Nuevo León, and Tamaulipas) increased nearly 60 percent, to more than 13 million people. Population movement northward during this period also helped to intensify the "twin cities" phenomenon, which was already well advanced on both sides of the border. Extending from the Pacific Coast to the Gulf Coast, the explosive growth of twin cities like Tijuana and San Diego (the combined populations of which increased from 974,000 in 1970 to 1.8 million in 1990), Ciudad Juárez and El Paso (which grew from 730,000 to 1.3 million over the same period), and Matamoros and Brownsville (which grew from a combined population of 190,000 to 365,000) all exemplified the powerful melding of the regional economy and the convergence of populations along the international frontier.[43] The trend continued, and in some cases intensified in the 1990s. For example, although the local birth rate among residents in Tijuana, Baja California, was similar to the annual rate of growth for the rest of Mexico in the 1990s, the lure of migrants to the border boomtown from elsewhere in Mexico contributed to a average rate of growth of 5.4 percent per year between 1990 and 2000. Together, Tijuana and Ciudad Juárez in Chihuahua, the two largest Mexican border cites, grew by an astounding 65,000 and 50,000 persons per year, respectively, throughout the decade.[44]

On the United States side of the international frontier, the continued expansion of the service sector, a concomitant growth in the informal economy, and the unexpected opening of new entry-level assembly, food-processing, construction, and manufacturing jobs in places like Nevada, Arizona, and Colorado, and in southern states such as Oklahoma, Arkansas, Georgia, and the Carolinas, drew millions of sanctioned and unsanctioned workers from the staging area on the border and from the Mexican interior. Census figures underscore the scope of the population shifts that occurred between 1990 and 2000. Overall, the aggregate ethnic Mexican population of the United States grew by nearly 53 percent in the 1990s, from 14.5 million to nearly 21 million. Of this population, almost 9 million were people born in Mexico. Although the ethnic Mexican proportion of the total national Latino population shrank a bit from 1990, when they constituted 60.4 percent of the total, in 2000 ethnic Mexicans still represented a majority (58.5 percent) of all Latinos—and 28 percent of all immigrants in the United States. The median age of ethnic Mexicans—just 24.2 years according to census data—guarantees that even if migration rates were to slow as a result of tightened U.S. border security after September 11, 2001, the population will continue to grow appreciably for the foreseeable future. As a result of this remarkable surge in population, more than 1 in 14 of all the inhabitants of the United States now claim Mexican origin or descent.[45]

The most striking feature to emerge from the 2000 census, however, may be the extent to which ethnic Mexicans have dispersed in significant numbers to new regional pockets of settlement. Most continue to reside in the Southwest (half of all ethnic Mexicans in the United States still live in the two states of California and Texas alone), but the trend toward dispersal that was becoming evident at the end of the 1980s had accelerated by 2000. Traditional destinations in the West continue to attract Mexican workers, but the rate of growth has cooled a bit from the 1970s and 1980s. Between 1990 and 2000, California and Texas's Mexican immigrant population grew by 35 and 47 percent, respectively. But other western states' rates of growth far exceeded the two Southwestern giants. For example, the Latino populations (again, which were overwhelmingly Mexican) of Arizona, Colorado, and Nevada jumped 53, 58, and an astonishing 300 percent, respectively, in the decade. Rates of growth outside the Southwest were even more spectacular. Latino populations in the American South, which are also predominantly of Mexican origin, grew by leaps and bounds during the 1990s. Drawn to work in agriculture, food processing, meat and poultry packing, and textile and carpet manufacturing, and fleeing from what has become a hypercompetitive job market along the border, Latino populations doubled in the states of Mississippi and Virginia, tripled in Alabama, Arkansas, Georgia, and South Carolina, and more than quadrupled in North Carolina. The 2000 census revealed similarly large increases in the Midwest (especially in Nebraska, Indiana, Illinois, Ohio, and Iowa), where the Latino population more than doubled.[46]

Thus, in summary, over the past decade the trend included slower but still steady population growth in existing Mexican population centers combined with explosive growth in new ones well away from the border. As existing barrios such as those in greater Los Angeles (which was 47 percent Latino in 2000), Tucson (36 percent), El Paso (77 percent), San Antonio (59 percent), and Chicago (26 percent) all expanded, new ones were created in a broad expanse of territory stretching from California's great central valley through Nevada, Utah, and Colorado, and all the way to the Brownsville-Harlingen–San Benito metropolitan area on the Texas Gulf Coast. In addition, New York City, whose Latino cultural landscape has long been dominated by Puerto Ricans and Dominicans, saw an influx in the 1990s whereby the ethnic Mexican population swelled to almost 200,000.[47] By 2000, major cities on or near the border had all experienced even higher densities of Latino residents, and again, of course, most were of Mexican descent.[48] More intriguingly, significant numbers of Mexican migrants began to leave the border region for more distant destinations where Mexicans had seldom been seen before, including the Pacific Northwest (and Alaska, where more than 45,000 ethnic Mexicans live), the industrial Midwest, and the American South. Decennial increases in places as different as Salt Lake City and Kansas City (up 133 percent and 105 percent, respectively, between 1990 and 2000), Seattle, Washington, and Grand Rapids, Michigan (up 105 percent and 136 percent), and Portland, Oregon, and Minneapolis–St. Paul, Minnesota (up 175 percent and 162 percent), underscore just how dramatic both ethnic Mexican population growth and dispersal have been in the 1990s. The fact that the top five highest decennial percentage increases in Latino populations all occurred in areas not previously known to be destinations for significant numbers of Latinos (ranging from an astounding 694 percent in Greensboro, North Carolina, to 262 percent in Las Vegas, Nevada) offers further evidence of the depth of the demographic shifts that have unfolded in recent years.[49]

SOCIAL AND CULTURAL IMPLICATIONS: AN UNCERTAIN FUTURE

Given the contradictory forces at work in this rapidly changing social and cultural environment, it is difficult to predict the future trajectory of the ethnic Mexican population in the United States. On the one hand, it is clear that the people who are already in the United States are very likely to stay—and consequently will continue to change American society in unexpected ways. In new places of settlement—especially in the U.S. South—the long term effect of new cultural actors in a social setting previously defined by the polarity between the black and white populations remains to be seen. Whatever occurs, southern cities may provide, for good or ill, a template for intercultural and interracial relations in the twenty-first century.

Nationally, the combination of the intertwined processes of massive demographic flux, economic restructuring, and the steady expansion of Latino domestic consumer spending to at least $560 billion per year as of 2001 has already radically transformed the social and cultural landscape of the United States to the extent that some regions of the country resemble places in Mexico. As predominantly Mexican neighborhoods have expanded in communities that already had sizable Mexican and Latino populations, the ethnic infrastructure that services these populations has grown apace. In traditional places of ethnic Mexican settlement in the border regions, like San Antonio, El Paso, Albuquerque, Tucson, and Los Angeles, existing belts of restaurants and bars, *panaderias* and *carnicerias*, nightclubs and dance halls, Roman Catholic parishes and storefront Protestant *iglesias* have all grown and become as ubiquitous as McDonald's restaurants—distinctive features on the American landscape.

At a less visible and yet no less important level, the demographic transformation of U.S. national territory has also begun to exert obvious changes in patterns of cultural expression and cultural exchange in the United States. Of course, cultural syncretism has been a prominent feature in zones of American/Mexican interaction since the early nineteenth century, but, until recently, the predominance of non-Mexicans in the demographic mix tended to push Mexican cultural practices to the margins of American society. This is clearly no longer the case. Over the past twenty years, the growth of the ethnic Mexican population (in most cases in concert with other Latino groups) in locales across the Southwest and Midwest, and now into the South, has created a new social dynamic characterized by new forms of cultural expression and everyday practice. Examples of such shifts include the realm of the prosaic, such as the circulation of Mexican comic books and scandal sheets, the growing audiences for scandalous Mexican *telenovelas* (soap operas), the establishment of Mexican weekend soccer leagues, the proliferation of restaurants featuring regional Mexican cuisine, and nightclubs catering to regional Mexican and Latino musical and dance forms such as *música norteña, conjunto*, *roc en español*, and *salsa*. But they also include the expansion of less visible but no less important complex cultural institutions such as *compadrazgo* (extended fictive kinship networks of godparents) and the growing observance in ethnic Mexican families of traditional rites of passage such as the *quinceañera*, a celebration that simultaneously marks a young girl's "coming of age" on her fifteenth birthday and a pledge to chastity until marriage.

These are but a few of the examples of the extent to which a deeply rooted bilingual, multinational cultural matrix has emerged and matured in the United States since the 1970s. As Frances Aparacio and Pierrette Hondagneu-Sotelo note in their contributions to this volume, there are many more examples of this. Among the most spectacular is the explosive growth of Spanish-language broadcast media. Spanish-language recording studios, radio programming, and film production have been important parts of the social landscape of the U.S.-Mexico borderlands for most of the twentieth century, but the recent demographic transformation of the United States has stimulated unprecedented growth in this sector of cultural expression and production. In 1974, for example, 55 American radio stations broadcast in Spanish at least half the time, and another 425 broadcast in Spanish less than half time. By 1980, these numbers had grown modestly to 64 and 436, respectively. By 1991, however, 185 AM stations and 68 FM stations were broadcasting full time in Spanish, and another 300 stations were broadcasting in Spanish for at least several hours each week.[50] By 2000, the number of radio stations offering full time Spanish-language programming had jumped to 533, and the top-rated radio shows in both the massive New York and Los Angeles radio markets were in Spanish. Broadcasting everything from radio evangelism, talk shows, and infomercials, to music formats including *salsa, conjunto, ranchera, technobanda*, and *roc en español*, it is likely that this upward trend will continue into the foreseeable future.[51]

Spanish-language print media and television broadcasting have also experienced dramatic upward trends. It is estimated that the Spanish-language press in the United States expanded from 355 to 550 dailies and weeklies between

1990 and 2000, an increase of more than 55 percent. Latino magazines (which are published in English, Spanish, and bilingual formats) showed similarly dramatic rates of growth from about 177 titles in 1990 to at least 352 in 2000. Over the same period, the number of Spanish-language or bilingual broadcast television stations jumped 70 percent to 53—and this number does not include cable or satellite outlets. The growth of Spanish and bilingual media outlets reflects more than simply an increasing demand for reading material, news, and entertainment in the burgeoning pan-Latino population. It also demonstrates a growing awareness among corporate advertisers of the steady growth of the Latino consumer market. At the level of Spanish-language print media alone, sponsors spent more than $253 million in 2000, an increase of 207 percent from a decade earlier. Overall, expenditures among the top sixty advertisers targeting Latino consumers topped $2.2 billion in 2001.[52]

In the realm of politics, powerful changes have also been evident over the past decade. As Louis DeSipio points out in his contribution to this volume, one of the most important developments stemming from these recent socioeconomic trends has been the steadily increasing level to which Mexican Americans and other Americans of Latino descent are participating in American electoral politics. Since the mid-1990s, unprecedented numbers of ethnic Mexicans and other Latinos have applied for naturalization, registered to vote, and gone to the polls to make their voices heard. Latinos together made up only 5.2 percent of the American electorate in 1998. That rose to 7 percent in the 2000 elections, and voter participation is expected to continue to rise. These numbers are being brought to bear in halls of power across the political spectrum. Whereas there were only about 1,400 elected and appointed Latino officials in the U.S. in 1973, this number had grown to nearly 3,800 by 1989. By 1994 the number had grown to more than 5,400.[53] In places like California and Texas, the rise in Mexican American and Latino political influence has been even more striking. For example, in the 2000 elections in California, Latino candidates picked up 4 more seats in the state assembly to bring their total to 20 (compared to only 4 in 1991), which means that Latinos now hold 25 percent of all seats in the lower house of the legislature. In contrast, African Americans have only four members in the lower house.[54]

As impressive as these gains have been, however, one should be extremely cautious about drawing uncritical conclusions about the future trajectory of ethnic Mexicans in American society. At the level of politics, while it is true that ethnic Mexicans and other Latinos have recently begun to get more involved in electoral politics, increasing political involvement must be seen at least in part as a defensive reaction to what is widely perceived as a negative political environment symbolized, most notably, by the passage of California's Proposition 187 in 1994, federal welfare-reform legislation in 1996, and the continuing national debate over language issues in the United States. While there is no question that the ongoing demographic revolution has in some instances helped to increase multicultural awareness and appreciation in some sectors of American society, the fierce and sometimes violent backlashes that have erupted against Mexicans, Latinos, and other immigrants—even before the events of September 11, 2001—provide an indication of the continuing tension that the presence of large numbers of immigrants has stimulated and is likely to continue to produce in the future.[55] It is also important to note that while voter registration rates and the number of Latinos actually voting are rising, ethnic Mexicans and Latinos still represent small political minorities, even in states where their populations are largest, ranging from a national high of 33 percent of the electorate in New Mexico to only 9 percent in the states of New York, Florida, Colorado, and New Jersey. The point is further illustrated when one notes that the Latino percentage of registered voters in the Southwestern giants of California, Arizona, and Texas are only 16, 10, and 19 percent, respectively.[56] Moreover, given the youth, low level of education, lack of English-language proficiency, and noncitizen status of much of the ethnic Mexican and larger pan-Latino population, very few actually participate in American electoral politics. According to latest census estimates, nationwide in 1998, only 33 percent of Latinos reported that they registered to vote, and only 20 percent reported actually voting in that year's elections.[57] Given the dispersal of ethnic Mexicans and other Latinos into new areas of the South, Midwest, and Northwest, where their proportional numbers are even smaller, the question remains as to whether these social laboratories will produce examples of new "melting pots," or whether the class and cultural differences that currently divide Latinos from resident white—and black—residents will spark a whole new series of racial, cultural, and class tensions.

The precarious socioeconomic profile of the ethnic Mexican population should also give one pause about the extent to which a kind of benign multiculturalism is inevitably changing American society for the better. It should also raise serious questions about blithe predictions that it is only a matter of time before ethnic Mexicans will "assimilate" into the "mainstream." Some commentators, notably journalist Gregory Rodríguez, political pundit Linda Chávez, political scientist Peter Skerry, and others have argued that the emergence of a vital and growing Mexican American (and Latino) middle class over the past quarter century provides evidence that ethnic Mexicans are well on the way to replicating the upward path of previous immigrant groups like the Irish and Italians on their way to "becoming Americans."[58] And to a certain extent they have a case. According to data from the 2000 Census, a significant middle class has in fact emerged among U.S.-born Mexican Americans. In Texas and California, the states with the highest concentrations of long-term ethnic Mexican residents, the emergence of a sizable middle class stratum has been even more pronounced.[59]

These important trends should not be ignored in any analysis of the ethnic Mexican population, but it is also crucial to consider such data in context because, as promising as these trends are to some observers, the fact remains that the overwhelming majority of ethnic Mexicans of both nationalities continue to toil in the bottom rungs of the American economy. Of course, the most obvious reason for this kind of skewing is the massive influx of undereducated and underskilled Mexican workers over the past twenty years. On the most obvious level, Mexican immigrants enter the country with levels of social capital (such as education, job skills, and English-language proficiency) that are lower than virtually any other identifiable national group. For example, in 1990, three-fourths of all Mexican immigrants had not completed high school and only 3.5 percent of all Mexican immigrants had attended college. Given this profile, it not surprising that the incomes of nearly 30 percent of the Mexican immigrant population placed them below the poverty line.

But as important as recent immigrants are in exerting downward pressure on Latino social and economic indicators, it is also critical to recognize just how drastically the larger socioeconomic context of the reception of immigrants has changed in the United States over the past forty years—a point that Jiménez-Muñoz and Santiago-Valles pursue forcefully in the chapter that follows. Migration clearly continues to serve as a safety valve for Mexico's unemployed, but the biggest difference recent immigrants face in the reconfigured U.S. economy is the changing nature of the job market and the larger opportunity structure they now face—and likely will face in the future. Whereas Mexican Americans and transnational Mexican migrants in the postwar era could reasonably expect to experience significant upward occupational mobility over the course of their working lifetimes due to the availability of relatively high-paying skilled blue-collar jobs, after the mid-1970s, the structure of both the regional economy and the global economy changed to the extent that this was no longer the case for an increasing number of poor immigrants and their children.[60] Today, Mexican immigrants enter a rapidly polarizing, tiered economy characterized by the simultaneous expansion at the top of highly skilled technical and professional jobs for highly educated people; the steady shrinkage in the number of semiskilled and skilled jobs in the manufacturing sector in the middle; and a dramatic expansion of semiskilled and unskilled occupations in the lowest echelons of the economy, particularly in the agricultural, service, garment-manufacturing, and basic assembly sectors, and especially in "casual" labor of all kinds—the low-end, part-time, and temporary work that has been an ever increasing part of the American economy since the 1970s.[61] Another important characteristic of the current period is the simultaneous expansion of "informal" activities at the bottom of the economy. The expansion of the informal economy (that is, both licit and illicit income-generating activities that operate largely outside the regulatory control of agents of the state) include smuggling and drug trafficking and an entire panoply of small scale "off-the-books" economic activities ranging from recycling, street vending and entertainment, house cleaning, and baby sitting, to gardening, landscaping, and nursery work, and casual day labor on construction sites.[62]

Given the powerful correlation between education and job skill levels and earnings potential, it is not surprising that in the context of this kind of polarized restructuring of the U.S. job market and larger shifts in the global economy, aggregate income levels for ethnic Mexicans (again, of both nationalities) have actually declined since the 1970s. Whereas mean household income for ethnic Mexicans had crept up slightly from $37,891 in 1979 to $38,741 in 1989, by 1999, the combination of a changing economy and mass migration had helped to erode this figure to $36,923.[63] In California, where the largest concentrations of ethnic Mexicans continue to live—and where nearly 16 percent of the state's population are noncitizens—the process of income and wealth polarization has been even more intense. Whereas in 1980 the top 5 percent of taxpayers (those earning at least $150,000 per year) received about 20 percent of the state's total personal income, by 2000 the top 5 percent now earned 42 percent of personal income. For immigrants, the trend worked in reverse. In a state where a third of all the immigrants in the United States live and nearly 40 percent of all Mexican immigrants reside, the hourly wages of the bottom 70 percent of the labor force have steadily decreased since the late 1970s.[64]

For many of the same reasons, poverty rates among Mexican immigrants and their children continue also to be alarmingly high. Although poverty nationwide dropped approximately 17 percent between 1993 and 2000, currently nearly 26 percent of all Mexican immigrants continue to live below the poverty line, and more than half have no form of health insurance. But the dire straits of so many immigrants represent only part of the story. More generally, economic restructuring in the United States has accelerated the bifurcation of the economy between a highly educated, highly skilled, and highly paid sector at the top and an increasingly dispossessed workforce at the bottom. Nationwide, this generalized polarization has resulted in a situation in which the bottom two quintiles of workers have actually seen their wages erode over the past twenty years.[65]

More ominously, recent research indicates that because of the cumulative, cascading effects of these structural changes, the children and grandchildren of immigrants may well be inheriting the disadvantaged structural position of their forebears. According to a study published by the Public Policy Institute of California, first-generation immigrants earned from 61 to 86 percent less than did non-Hispanic white Californians in 1999. Second-generation Mexican Americans were found to have 35 percent higher wages than their parents, but the third generation was shown to have not improved on the second, and on average earned 25 percent less than did non-Hispanic whites.[66] Of course, the daunting challenges that working-class ethnic Mexicans face have been exacerbated by the general erosion of the American public school system. As a result of the combination of deeply rooted patterns of "white flight" from inner cities to suburbs and the tendency of new immigrants to cluster in low-income residential areas, Latinos—and ethnic Mexicans in particular—are now the most educationally segregated students in the United States.[67] According to one important Harvard University study, between 1968 and 1995, the proportion of Latino students who attended schools whose student body comprised mainly minority students increased from less than 55 percent to 74 percent. Over the same period, the proportion of Latino students who attended hypersegregated schools that were 90–100 percent Latino increased from 23 percent to almost 35 percent.[68] These patterns of increasing segregation have had a series of serious interlocking cascading effects. At the most obvious level, since school funding is often tied to property taxes, and property taxes to local property values, schools in impoverished areas tend to be comparatively underfunded and situated in blighted, high-crime areas. In turn, these characteristics have made classroom conditions so difficult—and dangerous—that many school districts have been compelled to offer what amounts to "combat pay" to young teachers willing to take on the monumental task of simply trying to reach and teach inner-city Latino students under extremely trying circumstances.

These conditions have given rise to a number of troubling trends among the ethnic Mexican and Latino students who are trapped in such school environments. Although some students, with the support of their families, are able to exert the herculean effort it takes to overcome such constraints and continue their postsecondary educations, a great many others become socialized in underachievement and failure. In effect, such students, who often enter the education system with high hopes and aspirations, eventually succumb to the culture of underachievement and social alienation present both in their schools and their home environments. Recent research indicates that the result for too many immigrant and native children of Mexican descent or heritage has been a long slide into a downward spiral in which their life opportunities are constrained by the limits of their existence on the far margins of society, as underemployed high school dropouts, teenage mothers and fathers, or prisoners. As sociologists Alejandro Portes and Rubén Rumbaut have noted of this process in their sweeping recent study of the children of immigrants:

> Recently arrived immigrants confront these features of life in American cities as a fait accompli conditioning their own and their children's chances for success. Because of their poverty, many immigrants settle in close proximity to urban ghetto areas. In this environment, they and their families are often exposed to norms of behavior inimical to upward mobility as well as to an adversarial stance that justifies these behaviors. For second-generation youths, the clash of expectations is particularly poignant when the messages that education does not pay and that discrimination prevents people of color from ever succeeding are conveyed by native peers of the same race or ethnic origin.[69]

At very least, such patterns over several generations suggest a troubling pattern of nonintegration among significant segments of the ethnic Mexican population of both nationalities. The chronic problem of the emergence of oppositional subcultures like inner-city gangs and the tremendous expansion of Mexican and Latino incarceration over the past two decades are yet more indications that these sectors of the population may well be trapped in the process Portes and his colleagues call "segmented assimilation"—that is, a process in which immigrants enter a depressed segment of the socioeconomic structure and tend to languish there over time. Although previous generations of immigrants entered similar segments, the difference now appears to be the extent to which immigrants stay there and—because of a whole series of virtually impenetrable socioeconomic "ceilings"—pass on their disadvantaged position to their children.[70]

Whether the socially pathological environment described by Portes, Rumbaut, and other scholars continues to dominate the lives of working-class ethnic Mexicans of both nationalities in the coming years and decades is a question that will undoubtedly become an increasingly important issue not only to the growing ethnic Mexican population in the United States, but to all the inhabitants of both sides of the international frontier. Again, the social prognosis on this pressing question is unclear. On the one hand, despite the deep uncertainties generated by the events of September 11, 2001, there is very little evidence that the kind of global economic developments that stimulated mass international population movements in the first place are going to change appreciably any time soon. The momentum that has so inextricably combined the U.S. and Mexican economies over the past four decades shows no signs of abating. If those trends continue in the region and in the overarching international economy, it is likely that employers on both sides of the border will continue to seek to exploit the services of the ever-expanding pool of disenfranchised transnational workers.

And even if the events of September 11 do result in a permanent tightening of border controls, the rapid growth of the native ethnic Mexican population, combined with the presence of millions of ethnic Mexicans, their children, and their children's children on both sides of an increasingly integrated frontier zone will continue to present a vast social issue that will demand increasing international attention in the coming years. Still, at the same time, there are few signs that Americans yet view the explosive growth of the ethnic Mexican and greater Latino population with the sense of urgency that is so deeply felt in Mexico, in greater Latin America, and in expanding barrios across the United States. Whether the inhabitants of these communities are able to carve out a meaningful existence anywhere in the Western Hemisphere, or are socialized into what may well become a permanent underclass of marginalized, disaffected, and socially disenfranchised people is a critical question at the beginning of the twenty-first century—and will remain so for the foreseeable future.

NOTES

1. In this essay, I employ the term "ethnic Mexicans" to refer to the combined population in the United States of people of Mexican descent or heritage, regardless of their actual nationality or citizenship status. When referring to Mexican immigrants or migrants I use the terms "Mexican," "Mexican national," or simply "*mexicano.*" When referring to American citizens of Mexican descent, I use the term "Mexican American," except in cases where I utilize the term "Chicano," which denotes a Mexican American who has adopted a certain political positioning and sense of identity distinct from both Mexicans from Mexico and Mexican Americans in the United States. I hope that the text of the essay will make clear the significance of these different types of self-referents.
2. For thought-provoking discussions of the recent "Latinization" of the American South, see, for example, Esther Schrader, "Widening the Field of Workers," *Los Angeles Times*, 26 August 1999; Leah Beth Ward, "North Carolina's Trade in Foreign Farm Workers Draws Scrutiny," *Charlotte Observer*, 30 October 1999; Hector Tobar, "Living La Vida Buena in Georgia," *Los Angeles Times*, 29 December 1999; and Toni Lepeska and Ron Maxey, "Hispanics and Asians Changing Face of Memphis," *The Commercial Appeal* (Memphis, Tenn.), 1 January 2000.
3. For discussion of the establishment of these satellite populations, see Dionicio Nodín Valdés, *Al Norte: Agricultural Workers in the Great Lakes Region, 1917–1970* (Austin: University of Texas Press, 1991); Valdés, *Barrios Norteños: St. Paul and Midwestern Mexican Communities in the Twentieth Century* (Austin: University of Texas Press, 2000); and Zaragosa Vargas, *Proletarians of the North: A History of Mexican Industrial Workers in Detroit and the Midwest, 1917–1933* (Berkeley: University of California Press, 1993).

4. Accurately enumerating the ethnic Mexican population of the United States has always been a controversial issue. Because the U.S. Census Bureau constantly changed both its population categories and its enumerating techniques, historical demographers have been forced to estimate population trends over time. For population estimates and discussion of the statistical challenges involved in enumerating historic populations of ethnic Mexicans, see Charles Teller, ed., *Cuantos Somos: A Demographic Study of the Mexican American Population*, (Austin: Center for Mexican American Studies, University of Texas Press, 1977); Frank D. Bean and Marta Tienda, *The Hispanic Population of the United States* (New York: Russell Sage Foundation, 1987); and Myron Guttman, W. Parker Frisbie, and K. Stephen Blanchard, "A New Look at the Hispanic Population of the United States in 1910," *Historical Methods* 32, no. 1 (winter 1999): 5–19.
5. These population increases occurred despite another major repatriation campaign, "Operation Wetback," conducted by the U.S. Immigration and Naturalization Service (INS) in 1954. According to INS statistics, at least one million Mexicans were compelled to return to Mexico during this period. For discussion, see Juan Ramón García, *Operation Wetback: The Mass Deportation of Mexican Undocumented Workers in 1954* (Westport, Conn.: Greenwood Press, 1980).
6. From Richard Griswold del Castillo and Arnoldo De León, *North to Aztlán: A History of Mexican Americans in the United States* (New York: Twayne Publishers, 1996), 126, table 8.1.
7. For an excellent discussion of the persistence of these transnational ties, see Robert R. Alvarez Jr., *Familia: Migration and Adaptation in Baja and Alta California, 1800–1975* (Berkeley: University of California Press, 1987).
8. Leo Grebler, Joan W. Moore, and Ralph C. Guzmán, *The Mexican American People: The Nation's Second Largest Minority* (New York: Free Press, 1970), 30.
9. Mario Barrera, *Race and Class in the Southwest: A Theory of Racial Inequality* (Notre Dame, Ind.: University of Notre Dame Press, 1979), 131; Vernon M. Briggs, Walter Fogel, and Fred H. Schmidt, *The Chicano Worker* (Austin: University of Texas Press, 1977), 43–77.
10. Vernon M. Briggs, Walter Fogel, and Fred H. Schmidt, *The Chicano Worker* (Austin: University of Texas Press, 1977), 76.
11. For examples of these early observations, see Paul S. Taylor, *An American-Mexican Frontier: Nueces County, Texas* (Chapel Hill: University of North Carolina Press, 1934); Emory Bogardus, *The Mexican in the United States*, University of Southern California Social Science Series, no. 8 (Los Angeles: University of Southern California, 1934); Manuel Gamio, *Mexican Immigration to the United States: A Study of Human Migration and Adjustment* (Chicago: University of Chicago Press, 1930); and Ernesto Galarza, "Mexicans in the Southwest: A Culture in Process," in *Plural Society in the Southwest*, ed. Edward H. Spicer and Raymond H. Thompson (New York: Weatherhead Foundation, 1972), 261–97.
12. For perceptive analyses of the conflicting pulls young Mexican Americans felt in their encounters with American consumer culture see, Vicki L. Ruiz, "'Star Struck': Acculturation, Adolescence, and the Mexican American Woman, 1920–1950," in *Building with Our Hands: New Directions in Chicana Studies*, ed. Adela de la Torre and Beatríz M. Pesquera (Berkeley: University of California Press, 1993), 109–29;

Manuel Peña, *The Texas-Mexican Conjunto: History of a Working-Class Music* (Austin: University of Texas Press, 1985); José E. Limón, *American Encounters: Greater Mexico, The United States, and the Erotics of Culture* (Boston: Beacon Press, 1998); Matt García, *A World of Its Own: Race, Labor, and Citrus in the Making of Greater Los Angeles, 1900–1970* (Chapel Hill: University of North Carolina Press, 2002); and Marilyn Gardner, "New Country, Old Customs," *Christian Science Monitor*, 9 August 2000.

13. See Pierrette Hondagneu-Sotelo, "Overcoming Patriarchal Constraints: The Reconstruction of Gender Relations among Mexican Immigrant Women and Men," *Gender and Society* 6, no. 3 (September 1992): 393–415; and Hondagneu-Sotelo, chapter 7 of this volume.
14. For discussion of the dynamics of social alienation among ethnic Mexican youth, see Joan W. Moore, *Homeboys: Gangs, Drugs, and Prison in the Barrios of Los Angeles* (Philadelphia: Temple University Press, 1978); Martín Sánchez Jankowshi, *City Bound: Urban Life and Political Attitudes Among Chicano Youth* (Albuquerque: University of New Mexico Press, 1986); and James Diego Vigil, *A Rainbow of Gangs: Street Cultures in the Mega-City* (Austin: University of Texas Press, 2002).
15. Until fairly recently, naturalization rates among Mexican nationals were among the lowest of any identifiable population, ranging from only about 26 percent in 1950 (compared to a rate of 74 percent for all other nationality groups) to 14 percent in 1994. Although Mexicans represented by far the largest single immigrant group by nationality between the 1960s and 1990s, they accounted for only 7.5 percent of all naturalizations over that period. For discussion, see Elliott R. Barkan, *And Still They Come: Immigrants and American Society, 1920 to the 1990s* (Wheeling, Ill.: Harlan Davidson, 1996), 106–7, 211; and Leo Grebler, "The Naturalization of Mexican Immigrants in the United States," *International Migration Review* 1, no. 1 (autumn 1966): 17–32.
16. For good historical overviews of ethnic Mexican political involvement through this period see, Miguel David Tirado, "Mexican American Community Political Organization: The Key to Chicano Political Power," *Aztlán* 1 (1970): 53–78; and Juan Gómez-Quiñones, *Chicano Politics: Reality and Promise, 1940–1990* (Albuquerque: University of New Mexico Press, 1990). For an incisive recent examination of the contradictions involved in Mexican American activism during this era, see Stephen J. Pitti, *The Devil in Silicon Valley: Race, Mexican Americans, and Northern California* (Princeton, N.J.: Princeton University Press, 2002).
17. For discussion of these efforts see, Guadalupe San Miguel Jr., *Let All of Them Take Heed: Mexican Americans and the Campaign for Educational Equality in Texas, 1910–1981* (Austin: University of Texas Press, 1987); and San Miguel, *Brown, Not White: School Integration and the Chicano Movement in Texas* (College Station, Tex.: Texas A&M Press, 2001).
18. For compelling recent discussions of political developments outside the Southwest, see, for example, Dionicio Nodín Valdés, *Al Norte: Agricultural Workers in the Great Lakes Region, 1917–1970* (Austin: University of Texas Press, 1991); Valdés, *Barrios Norteños: St. Paul and Midwestern Mexican Communities in the Twentieth Century* (Austin: University of Texas Press, 2000); and Marc S. Rodríguez, "Obreros Unidos: Migration, Migrant Farm Workers' Activism, and the Chicano

Movement in Wisconsin and Texas, 1950–1980," (Ph.D. diss., Northwestern University, 2000).

19. See Peter Nabakov, *Tijerina and the Courthouse Raid* (Albuquerque: University of New Mexico Press, 1969); and Reies López Tijerina, *They Called Me "King Tiger": My Struggle for the Land and Our Rights* (Houston: Arte Público Press, 2000).
20. For good discussions of political events in Texas in the 1960s and 1970s, see Arnoldo De León, *Mexican Americans in Texas: A Brief History* (Arlington Heights, Ill.: Harlan Davidson, 1993), 122–35; and Armando Navarro, *Mexican American Youth Organization: Avant-Garde of the Chicano Movement in Texas* (Austin: University of Texas Press, 1995). See also Marc S. Rodríguez, "Obreros Unidos: Migration, Migrant Farm Workers' Activism, and the Chicano Movement in Wisconsin and Texas, 1950–1980," (Ph.D. diss., Northwestern University, 2000).
21. The shift from "Mexican American" to "Chicano" as a political self-referent during this period was analogous to the shift from "Negro" to "Black" among young African Americans at about the same time. For the significance of the school walkouts, see Juan Gómez-Quiñones, *Mexican Students por La Raza: The Chicano Student Movement in Southern California, 1967–1977* (Santa Barbara, Calif.: Editorial La Causa, 1978); Dolores Delgado Bernal, "Grassroots Leadership Reconceptualized: Chicana Oral Histories and the 1968 East Los Angeles School Blowouts," *Frontiers* 19, no. 2 (1998): 113–42; and Ian Haney López, "Protest, Repression, and Race: Legal Violence and the Chicano Movement," *University of Pennsylvania Law Review* 150, no. 1 (November 2001): 205–45.
22. The best single-volume analyses of these events remain Carlos Muñoz Jr., *Youth, Identity, and Power: The Chicano Movement* (London: Verso, 1989); and Gómez-Quiñones, *Chicano Politics*.
23. The best studies of the rise and demise of LRUP are Ignacio García, *United We Win: The Rise and Fall of the Raza Unida Party* (Tucson: MASRC, University of Arizona Press, 1989); and Armando Navarro, *La Raza Unida Party: A Chicano Challenge to the U.S. Two-Party Dictatorship* (Philadelphia: Temple University Press, 2000).
24. Indeed, after years in which Mexican Americans had successfully fended off government efforts to define them as "non-white," in 1970 MALDEF activists in Texas were able to convince a federal district court to rule in *Cisneros v. Corpus Christi Independent School District* (a ruling later upheld on appeal by the U.S. Supreme Court) that Mexican Americans constituted an "identifiable ethnic minority with a past pattern of discrimination" and thus were eligible for special federal protections and redress. The ruling proved useful in the fight against segregation, but it also had the paradoxical effect of "racializing" ethnic Mexicans in a new if largely unintentional way. For brief discussions of this important case, see Guadalupe San Miguel Jr., *Let All of Them Take Heed: Mexican Americans and the Campaign for Educational Equality in Texas, 1910–1981* (Austin: University of Texas Press, 1987); and Arnoldo De León, *Mexican Americans in Texas: A Brief History* (Arlington Heights, Ill.: Harlan Davidson, 1993), 120–21.
25. For an insightful recent analysis of the rise and decline of the Chicano movement in an important site, see Ernesto Chávez, *Mi Raza Primero! (My People First!): Nationalism, Identity, and Insurgency in the Chicano Movement in Los Angeles, 1966–1978* (Berkeley: University of California Press, 2002).

26. See, for example, Laura M. Padilla, "'But *You're* Not a Dirty Mexican': Internalized Oppression, Latinos, and Law," *Texas Hispanic Journal of Law & Policy* 7, no. 1 (fall 2001): 59–113.
27. For discussion of Chicana feminist responses to sexism in the movement—and in the ethnic Mexican community at large—see Alma García, *Chicana Feminist Thought: The Basic Historical Writings* (New York: Routledge, 1997); and Paula Moya, "Chicana Feminism and Postmodernist Theory" *Signs* 26, no. 2 (2001): 441–83. For a more general overview of some of the gendered dimensions and contradictions of the movement, see Ramón A. Gutiérrez, "Community, Patriarchy, and Individualism: The Politics of Chicano History and the Dream of Equality," *American Quarterly* 45 (March 1993): 44–72.
28. For discussion of some of the most important of these intraethnic conflicts, see Tatcho Mindiola and Max Martínez, eds., *Chicano-Mexicano Relations* (Houston: Mexican American Studies Program, University of Houston, 1986); and David G. Gutiérrez, *Walls and Mirrors: Mexican Americans, Mexican Immigrants, and the Politics of Ethnicity* (Berkeley: University of California Press, 1995).
29. For explication of this theme see David G. Gutiérrez, "Migration, Emergent Ethnicity, and the 'Third Space': The Shifting Politics of Nationalism in Greater Mexico," *Journal of American History* 86, no. 2 (September 1999): 481–517.
30. Robin Fields, "'90s Saw a Tide of New People," *Los Angeles Times*, 6 August 2001.
31. It should be noted, however, that some of the population increases that have been recorded since the 1970s are due to more sophisticated and accurate enumeration techniques.
32. For discussion of the impact of the period of postwar economic growth known as "Mexican Miracle," see Roger D. Hansen, *The Politics of Mexican Development* (Baltimore: Johns Hopkins University Press, 1971); and Colin M. MacLachlan and William H. Beezeley, *El Gran Pueblo: A History of Greater Mexico*, 2d ed., (Upper Saddle River, N.J.: Prentice Hall, 1999), 382–420.
33. Michael C. Meyer and William L. Sherman, *The Course of Mexican History*, 5th ed. (New York: Oxford University Press, 1995), 678–88.
34. Dale Hathaway, *Allies Across the Border: Mexico's "Authentic Labor Front" and Global Solidarity* (Cambridge, Mass.: South End Press, 2000), 112.
35. For an insightful historical analysis of these trends over the course of the century, see Raul A. Fernández and Gilbert González, "Chicano History: Transcending Cultural Models," *Pacific Historical Review* 63, no. 4 (1994): 469–97.
36. It is estimated that remittances sent to Mexico from nationals in the United States increased from less than $3 billion in 1990 to more than $6 billion in 2000. Before the events of September 11, 2001, Mexican expatriates in the United States were sending $750 million *per month*—and were thus on a pace to remit more than $9 billion to their communities in Mexico. Only international oil sales generated more foreign exchange. See Chris Kraul, "Mexican Immigrants Sending More Money Home," *Los Angeles Times*, 24 September 2001. For larger contextual discussions of transnational networks and the dynamics involved in migration circuits between the two countries, see Alejandro Portes and Robert L. Bach, *Latin Journey: Cuban and Mexican Immigrants in the United States* (Berkeley: University of California Press, 1985); Douglas Massey, Rafael Alarcón, Jorge Durand, and Humberto González, *Return to*

Aztlán: The Social Process of International Migration from Western Mexico (Berkeley: University of California Press, 1987); Roger Rouse, "Mexican Migration and the Social Space of Postmodernism," *Disapora* 1, no. 1 (1991): 8–23; and Bryan R. Roberts, Reanne Frank, and Fernando Lozano-Ascencio, "Transnational Migrant Communities and Mexican Migration to the United States," *Ethnic and Racial Studies* 22, no. 2 (March 1999): 238–267. Overall, immigrants in the United States remit to friends and family abroad at least $30 billion each year. See, Susan Sachs, "Immigrants Facing Strict New Controls On Cash Sent Home," *New York Times*, 12 November 2002.

37. Colin M. MacLachlan and William H. Beezeley, *El Gran Pueblo: A History of Greater Mexico*, 2d ed., (Upper Saddle River, N.J.: Prentice Hall, 1999), 460; David E. Lorey, *The U.S.-Mexican Border in the Twentieth Century* (Wilmington, Del.: Scholarly Resources, 1999); and Isidro Morales, "NAFTA: The Institutionalization of Economic Openness and the Configuration of Mexican Geo-Economic Spaces," *Third World Quarterly* 20, no. 5 (1999): 971–93.

38. See Jonathan J. Higuera, "Why Maquiladoras Endure," *Hispanic Business* (November 2000): 54; Chris Kraul, "Mexican Border Factory Output is Slowing," *Los Angeles Times*, 8 October 2001; and Diane Lindquist, "Maquiladora Mess," *San Diego Union-Tribune*, 28 October 2001. It is estimated that as a result of the 2001 global economic downturn, Mexico's maquiladora industry lost more than 200,000 jobs—many of which were relocated to Asian overseas markets with even lower labor costs. See Diane Lindquist, "A Boost for Baja," *San Diego Union-Tribune*, 22 February 2002. Still, while the maquiladora sector continues to adjust to global restructuring, post-NAFTA U.S.-Mexico trade has continued to grow, expanding from $81 billion in 1993 (the year before NAFTA was implemented) to $247 billion in 2000. See Chris Kraul, "Economic Downturn Deepens in Mexico," *Los Angeles Times*, 1 July 2001; Frank McCoy, "NAFTA Expansion Hits Traffic Jam," *Hispanic Business* (September 2001): 26; and Diane Lindquist, "Maquiladora Mess," *San Diego Union-Tribune*, 28 October 2001.

39. The practice of shifting production facilities to offshore sources has been a major feature of globalization. According to recent estimates, of all worldwide production, the share produced by workers employed by foreign firms increased from 11.6 percent in 1977 to 16.3 percent by 1990. See Evelyn Iritani, "In Global Economy, U.S. Job Gains, Losses Know No Borders," *Los Angeles Times*, 6 April 2001.

40. The proportion of Mexican goods exported to the United States after NAFTA has risen to 88 percent as of 2001. At the same time, the number of U.S. jobs lost to NAFTA since 1994 in the major industrial states of California, Michigan, New York, Texas, and Ohio is estimated to exceed 250,000. For discussion of the potentially profound social impacts of these trends, see Saskia Sassen, "U.S. Immigration Policy Toward Mexico in a Global Economy," *Journal of International Affairs* 43, no. 2 (winter 1990): 369–83; Dolores Acevedo and Thomas J. Espenshade, "Implications of the North American Free Trade Agreement for Mexican Migration to the United States," *Population and Development Review* 18, no. 4 (December 1992): 729–44; Enrique Dussel Peters, "Recent Structural Changes in Mexico's Economy: A Preliminary Analysis of Some Sources of Mexican Migration to the United States," in *Crossings: Mexican Immigration in Interdisciplinary Perspective*, ed. Marcelo Suárez-Orózco, (Cambridge, Mass.: David Rockefeller Center for Latin American Studies,

Harvard University, 1998): 53–74; and Evelyn Iritani, "Latino Immigrants Pay a Price for Free Trade," *Los Angeles Times,* 12 June 2001.

41. See María Patricia Fernández-Kelly, *For We Are Sold, I and My People: Women and Industry in Mexico's Northern Frontier* (Albany: State University of New York Press, 1983); Susan Tiano, *Patriarchy on the Line: Labor, Gender, and Ideology in the Mexican Maquila Industry* (Philadelphia: Temple University Press, 1994); Altha Cravey, *Women and Work in Mexico's Maquiladoras* (New York: Rowman and Littlefield, 1998); and Cirila Quintero Ramírez, "Migration and Maquiladoras on Mexico's Northern Border," *Migration World* 28, no. 3 (2000): 14–18. See also Alfred Corchado and Dianne Solís, "A Force of Change: Unprecedented Surge of Mexican Migrants Altering the U.S. Economy, Politics and Culture," *Dallas Morning News*, 19 September 1999.

42. As a partial consequence of such rapid population growth, the poverty rate in Mexico rose more than 70 percent between 1990 and 1996, with an estimated 27 percent of the Mexican population living in what one report called "extreme poverty." See "Census: Mexico Slows Population Growth," *San Diego Union-Tribune*, 22 June 2000; James M. Cypher, "Developing Disarticulation Within the Mexican Economy," *Latin American Perspectives* 28, no. 3 (May 2001): 11–37; and William A. V. Clark, *The California Cauldron: Immigration and the Fortunes of Local Communities* (New York: Guilford Press, 1998), 30.

43. See David E. Lorey, *The U.S.-Mexican Border in the Twentieth Century* (Wilmington, Del.: Scholarly Resources, 1999), 118, table 6–1, 126, table 6–2.

44. For discussion of the history of population booms in the border, see Oscar J. Martínez, *Border Boom Town: Ciudad Juárez since 1848* (Austin: University of Texas Press, 1978); and Martínez, *Troublesome Border* (Tucson: University of Arizona Press, 1988). For the contemporary era, see Sandra Dibble, "Boomtown," *San Diego Union Tribune*, 10 September 2000; and Tim Padgett and Cathy Booth Thomas, "Two Countries, One City," *Time*, 11 June 2001, 64–66.

45. See Patrick J. McDonnell, "Mexicans Change Face of U.S. Demographics," *Los Angeles Times*, 10 May 2001. Another way to gauge these population shifts is to consider the profound impact they have had on "sending" regions in Mexico. For example, although it remains an extreme case, officials have recently estimated that fully *one-half* of the entire population of the Mexican state of Zacatecas now resides in the United States. See Jennifer Mena, "Today in Santa Ana: Mexico's 2006 Race," *Los Angeles Times*, 5 July 2002; Jennifer Mena, "Zacatecans Strive to End Emigration," *Los Angeles Times*, 6 July 2002; Mary M. Kent, Kelvin M. Pollard, John Haaga, and Mark Mather, "First Glimpses from the 2000 U.S. Census," Population Bulletin 56, no. 2 (June 2001): 14; and Betsy Guzmán, *The Hispanic Population: Census 2000 Brief* (Washington, D.C.: U.S. Department of Commerce, U.S. Census Bureau, Economics and Statistics Administration, May 2001).

46. For regional and national population growth trends see Hector Tobar, "Deep in the Heart of Texas, the Popular Destination is Suburbia," *Los Angeles Times*, 13 March 2001; Tom Gorman, "Nevada Jumps 66.3% in Ten Years, Census Shows," *Los Angeles Times*, 14 March 2001; and Betsy Guzmán, *The Hispanic Population: Census 2000 Brief* (Washington, D.C.: U.S. Department of Commerce, U.S. Census Bureau, Economics and Statistics Administration, May 2001), 4, table 2.

47. For an insightful analysis of recent trends in New York City, see Michael Jones-Correa, *Between Two Nations: The Political Predicament of Latinos in New York City* (Ithaca: Cornell University Press, 1998).
48. In 2000, the border-state towns and cities with the highest proportion of Latino residents were: unincorporated East Los Angeles (an astonishing 97 percent); Laredo, Brownsville, McAllen, and El Paso, Texas (94, 91, 80, and 77 percent, respectively); and three other cities in California: Santa Ana (76 percent), El Monte (72 percent), and Oxnard (66 percent). See Hector Becerra and Fred Alvarez, "Census Reflects Large Gains for Latinos," *Los Angles Times*, 10 May 2001; and U.S. Census Bureau, *Statistical Abstract: 2001* (Washington, D.C.: U.S. Census Bureau, 2001), 39, table 36.
49. The five metropolitan areas with the highest decennial percent increases in Latino population were: Greensboro-Winston-Salem–High Point, North Carolina (Latino population—62,000, an increase of 694 percent); Charlotte-Gastonia–Rock Hill, North Carolina/South Carolina (77,000, a 622 percent increase); Raleigh-Durham–Chapel Hill, North Carolina (73,000—569 percent); Atlanta, Georgia (269,000—362 percent); and Las Vegas, Nevada (322,000—262 percent). For statistics and discussion of these trends, see U.S. Census Bureau, *Statistical Abstract of the United States: 2001* (Washington, D.C.: U.S. Census Bureau, 2001), 39, table 36; and William H. Frey, "Mini-Melting Pots: Census 2000," *American Demographics* 25, no. 6 (June 2001): 21–23.
50. See Frederico A. Subveri-Vélez, "Mass Communication and Hispanics," in *Handbook of Hispanic Cultures in the United States: Sociology*, ed. Nicolás Kanellos and Claudio Esteva-Fabregat (Houston: Arte Público Press, 1994), 329.
51. For the explosion in Spanish-language radio, see Alisa Valdes-Rodríguez, "Rocanroll!" *Los Angeles Times,* 8 August 2000; and Ernesto Lechner, "The Other Latin Music," *Hispanic Business* (July/August 2001): 88, 90, 92.
52. Tim Dougherty, "Breakout Year," *Hispanic Business*, December 2000: 46; Kim Campbell, "Demographics Drive the Latino Media Story," *The Christian Science Monitor*, 21 June 2001; Deborah Sharp, "Si Usted no Habla Español, Puede Quedarse Rezagado—If You Don't Speak Spanish, You Might Be Left Behind," *USA Today*, 9 May 2001; and "Spending Spree," *Hispanic Business*, December 2001: 38, 40, 56.
53. Teresa A. Sullivan, "A Demographic Portrait," in *Hispanics in the United States: An Agenda for the Twenty-First Century*, ed. Pastora San Juan Cafferty and David W. Engstrom, (New Brunswick, N.J.: Transaction Publishers, 2000), 19.
54. See Maurilio E. Vigil, "Latinos in American Politics," in *Handbook of Hispanic Cultures in the United States: Sociology*, ed. Felíx Padilla (Houston: Arte Público Press, 1994), 99; Mark Z. Barabak, "Blacks See a Shrinking Role in California," *Los Angeles Times*, 20 May 2001; and David S. Broder, "The Mobilization of New Americans," *San Diego Union-Tribune*, 23 May 2001.
55. See Juan F. Perea, *Immigrants Out! The New Nativism and the Anti-Immigrant Impulse in the United States* (New York: New York University Press, 1997).
56. See John Marelius, "In Pivotal States, Latinos' Impact May Ring Hollow," *San Diego Union-Tribune*, 8 October 2000.
57. See U.S. Census Bureau, *Statistical Abstract of the United States: 2001* (Washington, D.C.: U.S. Census Bureau, 2001), 40, table 37. See also, Manuel Pastór Jr., "Interde-

pendence, Inequality, and Identity: Linking Latinos and Latin Americans," in *Borderless Borders: U.S. Latinos, Latin Americans, and the Paradox of Interdependence*, ed. Frank Bonilla, Edwin Meléndez, Rebecca Morales, and María de los Angeles Torres (Philadelphia: Temple University Press, 1998), 29–30.

58. See, for example, Gregory Rodríguez, "The Democrats' Fixation on the Aggrieved Minority," *Los Angeles Times*, 13 August 2000; and "Don't Mistake the Parts for the Whole in L.A.," *Los Angeles Times*, 6 July 2001; Linda Chávez, *Out of the Barrio: Toward a New Politics of Hispanic Assimilation* (New York: Basic Books, 1991); and Peter Skerry, *Mexican Americans: Ambivalent Minority* (New York: Free Press, 1993).

59. According to a recent analysis in *Hispanic Business*, 34 percent of all Latino heads of household in California and 28 percent of Latino heads of household in Texas were "middle income" earners (i.e., with earnings of between $40,000 and $140,000 per year). For discussion of national trends see, Robert R. Brischetto, "The Hispanic Middle Class Comes of Age," *Hispanic Business* (December 2001): 21–30.

60. Between 1950 and 1996, such skilled jobs dropped from nearly a third of all jobs in the United States to less than 15 percent. Over the same period, the low-paid service sector expanded from less than 12 percent to nearly one-third of all jobs. Another gauge of the structural changes in the economy is the slowing rate of growth of wages, salaries, and fringe benefits. Between 1950 and 1960, wages, salaries, and fringe benefits grew by a robust 38.7 percent per full-time employee. In contrast, between 1984 and 1994, growth in these areas was 7.1 percent. For occupational shifts see Alejandro Portes and Rubén Rumbaut, *Legacies: The Story of the Immigrant Second Generation* (Berkeley: University of California Press; New York: Russell Sage Foundation, 2001), 57; and Steven Greenhouse, "Foreign Workers at Highest Level in Seven Decades, *New York Times*, 4 September 2000. For changing rates of compensation see Frank Levy, "How Big is the Income Dilemma?" in *America's Demographic Tapestry: Baseline for the New Millennium*, ed. James W. Hughes and Joseph J. Seneca (New Brunswick, N.J.: Rutgers University Press, 1999), 112. See also Gladys Jiménez-Muñoz and Kelvin Santiago-Valles, chapter 2, this volume.

61. See Michael D. Yates, *Longer Hours, Fewer Jobs: Employment and Unemployment in the United States* (New York: Monthly Review Press, 1994).

62. On the expansion and significance of the informal sector, see *Informalization: Process and Structure*, ed. Faruk Tabak and Michaeline A. Crichlow (Baltimore: Johns Hopkins University Press, 2000).

63. See Robert R. Brischetto, "The Hispanic Middle Class Comes of Age," *Hispanic Business*, December 2001: 21–32; and Robin Fields, "'90s Saw a Tide of New People," *Los Angeles Times*, 6 August 2001.

64. Dan Walters, "We May Have to Live with Stratification," *San Diego Union-Tribune*, 9 May 2000; Melissa Healy, "U.S. Children's Poverty Level Is Down 17% Since 1993," *Los Angeles Times*, 11 August 2000; Peter H. Hong and Patrick J. McDonnell, "Proportion of Immigrants in U.S. Population has Doubled since '70," *Los Angeles Times*, 7 February 2002.

65. See Portes and Rumbaut, *Legacies*, 57; Daniel T. Lichter and Martha L. Crowley, "Poverty in America: Beyond Welfare Reform," *Population Bulletin* 57, no. 2 (June 2002): 1–36; and Jorge Chapa, "The Burden of Interdependence: Demographic, Economic, and Social Prospects for Latinos in the Reconfigured U.S. Economy," in

Borderless Borders: U.S. Latinos, Latin Americans, and the Paradox of Interdependence, ed. Frank Bonilla, Edwin Meléndez, Rebecca Morales, and María de los Angeles Torres (Philadelphia: Temple University Press, 1998), 71–82.

66. See Mary C. Daly, Deborah Reed, and Heather N. Royer, "Population Mobility and Income Inequality in California," in *California Counts: Population Trends and Profiles* 2, no. 4 (May 2001) (San Francisco: Public Policy Institute of California). See William A. V. Clark, *The California Cauldron: Immigration and the Fortunes of Local Communities* (New York: Guilford Press, 1998), 74–82; and "California," *Migration News* 8, no. 6 (June 2002).
67. White flight has probably been most dramatic in California, which, coincidentally, has the largest immigrant population in the United States. Indeed, in a trend that has accelerated since the 1970s, the 2000 census reported that southern California's non-Hispanic white population shrank by nearly 12 percent. White flight from Los Angeles County was even more pronounced, with the non-Hispanic white population dropping by 18 percent over the same period. By 2000, non-Hispanic whites represented only 41.4 percent of southern California's population. Overall, the state of California saw its non-Hispanic white population drop by 7 percent between 1990 and 2000. See Robin Fields and Scott Martelle, "White Exodus Attributed to Economic Slump," *Los Angeles Times*, 31 March 2001; and Geoffrey Mohan and Phil Willon, "Population Abandons the Older Suburbs for Isolated, Affluent Fringe," *Los Angeles Times*, 30 March 2001.
68. Gary Orfield, Mark Bachmeier, David R, James, and Tamela Eitle, *Deepening Segregation in American Public Schools* (Cambridge: Harvard Project on School Desegregation, 1997), cited in Melissa Roderick, "Hispanics and Education," in *Hispanics in the United States: An Agenda for the Twenty-First Century*, ed. Pastora San Juan Cafferty and David W. Engstrom, (New Brunswick, N.J.: Transaction Publishers, 2000), 146.
69. Portes and Rumbaut, *Legacies*: 61. For a similar analysis, see Lichter and Crowley, "Poverty in America," 24–26.
70. In Los Angeles County alone, officials estimate that at least 112,000 young people are either members of gangs or are gang "wannabes." See Charlie LeDuff, "Los Angeles Police Chief Faces a Huge Challenge," *New York Times*, 24 October 2002.

TWO

SOCIAL POLARIZATION AND COLONIZED LABOR: PUERTO RICANS IN THE UNITED STATES, 1945–2000

KELVIN A. SANTIAGO-VALLES
AND GLADYS M. JIMÉNEZ-MUÑOZ

INTRODUCTION

During the last twenty-five years the perennial and disproportionately high indices of poverty among Puerto Ricans in the United States continued to puzzle both social scientists and policy makers. Despite the growing numbers of highly educated Puerto Ricans within the United States, this second-largest U.S. Latino group nevertheless still fails to conform to the "immigrant model" of upward mobility and the "ethnic paradigm" of socioeconomic development. Prominent scholars like Marta Tienda and others have argued from the late 1970s to the present day that a satisfactory explanation for the growing social disparities between most Puerto Ricans in the United States versus other Hispanic Americans and African Americans remains very much an open question.[1]

This essay suggests pursuing an alternate path that, with further research, could begin to satisfactorily unravel this riddle. By way of reconceptualization and extensive counterdemonstrations, we try to go beyond the limits of primarily concentrating on the continental U.S. arena, as most current research has done. Such barriers continue to confine even cutting-edge research that has identified the role of deindustrialization and the collapse of traditional manufacturing within the U.S. economy as the primary causes of widespread poverty among many Puerto Rican communities.[2] What we have done is to place these brutal social and economic processes within the broader context of the massive changes in the global economy, which have been most strongly influenced by the actions of the United States. Within this framework, we also suggest that the crude economic frameworks and short-term scope of most existing research models might be improved by examining Puerto Ricans in the U.S. mainland as part of a world-historical process of colonized labor formation framed by the conflicting ways that Puerto Ricans have been narrowly incorporated and reincorporated within a constantly shifting world-economy.[3]

We understand the structural position of Puerto Ricans within the United States as part of a racialized, indeed colonial, pattern of labor exploitation.[4] But we also believe it is necessary to explicitly link the subordinate racialization of Puerto Ricans in the United States to their feminization over the historical long term. One of the principal features of racially subordinate populations is that we are negatively associated with characteristics widely attributed to "women": that is being capricious, irrational, excessively emotional, wayward, infantile, and therefore in need of guidance, control, protection, supervision, instruction, and tutelage. Thus, whether male or female, the subordination of "lesser races" has included a complex process of feminization as well.[5]

Our emphasis here is on the colonial character of unevenly assembling global labor on the basis of deeply rooted sexual and racial hierarchies. What make such situations and populations *colonial* are the structural imbalances that reinforce and reproduce populations (in these markedly sexual and racial ways) as socially inferior or peripheral,[6] holding those of European descent as the norm. Such imbalances result in higher rates of return for the racially dominant elites and short-term social benefits for the racially dominant laboring populations. Hence, the colonial condition of Puerto Ricans in the United States is not a matter of simple negative stereotypes,[7] but is rather a component part of the larger historical and contemporaneous world-system.[8]

Being part of a colonized or peripheral labor force is a *relational and historical* condition, rather than an absolute situation marked by some universally fixed statistical threshold. The colonization or peripheralization of labor is defined by the deficit between the relatively larger amount of physical and mental energies spent during everyday socioeconomic survival versus the relatively lower formal income and the other relatively unfavorable living conditions of a racially subordinate population *when compared to* the general, and relatively privileged, conditions of the colonizer population. In the case of most Puerto Ricans, such inequalities have been historically documented with respect to lower earnings, second-rate education, inadequate food intake, poorer health conditions, substandard housing, and higher unemployment levels, vis-à-vis those of the racially normative populations across all of the United States and its imperial domains.[9]

THE BROADER CONTEXT OF THE POSTWAR ERA

In 1960, the population of Puerto Rico reached approximately 2,350,000, and its inhabitants abandoned the countryside and mountain regions in larger numbers, finally transforming the island by the end of that same decade into an urban society (USBC 1993a: 31). There were already almost 900,000 Puerto Ricans on the U.S. mainland by 1960, which amounted to a 200 percent increase when compared to island migrants identified by the 1950 census as living in the United States. According to this same 1960 census, over 600,000 Puerto Ricans in the United States had been born in the island, and this was 172 percent larger than the number of U.S. residents who had been island-born in 1950. Almost 300,000 Puerto Ricans in the United States in 1960 were of parents born in Puerto Rico, which represented a 262 percent increase from the figures for 1950 (tabulations based on: USBC 1963; USBC 1973).

Over the past two centuries, inhabitants of the island had polarized into a large mass of "mixed-race" laborers and small property owners (near-white, mulatto, and black) versus the insulated elites of European descent, mostly Spaniard, but also some French, British, German, and Anglo-American. Since the early nineteenth century, the peasants and artisans derisively referred to these elites (who controlled most of the landed estates and large businesses) and their parasitic intelligentsia as *blanquitos* or "little whites." By the 1800s, all Puerto Ricans—of whatever social background—had begun referring to themselves also as "*criollos*" (or Creoles) and *Boricuas*, the latter term deriving from the original indigenous name for this island (Borikén). These social, racial, and national markers nevertheless persisted after the island became a formal U.S. colony as a result of the War of 1898.

From the mid-1930s to the mid-1960s, U.S. corporate, export-oriented agriculture in the island (sugar and tobacco) went into crisis and decline. This process was accompanied by massive unemployment and a distinct shift on the island toward export-oriented, light, labor-intensive, machine-based industry; the uneven imposition of welfare-state reforms; and a mass market for low-income housing and individual mechanized transportation (Muñiz Varela 1983; Santiago-Valles 1994a). The reincorporation of Puerto Ricans within the restructured world-economy in this manner created the circumstances that led many manual day laborers, landless peasants, and devastated small-property owners to leave the island in unprecedented numbers. The migrants who left the island at this time moved into the dilapidated tenements vacated by Italians, Jews, and Poles in the northeastern U.S. seaboard and Chicago during the 1940s and 1950s, joining the similarly colonized populations from the U.S. South, U.S. Southwest, and Mexico who were nevertheless being incorporated within a much a broader spectrum of the U.S. economy (F. Padilla 1987: 58;

Torres 1995: 64–78). As opposed to island farm laborers during the 1898–1944 period, who produced consumer goods on the island, postwar Puerto Rican rural workers were increasingly repositioned as seasonal migrants in U.S. mainland farms.[10] In this manner, the use of low-wage Boricua labor began overlapping with other ways of exploiting peripheral labor in the United States—such as share-cropping, the convict-lease system, the *bracero* program (see Gutiérrez, chapter 1, this volume)—alongside higher-wage labor in the industrial production of capital and consumer goods.

To a large extent, the intensifying incorporation of most Puerto Ricans into the lowest strata of the restructured regional economy was masked by a simultaneous expansion of the propertied, educated, and almost exclusively white Puerto Rican minority (the *blanquitos*) on the island. Although the development of this minority was uneven, this sector has oscillated between one-fourth and one-third of the island's population since World War II. These historical and present-day partial beneficiaries of colonial domination in Puerto Rico were the heirs of the early twentieth century's *hacendados* (large landowners), bankers, great merchants, Euro-Caribbean intelligentsia, and "native" bureaucrats. By the mid to late twentieth century, they had evolved into the local junior partners of the new U.S. corporate investors and the upper strata of a rapidly expanding local state administration, as well as an overlapping array of highly skilled professionals, technicians, and managerial personnel across the financial, commercial, service, industrial, and public sectors. There was also an increase in government relief programs (1940–1973) and a saturation of the local market with cheap U.S. goods associated with the overall postwar economic expansion and subsequent economic restructuring, which coincided with the relative expansion and accommodation among the island's educated minorities from the 1970s to the 1990s.[11]

The social polarization structured by the colonial patterns just described has to be conceptually located within the even larger context of rising U.S. global economic hegemony, the continuing reconfiguration and polarization of the labor force in the United States, and the already mentioned reincorporation of Puerto Ricans within the world-economy. This combined process (which many academics and journalists have recently and ahistorically dubbed "globalization"[12]) involved increases in, the extension of "scientific management" and work discipline within U.S. enterprises; the accelerated degradation of wage workers' expertise levels when their skills were superseded by new technologies and speed-ups in the labor process; a corollary continuing demand for cheap labor—particularly within declining economic sectors such as food processing, the garment industry, and labor-intensive agriculture. Together, the various components of this process had the effect of locking in disproportionately higher numbers of workers long considered to be "disposable" or peripheral into even narrower tiers of dead-end jobs. The postwar phase of globalization also involved a veritable explosion in the capitalist production of new consumer goods (namely, electric household products, standardized housing, and the automobile) and of infrastructure projects enabling the rapid consumption of such goods (i.e., highway construction, urban renewal, suburban sprawl) in order to meet the further growth in the demand for just these goods, particularly among the skilled sectors of the working classes and the expanding professional-managerial middle classes. (Arrighi 1994: 273–81, 295–300; Aglietta 1979).

These reciprocal developments stimulated a gradual increase in the movement of Puerto Ricans to the U.S. mainland over the course of the century in three distinct eras of migration: 1898–1944, when an average of 2,681 people per year left the island; 1945–1968, when the yearly average increased to 31,020 people; and 1968–2000, when the migratory flow became much more cyclical, extremely variegated, and, hence, considerably more difficult to calculate.[13]

One of the main factors behind the enormous postwar emigration is once again associated with how Puerto Ricans were being reincorporated within the global economy. Older sources of income for ordinary Puerto Ricans—such as the sale of marginal farm produce and seasonal agricultural labor—rapidly disintegrated from the late 1940s to the early 1960s. As a result, between 1950 and 1960 the number of agricultural laborers dropped by 37 percent while the number of farmers and farm administrators decreased by 51 percent (Vázquez Calzada 1978: 376–77). This deterioration extended the protracted agrarian crisis of the interwar period (Gulick 1952; Augelli 1972), but now within the context of Puerto Rico's realignment within the evolving international division of labor, expressed most clearly in the new version of the rising use of "foreign" labor within the U.S. "domestic" economy.[14] Similar to the U.S. South (Hoover and Ratchford 1951; Wright 1986: 239–49) and large portions of Latin America (Cueva 1977) at that time, Puerto Rico was being transformed into a major enclave for light, labor-intensive, export-oriented industries dependent on peripheral labor. This narrow band of industries consisted primarily of subsidiaries of corporations from the northeastern U.S. from economic sectors (e.g., apparel and food processing) desperately in need of cheaper labor.[15]

In all these peripheral regions of the Americas, the forms of livelihood among populations deemed racially inferior perennially fell below the living standards of the racially dominant and colonizer populations. In the case of Puerto Rico, average hourly wages were only 28 percent of what they were in the United States in 1950 and still only 41 percent of the U.S. average in 1960 (USDC 1979: 2:56). This gap—while narrowing slightly—persisted into the late 1990s. Indeed, a convergence of average hourly wages in the United States and hourly wages in Puerto Rico has *not* taken place even today, nor does it seem likely in the immediate future. In addition, while new factories were a burgeoning source of employment on the island, as the armed forces and the emergency-relief agencies had been during the war, Puerto Rico still had relatively high, officially recorded unemployment levels: 15 percent in 1940 and 13 percent in 1950.[16] Thus, despite the relative decline in island unemployment rates between 1940 and 1950, at the end of the decade the unemployment level was still 2.4 times the overall unemployment rate for the United States (Bureau of Labor Statistics [BLS] 2002b). This was another significant feature of racial subordination and colonial feminization, and it endures to the present day.

But there were three additional important factors driving Puerto Ricans to seek work in the United States. For one thing, the plants established on the island relied more on machine tools, which meant jobs there carried intensified regulatory instruction, stricter work discipline, and higher skill levels, all of which clashed with a mostly unskilled and relatively uneducated labor force of landless-peasant background (Reynolds and Gregory 1965). To complicate matters further, these new industrial complexes were also established in urban zones far from the hills and mountains where most of the island's population lived (Young 1974; Tata 1980). Lastly, those light, labor-intensive U.S. industries which remained in the northeastern U.S. often belonged to the same declining economic sectors as those firms which had relocated to the Caribbean or the U.S. South, also sharing the lowest levels of machine use and a desperate need for cheap labor. This same narrow band of backward manufacturing companies, together with those leading corporate sectors riding the wave of the postwar economic boom, began attracting large masses of low-wage labor from all over the world in the early 1950s—especially to the northeast coast and Midwestern regions of the United States.[17] New York City's garment industry was a prominent example of this trend. These were some of the main forces compelling massive segments of the impoverished rural population of the island to relocate both to the urban areas in Puerto Rico and to the swelling metropolitan areas of the United States.

However, this monumental emigration of the island's laboring-poor majorities from the 1940s to the 1960s has to be framed within other larger contexts, specifically the contested developments unfolding inside the United States and the rest of its imperial domains.[18] The expulsion and mobilization of large masses of laborers is always something that the working classes and related subordinate sectors have tried to use to their advantage, however contradictorily. They have mainly done this by evading economic conscription into wage work whenever alternate forms of income, subsistence, or both were available (which usually has been nonwage activity) or by combining formal wage work with these alternate and usually illegal forms of income. There is nothing particularly "Puerto Rican," nor even mid-twentieth-century, about such responses.[19] Like subordinate populations everywhere, Puerto Rico's laboring-poor majorities on the move also experimented with forms of refusing a factory system that they understood as what one scholar has termed "the least favorable terrain of struggle" (Linebaugh 1981: 86–87). And as they had done during the first half of the twentieth century,[20] the authorities (in both North America and in the island) were forced to consider such "struggles . . . for the reappropriation of wealth" and the broader patterns of postwar "native" waywardness "as a major problem of 'crime and order.'"[21]

This was how growing numbers of Puerto Ricans ended up choosing migration (both internal and, particularly, external) as a way of escaping or disrupting capitalist control over their labor. Bourgeois interests had always sought to channel the migration of Boricua peasants and urban workers in a manner that addressed the needs of capital and the state. But as was true for Asian laborers in Hawaii and their African American and Mexican counterparts in North America,[22] Puerto Rican laborers simultaneously turned this very recourse, migration, into a device that short-circuited employers' ability to readily exploit colonized labor. Such practices followed the historical trend of capitalist development everywhere insofar as these demographic movements usually opened avenues to noncapitalist (and heavily criminalized) ways of making a living: that is, survival practices which partially interfered with both capital's ability to exploit labor and with the bourgeois rule of law.

Migration was made all the more attractive by the previously mentioned expansion of governmental services and relief programs in the island's towns and cities and, even more so, by the expansion of a mass market for standardized affordable housing, electronic domestic goods, and individual mechanized transportation in the United States. On both sides of the San Juan–U.S. routes, dispossessed Puerto Ricans attempted to turn such massive socioeconomic transformations to their own advantage. As a short-term solution they did this by shifting within and across different regional domains of the entire United States, trying to take advantage of variations in wages and general living conditions. In the U.S. setting, some of these "native" laborers tended toward jobs in light industry, lower-skilled services, and so on in these urban contexts. But many simultaneously tried their hand in the urban and mid- to late-twentieth-century versions of what Linebaugh (1981: 87) calls "the dwarf economy": that is, the elusive but always significant informal sector.

LABOR AND COMMUNITY SURVIVAL DURING ECONOMIC EXPANSION

As indicated above, most Puerto Ricans migrating from the island ended up working as unskilled or semiskilled laborers in the cities. The proportion of all Puerto Ricans in the United States (of both sexes) classified as factory operatives, nonfarm laborers, and domestic servants oscillated between 54 percent in 1950 and 56 percent in 1960; service workers fluctuated between 18 percent in 1950 and 15 percent in 1960. During this same period, the proportion of those categorized as sales and office workers rose from 10 percent to 13 percent for both sexes (tabulations based on: USBC 1953; USBC 1963). The overwhelming majority of these employees—even in the case of the latter, "white-collar" grouping—tended to be positioned in the lesser-skilled segments of the U.S. labor force. The principal difference between this occupational pattern and that of Puerto Ricans on the island at this time for both sexes was that agricultural laborers, while shrinking as a proportion of the overall labor force, still constituted a significant portion of all manual workers in Puerto Rico—31 percent in 1950 and 20 percent in 1960—while the proportion of service workers was only about a third of that for Puerto Ricans in the United States (Vázquez Calzada 1978: 376–377). This general occupational profile remained in place for most of the 1960s.[23]

In New York City during the immediate postwar decades, Boricuas continued to be heavily concentrated in certain economic niches. Indeed, as one observer noted at the time, "They *dominate* the hotel and restaurant trades *to such an extent* that these businesses would be helpless without them" (Fitzpatrick 1971: 60, our emphasis). This, once again, illustrates the continuing reincorporation of Puerto Ricans as peripheral labor—but now within core regions of the colonial capitalist world-system.

But it was the garment industry that became exemplary in employing large quantities of cheap, relatively unskilled Puerto Rican labor. In fact, by the late 1950s, this was the chief source of labor in the skirt, undergarment, and dressmaking sectors of the trade. The wages and working conditions of these workers—many of them women—remained degraded due, in part, to the persistent subcontracting and deskilling practices of the employer. It is true that these enterprises had been characterized by low-skilled labor since the nineteenth century, but garment manufacturing during the interwar and postwar periods was beleaguered even more by pressures from transnational clothing corporations: hence, the drive to save profit margins by driving down labor costs in the needle trades. Although unionization efforts brought initially positive results for these laborers, the racist and sexist practices of the union leadership (primarily the International Ladies Garments Workers Union) failed to adequately address the further corrosion of working conditions over the long run. Both situations led to labor mobilizations and protests on the part of these laborers (women, especially) together with their African American coworkers during the late 1950s and early 1960s. This was yet another example of Puerto Rican laborers toiling alongside other colonized workers in dead-end jobs that tended to continually reproduce themselves over time. Until the restructuring of the garment industry, beginning in the late 1960s and early 1970s, these labor and community struggles led to piecemeal governmental intervention and staunch opposition from business and trade-union bureaucrats.[24]

On balance, the postwar overrepresentation of Puerto Rican labor within New York City's garment industry was such that the importance of island labor in shoring up this economic sector cannot be underestimated. As one scholar (C. Rodríguez 1979: 213; emphasis added) pointed out for the 1950–1970 period,

> Puerto Ricans have, in a sense, *provided a "positive tipping point."* Without this source of cheap labor many more firms would have left the city; those that stayed have had to reduce their production. In this sense, New York's claim to be the garment capital of the world *rests upon Puerto Rican shoulders.*

However, part of this demographic profile, and its basis in New York City, started to change during the late 1960s and early 1970s with the beginning of the long-wave of global economic decline. By 1970 (and with a now mostly urban island population of about 2,700,000), the number of Puerto Ricans in the United States reached almost 1,400,000 (a 57 percent increase from 1960): approximately 810,000 of island birth (a 31 percent increase from 1960) and about 580,000 who were U.S.-born of Puerto Rican parents (a 114 percent increase from 1960).[25] It is true that between 1950 and 1970 over three-fourths of all Puerto Ricans in the United States were clustered within the larger urban industrial centers of the northeast (New York City in particular) and that most Boricuas continued to reside in this same metropolis. Nevertheless, their New York City proportions were already decreasing appreciably: from 81 percent of all Puerto Ricans in the United States in 1950 to 59 percent in 1970. By the late 1960s, this geographic dispersal appeared to be a partial response to the first signs of the prolonged downturn in the capitalist world economy that, in turn, accelerated the trend among Puerto Ricans and other characteristically low-wage laborers to find better paying work elsewhere. Thus, at the same time that New York was losing population, Puerto Ricans were moving in significant numbers to Illinois, Ohio, and Indiana. The percentage of all Puerto Ricans living in the U.S. Midwest—primarily concentrated in Chicago—increased from 4 to 10 during this same period. It should be noted, however, that the move to Chicago did not appear to be so much a qualitative shift toward different kinds of jobs than those available in New York City (the occupational contours of Boricuas in both cities were basically similar), but rather a quantitative shift: that is, an attempt to find more of the same kind of subsistence activities that were beginning to decline for Puerto Ricans and other such colonized workers in the northeast. Smaller pockets of Puerto Ricans could also be found at this time in Florida (Miami, primarily) and the West Coast (especially Los Angeles and San Francisco).[26]

From the early 1950s to the early 1970s, Puerto Ricans on the U.S. mainland continued to evince disproportionately elevated signs of indigence, once more confirming the peripheral location of Boricua populations even within core regions of the world economy. Although their official unemployment rates declined between 1950 (13.3 percent) and 1960 (9.7 percent), by 1972 these proportions had almost reached 1950 levels (12.6 percent).[27] And even more important than the absolute percentage is the ratio between official unemployment among Puerto Ricans in the United States and the corresponding rates for the whole U.S. population during the same period. Within this larger colonial context, Boricuas on the U.S. mainland represented 2.5 times (1950), 1.8 times (1960), and 2.0 times (1972) the general levels of unemployment across the United States (BLS 2002b). And—notwithstanding that average annual income among Puerto Rican families in the United States more than doubled between 1959 (when it was approximately $4,000) and 1974 (when it reached approximately $9,000)—the 1959 annual family income—71 percent of the U.S. average—had *declined* to 59 percent of the U.S. average by 1974. In 1970, 29 percent of all Puerto Rican families in the United States were still below the federal poverty level—versus 65 percent of the island's population living below this level at this same time (USCRC 1976: 52; USBC 1993b: 33).

It is also true that 14.3 percent of all Boricuas (twenty-five years or older) on the U.S. mainland had completed a high school education by 1960, but again, this lagged behind the 41.4 percent of all U.S. inhabitants with comparable schooling. The latter figures also failed to specify where these Puerto Ricans had received such education: in the English-only U.S. schools or in the island's Spanish-language public school system (USBC 1963; Cordasco and Bucchioni 1973: 134). By the early 1970s, almost 30 percent of these same Puerto Ricans had completed high school, but by that time 63 percent of the general U.S. population had reached this level of education (USCRC 1976: 106). Within New York City, the percentage of Puerto Ricans that completed high school rose from 9.9 (in 1960) to 16.6 percent (in 1970), but, again, the proportions among the city's general population were always twice the percentage for Boricua New Yorkers (BLS 1975: 50). Puerto Ricans throughout the 1960s proved to be the most destitute segment of the entire New York City population (even poorer than African Americans) in additional ways, including having the highest proportion of single-mother families in the Aid to Families with Dependent Children program (Fitzpatrick 1971: 59–60, 155, 158). The rise in professional-managerial and office jobs during the mid-1960s (even within the city's poorest districts) could not counteract Puerto Ricans' being the most destitute residents within these areas due to the lower occupational skill levels of Boricua New Yorkers (BLS 1968: 13). These markers of racially subordinate and feminized labor persisted into the late 1990s.

Spatially and socioeconomically compressed by racial segregation and limited affordable housing, the largest concentrations of Puerto Ricans in the United States established a series of identifiable barrios. This ghetto archipelago often materialized in close proximity to, or intermixed with, other Caribbean and African American populations: for example, East Harlem (El Barrio), New York City's Lower East Side (Loisaida), southern Brooklyn (Los Sures), the South Bronx, Roxbury in Boston, Northern Philadelphia, and the Division Street sector of Chicago.[28] While in 1950 only the South Bronx had an entire school population that was more than 50 percent Puerto Rican, sixteen years later there were four school districts—South Bronx, South Central Bronx, Manhattan's Lower East Side, and Brooklyn's Williamsburg—that were more than 50 percent Puerto Rican (Fitzpatrick 1971: 55).

Their disproportionately concentrated working-class composition, embattled living conditions, and the continuing economic expulsion from the island sometimes hardened social resentments between and among Puerto Ricans. Yet several factors counteracted these burgeoning social tensions, driving most Puerto Ricans in the United States to maintain their national and cultural affinities with the imagined community of Puerto Rico–as-nation. Sports, music, extended families, island-municipal associations abroad (the *asociaciónes de ausentes*), politics (both official moderate and radical nationalist), and U.S.-located island-government institutions like the Office of the Commonwealth of Puerto Rico continued to bring together Boricuas across socioeconomic, racial, and oceanic divides.[29] The material basis of such national and cultural affinities was the progressively cyclical character of this migration. Because most Puerto Ricans who lived in the United States—regardless of where they were born—continued to travel periodically back and forth between the island and the United States, many retained strong affective ties to the Puerto Rico. This pattern was increasingly similar to the Dominican, Mexican, and Filipino labor circuits of the late twentieth century (Sassen 1988). As suggested earlier, all these migratory shifts and waves (Puerto Ricans included) were partly the result of global forces and partly a recurrently disruptive popular response to these same forces. However, Puerto Rican cyclical-migration movements did differ notably from the traditionally one-way demographic displacements to the United States from Europe, South America, and Asia (Hernández Alvarez 1976; Hernández Cruz 1985).

As with other Latino migrant populations, the establishment of Puerto Rican barrios usually resulted in the rise of neighborhood "ethnic" associations, trade-union efforts, political circles, and cultural expressions, many of which were initiated by local Puerto Rican women. These were extremely complex and variegated efforts. Similar to the migratory process itself, these social survival practices not only represented accommodations to the constraints of both the capitalist market (global and local) and of the U.S. city and federal governments, but also at different times these same survival practices attempted to circumvent the constraints of capital and the state.[30]

Within New York City, this broader process of community-building gave birth to a plethora of legal and semilegal, mostly retail commerce that transplanted island patterns of exchange and sociality, mutating these same patterns while simultaneously transforming the city's vernacular architecture. These included corner minimarkets (*colmados*, *bodegas*) featuring "ethnic" food, both canned and fresh. The latter were complemented by local vendors and kiosks specializing in the trademarks of the West African–originated diet of laboring families on the island, namely rice-and-bean side dishes like pork fritters (*cuchifritos*), fried blood sausage (*morcillas*), stewed pork bits (*gandinga*), fried chicken (*pollo frito*), boiled, mashed tubers stuffed with meat and wrapped in plantain leaves (*pasteles*), cooked pig-stomach lining (*mondongo*), as well as desserts or treats like syrupy snow cones (*piraguas*), sesame-seed candy (*dulce de ajonjolí*), guava paste (*pasta de guayaba*), and fried coconut sweetened with molasses (*mampostiales*). Neighborhood religious shops (*botánicas*) catered to syncretic Caribbean expressions of Afro-Catholic and spiritualist derivation (*santería*, *espiritismo*, *santiguos*, etc.). There was even a transformed version of the gatherings of food merchants and traders in other perishable goods found throughout the Island (*plazas del mercado*) which was resurrected in New York City—between 111th and 116th Streets and Park Avenue, under the train tracks—and given the famously Spanglish appellation of *La Marqueta*. Some of these venues fell under the umbrella of the Puerto Rican Merchants Association (Wakefield 1959; Steiner 1974: 279–311).

In all these cases, the corresponding "native" microbusinesses were partly dependent on burgeoning Caribbean-based small-capitalist enterprises (e.g., Goya Foods Co., INDULAC, et al.), on their distribution chains, and on the favors of corrupt city politicians. Yet these same microbusinesses concurrently disrupted the operation of a number of citywide laws (e.g., sanitation and labor codes) and certain state and federal tax regulations. The immense network of self-employment thus created also provided a short-term alternative to wage work in the Manhattan garment industry or in the Brooklyn warehouses. Last but not least, these colloquial forms of commerce and petty production (and their subsequent incarnations up to the 1990s) *did not merely suggest and/or recall*—in the minds of the New York City population in general and Boricuas in particular—distinctly Puerto Rican practices of everyday life in the island. These "native" forms of everyday life *actually reproduced* such practices (and their distinctive Puerto Rican-ness) but now within the

U.S. metropole. This process eventually contributed to significant, albeit subtle, shifts in what it meant to be Puerto Rican (and even in what it meant to be an "American" or a "New Yorker").

A parallel and similarly contradictory process of cultural formation and community survival unfolded in the New York City of the mid- to late 1950s at the level of civic politics. This was how youth-education and cultural-nationalist organizations like the Puerto Rican Forum (a business-development and job-training program) and the Puerto Rican Association for Community Affairs (PRACA) came into being, the latter soon headed by the young social investigator Yolanda Sánchez. This was also how the national Puerto Rican and Latino youth-leadership and educational institution known as Aspira was organized in 1961 by the socially conscious educator Antonia Pantoja, whose successful guidance enabled the group to branch out into Chicago, Philadelphia, and several New Jersey cities by the late 1960s. This was also how political-action groups like the Puerto Rican Community Development Project (since the early 1960s) and community-based groups such as the Puerto Rican Traveling Theater (founded at this time by the actress and cultural worker Miriam Colón) and United Bronx Parents (organized by the neighborhood activist Evelina Antonetti) originated. In more mainstream circles, such efforts were echoed in the institutionalization of the Puerto Rican Day Parade (since 1959), the formation in 1963 of the Puerto Rican Family Institute (to facilitate "the integration of families" arriving from the island), and the puertorriqueñization of the major Spanish-language daily *El Diario de Nueva York* (which by the 1960s was mainly staffed—albeit not owned—by Puerto Ricans). Corollary events included the selection of a handful of municipal officials and city-hall appointments, as well as the election of Herman Badillo as the first Puerto Rican Congressman (1971–1977) to represent one of the city's congressional districts.[31] During this period, in other major cities, like Chicago, similar processes of struggle and community formation led to lay mutual-aid brotherhoods like the Caballeros de San Juan (established in 1954) and Spanish-language monthlies like *El Centinela* (1959–1960), *Prensa Libre* (1960), and *La Gaseta* (1964), which in 1965 became the weekly *El Puertorriqueño* (Padilla 1987: 126–44).

Some analysts (e.g.: Fitzpatrick 1971; C. Rodríguez 1991) have posited that these settlement patterns and the emergence of everyday practices in the United States signified the growing "Latinization" of Puerto Ricans as they developed deeper affinities with other "Hispanic" peoples within U.S. society. But this phenomenon can be understood likewise as a central component of an emerging, new, postwar colonized labor force composed of populations from extremely varied cultural and linguistic backgrounds. Indeed, from this vantage point, the "Latinization" of the U.S. can be seen as a process in which populations are still being socially produced as "lesser races" in order to regulate, differentiate, and distribute labor (across the United States and the Caribbean, across all of the Americas, as well as globally). What has been unprecedented in the current period is *the scale and the diversity* of the peripheral populations being recruited, uprooted, and relocated for the purpose of capital accumulation within the United States. Puerto Ricans at this time tended to blur into the full spectrum of Pan-Caribbean and Afro-diasporic populations within the large metropolitan areas of the northeastern seaboard and the Midwest. These were the racialized (i.e., colonial) conditions that located all of these populations as subordinate with respect to the Euro-American population within the United States as a whole. This is not to deny the recurring frictions within Pan-Caribbean and Afro-diasporic laboring-poor sectors: for example, between Puerto Ricans and African Americans or between Puerto Ricans and Dominicans.[32] Rather, the point is that for much of the postwar period (and up to the 1990s) most Puerto Ricans in the United States were inclined to live with—and to live as part of—larger urban communities more on the basis of shared social conditions (i.e., racialized poverty) than on the basis of any common "Hispanic" linguistic identification.[33]

Impoverished Puerto Rican barrios also emerged as places where racially subordinate laborers, in particular unemployed youth, sought out alternate ways of everyday survival. As they wove in and out of what amounts to labor-market conscription, they found self-expression by recuperating, directly influencing, and transforming various aspects of African American and Caribbean popular culture into an amalgam imbued with new meanings. Among official circles, such practices were often viewed as "deviant behavior" and part of the "culture of poverty" theorized and taxonomized with morbid fascination by so many Anglo-American sociologists, anthropologists, and journalists furthering their careers since the 1950s. Thus, the clandestine lottery (*bolita*), on-the-job pilfering, social violence, illegal betting, gang activity, performing "off-the-books" labor, Afro-Caribbean spirit cults (*santería* and *espiritismo*), drug addiction, prostitution, moonlighting as Latin-Caribbean musicians and/or as street-corner doo-wop singers were all seen as part of the specific pathology of Puerto Ricans.[34]

The alternative to this pathologizing is to understand and research such wayward practices and transgressions among Puerto Ricans in the postwar United States (especially barrio-based young adults) as what one scholar has called "the way many of us stylized our work . . . turned work into performance," where "the terrain was often cultural, centering on identity, dignity, and fun" (Kelley 1994: 2, 3). This included everyday-life situations where "theft at the workplace is also [a] strategy to recover unpaid wages and/or compensate for low wages and mistreatment" and involved other schemes to "minimize labor with as little economic loss as possible." This all took place within the larger-scale, longer-term patterns of historical capitalism whereby "changes in the law in response to workers' actions often turned accepted traditions—what [E. P.] Thompson called 'the moral economy'—into crime" (Kelley 1994: 19, 20, 22). As indicated above, this extensive criminalization of the everyday-life survival practices among Puerto Rican laboring populations had already been taking place on the island itself after the turn of the previous century.

One glaring example of how bourgeois "American" values were unsettled and challenged by popular illegalities among Puerto Ricans in the United States through the late 1950s and mid-1960s was the press coverage and court case against Salvador Agrón (aka "Dracula" or "The Capeman"). The otherwise turbulent summer of 1959 climaxed with the killing of Theresa Agee in the Lower East Side and, especially, when sixteen-year-old Agrón, decked in an extravagant black cape and captaining a gang called The Vampires, stabbed to death two white Anglo teenagers during his gang's assault on a midtown Manhattan playground. At trial's end he became the youngest person in New York State's history to be condemned to death, though this sentence was subsequently commuted (Dubner 1997: 45). Agrón rehabilitated in prison and later became a writer, dying in 1986. His cause célèbre was intermittently revived from the late 1970s to the late 1990s, including the short-lived 1998 Paul Simon Broadway musical *The Capeman.* Yet during the second half of 1959 and early 1960, what could have been more haunting to the sanctity of white Anglo propriety, middle-class morality, and the Western work ethic than reading about or listening to a young Puerto Rican migrant turned gang leader like Agrón being flamboyantly unrepentant throughout his arrest and murder conviction?[35]

Such abhorrent behavior was seen as the epitome of the juvenile-delinquency wave sweeping the United States during the decades immediately following the Second World War. New York was such a prominent site of this kind of social disorder that a U.S. Senate subcommittee was convened during the late 1950s and held hearings to, among other things, see how the problem could be addressed within the Empire State (U.S. Congress, Senate Committee on the Judiciary, Subcommittee to Investigate Juvenile Delinquency [USCSCJ-SIJD] 1957). Corollary examples of such moral panic at this time included media melodramas and Hollywood cautionary tales such as *City Across the River* (1949), *The Blackboard Jungle* (1955), *So Young, So Bad* (1956), *Cry Tough* (1959), *West Side Story* (1961, after having been a 1957 Broadway hit), *The Pusher* (1960), *The Young Savages* (1961), *The Pawnbroker* (1965), and the mid-1960s television series *East-Side, West-Side*, set in New York City. Here Puerto Ricans, like African Americans, personified the "Barbarians at the Gate" menacing northeastern cities—New York in particular—

and Chicago (Pérez 1990; L. Ortíz 1998). Within this context, the publicity surrounding something like the 1959–1960 Agrón case could be read as an instance of life imitating art imitating life.

Consequently, it made perfect sense for somebody like Leonard Bernstein in the mid-1950s, then agonizing over how to update "Romeo and Juliet" as a Broadway musical set in New York City, to shift smoothly from feeling captivated by the headline-grabbing gang wars between Chicanos and whites in Los Angeles (where Bernstein and his collaborators were meeting) to hitting upon the plot device of the East Coast equivalent of Chicano hoodlums: "In New York we had the Puerto Ricans, and at that time the papers were full of stories about juvenile delinquents and gangs" (Guernsey 1985: 42; E. Wells 2000: 1). This U.S. racist characterization resonated with the homegrown racialized fears of "native" propertied and educated circles on the island, where destitute Puerto Ricans returning from the United States were being blamed for rising crime and drug-addiction rates from the late 1950s to the late 1960s (Wagenheim 1970: 10; H. Wells 1969: 188).

From the mid-1960s to the early 1970s the worsening conditions (including police brutality) in poor communities of color clashed—sometimes violently—with the rising expectations spurred by the unprecedented generalization of mass-market goods and affordable housing for most of the U.S. (white) population during the postwar economic boom. Puerto Ricans too came to embody that famous line from the Langston Hughes poem: "Nothing lights a fire like a dream deferred." As with African American ghettos (in Harlem, Watts, Detroit, Philadelphia, Omaha, Dayton, and Atlanta) at this time, riots also erupted in a number of Puerto Rican ghettos in the United States. New Jersey was particularly prominent in this regard, with mass violence taking place in Puerto Rican barrios in Perth Amboy (1966), Paterson (1968), Passaic (1969), and Jersey City (1970) (Fitzpatrick 1971: 74–75).

One of the earliest, most typical, and significant of these urban uprisings was the Chicago Riot of June 1966, when three days of rioting and violent demonstrations in the Division Street sector occurred as local residents protested police brutality and targeted local Euro–North American businesses (F. Padilla 1987: 144–55) To a large extent, such phenomena corresponded to the politicization of community struggles among low-wage, peripheral laborers across the United States (Sassen 1988: 57, 146). In Chicago, for example, the riot's aftermath gave rise to a whole new generation of socially active organizations, from the radicalization of youth gangs (e.g., the Young Lords) to the institutionalization of Community Action Programs and the Spanish Action Committee of Chicago (F. Padilla 1987: 155–68).

This was the type of effort that resulted in the uneven emergence of social-welfare and job programs (including vocational training), as well as civil-rights reforms, for Puerto Rican barrios in the United States. In New York City, similar developments during the late 1960s and early 1970s materialized as militant and antiracist trade unionism, especially in public sectors such as hospitals and sanitation, and a leftist nationalist revival (Puerto Rican Student Union, Young Lords Party, Movimiento de Izquierda Nacional Puertorriqueña-El Comité, Partido Socialista Puertorriqueño, et al.), and demands for the community control of schools (Ocean Hill-Brownsville, Two Bridges). In addition, New York Puerto Ricans began resisting the destructive elements of urban renewal and demanding rent controls. But the movement also included mobilizations for welfare rights, greater access to health services and higher education—such as the struggle for open admissions within the City University of New York (CUNY)—and socioculturally affirmative educational programs (such as bilingual secondary education and Puerto Rican studies college programs).[36]

SECTORIAL DECLINE, URBAN FISCAL CRISIS, AND GENERALIZED POVERTY

Between the late 1960s and the early 1970s, the long-term slump in the world-systemic cycle of accumulation was beginning to make itself manifest (Castells 1978; Arrighi 1994: 300–313). Puerto Ricans were deeply affected by this slowly evolving crisis at several levels across the entire domains of the United States. Traditional manufacturing—especially the declining light industries most dependent on cheap, lesser-skilled labor—began to be reorganized or replaced according to the logic of deskilled assembly-line production and offshore production facilities. These were precisely the forms of production wherein Puerto Ricans were overrepresented in both the United States and the island, given their continuing incorporation (as peripheral labor) into the postwar world economy in both locations. During the 1970s, the trend was toward the generation of a denser and wider network of increasingly capital-intensive plants, the expansion of high-tech coordination centers, and the steady downgrading of manufacturing enterprises in the United States. This massive economic transformation spurred a concomitant expansion of the informal economy and other illegal practices. This was manifest, on the one hand, in an expansion both on the part of capital (e.g., sweatshops) and, on the other hand, in a continuation of the already described responses from poverty-stricken people themselves. Hence, structural adjustment throughout the U.S. economy (Puerto Rico included) and the general process of socioeconomic polarization inherent to it depended on new colonial configurations of racially structured labor: highly skilled and full-time work (usually Euro–North American at the top) combined, at the bottom, with growing levels of temporary, low-income, peripheral labor (wage and nonwage) working extended and intensified hours corresponding to increasingly nonwhite, female, and less-unionized labor.[37]

The key sites of this massive corporate restructuring were—and still are—the global cities (e.g., New York City, Los Angeles) and the large urban hubs of U.S. regional capitalist command and interaction within the world economy (e.g., Houston, Boston, Denver, Atlanta, Miami).[38] Economic restructuring in these cities brought about a drastic decline in office work and, in particular, of shop-level industrial jobs—principally affecting those who, like Puerto Ricans in the United States, were the "last hired, first fired."[39] This contraction was especially evident in New York City's industries, and Puerto Ricans—male workers, mostly—were among the groups hardest hit.[40] The proportion of all Puerto Ricans of both sexes working as factory operatives at this time plummeted from 50 percent to 36 percent between 1960 and 1970, and then from 31 percent in 1980 to 19 percent in 2000. There was a boom in clerical and other low-end (often low-wage) jobs associated with business services and consumer services (technical, sales, and administrative support, and related service occupations): from 12.7 percent to 20.8 percent between 1960 and 1970, and then from 27.7 percent to 34.9 percent between 1980 and 2000. By comparison, those Puerto Ricans employed as professional-managerial personnel experienced only a relative increase: from 5.9 percent to 8.8 percent between 1960 and 1970, and then from 12.2 percent to 17.1 percent between 1980 and 2000. The proportions of those working in the remainder of the services rose even more gradually, from 15.2 percent to 16.3 percent between 1960 and 1970, and then from 16.5 percent to 18.2 percent between 1980 and 2000.[41] As is clear from the statistical trend, it was working-class Puerto Ricans who suffered the brunt of this economic restructuring and social polarization. Similar conditions predominated in Puerto Rico, where industrial employment also plunged. The proportion of both sexes employed in labor-intensive industries in Puerto Rico decreased from 93 percent in 1958 to 81 percent in 1970 then to 63 percent in 1980, while the percentages of factory operatives on the island virtually remained the same at this time (18–19 percent) (USDC 1979: 2:29–40; Vázquez Calzada 1978: 376–77).

The subsequent fiscal crisis in cities like New York brought about an uneven polarization across the full "ethnic" spectrum of racially depreciated labor. On the one hand, there were those who made significant gains (African Americans more than Puerto Ricans) due to the short-term expansion in access to higher education and government employment (A. Torres 1995: 46, 57, 76–77, 87–88, 135–36; Navarro 2000) and the selective growth of elite public schooling. This contributed to the legitimation of mainstream politics among some Puerto Ricans in the United States. In this sense, it created a wider base for moderate cultural nationalism: extensions of island government institutions, party affiliations, civic organizations, and corporatist groups of Latino professionals. As will be detailed below, the latter phenomenon would eventually dovetail with the ascending numbers of "white-collar" and/or propertied migrants from the island to the United States from the late 1970s to the late 1990s.

On the other hand, however, most of these colonized populations were crushed by the capitalist "remedies" to New York City's fiscal crisis. This meant a contraction of welfare-state coverage and access to consumer goods by the working classes, epitomized by municipal retrenchment and especially deteriorating public services: under staffing, lower salaries, and outdated facilities within most public schools and health-delivery units. This degradation of government services and social cutbacks, in turn, seriously affected the physical well-being of impoverished communities in the city. By 1980, the three boroughs with the highest concentration of Puerto Ricans (the Bronx, Manhattan, and Brooklyn) had infant mortality rates comparable to Malaysia, El Salvador, and the Dominican Republic. Decaying public services also affected the skill levels and job opportunities of Puerto Ricans.[42]

The reason the capitalist restructuring process impacted Puerto Ricans in the United States so severely was because, until the early 1970s—and even more so than other Latino and Afro-diasporic populations—Boricuas were overrepresented within extremely constricted tiers of otherwise traditionally declining economic sectors, particularly in northeastern U.S. cities.[43] During the entire 1945–1970 period, the largest concentrations of Puerto Ricans in the United States tended to be characterized by manual, unskilled production laborers and low-end service workers, together with the broadest masses of unemployed (History Task Force 1979: 145–47, 159; C. Rodríguez 1979). But such an unequal impact also occurred because, in the historical long term, this has been the colonial pattern whereby Puerto Ricans (including those on the island) have always been incorporated in peripheral labor within the world-economy, especially since the Second World War.[44]

This colonial concentration of occupational niches and skill levels—one that objectively guarantees the social construction and reproduction of a feminized and racially subordinate labor force and structurally restricts this labor to a very narrow band of economic sectors—would seem to be one of the main reasons why, during the late 1970s and 1980s, disproportionately high numbers of Puerto Ricans remained an integral part of the laboring poor within the entire domains of the United States. On the island itself, the percentage of families below the federal poverty level continued its slight descent from 63 percent in 1979 (a 2 percent drop from 1972) down to 60 percent in 1989. The median annual family income rose even more moderately, from

$9,925 in 1979 to $9,988 in 1989. But official unemployment rates in Puerto Rico continued to oscillate between 15.4 percent in 1975 to 20.7 percent in 1990, reaching a high of 23.5 percent in 1983. As in the 1950–1970 period, Puerto Rico's unemployment rates persisted between 1.8 times (1975) and 3.4 times (1990) the corresponding rates for the entire United States. Meanwhile, 42 percent of Boricua families in the U.S. mainland lived below poverty between 1984 and 1986—already the highest level among all U.S. Latinos. Official unemployment rates among Puerto Ricans in the United States at that time fluctuated between 11.4 percent (1980), 14.3 percent (1985), and 12.1 percent (1990). Again, and very similar to what we already saw for the 1950–1972 period, these rates were still 1.6 times (1980) to 2.0 times (1985), and up to 2.2 times (1990), the overall U.S. average. And although the median annual income for Puerto Rican families in the United States continued to rise up to the late 1980s (approximately $11,000), this was still 33 percent of the median annual income for non-Latino U.S. families (approximately $33,000).[45]

By this time the alarming proportions and tenacity of Puerto Rican poverty in the United States gnawed at the apprehensions and imaginations of official and academic U.S. circles. Renowned economic sociologist Marta Tienda published a 1989 journal article on "Puerto Ricans in the Underclass Debate," while by 1990 Puerto Rican families in the United States were twice as likely as African American families to be on welfare and 50 percent more likely to be poor. In 1991, the *Journal of the American Medical Association* noted that infant mortality rates among Boricuas on the U.S. mainland were 50 percent higher than was the case for Mexican Americans. That same year, *The Atlantic Monthly* ran a lead article focusing on Puerto Ricans in the United States entitled "The Other Underclass," and a year later a special issue of the *Congressional Quarterly*'s *CQ Researcher* on "Hispanic Americans" included a sidebar whose title significantly asked "Why Are Puerto Ricans in Such Dire Straits?"[46]

The situation of Puerto Rican New Yorkers from the late 1970s to late 1980s was considerably worse. While still more than 50 percent of the city's entire Latino population, Boricuas in 1981 already constituted the majority in ten of the city's school districts (up from four in 1966). By the end of that decade, the average annual income of New York City's Puerto Rican families had risen to approximately $19,000, but this was still little over half of the average annual income for all the city's families at that time (approximately $34,000). Puerto Ricans remained the poorest "ethnic" group in the city—even when compared to Dominicans, Mexicans, and African Americans. In 1989, 38 percent of all Puerto Ricans struggled to survive on income below the poverty level, compared to 19 percent for all New Yorkers.[47] In this regard, the Department of City Planning's report clarified that "the gap in the percent of the population below the poverty line remained substantial at each point in the life-cycle.

When the threshold is increased to 150 percent of the poverty line, close to one-half of all Puerto Ricans in the city can be categorized as poor" (DCP 1994: 56). And despite the increase in their levels of educational attainment during the 1980s—high school graduates increased from 35 percent in 1980 to 46 percent of the total in 1990—Puerto Rican New Yorkers continued to lag behind the city's average of 69 percent (1990) (DCP 1994: 40; and Fitzpatrick 1987: 142). In addition, two other pertinent factors were eventually documented: (1) that there was an overrepresentation of Puerto Ricans in the city's vocational schools, and (2) that the training in these schools was scandalously substandard (Oakes 1985; Educational Priorities Panel [EPP] 1985). Not surprisingly, this overrepresentation also extended to the percentage of Puerto Ricans within the state penal population, which by the early 1980s was more than triple the proportion of New York State's general population (19.0 percent versus 5.6 percent). Again, all this strongly suggests a structural (i.e., colonial) relationship between the institutionalization of low skill levels and the social regulation of a racially subordinate and feminized laboring population historically constructed to work for low wages.

These dismal circumstances did not qualitatively shift during the 1990s, when almost half of all Puerto Ricans everywhere lived on the U.S. mainland: the numbers of those living stateside had more than doubled since 1970, reaching 3,100,000 by the year 2000. Close to 50 percent of all Boricua children in the United States in 1998 still lived below poverty level, while unemployment rates for Puerto Ricans in the United States continued to oscillate between 2.17 times (1990) and 2.38 times (2000) general U.S. percentages. By the year 2000, Puerto Ricans still had one of the highest unemployment rates (8.3 percent) and most elevated poverty levels (30.4 percent) among all of the U.S. "Hispanic" population groups—surpassed on both counts only by Dominicans—notwithstanding the relative decline in the corresponding rates since the 1980s. By 1999, although 64 percent of all Boricuas on the U.S. mainland had obtained a high school diploma or more education (up from 58 percent in 1991)—in one of the few indices in which they surpassed Chicanos and Mexicans (49.7 percent)—but Boricuas still lagged behind the corresponding proportions for U.S. whites, which had risen to 87.7 percent by this time (USBC 2000a; Logan 2001: 3).

As the data and arguments in the rest of this chapter suggest, part of this dramatic increase in educational attainment appears to be associated with the increasing social polarization among Puerto Ricans in the United States since the 1980s, rather than any single statistical anomaly between Puerto Ricans and Chicanos and Mexicans. For instance, despite having *higher poverty levels* than U.S. Mexicans, by 1999 there were proportionally more Puerto Ricans than Mexicans in the U.S. mainland *who were full-time, year-round workers* *with annual earnings of $35,000 or above* (USBC 2000a). This relatively better-off segment threw off the curve and contrasted sharply with the continuing bleak conditions among most Puerto Ricans in the United States during the 1990s. For instance, a 1996 Yale study revealed that Boricua children had the highest asthma rates in the U.S. mainland, above any other Latino and racial group—and more than twice the rate for white Anglos (Reuters 1996). In turn, the National Center for Health Statistics disclosed in 2000 that "Puerto Rican persons in the mainland U.S. fare significantly worse than other U.S. Hispanics on a number of health indicators" (NCHS 2000). Not surprisingly, the latter findings drew sharp criticism from the organizations of propertied and highly educated U.S. Puerto Ricans, like the Puerto Rican Professional Association of South Florida and the Puerto Rican Chamber of Commerce at Coral Gables, who were worried that "the report might create a stereotype, possibly causing health insurance providers to raise Puerto Ricans' rates" (Associated Press [AP] 2000). Meanwhile, a Population Resource Center document on Latina teen pregnancy found that young Puerto Rican mothers—most of whom probably could not afford private health insurance—"were worse off than other Latino groups: they are less likely to be married or to be living with parents or other adults, and more likely to be living in poverty and receiving welfare" (Population Resource Center [PRC] 2001).

Once again, social conditions for Puerto Ricans in New York City continued to leave much to be desired throughout the 1990s, where Boricuas (by then mostly U.S. born) were the largest Latino group in every city borough except Manhattan (where they had been surpassed by Dominicans). The *New York Times* reported that "in the 1990s, the percentage of Puerto Rican households in the city living at or below the poverty line increased despite the strong local economy, to a rate greater than any other group. According to the most recent data, about 40 percent of New York's Puerto Ricans qualified as poor, a figure considerably higher than that of African-Americans and worse than the average rate for all Hispanics" (Navarro 2000). An annual survey of Hispanic New Yorkers—issued at the end of that decade by the Hispanic Federation (1999)—poignantly asked "Why are Puerto Ricans who have lived in the U.S. for generations not doing better than other Hispanics who are recent immigrants?" As in the previous two decades, the 1990s confirmed the structural link between, on the one hand, the decline of traditional manufacturing and rising employment among highly skilled workers and, on the other hand, Boricua New Yorkers' leaving the formal labor market due to the persistence of deficient inner-city public schools, employer racism, and residential segregation,[48] all compounded by the already mentioned socially polarized demographic shifts among Puerto Ricans themselves. The veteran Puerto Rican activist and city educator Antonia Pantoja concluded as much in a February

2000 newspaper interview: "The underlying problem," she noted, "is indifference by both government and the public, including economically comfortable Puerto Ricans, to 'a society where children are not taught by the schools they attend, families do not have decent housing to live in, where the color of your skin will keep you out of the services and resources all citizens are entitled to'" (Navarro 2000).

In 1999 and 2000, Puerto Rico's population numbered 3,809,000 (a 71 percent increase from 1970), and virtually all socioeconomic indicators remained grim. Of all school-age children, 84 percent persisted in poverty. And depending on how and where the calculation is carried out,[49] between half and two-thirds of the island's entire population remained below the poverty level in 2000—which had been the case since at least the early 1970s.[50] This type of chronic social distress was akin to the fluctuations in official unemployment levels during the 1990s in Puerto Rico, oscillating between 17 percent (1992) and 10 percent (2000). As had already occurred between 1950 and 1990, unemployment rates in Puerto Rico at the turn of this century remained consistently higher than was the case for the general population of the United States: concretely, between 2.2 times (1992) and 3.1 times (2000) the overall U.S. rates.[51] And despite the steady rise in per capita income since the 1970s, during the 1990s this figure continued to be one-third of the per capita income within the United States.[52] By the year 2000, the island's average hourly wages were still 58 percent of the corresponding rates in the United States at that time (up from 41 percent of the U.S. average in 1960) (Rivera 2002; BLS 2002c). Similar to what was already indicated for most Puerto Ricans in the United States, a feedback loop also existed in the island between generalized poverty and diminished well-being. For instance, the U.S. Center for Disease Control observed that "the continued low per capita income in Puerto Rico adversely affects Puerto Ricans' mental and physical health and their overall quality of life. . . . In some cases, low HRQOL [health-related quality of life] might affect socioeconomic status (e.g., by reducing one's productivity and associated earnings)" (CDC 2002). As a result, the island's infant mortality rate in 2000 remained twice as high as that of the entire United States (NCHS 2001).

SOCIAL RESISTANCE, RACIAL PROFILING, AND THE NEW EXPANDING SERVICE SECTORS

Out of the entire Boricua population (on the island and in the United States), young adults—males, in particular—from laboring-poor U.S. barrios have been among the groups hardest hit by this brutal structural adjustment and general socioeconomic polarization process across the United States since the early 1970s (Cordero Guzmán 1992–1993). Largely as a result, this was the demographic sector that spearheaded the new forms of expression, protest, and resistance that proliferated from the late 1970s to the mid-1990s, especially in cities like New York (where almost half of this population was under 17 years of age by 1981) and in conjunction with other colonized youths like African Americans, as well as Dominicans and other Caribbeans (for a similar line of analysis, see Aparicio, this volume). The result was the creation among them of a sense of larger communities of struggle and desire, where—to again quote Robin Kelley—they tried "to turn [their] bodies into instruments of pleasure," and "generational and cultural specificity had a good deal to do with [their] unique forms of resistance" (1994: 2, 3).

In this manner, the block-party music and dance (rap, dancehall, breaking) and the visual imagery ("bombing" subway cars and buses, "tagging" city walls with graffiti, and spray painting memorial murals on tenement walls) of the Puerto Rican ghetto kids who participated in the rise of hip-hop culture blurred the sociocultural differences in New York between African American West Harlem and Puerto Rican East Harlem (aka El Barrio), or between Loisaida (Lower East Side) and the Dominican bastion of Washington Heights. But these emergent cultural forms also metaphorically and literally bridged the gap between the South Bronx and Los Sures (in Brooklyn), from there establishing links with Puerto Rican barrio teens in Boston's Roxbury, in North Philly, and in the housing projects of San Juan. Some of these same unemployed Boricua youth and university activists indelibly marked the city's swelling gay and lesbian insubordinate geographies (historically symbolized in the Stonewall rebellion, gay fashion houses and performance balls, Gay Pride marches, and ACT-UP) while helping form autonomous sites (Comité Homosexual Latino, gay/lesbian contingents in the Puerto Rican Day parades, La Casita, Hispanic AIDS Forum, Las Buenas Amigas). Both urban forms of expressive culture and ad hoc political coalitions crossed social-class and racial divides between gay/lesbian New Yorkers and city-health professionals, and helped bridge sexual and age divides among communities of color in the city and the region, as well as between the latter and Puerto Rico.[53]

Barrio youth from one or both of these hip-hop and gay/lesbian scenes, in turn, blurred into new and old local politicocultural expressions (such as the Museo del Barrio, the Puerto Rican Traveling Theater, Pregones, leftist nationalist organizations, and, again, the Puerto Rican Day Parade). Some of these same Puerto Rican ghetto kids also went on to participate in the militant CUNY student strikes of 1989–1992, resisting the administration's attempts to roll back the gains of the late 1960s and early 1970s, like the dismantling of bilingual education, open-admissions policies, and Puerto Rican studies college programs. These struggles likewise embraced the resurgence of politicized gangs that operated within both the penal system and the neighborhoods, in particular the Asociación de Confinados (aka *ñetas*) and the Almighty Latin King and Queen Nation. But they also included the massive, anti–police brutality street demonstrations of the late 1980s and early 1990s (giving rise to organizations such as the Coalition for Racial Justice) and the youth conferences organized by new groups like the National Congress for Puerto Rican Rights (founded in 1981), Fuerza Latina, and MUEVETE: The Boricua Youth Movement. The relevance of such issues was confirmed by a 1999 annual survey of Latino New Yorkers, which found that "for the first time since 1993, crime is not the number one problem for all Latinos. . . . Now the number one problem is police brutality. For Puerto Ricans, however, crime and police brutality are tied for the number one problem, . . . followed by racism/discrimination (13 percent)" (Hispanic Federation 1999). This type of more combative, cross-district, grassroots activism eventually overlapped with wider social movements that brought together many of the same ghetto kids and their parents, along with other sectors from communities of color mobilizing around an entire array of issues: housing, education, police violence, working conditions, immigrants' concerns and other legal rights, environmental racism, and so on.[54]

These were some of the ways in which, however unevenly, the downward phase in the long-term world-systemic economic crisis did not merely generate a legitimation of mainstream "Hispanic" politics. It simultaneously seemed to provoke political practices among racially subordinate sectors that partially disrupted the colonial social order within pivotal world cities like New York. This seems to have been the particular case of the more militant interneighborhood activism and young-adult protagonism just described. Here the lines were more clearly drawn between, on the one hand, the police and city hall and, on the other hand, nonwhite laboring-poor communities where Puerto Ricans were more prone to transcend divisions of citizenship, language, or color (which at times have also partially separated most Puerto Ricans from most Dominicans, African Americans, and Anglo-Caribbeans). Unfortunately, the neighborhood bases of this type of militancy also became the principal targets of city- and state-based co-optation(e.g., indulging certain families and favoring entire blocks that denounced such forms of struggle) and selective abuse (both in terms of even higher levels of officer brutality and social-service neglect). As the economic restructuring unfolded and its long-term effects made themselves felt, this kind of activism became increasingly harder to sustain.[55]

Grassroots movements and activism were also disorganized by the massive reorientation of New York City's political economy in the late 1980s and 1990s. In a marked shift from 1960s poverty programs, the city now began an urban renewal campaign that dwarfed previous efforts. Factory buildings were converted into residential lofts. Tenements and industrial districts were turned into high-end restaurants, exclusive night clubs, boutiques, performing arts centers, museums, and galleries. Although such measures resulted in the return of some corporate headquarters, the rising levels of gentrification created a real estate feeding frenzy that continued into the 1990s. Skyrocketing rents and housing prices contributed to the protracted dismantling and atomization of the already impoverished Puerto Rican barrios of East Harlem, the Lower East Side of Manhattan, and especially the South Bronx. This physical devastation of Boricua-lived environments was another factor behind the growing appeal of more cautious political action among many Puerto Ricans in the United States. In New York City, desperate times in part continued to lead to desperate measures, but these now followed a tendency toward restraint and moderation. Combative outrage caved in to the politics of fear.[56]

This growth of mainstream politics (electoral and cultural) had two extremely contradictory social roots. On the one hand, there was the more conservative version of the politics of desperation in light of the razing of Puerto Rican slums and the corresponding ruthless measures of economic structural adjustment inside the United States. On the other hand, the spreading influence of mainstream politics unevenly converged with the relative expansion of professional-managerial Boricuas in the United States, especially as a result of the new wave of migration coming from the island since the late 1970s (discussed at the end of this chapter).

However, the disparate social bases of the two phenomena should not be confused. One was the *defensive* retreat into more cautious politics on the part of ghetto refugees desperately trying to recuperate from bombed-out tenements and a bombed-out "blue-collar" economy. The other force was the *forward and aggressive*—often triumphant—careerism (social and political) of middle-class and highly qualified Puerto Ricans. This was true, regardless of whether this professional-managerial condition was of island origin (e.g., Kileen,Texas, mayor Raúl Villaronga and Tampa candidate for Hillsborough Commissioner Rock Roque) or came from those who were mostly U.S.-born or raised (e.g., New York City's now-perennial mayoral candidate Herman Badillo and Lower East Side Councilman Antonio Pagán). In the case of laboring-poor Puerto Ricans, and depending on the stakes and correlation of forces, the indigent majority always oscillates paradoxically between insurgency and co-optation. The second, intermittently more guarded position, has contributed to the rise of careerist politicians. Whether in the United States or in Puerto Rico, middle-class and highly educated Puerto Ricans have historically been—and still are—a minority among all Boricuas, and most tend to fulfill their historical role as colonial(ist) and social-class intermediaries.[57]

In summary, such were the social transformations unfolding from the late 1970s to the late 1990s (in the United States and Puerto Rico, as well as globally): retrenchment, downsizing enterprises, increased automation and part-time employment, elongated working hours and an intensification of the labor process, severe erosion of "real" wages, fiscal conservatism, privatization of the state sector, bigger tax breaks for capital and the middle classes, deregulation of the economy, erosion of trade unions, and an expanding criminalization of racially subordinate destitute communities. But this entire array of socially ruthless measures pursued by capital and the state produced contradictory and complex results. On the one hand, such measures restored—and, at best, optimized—previous levels of capital accumulation by stabilizing or even reducing labor costs and government social expenditures, collaterally increasing the acceptance of political moderation among the laboring classes. On the other hand, this assault also propelled a plethora of "refusals from below" that interfered with the orderly reproduction of colonial-capitalist relations.[58]

In the large U.S. cities of the northeast, these socially ruthless measures were also accompanied by a heightened police surveillance and repression targeting the residents of the Boricua ghetto archipelago from the 1980s to the early twenty-first century[59] and the concomitant blurring of the African American, Dominican, Haitian, Jamaican, Mexican, Central American, and Southeast Asian into a collective, generic "colored" urban threat.[60] Although the incidence of serious criminal activity in the United States has been declining since the late 1980s, incarceration rates have been rising dramatically in part due to the so-called War on Drugs and its harsher fixed-sentencing laws and racial-profiling techniques targeting racially subordinate populations (Human Rights Watch (HRW) 2000). For instance, during the 1996–97 fiscal year, the states with the highest indices of overrepresentation for Latino youth in detention (Connecticut, New York, Massachusetts, and New Jersey) also happened to be those states where Puerto Ricans were the largest Latino group. These were also the same states where Latino youth had three to eight times the judicial custody rate of white youths during this same period (Poe-Yamagata and Jones 2000; Villaruel et al. 2002).

For New York City (where Puerto Ricans continued to represent the main Latino group), "a December 1999 report by the New York State Attorney General found that of the 175,000 'stops' engaged in by the NYPD officers from January 1998 through March 1999, almost 84 percent were of blacks and Hispanics, despite the fact that those groups comprised less than half of the city's population." Evidently associated with the NYPD's "Stop and Frisk" campaigns and "Tough-On-Crime Movement" during that decade, that same report found that "of the 10 police precincts with the most stops, seven were majority black/Hispanic districts" (Weich and Angulo 2000: 4–5. For similar nationwide trends see Johnson, this volume). Once again, such measures should be understood in light of the fact that throughout the 1990s, Puerto Ricans continued to have the highest unemployment rates and most elevated poverty levels among all U.S. "Hispanics," itself an indication of the forces compelling Boricua barrio youths into the informal economy and other criminalized survival practices.

These official punitive measures dovetailed with the sensationalist reinscription of Puerto Rican neighborhoods as the racially coded "combat zones," which populated the middle-class, Euro–North American imaginary over the past twenty-five years. Within these mass-media mental landscapes, such ideological representations could be found in Hollywood-made or Hollywood-marketed films like *The New Centurions*, *The French Connection*, *Death Wish*, *Fort Apache, the Bronx*, and *Badge 373* in the 1970s, and *The Police Tapes*, *Carlito's Way*, *Q. & A.*, and *Bonfire of the Vanities* during the 1980s and 1990s, as well as within more recent independent productions like *Do the Right Thing*, *Hangin' with the Homeboys*, *I Like It Like That*, *Basquiat*, *Clockers*, and *He Got Game*. But these images were also recurring and interchangeable tropes of cop shows—both explicitly fictional (e.g., *NYPD Blue*, *New York Undercover*) and "reality" TV—and the eleven o'clock news.[61]

Although these kinds of representations were partially mitigated by the commercial success of the most recent "Latin Craze" in the United States from the late 1980s to the present (see below), the overwhelming Anglo media characterization of Puerto Ricans in particular (and, to a lesser extent, Latinos in general) within the United States continues to be disproportionately peppered—when not outright suffused—with vermin infestations (biological and social), crime-ridden neighborhoods, and shady figures. It bears remembering that the previous wave of U.S.-white moral panic during the 1950s and early 1960s regarding "naturally" crime-prone Puerto Ricans also coincided with the phenomenal marketing triumph of the mambo and the cha-cha-chá exemplified by Puerto Rican media stars like Tito Puente, Tito Rodríguez, Rita Moreno, and Chita Rivera. *West Side Story*, once again, personifies both contradictory tendencies (Wells 2000; Aparicio, chapter 9, this volume).

The social dislocation caused by ongoing economic restructuring and the general process of polarization in North America and the rest of the world-economy all tended to reinforce and reproduce the racial profiling of Puerto Ricans in the United States carried out by the police and the mass media. As skilled, higher-wage jobs disappeared and the menial service sector expanded, Puerto Ricans joined other people of color in a "race to the bottom" within this last phase of capitalist globalization. Some of these low-income laborers became intimately linked to the low end of export-oriented sectors, the parceling out of delivery services via multiple global outlets (as has been happening within hotels, repair services, car rentals, retail outlets for high-end consumer goods, and so on). But these downgraded laborers also serviced the life-style needs of the growing sector of professional technical and managerial personnel, as in traditional domestic service, and likewise worked in the high-end service sector described previously. Another outcome of this kind of restructuring has been the increasing Puerto Rican involvement in the production of low-end goods and services for their own communities and for other colonized populations—for example, food stands, corner markets, and neighborhood repair shops—but now increasingly financed or merchandised via corporate enterprises like the transnational fast-food corporations. Meanwhile, the expansion of these low-wage service jobs simultaneously increased the number of job opportunities for professional-technical personnel in public and private institutions involved in socially regulating these very same low-income populations. Such was the case of curtailed social-service agencies, religious-based charities, and "poverty experts"—community planning boards, shelters, youth programs, and neighborhood development commissions.[62]

Thus, proportional Puerto Rican employment in these continental U.S. sectors—service, technical, sales, administrative support, and office workers—had increased from 28 percent (9 percent of whom were female) in 1960 to 37 percent (17 percent of whom were female) in 1970. By 2000, proportional employment in these same sectors had soared to 70 percent, and by then 61 percent were female.[63] In the area where Puerto Ricans were most heavily concentrated (the U.S. mid-Atlantic states), the percentage of women working in these sectors has risen from 61 percent in 1970 to 71–72 percent between 1980 and 1990 out of all Puerto Rican female employment in the United States, while Puerto Rican men's employment within these sectors oscillated between 36 and 43–47 percent for these same decades, respectively. Likewise, the joint percentages of Puerto Ricans in the U.S. mid-Atlantic states working in wholesale and retail trade, finance, insurance, real estate, business and repair services, professional and related services (health, education), personal services, and public administration rose from 35 percent in 1960 to 57 percent in 1980 and then to 66 percent in 1990 (Colón-Warren 1997: 142). This shift in employment patterns was no less dramatic in Puerto Rico itself, insofar as the island too was part of the global process of capitalist restructuring. There, the proportion of people (both sexes) employed in commerce and trade, finance, insurance, real estate, all services, professional, and public administration rose from 44 percent in 1960 to 64 percent in 1980 and then to 77 percent in 2000.[64]

Although much more detailed and long-term research needs to be done in this regard, the preliminary data suggests that, rather than a simple and clear-cut case of upward mobility,[65] most Puerto Ricans tended to exhibit a horizontal displacement from low-wage employment in manufacturing and traditional services to still relatively devalued labor within the low-end of corporate business services and transnational consumer services, rather than a uniform and across-the-board upward mobility. This in no way denies the expanding minority of Boricuas (mostly from the island, but some U.S.-born) who enjoyed substantially higher income levels within the United States, but it is important to note that such gains usually are relative to what they would have been earning in similar jobs within Puerto Rico.

The downgraded manufacturing sector—emerging out of this same economic restructuring general process of polarization up to the mid-1990s—went hand in hand with an expansion of sweatshops and industrial homework among subcontractors for the older labor-intensive industries (e.g., apparel, footwear, toys), as well as among subcontractors for high-tech industries (e.g., certain electronics sectors). In both cases, this growth again depended on the colonial structuring of different forms of peripheral labor in the lowest income levels (Sassen 1998: 111–31; Glover 2001). Preliminary evidence seems to suggest that the U.S. jobs formerly held by Puerto Rican men in this sector were being filled by females, albeit not necessarily Puerto Rican women. Especially in sites like New York City, the tendency seemed to be towards immigrant (legal and illegal), nonunionized, female employment within downgraded manufacturing enterprises. In the case of Dominican immigrants to the United States, these low-wage (often undocumented) laborers usually entered the United States by air via Puerto Rico, where they had originally arrived by water.[66]

As we already saw above, apparel manufacture has been one of the quintessentially backward economic sectors since the early twentieth century. But in New York City during the 1990s, this was still a four-billion-dollar-per-year industry representing almost a third of the city's manufacturing jobs and at least 60 percent of its factories are sweatshops. Similar to what was also taking place in Los Angeles at that time, New York City's garment industry was annexed to the multibillion-dollar-per-year transnational retail powerhouses that had mushroomed since the 1970s. Such firms have learned to deploy their own version of flexible accumulation (known as "lean retailing") in the face of growing competition from elsewhere in the world economy. As had been the case from the 1940s to the late 1960s (when Puerto Rican labor played a crucial role), the garment industry remained extremely dependent on cheap labor in order to secure comfortable profit margins. After the 1970s, this dependence became even more acute: subcontractors (who actually ran the sweatshops) competed fiercely, trying to outbid each other for the business of big-name manufacturers.[67] By the late 1970s to mid-1980s, this was how and why wage levels in New York City's apparel manufacture dropped below what they were in Puerto Rico (Ross and Trachte 1990: 162). Under these conditions, it became more profitable to replace Puerto Rican wage laborers (the male workers, especially) with, for example, illegal Chinese immigrant women and girls. As unemployment levels in the overwhelmingly Boricua Lower East Side of Manhattan reached 45.4 percent during the mid-1990s, a few blocks away in the dilapidated tenement-factories of Chinatown's Mott Street, the hourly earnings—even within unionized garment shops—were only between $1.00 and $3.00. At that time, average hourly wages in apparel industries within Puerto Rico were $5.42, compared to $8.21 across the U.S. mainland (National Mobilization Against Sweatshops [NMASS] 2001; Puerto Rico U.S.A. [PRUSA] 2002).[68]

Especially in places like New York City and other major urban hubs in the East Coast and central Florida, these displaced Puerto Rican men and women partly shifted towards three overlapping sectors: low-paying service jobs,[69] transient work in the downgraded manufacturing sector, and a wide range of activities in the informal economy, including " odd jobbing," street vending, trading in stolen car parts, and illegal drug trafficking.[70] Therefore, from the 1970s to the present, global structural adjustment and its far-reaching social polarization enabled the U.S. industrial sector and the services to attract or capture many Puerto Ricans as an integral component of a much broader spectrum of low-income colonized labor than ever before: across North America and from all corners of the earth, but in every case subject to the same restructuring of global U.S. capital. This racially depreciated peripheral labor could be found not only *within U.S. global cities* (New York, Los Angeles), but also *within the hinterlands of all U.S. domains*—that is, the smaller, up-state urban zones of the northeastern seaboard, the north-central Midwest, and the so-called Sunbelt (the U.S. South, portions of the West Coast, and Puerto Rico itself). On the other hand, these U.S. transnational industries and business or consumer services lured and trapped such colonized labor *within peripheral spaces formally outside U.S. jurisdiction*: Mexico (with the maquiladora system), the rest of the Caribbean Basin (in the "export-processing zones" or "free-trade zones"), as well as Southeast Asia and China (in the "special economic zones").[71]

THE NEW MIGRATORY PATTERNS

The monumental capitalist reorganization that began globally in the 1970s, therefore, not only had profound effects on *how* Puerto Ricans made a living, it also had a profound effect on *where* they lived across the entire domain of the United States from the late 1970s to the late 1990s. In terms of migratory flows, this was how the current "circular" or "cyclical" migration originated, albeit the phenomenon itself has existed (at lower levels) since the 1960s.[72]

As economic restructuring advanced on the island and federal minimum wage levels were extended to Puerto Rico, given the increase in capital's need (both within U.S. jurisdictions and internationally) for cheaper labor from the early 1980s onwards, employers began substituting variegated segments of Puerto Rican labor on the island with immigrant labor from around the world, especially Asia and the rest of the Caribbean Basin (Sassen-Koob 1985; Duany 1995). Simultaneously, many Puerto Ricans in the United States began using outward migration in ways similar to the postwar years, but now leaving their older and more established barrios in major cities (New York City, Chicago, Philadelphia) besieged by the restructuring process. Most Puerto Ricans on the U.S. mainland nevertheless remained concentrated in the northeast. In 1990, New York City still accounted for 33 percent of all Puerto Ricans in the United States, while an additional 17 percent lived in other cities in New England, New York state, New Jersey, and Pennsylvania. But as early as 1980, the U.S. cities with the highest numbers of Puerto Ricans as percentages of the total city population were in Connecticut (Hartford and Bridgeport) and New Jersey (Camden, Passaic, and Paterson) rather than in New York state: by 1990 the relative dimensions of the Boricua population in Hartford and Camden were twice as large as that of New York City (C. Santiago and Rivera-Batiz 1994: 22–23). Puerto Ricans continued to move in search of a better life (*buscando ambiente*), albeit not necessarily within the formal labor market. This shift not only meant moving back to the island for some, but also involved a growing relocation towards smaller U.S. urban areas in New England and the Mid-Atlantic states, as well as towards larger cities in the South, Midwest, and West Coast. For most Puerto Ricans, the persisting trend was to move into neighborhoods with other racially subordinate and feminized populations: African Americans, Dominicans, Haitians, Mexicans, Chicanos, Central Americans, and so on (J. Morales 1986: 162–82, 184–99; Bonilla 1994).

It is no accident that some of these exact same geographical areas began exhibiting a relative growth in the industrial sector (automated operations, but especially downgraded manufacturing), services (upper-level or not), and the informal economy. Massachusetts is a case in point: high-tech sectors like electronics experienced a spectacular expansion there throughout the 1970s and 1980s, generating an increase in the availability of very skilled and high-income personnel and, even more so, in the proportions of low-wage production labor. During this same period, though, the most rapidly growing economic niches in the area were low-wage, wholesale and retail trade, and the services. Not coincidentally, the Puerto Rican population of smaller cities like Worcester, Springfield, and Lawrence-Haverill in Massachusetts almost tripled between 1980 and 1990, now collectively representing close to 2 percent of all Puerto Ricans in the United States at a time in which the entire state accounted for almost 6 percent of all Boricuas living on the U.S. mainland. These three cities had among the highest poverty rates (between 56 and 62 percent) of all U.S. metropolitan areas and the largest Puerto Rican populations.[73]

Between 1990 and 2000, the rate of growth of the Puerto Rican populations in some of these northeastern urban areas continued at the same pace or leveled off. However, the most dramatic shifts at this time took place in the number of Boricuas relocating to Florida's towns and cities, especially the Tampa–St. Petersburg–Clearwater corridor and Orlando (Logan 2001: 9–10). Similar to Massachusetts from the late 1970s to late 1980s, Florida in the 1990s was undergoing a major growth in high-tech industries and in consumer and business services, all in dire need of low-wage labor (usually from out-of-state). Two cases in point were Tampa's technology boom (once again, in automated operations and downgraded manufacturing) and the expanding hospitality and tourist services tied to central Florida's mega theme parks and mass-media spectacles.[74] That was how Florida doubled its Puerto Rican population during this decade, almost tripling in the Orlando and Tampa–St. Petersburg–Clearwater areas alone. Florida now has the second largest concentration (16 percent) of Puerto Ricans on the U.S. mainland and Boricuas are now the second largest Latino group in the state—representing 19 percent of all of Florida's "Hispanics"—Cubans remain in first place with 32 percent (Logan 2001: 8, 10; de Valle and Henderson 2002). Yet this was a much more complex demographic shift than otherwise meets the eye. According to Darío Ruíz, past president of the League of United Latin American Citizens (LULAC) and a manager in the Human Resources Department of Hillsborough County, "Puerto Ricans have migrated to Florida in recent years in two streams. . . . One stream is a largely professional group coming directly from Puerto Rico; the second is a less-skilled wave of second- and third-generation Puerto Ricans moving from the northeastern United States" (Coats 2001).

This last quotation illustrates the extent to which the rising proportions of Puerto Ricans in U.S. areas outside New York City, Chicago, and Philadelphia were not merely a *geographic* polarization among Puerto Ricans in the U.S. mainland: this exodus also represents a *social* polarization among Boricuas in the United States, and it is part and parcel of the general socioeconomic polarization occurring across North America and the rest of the world economy. This was a direct outcome of the already described deterioration of public education (especially, inner-city schools) within northeastern U.S. urban zones since the mid-1970s, itself resulting from global neoliberalism's economic restructuring. Not coincidentally, this latter process also repositioned Puerto Rico within the world economy over the last two decades, thus giving rise to a new type of Puerto Rican migration from the island to the United States.

From the 1970s to the early 1990s, cash-strapped, capital-intensive heavy industries (petrochemicals, pharmaceuticals, some electronics sectors) in the United States, together with international finance corporations, began transferring operations to Puerto Rico on a large scale. These companies manipulated global price differences in raw materials and benefited from federal tax-shelter legislation, specifically Section 936 of the U.S. Internal Revenue Code (from the early 1970s to the mid-1990s). The latter legislation enabled these corporations to repatriate to the continental United States—via Puerto Rico—the profits generated by their subsidiaries internationally.[75]

Together with older light-industry sectors (apparel, footwear, furniture), this shift also corresponded to the uneven extension of new, "off-shore" production projects toward the Caribbean. As with Mexico in the 1980s (see Gutiérrez, chapter 1, this volume), this approach became known as the "Twin-Plant Concept" or "*fábricas de producción complementaria.*" Similar to the economically colonial role South Korea was playing in the Pacific Rim at this time, Puerto Rico was partially relocated as an intermediate link (in industrial production as well as in business services) between the corporate headquarters, most capital-intensive and high-wage operations, with research and development within U.S. global cities, and regional-coordination centers; and the most labor-intensive, least-skilled, and low-wage end of this chain in the export-processing free-trade zones elsewhere in the Caribbean (e.g., Haiti, the Dominican Republic, Jamaica, Barbados). In both the "Section 936"case and the "Twin-Plant" strategy, such companies took advantage of the local nuclei of skilled manual labor and of the growing numbers of upper-level, producer- and consumer-service workers and professional technical personnel on the island—most of whom usually ended up with smaller blocks of take-home pay than their counterparts in the United States.[76]

There are three overlapping migratory components worth referencing in this context, beginning with the larger and more cyclical migration of semi- and lower-skilled labor from the island to the United States and back to the island again, described above. This working-class makeup has continued to characterize most of the migratory circuit, in particular from Puerto Rico to the United States.[77] The same process also produced a second—considerably smaller—wave of very skilled labor migrating to the island, namely clusters of high-level, professional technical and managerial personnel from the United States (mainly, Anglo-American and Cuban) and from other parts of the world (e.g., South America, Europe, Israel, Asia).[78]

Yet there has also been a third layer of migration, the so-called brain drain from the island to the United States.[79] The reader should bear in mind, on the one hand, that this "brain drain" in no way denies the continuing working-class configuration of most emigration from Puerto Rico to the United States. On the other hand, we feel the indicators for this new trend are significant enough to warrant our current conclusions—particularly when such conclusions are seen within the context of the long-term trends, relational patterns, and global structures examined above.

Some scholars (e.g., Santiago and Rivera-Batiz 1994: 43, 59, 67) have recently insisted that Puerto Ricans in the United States "have come a long way" from the slum backgrounds which characterized the Boricua U.S. population in the past and have partly based this argument on the official statistics confirming the higher educational levels over the past twenty years for both Puerto Ricans living in the United States and especially for Puerto Ricans migrating from the island to the United States. As with the upward-mobility theses mentioned above, this corollary claim does not seem to fully consider either the long-term impact of global economic restructuring in the United States and Puerto Rico or the persistence of the colonized character of Puerto Rican labor. A key development in this regard was the contradiction between, on the one hand, the growth of professional technical personnel (resulting from the prodigious expansion of higher education on the island since the mid-1970s) and, on the other hand, the limits of the existing local job market. This discrepancy, combined with the higher U.S. salary levels, generated a sharp rise in the numbers of higher-skilled, "white-collar" workers migrating to the United States starting in the late 1970s and early 1980s and continuing throughout the 1990s.[80]

As early as 1983, for instance, 80 percent of those graduating from the most important engineering school on the island did not even bother to look for employment in Puerto Rico but went directly to the United States, a trend that has continued up to the present. A similar pattern emerged among the majority of the medical school graduates in Puerto Rico, given that, by the mid-1990s, annual beginning salaries for resident physicians on the island were less than half the U.S. average. Soon the island became a fertile ground for the recruitment efforts of U.S. companies and municipal governments seeking highly credentialed, skilled, and bilingual professional technical labor.[81] As in other formally colonized and neocolonized contexts, this particular exodus epitomized yet another unequal exchange whereby the training and educational costs were shouldered by the island's residents while the economic benefits generated and the services rendered by this same professional-technical "native" labor were transferred to the U.S. metropole (Dietz 1986: 286). Despite the dearth of "hard" data and qualitative studies focusing on this phenomenon (given what exists, for example, for middle-class African Americans in the United States),[82] preliminary information suggests one way to explain why this new kind of—still colonized—labor is so attractive to U.S. employers, public and private.

In the early 1990s school districts and municipal hospitals everywhere from Hartford, Connecticut, and Miami to Houston and Los Angeles were actively drafting Puerto Rican school teachers, social-service workers, and nurses from the island, most of them women. By the mid-1990s, school teachers constituted the largest group (33 percent) of professionals, almost a third of whom moved to Texas and Florida (Pascual Amadeo 1994e; Glasser 1995: 58). The immediate personal economic rationale behind this migration is hardly a mystery: even after the island's short-term economic expansion of the 1990s, Puerto Rico during 1999 and 2000 still had both the lowest average teachers' salaries and the worst average beginning teachers' salaries within all U.S. jurisdictions (American Federation of Teachers [AFT] 2001). Such factors contributed to an almost fourfold increase of Florida's Puerto Rican population between 1980 and 2000, with a growing percentage of them coming from the middle classes. The Tampa–St. Petersburg–Clearwater metropolitan sprawl, for instance, had the second-highest median income levels and one of the most elevated percentages of higher education among Puerto Ricans in all U.S. metropolitan areas by 1990—the highest was the Los Angeles–Long Beach zone (for similar reasons).[83] Still, as late as 2002, Florida's state legislature was actively promoting the recruitment of nurses and teachers (*Tallahassee Democrat* [*TD*] 2002). This influx of highly educated professionals made it perfectly logical for Puerto Rico's Chamber of Commerce to open a chapter in southern Florida during the mid-1990s, despite the fact that over 200 Puerto Rican businesspeople and professionals in Florida's Gulf area had already established their own Chamber of Commerce in 1992.[84]

But these trends do not necessarily mean that Puerto Ricans generally had escaped the racialized socioeconomic constraints with which historically they have been shackled. The main point here is that although Puerto Rican professionals on the U.S. mainland are much more credentialed and relatively better off than both preceding generations of Boricua migrant labor and most Puerto Ricans everywhere today, this professional technical labor sector continues to occupy a racially subordinate and economically depreciated niche when compared to that of racially dominant and colonizer personnel performing the same tasks. In other words, like previous colonized and neocolonized migrants before them, what most middle-class Puerto Ricans since the 1970s primarily see (and continue to see to this day) when they arrive in the United States is that, *in absolute terms*, they have greater incomes and better working conditions than they had back home, *not* that they are being paid *relatively* less and working under *relatively* worse conditions than their U.S.-white counterparts while carrying out comparable labor. For instance, even the famously mainstream *Puerto Rico Herald* acknowledged recently that the state legislature of Florida in 2002 continues to enthusiastically promote the recruitment of school teachers from Puerto Rico "willing to work for low pay and under extremely trying conditions" (PRH 2002). These same conditions apply to virtually all other highly trained Puerto Ricans in professional occupations, even when compared to other "Hispanic" groups (Babco 1999).

The results of such polarizations have not yet become decisively explosive within the United States any more than they have done on the island—another phenomenon that requires further inquiry. Even more than in Puerto Rico, cultural nationalism (via music, sports, and mainstream politics) has played a significant role in suturing the looming disparities we have described among Puerto Ricans in the United States, as well as between Puerto Ricans and the racially dominant and U.S.-white colonizer population. One important and recently added factor is that, despite its higher skill levels, significant portions of this "brain drain" continue to be concentrated in the so-called "petit professions" (school teachers in particular, but also nurses and social workers), with usually female labor. In other words, these were employees frequently placed in lower-salary scales and subject to the same traditional "glass ceilings" as other non-Euro–North Americans working in the United States. Such complex mediations have now been joined by hegemonically middle-class and highly commodified instances of pan-"Hispanic" identification analyzed by Frances Aparicio in this volume: Univisión, telenovelas, "Hispanic" *belle lettres*, the sanitized Latino music boom—from Menudo and Gloria Estefan to "lite salsa" (*salsa monga*) and Ricky Martin—and other corollary mass-media moments.[85] Whether such mediations continue to operate effectively in the twenty-first century remains to be seen.

However, during the 1980s and 1990s, the greater economic polarization brought about by global structural adjustment has promoted a greater social distancing between Puerto Rican *blanquitos* (and their U.S. proxies), on the one hand, and the destitute majority of Puerto Ricans, on the other. This has been especially true within U.S. regions with already existing, historically large "white-collar" Latinos and bourgeois "Hispanic" populations, such as Florida (with its Cuban, South American, and Central American populations) and Texas and California (Mexicans and Chicanos). Here, highly educated and propertied Boricuas tend to define "Latino-ness"—and, indeed, Puerto Rican-ness—in the genteel terms of middle-class respectability and moderation.[86] This new wave of migrants has tended to reproduce the disavowals already mentioned in the case of the Puerto Rican Professional Association of South Florida and the Puerto Rican Chamber of Commerce at Coral Gables, which vociferously took issue with being confused in any way with laboring-poor Boricuas in the United States (AP 2000).

Such disavowals are also reflected in the settlement patterns of these very educated and highly propertied U.S. Puerto Ricans: "There is no distinctive middle-class Puerto Rican neighborhood in the United States" (Lemann 1991: 107). Prosperous retirees and professionals from the island move to majority-white-Anglo suburbs in the U.S. Sunbelt, whereas their mainland-born or raised Boricua counterparts (many of them from the northeast or Chicago) tend to move to the exclusive suburbs of Puerto Rico.[87] This contrasts markedly with "white-collar" and moneyed U.S. Mexicans and Chicanos, more than a third of whom live in their own majority-ethnic affluent urban developments—especially within greater Los Angeles, as well as Orange and Ventura counties (G. Rodríguez 1996: 16, 18).

Puerto Rican professionals, managers, and large-property owners have been able to branch out as never before and expand their assets (now, usually in the business services), remaining the often Hispanophile junior partners of U.S. capital firms, and/or joining the upper strata of local and state administrations. This has given birth since the 1990s to a profusion of local mayors, judges, public policy makers, and legislators, as well as academics across North America (although mostly within the behavioral sciences). Yet some of the disparities examined above have persisted even among the formal housing and property patterns of these professional-managerial and wealthy U.S. Puerto Ricans. Although in 1990 Puerto Ricans were 12 percent of the entire "Hispanic" population in the United States, they were only 2.6 percent of the U.S. Latino middle class (USCB 1993b; G. Rodríguez 1996: 13).[88]

This was how the current socioeconomic split among Puerto Ricans in the United States came into being, a development that requires a considerably more in-depth examination than we have space for here. The transformations of the 1980s and 1990s have meant that Puerto Ricans in the United States no longer tend to be a homogeneously laboring-poor population, but now increasingly reflect the general socioeconomic polarization of the current phase of globalization—even within the U.S. mainland. Seen as a whole (both in Puerto Rico and in the United States), there has been a greater divergence among the modes of economically depreciated labor, from previous forms of colonized labor (lower-skilled, manual) to more recent forms of colonized labor (higher-skilled, "white-collar"). But the structural disparities which characterize Puerto Ricans were and are still colonial: Boricuas were and are still epitomized by persistent disadvantages in the preparation of the labor force, constrictions in the available sources of employment, and relatively inferior conditions compared to those that exist among the racially dominant sectors of the population within the North American metropole.

NOTES

1. See, for example: Cooney and Colón 1979; Association of Puerto Rican Executive Directors (APRED) 1985; Fitzpatrick 1987; Tienda and Lii 1987; Tienda and Jensen 1988; Tienda 1989; Lemann 1991; Congressional Quarterly 1992; H. Rodríguez 1992; Falcón and Hirschman 1992; Darder 1992; Meléndez 1993b; Department of City Planning (DCP) 1994; Rivera-Batiz 1994; Canabal 1997; Hispanic Federation 1999; Navarro 2000.
2. See, for example: Tienda 1989; H. Rodríguez 1992; Meléndez 1993b; Canabal 1997.
3. In this sense, we carry on the research strategy advanced by the History Task Force (1979) of the Centro de Estudios Puertorriqueños at Hunter College—especially Frank Bonilla (1994) and Ricardo Campos (Campos and Bonilla 1981; Bonilla and Campos 1986)—as well as by Colón-Warren (1997) and Benson Arias (1996; 1997).
4. From this perspective (Quijano 2000), "race" has been and continues to be one of the pivotal factors enabling all the power relations inherent to historical capitalism (e.g., "gender," "class," "nation," "ethnicity"), and it does this by racially organizing the ways in which labor is regulated, differentiated, and distributed across the entire world (Quijano and Wallerstein 1992). This is also what makes "race" historically contingent. If "race" had not emerged during the period from 1450–1640 and developed systematically since then to cover eventually the whole planet, the capitalist global order would not be in place today: hence the *colonial* character of the modern world-system (Quijano 2000).
5. Evidence for this process may be seen in the recent work of Sassen (1988; 1991; 1998); we have also documented this process elsewhere (Jiménez-Muñoz 1991b; Jiménez-Muñoz 1993a; Santiago-Valles 1994a; Santiago-Valles 1999).
6. The concepts of "peripheral" and "periphery" within this essay follow one of Fernand Braudel's uses of this term (1992: 40): namely, to describe populations and regions characterized by constrained socioeconomic growth and the most degraded forms of labor. By not reducing the term merely to the relationship *between* specific nation-states, he was able to see that such conditions have existed *within* otherwise core countries since the origins of the modern world-system (Braudel 1992: 44). The latter usage is akin to Sassen-Koob's (1982) notion of the "peripheralization of the core," though she only employs this term to describe late-twentieth-century global cities like New York and Los Angeles.
7. Examples of this perspective may be found, for instance, in Grosfoguel and Georas 1996: 195–96; Grosfoguel, Negrón-Muntaner, and Georas 1997: 19–23.
8. Neither do we reduce "colonial situations" to territorial questions, that is, the desire for a nation-state of one's own (e.g., Nieves Falcón 1990; Dietz and Pantojas-García 1993).
9. U.S. Civil Rights Commission (USCRC) 1976; U.S. Department of Commerce (USDC), 1979: 1:313, 353–55, 705–8, 722; C. Rodríguez 1991; Colón-Warren 1997; Muñiz Varela 1999.
10. History Task Force 1979: 93–112; F. Rivera 1979; Santiago-Valles 1994a.
11. Cochran 1959: 70–148; Reynolds and Gregory 1965: 117–138; Alva Forde 1979; Santiago-Valles 1991; Santiago-Valles 1994b.

12. Such a characterization is ahistorical because it assumes that a single, "global" economy is the result of only the past fifteen to thirty years of socioeconomic shifts, rather than being synonymous with a complex and asymmetrical, *world-systemic* process, beginning in the period from 1450 to 1640 and continuing—albeit transformed—up to the present.
13. Perloff 1950; History Task Force 1979; Bonilla 1994; Duany 1995.
14. This use was "new" inasmuch as it could be distinguished from the previous periods of what eventually became the United States (1607–1800, 1800–1865, 1865–1924, 1924–1945), which also relied on a variety of "foreign" labor: that is, African, Irish, Mexican, Chinese, German, Southern and Eastern European, Japanese and Pacific Islander, and Caribbean.
15. Perloff 1950: 60; Vernon and Hoover 1959: 65; Keller 1983: 61–62; Dietz 1986: 206–12.
16. Perloff 1950: 146; Descartes 1972: 61; Junta de Planificación de Puerto Rico (JPPR) 1980b: 1, 7.
17. Herberg 1953; Helfgott 1959; Fleisher 1961; Keyserling 1963.
18. See Santiago-Valles 1991.
19. As Linebaugh (1981) demonstrated in the case of nineteenth-century, central European, rural proletariat.
20. See: Santiago-Valles 1994a; Jiménez-Muñoz 1999.
21. Linebaugh 1981: 86–87; in the case of Puerto Rico, see: Silvestrini 1980; Santiago-Valles 1994b.
22. Takaki 1983; Kelley 1994; Gutiérrez 1995.
23. Tobier 1984; Waldinger 1985; Sassen-Koob 1985.
24. Herberg 1953; Helfgott 1959; Wakefield 1959: 191–212; Hill 1974; Laurentz 1980: 186–87, 230–307; V. Ortíz 1990: 115–25.
25. See: USBC 1963; USBC 1973; USBC 1993a.
26. USBC 1963: 103–4; Fitzpatrick 1971: 72–76; U.S. Department of Labor (USDL) 1975: 32; Padilla 1987: 104–116; Sassen 1988: 149.
27. See: USBC 1953; USBC 1963; USBC 1973.
28. Handlin 1959; Cordasco and Buchioni 1973; Steiner 1974; F. Padilla 1987.
29. Estades 1978: 37–44; History Task Force 1979: 151–60; Fitzpatrick 1987: 50–52; Torres 1995: 73–74.
30. E. Padilla 1958; Wakefield 1959; López 1980; Morales 1980; Rodríguez-Morazzani 1995.
31. Fitzpatrick 1971: 62–70; I. Santiago 1978; History Task Force 1979: 151–55; Estades 1980; Rodríguez-Fraticelli and Tirado 1989: 38–43; Rodríguez-Morazzani 1991–1992: 101–106; Torres 1995: 79.
32. J. Morales 1986: 45–61; Jiménez-Muñoz 1993b; Laó 1997: 178; Newman 1999: 223–25, 234–45.
33. Handlin 1959; Hill 1974; Massey and Denton 1989: 73, 75; Luciano 1980; Grasmuck and Pessar 1991; Thomas 1991: 95–104, 142–48; Torres 1995; Rodríguez-Morazzani 1995; Grosfoguel and Georas 1996; Rodríguez-Morazzani 1996; Guzmán 1998.
34. Wertham 1958; Rand 1958; Wakefield 1959; Lait and Mortimer 1959; Lewis 1966; Sexton 1965; Fitzpatrick 1971: 170–78; Cooper 1972; Steiner 1974: 327–63, 475–86; Rodríguez-Morazzani 1991–1992: 110; L. Ortíz 1998.
35. Breslin 1986; MacNamara 1989; Schneider 2001.

36. Piven and Cloward 1977; Fuentes 1980; Katznelson 1981; Shefter 1987: 75, 90; Rodríguez-Morazzani 1991–1992: 111–14; A. Torres 1995: 77–82; Torres and Velázquez 1998.
37. Campos and Bonilla 1981; U.S. Congress, House Committee on Education and Labor—Subcommittee on Labor Standards (USCHCEL—SLS) 1982; Bonilla and Campos 1986; Lipietz 1987; Sassen 1988; Ross and Trachte 1990; Santiago-Valles 1991; Benson Arias 1996; Benson Arias 1997: 86–87; Colón-Warren 1997; Newman 1999; New York State Legislature Assembly's Standing Committee on Labor—Subcommittee on Sweatshops (NYSASCL—SoS) 1999.
38. O'Connor 1973; Melguizo and Tablas 1981; Cohen 1981; Tabb 1982; Soja, Morales, and Wolff 1983; Sassen 1988; Ross and Trachte 1990: 156–57; Sassen 1991.
39. North American Congress on Latin America (NACLA) 1978; C. Rodríguez 1979; Sassen 1988: 148, 153, 160, 162.
40. B. Early 1980; Stafford 1981; Bonilla and Campos 1986: 9–14.
41. Tabulations based on: USBC 1963; USBC 1973; USBC 1983; USBC 1993a; USBC 2000b. The categories excluded in the previous tabulations are farming, forestry, and fishing workers.
42. USCRC 1976: 55–71, 105–46; C. Rodríguez 1979; Katznelson 1981; Stafford 1985; Fitzpatrick 1987: 141–78; Ross and Trachte 1990: 168; Jiménez-Muñoz 1991a; C. Rodríguez 1991: 120–38; H. Rodríguez 1992; A. Torres 1995; Canabal 1997.
43. Tienda 1989; H. Rodríguez 1992; Falcón and Hirschman 1992; Canabal 1997.
44. Seen in isolation, this situation would seem to mark a sharp contrast with what had been the case on the island since the late 1940s, where social polarization had been occurring at a much faster pace. But, taken within the context of the totality of U.S. domains—themselves a significant component of the shifting global capitalist economy—the disproportionately elevated laboring-poor composition of Puerto Ricans in the United States could be understood as the most destitute pole of the entire Puerto Rican population (the island included), constituting a fragment of all the depreciated labor being economically restructured on a world scale since the early 1970s.
45. See: USBC 1986; USBC 1990; USBC 1993a.
46. Tienda 1989; Becerrraet al. 1991: 217; Lemann 1991; Congressional Quarterly 1992: 944.
47. Fitzpatrick 1987: 40, 142; DCP 1994: 56, 59; Rivera-Batiz 1994: 44.
48. H. Rodríguez 1992; Falcón and Hirschman 1992; Canabal 1997.
49. By the 1990s there were discrepancies in how poverty levels were calculated between federal agencies and the island's government: "Puerto Rico uses its own poverty level which is significantly lower than the [federal standard] roughly equal to half of it. It also does not change on an annual basis" (National Association of State Medicaid Directors (NASMD) 1999). "The poverty guidelines are not defined for Puerto Rico [et. al.] . . . In cases in which a Federal program using the poverty guidelines serves any of those jurisdictions [i.e., Puerto Rico, the U.S. Virgin Islands, American Samoa, Guam, the Marshall Islands, Micronesia, the Marianas, and Palau], the Federal Office which administers the program is responsible for deciding whether to use the contiguous-states-and-D.C. guidelines for those jurisdictions or to follow some other procedure" (Health and Human Services (HSS) 2002).
50. USBC 1973; USCRC 1976; USBC 1993; Acevedo-Vila 2001; NCCIC 2002.
51. BLS 2002a; BLS 2002b; USBC 1999; USBC 2000b.

52. USBC 1993; Federal Student Aid (FSA) 2001; Bureau of Economic Analysis (BEA) 2002.
53. Flores 1988; Pomales 1992–1993; Flores 1992–1993; Bravo 1996; M. Guzmán 1997; Aponte-Parés and Merced 1998; R. Rivera 2001; Cardalda Sánchez and Tirado Avilés 2001; Aponte-Parés 2001.
54. Such was the case of the political alliances composed mostly of Puerto Ricans and Dominicans (e.g., Latinos United for Political Action, Coalition for Latino Empowerment, Southside Political Action Committee) and parallel instances of neighborhood social activism (like Brooklyn's Música Against Drugs, the Latino Parent Coalition Against Police Brutality, Latino Committee of Relatives of Victims of Police Brutality, United Bronx Parents, Ciudadanos Concientes de Queens, and the Committee to Save East Harlem). Totti 1987; Rodríguez-Fraticelli and Tirado 1989; Rodríguez-Morazzani 1991–1992: 97; A. Torres 1995: 135; *Stress* 1996; Trim-TNC 1996; Hispanic Federation 1999; Laó 2001: 119–20, 127–32.
55. Mollenkopf 1993; A. Torres 1995; Laó 2001.
56. Sternlieb, Roistacher, and Hughes 1976; Tobier 1979; Katznelson 1981; Zukin 1982; Marcuse 1986; Fainstein and Fainstein 1987; Fainstein 1989; Ross and Trachte 1990: 154–63; Massey 1990; Mollenkopf and Castells 1991; C. Rodríguez 1991: 106–16; A. Santiago 1992; A. Torres 1995; Glover 2001.
57. Cochran 1959; Estades 1978; Fitzpatrick 1987; Rodríguez-Fraticelli and Tirado 1989; C. Rodríguez 1991; Rodríguez-Morazzani 1991–1992; Santiago-Valles 1992; Pascual Amadeo 1994c; Pascual Amadeo 1994h; Santiago-Valles 1994b; Santiago-Valles 1995; Muñiz Varela 1995; A. Torres 1995; Muñiz Varela 1996; Rodríguez-Morazzani 1995; Laó 1997; Torres and Velázquez 1998; L. Ortíz 1998; Muñiz-Varela 1999; Laó 2001: 133–37.
58. Bluestone and Harrison 1982; Sassen 1988: 57, 146; Piven and Cloward 1988; Harrison and Bluestone 1990; Santiago-Valles 1991; Santiago-Valles 1995; Benson Arias 1996; Muñiz Varela 1996; Colón-Warren 1997.
59. Criminological anthropologies and psychological microstudies of the relationship between social disorder, crime, and Puerto Ricans in the United States (1940s to 1990s) already exist: e.g., Mobilization for Youth (MfY) 1963; Malzberg 1965; Lewis 1966; Sullivan 1989; Bourgois 1995; Schneider 2001. However, in-depth social histories addressing such issues and covering this same period—comparable to the existing historical studies focusing on Puerto Rico itself (Silvestrini 1980; Santiago-Valles 1994a; Santiago-Valles 1995)—still remain to be done. Our present observations are based on the patterns suggested by current social trends.
60. Morín 1989; Kamber 1989; Lemann 1991; James 1992; Pérez 1996; Laó 2001.
61. Pérez 1990; L. Ortíz 1998; Dorfman and Schiraldi 2001.
62. Sassen 1988: 22–25; USDL 1997: 4–6; Newman 1999: 76, 263–66; Glover 2001.
63. See: USBC 1963; USBC 1973; USBC 2000b.
64. Vázquez Calzada 1978: 376–77; JPPR 1980a: 22–23; JPPR 1999:A-38; M. Rivera 2002.
65. The upward-mobility argument seems to overlook two additional overlapping issues. As Saskia Sassen (1988; 1991; 1998) has demonstrated more generally and other scholars have documented in the case of Puerto Ricans in the United States (but also on the island), this shift towards greater employment for higher-skilled and more credentialed laborers did not compensate for all of the lower-skilled, manual

jobs Puerto Ricans have lost to economic restructuring across the United States and Puerto Rico. On the other hand, this same shift is inseparable from the marked growth in the proportions of Puerto Ricans increasingly stuck in deskilled, dead-end jobs in the new sweatshops and business services linked to this boom in the production of emergent technology and in the high-tech service sectors. See Tienda 1989; Santiago-Valles 1991; H. Rodríguez 1992; Falcón and Hirschman 1992; Darder 1992; Canabal 1997; Colón-Warren 1997.

66. Waldinger 1985; Duany 1995; Colón-Warren 1997: 172–73.
67. USBC 1997; Pugatch 1998; Weil 2000; Glover 2001.
68. The mostly undocumented Chinese laborers in New York City's apparel sweatshops not only worked for rock-bottom wages, but often labored under indentured-servant conditions or other types of bonded-labor contracts, wherein their back-pay was docked by the subcontractors or by the "snakehead" rings who had smuggled these workers from China. See USCHCEL—SLS 1982; NYSASCL-SoS 1999; Kwong 2001; Glover 2001.
69. However, this differed from the interwar and postwar periods, when Boricuas usually worked in, for instance, small restaurants, individually owned hotels, government buildings, and minor businesses. Now such employment tended toward the rapidly expanding new business services and consumer services, namely: transnational conglomerates and company chains linked to major advertising firms or to building maintenance, hospitality services, legal counsel, research and development, and management and consulting services.
70. Russell 1982; Ghigliotty 1982; Sassen-Koob 1982; Weisskoff 1985: 55, 63–64; Petrovich and Laureano 1987; Sassen 1988: 87, 157–58, 200; Bonilla 1994: 135–38; Santiago-Valles 1995; A. Torres 1995: 28, 58, 131–32; Colón-Warren 1997: 139–41, 168–71; Newman 1999: 26–27, 46, 199, 218, 297–98.
71. Fernández-Kelly 1984; Sassen 1988; Ross and Trachte 1990: 88–110, 160–61; Ríos 1993; Dietz and Pantojas-García 1993; Colón-Warren 1997; NMASS 2001; Kwong 2001; Glover 2001.
72. Hernández Alvarez 1976; Hernández Cruz 1985; Bonilla and Campos 1986; Bonilla 1989; Meléndez 1993a; C. Rodríguez 1993; Hernández Cruz 1994; Duany 1995.
73. E. Rivera 1984; J. Morales 1986: 90–132; Ross and Trachte 1990: 181–88; Borges-Méndez 1993; C. Santiago and Rivera-Batiz 1994: 22, 48; Inter-University Program for Latino Research (IUPLR) 2000.
74. Williams 2001; Fechter and Stanley 2001; Caldwell and Waite 2002.
75. Weisskoff 1985: 162; Martínez 1988; Dietz and Pantojas-García 1993; Muñiz Varela 1995.
76. Sassen-Koob 1982: 99; Castañer 1988; Santiago-Valles 1991; Benson Arias 1996; Muñiz Varela 1996.
77. V. Ortíz 1986; Nieves Falcón 1990; Meléndez 1994.
78. Vázquez Calzada and Morales del Valle 1979; Cobas and Duany 1995.
79. For arguments to the contrary, see: Duany 1995: 62; Santiago and Rivera-Batiz 1996: 185–90.
80. Turner 1982a; Turner 1982b; Alameda 1983; Lidin 1983a; Lidin 1983b; Latortue 1983; Licha 1984; Alameda and Ruíz Oliveras 1985; Gaud 1988; Pagán Irizarry 1989; Blasor 1990; Santiago-Valles 1991; Vega López 1992.

81. Olavarría 1983; Duany 1995: 62; Pascual Amadeo 1994a; Pascual Amadeo 1994f; Santiago and Rivera-Batiz 1996: 190; MITRE 1999.
82. The Puerto Rican middle class in the United States—and, more broadly, the U.S. Latino middle class—is a famously understudied phenomenon (G. Rodríguez 1996; Kirschten 1999).
83. USBC 1983: 6; C. Santiago and Rivera-Batiz 1994: 35, 112; Logan 2001: 10.
84. Pascual Amadeo 1994b; Pascual Amadeo 1994c; Pascual Amadeo 1994d; L. Torres 1994a; L. Torres 1994b.
85. C. Rodríguez 1991: 158–74; Santiago-Valles 1995: 38; Flores 1996; Laó 1997: 170–171; Hernández and Scheff 1997.
86. Pascual Amadeo 1994b; Pascual Amadeo 1994c; L. Torres 1994a; L. Torres 1994b; Pascual Amadeo 1994d; Pascual Amadeo 1994g; Pascual Amadeo 1994h.
87. Newman 1991: 107–8; Pascual Amadeo 1994b; Pascual Amadeo 1994c; L. Torres 1994a; L. Torres 1994b; Pascual Amadeo 1994d; Pascual Amadeo 1994g; Pascual Amadeo 1994h; Navarro 2000.
88. Bearing in mind that officially these "percentages correspond almost exactly to those for the overall U.S.-born Latino householder population" (G. Rodríguez 1996: 13), it is significant that by the year 2000 only 35 percent of Puerto Ricans in the United States actually owned their homes: in spite of the fact that the latter percentage was up from 26 in 1990, it was still below the corresponding rates for African Americans (46 percent), Mexicans (48 percent), Asians (53 percent), Cubans (58 percent), and White-Anglos (72 percent) (Armas 2002). Likewise, the official average receipts from firms owned by U.S. Boricuas in 1997 ($107,100) trailed well behind the average for all U.S. Latinos ($155,200), especially when compared to those for Cuban-owned ($211,500) and Mexican-owned ($156,100) businesses (USBC 2001).

REFERENCES

Acevedo-Vila, Anibal. 2001. *"No Child Left Behind": Statement Submitted for the Record of Representative Anibal Acevedo-Vila*. Washington, D.C.: U.S. House of Representatives, Hearings of Committee on Education and the Workforce, March 28, Government Printing Office.

Aglietta, Michel. 1979. *A Theory of Capitalist Regulation: The U.S. Experience*. London: New Left Books.

Alameda, José. 1983. "Efectos y consecuencias del éxodo de profesionales en Puerto Rico." *El Reportero*, 19 July.

Alameda, José, and Wilfredo Ruíz Oliveras. 1985. "La fuga de capital humano en la economía de Puerto Rico: Reto para la actual década." *Revista de Ciencias Sociales* 24, nos. 1–2 (January-June): 3–36.

Alva Forde, Errol. 1979. "Labor Absorption in the Service Sector of a Developing Economy: The Case of Puerto Rico." Ph.D. diss., University of Illinois, Urbana.

American Federation of Teachers (AFT). 2001. "Teachers Salaries Fail to Keep Up with Inflation." AFT Press Release, 17 May. http://www.aft.org/press/2001/051601.html. Accessed 10 July 2002.

Aponte-Parés, Luis. 2001. "Outside/In: Crossing Queer and Latino Boundaries." In *Mambo Montage: The Latinization of New York*, ed. Agustín Laó and Arlene Dávila, 363–85. New York: Columbia University Press.

Aponte-Parés, Luis, and Jorge Merced. 1998. "*Páginas Omitidas*: The Gay and Lesbian Presence." In *The Puerto Rican Movement: Voices from the Diaspora*, ed. Andrés Torres and José Velázquez, 296–315. Philadelphia: Temple University Press.

Armas, Genaro C. 2002. "Hispanic Ownership Soared During Nineties." Newszine. Gainsville Sun.com. http://iml.jou.ufl.edu/Newszine/national/5.htm. Accessed 2 July 2002.

Arrighi, Giovanni. 1994. *The Long Twentieth Century: Money, Power, and the Origins of Our Times*. London: Verso.

Association of Puerto Rican Executive Directors (APRED). 1985. *A Call To Action: Puerto Rican New Yorkers*. New York: Association of Puerto Rican Executive Directors.

Associated Press (AP). 2000. "Some Puerto Ricans Reject Result of Government Health Study." http://www.polkonline.com/stories/030100/hea_hispanic-health.sthml. Accessed 3 July 2002.

Augelli, John P. 1972. "San Lorenzo: A Case Study of Recent Migrations in Interior Puerto Rico." In *Portrait of a Society: Readings in Puerto Rican Sociology*, ed. E. Fernández Méndez, 201–7. Río Piedras: University of Puerto Rico Press.

Babco, Eleanor. 1999. "Limited Progress: The Status of Hispanic Americans in Science and Engineering" *Making Strides: Report no. 2*. Alliance for Graduate Education and the Professorate Program. http://ehrweb.aaas.org/mge/Reports/Report2/Report2.html. Accessed 10 July 2002.

Becerra, José, Carol J. Hogue, Hanik Atrash, and Nilsa Pérez. 1991. "Infant Mortality Among Hispanics: A Portrait of Heterogeneity." *Journal of the American Medical Association* 265, no. 2 (9 January): 217–21.

Benson Arias, Jaime. 1996. "Postfordismo Puerto Rico-USA." *Bordes* 3: 29–40.

——. 1997. "Puerto Rico: The Myth of the National Economy." In *Puerto Rican Jam: Essays on Culture and Politics*, ed. Frances Negrón Muntaner and Ramón Grosfoguel, 77–92. Minneapolis: University of Minnesota Press.

Blasor, Lorraine. 1990. "Puerto Rico's Brain Drain: Curse or Blessing?" *Caribbean Business*, 4 August.

Bluestone, Barry, and Bennett Harrison. 1982. *The Deindustrialization of America*. New York: Basic Books.

Bonilla, Frank. 1989. "La circulación migratoria en la década actual." *Centro* 2, no. 6 (summer): 55–59.

——. 1994. "*Manos que sobran*: Work, Migration, and the Puerto Rican in the 1990's." In *The Commuter Nation: Perspectives on Puerto Rican Migration*, ed. Carlos Antonio Torre, Hugo Rodríguez Vecchini, and William Burgos, 115–52. Río Piedras: Editorial de la Universidad de Puerto Rico.

Bonilla, Frank, and Ricardo Campos. 1986. *Industry and Idleness*. New York: Centro de Estudios Puertorriqueños, Hunter College.

Borges-Méndez, Ramón. 1993. "Migration, Social Networks, Poverty, and the Regionalization of Puerto Rican Settlements: Barrio Formation in Lowell, Lawrence, and Holyoke, Massachusetts." *Latino Studies Journal* 4, no. 3 (May): 3–21.

Bourgois, Philippe. 1995. *In Search of Respect: Selling Crack in El Barrio*. Cambridge and New York: Cambridge University Press.

Braudel, Fernand. 1992. *Civilization and Capitalism, Fifteenth–Eighteenth Century*. Vol. 3, *The Perspective of the World*. Berkeley: University of California Press.

Bravo, Vee. 1996. "Street Bombing." *Stress* (summer): 14–18.

Breslin, Jimmy. 1986. "The Beauty of His Death in the Bronx." *Daily News*, 24 April.

Bureau of Economic Analysis (BEA). 2002. *Per Capita Personal Income by State*. Washington, D.C.: Government Printing Office, U.S. Department of Commerce.

Bureau of Labor Statistics (BLS). 1968. *Labor Force Experience of the Puerto Rican Worker*. New York City: Regional Report, No. 9. New York: U.S. Department of Labor, Middle Atlantic Region.

——. 1975. *A Socio-Economic Profile of Puerto Rican New Yorkers*. Regional Report no. 46. New York City: Bureau of Statistics, Middle-Atlantic Regional Office.

——. 2002a. *Bureau of Labor Statistics Data: Local Area Unemployment Statistics—Puerto Rico*. Washington, D.C.: Government Printing Office.

——. 2002b. *Bureau of Labor Statistics Data: Labor Force Statistics from the Current Population Survey: Unemployment Rate, Civilian Labor Force—United States*. Washington, D.C.: Government Printing Office.

——. 2002c. *Bureau of Labor Statistics Data: National Employment, Hours, and Earnings*. Washington, D.C.: Government Printing Office.

Caldwell, Alicia, and Matthew Waite. 2002. "New Census Figures Show Colombians, Dominicans, and Asians Pouring Into Florida." *The St. Petersburg Times*, 24 April.

Campos, Ricardo, and Frank Bonilla. 1981. "A Wealth of Poor: Puerto Ricans in the New Economic Order." *Daedalus* 110, no. 2 (Spring): 133–176.

Canabal, María, E. 1997. *Poverty Among Puerto Ricans in the United States*. East Lansing, Mich.: JSRI Working Paper 32, The Julian Samora Research Institute, Michigan State University, June.

Cardalda Sánchez, Elsa B., and Amilcar Tirado Avilés. 2001. "Ambiguous Identities! The Affirmation of Puertorriqueñidad in the Community Murals of New York City." In *Mambo Montage: The Latinization of New York*, ed. Agustín Laó and Arlene Dávila, 263–86. New York: Columbia University Press.

Castañer, Juan. 1988. "Las fábricas de producción complementaria en Puerto Rico: Su evaluación y posibilidades como centro de alta tecnología para el resto del Caribe." In *Puerto Rico en los 1990*, ed. Carmen Gautier Mayoral and Nestor Nazario Trabal, 1–31. Río Piedras: Centro de Investigaciones Sociales, Universidad de Puerto Rico.

Castells, Manuel. 1978. *La crisis económica mundial y el capitalismo norteamericano*. Barcelona: Editorial Laia.

Centers for Disease Control (CDC). 2002. "Health-Related Quality of Life—Puerto Rico, 1996–2000." *MMWR Weekly*, 51, no. 8 (March 1): 166–68.

Coats, Bill. 2001. "County's Hispanic Population Changes." *St. Petersburg Times*, 23 May.

Cobas, José, and Jorge Duany. 1995. *Los cubanos en Puerto Rico: Economía étnica e identidad cultural*. Río Piedras: Editorial de la Universidad de Puerto Rico.

Cochran, Thomas. 1959. *The Puerto Rican Bussinesman: A Study of Cultural Change*. Philadelphia: University of Pennsylvania Press.

Cohen, Robert. 1981. "The New International Division of Labor: Multinational Corporations and Urban Hierarchy." In *Urbanization and Urban Planning in Capitalist Society*, ed. Michael Dear and Allen Scott, 287–315. New York: Methuen.

Colón-Warren, Alice. 1997. "Reestructuración industrial, empleo y pobreza en Puerto Rico y el Atlántico Medio de los Estados Unidos: La situación de las mujeres puertorriqueñas." *Revista de Ciencias Sociales-Nueva Epoca* 3 (June): 135–88.

Congressional Quarterly. 1992. "Hispanic Americans." *The CQ Researcher* 2, no. 4 (30 October): 929–52.

Cooney, Rosemary Santana and Alice Colón. 1979. "Declining Female Participation Among Puerto Rican New Yorkers: A Comparison with Native White Non-Spanish New Yorkers." *Ethnicity* 6, no. 3: 281–297.

Cooper, Paulette. 1972. *Growing Up Puerto Rican.* New York: Arbor House.

Cordasco, Francesco, and Eugene Bucchioni, eds. 1973. *The Puerto Rican Experience: A Sociological Sourcebook.* Totowa, N.J.: Towman and Littlefield.

Cordero Guzmán, Héctor. 1992–1993. "The Structure of Inequality and the Status of Puerto Rican Youth." *Centro* 5, no. 1 (winter): 100–115.

Cueva, Agustín. 1977. *El desarrollo del capitalismo en América Latina.* Mexico City: Siglo XXI Editores.

Darder, Antonia. 1992. "Problematizing the Notion of Puerto Ricans as 'Underclass': A Step toward a Decolonizing Study of Poverty." *Hispanic Journal of Behavioral Science* 14, no. 1 (February): 144–56.

Department of City Planning (DCP). 1994. *Puerto Rican New Yorkers in 1990.* New York: Department of City Planning, City of New York, September.

Descartes, Sol Luis. 1972. "Historical Account of Recent Land Reform in Puerto Rico." In *Portrait of a Society*, ed. E. Fernández Méndez, 183–200. Río Piedras, University of Puerto Rico.

de Valle, Elaine, and Tim Henderson. 2002. "More Puerto Ricans Are Making Their Homes in Florida?" *Puerto Rico Herald* 16, no. 17 (April): 19.

Dietz, James. 1986. *Economic History of Puerto Rico.* Princeton, N.J.: Princeton University Press.

Dietz, James, and Emilio Pantojas-García. 1993. "Puerto Rico's New Role in the Caribbean: The High-Finance/*Maquiladora* Strategy." In *Colonial Dilemma: Critical Perspectives on Contemporary Puerto Rico*, ed. Edwin Meléndez and Egardo Meléndez, 103–15. Boston: South End Press.

Dorfman, Lori, and Vincent Schiraldi. 2001. *Off Balance: Youth, Race, and Crime in the News.* Washington, D.C.: Youth Law Center, Building Blocks for Youth, April.

Duany, Jorge. 1995. "Common Threads or Disparate Agendas? Recent Research on Migration to and from Puerto Rico." *Centro* 7, no. 1: 60–77.

Dubner, Stephen J. 1997. "The Pop Perfectionist." *New York Times Magazine* (9 November): 42–49, 56, 63–66, 83.

Early, Brian. 1980. "Puerto Ricans in the New York City Labor Market, 1970: A Structural Analysis." Ph.D. diss., Fordham University.

Educational Priorities Panel (EPP). 1985. *Ten Years of Neglect: The Education of Children of Limited English Proficiency in New York Public Schools.* New York: Interface.

Estades, Rosa. 1978. *Patterns of Political Participation of Puerto Ricans in New York City.* Río Piedras: Editorial Universitaria.

——. 1980. "Symbolic Unity: The Puerto Rican Day Parade." In *The Puerto Rican Struggle: Essays on Survival in the U.S.*, ed. Clara Rodríguez, Virginia Sánchez-Korrol, and José Oscar Alers, 82–89. New York: Puerto Rican Migration Research Consortium.

Fainstein, Susan. 1989. "Economics, Politics, and Development Policy: New York and London." Paper presented at the Conference on Urban Policy and Economic Restructuring in Comparative Perspective, State University of New York at Albany, 7–8 April.

Fainstein, Susan, and Norman Fainstein. 1987. "The Politics of Land Use Planning in New York City." *Journal of the American Planning Association* 53: 237–48.

Falcón, Luis M., and Charles Hirschman. 1992. "Trends in Labor Market Position for Puerto Ricans in the Mainland, 1970–1987." *Hispanic Journal of Behavioral Sciences* 14, no. 1 (February): 16–51.

Fechter, Michael and Doug Stanley. 2001. "Census Shows Ethnic Shifts." TBO.Com News. 23 May. http://news.tbo.com/news/MGAXWTWKARC.html. Accessed 18 July 2002.

Federal Student Aid (FSA). 2001. "Estimated State Median Income for 4-Person Families, By State, Fiscal Year 2001." www.ed.gov/offices/OSFAP/Students/medianincomes.pdf. Accessed 4 July 2002.

Fernández-Kelly, María Patricia. 1984. *For We Are Sold, I and My People: Women and Industry in Mexico's Frontier*. Albany: State University of New York Press.

Fitzpatrick, Joseph P. 1971. *Puerto Rican Americans: The Meaning of Migration to the Mainland*. Englewood Cliffs, N.J.: Prentice-Hall.

——. 1987. *Puerto Rican Americans: The Meaning of Migration to the Mainland*. 2d ed. Englewood Cliffs: Prentice-Hall.

Fleisher, Belton M. 1961. "Some Economic Aspects of Puerto Rican Migration to the United States." Ph.D. Diss., Stanford University.

Flores, Juan. 1988. "Rappin', Writin', and Breakin.'" *Centro* 2, no. 3 (spring): 34–41.

——. 1992–1993. "'Puerto Rican and Proud, Boyee!': Rap, Roots, and Amnesia." *Centro* 5, no. 1 (winter): 22–32.

——. 1997. "Pan-Latino/Trans-Latino: Puerto Ricans in the 'New Nueva York,'" *Centro* 8, nos. 1–2: 170–186.

Fuentes, Luis. 1980. "The Struggle for Local Political Control," In *The Puerto Rican Struggle: Essays on Survival in the U.S.*, ed. Clara Rodríguez, Virginia Sánchez-Korrol, and José Oscar Alers, 111–20. New York: Puerto Rican Migration Research Consortium.

Gaud, Frank. 1988. "Exhortan a detener el éxodo de ingenieros." *El Mundo*, 28 March.

Ghigliotty, Julio. 1982. "Their Subsistence Comes from Discarded Cans." *The San Juan Star*, 19 December.

Glasser, Ruth. 1995. "*En Casa en Connecticut*: Towards a Historiography of Puerto Ricans Outside New York City," *Centro* 7, no. 1: 50–59.

Glover, Hannah. 2001. "Hemmed In: Times Change, Conditions Don't." In *Under the Radar: The World of the Undocumented Immigrant In New York City*, ed. The Investigative Project. New York: Columbia University Graduate School of Journalism, The Investigative Project.

Grasmuck, Sherri, and Patricia Pessar. 1991. *Between Two Islands: Dominican International Migration*. Berkeley: University of California Press.

Grosfoguel, Ramón, and Cloé S. Georas. 1996. "The Racialization of Latino Caribbean Migrants in the New York Metropolitan Area." *Centro* 8, nos. 1–2: 190–201.

Grosfoguel, Ramón, Frances Negrón-Muntaner, and Cloé S. Georas. 1997. "Beyond Nationalist and Colonialist Discourses: The Jaiba Politics of the Puerto Rican Ethno-

Nation." In *Puerto Rican Jam: Essays on Culture and Politics*, ed. Frances Negrón Muntaner and Ramón Grosfoguel, 1–36. Minneapolis: University of Minnesota Press.

Guernsey, Otis L. 1985. *Broadway Song and Story: Playwrights/Lyricists/Composers Discuss Their Hits.* New York: Dodd, Mead.

Gulick, Luther H. 1952. *Rural Occupance in Utuado and Jayuya Municipios, Puerto Rico.* Research no. 23. Chicago: Department of Geography, University of Chicago.

Gutiérrez, David G. 1995. *Walls and Mirrors: Mexican Americans, Mexican Immigrants, and the Politics of Ethnicity.* Berkeley: University of California Press.

Guzmán, Manuel. 1997. "Pa' La Escuelita con Mucho Cuida'o y por la Orillita: A Journey through the Contested Terrains of the Nation and Sexual Orientation." In *Puerto Rican Jam: Essays on Culture and Politics*, ed. Frances Negrón Muntaner and Ramón Grosfoguel, 209–28. Minneapolis: University of Minnesota Press.

Guzmán, Pablo. 1998. "*La Vida Pura*: A Lord of the Barrio," In *The Puerto Rican Movement: Voices from the Diaspora*, ed. Andrés Torres and José Velázquez, 155–72. Philadelphia: Temple University Press.

Handlin, Oscar. 1959. *The Newcomers: Negroes and Puerto Ricans in a Changing Metropolis.* Cambridge, Mass.: Harvard University Press.

Harrison, Bennett, and Barry Bluestone. 1990. *The Great U-Turn: Corporate Restructuring and the Polarizing of America.* New York: Basic Books.

Health and Human Services (HSS). 2002. *The 2002 HHS Poverty Guidelines.* Washington, D.C.: U.S. Department of Health and Human Services, Office of the Assistant Secretary for Planning and Evaluation.

Helfgott, Roy B. 1959. "Women and Children's Apparel," In *Made in New York: Case Studies in Metropolitan Manufacturing*, ed. Max Hall, 21–134. Cambridge: Harvard University Press.

Herberg, Will. 1953. "The Old-Timers and the Newcomers: Ethnic Group Relations in a Needle Trades Union." *Journal of Social Issues* 9, no. 1 (summer): 12–19.

Hernández, David, and Janet Scheff. 1997. "Puerto Rican Geographic Mobility: The Making of a Deterritorialized Nationality," *The Latino Review of Books* 2, no. 3 (winter): 2–8.

Hernández Alvarez, José. 1967. Reprint, 1976. *Return Migration to Puerto Rico.* Westport, Conn.: Greenwood Press.

Hernández Cruz, Juan. 1985. "¿Migración del retorno o circulación de obreros boricuas?" *Revista de Ciencias Sociales* 24, no. 12: 81–112.

——. 1994. *Corrientes migratorias en Puerto Rico.* San Germán: Centro de Publicaciones, Universidad Interamericana de Puerto Rico.

Hill, Herbert. 1974. "Guardians of the Sweatshops: The Trade Union, Racism, and the Garment Industry." In *Puerto Rico and the Puerto Ricans*, ed. Adalberto López and James Petras, 384–416. New York: Schenkman Publishing.

Hispanic Federation. 1999. *Hispanic New Yorkers on Nueva York: Seventh Annual Survey—Report 3: Profile of the Puerto Rican Community.* http://www.hispanicfederation.org/sv99–3.htm. Accessed 3 July 2002.

History Task Force, ed. 1979. *Labor Migration Under Capitalism: The Puerto Rican Experience.* New York: Monthly Review Press.

Hoover, Calvin, and B. U. Ratchford. 1951. *Economic Resources and Policies of the South.* New York: Macmillan.

Human Rights Watch (HRW). 2000. *Punishment and Prejudice: Racial Disparities in the War on Drugs*. New York: Human Rights Watch Report 2, no. 2 (May).

Inter-University Program for Latino Research (IUPLR). 2000. *Census 2000 Latino Population Counts: Population Changes for Puerto Ricans by State*. http://www.nd.edu/~iuplr/cic/origins_html/5.html. Accessed 18 July 2002.

James, Joy. 1992. "Media Convictions, Fair-Trial Activism, and the Central Park Case." *Zeta Magazine* 5, no. 2 (February): 33–37.

Jiménez-Muñoz, Gladys M. 1991a. "Latinas in the U.S.: A Profile." Paper presented at The New York State Latino Collegiate Conference, 9 March, at SUNY—Albany, Albany, New York.

——. 1991b. "Wanting Identities: Citizenship and Women's Rights in Puerto Rico, 1898–1929." Paper presented at the 16th International Congress of the Latin American Studies Association, 4–6 April, Washington, D.C.

——. 1993a. "Deconstructing Colonialist Discourses: Links Between the Women's Suffrage Movements in the United States and Puerto Rico." *Phoebe* 5, no. 1 (spring): 9–34.

——. 1993b. "The Elusive Signs of African-Ness: Latinas in the United States." *Border/Lines* 29–30: 9–15.

——. 1999. "Literacy, Class, and Sexuality in the Debate on Women's Suffrage in Puerto Rico During the 1920s." In *Puerto Rican Women's History*, ed. Félix V. Matos and Linda Delgado, 143–70. New York: M. E. Sharpe.

Junta de Planificación de Puerto Rico (JPPR). 1980a. *Informe económico al Gobernador-1980*. San Juan: Oficina del Gobernador.

——. 1980b. *Serie histórica de empleo, desempleo, y del grupo trabajador*. San Juan: Oficina del Gobernador.

——. 1999. *Informe económico al Gobernador-1998*. San Juan: Oficina del Gobernador.

Kamber, Michael. 1989. "Do the Right Thing?" *Zeta Magazine* 2, no. 10 (October): 37–40.

Katznelson, Ira. 1981. *City Trenches*. Chicago: University of Chicago Press.

Keller, John F. 1983. *Power in America: The Southern Question and the Control of Labor*. Chicago: Vanguard Books.

Kelley, Robin D. G. 1994. *Race Rebels: Culture, Politics, and the Black Working Class*. New York: The Free Press.

Keyserling, Leon. 1963. *The New York Dress Industry: Problems and Prospects*. Washington, D.C.: n.p.

Kirschten, Dick. "Hispanics: Beyond the Myths." *Puerto Rico Herald*, 14 August.

Kwong, Peter. 2001. "The Politics of Labour Migration: Chinese Workers in New York." In *Socialist Register-2001: Working Classes, Global Realities*, ed. Leo Patnitch and Colin Leys, 293–313. New York: Monthly Review Press.

Lait, Jack, and Leo Mortimer. 1959. "Little Puerto Rico . . . Love and Votes for Sale." *New York Confidential* 1, no. 1.

Laó, Agustín. 1997. "Islands at the Crossroads: Puerto Ricanness Traveling between the Translocal Nation and the Global City." In *Puerto Rican Jam: Essays on Culture and Politics*, ed. Frances Negrón Muntaner and Ramón Grosfoguel, 169–88. Minneapolis: University of Minnesota Press.

——. 2001. "Niuyol: Urban Regime, Latino Social Movements, Ideologies of Latinidad." In *Mambo Montage: The Latinization of New York*, ed. Agustín Laó and Arlene Dávila, 119–57. New York: Columbia University Press.

Latortue, Paul. 1983. "La migración de los profesionales." *El Reportero*, 21 June.

Laurentz, Robert. 1980. "Racial-Ethnic Conflict in New York City Garment Industry, 1933–1980." Ph.D. diss., State University of New York at Binghamton.

Lemann, Nicholas. 1991. "The Other Underclass." *The Atlantic Monthly* (December): 96–110.

Lewis, Oscar. 1966. *La Vida: A Puerto Rican Family in the Culture of Poverty—San Juan and New York*. New York: Random House.

Licha, Silvia. 1984. "Vuelve la emigración a EE.UU." *El Nuevo Día*, 6 May.

Lidin, Harold. 1983a. "Puerto Ricans Altering Move." *The San Juan Star*, 31 January.

——. 1983b. "Is Job Mart Pressure Squeezing the 'Liberal' Out of Education?" *The San Juan Star*, 29 May.

Linebaugh, Peter. 1981. "Karl Marx, the Theft of Wood, and Composition." In *Crime and Capitalism: Readings in Marxist Criminology*, ed. D. Greenberg, 76–97. Palo Alto, Calif.: Mayfield Publishing.

Lipietz, Alain. 1987. *Mirages and Miracles: The Crises of Global Fordism*. London: Verso.

Logan, John R. 2001. *The New Latinos: Who They Are, Where They Are*. Albany: Lewis Mumford Center for Comparative Urban and Regional Research, SUNY Albany.

López, Adalberto. 1980. "The Puerto Rican Diaspora: A Survey." In *The Puerto Ricans: Their History, Culture, and Society*, ed. Adalberto López, 313–44. Cambridge, Mass.: Schenkman Publishing.

Luciano, Felipe. 1980. "'America should never have taught us to read, she should never have given us eyes to see.'" In *The Puerto Ricans: Their History, Culture, and Society*, ed. Adalberto López, 446–51. Cambridge, Mass.: Schenkman Publishing.

MacNamara, Joseph. 1989. "The Justice Story Full of Hate" *Daily News Magazine*, August, 18.

Malzberg, Benjamin. 1965. *Mental Disease Among the Puerto Rican Population of New York State, 1960–61*. Albany: Research Foundation for Mental Hygiene.

Marcuse, Peter. 1986. "Abandonment, Gentrification, and Displacement: The Linkages in New York City." In *Gentrification of the City*, ed. Neil Smith and Peter Williams, 153–77. Boston: Allen and Unwin.

Martínez, Francisco. 1988. "Los centros bancarios internacionales y las posibilidades de las zonas de incentivos económicos." In *Puerto Rico en los 1990*, ed. Carmen Gautier Mayoral and Nestor Nazario Trabal, 80–107. Río Piedras: Centro de Investigaciones Sociales, Universidad de Puerto Rico.

Massey, Douglas. 1990. "American Apartheid: Segregation and the Making of the Underclass." *American Journal of Sociology* 96: 329–57.

Massey, Douglas, and Nancy Denton. 1989. "Residential Segregation of Mexicans, Puerto Ricans, and Cubans in Selected U.S. Metropolitan Areas." *Sociology and Social Research* 73, no. 2 (January): 73–83.

Meléndez, Edwin. 1993a. *Los Que Se Van, No Regresan: Puerto Rican Migration to and from the United States, 1982–1988*. New York City: Political Economy Working Papers Series, no. 1, Centro de Estudios Puertorriqueños.

——. 1993b. "The Unsettled Relationship Between Puerto Rican Poverty and Migration." *Latino Studies Journal* 4, no. 3 (May): 45–55.

——. 1994. "Puerto Rican Migration and Occupational Selectivity, 1982–1988." *International Migration Review* 28, no. 1: 49–67.

Melguizo, A., and A. Tablas. 1981. "Entrevista con Ian Gough y James O'Connor: Crisis fiscal y crisis del Estado-Providencia." *Transición* 4, nos. 31–32 (April–May): 36–45.

MITRE. 1999. "Uniquely MITRE—Angelo Colón." MITRE: News and Articles. http://www.mitre.org/news/articles_99/uniquely_m_angel_colon.shtml. Accessed 10 July 2002.

Mobilization for Youth (MfY). 1963. *Record Material on the Spanish Kings: A Puerto Rican Youth Gang*. Glen Rock, N.J.: Microfilming Corporation of America.

Mollenkopf, John. 1993. *A Phoenix in the Ashes: The Rise and Fall of the Koch Coalition in New York City*. Princeton: Princeton University Press.

Mollenkopf, John, and Manuel Castells, eds. 1991. *Dual City: Restructuring New York*. New York: Russell Sage Foundation.

Morales, Iris. 1980. "I Became the One that Translated . . . The Go-Between." In *The Puerto Ricans: Their History, Culture, and Society*, ed. Adalberto López, 439–45. Cambridge, Mass.: Schenkman Publishing.

Morales, Julio. 1986. *Puerto Rican Poverty and Migration: We Just Had to Try Elsewhere*. New York: Praeger.

Morín, José Luis. 1989. "A Community Under Siege: Racial Violence and Police Brutality Against Latinos." *Centro* 2, no. 5 (spring): 95–102.

Muñiz Varela, Miriam. 1983. *Crisis económica y transformaciones sociales en Puerto Rico, 1973–1983*. Río Piedras: Centro de Investigaciones Sociales, Universidad de Puerto Rico.

——. "Más allá de Puerto Rico 936, Puerto Rico USA, Puerto Rico, INC.: Notas para una crítica al discurso del desarrollo." *Bordes* 1: 41–53.

——. 1996. "De Levittown a La Encantada: 'Más acá' de las 936." *Bordes* 3: 41–50.

——. 1999. "Puerto Rico Post-936: Miracle and Mirror or Savage Anomaly." Paper presented at the 2d Annual Conference of the Coloniality Working Group: "World Historical Sites of Colonial Disciplinary Practices: The Nation-State, the Bourgois Family, and the Enterprise." 22–24 April. Binghamton University.

National Association of State Medicaid Directors (NASMD). 1999. *Puerto Rico CHIP Plan*. Washington, D.C.: National Association of State Medicaid Directors.

National Center for Health Statistics (NCHS). 2000. "Puerto Ricans' Health Fares Worse Than Other U.S. Hispanics." http://www.cdc.gov/nchs/releases/oofacts/hispanic.htm. Accessed 3 July 2002.

——. 2001. "Puerto Rico Health Facts." http://www.cdc.gov/nchs/fastats/puerto.htm. Accessed 3 July 2002.

National Childcare Information Center (NCCIC). 2002. *State Profiles: Puerto Rico*. Washington, D.C.: The Administration for Children and Families, U.S. Department of Health and Human Services. 13 March.

National Mobilization Against Sweatshops (NMASS). 2001. *The Global Sweatshop*. http://www.nmass.org/nmass/articles/global.html. Accessed 5 July 2002.

Navarro, Mirega. 2000. "Peurto Rican Presence Wanes in New York." *New York Times*, 28 February.

Newman, Katherine S. 1999. *No Shame in My Game: The Working Poor in the Inner City*. New York: Vintage Books.

New York State Legislature Assembly's Standing Committee on Labor—Subcommittee on Sweatshops (NYSASCL—SoS). 1999. *Behind Closed Doors II: Another Look into the Underground Sweatshop Industry*. Albany: The Subcommittee on Sweatshops.

Nieves Falcón, Luis. 1990. *Migration and Development: The Case of Puerto Rico*. Washington, D.C.: Economic Development Working Papers, no.18, Wilson Center.

North American Congress on Latin America (NACLA). 1978. "Capital's Flight: The Apparel Industry Moves South." *Latin America and Empire Report* 11, no. 3 (March): 2–33.

Oakes, Jeannie. 1985. *Keeping Track: How Schools Structure Inequality*. New Haven: Yale University Press.

O'Connor, James. 1973. *The Fiscal Crisis of the State*. New York: St. Martin's Press.

Olavarría, Bienvenido. 1983. "Preocupa el éxito de profesionales y técnicos." *El Nuevo Día*, 31 May.

Ortíz, Laura. 1998. "Disrupting the Colonial Gaze: A Critical Analysis of the Discourses on Puerto Ricans in the United States (Other)." Ph.D. diss., City University of New York.

Ortíz, Vilma. 1986. "Changes in the Characteristics of Puerto Rican Migrants from 1955 to 1980." *International Migration Review* 20, no. 3: 612–28.

——. 1990. "Puerto Rican Workers in the Garment Industry in New York City, 1920–1960." In *Labor Divided: Race and Ethnicity in United States Labor Struggles, 1835–1960*, ed. Robert Asher and Charles Stephenson, 105–25. Albany: State University of New York Press.

Padilla, Elena. 1958. *Up from Puerto Rico*. New York: Columbia University Press.

Padilla, Félix. 1987. *Puerto Rican Chicago*. Notre Dame, Ind.: University of Notre Dame Press.

Pagán Irizarry, Javier Francisco. 1989. "El drenaje de talento: la nueva emigración de puertorriqueños hacia los Estados Unidos." Master's thesis, Universidad de Puerto Rico, Recinto de Río Piedras.

Pascual Amadeo, Aixa. 1994a. "Hora de consulta." *El Nuevo Día—A Fondo: Suplemento Educativo* 3 (17 May): 48–49.

——. 1994b. "Al otro lado del arcoiris." *El Nuevo Día—A Fondo: Suplemento Educativo* 3 (17 May): 50–51.

——. 1994c. "En el horno y con levadura." *El Nuevo Día—A Fondo: Suplemento Educativo* 3 (17 May): 52–53.

——. 1994d. "Allí donde calienta el dólar." *El Nuevo Día—A Fondo: Suplemento Educativo* 3 (17 May): 54–55.

——. 1994e. "Lo selecto no quita lo valiente." *El Nuevo Día—A Fondo: Suplemento Educativo* 3 (17 May): 69–70.

——. 1994f. "La hemorragia que no cesa." *El Nuevo Día—A Fondo: Suplemento Educativo* 3 (17 May): 77.

——. 1994g. "A resguardo el rescoldo boricua," *El Nuevo Día—A Fondo: Suplemento Educativo* 3 (17 May): 46–47.

——. 1994h. "Alcalde con toda la fuerza de la ley." *El Nuevo Día—A Fondo: Suplemento Educativo* 3 (17 May): 47–48.

Pérez, Richie. 1990. "From Assimilation to Annihilation: Puerto Rican Images in U.S. Films." *Centro* 2, no. 8 (spring): 8–27.

——. 1996. "My People Brutalized." *Stress* (summer): 76–78.

Perloff, Harvey S. 1950. *Puerto Rico's Economic Future: A Study in Planned Development*. Chicago: University of Chicago Press.

Petrovich, Janice, and Sandra Laureano. 1987. "Towards an Analysis of Puerto Rican Women and the Informal Economy." *Hómines* 10, no. 2: 70–81.

Piven, Frances Fox, and Richard Cloward. 1977. *Poor People's Movements*. New York: Vintage Books.

——. 1988. *The New Class War: Reagan's Attack on the Welfare State and its Consequences*. New York: Pantheon Books.

Poe-Yamagata, Eileen, and Michael Jones. 2000. *"And Justice for Some": Differential Treatment of Minority Youth in the Justice System*. Washington, D.C.: Youth Law Center, Building Blocks for Youth, April.

Pomales, Greg. 1992–1993. "The Language of Memorial Murals: An Interview." *Centro* 5, no. 2 (spring): 18–24.

Population Resource Center (PRC). 2001. "Executive Summary. Latina Teen Pregnancy: Problems and Prevention." Available at http://www.prcdc.org/summaries/latinapreg/latinapreg.html.

Puerto Rico Herald (PRH). 2002. "New Teachers Hard to Find: Palm Beach To Recruit Teachers in Puerto Rico." *Puerto Rico Herald*. Editorial, 10 April.

Puerto Rico U.S.A. (PRUSA). 2002. *Average Hourly Wages in Puerto Rico vs. U.S. Average*. http://www.bizsites.com/stateads/PuertRico/prworkforcewage.html. Accessed 25 June 2002.

Pugatch, Todd. 1998. "Historical Development of the Sweatshop." University of North Carolina—Chapel Hill, on-line seminar INTS 92: The Nike Seminar, 30 April. http://www.unc.edu/courses/ints092/sweat.html.

Quijano, Aníbal. 2000. "Coloniality of Power and Eurocentrism in Latin America." *Nepantla* 1, no. 3: 533–80.

Quijano, Aníbal, and Immanuel Wallerstein. 1992. "Americanity as a Concept of the Americas and the Modern World-System." *International Journal of the Social Sciences* 134 (November): 549–57.

Rand, Christopher. 1958. *The Puerto Ricans*. New York: Oxford University Press.

Reuters. 1996. "Asthma Rate Higher In Puerto Ricans." http://www.personalmd.com/news/a1996101809.shtml. Accessed 3 July 2002.

Reynolds, Lloyd, and Peter Gregory. 1965. *Wages, Productivity, and Industrialization in Puerto Rico*. Homewood, Ill.: Richard D. Irwin.

Ríos, Palmira. 1993. "Export-Oriented Industrialization and the Demand for Female Labor: Puerto Rican Women in the Manufacturing Sector, 1952–1980." In *Colonial Dilema: Critical Perspectives on Contemporary Puerto Rico*, ed. Edwin Meléndez and Edgardo Meléndez, 89–101. Boston: South End Press.

Rivera, Elaine. 1984. "Hispanics Face Greatest Social Gap in Boston." *The San Juan Star*, 18 March.

Rivera, Felipe. 1979. "The Puerto Rican Farmworker: From Exploitation to Unionization." In *Labor Migration Under Capitalism: The Puerto Rican Experience*, ed. History Task Force, 239–51. New York: Monthly Review Press.

Rivera, Magaly. 2002. *Welcome to Puerto Rico: The Economy*. http://welcome.topuertorico.org/economy.shtml. Accessed 18 July 2002.

Rivera, Raquel. 2001. "Hip-Hop, Puerto Ricans, and Ethno-Racial Identities in New York." In *Mambo Montage: The Latinization of New York*, ed. Agustín Laó and Arlene Dávila, 235–61. New York: Columbia University Press.

Rivera-Batiz, Francisco. 1994. "The Multicultural Population of New York City: A Socioeconomic Profile of the Mosaic." In *Reinventing Urban Education: Multiculturalism and the Social Context of Schooling*, ed. Francisco Rivera-Batiz, 23–67. New York: June Press Insititute for Urban and Minority Education, Teachers College, Columbia University.

Rodríguez, Clara. 1979. "Economic Factors Affecting Puerto Ricans in New York." In *Labor Migration Under Capitalism: The Puerto Rican Experience*, ed. History Task Force, 197–222. New York: Monthly Review Press.

——. 1991. *Puerto Ricans: Born in the U.S.A.* Boulder, Col.: Westview Press.

——. 1993. "Puerto Rican Circular Migration Revisited." *Latino Studies Journal* 4, no. 2: 93–113.

Rodríguez, Gregory. 1996. *The Emerging Latino Middle Class*. Los Angeles: Pepperdine University, Institute for Public Policy.

Rodríguez, Havidan. 1992. "Household Composition, Employment Patterns, and Income Inequality: Puerto Ricans in New York and Other Areas of the United States Mainland." *Hispanic Journal of Behavioral Sciences* 14, no. 1 (February): 52–75.

Rodríguez-Fraticelli, Carlos, and Amilcar Tirado. 1989. "Notes Towards a History of Puerto Rican Community Organizations in New York City." *Centro* 2, no. 6 (summer): 35–47.

Rodríguez-Morazzani, Roberto. 1991–1992. "Puerto Rican Political Generation in New York: Pioneros, Young Turks, and Radicals." Centro 4, no. 1 (winter): 96–116.

——. 1995. "Linking a Fractured Past: The World of the Puerto Rican Old Left." *Centro* 7, no. 1: 20–30.

——. 1996. "Beyond the Rainbow: Mapping the Discourse on Puerto Ricans and 'Race.'" *Centro* 8, nos. 1–2: 150–69.

Ross, Robert, and Kent Trachte. 1990. *Global Capitalism: The New Leviathan*. Albany: State University of New York Press.

Russell, Tom. 1982. "Underground Economy Here is a Huge Activity." *Caribbean Business*, 21 April.

Santiago, Anne. 1992. "Patterns of Puerto Rican Segregation and Mobility." *Hispanic Journal of Behavioral Sciences* 14, no. 1 (February): 107–33.

Santiago, Isaura. 1978. *A Community's Struggle for Equal Opportunity: ASPIRA vs. Board of Education*. Princeton, N.J.: Educational Testing Service.

Santiago, Carlos, and Francisco Rivera-Batiz. 1994. *Puerto Ricans in the United States: A Changing Reality*. Washington, D.C.: National Puerto Rican Coalition.

——. 1996. "La migración de los puertorriqueños durante la década de 1980." *Revista de Ciencias Sociales, Nueva Epoca* 1 (June): 178–206.

Santiago-Valles, A. Kelvin. 1991. "Economic Transformation and Social Unrest in Puerto Rico, 1898–1985." Unpublished manuscript.

——. 1992. "Dances with Colonialism: The Current Plebiscite Debate in Puerto Rico as Crisis Management." *Centro* 4, no. 2 (spring): 12–26.

——. 1994a. "*Subject People" and Colonial Discourses: Economic Transformation and Social Disorder in Puerto Rico, 1898–1947*. New York: State University of New York Press.

——. 1994b. "The Unruly City and the Mental Landscape of Colonized Identities: Internally Contested Nationality in Puerto Rico, 1945–1985." *Social Text* 38 (spring): 149–63.

——. 1995. "Del cuerpo del delito al delito de los cuerpos en la crisis del Puerto Rico urbano contemporáneo." *Bordes* 2: 28–42.

——. 1999. "The Sexual Appeal of Racial Differences: U.S. Travel Writing and Anxious American-ness in Turn-of-the-Century Puerto Rico." In *Race and the Invention of*

Modern American Nationalism, ed. Reynolds Scott-Childress, 127–148. New York: Garland Press.

Sassen, Saskia. 1988. *The Mobility of Labor and Capital.* Cambridge, U.K.: Cambridge University Press.

——. 1991. *The Global City: New York, London, Tokyo.* Princeton, N.J.: Princeton University Press.

——. 1998. *Globalization and Its Discontents.* New York: The New Press.

Sassen-Koob, Saskia. 1982. "Recomposition and Peripheralization at the Core." *Contemporary Marxism* 5 (summer): 88–100.

——. 1985. "Changing Composition of Labor Market Location of Hispanic Immigrants in New York City, 1960–1985." In *Hispanics in the U.S. Economy*, ed. George Borjas and Marta Tienda, 299–322. Orlando: Academic Press.

Schneider, Eric C. 2001. *Vampires, Dragons, and Egyptian Kings: Youth Gangs in Postwar New York.* Princeton, N.J.: Princeton University Press.

Sexton, Patricia Cayo. 1965. *Spanish Harlem: Anatomy of Poverty.* New York: Harper and Row.

Shefter, Martin. 1987. *Political Crisis, Fiscal Crisis.* New York: Basic Books.

Silvestrini, Blanca. 1980. *Violencia y criminalidad en Puerto Rico, 1698–1973: Apuntes de un estudio de historia social.* Río Piedras: Editorial Universitaria.

Soja, E., R. Morales, and G. Wolff. 1983. "Urban Restructuring: An Analysis of Social and Spatial Change in Los Angeles." *Economic Geography* 58, no. 2 (April): 195–230.

Stafford, Walter. 1981. *Closed Labor Markets: Underrepresentation of Blacks, Hispanics, and Women in New York City's Core Industries and Jobs.* New York: Community Service Society of New York.

Steiner, Stan. 1974. *The Islands: The Worlds of the Puerto Ricans.* New York: Harper and Row.

Sternlieb, George, Elizabeth Roistacher, and James Hughes. 1976. *Tax Subsidies and Housing Investment.* New Brunswick, N.J.: Center for Urban Policy Research, Rutgers University.

Stress. 1996. "Moves and News." *Stress* (spring): 12.

Sullivan, Mercer. 1989. *Getting Paid: Economy, Culture, and Youth Crime in the Inner City.* Ithaca: Cornell University Press.

Tabb, William. 1982. *The Long Default.* New York: Monthly Review Press.

Takaki, Ronald. 1983. *Pau Hana: Plantation Life and Labor in Hawaii.* Honolulu: University of Hawaii Press.

Tallahassee Democrat (*TD*). 2002. "Bill to Recruit Nurses a Must for Florida: A Democrat Editorial." *Tallahassee Democrat.* Editorial, 31 May.

Tata, Robert. 1980. *Structural Changes in Puerto Rico's Economy, 1947–1976.* Athens, Ohio: Center for Information Studies, Ohio University.

Thomas, Piri. 1967. Reprint, 1991. *Down These Mean Streets.* New York: Vintage Books.

Tobier, Emanuel. 1979. "Gentrification: The Manhattan Story." *New York Affairs* 5 (summer): 13–25.

Tienda, Marta. 1989. "Puerto Ricans and the Underclass Debate." *The Annals of the American Academy of Political and Social Science* 501 (January): 105–119.

Tienda, Marta, and Leif Jensen. 1988. "Poverty and Minorities: A Quarter-Century Profile of Color and Socioeconomic Disadvantage." In Marta Tienda and Gary Sandefur, eds., *Divided Opportunities: Minorities, Poverty, and Social Policy*, 23–61. New York: Plenum Press.

Tienda, Marta, and Ding-Tzann Lii. 1987. "Minority Concentration and Earnings Inequality: Blacks, Hispanics, and Asians Compared." *American Journal of Sociology* 93, no.1 (July): 141–165.

Tobier, Emanuel. 1984. *The Changing Face of Poverty: Trends in Population in Poverty, 1960–1990*. New York: Community Service Society of Greater New York.

Torres, Andrés. 1995. *Between Melting Pot and Mosaic: African Americans and Puerto Ricans in the New York City Political Economy*. Philadelphia: Temple University Press.

Torres, Andrés, and José E. Velázquez, eds. 1998. *The Puerto Rican Movement: Voices from the Diaspora*. Philadelphia: Temple University Press.

Torres, Luisangeli. 1994a. "Fascinación se escribe con la F de Florida." *El Nuevo Día—A Fondo: Suplemento Educativo* 3 (May 17): 53.

——. 1994b. "Miami, puente de plata," *El Nuevo Día-A Fondo: Suplemento Educativo* 3 (May 17): 55–56.

Totti, Xavier. 1987. "The Making of a Latino Ethnic Identity." *Dissent* (fall): 537–42.

Trim-TNC. 1996. "Tales from the Rock." *Stress* (summer): 21.

Turner, Harry. 1982a. "Brain Drain: New Kind of Migration from P.R. Heads North." *San Juan Star*, 31 January.

——. 1982b. "More P.R. Professionals Leaving Island for the U.S." *San Juan Star*, 1 February.

U.S. Bureau of the Census (USBC). 1953. *U.S. Census of Population: 1950: Subject Reports: Puerto Ricans in the United States*. Washington, D.C.: Government Printing Office.

——. 1963. *U.S. Census of Population: 1960: Subject Reports: Puerto Ricans in the United States*. Washington, D.C.: Government Printing Office.

——. 1973. *U.S. Census of Population: Persons of Spanish Origin in the United States: March 1972 and 1971*. Washington, D.C.: Government Printing Office, P-20 Series, no. 259, April.

——. 1983. *Census of Population and Housing: 1980: Public Use of Microdata Samples, Technical Documentation*. Washington, D.C.: Government Printing Office, March.

——. 1986. *Characteristics of the Population Below the Poverty Level: 1984*. Washington, D.C.: Government Printing Office, June.

——. 1990. *The Hispanic Population in the United States: March 1989*. Washington, D.C.: Government Printing Office, May.

——. 1993. *Current Population Reports: Population Characteristics: Hispanic Americans Today*. Washington, D.C.: Government Printing Office, P23–183.

——. 1997. *Economic Census–Manufacturing–1997: New York*. Washington, D.C.: Government Printing Office.

——. 1999. *The Hispanic Population in the United States: Population Characteristics*. Washington, D.C.: Government Printing Office, P20–527 Series.

——. 2000a. *The Hispanic Population in the United States: Population Characteristics*. Washington, D.C.: Government Printing Office, P20–535 Series.

——. 2000b. *Hispanic Population in the United States: Current Population Survey—March 2000*. Washington, D.C.: Government Printing Office.

——. 2001. *Hispanic-Owned Business: 1997. Census Brief: Minority-Owned Business Enterprises*. Washington, D.C.: Government Printing Office, October.

U.S. Civil Rights Commission (USCRC). 1976. *Puerto Ricans in the Continental United States: An Uncertain Future.* Washington, D.C.: Government Printing Office.

U.S. Congress, House Committee on Education and Labor—Subcommittee on Labor Standards (USCHCEL—SLS). 1982. *The Re-emergence of Sweatshops and the Enforcement of Wage and Hour Standards.* Washington, D.C.: Government Printing Office.

U.S. Congress, Senate Committee on the Judiciary, Subcommittee to Investigate Juvenile Delinquency (USCSCJ-SIJD). 1957. *Juvenile Delinquency: New York Programs for the Prevention and Treatment of Juvenile Delinquency. Hearings Before the Subcommittee to Investigate Juvenile Delinquency of the Committee on the Judiciary.* Washington, D.C.: Government Printing Office (December 4).

U.S. Department of Commerce (USDC). 1979. *Economic Study of Puerto Rico.* 2 vols. Washington, D.C.: Government Printing Office.

U.S. Department of Labor (USDL). 1997. *Facts on Working Women: Women of Hispanic Origin in the Labor Force.* No. 97–2, February. Washington, D.C.: Government Printing Office.

Vázquez Calzada, José. 1978. *La población de Puerto Rico.* Río Piedras: Centro Multidisciplinario de Estudios Poblacionales.

Vázquez Calzada, José, and Zoraida Morales del Valle. 1979. "Características sociodemográficas de los norteamericanos, cubanos y dominicanos residentes en Puerto Rico." *Revista de Ciencias Sociales* 21, nos. 1–2: 1–34.

Vega López, Carlos. 1992. "Perfil del puertorriqueño: Razones por las que emigra y su opinión con respecto a la ingerencia del gobierno en la problemática social de la Isla." Master's thesis, Universidad de Puerto Rico, Recinto de Río Piedras.

Vernon, Raymond, and Edgar Hoover. 1959. *Anatomy of a Metropolis: The Changing Distribution of People and Jobs Within the New York Metropolitan Region.* Cambridge, Mass.: Harvard University Press.

Villaruel, Francisco A., et al. 2002. *¿Dónde está la justicia? A Call to Action on Behalf of Latino and Latina Youth in the U.S. Justice System.* Washington, D.C.: Youth Law Center, Building Blocks for Youth and Michigan State University, Institute for Children, Youth, and Families.

Wagenheim, Kal. 1970. *Puerto Rico: A Profile.* New York: Praeger.

Wakefield, Dan. 1959. *Island in the City: The World of Spanish Harlem.* New York: Corinth Books.

Waldinger, Roger. 1985. "Immigration and Industrial Change in the New York City Apparel Industry." In *Hispanics in the U.S. Economy*, ed. G.J. Borjas and M. Tienda, 323–67. Orlando: Academic Press.

Weich, Ronald H., and Carlos T. Angulo. 2000. *Justice on Trial: Racial Disparities in the American Criminal Justice System.* Washington, D.C.: Leadership Conference on Civil Rights, Leadership Conference Education Fund, May.

Weil, David. 2000. "Everything Old Is New Again: Regulating Labor Standards in the U.S. Apparel Industry." Paper presented at the Annual Meeting of the Industrial Relations Research Association, Boston, Mass., 8 January.

Weisskoff, Richard. 1985. *Factories and Food Stamps: The Puerto Rico Model of Development.* Baltimore: The Johns Hopkins University Press.

Wells, Elizabeth. 2000. "West Side Story and the Hispanic." *Echo* 2, no. 1 (spring): http://www.humnet.ucla.edu/echo/Volume2-Issue1/wells/wells-article.

Wells, Henry K. 1969. *The Modernization of Puerto Rico*. New Haven. Yale University Press.

Wertham, Frederic. 1958. *The Circle of Guilt*. London: Dennis Dobson.

Williams, Mike. 2001. "Florida's Latin Flavor Spreads North to Orlando." Cox Washington Bureau, August 30. http://www.coxnews.com/washingtonbureau/staff/williams/083001FOREIGN-FLORIDA30html. Accessed 18 July 2002.

Wright, Gavin. 1986. *Old South, New South: Revolutions in the Southern Economy Since the Civil War*. New York: Basic Books.

Young, Frank. 1974. "New Communities and Industries in Puerto Rico, 1940–1970." *Caribbean Studies* 4, no. 1 (April): 131–53.

Zukin, Sharon. 1982. *Loft Living*. Baltimore: Johns Hopkins University Press.

Documentary

- anger
- change
- poor living conditions
- garbage protest
  - police brutality
- Lords - Party
- History-making - Europeans
  Tainos
  Africans
- Spanish colony → U.S freedom? no. US Free colony

Young lords would push for complete independence.
crack down

1970's Y.L's break up.

IDENTITY → multi-ethnic, defined through history-making

- one of the 1° groups who acknowledged homosexuality.
- gender equality
  vs. Black Panthers. → Military organization (government rxn)

Chicago Y.L.
Church, hospital "doing"

THREE

EXILES, IMMIGRANTS, AND TRANSNATIONALS: THE CUBAN COMMUNITIES OF THE UNITED STATES

MARÍA CRISTINA GARCÍA

THE MAJORITY of the 1.3 million Cuban Americans presently in the United States arrived after 1959, when revolutionaries led by Fidel Castro assumed control of the Cuban government. Over the next forty years, more than one-tenth of Cuba's present-day population migrated to the United States, and thousands more migrated to other countries in the Caribbean, Latin America, and Europe. Unlike other migrations from the Americas, however, Cuban immigration to the United States is not merely a late-twentieth-century phenomenon. It is a pattern that was established several centuries earlier, the product of commercial ties and geographic proximity. Distinct Cuban communities in the United States were first noticed in the nineteenth century.

THE EARLY CUBAN COMMUNITIES

During the first half of the 1800s, Cuban merchants and businessmen conducted business and settled in the United States, in cities as diverse as Boston, New York, Philadelphia, Wilmington, and Baltimore. Many assumed U.S. citizenship, and even promoted the political goal of Cuba's annexation. It was also common during the nineteenth century for the *criollo* elites to send their children to boarding schools and colleges and universities in the United States rather than to Europe.

Prior to the 1860s, Cuban immigration was largely white and professional, and never totaled more than one thousand people.[1] A larger and more diverse migration occurred during the final decades of the nineteenth century as a result of the Ten Years' War (1868–1878.) The destruction of property and the loss of traditional economic markets during the war, as well as the economic recession provoked by the drop in world-wide sugar prices in the following years, devastated Cuba's major industry and hence Cuban society. Political turmoil and high unemployment pushed thousands of Cubans of all races and social classes to the United States.

Concurrently, the growth of the cigar industry in the U.S. also lured Cubans to the United States, particularly to Florida, Louisiana, and New York. By 1895, distinct and fairly large Cuban communities existed in Key West, Tampa, and New Orleans. For example, one-third of Key West's population—some 5,000 people—were Cuban, mostly cigar workers employed in the more than one hundred factories on the key.[2] Interestingly, the first Cuban elected to public office in the United States was elected in the nineteenth century, not the late twentieth century as has been generally assumed: Carlos Manuel de Céspedes y Castillo, the son of the Cuban insurgent leader of the Ten Years' War, was elected mayor of Key West in 1876. In Florida, other Cuban cigar-making communities emerged in Martí City (Ocala) and Jacksonville. However, by 1900 Tampa and the neighboring Ybor City were the heart of the Cuban expatriate community. Tampa became the most important cigar-producing center in the United States thanks, in large part, to thousands of Cuban workers who had relocated to this area. All in all, more than 100,000 Cubans expatriated themselves over the second half of the nineteenth century, most of them to the United States.[3] This U.S.-based population, particularly in Florida and New York, became the backbone of José Martí's popular nationalist movement of the 1880s, which led to the second—and ultimately successful—Cuban war of independence.[4]

Migration continued during the first half of the next century. Because of the close proximity of the two countries and the higher incomes across the Florida straits, it was not uncommon for some Cuban workers to spend at least part of their adult working lives in the United States. Records show that from 1921 to 1930, 16,000 Cubans immigrated to the United States, but these figures are probably an undercount. Migration decreased temporarily during the 1930s as a result of the Great Depression, as it did for most other immigrant groups: only 9,000 Cubans are registered to have immigrated to the United States during this decade. Migration expanded once again during the 1940s and 1950s. From 1941 to 1950, some 26,000 Cubans immigrated to the United States, followed by 79,000 in the next decade. They came from all different classes, motivated by a variety of concerns. Some came as political exiles, people victimized by the *gangsterismo* so prevalent in Cuban politics after 1930. Others came as sojourners, hoping to make a better living in the United States so that they and their families could eventually live more comfortable lives when they returned to the homeland. By the 1940s the working class held a precarious position in Cuban society. Low wages affected their purchasing power, and more than half of workers had no disability or unemployment insurance. Colonialist economic policies discouraged industrialists and entrepreneurs from expanding or creating new enterprises that would have provided the unemployed and underemployed with new work opportunities.[5] Whether they came for political or economic reasons, the majority of Cubans who migrated to the United States came with the intention of one day returning to their homeland. In addition to these expatriates, thousands more came temporarily to the United States to vacation, to study, to invest, or to transact business, all contributing to a growing Cuban presence in the United States.

The world these migrants and visitors entered was not completely foreign to them because of the intense cultural, economic, and political contacts between Cuba and the United States since 1898. By the 1950s, Pan American airlines scheduled as many as twenty-eight daily flights between Miami and Havana. Cubans were vast importers of U.S. consumer goods and cultural forms, from New York fashions to Hollywood movie features. Vacationing in Miami Beach or New York City was as popular for middle-class Cubans before the Castro revolution as vacationing in Havana was for middle-class Americans. The large American presence and financial investments on the island and the close commercial ties between both countries shaped the evolution of Cuban politics. It also influenced language, customs, and traditions.[6] However, this familiarity with American culture and institutions did not guarantee that life for the exiles and immigrants would evolve smoothly in the United States, nor did it exempt them from discrimination, racial violence, and abuse in the workplace. Black and mulatto Cuban workers were particularly harassed, especially those who were involved in labor organizing, and there is evidence that many were intimidated into returning to the island.[7]

Cubans on opposite sides of the Florida straits maintained contact with each other in multiple ways, and those who lived in the United States strove to maintain a strong sense of *cubanidad.* They kept Cuban traditions alive through cultural pageants and celebrations; they published Spanish-language newspapers with news of the homeland; they wrote novels, plays, and poetry and composed music that spoke of their ties to both Cuba and the United States. Cigar workers, in particular, in both countries, supported one another's labor struggles. Remittances traveled easily across the border. Up until 1959, Cubans on the island and on the mainland were able to travel back and forth relatively freely, exchanging ideas, importing and exporting one another's goods, investing in one another's future. Like their nineteenth-century forebears, the Cubans on the mainland played an active role in the politics of their homeland, raising money for political causes and candidates.

Ironically, the revolutionary movement that produced the most expansive economic and political reform on the island also scared away the greatest number of people by its radicalism. Some of those who chose—or were forced—to leave Cuba after Castro took power were supporters of the U.S.-backed dictator, Fulgencio Batista. But many more were not: rather, they were the silent majority whose fear, apathy, resignation, or victimization had prevented them from assuming a more active role in the political affairs of their country. As in many colonial and authoritarian societies with a history of corruption, the population had long hoped that an idealistic politician would come along and initiate the necessary reforms to create a truly egalitarian society. During the 1950s, many cautiously hoped that Fidel Castro and his July 26th Movement would provide that leadership and restore José Martí's vision for Cuba: a vision that had been thwarted by U.S. military and political intervention in 1898. Thus, when Castro proved successful in ousting Batista from power, many Cubans were euphoric, but that enthusiasm slowly waned in the years that followed. It is unclear if Castro was a communist when he took power in 1959, or if he was compelled to become so because of aggressive U.S. diplomatic and economic policies. Whatever the case, many Cubans became disillusioned with the marxist orientation their nationalist revolution ultimately took. They believed that under Castro, Cuba remained a colony, only this time of the Soviet Union. Cubans who now came to the United States perceived themselves as "exiles" rather than immigrants: people who had been displaced by a government that became increasingly hostile to their basic beliefs about democratic government, commercial enterprise, and equal opportunity. Over one-tenth of Cuba's population ultimately chose to express their displeasure by emigrating.

Cuba's historic ties to the United States made it logical that most exiles would turn to their former American patrons for help, and until the mid-1970s, daily flights between Havana and Miami allowed Castro to export dissent. Arriving during the midst of the Cold War, the Cubans became powerful symbols for Americans of the clash between democracy and authoritarianism, between free enterprise and communism. Popular U.S. magazines like *Time*, *Life*, *Newsweek*, and *Fortune* celebrated the refugees' courage, love of freedom, and entrepreneurial spirit. Laws were bent or broken to facilitate the Cubans' entrance into this country and their accommodation and naturalization. No other immigrant group in the second half of the twentieth century received as expansive a welcome as the Cubans.

THE MIGRATION BEGINS

Cuban migration to the United States in the Castro years occurred in distinct "waves." The first occurred from 1 January 1959 to 22 October 1962 and brought approximately 248,070 Cubans to the United States.[8] The first people to leave were those who were in some way connected to the old regime: political leaders, high government officials, and military officers of Fulgencio Batista's government. Associated with the corruption and abuses of the Batista years, these individuals were eager to leave Cuba since they faced retribution from a resentful population. Their only option was to emigrate until time healed political wounds or until a more sympathetic government was in place.

However, not all who left during this first wave were affiliated with the Batista government. Thousands became alienated by the social upheaval that followed Castro's rise to power.[9] Cuban society underwent radical transformation in the 1960s. Agrarian and urban reform laws changed the character of ownership and production and placed most properties under the control of the state. The nationalization of U.S. properties on the island—a considerable investment ranging from sugars mills and factories to railroads and public utilities—angered the Eisenhower administration and led to a severing of diplomatic relations between the two countries and, eventually, an economic embargo. Fidel Castro correctly assumed that the United States would try to overthrow his government, and he proceeded to create a police state obsessed with weeding out any counterrevolutionary activity, real or imagined. Cubans who left their country during the 1960s described the country as a violent, even paranoid, state that denied basic civil liberties such as freedom of speech, religion, and assembly. It was a society where neighborhood watch committees (the Committees for the Defense of the Revolution, or CDRs) monitored the population's every move. It was a society characterized by political indoctrination in schools, restrictions on religious observances, and mandatory "volunteer" labor. Shortages in basic food staples and consumer goods, brought on by the restructuring of the Cuban economy and later by the trade embargoes imposed by the United States and several other nations also affected Cubans across society.[10]

These and other factors proved to be the decisive points that forced many people to leave their country. For those who left Cuba, the general feeling was that their popular nationalist revolution had been betrayed in favor of a communist one. The migration out of Cuba followed a logical socioeconomic progression. Cubans of the elite classes were the first to leave, followed by member of the professional middle class. By 1962, Cubans of the working class also left: office and factory employees, artisans, and skilled and semi-skilled laborers.

Most Cubans who traveled to the U.S. did so under the assumption that they would soon return to their homeland. Because of the United States' long history of involvement in Cuban affairs, most exiles believed that it was merely a matter of time before the United States intervened to replace Castro. Only a few years earlier, the CIA had successfully arranged the overthrow of Jacobo

Arbenz Guzmán in Guatemala when the latter's socialist policies threatened U.S. corporate interests in that country. Exiles knew that Cuba was even more valuable to U.S. interests, and the Castro government's nationalization of U.S. properties guaranteed a more active response from the United States. Thus, during the early 1960s, most exiles came to the U.S. under the assumption that their stay was temporary.

South Florida became the principal place of settlement for a variety of reasons. Flights between Havana and Miami were the most readily available. Since the first arrivals came primarily from the middle class, Miami was also a place with which they were familiar because they had either vacationed or conducted business there. There was also a fairly large Cuban community in south Florida by 1959—some 30,000—many of whom had migrated a generation or two earlier as exiles from other political regimes.[11] For homesick, snow-fearing Cubans, Florida's climate and topography were also important considerations; and, as an added incentive, the plane ride from Havana to Miami was a short one (fifty-five minutes) and inexpensive (approximately twenty-five dollars), making a return easy when conditions in Cuba changed. However, despite south Florida's many attractive features, Cubans ultimately settled wherever they found jobs, even if it meant relocating way up north in cities such as Chicago, St. Louis, or New York. Taking care of one's family was always the primary consideration. The Miami of the early 1960s was a small resort town that could hardly accommodate the thousands of Cubans who arrived each week. If the majority of Cubans eventually stayed in south Florida it was because, over time, they assisted in the area's economic transformation.

Acquiring permission to leave Cuba, as well as to travel to the United States, was a long, complicated affair. In order to leave their country legally, Cubans had to acquire an exit permit from one of the government ministries, which allowed the government to screen travelers before they left. Cubans had to fill out numerous forms and submit to lengthy interrogations. While the government wanted to rid the country of dissenters, they also wished to prevent a "brain-drain"; those with skills considered vital to the revolutionary society (particularly in the sciences) and who did not pose a security threat were prohibited from leaving. Those suspected of "crimes against the revolution" were also detained for appropriate punishment. Cubans who could not secure exit permits, or who feared for their safety, took refuge in foreign embassies or sailed clandestinely to the Florida Keys, often on homemade rafts. Those unable to get a seat on a plane to the United States also had the option of traveling to a third country—if they were fortunate enough to acquire the appropriate visas—and either stay in those countries or apply for immigrant visas at the U.S. embassy there. If they did not return within a certain period of time—in most cases, one year—their property was confiscated by the state.

The U.S. bureaucracy was somewhat easier to navigate. Visas to travel to the United States could be acquired at the U.S. Embassy in Havana or at the American consulate at Santiago, and officials there regularly granted over a thousand "tourist" visas each week to allow Cubans to come to the United States. Once in the U.S., the Cubans were granted "indefinite voluntary departure" or "parole" status. After the United States severed relations with Cuba in January 1961, U.S. officials inaugurated a procedure of " visa waivers," which could be obtained through the Swiss embassy in Havana. Airline tickets had to be purchased with U.S. currency, and if Cubans did not have U.S. dollars, which were increasingly scarce after 1961, they had to wait until friends or relatives in the U.S. assisted them in purchasing the tickets. Even after purchasing a ticket, there was a waiting list for seats on airlines. Once you secured a seat and got to the airport, members of the state police carefully inspected every piece of luggage and often submitted passengers to dehumanizing personal searches. After 1961, Cubans were not allowed to take more than five dollars out of the country and more than thirty pounds of luggage per person. In the most fortunate of cases, Cubans arrived in Miami and stayed with already-established relatives or friends who assisted them in finding housing and jobs and enrolling their children in school. Or they took a train or bus to cities where they knew people who could help them. Some of the more fortunate emigrés (usually the wealthier) had some money invested in U.S. banks before the revolution and were able to draw on these reserves. The majority of exiles, however, arrived at Miami International Airport with just a few U.S. dollars and with no clue as to what to do next.

During the first years of the migration, the Catholic Church was their major source of assistance. Since the majority of Cubans were at least nominally Roman Catholic, they logically turned to the Church in their time of need. The newly established Diocese of Miami created a social welfare agency to assist the Cubans, the Centro Hispano Católico.[12] Located in a remodeled wing of a parochial school in downtown Miami, the Centro provided housing and job referrals, English classes, a day nursery, educational programs for children, an outpatient and dental clinic, home visits to the sick, food, toiletries, used clothing, and small loans to cover miscellaneous expenses such as eyeglasses and dentures. By December 1961, the Diocese of Miami had spent over $1.5 million in assisting the Cubans.[13] Voluntary relief agencies (VOLAGS) such as the Catholic Relief Services, the International Rescue Committee, and the United HIAS Service, among many others, also assisted the arrivals from Cuba. By late 1960, representatives of these different VOLAGS met each plane coming from Havana to answer the Cubans' questions and to inform them on the resources available to help them.

By the end of 1960, almost forty thousand Cubans had arrived in the United States, and their numbers increased by one thousand to fifteen hundred per week.[14] Residents of south Florida panicked, since they knew that their city could not accommodate such sudden population growth. Most jobs were in the low-paying service sector, and Cubans had to compete with a large pool of unemployed workers, mostly African American, as well as northerners that traveled south each winter in search of jobs in the resort economy. The public school system, one of the poorest in the country, was ill-equipped to deal with the hundreds of children who arrived in their classrooms each month.

Not surprisingly, the early arrivals from Cuba experienced radical downward mobility. Approximately 36 percent of Cubans of the first wave were professionals (e.g. doctors, lawyers, engineers, and educators) but were unable to practice their professions because they lacked English fluency or did not meet other state licensing requirements. They worked at whatever jobs they could get, in construction, maintenance, and service occupations. It was common to see doctors, lawyers, and teachers working as hospital orderlies, dishwashers, and janitors. Women often found jobs more easily than men because employers could pay them even lower wages. Women found jobs as seamstresses (many doing piecework at home), domestics, janitors, cooks, dishwashers, waitresses, cashiers, manicurists, and other unskilled or semiskilled labor that did not require experience or fluency in English and had limited contact with the general public. Some were fortunate to find employment in Miami's expanding garment industry. Others found jobs sorting fish in warehouses by the Miami River or as agricultural workers in the fruit and vegetable fields outside the city.

The Eisenhower administration left the task of accommodating the Cubans to local communities and charitable organizations. Like the exiles, the Eisenhower administration believed that it was only a matter of time before the Cubans returned to their homeland, and thus a comprehensive assistance program was not considered necessary. As early as March 1960, Eisenhower authorized the CIA to begin preparing an invasion of Cuba that would overthrow the Castro government and replace it with a coalition of leaders chosen directly by the United States. However, after many complaints from south Florida residents, who wanted the Cubans moved out of the area, the president finally released one million dollars from the contingency funds of the Mutual Security Act to assist in resettlement efforts. This act had tremendous significance, since in invoking the Mutual Security Act, Eisenhower officially recognized that Cuba was a communist state, and thus the Cuban exiles were refugees. The administration also established a "Cuban Refugee Emergency Center" in downtown Miami to coordinate the relief efforts of all the voluntary relief agencies and oversee a resettlement program. However, most of the financial burden of the Cubans' accommodation continued to rest with the volunteer agencies.

It was not until the Kennedy administration that the federal government assumed a more assertive role in refugee relief efforts. Kennedy established a "Cuban Refugee Program" (CRP) under the umbrella of the Department of Health, Education, and Welfare (HEW).[15] The CRP provided funding for resettlement, monthly relief checks, health services, job training, adult educational opportunities, and surplus food distribution (e.g. canned meat, powdered eggs and milk, cheese, and oatmeal).[16] The government also provided partial funding to the Dade County Public School System to help it accommodate the more than 3,500 Cuban refugee children who attended public schools by January 1961.

One major problem the Kennedy administration had to deal with was the over 14,000 children who arrived unaccompanied during this first wave. Many parents unable to leave Cuba sent their children ahead, hoping to be reunited with them at a later date. These parents feared the political indoctrination in the schools and the military draft, and so they took part in what is now known as Operation Peter Pan, an underground network that emerged on the island to send children to the United States.[17] Over half of the children who arrived unaccompanied in Miami were between the ages of 13 and 17, and over two-thirds were boys. Many arrived in Miami with only an identification tag pinned to their clothes or a letter in their pocket requesting assistance; some arrived carrying infants and younger siblings. Bryan O. Walsh, a Catholic priest and director of the Catholic Welfare Bureau in Miami initially assumed responsibility for their care, finding lodging for the children in homes or dormitories around the city. However, the Kennedy administration assumed financial responsibility for the children, providing foster families and institutions with funding for their care.[18]

The Kennedy administration also became involved in a number of other projects to assist the exiles. Skills and talents remained untapped within the largely middle-class refugee community because the language barrier made it difficult to meet state licensing requirements. The Castro government also prohibited teachers and other professionals from bringing their diplomas or transcripts of university records to the United States, thus making it nearly impossible for potential employers to verify their educational training. Working with community groups, the administration funded programs to assist Cuban professionals to prepare for their state licensing boards or to retrain for other types of employment. Programs were established at local universities to assist doctors, lawyers, teachers, and other professionals in their efforts to become certified for practice in the United States.

A number of federally funded vocational training programs targeted the working class. One program in particular entitled "Aprenda y Supérese," or "Training for Independence," helped unskilled Cuban women become self-supporting. Women received intensive English-language instruction and training in any of a number of skills: hand-sewing, sewing-machine work, office machine operation, clerical work, nursing, domestic service, and even silk-screen art work. Women were later resettled to cities where jobs were available for them. Aprenda y Supérese was so successful that it became a model for the amended "Aid to Families with Dependent Children" (AFDC) program in 1968.[19]

Cuban migration to the United States continued even in the wake of the Bay of Pigs invasion of 1961, when the United States unsuccessfully carried out CIA plans to overthrow the Castro government.[20] Migration continued until October 1962, when the Cuban Missile Crisis finally severed all air traffic between the two countries.[21] In just three short years the city of Miami had undergone dramatic change as it accommodated over two hundred thousand "temporary visitors." While the government had resettled a few thousand Cubans out of south Florida, the majority preferred to remain in the area, even if it meant forfeiting any government assistance. They preferred to stay as close to the homeland as possible and within the more familiar and nurturing exile enclave.

Even though air traffic between the two countries ceased after the missile crisis, approximately 56,000 Cubans arrived in the United States from 22 October 1962 to 28 September 1965.[22] The majority came via third countries, particularly Spain or Mexico, arriving with immigrant visas acquired at the U.S. embassies in those countries. During this period many Cubans also sailed clandestinely from Cuba, arriving on small boats, rafts, and even inner tubes. By 1963, approximately 4,000 men, women, and children successfully crossed the Florida Straits in such craft and either arrived at Key West or were rescued by the U.S. Coast Guard.[23] How many drowned, or were forced to return by Cuban authorities, is unknown.

THE FREEDOM FLIGHTS

Wishing to export even more dissenters, on 28 September 1965, Fidel Castro announced that Cubans with relatives in the United States who wished to leave the island would be permitted to do so. He designated the small fishing port of Camarioca as a possible gathering place and port of departure and he pledged "complete guarantees and facilities" to exiles returning to Cuba by their own means to get their families out.[24]

Within days of Castro's announcement, hundreds of Cuban exiles sailed to Cuba, mostly on rented craft, to pick up their relatives. The Johnson administration was caught completely by surprise. While the administration agreed to assist all those who wanted to leave communist Cuba, the last thing it wanted was an uncontrolled migration. Johnson announced that the United States would accept more Cuban refugees, but the migration had to be monitored; the State Department was instructed to negotiate the terms of the migration with the Castro government through the Swiss Embassy in Havana. The crisis coincided with the passage of the 1965 Immigration Act that abolished the national quota system in favor of a seven-category preference system that stressed family reunification. Thus, under the terms of the new law, migration preference was given to those Cubans who already had immediate family in the United States. In a "memorandum of understanding" between the two countries, the U.S. agreed to send chartered planes to Varadero twice each day, transporting between 3,000 and 4,000 Cubans each month. Men of military age and political prisoners were prohibited from emigrating. The flights continued until April, when the Castro government once again prevented emigration to the United States. By this date, 3,048 flights had carried 297,318 refugees to the United States.[25]

This "second wave" of Cuban refugees was distinct from the first in several ways. First, both the United States and Cuba were able to exert more control over this migration. The United States limited immigration to the immediate families of those Cubans already in the country, thereby upholding its new immigration laws, and the Cuban government protected its own interests by more thoroughly screening the emigrant pool and prohibiting the emigration of those with skills or military service vital to the regime. Secondly, the refugees differed from the earlier arrivals in socioeconomic status: the "second wave" was much more representative of Cuba's working class. During the first wave, 31 percent of the Cubans who arrived in the United States were professionals or managers. By 1970, only 12 percent were professionals or managers, and 57 percent were blue-collar, service, or agricultural workers.[26] Women were also overrepresented in this migration, as were the elderly: a consequence of the emigration restrictions placed on certain types of skilled labor and men of military age.

By the end of the freedom flights, the Cuban exile community was a fairly heterogeneous population. While the emigrés came predominantly from Havana province, Cuba's most populated region, all of Cuba's provinces were represented in the exile population (the westernmost provinces more so than the poorer eastern provinces.) Cubans of every social class and profession were represented in the population, as were its various ethnic and religious groups. For example, the majority of Cuba's Chinese and Jewish populations settled in the United States.[27]

Of all the groups, however, blacks remained underrepresented. The 1953 Cuban census revealed that 27 percent of Cuba's population was black or of mixed race, and yet in 1970, less than 3 percent of the Cubans in the United States were black.[28] This underrepresentation was attributed to three factors. Since racial equality was one of the goals of the revolution, black Cubans were generally optimistic about the future. As the poorest and most discriminated segment of Cuban society, they also stood to gain the most from the revolution's social and economic policies and generally became enthusiastic supporters of the Castro government. Secondly, blacks feared emigrating to the United States due to its history of Jim Crow segregation, lynching, race riots, and other types of race-related violence. During the 1960s, the photographs and news stories coming out of the United States showed a society in violent confrontation over civil rights, and this frightened many Cubans considering emigration. Radio interviews with members of more radical groups such as the Black Panthers also reinforced the perception of the United States as a society hostile to equal opportunity. Third, since U.S. immigration policy gave preference to those with relatives already in the United States, this policy tended to benefit whites—the first to leave—rather than blacks.[29] Consequently, it was not until the Mariel boatlift of 1980 that a larger number of black Cubans emigrated to the United States (by the 1990 census, however, only sixteen percent of the Cuban exile population identified themselves as black, Chinese, or of another race). The small number that did choose to emigrate during the 1960s and 1970s were more likely to settle outside of Florida to escape the heightened racial tension in the South and the discrimination from their own white compatriots.[30]

By 1974, the Cuban Refugee Program had resettled 299,326 of the 461,373 Cubans who had registered with them. They were resettled around the country (as well as in Puerto Rico and the U.S. Virgin Islands), but the areas to receive the largest percentages were New York (27.1), New Jersey (19.8), California (13.2), Puerto Rico (8.5), Illinois (7.5), and Louisiana (2.8).[31] By the mid-1970s, the Cuban Refugee Program had spent over $957 million in resettlement, relief, and other services, and a gradual phaseout of the program began.[32]

The end of the "freedom flights" did not stall Cuban migration to the United States. Several thousand more Cubans immigrated to the United States over the next few years, mostly via third countries. Clandestine emigration continued even though Cubans risked their lives crossing the shark-infested waters of the Florida straits and risked imprisonment if caught leaving the country illegally. By September 1977, the total number of Cubans to arrive in the United States (since 1 January 1959) through legal and illegal channels reached 665,043.[33]

THE MARIEL BOATLIFT

In 1980, the Castro government once again allowed Cubans to emigrate to the United States. Echoing his actions fifteen years earlier, Castro announced in April that all who desired to leave Cuba were permitted to do so, and once again he invited Cuban exiles to sail to Cuba—this time to the port of Mariel—to pick up their relatives. One more time, thousands of exiles sailed across the Florida straits on yachts, sailboats, shrimp boats, and even freighters to pick up their relatives and any other compatriots who wished to leave the island. 124,776 Cubans arrived in the United States from April to October 1980, constituting the third official wave of post-Castro Cuban migration.[34] However, unlike the previous two waves, the U.S. government played no role in sponsoring the migration. This third wave of migration was highly controversial, its legacy still evident in immigration policy today, and national perceptions of the Cuban exile community were forever altered.

While this migration was the consequence of unilateral actions taken by Castro in 1980, it can be best understood in light of the series of events that took place a few years earlier. During the late 1970s, there was a general thawing in tensions between Cuba and the United States. In 1977, for the first time in almost twenty years, both countries established limited diplomatic representation through the creation of "interests sections" in Washington and Havana. A number of cultural exchanges followed this rapprochement, and hundreds of Americans and Cubans traveled to one another's countries for sports competitions, scientific conferences, artistic exhibitions, and other cultural exchanges. In a gesture of goodwill, the Castro government released over four thousand long-term political prisoners in the late 1970s and allowed them to emigrate with their families. In 1978, also for the first time, a few hundred Cuban exiles were allowed to return to their homeland to visit; the following year, over 100,000 exiles were allowed to return to their homeland to visit their families and friends.

These developments had profound consequences for Cuban society. For the first time in almost twenty years, Cubans on the island were able to have steady contact with Americans, and especially with their former compatriots, the people their government had long—and angrily—called "*los gusanos*" (the worms.) Through the visits of the Cuban exiles, Cubans on the island, especially those born and raised under the revolutionary system, became aware of different interpretations of history, politics, and international relations that challenged the standard interpretations promoted within their political system. They also became aware of the latest developments in American popular culture, through the records, books, magazines, and other consumer goods the exiles brought as gifts for their relatives and friends. These new perspectives, whether ideological or cultural, aroused curiosity and challenged many Cubans' most basic beliefs about their society and about life in the United States. For those already resentful of Castro's communism, contact with the exiles only exacerbated their disaffection; for others, it provoked a serious reevaluation of what they held to be true.

These developments also coincided with one of Cuba's periods of economic austerity. Indeed, Castro's decision to allow Cuban exiles to visit their homeland was a move calculated to increase needed revenues. Each Cuban exile wishing to visit his family and friends had to spend thousands of dollars in inflated fares for air travel, hotel accommodations, and meals, whether they used them or not. However, Castro's plan ultimately backfired, since it contributed instead to the growing discontent on the island that was clearly demonstrated by the number of people who tried to leave the island illegally during this period. The number of people who successfully fled the country on homemade rafts increased, as did the number of people apprehended by the Cuban Coast Guard. Beginning in May 1979, Cubans also began smuggling themselves into Latin American embassies to request political asylum. By March 1980, close to thirty Cubans had crashed their vehicles through embassy gates and had taken refuge within the compounds. The "blue-jean revolution," as journalists called this phenomenon, was underway.

The tension climaxed on March 28, when a group of six Cubans stole a city bus and crashed through the gates of the Peruvian embassy. The Cuban guards stationed at the three entrances to the compound shot at the bus, and one of the guards was caught in the crossfire and killed. When the Peruvian ambassador refused to turn these gate-crashers over for criminal prosecution, the Castro government took action. On April 4, Castro pulled all Cuban guards from around the embassy compound, and sent in steamrollers to tear down the embassy gates. In a radio broadcast later that afternoon, Castro stated that his government would no longer risk the lives of its soldiers to protect "criminals."

As news of the event spread through the city of Havana, people left their homes and jobs to go to the embassy to observe. Realizing that they could freely walk into the embassy, many quietly entered the compound and requested asylum. Within 48 hours, approximately 10,800 men, women, and children were standing inside the Peruvian embassy.[35] On April 6, Cuban police finally put up barricades all around the perimeter of the embassy—and for several blocks around—and prohibited more people from entering. For days the fate of the 10,800 was uncertain. The Peruvian government announced that it was unable to accept all the Cubans as asylees and requested international assistance. While they waited to know their fate, conditions in the camp steadily worsened. The Cubans were so densely packed inside the lot that they sat and slept on tree branches and roof tops. There was little food or water, and they had no protection from inclement weather. Cuban officials eventually sent in cartons of food, but never enough to feed all the people housed there, and this provoked fights among the tired and frightened residents. Portable toilets were eventually provided, but not before the lot became covered with mud, urine, and excrement. Thousands of onlookers gathered around the compound each day, some hoping to be allowed into the compound; others, as an act of support for the government. *Granma,* the official state newspaper, called the asylees "delinquents, social deviants, vagrants, and parasites," and blamed them for all the ills that plagued Cuban society.[36] Editorials in the Cuban press fueled the passions of loyal citizens. The Peruvian embassy became a symbol of everything that was wrong with their country, and many Cubans vented their anger against those who took refuge there. People taunted and insulted the refugees and threw stones and rotted food at them. The Cuban police participated in the harassment, beating those refugees on the outer periphery of the compound, unleashing their dogs on them, and blinding the refugees with reflector lights at night.

The 10,800 remained in the compound for two weeks until an emigration plan was negotiated. Peru agreed to take one thousand asylees, and Costa Rica, Spain, Ecuador, Argentina, Canada, France, and West Germany pledged to accept a total of 2,500.[37] The U.S. accepted a total of 6,200 refugees.

The airlift began on April 16. Under the terms of the negotiations, the refugees flew first to Costa Rica before continuing on to their final destination. This stopover, however, presented a new set of problems for Cuba. Journalists from around the world converged at the airport in San José to document the refugees' arrival. They filmed the refugees unboarding from their flights defiantly shouting "Freedom!" and "Down with Castro!" They showed poignant scenes of Cubans kissing the airport tarmac and tearfully embracing the relatives who had flown to Costa Rica to greet them. These simple yet powerful images ultimately did more harm to Castro's regime than any counterrevolutionary plot. After years of promoting an image abroad as the model socialist state, it became clear that Cuba was a society in turmoil. Despite the government's claims that these were the delinquents of Cuban society, the journalists' interviews showed that they were ordinary citizens who preferred exile to the repression and economic hardships in Cuba.

Angered by all the negative publicity, Castro abruptly suspended the flights to Costa Rica four days after they began. A few days later, Castro substituted a new plan to rid the island not only of the remaining asylees at the Peruvian embassy, but of thousands of other dissidents and troublemakers as well. On April 20, the government announced that all Cubans who wished to leave the island were permitted to do so, and urged them to call their relatives in the

United States to come pick them up. He declared the port of Mariel, located some twenty miles west of Havana, as the port of departure and instructed officials to quickly set up camps around the port to process the thousands of Cubans expected to leave.

On hearing the news, hundreds of Cuban exiles in south Florida rushed to the nearest marina to rent any available boat to sail Mariel. By the end of the week, an estimated five hundred boats had arrived in Mariel, and hundreds of others followed over the next few weeks. Those that did not know how to sail found a large population of fishermen in Key West who were willing to transport any number of Cubans for the right fee. The U.S. Coast Guard, the INS, and other federal authorities tried to discourage the boats from sailing out to Cuba, warning them that their actions violated U.S. immigration laws. However, as in Camarioca, these warnings had little effect. Cuban exiles were not about to forfeit this chance to bring their relatives to the U.S.

Although most were aware that there were risks in sailing to Cuba, no amount of precaution prepared them to deal with the events they encountered at Mariel. As each boat arrived at the port, each ship captain presented a Cuban official with a list of relatives they wished to pick up. In most cases, they had to wait several days before they received any response from the government. As they waited for authorization to pick up their relatives, they ran out of fuel, food, and water, and they had to pay the outrageous prices the Cuban government charged for these services. When their relatives finally arrived at the port, Cuban officials informed the ship captains that they had to transport additional passengers—whomever the Cuban government told them to take. If they refused to cooperate they were detained and their ships confiscated. Each boat was packed full of passengers—the majority of them total strangers; many of the boats broke down at sea and had to be rescued by the U.S. Coast Guard. By the end of May, the Coast Guard had rescued thousands of people.[38]

As in the previous Cuban migrations, a large and complex bureaucracy developed in south Florida to register and assist the new immigrants. The first arrivals were processed in Key West, but as the numbers increased, two other processing centers were opened. The refugees were questioned, photographed, fingerprinted, and given medical tests. Voluntary relief agencies provided the Cubans with medical care, food, clothing, and toiletries. While the Cubans waited to be processed and released to relatives or sponsors, they were housed in churches, recreation centers, armories, and even the Orange Bowl Stadium. Officials worked around the clock to register the Cubans and release them to their families or sponsors as quickly as possible. The Federal Emergency Management Agency (FEMA), best known for managing crises caused by natural disasters, assumed responsibility for coordinating the relief efforts.

Finding sponsors became an especially difficult task during this third wave, however, since close to half of the Cubans had no friends or family in the United States. The government eventually had to build "tent cities" in parks and underneath expressways to house those who had little chance of immediate sponsorship. The federal government also opened up three additional camps to house the Cubans: Fort Chaffee, Arkansas; Fort Indiantown Gap, Pennsylvania; and Fort McCoy, Wisconsin. 62,541 Cubans, or almost half of the Mariel immigrants, waited for sponsorship in one of these camps; some stayed a few days, others remained for over a year.[39]

As officials registered the Cubans, they heard disturbing tales. For years, international organizations such as Amnesty International had reported an increase in human-rights violations in Cuba, and the tales they heard in the registration centers verified these reports. INS officials heard, for example, that the Cuban government encouraged *actos de repudio* (acts of repudiation) against those who applied to leave the country, and gangs of people accosted them at home and in public places.[40] At the holding camps near Mariel they endured more insults. Many were not given food, and, before they could leave the country, they had to sign documents confessing that they were social deviants or had committed crimes against the state. With one signature, decent, hard-working citizens established fictional records as burglars, arsonists, murderers, rapists, and CIA agents: records which were later publicly displayed in a new museum—*el museo del pueblo combatiente*—to discredit those who had chosen to leave revolutionary Cuba. At the pier, officials forced them to board any available boat, but not before they took away all their personal belongings: money, suitcases, jewelry, wedding rings, and even their address books with the names and phone numbers of relatives living in the United States. By the time they arrived at Key West, they were sick or malnourished, frightened, and without any personal belongings or identification.

Over the weeks, it became clear that the Castro government was using the boatlift to rid the country of its "undesirables." Cuban police removed people from hospitals, jails, and other institutions and forced them to board the boats against their will. An estimated 1,500 of the new arrivals had serious mental illness or mental retardation. An estimated 1,600 had chronic medical problems such as drug and alcohol abuse or infectious diseases such as tuberculosis. Most distressing to U.S. officials, however, was the discovery that thousands of Mariel emigrants—26,000 by the end of the boatlift—had criminal records. Estimates varied, but of these 26,000, approximately 2,000 had committed serious felonies in Cuba, and most of these were sent directly to the correctional institutions in the United States to await deportation.[41] The majority of the offenders, however, served time for lesser crimes. Under Cuba's *ley de peligrosidad* (the law of dangerousness), Cubans could be incarcerated for gambling, drug addiction, homosexuality, prostitution, and buying or selling on the black market. A percentage of the “criminals” fell under this category and served terms ranging from a few months to a few years at a work farm. Others served time for political crimes as counterrevolutionaries or dissidents. Still others served time because they refused to conform to revolutionary norms; these included members of religious groups such as the Jehovah’s Witnesses and the Seventh Day Adventists (who discouraged military participation). Since the majority of “criminals” served time for crimes not recognized in the United States, they were not considered a threat to U.S. society and were released to sponsors.

The Carter administration tried to communicate with the Castro government through diplomatic channels, requesting that they take back the hard-core felons; all notes went unanswered. Forcible deportation was ruled out because of a possible military confrontation with Cuba. The United States had no choice but to accommodate this prison population until the Castro government agreed to take them back. Throughout the 1980s, Cuban “entrants” who committed misdemeanors or felonies in the United States were handed over to federal custody upon completion of their jail terms to await the day when they could be deported to Cuba. By March 1986, federal authorities held close to 2,000 Cubans in the Atlanta federal penitentiary, and another 700 in prisons and detention centers around the country to await the day when deportation became possible. Detainees remained in U.S. prisons until after 1987, when the Castro finally agreed to take some of them back.

Unfortunately, the U.S. press focused an exaggerated amount of attention on the hard-core felons. While the latter constituted less than 2 percent of the total number of entrants, they commanded almost all of the media attention. Few journalists ever mentioned the fact that the overwhelming majority of Mariel Cubans had no criminal history and were hard-working citizens yearning for a better life. Instead, popular news magazines such as *Newsweek* and *Time,* as well as major newspapers such as the *New York Times,* focused on the disturbing details of Castro’s plan to rid the island of its criminals and mentally ill. In August 1980, the *National Catholic Reporter* commented that the “bad press” was making it difficult to resettle the Cubans.[42] As late as 1984, *U.S. News and World Report* reported on Castro’s “crime bomb.”[43] Unfortunately, the Cubans of Mariel suffered for this sensationalism.

Most Americans initially sympathized with the Cubans’ plight, and they applauded the refugees’ courage at the Peruvian embassy. Those sentiments changed, however, when it became clear that the United States was to play host again to thousands of Cuban refugees, this time during an economic recession when they could ill afford to do so. In just one month, over 80,000 Cubans entered the United States: more people than in any previous year of Cuban immigration.[44] The discovery of the criminal element, however, proved the principal factor in turning public opinion against the boatlift. Never before, according to public opinion, had a neighboring country committed such an act of aggression against the United States. Americans resented that once again Castro was dictating U.S. immigration policy, and the Carter administration was criticized for its inability to control the situation. The Mariel crisis haunted Carter throughout the rest of the year and proved to be one of the factors that led to his electoral defeat later that year.

In reality, the Carter administration did try to protect U.S. interests. Carter was sensitive to the exiles' desire to be reunited with their family members but, understandably, wanted control over who came to the United States, and in what numbers. Administration officials contacted the Castro government, offering a compromise: the administration proposed a new series of airlifts similar to the "freedom flights" of the late 1960s, but which would last approximately twelve months. The Castro government rejected the offer; instead, the Carter administration was forced to rely on the Coast Guard as well as threats of penalties to deter exiles from rushing out to Mariel to pick up their relatives. The U.S. Coast Guard increased its patrol teams off the Florida coast and warned all captains on out-going vessels that those caught transporting Cubans illegally would be fined up to $1,000 for each person brought to the United States and have their ships confiscated. While the warnings deterred some, others continued with their plans. Many were willing to pay any price to get their families out of Cuba. By the end of the summer, however, this stricter policy ultimately succeeded in reducing the flow from thirteen thousand a week to less than seven hundred.[45] The Cuban government finally closed the port of Mariel to further emigration on September 25, and the last boat arrived in Key West four days later. By this date, over 124,000 Cubans had made it to the United States.

Demographically, the Cubans of Mariel were different from the Cubans who arrived during the 1960's. The Mariel population was younger by about ten years (averaging thirty years of age), contained a higher percentage of blacks and people of mixed race (roughly twenty percent), and reflected a wider geographic distribution. Almost seventy percent were male.[46] Despite these differences, the Cubans of Mariel had much in common with the working-class Cubans who emigrated during the "freedom flights," especially in their occupational history. In education, they rated slightly higher, having completed more years of schooling than their earlier working-class compatriots.[47]

The Mariel migration was most distinctive, however, in how it was perceived by the federal government and the larger U.S. society. Unlike the Cubans who immigrated from 1959 to 1973, the Cubans of Mariel were not considered legitimate refugees. The majority cited political reasons for their emigration, and administration officials commonly referred to them as "refugees." But the Justice department determined that under the terms of the 1980 U.S. Refugee Act (which came into effect a month before the boatlift), the Cubans did not qualify for refugee status nor for the special assistance that that status entitled them to receive. This marked the first time since the Cold War began that the government denied refugee status to individuals leaving a communist state. Instead, the government categorized the Cubans with the rather ambiguous term "entrant: status pending," which was a political compromise: an undetermined status that allowed the United States to symbolically uphold its "open-door" policy, while appearing to take a harsher stand against "illegal" immigration. It was not until 1984 that the Cubans of Mariel were able to regularize their status.

The Mariel Cubans became the most stigmatized group of immigrants in recent history. No articles or editorials praised their patriotism, their democratic spirit, or their "Horatio Alger" drive to succeed as they had the earlier arrivals from Cuba. Instead, they were described as troublemakers and opportunists who were taking the place of more worthy immigrants. Ironically, the reaction of the Cuban exile community paralleled that of the larger society. The older, more established Cuban exiles initially felt a moral responsibility to assist their compatriots, and they pooled their resources to help them adapt to the United States. By the end of April, the exile community of Dade County had raised over $2 million to assist the Cubans in their immediate needs. Local businesses donated flood and clothing, and exiles volunteered as sponsors and served as doctors, nurses, teachers, and translators in the temporary camps. However, currents of fear ran beneath these feelings of obligation. Many worried that the new immigrants, raised under an authoritarian socialist system, would never adapt to their new society. Like most Americans, they were scandalized by the news that Castro had released criminals into the boatlift population. Angered that their reputation as "golden immigrants" was now tarnished, the exiles took great care to distinguish themselves from the new immigrants. They coined a special term for the Cubans—*los marielitos*—that quickly became a pejorative in the community. As fear spread, exiles became reluctant to sponsor the Cubans and even to offer them jobs. This came as a surprise to the new immigrants, who did not expect such behavior from their compatriots.

Ethnic relations in south Florida deteriorated in the wake of the boatlift. During the summer of 1980, African Americans in nearby Liberty City rioted. While the riot was a response to a specific act of police brutality, it expressed the larger frustration in this community. For decades African Americans complained of having to compete with "foreigners" for jobs and political power, and the 1980s riot was the latest in a series of civil actions where citizens vented their rage against a system they felt had shut them out. In November 1980, in another demonstration of anti-Cuban sentiment, voters repealed the

Bilingual-Bicultural Ordinance (originally passed in 1973) and made it unlawful to use county funds "for the purpose of utilizing any language other than English, or promoting any culture other than that of the United States."[48] A popular bumper sticker sported on the cars of many non-Latinos read "Will the last American out of south Florida please bring the flag?" The television and film industry capitalized on the anger and resentment, portraying Cubans as drug dealers, pimps, and psychopaths. Nowhere were the stereotypes plainer than in Universal Studio's 1983 remake of *Scarface*, wherein the mobster made famous by James Cagney was now a *marielito* cocaine smuggler played by Al Pacino. To combat the negative images that now dominated the media, Miami Cubans founded the organization "Facts About Cuban Exiles" (FACE) in 1982. Like the NAACP, the League of United Latin American Citizens (LULAC), and other minority rights groups, FACE's goal was to educate Americans about the exile community through conferences and publications, and to celebrate the Cubans' accomplishments.

Since 1980, south Floridians have lived with the knowledge that Castro could, at any moment, allow another large-scale migration. Rumors of another boatlift periodically circulated in Miami. In 1983, the federal government and state of Florida compiled a list of emergency procedures in case of such an event.[49] The *Miami Herald* regularly interviewed sociologists and political scientists for their "migration forecasts": analyses of social and economic conditions in Cuba which might foster another migration.

Despite the tremendous odds against them, the Cubans of Mariel made economic gains over the next decade and revealed the same entrepreneurial spirit as those who arrived earlier. By 1986, over one-fourth of the immigrants were self-employed. By 1990, only 5.6 percent were unemployed: a figure comparable to the rest of the nation.[50] The children of Mariel exhibited the most astounding success of all. Over 11,000 children enrolled in Dade County schools in the wake of the boatlift, and while none of them spoke English when they arrived, by 1987 only 8 percent required instruction in the bilingual education program known as ESOL (English for Speakers of Other Languages). In 1987, Cubans of Mariel presented the valedictory speeches at two Dade County high schools, and the proportion of students going on to college was comparable to that of emigrés who arrived earlier.[51] Ten years after the boatlift, the term *marielito* had ceased to be pejorative.

THE ONGOING FOURTH WAVE OF CUBAN MIGRATION

In 1984, the Reagan administration and the Castro government signed a new immigration accord in which the United States agreed to accept up to 20,000

Cuban immigrants per year. In return, the Cuban government agreed to take back 2,746 criminal and mentally ill detainees of the Mariel boatlift. However, in May 1985 the Castro government suspended the accords in response to the Reagan administration's installation of *Radio Martí*, a radio network founded with the specific purpose of beaming news, music, and sports to the island, twenty-four hours a day, from an undisclosed location in the Florida Keys. By the time of the suspension, only 201 Mariel detainees had been returned to Cuba. It was not until 1987 that both governments once again reinstated the terms of the migration accords. But over the next decade both countries moved slowly on their ends of the agreement: Cuba stalled on taking back the detained felons, and the United States never accepted the total number of immigrants it had committed itself to accept.

The number of Cubans who emigrated clandestinely on rafts and small boats increased dramatically during the 1990s as a result of the worsening economic conditions in Cuba. After the dismantling of the Soviet Union, Cuba could no longer rely on its former patron for the estimated $6 billion in assistance that it received each year.[52] The lack of external funding, together with a series of agricultural crises, caused even greater shortages in basic consumer goods. Limited efforts to restructure the economy meant that Cuba became increasingly dependent on tourism and remittances to keep its economy afloat. Cubans, desperate to improve their situation, took to the seas on homemade rafts. During 1990, the U.S. Coast Guard rescued 467 *balseros* (rafters), and the number the number doubled in the first six months of 1991 alone. In 1993, the Coast Guard picked up 3,656 *balseros*.[53] Cuban American pilots founded an organization called "Hermanos al Rescate" ("Brothers to the Rescue") to patrol the Florida straits by helicopter and assist the Coast Guard with the rescue missions.

The *balsero* crisis peaked during the summer of 1994. Rumor spread through island that, due to gasoline shortages, the Cuban Coast Guard was no longer patrolling the waters as vigilantly as it had in the past. Thousands took to the seas. Unlike other undocumented immigrants, Cubans caught entering the United States illegally were allowed to stay under the terms of the 1966 Cuban Adjustment Act. Fearing another Mariel, the Clinton administration suspended this thirty-year policy: he announced that Cubans detained at sea would not be admitted to the United States and, instead, would be sent to the Guantánamo naval base until the Cuban government accepted them or the *balseros* received admittance to a third country, if that was their choice. The Clinton administration also tried to pressure the Castro government to restrict illegal emigration. U.S. officials announced that the sending of remittances to relatives on the island was prohibited, and charter air traffic from Miami to Cuba, available since 1979 to allow Cuban exiles the opportunity to visit their relatives in Cuba, was now indefinitely postponed. Despite these reversals in policy, the *balseros* kept coming. During the last two weeks of August 1994, the U.S. Coast Guard picked up an average of 1,500 *balseros* each day.

Finally, the U.S. was forced to go back to the negotiating table. Officials from both countries met in a series of meetings in New York, Washington, and Havana to iron out the details of another migration accord. Under the terms of the 1994 agreement, the United States committed itself to accept a *minimum* of 20,000 per year, and the Castro government agreed to intercept any *balseros* and to accept the Cubans detained at Guantánamo without reprisals. However, the majority of the Cubans at Guantánamo refused to return to Cuba, and few were able to find admittance into a third country. They chose to remain indefinitely at Guantánamo, hoping that the United States would eventually take pity and allow them to enter the country. The Clinton administration was determined to maintain its hard-line policy, but providing for the tens of thousands of camp residents cost U.S. taxpayers an estimated one million dollars a day. Finally, in 1995, the Clinton administration agreed to begin processing the camp residents for admittance into the United States.

The 1994 accords has not stopped illegal boat traffic to the United States or to other countries. Instead, for the first time, U.S. Coast Guard officials found evidence of smuggling operations involving Cubans. For years, law enforcement agencies have encountered such smuggling operations along the U.S.-Mexico and U.S.-Canada border involving immigrants from other countries, but never had they encountered such operations involving Cubans, primarily because the Cuban Adjustment Act and other immigration laws facilitated the Cubans' entrance. Under the new U.S. policy, however, those apprehended at sea are deported back to their country if an immigration official determines that their petitions for asylum are frivolous. The goal of smugglers, then, is to facilitate the Cubans' landing on U.S. territory, where, like other undocumented aliens, they can try to remain anonymous within ethnic enclaves. Those who decide to petition for asylum on U.S. soil are guaranteed a hearing, and since the process can drag on for years, it increases their chances of making a successful plea.

However, U.S. policy regarding the Cubans remains highly inconsistent, as was seen in the case of Elián González. This six-year-old boy was rescued at sea by the U.S. Coast Guard on Thanksgiving Day 1999, one of two survivors of an illegal expedition that claimed the lives of eleven defectors, including Elián's mother. Under the new policy, the young boy should have been deported back to Cuba and to the father and grandparents who wanted him back. In this particular case, the United States allowed the boy to stay to live with his relatives (a great-uncle and his family) in Miami, prompting a political tug-of-war between Cuba and the United States—and the families in each country—over who had legitimate rights to care for the boy. Elián's relatives in Florida, as well as many in the Cuban exile community, claimed that he was entitled to a life in the United States given the fact that his mother had lost her life trying to reach this country. His father in Cuba, on the other hand, demanded his return based on his rights as the now custodial parent, and traveled to Washington, D.C., to make his appeal. Polls showed that most Americans supported his claim. Editorials and op-ed pieces in the U.S. press criticized the United States for its inconsistent immigration policies and for bowing to pressure from the conservative and vocal elements in the Cuban exile community.

Finally, in April 2000, the INS stormed the house in Little Havana in a predawn raid, seized the six-year-old at gun point, and transported him to Washington, D.C., to await the legal resolution of his case with his father, Juan Manuel. In June, the Supreme Court denied the Miami relatives' claims to keep Elián in the United States, and the boy returned with his father to a hero's welcome in Cuba.

Cases such as this one proved yet again how politicized the immigration and asylum process has become, as have the many parties that have a claim in the policy making. Ironically, a custody case later that year, that in some ways mirrored the Elián case, failed to attract as much international attention. In this particular case, a five-year-old U.S.-born boy was taken to live in Havana, by his Cuban mother, against the wishes of the boy's American father.[54] Once again, two countries and two families clashed and revealed the limitations of immigration law as well as custodial and family law.

IDENTITY, ADAPTATION, AND THE "CUBAN SUCCESS STORY"

The Cubans are often portrayed as one of the most successful immigrant groups in the United States, at least in recent history. In a fairly short time, they have come to occupy leading positions in the key institutions of south Florida: in labor unions, universities, political parties, the news media, cultural organizations, as well as city governments. As early as 1980, they exhibited the highest income and educational levels of the three largest Latino groups—levels that were only slightly below the national average. 16.2 percent of Cubans had completed four or more years of college, compared to 4.9 and 5.6 percent of Mexicans and Puerto Ricans, respectively; by 1990, 20.3 percent of Cubans had completed four or more years of college compared to 9.3 percent for the Latino population in general.[55] In 1980, Cubans earned a median family income of $18,245, compared to $14,765 and $10,734 for Mexicans and Puerto Ricans, respectively; by 1989, Cuban American income stood at $27,890, compared to $21,922 for Latinos in general (and slightly below the national average of $28,905).[56]

Cubans did particularly well in Florida, especially the immigrant enclave of Miami. According to the 1990 census, 65 percent (657,786) of the Cuban-origin population (then counted at 1,043,932 or 4.2 percent of the Latino population of the United States) lived in the state of Florida, concentrated in the Miami metropolitan area. As early as 1980, Miami was home to the wealthiest Latino business community in the nation, a thriving economic enclave that absorbed each new wave of immigration from Cuba, as well as thousands from other countries in Latin America. By 1980, Cuban exiles in Dade County generated close to $2.5 billion in income each year. 18,000 businesses were Cuban-owned, and 63 percent owned their own homes.[57] Over 44 percent of the nearly 500,000 Cubans living in greater Miami were either professionals, company managers, business owners, skilled craftsmen, or retail sales and clerical personnel. The figures improved with each year. In 1985, 19,700 businesses were Cuban-owned.[58] In 1987, the Department of Commerce's Survey of Minority-Owned Business Enterprises counted 61,470 small, nonincorporated, Cuban-owned firms across the country generating $5.5 billion in annual sales and employing 47,000 people.[59] These were notable accomplishments for a community of largely first generation immigrants.

The Cubans' success could be attributed to several factors. On the individual or family level, the structure of the Cuban family ensured success because it was built around economic cooperation.[60] Women had a high rate of participation in the labor force. As early as 1970, they constituted the largest proportionate group of working women in the United States.[61] Many Cuban households also contained three generations, and the elderly contributed to the family's economic well-being directly, by salaries or Social Security benefits, or indirectly, by raising children and assuming household responsibilities. These factors, along with the Cubans' low fertility rates and high levels of school enrollment facilitated the family's comparatively quick economic integration.

On the broader community level, the Cubans created prosperous businesses, built with the skills and capital of the middle- to upper-class exiles that constituted the first wave of immigrants. Some of the wealthier Cubans were fortunate to have money invested in U.S. banks at the time of the revolution, and when they settled in Miami or other cities they invested that capital in new business ventures. The middle class did not have that type of capital, but they did have the skills and business "know-how" with which to create lucrative businesses. They identified the needs in the community and built businesses catering to those needs. While the major banks would not lend start-up money to Cuban entrepreneurs without collateral—which only the wealthier emigrés had—the smaller banks in the area (some Cuban- or Latin American–owned) lent applicants money on the basis of their "character."[62] Cubans who had a solid history of entrepreneurship in Cuba, or who had strong personal references, usually qualified for these loans. By the late 1960s, Cuban entrepreneurs also had access to loans from the Small Business Administration (SBA). As their businesses expanded, these entrepreneurs hired more employees, almost always their fellow countrymen. Thus, south Florida became home to a thriving business community, which provided job opportunities for the new immigrants arriving each year, assisting their assimilation into the economic mainstream.[63]

The Cuban presence attracted domestic and international investments and helped convert Miami into a major production, trade, and commercial center linking North and South America. Many U.S. industries, particularly the garment and textile industries, relocated to south Florida to take advantage of the large, initially nonunion labor pool. By 1980, workers of "Spanish origin" (mostly Cuban women) constituted 83 percent of workers in the garment industry. By 1980, thirteen major banks and over one hundred multinational corporations had established regional offices in the Miami area, eager to take advantage of a large Cuban middle class adept at doing business with both the United States and Latin America. The Port of Miami replaced New Orleans as the chief port of trade with Latin America, and Miami International Airport became one of the busiest airports in the world.[64]

As early as the 1960s, the national news media, specifically popular magazines such as *Life* and *Fortune,* circulated the myth of the "Cuban success story." While the community, as a whole, had fared well, and many individual Cubans had achieved spectacular success in the United States in a short period of time, the myth overlooked the fact that many Cubans did not share in the community's overall wealth. In 1980, 11.7 percent of Cuban families lived below the poverty level, and in 1993, 17 percent lived below the poverty level.[65] The myth of the Cuban success story overlooked most Cubans' successes in the United States being modest, certainly less spectacular than the rags-to-riches stories promoted by the popular media. Despite the presence of a large middle-to-upper class, and the comprehensive federal assistance pumped into the community, Cuban income still remained below the national average (albeit slightly), and there was a significant percentage of elderly poor.[66] The elderly, for example, were less likely to speak English, hold full-time, higher-paying employment, or receive adequate health care, especially if they lived alone.[67] Working-class Cubans, like other Americans, struggled for better wages, benefits, working conditions, as well as job security, particularly if they were women. Black Cubans experienced the most discrimination in the workplace. As late as 1990, their income lagged behind that of white Cubans by almost 40 percent.[68]

But Cubans themselves internalized the myth of the Cuban success story and took pride in it. Aside from their anticommunism, it was the one feature they most promoted about themselves. To admit that not all who had come to the United States had done well was to give the Castro government ammunition against them. They felt they had to be symbols for their countrymen on the island of Cuba's political and economic alternatives.

Maintaining a sense of *cubanidad* in the United States was crucial to the first generation. They asked themselves whether Cuban culture could thrive in a society that celebrated ethnic pluralism and yet rewarded Anglo-conformity. Could one be both a Cuban exile and a U.S. citizen? Would their children be able to adapt to Cuban society once Castro was overthrown? These and other questions became increasingly important with each year, as the chances of returning to Cuba became increasingly remote.

To maintain a sense of *cubanidad* meant to preserve those customs, values, and traditions that they associated with being Cuban, and the exiles created literally hundreds of organizations to reinforce those values in exile. Maintaining a sense of *cubanidad* was easier in Miami and south Florida because it was home to the largest concentration of Cubans. The Cuban Refugee Program tried to resettle Cubans around the country, to ease the pressure on the local community, but the majority of exiles refused to move; many of those resettled eventually returned to live in south Florida. Census figures showed that in 1970, 299,217 Cubans lived in Dade County, but by 1980 the number had almost doubled to 581,030. In 1990, their numbers dropped somewhat to 563,979, or 29 percent of Dade County's total population.[69] Still, the only city with a larger Cuban population was Havana.

The symbolic heart of Cuban Miami is "Little Havana," a four-square-mile area southwest of the central business district. Here the Cubans renovated the old buildings and established their own businesses along the principal thoroughfares, especially Flagler Street and Southwest Eighth Street (Calle Ocho). The Cubans turned an economically depressed area into a lucrative commercial and residential district. But the majority of Cubans moved west and south into other residential areas, so that Cubans were dispersed throughout the entire city. Exiles joked—and took pride in the fact—that in many ways all of Miami was a Little Havana. The Cubans settled in neighboring cities in Dade County as well. The nearby city of Hialeah drew many Cubans; by 1970, Cubans comprised 42 percent of its population, and by 1980, 74 percent. The city of Sweetwater also grew with the Cuban migration, acquiring a Latino population of 81 percent by 1980.[70] It became the first city in south Florida (in the Castro era) to elect a Cuban-born mayor. Coral Gables and Miami Beach also attracted Cubans, especially those with higher incomes.

Reinforcing *cubanidad* became something of an obsession for the exiles, particularly during the 1960s and 1970s. Life in exile made them nostalgic, even depressed, and they looked for ways to remember and celebrate the past, reinforce their feelings of nationalism, and assert their identity. Of particular concern to the exiles was the second generation: those who were born in the United States, or who came here as children, and knew little about Cuba or their heritage. To help parents educate their children on the essentials of *cubanidad,* schools and churches in Little Havana established after-school programs that offered courses on Cuban history, geography, and culture each day. Those who wanted a more intensive Cuban education could attend one of the dozens of small private schools that emerged in Miami and Hialeah, nicknamed *las escuelitas cubanas* (the little Cuban schools). Several of Havana's best private schools also reopened in exile, including Belen Jesuit High School, Fidel Castro's alma mater, offering a consoling continuity.

Exile organizations sponsored lectures and seminars on Cuban history and culture and organized rallies, festivals, concerts, and parades to celebrate patriotic holidays such as *el veinte de mayo* (May 20) and *el diez de Octubre* (October 10). Cuban-owned book stores organized *peñas literarias* (literary circles) to discuss the works of Cuban authors. On the shores of Biscayne Bay, Cubans constructed a shrine to Cuba's patron saint, *la Virgen de la Caridad del Cobre.* They named parks, monuments, streets, and businesses after long-dead heroes of Cuba's wars of independence or their own heroes, such as the veterans of the Bay of Pigs invasion, as well as figures of the sports and entertainment world. Cubans produced a vital news media, consisting of hundreds of Spanish-language periodicals as well as dozens of radio and television stations, which kept the community informed on news from Cuba as well as domestic issues that were important to them.

In expressing their *cubanidad,* they asserted an identity that was political as well as cultural. As exiles, they perceived complete assimilation as a rejection of their heritage, as well as a denial of those forces that had compelled them to come to the United States. But in the long term, ironically, their *cubanidad* assisted them in their adaptation to the United States, since it psychologically empowered them to deal with life in exile and gave their hardships a larger meaning. Starting over was difficult for the first generation. Many had left behind rewarding careers, home, and property, as well as friends and family. They now had to begin again, in most cases at middle age (in 1980 the median age was 37.7 years; in 1994, 43 years),[71] and they had to adapt to a new society and a new way of living. When life in the United States became overwhelming, these Cubans took some comfort in the fact that their struggles had a larger meaning.

As early as the 1970s there was evidence of a shift in self-perception in the exile community from that of "temporary visitor" to that of permanent resident. This shift was attributable, in part, to the termination of the "freedom flights," which forced many Cubans to come to terms with the reality of their situation. By the end of the decade, contact with the Cubans of Mariel along with the new travel opportunities to Cuba (the so-called family reunification trips) also contributed to this shift in self-perception. Many realized that the Cuba they remembered no longer existed and their future role in their homeland was uncertain. This increased contact with the "new" Cuba forced them to reanalyze their ties to the United States and to view it as home. This shift in consciousness was especially evident in the growing number seeking naturalization as well as their increased involvement in civic affairs. From 1971 to 1980, for example, Cubans accounted for twelve percent of total naturalizations in the United States, compared to six percent for Mexican immigrants, who constituted a much larger number of legal immigrants (178, 374 Cubans naturalized compared to 68,152 Mexicans).[72]

By the 1990s there were several intersecting political generations in the Cuban community. They are defined not by age or time of entry into the United States, but rather by experience. The first generation—the exile generation—more clearly identifies with the homeland. They identify themselves as Cuban and choose Spanish as their principle language of communication, and they are more likely to engage in exile politics. The next generation—what some have called the "one-and-a half-generation"—were born in Cuba but came of age in the United States; they regard themselves as both Cuban and American, feel equally comfortable with both cultures and languages, and make both an integral part of their lives.

The so-called second generation, the first to be born in the United States, is very different. They feel a connection to Cuba because their parents and grandparents have encouraged that connection, but they are not as passionately committed to exile politics or as emotionally bound to Cuba as their elders. Nor could they be. Most of them have never visited Cuba except through photographs and through the memories of others. They have never lived through revolutionary change or been forced to seek refuge in another country. Statistics show that U.S.-born Cuban Americans are wealthier and better educated. While socioeconomic statistics for Cuban exiles are comparable to that of other Hispanics/Latinos, U.S.-born Cuban Americans fare better than even the "Anglo" population: 26.1 percent of second generation Cuban Americans were educated beyond the high school level as compared to 20.6 percent of "Anglos." Also, 36.9 percent of U.S.-born Cuban Americans had incomes above $50,000 as compared to 18.1 percent of Anglos.[73] The Latino National Political Survey also revealed that U.S.-born Cuban Americans are more likely to identify themselves as "American" or with a pan-ethnic label such as "Hispanic" or "Latino."[74] Ironically, U.S.-Born Cubans are less likely to vote than their elders; although turnout in elections has reached over ninety percent, in some presidential elections only thirty percent of Cuban Americans under the age of twenty-five show up to vote, and only 50 to 60 percent of Cuban Americans between the ages of twenty-five and thirty-four vote.[75] English is the language of choice in personal and business interactions outside the home, though 36.9 percent of U.S.-born Cuban Americans use both languages.[76]

Despite these obvious linguistic and cultural changes in the Cuban community, Spanish will always be as important as English in Dade County due to the continued migration from Cuba and other parts of Latin America, as well as the high volume of tourists from Spanish-speaking countries. But just as Cuban culture in Cuba has changed over the past forty years in response to changing socioeconomic and political realities of that country, Cuban culture on this side of the Florida straits has continually redefined itself as well. In many ways, there are multiple Cuban cultures.

Cuban immigration continues to influence U.S. popular culture, as well. Nowhere is this influence more evident than in the sport of baseball. Since 1911, when Rafael Almeida and Armando Marsans joined the Cincinnati Reds, Cuban players have played in major league baseball teams and set a number of records. In the pre-Castro era, Minnie Minoso, Camilo Pascual, Luis Tiant, and Tony Pérez, were just some of the Cuban names in the sport. More recently, José Canseco, Rey Ordoñez, Orlando "El Duque" Hernández, Livan Hernández, Alex González, and Omar Linares top the long roster of Cuban-born (some of them recent defectors to the United States) and Cuban American players.

Since the 1930s, Cuban music and dance have fascinated Americans. The *mambo* and *cha-cha-chá* were just two of the forms imported from Cuba prior to the revolution, and musicians such as Desi Arnaz, Beny More, and Machito found a welcoming audience in the United States. More recently, Americans have rediscovered Cuban music as seen in the popularity of musicians such as Los Van Van, Silvio Rodríguez, and the Buena Vista Social Club, each representing a very different musical style. Cuban American musicians have also attracted a great deal of attention including Paquito D'Rivera, Israel "Cachao" López, Albita, Willie Chirino, and especially Gloria Estefan, who was among the first of the Latino artists to "cross over" in the popular market.

Cuban exile writers such as Guillermo Cabrera Infante, Lydia Cabrera, Heberto Padilla, and Reinaldo Arenas have produced some of their best work outside their homeland. However, a new and distinctly Cuban American generation of writers and poets has demonstrated that ethnic or immigrant literature in this country is not solely an exercise in nostalgia or an exploration of alienation. Pulitzer prize–winning Oscar Hijuelos, Achy Obejas, Virgil Suárez, Roberto G. Fernández, Gustavo Pérez-Firmat, Cristina García, Pablo Medina, and Elias Miguel Muñoz are just some of the Cuban-born or Cuban American writers and poets that have generated interest from mainstream publishing houses and academia. In journalism, the *Miami Herald*'s Liz Balmaseda was recognized with a Pulitzer prize; in television, Cristina Saralegui has been called the "Cuban Oprah Winfrey" because of her syndicated talk show's impact in the United States and Latin America. In theater, Ivan Acosta, María Irene Fornés, Nilo Cruz, Luis Santeiro, and Eduardo Machado have staged their plays throughout the United States, Europe, and Latin America. In the visual arts, Ana Mendieta, Julio Larraz, and José Bedía are just three of the artists whose works form part of the collections of museums and private estates. In film, the late Nestor Almendros won the coveted Academy Award for cinematography. In acting, Andy García, Elizabeth Peña, Cameron Díaz, and Steven Bauer are among the more popular Cuban actors.

CUBAN EXILE AND CUBAN AMERICAN POLITICS

The political culture of the Cuban community evolved in response to events in both Cuba and the United States. Cubans engaged in both exile politics and ethnic politics: as exiles, they tried to shape the political reality in the homeland; as immigrant-citizens, they tried to shape their local environment. The line between the two often blurred.

During the 1960s, Cubans were almost exclusively concerned with overthrowing Castro and returning to the homeland, and they created hundreds of organizations dedicated to *la causa cubana.* As early as 1963, there were so many exile political organizations in south Florida that the Department of Justice was unable to keep track of all of them.[77] The majority of these organizations emerged in Miami, but others emerged wherever Cubans settled: in Union City, N.J., Chicago, New York, Los Angeles, and San Juan. Most were propaganda organizations that tried to discredit the Castro government through a variety of measures: they organized conferences, marches, boycotts, and published reports on human rights abuses in Cuba, and they pressured Congress, the United Nations, and the OAS to enact more punitive policies towards the Castro government.

A small percentage of these organizations were paramilitary groups that launched attacks on Cuban property and on the property of countries that traded with Cuba. While these groups were the minority, they naturally commanded most of the media attention. These groups tried to present themselves as well-manned and well-armed, but in reality, most conducted operations with just a few dozen volunteers. Some of these groups received funding from the CIA and were used in a variety of covert operations against Castro, including the Bay of Pigs invasion, Operation Mongoose, and the "secret war" of the 1960s. A few others received funding from foreign governments, which then expected them to serve as mercenaries in their own covert operations. But most operated independently, relying on donations from sympathetic Americans to buy their boats and armaments. They trained in secret camps in the Florida Everglades and around the Caribbean, trying to avoid detection. On a number of occasions these paramilitary guerrillas infiltrated Cuba and bombed rail lines, shipping vessels, sugar refineries, and other centers of production, as well as cargo ships from the Soviet Union and the eastern bloc countries. Their logic was that if they destabilized the country, their countrymen would tire of the Castro government and rise up to overthrow him. They also hoped to turn Cuba into a liability for the Soviet Union and thereby undermine its control, in much the same way that the Irish Republican Army used bombings and other terrorist tactics to try to force Great Britain to relinquish its control of Northern Ireland.

At first, the U.S. Justice Department looked the other way. They realized these raids served a purpose within U.S. foreign policy: that is, they harassed the Cuban government, undermined their economy, and perhaps distracted Castro from exporting revolution by committing the military to domestic defense. It also gave Cuban exiles an outlet for their anger and frustration. By the late 1960s, however, the government had cracked down on these operations because they strained an already tense relationship with the Soviet Union, as well as with neighboring allies who feared an escalation of regional tensions. By the late 1960s, the U.S. government was also focusing most of its attention on Southeast Asia, and unseating Castro became less important. The Cuban paramilitary groups found themselves isolated, both by the U.S. government and, eventually, the exile community who increasingly doubted the wisdom of their strategies. In the 1970s only a handful of these paramilitary organizations continued to operate.

For most Cuban exiles, each passing year was a reminder that returning to Cuba permanently was unlikely, and so they focused their attention on improving their lives in the United States. This led to their growing naturalization rates and their involvement in local, state, and national politics. The Cubans demonstrated high voter turnouts in elections. By the Bicentennial celebrations of 1976, Cubans constituted 8 percent of registered voters in Dade County and had been elected to important offices in city and county governments. Seven years later they constituted 20 percent of registered voters in Dade County, and their voting participation exceeded that of the general population.[78]

There were indications that they were developing an *ethnic* identity as well, as seen in their growing membership in pan-Latino organizations such as LULAC, as well as in the creation of groups such as the Cuban National Planning Council, the Spanish American League Against Discrimination (SALAD), and the National Coalition of Cuban Americans, which focused on domestic concerns such as voting rights, employment, housing, education, and health. All signs seemed to indicate that the Cubans had unpacked their bags and settled into their new society, and, as mentioned earlier, U.S.-born Cuban Americans were even more likely to identify with the United States.

The exile generation never completely abandoned their war against Castro, but they did alter their tactics in ways that reflected their growing accommodation to the United States. They continued to try to influence Cuban affairs, but more and more they did so by working within the U.S. political system rather than independently of it. By the 1980s, Cubans registered largely as Republicans and voted Republican more consistently than any other ethnic group. Their loyalty to the Republican party had less to do with domestic policy issues, however, than with their foreign policy agenda. Even though the Cubans were indebted to Democratic administrations for a liberal immigration policy, and even though they supported traditionally "Democratic" issues such as workers' rights and a woman's right to choose, they nevertheless overwhelmingly gave their support to the Republican Party—at least during the 1980s—because the latter was perceived to be more anticommunist. However, the Republican Party realized that it could not take the Cuban vote for granted. On the local and state level, Cubans voted as readily for Democrats as for Republicans, taking into account not only the candidates' views on Cuba, but their positions on health care and education and other domestic issues that affected their day-to-day lives. Even Republican presidential candidates could not always rely on the Cuban vote. The Cubans voted for Reagan by over 90 percent in 1980 and 1984, but failed to give the Republicans that edge in 1996 because of the party's support of revoking welfare benefits for legal immigrants and the Republicans' support of the English-only amendment. Back in 1992, only 20 percent of Cubans in Florida voted for Bill Clinton; but four years later almost as many Cubans voted for Clinton as for the Republican candidate, Bob Dole.[79]

Exile politics were never monolithic either. Within the general sphere of anti-Castroism, the Cubans exhibited a broad range of political perspectives, which is one of the reasons why no one single organization ever emerged in this community that represented the interests of the population as whole. The most influential of the " hard-line" organizations is the Cuban American National Foundation, founded in 1981 by a group of wealthy Cuban American businessmen with the goal of shaping a more "realistic" foreign policy toward

Cuba. CANF created a bipartisan political-action committee, the "Free Cuba PAC," that donated to the campaigns of politicians who favored tougher sanctions against Cuba. As a result of CANF's intensive lobbying, Congress passed a number of laws that tried to pressure the Castro government into enacting democratic reforms. These included the bills to create *Radio Martí* and *Televisión Martí,* as well as the Cuban Democracy Act and the Helms-Burton bill that further tightened the economic embargo on Cuba by eliminating loopholes in the existing laws and sanctioning foreign corporations that conducted business in Cuba.

Hard-liners in the community believe that a political accommodation of the Cuban government is an endorsement of Castro communism. They cannot understand why a Cuban exile would choose to negotiate with the individuals who have tortured, imprisoned, and executed tens of thousands of their compatriots. They prefer to see Castro pushed out of power—by a coup organized by their countrymen on the island rather than a U.S.-backed invasion—and they favor all measures, including the trade embargo, that will create the political climate necessary for such an event. Some of those who espouse these hard-line views are opposed to the sending of remittances to the island, which, they argue, help to maintain Castro's power; and they even object to any artist or musician from Cuba exhibiting or playing in a Miami venue unless they publicly denounce the Castro government.

But just as the Cuban American community is diverse socioeconomically, they are ideologically diverse as well. Cuban exiles differ in their visions of a post-Castro Cuba, and they disagree about the tactics they consider legitimate in the war against Castro. Some Cubans even favor abandoning the "war" completely, arguing for the reestablishment of full diplomatic and trade relations with Cuba. A handful of organizations have emerged over the past four decades to lobby for this cause, arguing that dialogue and forgiveness are always preferable to conflict. One of the most influential organizations to lobby for this cause is the Cuban Committee for Democracy, with offices in Washington, D.C. As with other issues, there are generational differences: U.S.-born Cubans are more likely to favor dialogue and to oppose the censorship of those who articulate opposing views.[80]

A CONCLUDING NOTE

Those who read about the Cuban exile and Cuban American population frequently want to know what will happen once there is a political shift in Cuba toward democratic reform and free-market capitalism, if this indeed ever happens once Fidel Castro no longer rules Cuba. Will the U.S. Cubans return en masse to their homeland or will most of them stay in their adopted home? It is difficult to predict what will happen. Despite the attempts to neatly categorize the Cubans (e.g., that they are wealthy, politically conservative, and that they refuse to assimilate), the truth is their population has always been diverse. To assume that a population of over one million people all think and act the same is, of course, absurd.

However, one can outline some *possible* scenarios. As happens in most countries undergoing structural change, no matter how positive those changes in the long term, migration is usually an initial response to any political or economic shift. In the case that there is democratic reform and an expansion of capitalism in a post-Castro Cuba, it is very likely that the United States will once again have to deal with an increase in boat traffic from the island, as people try to leave behind the political and economic instability created by such a transition. Cubans on the island may wish to take advantage of this instability, and perhaps the liberalized travel and migration policies, to come to the United States, legally and illegally, as students, tourists, and immigrants.

It is also likely that some U.S. Cubans will return to their homeland, but perhaps not in the numbers that some might expect. Surveys conducted over the past thirty years have demonstrated that Cuban exiles have established ties to the United States in spite of their original intentions. They have established careers and businesses here, bought homes, and adopted the language and citizenship of the country that gave them refuge. They have raised families here. Many who arrived in the early 1960s are now grandparents and great-grandparents, and these new generations in their family are more American than Cuban. Returning to Cuba, then, would mean uprooting themselves a second time and once again leaving behind family, friends, and home. Few will be willing to do this.

Those who will choose to return to Cuba will more likely be the more recent arrivals, who have yet to establish ties to their host country, as well as the disaffected, who never felt quite comfortable here. Some elderly may also wish to return to Cuba to spend their last days in their country of origin. A more likely scenario, however, will be that Cubans in the United States will travel back and forth between the two countries for business as well as for pleasure, in much the same way that their forebears did in pre-Castro Cuba. Many Cuban exiles would like to play a role in Cuba's "reconstruction," helping to create economic enterprises and investing in businesses that will assist their homeland in becoming truly independent. This is what many Americans of Polish, Czech, and other Eastern European descent have done in the decade following the Velvet Revolution and the dismantling of the Warsaw pact countries. And it is a very likely scenario among the Cubans. Whatever ultimately happens, a Cuban presence in the United States is guaranteed, as has been the case for the past two centuries.

NOTES

1. Gerald E. Poyo, *With All and For the Good of All: The Emergence of Popular Nationalism in the Cuban Communities of the United States, 1848–1898* (Durham: Duke University Press, 1989), 1.
2. Poyo, *With All*, 53–55.
3. Louis A, Pérez, *Cuba and the United States: Ties of Singular Intimacy*, 2d ed. (Athens: University of Georgia Press, 1997), 65–73.
4. Poyo writes about José Martí's relationship with the Cuban workers in the United States, and their role in the *Partido Revolucionario Cubano.* See also Louis A. Pérez, *Cuba: Between Reform and Revolution* (New York: Oxford University Press, 1988).
5. Pérez, *Cuba and the United States*, 230.
6. Pérez provides the most detailed examination of U.S.-Cuban cultural exchange in *Cuba and the United States.* See also his *On Becoming Cuban: Identity, Nationality, and Culture* (Chapel Hill: University of North Carolina Press, 1999).
7. Pérez, *Cuba and the United States*, 214–18.
8. Juan Clark, "The Exodus from Revolutionary Cuba (1959–1974): A Sociological Analysis." Ph.D. diss., University of Florida, 1975, 75.
9. Among the first to study the emigrés and the reasons for their disaffection were Richard R. Fagen, Richard A. Brody, and Thomas J. O'Leary, *Cubans In Exile: Disaffection and Revolution* (Stanford: Stanford University Press, 1968).
10. On 20 October 1960, the State Department announced an embargo on most U.S. exports to Cuba (except medicines, medical supplies, and certain foods). A more comprehensive U.S. trade embargo was imposed on 3 February 1962, under the authority of section 620(a) of the Foreign Assistance Act of 1961 (75 Stat. 445). The embargo now prohibited the importation into the United States of all goods of Cuban origin and all goods imported from or through Cuba. In May 1964, the government also issued an order requiring export licenses for sales of food and drugs to the island (previously exempted for humanitarian reasons); gift parcels became the only means of exporting these products without export licenses. See President John F. Kennedy, White House Press Release, 3 February 1962, in Papers of President Kennedy, President's Office Files, Countries (Costa Rica–Cuba), Box 114a, John F. Kennedy Presidential Library.
11. United States Department of Health, Education, and Welfare, *The Cuban Immigration, 1959–1966, and Its Impact on Miami–Dade County, Florida* (Washington, D.C.: Government Printing Office, 10 July 1967); Bryan O. Walsh, "Cubans in Miami," *America* 119 (26 February 1966): 286–89.
12. For a discussion of the role the Diocese of Miami played in assisting the refugees see Michael J. McNally, *Catholicism in South Florida, 1868–1968* (Gainesville: University of Florida Press, 1982).
13. "Operations of the Cuban Refugee Emergency Center," 28 March 1961, Records of Health, Education, and Welfare (HEW), JFK Library.
14. Tracy Voorhees, "Final Report on the Cuban Refugee Problem," *Department of State Bulletin* 44 (13 February 1961): 220.
15. Memorandum from W. L. Mitchell, Commissioner of Social Security, 20 February 1961, Records of HEW, JFK Library.

16. White House Statement, February 3, 1961, Records of HEW, JFK Library; see also "President Outlines Measures for Aiding Cuban Refugees," *Department of State Bulletin* 44 (27 February 1961): 309–310. Bryan O. Walsh, "Cubans in Miami."
17. Department of Health, Education, and Welfare, *Cuba's Children in Exile* (Washington, D.C.: Government Printing Office, 1967).
18. For a more detailed account of Operation Peter Pan, see María Cristina García, *Havana USA: Cuban Exiles and Cuban Americans in South Florida, 1959–1994* (Berkeley: University of California Press, 1996); see also Yvonne M. Conde, *Operation Peter Pan: The Untold Story of 14,000 Cuban Children* (New York: Routledge, 1999); Victor Andres Triay, *Fleeing Castro: Operation Peter Pan and the Cuban Children's Program* (Gainesville: University Press of Florida, 1999).
19. U.S. Cuban Refugee Program, *Training for Independence: A New Approach to the Problems of Dependency* (Washington, D.C.: Social and Rehabilitation Service, 1968).
20. Some of the more interesting studies of the Bay of Pigs invasion are: Trumbull Higgins, *The Perfect Failure: Kennedy, Eisenhower, and the C.I.A. at the Bay of Pigs* (New York: W. W. Norton, 1987); Haynes Johnson, *The Bay of Pigs: The Leaders' Story of Brigade 2506* (New York: Dell Publishing, 1964); Karl Eernest Meyer and Tad Szulc, *The Cuban Invasion: The Chronicle of a Disaster* (New York: Ballantine Books, 1962); Peter Wyden, *Bay of Pigs: The Untold Story* (New York: Simon and Schuster, 1979).
21. A number of new analyses were published on the thirtieth anniversary of the Missile Crisis, which are particularly useful in understanding it: James G. Blight, *On the Brink: Americans and Soviets Reexamine the Cuban Missile Crisis* (New York: Hill and Wang, 1989); Dino A. Brugioni, *Eyeball to Eyeball: The Inside Story of the Cuban Missile Crisis* (New York: Random House, 1991); Robert Smith Thompson, *The Missiles of October: The Declassified Story of John F. Kennedy and the Cuban Missile Crisis* (New York: Simon and Schuster, 1992).
22. Clark, "The Exodus from Revolutionary Cuba," 75.
23. E. M. Martin, "U.S. Outlines Policy Toward Cuban Refugees," *Department of State Bulletin* 48 (24 June 1963): 984.
24. "Why Castro Exports Cubans," *New York Times Magazine* (7 November 1965): 30.
25. Clark, "The Exodus from Revolutionary Cuba," 75.
26. Silvia Pedraza Bailey, "Cuba's Exiles: Portrait of a Refugee Migration," *International Migration Review* 19 (spring 1985): 18.
27. Seymour Liebman, "Cuban Jewish Community in South Florida," in *American Jewish Yearbook* (New York: American Jewish Committee, 1969), 283; Abraham J. Dubelman, "Cuba," in *American Jewish Yearbook* (New York: American Jewish Committee, 1962), 482; Benigno E. Aguirre, "The Differential Migration of the Cuban Social Races," *Latin American Research Review* 11 (1976): 103–24.
28. República de Cuba, *Censo de Población, Viviendas, y Electoral, Informe General, 1953* (n.p.), 48–49; Aguirre, "The Differential Migration," 103–24. Also see Lourdes Casal and Yolanda Prieto, "Black Cubans in the United States: Basic Demographic Information," in *Female Immigrants to the United States: Caribbean, Latin American, and African Experiences*, ed. Delores M. Mortimer and Roy S. Bryce-Laporte, *RIIES Occasional Papers No. 2* (Washington, D.C.: Research Institute on Immigration and Ethnic Studies, Smithsonian Institution, 1981).

29. Aguirre, "The Differential Migration," 103–24.
30. Heriberto Dixon, "Who Ever Heard of a Black Cuban?" *Afro-Hispanic Review* 1 (September 1982): 10–12; Heriberto Dixon, "The Cuban American Counterpoint: Black Cubans in the United States," *Dialectical Anthropology* 13 (1988): 227–39.
31. Clark, "The Exodus from Revolutionary Cuba," 128–30.
32. Rafael J. Prohías and Lourdes Casal, *The Cuban Minority in the U.S.: Preliminary Report on Need Identification and Program Evaluation: Final Report for Fiscal Year 1973*, 2d ed. (Washington, D.C.: Cuban National Planning Council, 1974).
33. Domestic Policy Staff, Civil Rights and Justice, *Briefing Paper: Procedures for Admitting Refugees, Parolees, and Asylees: Miami Regional Hearing, December 4, 1979*, in "Refugees—Select Commission Papers" file, Box 25, staff offices, Papers of Franklin E. White, Carter Presidential Library.
34. Robert L. Bowen, ed., *A Report of the Cuban-Haitian Task Force*, draft (1 November 1980), 78, in box 8, Records of the Cuban-Haitian Task Force, Carter Presidential Library.
35. U.S. Department of State, "Exodus from Cuba," *Department of State Bulletin* 80 (July 1980): 80.
36. See, for example, "Editorial: Hay que mostrale al imperialismo yanqui quee es Cuba," *Granma* 27 (April 1980).
37. "The Flight from Havana," *Newsweek*, 28 April 1980, 38; "Start of a Mass Exodus," *Time*, 28 April 1980, 32.
38. Memo from William J. Beckham to Jimmy Carter, May 30, 1980, in File 6/3/80 [2], Box 189, Staff Offices: Office of the Staff Secretary, Carter Library. See also "Cuban Refugees," *Department of State Bulletin* 80 (August 1980): 74.
39. Bowen, ed., *A Report of the Cuban-Haitian Task Force*, 4.
40. Néstor Almendros and Orlando Jiménez-Leal, *Conducta Impropia* (Madrid: Editorial Playor, 1984);
41. Bowen, ed., *A Report of the Cuban-Haitian Task Force*, 55–58.
42. Mark Neilsen, "Bad Press Creating Difficulties in Resettling Cuban Refugees," *National Catholic Reporter* 16 (15 August 1980): 22–23.
43. "Castro's Crime Bomb," *U.S. News and World Report*, 16 January 1984, 27–30.
44. U.S. Department of State, "Exodus from Cuba," 80.
45. Cuban-Haitian Task Force, "Enrants vs. Refugees," Records of the Cuban-Haitian Task Force, Box 21, Carter Presidential Library.
46. Bowen, ed., *A Report of the Cuban-Haitian Task* Force, 70; Thomas D. Boswell, Manuel Rivero, and Guarioné M. Díaz, eds., *Bibliography for the Mariel-Cuban Diaspora, Paper No. 7* (Gainesville: Center for Latin American Studies, the University of Florida, 1988), 1–22; Heriberto Dixon has written that the percentage of blacks and mulattos may have been as high as 40 percent because of the difficulties of classifying mulattos. "Undoubtedly," he writes, "many of the lighter mulattoes will attempt to 'pass' for white in the United States." See "The Cuban-American Counterpoint," 227–39; and Dixon's "Who Ever Heard of a Black Cuban?" 49–51.
47. See Robert L. Bach, Jennifer B. Bach, and Timothy Triplett, "The Flotilla 'Entrants': Latest and Most Controversial," *Cuban Studies/Estudios Cubanos* 12 (July 1982): 29–48; Gastón A. Fernández, "The Flotilla Entrants: Are they Different?" *Cuban Studies/Estudios Cubanos* 11/12 (July 1981–January 1982): 49–54; Alejandro Portes,

Juan M. Clark, and Robert D. Manning, "After Mariel: A Survey of the Resettlement Experiences of 1980 Cuban Refugees in Miami," *Cuban Studies/Estudios Cubanos* 15 (summer 1985): 37–59; Bowen, ed., *A Report of the Cuban-Haitian Task Force*, 70–71.

48. Frederic Tasker, "Anti-Bilingualism Approved in Dade County," *Miami Herald*, 5 November 1980.
49. Roberto Fabricio, "Mariel Boatlift Still Raising Waves of Fear," *Miami Herald*, 28 May 1983. For federal recommendations, see Cuban-Haitian Task Force, "Mariel II," Records of the Cuban-Haitian Task Force, Box 12, Carter Presidential Library.
50. Derek Reveron, "Se disipó el temor de que refugiados fueran carga," *El Nuevo Herald*, 22 April 1990.
51. Helga Silva, *The Children of Mariel: Cuban Refugee Children in South Florida Schools* (Washington, D.C.: Cuban American National Foundation, 1985); Guillermo Martínez, "The Children of Mariel Turn School Into Success Story," *Miami Herald*, 15 January 1987.
52. "Cuba's Decline Continues," *The American Enterprise* 10 (January/February 1999): 89.
53. Ana E. Santiago, "Bajo revisión plan de emergencia ante ortro Mariel," *El Nuevo Herald*, 25 May 1991. Lizette Alvarez, "Exodo Cubano: De asunto político a económico," *El Nuevo Herald*, 21 April 1991.
54. "Father Goes to Cuba, Hoping to Get Son Back," *The St. Petersburg Times*, 19 December 2000.
55. Alejandro Portes, "From South of the Border: Hispanic Minorities in the United States," in *Immigration Reconsidered: History, Sociology, and Politics*, ed. Virginia Yans-McLaughlin (New York: Oxford University Press, 1990), 168; Alejandro Portes, "The Cuban American Community Today: A Brief Portrait," Memorandum, Cuban Committee for Democracy, n.d.
56. Portes, "From South of the Border," 168; Portes, "The Cuban American Community Today." See also Alejandro Portes and Robert L. Bach, "Immigrant Earnings: Cuban and Mexican Immigrants in the United States," *International Migration Review* 14 (fall 1980): 315–40.
57. Carlos Arboleya, *The Cuban Community, 1980: Coming of Age as History Repeats Itself* (Miami: Self-published, 1980); "Cuban and Haitian Arrivals: Crisis and Response," 30 June 1980, White House Central File, Subject File: National Security-Defense, file ND16/CO 38 1/20/77–1/20/81, Box ND-42, Carter Presidential Library, 6.
58. Carlos Arboleya, *El impacto cubano en la Florida* (Miami: Self-published, 1985). See also "Dade Latin Businesses Top U.S.," *Miami Herald*, 23 October 1986.
59. Portes, "The Cuban American Community Today," 1.
60. Lisandro Pérez, "Immigrant Economic Adjustment and Family Organization: The Cuban Success Story Re-Examined," *International Migration Review* 20 (spring 1986): 4–20.
61. Myra Marx Ferree, "Employment Without Liberation: Cuban Women in the U.S." *Social Science Quarterly* 60 (January 1979): 35–50. See also Dorita Roca Mariña, "A Theoretical Discussion of What Changes and What Stays the Same in Cuban Immigrant Families," in *Cuban Americans: Acculturation, Adjustment, and the Family*, ed. José Szapocznik and María Cristina Herrera (Washington, D.C.: The National

Coalition of Hispanic Mental Health and Human Services Organization, 1978); María Cristina García, "Adapting to Exile: Cuban Women in the United States, 1959–1973," *Latino Studies Journal* 2 (spring 1991): 17–33.

62. Hector Cantu, "Building a Bridge to Success," *Hispanic Business* 15 (September 1993): 16.
63. Alejandro Portes and Leif Jensen, "The Enclave and the Entrants: Patterns of Ethnic Enterprise in Miami Before and After Mariel," *American Sociological Review* 54 (December 1989): 929–49.
64. See Arboleya, *The Cuban Community, 1980.*
65. Portes, "From South of the Border," 168; U.S. Census Bureau, "Statistical Brief," September 1985.
66. Pérez, "Immigrant Economic Adjustment and Family Organization." See also Lisandro Pérez, "The Cuban Population of the United States: The Results of the 1980 U.S. Census of Population," *Cuban Studies/Estudios Cubanos* 15 (summer 1985): 1–18; Alejandro Portes, "Dilemmas of a Golden Exile: Integration of Cuban Refugee Families in Milwaukee," *American Sociological Review* 34 (August 1969): 505–18; Alejandro Portes, "¿Quienes Somos? ¿Que Pensamos? Los Cubanos en Estados Unidos en la Década de los Noventas," *Cuban Affairs/Asuntos Cubanos* 1 (spring 1994): 5.
67. Margaret W. Linn, Kathleen I. Hunter, and Priscilla R. Perry, "Differences by Sex and Ethnicity in the Psychosocial Adjustment of the Elderly, " *Journal of Health and Social Behavior* 20 (September 1979): 273–81; Margaret W. Linn, Kathleen I. Hunter, and Bernard Linn, "Self-Assessed Health, Impairment, and Disability in Anglo, Black, and Cuban Elderly, " *Medical Care* 18 (1980): 282–88.
68. Alfonso Chardy, "'Invisible Exiles': Black Cubans Don't Find Their Niche in Miami," *Houston Chronicle*, 12 September 1993.
69. These figures were provided by the Metro-Dade County Planning Department, Research Division. According to the 1990 census, the total Latino population in Dade County was 953,407. Cubans comprised 59 percent of this number. See also Thomas D. Boswell and James R. Curtis, *The Cuban-American Experience* (Totowa: Rowman and Allanheld, 1983).
70. Boswell and Curtis, *The Cuban-American Experience*, 78–79
71. Portes, "From South of the Border," 168; U.S. Bureau of the Census, "The Nation's Hispanic Population—1994," Statistical Brief (Washington, D.C.: Bureau of the Census, 1994), 1.
72. Portes, "From South of the Border," 178.
73. Kevin A. Hill and Dario Moreno, "Second-Generation Cubans," *Hispanic Journal of Behavioral Sciences* 18 (May 1996): 177.
74. Hill and Moreno, "Second-Generation Cubans," 178.
75. Ivan Román, "The Cuban Vote," *Hispanic* 9 (August 1996): 24.
76. Hill and Moreno, "Second-Generation Cubans," 178; Isabel Castellanos, "The Use of English and Spanish Among Miami's Cubans," *Cuban Studies/Estudios Cubanos* 20 (1990): 49–63.
77. Martin, "U.S. Outlines Policy," 983–90; Arthur M. Schlesinger Jr., "Major Cuban Exile Organizations" [1962], in file "Cuba, 11/1/62–12/29/62," Papers of Arthur M. Schlesinger Jr., White House Files, Box WH-5, JFK Library; Al Burt, "Cubans Split, Action Could Unite Them," *Miami Herald*, 11 March 1963.

78. Genie N.L. Stowers, "Political Participation, Ethnicity, and Class Status: The Case of Cubans in Miami," *Ethnic Groups* 8 (1990): 76–77; Eleanor Meyer Rogg and Rosemary Santana Cooney, *Adaptation and Adjustment of Cubans: West New York, New Jersey*, Monograph no. 5 (New York: Hispanic Research Center, Fordham University, 1980), 18; Boswell and Curtis, *The Cuban-American Experience*, 174.
79. Lissette Alvarez, "G.O.P. Tries to Win Hispanic Support Reagan Once Had," *New York Times*, 21 November 1997; Mireya Navarro, "Alliance of G.O.P. and Cuban Americans Shows Rift," *New York Times*, 22 October 1996; Ivan Roman, "The Cuban Vote," *Hispanic* (August 1996): 24.
80. María de los Angeles Torres, "Autumn of the Cuban Patriarchs," *The Nation* 1 December 1997, 24–26.

glorification of 1st wave, Rich left to keep all of their shit because Castro was working for the poor.

FOUR

CENTRAL AMERICAN IMMIGRANTS: DIVERSE POPULATIONS, CHANGING COMMUNITIES

NORMA STOLTZ CHINCHILLA AND NORA HAMILTON

INTRODUCTION

Central Americans have been coming to the United States since the nineteenth century, but large-scale immigration is a relatively recent phenomenon. According to the 1990 census, there were 1,323,800 persons of Central American ancestry in the United States, the majority of them foreign born. Over two-thirds of these had come during the 1980s.[1] By 2000, the number of those who claimed Central American ancestry was 1,686,973.[2]

Central American immigration is distinctive for two reasons. The first is its diversity; Central Americans in the United States come from seven different countries. In 1990, over half of those of Central American ancestry were Salvadorans, followed by Guatemalans, Nicaraguans, and Hondurans and smaller numbers of Costa Ricans, Panamanians, and Belizans. In 2000, Salvadorans continued to be the largest group, but the numbers of Guatemalans and Hondurans had increased substantially.

Aside from the distinctions based on countries of origin, there are differences based on socioeconomic status—which ranges from rural and urban workers to middle-class professionals and landowning elites—and ethnicity. Mestizos constitute the major ethnic group, but there are substantial numbers from indigenous groups in the migrant stream, primarily Maya, Afro-Caribbean populations from Belize and the Caribbean coast of other Central American countries, and Garifuna, a group that traces its ancestry to both indigenous and African roots.

The second defining characteristic of Central American immigration is the way it has been shaped by the experience of the cohort arriving in the 1980s. This cohort was significant not only due to its size, but also due to its political character. Many, if not most, of the immigrants coming during this decade, particularly those from El Salvador, Guatemala, and Nicaragua, came escaping war and violence in their respective countries, and some were fleeing persecution. Many considered themselves, and were considered by others, to be refugees, even if not accepted as such by the U.S. government. This cohort included a small but highly influential core of political activists who played a significant role in U.S.-solidarity, anti-intervention, and immigrant-rights movements in the 1980s and have subsequently been involved in organizing around political, social, and community issues. Because the political character of this cohort tends to obscure the diversity of the Central American experience, it is important to keep both characteristics in perspective.

The majority of Central American immigrants have settled in urban areas, with major concentrations in Los Angeles, Houston, Miami, New York, San Francisco, and Washington. In 1990, Salvadorans constituted the largest number of Central Americans in Los Angeles, Houston, Dallas, San Francisco, New York, Anaheim, and Washington, D.C. Nicaraguans were the dominant Central American group in Miami, and Guatemalans and Hondurans were the most significant groups in Chicago and New Orleans, respectively, although their numbers are larger in Los Angeles and New York.

By the time of the 2000 census, the Central American population had again increased, reflecting the continuing immigration during the 1990s, and was more dispersed. The availability of jobs has drawn Central Americans from earlier settlement areas as well as some new immigrants to cities such as Las Vegas and states such as Iowa, North Carolina, and Arkansas. A particularly interesting case is that of the Q'anjob'al Maya in Indiantown, Florida, who initially came to the United States fleeing the scorched-earth policy of the Guatemalan government in the early 1980s, which destroyed numerous indigenous settlements in the Guatemalan highlands. A small nucleus found jobs in Indiantown in Southern Florida and formed the basis of a Q'anjob'al community that expanded throughout the state of Florida and into other parts of the southeast (Burns 2000).

ORIGINS AND CHARACTERISTICS

Although Central America consists of seven different countries, analyses of Central America as a region have tended to focus on the five countries that emerged from the United Provinces of Central America in the postcolonial period. These five nations, Guatemala, El Salvador, Honduras, Nicaragua, and Costa Rica, share certain common historical experiences and were also joined in various (ultimately unsuccessful) attempts to reunify. In contrast, Panama was part of Colombia for much of its nineteenth-century history. Subsequently, its trajectory has been shaped by its special relationship with the United States and the role of the Panama Canal. Prior to 1981, Belize was British colony with a predominantly Afro-Caribbean population, but increasing number of Guatemalans, including Maya, moved into Belize in the 1980s and 1990s.

With the exceptions of Guatemala and Belize, is the population of most of Central America is mestizo, a mixed race people that was the product of European colonization and the mingling of European and indigenous populations. However, indigenous Maya, or people of Mayan ancestry, constitute approximately half of the Guatemalan population and represent some twenty-eight distinct language groups. Maya also live in Belize, Honduras, and southern Mexico. Central America also includes other indigenous groups, such as the Cuna and Guarani in Panama and the Miskitu in Nicaragua, as well as Afro-Caribbean populations in Belize and along the Caribbean coast of the larger countries. The Garifuna have been a source of significant migration to the United States. They are descendants of two distinct groups: indigenous populations from South America, who migrated to the Caribbean islands of St. Vincent and Dominica, and Africans, who escaped and managed to flee to these islands when the ships bringing them to slavery in the Americas were shipwrecked. This population settled along the Caribbean coast of Central America beginning in the late eighteenth century.

MIGRATION PATTERNS

HISTORICAL TRAJECTORIES

The Central American countries have a long history of internal and intraregional migration that can be traced to the patterns of land concentration and forced-labor recruitment that evolved during the colonial period.[3] At the time of the Spanish conquest in the early sixteenth century, much of the region was inhabited by indigenous groups, particularly Maya, who were concentrated in Guatemala, Southern Mexico, parts of El Salvador, and northern Honduras. Another significant group was the Pipil in El Salvador. In contrast, the southern areas of Central America were more sparsely populated, and conquest, diseases brought by the Spaniards, and enslavement resulted in the eradication of many of the smaller indigenous groups.

Over the next 300 years the Spanish colonists and their descendants established commercial estates for the cultivation of export products, taking over the land of indigenous communities, a process that was particularly advanced in the area that is now El Salvador, where many of those expelled from these communities migrated to other parts of the country. Permanent and seasonal labor was secured through forced recruitment of indigenous workers. Ranches and small farms were established in more sparsely populated areas.

Following independence in the early nineteenth century, the process of land concentration and labor recruitment intensified as several Central American economies were drawn into coffee production and export. The implications for migration varied among the different countries. In Costa Rica, which had abundant land and a relatively small population, coffee production opened up new frontier regions, which resulted in the migration of workers from the province of Cartago, where the population was centered, to coffee regions in the western part of the country. In El Salvador, the expansion of coffee production involved the forced takeover of land cultivated by indigenous communities and small farmers in the western part of the country, again resulting in the expulsion of these populations to other areas of the country where they engaged in subsistence production. In some cases, displaced people also migrated on a seasonal basis for work on the coffee harvest. In Guatemala, the government and growers instituted forms of coerced labor, such as debt peonage, to recruit seasonal labor for the harvest, reinforcing patterns of cyclical migration between the indigenous communities in the highlands and the areas of export production.

These patterns of regional migration were reinforced by the subsequent expansion of coffee production and export to other countries and the introduction of other export products: the extension of coffee production into Nicaragua; the introduction of banana production and export, particularly in the Caribbean coastal areas, as well as its takeover by U.S. companies in the early twentieth century; and the introduction of cotton and livestock in the mid-twentieth century. The takeover of land in the populous regions, as in the case of coffee in El Salvador, led to net emigration from these regions, often followed by seasonal migration for work on harvests. In contrast, areas of export production in sparsely populated parts of Honduras attracted migrants from other parts of the country, both to work on the plantations or estates and to establish small and medium holdings on available land.

Seasonal and in some cases permanent migration also extended across borders, particularly in the case of El Salvador, where land concentration had pushed small producers to marginal areas barely capable of sustaining subsistence production. Salvadorans migrated seasonally to cotton-growing areas in Guatemala and Nicaragua or to the banana plantations in Honduras. Indigenous Guatemalans in the northern highlands migrated to Chiapas in Southern Mexico to harvest coffee; some settled there, mingling with the Mayan population and passing as Mexicans.

As suggested above, legal and extralegal coercion often accompanied the process of land concentration and labor recruitment. The introduction and expansion of coffee export in the nineteenth century was made possible by the emergence of a strong state that could establish the necessary infrastructure, grant (and enforce, if necessary) land concessions, obtain foreign loans, and enforce laws safeguarding labor contracts and private property (often at the expense of communal forms of land tenure). In Guatemala, and later in Nicaragua, vagrancy laws were introduced in order to secure a labor force for the coffee harvest. In El Salvador, strong resistance by communal and small farmers to the takeover of their land for coffee production led to the formation of a rural police force to repress revolts.

When urban and rural workers began to organize and protest against inadequate wages or poor working conditions, they were often met by the repressive apparatus of the state, notably in Guatemala, El Salvador, and Nicaragua. The most extreme example (prior to the 1970s) was the *matanza* of 1932 in El Salvador, the systematic slaughter of 10,000 to 30,000 peasants in response to an uprising by rural workers protesting layoffs and wage cutbacks in the western coffee region during a depression. Those who escaped fled to eastern El Salvador or across the border to Honduras.

With the growth of industry, rural to urban migration became increasingly important and outpaced migration between rural areas by the 1950s, in the case of El Salvador, and somewhat later in other Central American countries. In Central America (as in much of Latin America), women were important in rural to urban migration. Particularly in the case of El Salvador, the high level of internal migration has been a factor in the separation and disintegration of families and in the number of households headed by women (approximately 40 percent of the households in San Salvador), which in turn explains the frequent migration of women to find work.

CENTRAL AMERICAN IMMIGRATION TO THE UNITED STATES

Central American migration to the United States began to grow as a result of increased U.S. economic and strategic involvement in the region in the late nineteenth and early twentieth centuries. This included the establishment and growth of trade relations between Central America and the United States; the investment of U.S. corporations in the production and export of bananas along the Caribbean coast, often accompanied by substantial intervention in the political affairs of the respective countries; the building of the Panama

Canal during the first decade of the century; and the occupation of Nicaragua by the U.S. Marines during much of the period between 1912 and 1933.

The interaction of Salvadoran coffee growers and U.S. corporate interests in coffee processing and trade resulted in the migration of upper-class Salvadorans to San Francisco, a major center for the processing of Central American coffee, in the early part of the twentieth century. Some migrants became permanent settlers; San Francisco also became a major vacation spot for wealthy Salvadorans. Central Americans, especially Salvadorans and Nicaraguans who had worked on the Panama Canal and subsequently on the shipping lines, also made their way to San Francisco. During World War II, Central Americans were also recruited to work in shipyards in San Francisco, and many remained in the city (Córdova 1996).

Similarly, with the expansion of commerce between Honduras and U.S. ports as a result of the banana trade, Hondurans began to emigrate to the United States.[4] During World War II, the United Fruit Company hired many Hondurans for its merchant marine, enabling them as well as other Hondurans in the company to have access to the United States through New Orleans, New York, New Jersey, and Boston. The Garifuna migration became important in the postwar period; it is currently estimated that as much as one-quarter of the total Garifuna population is in the United States, including Garifuna from Belize and other Central American countries as well as Honduras.

For the most part, the majority of the Central Americans who came to the United States during the early years of the twentieth century were middle- or upper-class individuals who came initially to visit or had married U.S. citizens or were immigrants drawn to educational and work opportunities in the United States. Although the number of immigrants increased substantially following a decline during the Great Depression, the official number of Central Americans in the United States remained small prior to the second half of the century.

Central American immigration began to accelerate in the 1960s, a period when the Central American countries were trying to attract foreign, especially U.S., investment in industry, partly on the basis of a Central American common market that would eventually eliminate tariffs and other trade barriers between the countries of the region and thus expand the market for industrial products. Investment from the United States, and subsequently other countries, especially Japan, did increase during this period. Some Central Americans who had worked in U.S.-owned factories in Central America eventually migrated to the United States to seek more remunerative work. Prior to 1980, women immigrants, drawn to jobs as domestics or in other types of services, outnumbered the men. In some cases they had worked for U.S. families who had held foreign-service posts or corporate jobs in Central America, and the immigrants returned with them to the United States.[5]

During the 1960s, 101,330 Central Americans were legally admitted to the United States, and in the 1970s the number increased to 174,640. In 1970, the largest group of Central Americans in the United States were the Panamanians. By this time, however, a growing number of Central Americans, especially Salvadorans and Guatemalans, were entering illegally, sometimes passing themselves off as Mexicans. By 1980, the composition of the Central American immigrant population had shifted: Salvadorans had become the majority, followed by Guatemalans, and workers began to outnumber middle-class immigrants.

The trajectories of different immigrant groups often resulted from the contacts established by a "pioneer" in the United States, an immigrant from a particular town or village who, after obtaining a job in the United States, was able to secure work for family members and friends in the same location and often at the same workplace. Juan Xuc, a young Maya from San Pedro, Totonicapán, in Guatemala, came to Houston in 1978, where he found a job at a supermarket. Subsequently he was able to obtain jobs for relatives and friends from San Pedro, and eventually neighboring villages, in the same supermarket chain. In a number of cases, wives and sisters joined them to work as domestics for Houston families (Hagan 1994). Q'anjob'al from San Miguel Acatán and neighboring towns in Huehuetenango, Guatemala, who for decades had migrated to Chiapas for seasonal work, became aware of opportunities for work in California's San Joaquin valley. From there, some migrated to Los Angeles, where they found jobs for themselves and subsequent arrivals from the region in the city's garment industry (Loucky 2000).

Similar cases of network formation and chain migration following the trajectory of a "pioneer" or "godfather" occurred with Salvadoran immigrants. Migrants from Concepción de Oriente in the eastern department of La Unión came to Westbury, Long Island, following a trajectory established by Don Miguel Yanes, the head of sanitation and public health in his town, who had migrated to Long Island in 1971 at the instigation of a friend who had relatives there. Don Miguel obtained a job at a plastics factory and later married a Puerto Rican woman. On a visit to Concepción de Oriente at the end of the 1970s, he informed family and friends of job opportunities in Westbury, and soon emigrants from Concepción began to arrive in the town, where they numbered in the hundreds by the mid-1990s (Mahler 1995: 53). As these cases suggest, networks may eventually connect sending countries in Central America with specific neighborhoods or towns in the United States.

MIGRATION DURING THE 1980S

The 1970s was a period of increasing political activism and turmoil in Central America. In Nicaragua, the forty-two-year-old Somoza regime was overthrown in 1979 as a result of the Sandinista revolution and a massive uprising of the Nicaraguan population. In El Salvador and Guatemala, workers, peasants, students, and other groups, including indigenous groups in Guatemala, formed organizations and expanded and accelerated their activities in opposition to recalcitrant military regimes, which responded by increasing the levels of repression and counterinsurgency campaigns. Death squads as well as security forces targeted opposition party leaders, peasant and labor activists, student organizers, and priests and catechists,[6] who were often tortured and killed. Support grew for guerrilla organizations in both countries, which grouped into revolutionary armies in the early 1980s: the FMLN (Farabundo Martí Front for National Liberation) in El Salvador, and the URNG (Guatemalan National Revolutionary Unity). Following the 1980 election of Ronald Reagan as U.S. president, U.S. support for the Salvadoran government forces and anti-Sandinista counterrevolutionaries, or contras, in Nicaragua increased. Honduras was drawn into the conflicts when Nicaraguan contras massed at the Honduran border for incursions into Nicaragua, sometimes assisted by the Honduran military. Honduras also became a major base for U.S. support for both the contra war in Nicaragua and the government forces in El Salvador.

As violence in El Salvador and Guatemala increased, populations from affected communities fled to other parts of their respective countries and across borders to other Central American nations and to Mexico. Refugee communities were established in several countries, particularly of Salvadorans in Honduras and of indigenous Guatemalans in Mexico. Other Salvadorans and Guatemalans made their way to other parts of Mexico or the United States, in some cases taking advantage of existing trajectories and networks, as indicated above. The vast majority of these were undocumented and, because crossing the Mexico-U.S. border became increasingly difficult and dangerous during the 1980s, many of them relied on smugglers, or coyotes, who charged up to $2,000 to escort them through Central America and Mexico into the United States. A few were assisted by the U.S.-based Sanctuary movement, which brought Central Americans across the border and to safehouses in the United States through an "underground railroad."

During the 1980s, increasing numbers of Nicaraguans fled their country as a result of opposition to the Sandinistas or the contra war, and while many of them went to Costa Rica, the number coming to the United States increased throughout the decade. Most went to Miami, where there was already an established Cuban and Cuban American enclave. Analysts have identified three waves of Nicaraguan migrants. The first wave of Nicaraguan immigrants fled the Sandinista revolution and consisted of the Somoza family and their close associates, wealthy business groups, and members of the National Guard who began arriving in the late 1970s. The second wave, in the early 1980s, consisted of middle-class professionals and businesspeople. The final group was composed of poorer workers as well as young men from different classes who emigrated after escaping the draft as the contra war became widespread and U.S. involvement in it increased in the mid-1980s. This movement accelerated in the last years of the decade (Portes and Stepick 1993). The city of Miami also drew wealthy Central Americans from other countries, including Salvadoran landowning families affected by the agrarian reform of the 1980s, some of whom financed death squads and the new right-wing Arena party in El Salvador from their temporary exile in Miami. The number of Honduran immigrants also increased, reflecting in part the destabilization of that country as a center of the U.S.-backed counterinsurgency effort. Political instability also resulted in economic deterioration, particularly in the affected countries, but also in Central America as a whole, and this was an added factor in the large numbers leaving the region. The debt crisis and deep recession experienced by Mexico during the 1980s prevented many immigrants from finding work there, which may have been an added factor in migration to the United States.

As indicated above, Central Americans coming to the United States in the 1980s differed from previous Central American immigration flows in several respects. First, the number arriving in the 1980s was significantly higher than all previous flows. According to census figures, people of Central American ancestry in the United States increased from 331,219 in 1980 to 1,323,380 in 1990. Of these, 1,046,099 were immigrants, and 730,213—that is, 55 percent of the total Central American–origin population and 70 percent of the foreign-born—had come during the 1980s. Second, although Central American immigration flows continued to include middle-class groups, a much larger percentage of those coming in the 1980s were low-income groups from both rural and urban areas. Third, although women migrants had outnumbered men in previous decades, men outnumbered women among the Central Americans who came in the 1980s, reflecting, in part, the fact that men were more likely to be targeted as a result of activism in their respective countries or to face recruitment into government or guerrilla armies.

There were also significant differences within the Central American populations by 1990. While 28 percent of the Panamanian-ancestry population and 29 percent of those of Costa Rican origin had come to the United States during the 1980s, over half of those of Guatemalan and Honduran origin, and 60 percent of Nicaraguan and Salvadoran groups, immigrated in the 1980s. While immigration from Costa Rica and Panama increased during the decade, it was at rates suggesting a continuity with previous patterns of a gradual increase over time. In contrast, immigration from El Salvador, Guatemala, Honduras, and Nicaragua reflected an abrupt break with previous patterns, as one would anticipate given the upheavals in those countries.

Finally, many immigrants from El Salvador, Guatemala, and Nicaragua, and to some extent Honduras, differed from other immigrant groups in that they emigrated for political reasons—or a combination of political and economic reasons—rather than strictly economic or personal considerations. At the same time, they differed from other refugee groups, such as Cubans and Vietnamese, in that they were not accepted as refugees and enjoyed none of the benefits provided for refugees in U.S. policy.[7] Since many of them were undocumented, fear of apprehension by the INS was magnified by fear of being returned to countries where conditions were dangerous, particularly for those who had been targeted by military or security forces or by death squads.

MIGRATION IN THE 1990S

Many of the Central Americans coming in the 1980s assumed that their stay would be temporary and that they would return when conditions improved in their countries of origin. A study by the authors in 1995 of 300 Salvadorans and Guatemalans in Los Angeles found that at the time of arrival, nearly half had planned on a temporary stay and less than 14 percent had planned to remain permanently. By the mid-1990s, however, many had become settled, and 50 percent now had definite plans to remain in the United States. Although some Nicaraguans returned after the electoral defeat of the Sandinistas in 1990, the majority of Nicaraguans remained, and the peace agreements in the early to mid-1990s in El Salvador and Guatemala did not result in substantial return migration by Salvadorans and Guatemalans (Hamilton and Chinchilla 2001).

Indeed, Central Americans continued to migrate to the United States in the 1990s for a number of reasons. First, the end of hostilities did not result in conditions of security. In Nicaragua, former contras as well as previous members of the Sandinista army continued to fight, or they operated as bandits in rural areas of the country. In El Salvador and Guatemala, death squads and vigilante groups also persisted. In all three countries, crime became an alternative for some demobilized troops from both sides of the respective conflicts who lacked economic opportunity but had easy access to guns. El Salvador had the highest per capita crime rate in the western hemisphere.

Undoubtedly contributing to crime and insecurity, as well as continued migration, was the precarious economic situation of many Central Americans. It has been estimated that at least half of all Central American households are characterized by poverty or extreme poverty, and opportunities for well-paying jobs are limited. In Nicaragua, unemployment and underemployment are estimated at 60 percent, a factor in continued high levels of migration into Costa Rica and the United States. In the latter part of the decade, natural disasters aggravated the situation. In November 1998, Hurricane Mitch resulted in an estimated fifteen thousand deaths, while millions more lost homes or jobs, particularly in Honduras and Nicaragua. In January and February 2001, two massive earthquakes devastated several towns in El Salvador, leaving over one thousand people dead and over one million homeless.

Finally, by the early 1990s migrant networks linking Central Americans in the United States to their communities and neighborhoods of origin were well established. This was particularly true of El Salvador, where in 1999 approximately 20 percent of all households were receiving remittances from Salvadoran emigrants, most of them in the United States. In some regions, conditions were similar to that of many Mexican towns where young men and women joined the migration circuit. As a result, Salvadorans and Guatemalans continued to come in record numbers throughout the 1990s, and they have been joined by increasing numbers of Hondurans and Nicaraguans.

SETTLEMENT AND EMPLOYMENT

Literature on migration has attributed the experience and degree of success of immigrants in the United States to several factors: the characteristics of the immigrants themselves (such as level of education and skills), conditions of migration (e.g., economically motivated vs. refugee, documented or nondocumented), the context of reception (including U.S. immigration and refugee policies, receptivity by native populations, and economic conditions and the structure of the labor market in the host country), and what is sometimes referred to as social capital (e.g., the extent and nature of networks among immigrant and ethnic groups and between immigrants and other groups) (Portes and Rumbaut, 2001). Among Central American immigrants, we can see all of these factors at work, with considerable variation based on the timing of migration and nationality.

Costa Rican and Panamanian immigrants differ from other Central American groups in that they are predominantly middle class, and their numbers have increased only gradually. Prior to the 1970s this was true of other Central American groups as well. The 1970s and particularly the 1980s resulted in substantial change in the socioeconomic characteristics of Central American immigrants as well as the conditions of migration and their experience in the United States. During the 1970s, an increasing proportion of immigrants were of working-class origins and were economically motivated. Many were undocumented, although legal status was less significant than it became in the 1980s and 1990s. Most of them were from El Salvador and Guatemala, and the number from these countries increased substantially in the 1980s. In contrast to earlier cohorts, the new arrivals were less educated. Those coming in the 1980s were in some cases politically motivated, and they faced increasingly stringent conditions with respect to legal status.

These distinctions are reflected in socioeconomic characteristics and settlement patterns. In 1990, 36 percent of the Panamanians and 31 percent of the Costa Ricans in the United States had some college education, compared to only 13 percent of the Salvadorans and 16 percent of the Guatemalans. Only 13 percent of Costa Rican and Panamanian families were below the poverty level, while poverty rates of Guatemalans, Salvadorans, Hondurans, and Nicaraguans ranged from 20 to over 25 percent. Finally, Costa Ricans and Panamanians tended to be more dispersed, with only half of their populations in major metropolitan areas, perhaps reflecting their greater integration into mainstream society as well as the larger percentage of professionals or white-collar workers in these national groups (Rodríguez and Hagan 1999).

For the most part, however, Central American immigrants in the United States tended to be concentrated in urban areas, particularly metropolitan areas in the larger cities. According to the 1990 census, approximately one-third of all people of Central American origin or ancestry were in Los Angeles (453,048 of a total of 1,325,830). Other major centers of Central American settlement were Miami (119,534), New York (109,560) and Washington, D.C. (78,527). The largest concentration of Salvadorans was in Los Angeles, and Salvadorans were also the major Central American population in Houston, Dallas, San Francisco, Anaheim, and Washington, D.C. Los Angeles also had (as of 1990) the largest concentration of Guatemalans, Hondurans, and Costa Ricans. The major concentration of Nicaraguans was in Miami, where over 60 percent of the Nicaraguan-ancestry population had settled. Despite the increased dispersion of population of Central American ancestry during the 1990s, the majority continue to reside in Los Angeles and other major cities.

As with other immigrant groups, Central Americans are attracted to specific areas as a result of job opportunities, the presence of an ethnic community (in this case, Latinos or specific national groups), and the existence and expansion of networks. These factors are clearly related, since it is generally through networks that the availability of certain types of jobs become known and (at least in some cases) an ethnic community is formed; the availability of jobs is also a factor in network creation. By the 1980s, many Central American immigrants had a relative, friend, or neighbor who had migrated ahead of them and whom they counted on for temporary housing or job contacts when they came to the United States. In some cases, early arrivals provide job opportunities at their own workplace, as at the above-mentioned supermarket chain in Houston, or can help new arrivals obtain similar jobs, which has been widespread among women in domestic work who were able to inform their relatives and friends about opportunities for domestic work among friends of their employers.

The shift in the U.S. economy beginning in the 1970s, from manufacturing to service industries in areas such as communications and information, finance, and real estate, changed the structure of job opportunities. Middle-level manufacturing jobs declined and opportunities increased in technical and professional services, real estate, and finance, which in turn resulted in an expansion of employment in low-wage services, including janitors, hotel and restaurant workers, and construction workers. The increase in the number of women in the labor force also resulted in an increased demand for domestic and child-care workers at a time when African American women were leaving domestic service for government and other types of white-collar jobs. The changing structure of the American job market opened up opportunities for employment for new immigrants, including Central Americans, who were willing to work at relatively low wages. Most Central Americans arriving in the 1980s found jobs in low-wage factory work, particularly the clothing industry, in cleaning and janitorial services, in restaurants and hotels, in construction work, and as gardeners, domestics, and child-care workers. Some became day laborers or street vendors, replicating or adapting practices from their home countries.

Many of the new Central American and Mexican immigrants were undocumented, and they were often in danger of apprehension and deportation. INS sweeps of immigrant workplaces, such as garment factories or street corners where day laborers waited for work, were frequent during the 1980s. The Immigration Reform and Control Act (IRCA), passed in 1986, called for penalties for employers who hired illegal immigrants. It also provided amnesty for those undocumented immigrants who could demonstrate that they had been in the United States since January 1981. Although some Central Americans arrived prior to that date, many came afterwards, and others who might be eligible had difficulty obtaining the necessary documentation given the irregularity of their work situation. Relatively few employers were penalized under IRCA, but it had the effect of making conditions of work more precarious for undocumented immigrants, and some unscrupulous employers took advantage of these conditions to extract more work at lower wages.

CENTRAL AMERICANS IN LOS ANGELES

Central Americans who came to the United States in the 1980s tended to be attracted to areas where they could find concentrations of their own compatriots or other Latinos, in part due to established migration networks and in part because these areas were characterized by relatively low-cost housing and in some cases proximity to job opportunities. As noted above, the major concentrations of both Salvadorans and Guatemalans, and, increasingly, Hondurans, can be found in Los Angeles, where many settled initially in Westlake (sometimes referred to as Pico Union, which in fact is a neighborhood that encompasses the southeastern part of Westlake), a major immigrant entry area directly west of downtown Los Angeles. Others live west and north of Westlake in Hollywood, Echo Park, and Silverlake; some moved south to towns along the Alameda corridor, previously a manufacturing hub; into South Central, where in some areas Latinos (chiefly Mexicans and Central Americans) displaced African Americans as the major population group; and east into East Los Angeles, where Mexicans and Mexican Americans are the dominant population group. By the end of the 1980s there were substantial Central American settlements in the San Fernando Valley as well as in Anaheim and Santa Ana in Orange County.

Among the Central Americans who came to Westlake in the 1970s and 1980s were several Guatemalan Mayan groups, particularly Q'anjob'al who had fled from their villages in Huehuetenango in the Guatemalan highlands and settled in the area northeast of MacArthur Park, a major neighborhood center. Early arrivals provided assistance to those who came later and helped them find jobs, often in the nearby garment industry in downtown Los Angeles. In some cases, Q'anjob'al from a particular village or community lived in apartments in the same building. Over time, other Mayan groups have settled in the Los Angeles area as well as other parts of the country.

During the 1980s conditions became increasingly depressed in many parts of Westlake. The area already suffered from an acute housing shortage, aggravated by the new immigrant influxes (including Mexicans and other groups as well as Central Americans) and the tendency of many immigrants to share housing, with the result that a single-family unit might be home to as many as two dozen people. Westlake was also known as a high-crime area, with substantial gang activity, and, by the end of the decade, a major center for drugs. Some Central American youths were recruited into gangs, such as the 18th Street gang, or formed their own gangs, such as the Mara Salvatrucha, which quickly gained the reputation of one of the most dangerous in the city.[8]

Despite the depressed conditions in the area, Westlake became a major center of Central American activities and institutions, and the presence of new immigrants became increasingly evident throughout the decade. By the mid-1980s, Salvadoran, Guatemalan, and Nicaraguan restaurants, markets, grocery stores, pupusa stands, and other small businesses appeared in the area, including travel agencies advertising trips to Guatemala City, San José, and other Central American destinations, and express courier services offering secure transit for letters, money, and packages to different locations in the home countries. Many of these businesses were established by Central Americans who had come prior to the 1980s and had saved enough money to invest in ethnically oriented enterprises when the growth of a Central American population created a new market.

Churches in the area began to increase their services in Spanish, and several churches provided space for groups and organizations seeking to meet the needs of new refugees and immigrants. Christian Base Communities were formed in some churches, reflecting a practice that had become widespread in many Central American countries as a result of the changes in the Catholic Church in the 1960s and 1970s, and evangelical churches appeared in the area in response to the growing number of Central American immigrants who were already adherents or were drawn through the successful recruiting efforts of members. New institutions were formed to meet the particular needs of Central American refugees and immigrants.

The difficult conditions in Westlake prompted many Central American families to move out of the area as soon as possible, and, as noted above, the Central American population can now be found throughout the region. By the 1990s, some immigrants were going directly to these newer areas of settlement. However, many new immigrants still go directly to Westlake, which continues to be a major center of Central American institutions, cultural events, and community life.

CENTRAL AMERICANS IN OTHER PARTS OF THE COUNTRY

The conditions confronted by Central Americans in Los Angeles, and their contributions to its cultural life and institutional development, can be found in other cities where Central Americans or particular national groups have settled. In San Francisco, the Mission District became the major center of the Central American population, which already outnumbered Mexicans in the area in the 1950s. By the 1990s, Central Americans constituted 35 percent of the Latino population and the largest Latino group in San Francisco. This situation contrasts with that of cities like Los Angeles, where Mexicans and Mexican Americans have always been and continue to be the major Latino population group, and Miami, where Nicaraguans entered a predominantly Cuban community.

As with other U.S. cities, the decade of the 1980s saw dramatic growth in the number of Central Americans, particularly Salvadorans, coming to San Francisco, and the Mission District experienced a proliferation of restaurants, shops, and services oriented toward Central Americans, as well as the expansion of existing services and institutions to incorporate the needs of the new Central American population. Although the "gentrification" of the district and the increased presence of Asian businesses have resulted in rising rents and new cultural influences, the Mission District continues to be a predominantly Latin American community (Menjívar 2000).

In Washington, D.C., Central Americans settled initially in the inner-city areas of Mount Pleasant and Adams Morgan, previously dominated by African Americans. They were displaced in turn when the area became "gentrified," pushing rental rates up.[9] Many Central Americans moved to suburbs in Maryland and Virginia, although, as in Los Angeles and San Francisco, Adams Morgan and Mount Pleasant continued to be the center of social-service agencies oriented toward Latinos, as well as Latino festivals and celebrations.

Houston, Texas, attracted some Central American as well as Mexican immigrants during the oil-related boom of the 1960s and 1970s. Most of the migrants settled in the predominantly Mexican barrios in the eastern part of the city. The growth of Central American immigration in the 1980s, however, coincided with a recession in the mid-1980s, which had severe repercussions not only in the industries where Mexicans and Mexican Americans had worked, but also in the predominantly middle-class western section of the city. Losing their jobs led many of the young, white, middle-class tenants of the area to leave, which, combined with the influx of new immigrants, prompted the landlords of apartment complexes to restructure some units for lower-income immigrant renters. The new immigrants differed from earlier Mexican and Central American immigrants in that they were more heterogeneous in both national and ethnic composition, incorporating Salvadorans, Guatemalans (including Maya), Hondurans (including Garifuna), Nicaraguans, and Belizans. And in contrast to the earlier concentration of Mexicans and other Latinos in the eastern section of the city, most of the new immigrants settled in the western section, where their neighbors might include Iranians, Nigerians, Indians, and other immigrant groups (Rodríguez 1993).

Although there were Nicaraguans in cities such as Los Angeles and San Francisco prior to the 1980s, and they have continued to come to these cities, most of the Nicaraguans coming to the United States during the decade tended to settle in Miami. As indicated above, the Nicaraguan migrants to Miami included three groups or waves: elite groups associated with the Somoza regime, followed by middle-class professionals and businesspeople, and a third wave of working-class groups beginning in the mid-1980s. They were welcomed initially as "ideological brothers" by the Cuban American community, which provided jobs for them in their own enclaves, helped them to establish their own business and professional careers, and pressured the government on their behalf. Nicaraguans in Miami continue to be divided along class lines, with Nicaraguan professionals and business groups associated with the first two waves of Nicaraguan immigrants concentrated in the upscale neighborhood of Sweetwater, while poorer Nicaraguans, as well as some downwardly mobile middle-class immigrants, live in Little Havana (Portes and Stepick 1993).

New York is the major center of the Honduran immigrant population, and, here as elsewhere, the Garifuna and mestizo populations have distinct settlement patterns. While the mestizo population has tended to settle in neighborhoods with Salvadoran and other Central American groups in Queens, Brooklyn, and Long Island, the Garifuna tend to be concentrated in the South Bronx among a predominantly Dominican and Puerto Rican population. New York has the oldest and largest concentration of Garifuna in the United States, most of them from Honduras. The second largest is in Los Angeles, where for most part they are from Belize, but there are also Garifuna from Honduras and Guatemala. The Belizan population in Los Angeles also includes a large number of Creoles, descendants of the African population. In the United States as a whole, it has been estimated that approximately 75 percent of the Belizan population is Creole, the remaining 25 percent Garifuna, who, as noted above, trace their roots to a particular group of Afro-Amerindians from the Caribbean islands of St. Vincent and Dominica who came to Central America in the eighteenth century (England and Kroghmal 1997).

In the 1990s, many Central Americans already in the United States moved to secondary locations where jobs were available, in some cases joining Mexican immigrants and forming new immigrant concentrations in such places as Morganton, North Carolina, and new migrants sometimes went directly to these locations. Maya who lived and worked in Indiantown, Florida, in the 1980s and 1990s could be found throughout the state and in other areas of the southeast by the late 1990s, drawn by work in construction or low-wage industry such as the poultry business (Burns 2000; Fink and Dunn 2000). Although Central Americans continue to be concentrated in such states as California, Florida, and New York, there are increasing numbers in nontraditional locations in the southeast and West, reflecting a continuing response to job opportunities for low-wage workers in these areas.

RELATIONS WITH OTHER ETHNIC GROUPS

In large metropolitan areas and increasingly in smaller cities and some rural areas, Central Americans often found themselves living in close proximity to other ethnic groups and in some cases working in the same factories or otherwise relating to them on a frequent basis. This has on occasion led to tensions, sometimes resulting from a perceived threat or injustice. In Los Angeles, the predominantly Latino neighborhood in Westlake is adjacent to Koreatown, and Central Americans often shop at stores owned by Koreans or rent from Korean landlords. Some Central American business owners have complained of high rents charged by Koreans, although others, and in some cases the same individuals, have praised their industry and cohesiveness. Tensions also emerged in South Central Los Angeles, as more and more Latinos moved into the area during the 1980s and 1990s, often displacing African Americans as the predominant group in many schools, neighborhoods, and housing developments.

A major cause of tension between Latinos, particularly new immigrants, and African Americans is the perception that newcomers willing to work for low wages are taking their jobs or driving down wages in occupations in which African Americans have traditionally predominated. Although the record is mixed, the perception persists, particularly in areas where African American unemployment is higher than that of other groups, and during periods of recession.[10] In other cases, tensions have developed over neighborhood conditions or community resources. In Washington, D.C., for example, African Americans in the Adams Morgan area have complained of immigrant crowding leading to a deterioration of buildings in the neighborhood, while Latino leaders have complained of African American control of affirmative-action plans and most city social-service agencies.

There are also numerous instances of individual interethnic cooperation and institutional collaboration in multiethnic initiatives. In Houston, for example, nonimmigrants assisted Central Americans and Mexicans in the same apartment complex in obtaining documentation and English-language skills necessary to apply for the amnesty available to pre-1982 immigrants in the Immigration Reform and Control Act of 1986. In Los Angeles, KIWA, the Korean Immigrant Workers' Association, organizes both Latino and Asian workers, including those in Korean firms. In the wake of the 1992 riots in Los Angeles, leaders from the African American, Asian American, and Latino communities have promoted various initiatives designed to reduce tensions and encourage interethnic respect and cooperation, such as the Multiethnic Youth Leadership Collaborative, which provides youths from different ethnic communities with leadership training in interethnic relations. There is some evidence that such initiatives have been successful in increasing understanding and reducing tensions among affected individuals from different ethnic groups, although the general population may be more affected by contextual factors, such as the condition of the economy and the availability of jobs.

The relations between Central Americans and different national-origin populations of the same ethnic groups are often complex. Although Salvadorans and/or Central Americans as a whole sometimes represent the largest Latino group in certain cities, such as San Francisco, in most cases they enter Latino neighborhoods and communities dominated by other groups, such as Mexicans in Los Angeles or Cubans in Miami or, in the case of the Creole populations, African Americans. This often has important advantages for new immigrants, given affinities of language and culture and in some cases the proximity of available jobs. Individuals and institutions from the established groups may assist new arrivals with housing, jobs, and immigration documents, as has occurred in the case of predominantly Mexican American organizations in Los Angeles. Cuban Americans in Miami welcomed new Nicaraguan immigrants, whom they perceived as escaping a Communist regime. Mexican Americans in Los Angeles and other cities have been active in agencies specifically targeting Central American immigrants and during the 1980s were involved in solidarity initiatives challenging U.S. policy in the region. Central American, Mexican, and Mexican American workers and labor organizers often work together in organizing workplaces and fighting for better wages, benefits, and working conditions.

But intraethnic tensions may also develop. In the Los Angeles area, having a claim to the region that predates the coming of the Anglos in the nineteenth century and accustomed to their hegemony within the Latino population, Mexican Americans have sometimes been resentful of the massive influx of Central Americans in the 1980s and 1990s, and Central Americans in turn sometimes resent Mexican American control and accuse Mexican Americans of being "*prepotente*" (arrogant). Tensions have also emerged in Miami, in some cases due to resentment at the very different reception given the Nicaraguans by the United States, in comparison with the Cubans, or the experience or perception of discrimination by Cubans and Cuban Americans.

SOCIOECONOMIC CONDITIONS

While it is important to keep in mind the occupational and financial differences among Central American immigrants, as well as the ability of some to improve their economic situation over time, Central Americans as a whole, particularly recent migrants from El Salvador, Guatemala, Nicaragua, and Honduras, are among the most impoverished groups in the United States. Few of the factors allegedly leading to immigrant success are in their favor. Most Central American immigrants have low levels of education, and many lack basic English-language skills. Although some have obtained temporary or permanent legal status, the majority of new migrants are undocumented and often live with the fear of detention and deportation, which is a further deterrent to their ability to obtain relatively well-paid employment and job security. The context of reception in the United States has become increasingly negative with the heightened security measures following the attacks of September 11, 2001, and the subsequent deterioration of economic conditions. And while networks within the different Central American groups have been important in securing jobs and other resources, few immigrants have access to the kinds of contacts that can facilitate mobility.

ISSUES AND INITIATIVES IN THE 1980S

As the Central American population grew, so did the quantity and variety of its organizational expressions: cultural and religious groups, soccer (and, in the case of Nicaraguans, baseball) clubs, social-service organizations, self-help networks, economic-advancement programs—including entrepreneurial training and labor organizing—and activities on behalf of U.S. and home-country political parties.

POLITICAL ORGANIZING

By far the most visible and politically important Central American–oriented organizing effort in the 1980s occurred within Salvadoran and Guatemalan immigrant populations in the urban areas of their greatest concentration—Los Angeles, San Francisco, Chicago, New York, Washington, D.C., and Houston. Supplemented by the efforts of others throughout rural and urban areas of the United States where the number of Central Americans was relatively small, a core of Salvadoran and Guatemalan activist immigrants, some with grassroots organizing experiences in peasant and labor movements, student and teacher organizations, Christian Base Communities, and human-rights organizations, linked up with more established compatriots, other Latinos, and sympathetic North Americans (including former missionaries, former Peace Corp volunteers, and anthropologists and students who had lived in Central America) to provide protection against deportation, educate North Americans about the causes of the political upheaval that propelled them to migrate, and advocate change in U.S. policies toward Central America.

With support from religious-sector allies, academics, and others, these activists created prototypical solidarity organizations such as Casa Nicaragua, established in several U.S. cities, and CISPES (Committee in Solidarity with the People of El Salvador), which became the major national organization for solidarity with El Salvador. They also formed social-service institutions such as El Rescate in Los Angeles, the Central American Resource Center (CARECEN) in Los Angeles, Washington, and New York, and the Oscar Romero Clinic in Los Angeles. They formed refugee committees connected to the multiservice organizations, such as the Santiago Chirino Amaya Committee, linked to El Rescate, and the Central American Refugee Committee (CRECEN), linked to CARECEN in Los Angeles, and activists participated in multifunctional mixed committees made up of Central Americans and others, such as the Guatemala Information Center in Los Angeles. They incorporated the Christian Base Community model from their home countries in religious institutions and organized support groups for grassroots and political party organizations in those countries.

The organizations, committees, and social-service agencies formed during this period dispensed emergency food, provided free medical care, encouraged co-ops and community gardens, educated their members and helped them to find work, raised funds, organized car caravans which traveled around the country to dramatize the need for a change in U.S. immigration and foreign policies, cooperated with the Sanctuary movement, in which churches, synagogues, and university campuses defied federal law and publicly declared they would provide safe haven for the unofficial refugees. They also participated in multiracial, progressive, anti-interventionist, and pro-peace coalitions with other progressive groups. Individual refugees also "testified" (i.e., gave "testimonios") at local churches, synagogues, and schools about their experiences. The presence and creative grassroots organizing of these Guatemalans and Salvadorans helped catalyze a dynamic national movement opposing official and indirect U.S. support for the regimes of El Salvador and Guatemala and the counterrevolutionary groups in Nicaragua, and the groups challenged U.S. policies that opposed movements advocating greater social and economic equality in Central American countries.

LEGAL ISSUES AND INITIATIVES

As noted above, for most part Central Americans were not accepted as refugees in the United States, and their applications for asylum were routinely denied. Although the U.S. Refugee Act of 1980 established "a well-founded fear of persecution" due to belief or membership in a particular group as grounds for asylum, U.S. asylum policy during much of the 1980s favored those fleeing from Communist or certain Middle Eastern countries, and asylum decisions with respect to Salvadorans and Guatemalans reflected U.S. foreign policy, which supported their governments.

Nicaraguans were only slightly more successful; during the early 1980s, approximately 10 percent of Nicaraguan applicants, compared to 2 to 3 percent of those from El Salvador and Guatemala, received asylum. That they were unable to receive asylum, let alone receive the extensive assistance available to earlier Cuban arrivals, was a source of considerable bitterness to many Nicaraguan immigrants, who had anticipated being welcomed as refugees fleeing a Communist country. As in the case of Guatemalans and Salvadorans, U.S. immigration policy toward Nicaraguans partly reflected foreign policy. In this case, however, the intensification of the U.S.-financed contra war in Nicaragua convinced U.S. officials that Nicaraguans who could oppose the regime were more useful back home than in Miami.[11]

Denied the right to legal-resident or refugee status before entering the United States, or to receive asylum after they had arrived, more and more Salvadorans, Guatemalans, Nicaraguans, and Hondurans attempted to cross the border without papers. If caught by INS officials they faced detention and often pressure to waive their right to have a hearing or to apply for political asylum, or officials made it difficult for them to have access to a low-cost lawyer or to accurate information about their rights, with the goal of returning them as rapidly and cheaply as possible to their countries of origin. The tactics used to accomplish this goal of rapid "voluntary" return often included intimidation and psychological and physical deprivation and constituted violations of due process, U.S. immigration law, and international protocols for civilians fleeing armed conflict (Kahn 1996).

Salvadoran and Guatemalan immigrant activists, followed later by Hondurans and Nicaraguans, worked closely with sympathetic lawyers in the 1980s to remedy inhumane conditions and massive violations of rights in INS detention centers, especially on the Texas and California borders. *Orantes-Hernández v. Smith*—a case originally filed by attorneys associated with the National Center for Immigrants' Rights (a project of the Legal Aid Foundation of Los Angeles) and supported by a coalition of immigrant-related organizations—succeeded in gaining a preliminary injunction against these practices by requiring the INS to inform Salvadoran detainees of their right to receive counsel and to apply for political asylum. The case went to trial in December 1985, however, when attorneys presented evidence that INS agents were not complying with the original injunction. The lengthy judicial process finally concluded in 1987, after 20,000 pages of trial transcripts, 140 witnesses, and 10,000 pages of exhibits. The presiding judge, David V. Kenyon, ordered the INS to "stop using threats and coercion to dissuade Salvadoran refugees from applying for political asylum in this country" (Ramos 1988). He forbade the transportation of deportees to remote locations in the absence of ample notice to interested relatives or lawyers.

By the time of the judge's decision, members of the immigrant community were much better informed about their rights in general, and how to apply for asylum in particular, than they were in the late 1970s and early 1980s when the massive influx began. Although U.S. foreign-policy considerations continued to make the chances of receiving asylum slim for Guatemalans and Salvadorans, the unexpectedly large number of asylum applications generated during the first half of the decade virtually overwhelmed the system, delaying many hearings for years, which meant, in turn, that applicants had access to a legal work permit in the meantime.

Beginning in 1986, the Nicaraguans received a brief respite when the district director of the INS, Perry Rivkind, announced he had stopped deporting Nicaraguan aliens from Miami, although Nicaraguans in other parts of the country continued to be deported. By this time, the earlier waves of Nicaraguan business elites and professionals had established roots in Miami and cemented their ties with influential Cuban American organizations, making the Nicaraguans prime recruits as supporters of the administration's Central American policies and a source of potential members for the Republican party when they achieved U.S. citizenship. In July 1987, Attorney General Edwin Meese declared that all qualified Nicaraguans were entitled to work permits and those who had been denied asylum could reapply. More than 30,000 Nicaraguans applied for asylum in Miami as a result, and the approval rate for Nicaraguan asylum requests climbed to over 50 percent.

But concern by government officials as well as the Miami community, including some Cuban Americans, over the growing number of Nicaraguans entering the country and applying for asylum, as well as its economic costs at a time that the budget deficit in Washington was growing, resulted in another reversal as U.S. Justice officials reverted to a more repressive policy, stripping undocumented Nicaraguans of their right to work permits, accelerating the review of their asylum applications in order to accelerate the deportation process, stepping up border enforcement, and calling for Contra directors and others to return home after the Sandinistas were defeated in the 1990 elections.

Finally, in 1990, Central American immigrants achieved two significant if partial victories. In November, after considerable pressure from immigrant-rights organizations and their supporters in Congress, Salvadorans and Nicaraguans received temporary protected status (TPS) for eighteen months (subsequently renewed), as part of the 1990 Immigration Rights bill (although other Central Americans, including Guatemalans, were not affected). And on December 20, a settlement was reached in the landmark immigration case *American Baptist Churches v. Thornburgh* (sometimes referred to as the ABC decision), which had been filed in May 1985 and supported by over eighty religious, refugee, and refugee legal-assistance organizations. This case had challenged the low asylum-approval rate for Guatemalans and Salvadorans, alleging discrimination in the adjudication process based on nationality, U.S. foreign policy and border-enforcement considerations, and the U.S. government's views of the ideological beliefs of the applicant. In the settlement, widely seen as a vindication for the arguments of the Sanctuary movement, the INS was required to reopen 150,000 previously filed Guatemalan and Salvadoran asylum cases and hear petitions

from potentially 350,000 more who became eligible to file for asylum under special procedures, during which time both groups could enjoy temporary legal status and suspension of deportation hearings.

According to those involved, this was the largest case the INS had ever agreed to settle and the largest number of asylum cases ever reopened. The government was undoubtedly motivated to settle partly by the cost of pursuing the case and also the fact that new immigration regulations consistent with the settlement had already been adopted. But there can be no doubt that the tireless organizing efforts of the immigrants themselves and their supporters facilitated a settlement by highlighting certain contradictions in U.S. policies, for example between U.S. claims to support democracy abroad versus its support for regimes that repressed democratic movements in Central America, and claims that U.S. asylum policies were neutral with respect to national origin versus their discriminatory application to different national groups.

ISSUES AND INITIATIVES IN THE 1990S

The 1990s brought significant changes and new challenges for Central American immigrants in the United States. Despite the peace process in Central America, relatively few returned to their countries of origin, and Central Americans facing limited economic opportunities in their home countries continued to migrate. At the same time, however, the context of reception in the United States also deteriorated with the economic recession of the early 1990s, adding to tensions in many inner-city areas where migrants lived. Growing hostility toward immigrants was manifested in California's Proposition 187 (passed in 1994) and new immigration legislation at the national level in 1996.

By the early 1990s it was evident to Central American activists and others working with Central Americans that what had been considered a temporary refugee population had become largely permanent. This recognition, and particularly the failure of the peace process to result in the return of a significant number of immigrants to their home countries, led Central American organizations and activists to rethink the direction and emphasis of their activities and programs. Many focused increasingly on the long-term needs of Central Americans in the United States, including their economic and political empowerment, while continuing to attend to the needs of new, often undocumented, immigrants. Some who had worked in solidarity or refugee institutions in the 1980s shifted their orientation to initiatives such as citizenship training, the registration of new citizens as voters and the political representation of their interests, programs to provide inner-city youth—many of them children of the earlier immigrant cohort—with education and job-related skills, and labor organizing and other initiatives to inform workers of their rights. Legal initiatives continued to be important not only for new immigrants, but also for many from the earlier cohorts who had not yet succeeded in obtaining documentation.

Many Central American immigrants who had not necessarily been active in the 1980s also participated in these initiatives, which brought them into contact with a growing number of city officials, union leaders and organizers, educators, and community leaders at the local level and, in some cases, at the national level. Central American communities in many parts of the country had been polarized during the 1980s, particularly as a result of political conflicts, and ethnic differences also prevented many groups, such as the indigenous and nonindigenous Guatemalans, from working together. Although suspicion and distrust among these groups continue to exist, there have been concerted efforts to work across political and ethnic differences on issues of common interest.

Similar to other immigrants, Central Americans continued to support their families at home through remittances, which by this time were making a substantial contribution to the economies of their respective countries, even surpassing exports in some cases. In several U.S. cities, Central Americans from a particular locality formed hometown associations that raised funds for civic projects and developed initiatives in their communities of origin. In the meantime, Central American businesses and governments became increasingly aware of the significance of their compatriots in the United States as both a source of financial resources and a market for goods and services produced at home, ranging from familiar food products to real estate and new homes in their home communities, to which many immigrants hoped to return some day. This has resulted in a number of initiatives on the part of these businesses and governments to take advantage of these potential resources through trade conventions and fairs and the establishment of banks and other businesses in relevant U.S. cities.

Related to the continued and renewed contacts with home communities are cultural practices and ceremonies brought from Central America and in some cases adapted to the U.S. environment. Many of these activities predate the large influx of Central Americans in the 1980s. But cultural initiatives have been given additional impetus in the past ten years as a result not only of the size of the 1980s cohort, but also of many immigrants' fear that their children, growing up in the United States and socialized in U.S. schools and communities, were forgetting their roots. Children of immigrants as well as those immigrants who migrated at an early age tend to become more "Americanized," as indicated by factors such as music and entertainment preferences as well as a much greater inclination among younger immigrants to remain in the United States, compared with older cohorts who indicate a desire to return at some point in the future (Hamilton and Chinchilla 2001). At the same time, some of these children who were in high school or entering college by the 1990s were themselves confronting questions of their origins and identity. The result has been a proliferation of new cultural, educational, and community initiatives over the past decade.

Although some of these programs are similar to those of other immigrant communities, the rapid proliferation of organizations and activities oriented both to Central Americans in the United States and to their home communities in the 1990s undoubtedly owes much to the continued role and organizing skills of political activists from the 1980s cohort and to the institutional base established during that decade (Chinchilla and Hamilton 1999; Hamilton and Chinchilla 2001). In the following sections, we examine changes and initiatives in legalization and civic education, workplace organizing, transnational ties, and social and cultural practices, concluding with a discussion of the next generation.

LEGAL ISSUES AND CIVIC EDUCATION

By the early 1990s, some undocumented Central Americans had won a legal reprieve through congressional approval of a temporary protected status (TPS) for Salvadorans and Nicaraguans as a result of war and political instability in their respective countries and through the landmark ABC decision, which gave those Guatemalans and Salvadorans whose asylum applications had been rejected, or who had failed to apply due to their probable rejection, an opportunity to apply again. Central American– and other immigrant-rights organizations worked to register eligible immigrants under TPS, lobbied to extend it annually, and counseled former asylum applicants wishing to reapply. TPS (later designated DED—delayed enforced departure) was extended until 1996. With its expiration, legal initiatives concentrated increasingly on preparing those eligible for asylum hearings under ABC and counseling candidates for stays of deportation, which enable those immigrants "of good character" who could prove residency in the United States for seven consecutive years, and whose deportation would result in personal hardship, to remain in the United States and eventually apply for permanent residency and citizenship.

In the meantime, the intense debate over "illegal immigrants" in California culminated with the passage of the so-called SOS (Save Our State) initiative, or Proposition 187, which would have denied services, including education and all but emergency health care, to undocumented immigrants. The measure was eventually repealed as unconstitutional by a federal district court, but in the meantime the campaign had galvanized immigrants and their supporters who organized against it. The struggle also significantly raised the political profile of Latinos in the state. Two years later, however, the U.S. Congress passed the Illegal Immigration Reform and Immigrant Responsibility Act of 1996, which, among other provisions, stiffened conditions for a stay of deportation: applicants had to have spent ten consecutive years in the United States, and their deportation would have to result in "exceptional and extremely unusual" hardship for a close family member (spouse, parent, or child) who was a U.S. citizen or permanent resident.

Conditions were eased for some Central American immigrants with the passage of NACARA, the Nicaraguan Adjustment and Central American Relief Act, in 1997, which in effect reinstated previous conditions for a stay of deportation (now called cancellation of deportation) for those Salvadorans and Guatemalans who arrived prior to 1990. At the same time, it provided automatic cancellation of deportation for those Nicaraguans and Cubans who arrived prior to 1995, and subsequently Central American advocates and organizations have focused lobbying efforts on obtaining the same or similar conditions for Salvadorans, Guatemalans, Hondurans, and Haitians. These efforts gained substantial congressional support and legislative bills to this effect have been proposed in both the House and Senate, but have not to date obtained sufficient votes for passage. In January 1999, following Hurricane Mitch, which devastated significant areas of Honduras and Nicaragua the year before, TPS was extended to Hondurans and Nicaraguans who had been in the United States from December 1998. Due to expire in June 2000, it has subsequently been renewed.[12] Similarly, TPS was again extended to Salvadorans after the two massive earthquakes in El Salvador in January and February 2001.

Central American and immigrant-rights' organizations have engaged in extensive advocacy, organizing and lobbying around these initiatives on the local and national levels, individually and collectively. In Los Angeles, for example, organizations such as CARECEN, El Rescate, Asociación Salvadoreños de Los Angeles (ASOSAL), Casa Nicaragua, and the Coalition for Humane Immigrant Rights of Los Angeles (CHIRLA), dating from the 1980s, formed the Central American Coalition, which also included several new organizations such as GUIA (Guatemala Unity Information Agency) and HULA (Hondureños Unidos de Los Angeles), established in the late 1990s to respond to the needs of Guatemalan and Honduran populations, respectively. Several of these organizations are also part of national coalitions. The most enduring of these is SANN, the Salvadoran American National Network, formed of several activist organizations, many dating from the 1980s, to promote the well-being of Salvadoran Americans and other Central Americans and Latinos in the United States.

Recognition of the permanence of the Central American population in the United States has led these and other organizations to undertake initiatives aimed at the political and economic empowerment of Central American immigrants, and some new organizations have been formed for this purpose, such as SALEF—the Salvadoran American Leadership and Education Fund, focusing on civic-education programs, voter registration, and internships for Latino youth—and SALPAC, the Salvadoran Political Action Committee, which supports candidates based on their responsiveness to the needs of Central Americans and other Latinos and campaigns on behalf of relevant voter initiatives. Thus, increasing numbers of Central Americans and their children are becoming integrated into the political process, although some continue to maintain ties with their home countries, reinforced by their cultural traditions and in some cases by the continued immigration of Central Americans.

ORGANIZING AT THE WORKPLACE

Some politicians and many in the general population assumed that immigrants, particularly those without documents, were responsible for job loss and the drop in wages affecting U.S.-born workers beginning in the 1970s. A corollary of this assumption was the widespread belief among union leaders that undocumented immigrants were impossible to organize, further undermining the ability of workers and unions to retain the wages and benefits they had won through years of organizing. In fact, the first assumption was only partially true and tended to be specific to particular industries or to jobs that would have been exported if low-wage labor were not available. The second assumption was something of a self-fulfilling prophecy; once unions (and other groups) began to address the issue they found that immigrants, including the undocumented, could be quite militant in demanding and defending their rights.

The turnaround began in the mid-1980s with the election of John Sweeney as head of the SEIU (Service Employees International Union), a transition in leadership that led to a renewed emphasis on organizing, including the organization of immigrants. This was reinforced when Sweeney became president of the AFL-CIO in the mid-1990s. The SEIU covered several areas in which immigrants, including Central Americans, tended to be concentrated, including hotel and restaurant workers and building cleaners (janitors). The latter had indeed suffered a sharp drop in wages as well as declining union membership in some cities, such as Los Angeles, by the 1980s, and they were targeted for organization by the SEIU's dramatic Justice for Janitors campaign.[13] SEIU organizers began to draw immigrant workers into this campaign in the late 1980s, and by the turn of the century they had achieved significant victories in reversing the previous downward spiral of wages and benefits.

Organizers and workers in areas such as construction, building cleaning, and hotel and restaurant work had certain advantages in that although workers could be fired, jobs could not be altogether eliminated, as was sometimes the case in more mobile lines of work, such as the garment industry. Other typical immigrant jobs were difficult to organize because of the isolation of workers (domestic work), the illegality of the work itself (street vending, particularly in Los Angeles), or the occasional and temporary nature of the available jobs (day laborers). Organizing initiatives in these areas took different forms.

In the garment industry, UNITE (United Needletrades, Industrial and Textile Employees), while continuing unionization efforts, also used other tactics such as consumer boycotts of clothing produced in nonunion shops, and the union formed Justice Centers in several cities to inform workers of their rights. Street vendors in Los Angeles, many of them undocumented immigrants, formed the Street Vendors Association (Asociación de Vendedores Ambulantes) in the mid-1980s, which, with the assistance of North American advocates, established contacts with city officials in efforts to end police abuses against vendors and to become informed regarding health regulations and other issues that affected their work. In 1987, City Councilman Michael Woo formed the Street Vendors' Task Force, incorporating the Street Vendors Association as well as lawyers, educators, and businesspeople to work for the legalization of street vending in Los Angeles. The task force achieved limited success with a bill finally approved by the City Council in 1994 that permitted vending in certain districts, but subject to a formidable set of preconditions that limited implementation.

Several organizations worked with other difficult-to-organize sectors, such as day laborers. These efforts focused on organizing workers at hiring sites to achieve some order in the recruiting process, fair wages, and accountability of contractors who were sometimes guilty of not paying or underpaying their workers. Central Americans have been integrated into unionization efforts as well as other organizing initiatives as members and militants. By the end of the 1990s, several had become leaders in unions and other work-related organizations.

Some Central American workers have achieved a certain level of mobility. Middle-class immigrants, including professionals who initially experienced downward mobility, improved their language skills and in some cases were able to obtain the necessary credentials to practice their profession in the United States. Some who lacked the education or skills to shift to higher-level jobs were able to improve conditions within a particular job category. Women in domestic service, for example, often began as live-in domestic or child-care workers, which provided room and board in exchange for low wages, cultural isolation, and often extreme exploitation. Over time they managed to shift to day jobs which provided better wages and more control over their hours of work and their working conditions. Immigrants also managed to stretch their resources by pooling them and sharing living arrangements to cut costs.

Although many Central Americans in the United States have improved their situation as a result of organizing efforts or their own initiatives, they continue to be among the lowest-paid workers with the highest levels of poverty. The continued influx of new immigrants is undoubtedly a factor, since these are the most likely to be undocumented and to lack English-language and other skills. In addition, Central Americans and other new immigrants have had mixed success in their efforts to organize and obtain basic rights. Personal rivalries and substantive differences have split some organizations; hard-fought victories must be defended to ensure their continuity, and the vicissitudes of the U.S. economy, in addition to the economic restructuring occurring at the global level, have resulted in new insecurities and uncertainties for immigrant as well as U.S.-born workers.

SOCIAL AND CULTURAL LIFE

On weekends, Central American men gather in parks, school playgrounds, or wherever they can find sufficient space for soccer games. Most Central American communities in the United States of any size have their own soccer teams, or baseball teams in the case of Nicaraguans, and often their own leagues. In some cases, immigrants from a particular town or community form teams that travel to their communities of origin to play the home teams, or they host the Central American team in the United States.

Once the Central American immigrant community in a given location reaches a certain size, its presence is manifested through the proliferation of restaurants, *pupusa* stands, and markets selling Central American food; travel agencies advertising trips to Central American cities; and express courier and transport services for sending letters, remittances, and packages to major cities and even remote villages back home. In several cities, Central Americans from particular countries have established their own newspapers and even rival newspapers, and Central American businesspeople have their own chambers of commerce in some U.S. locations.

The church is a major social and cultural as well as spiritual center. As noted above, churches in Central American communities made efforts to incorporate new immigrants and refugees as these populations grew in the 1980s. As noted by Anthony Stevens-Arroyo in his contribution to this volume, although most Central Americans are Catholic and attend services at Catholic churches, churches of Protestant denominations in areas with large Central American populations also provided space for Central American organizations, as well as services such as English-language training. The increased presence of evangelical churches in these neighborhoods reflected widespread membership among Central Americans, particularly Guatemalans.

Because many Central American holidays are based on religious traditions, they are often centered at churches and may include a mass or other services. La Purissima, which commemorates the conception of the Virgin Mary, is celebrated annually with prayers, songs, and religious processions over several days in late November and early December in Nicaraguan American communities as well as in Nicaragua itself. Salvadorans celebrate the Feast of the Divine Savior in August. In 2001, SANA (the Salvadoran American National Association), formed in Los Angeles the previous year, commissioned a replica of the statue of the Savior in the Cathedral of San Salvador, which was then brought on a ten-day pilgrimage from El Salvador through Mexico and Guatemala to Los Angeles, where it was the center of a week of celebrations. Central American groups have particular traditions for commemorating Holy Week and Christmas, as well as for specific events such as births, baptisms, and deaths.

Many Central American communities in the United States celebrate Independence Day. For Guatemala, El Salvador, Honduras, Nicaragua, and Costa Rica, this is in mid-September, the same time as Mexico's, commemorating their independence from Spain in 1821. For Panama, however, independence came in 1903 when it broke with Colombia and is celebrated on 3 November. In some U.S. cities, Central American groups have a parade that may include elaborate floats and celebrities as well as bands and dancers.

The Garifuna celebrate Arrival Day, which commemorates the initial arrival of the Garifuna to the Caribbean coast of Central America after they were driven from the island of St. Vincent by the British. In New York, the Honduran American Cultural Association has sponsored an enactment of the arrival of Garifuna in Honduras with both Garifuna and mestizo performers. Settlement Day, which commemorates the settlement of some of the Garifuna from Honduras in British Honduras (now Belize), is celebrated by the Garifuna from Belize; the first commemoration in the United States was in Los Angeles in 1970.

Because their languages and culture distinguish them not only from the majority U.S. population, but also from the dominant groups in their countries of origin, the Maya and Garifuna in the United States have made particular efforts to preserve their culture. One vehicle has been the adaptation of their musical traditions to music forms, such as rock, reggae, rap, and others, popular with youth in the United States. Both Maya and nonindigenous Guatemalan musicians have experimented with syntheses of traditional and modern music such as marimba and hip-hop. The Garifuna have developed a musical form combining punta, a traditional sacred music involving drumming, with rock music to form punta rock. Efforts have also been made to create a standard, written Garifuna language, and both Maya and Garifuna sponsor cultural events, language classes, music lessons, and other programs oriented to the younger generation.

CHANGING TRANSNATIONAL TIES

The growth of Central American migration to the United States has resulted in a significant increase in transnational interaction. In part this reflects the process of globalization and particularly the development of transportation and communication over the past several decades, which facilitate the establishment and maintenance of transnational networks. But transnationalism[14] is a multifaceted and dynamic process, involving nonmigrants as well as migrants, whose initiatives have a profound effect on their home communities and societies and often result in new transnational practices and a cumulative increase in the transnational sphere of action. This is turn may result in the development of new transnational institutions and infrastructure (Chinchilla and Hamilton 1999; Landolt, Autler, and Baires 1999).

As a result of prior migration, many Central Americans who migrate today can take advantage of existing networks of families or friends in the United States, which sometimes help to finance their journey and may provide temporary housing or other assistance once they arrive, although the economic difficulties in which many Central American immigrants live may reduce the effectiveness of these networks (Mahler 1995; Menjívar 2000). The process of migration itself and the growing difficulties of this process, which may involve crossing three or four borders, has generated an "industry" of smugglers who charge as much as $5,000 to conduct would-be migrants through a series of established routes and safe houses to their U.S. destinations. Once in the United States, Central Americans maintain contact with families and friends in their countries of origin through letters, telephone calls, and Internet chat groups; some return to their home countries for periodic visits. One result is a significant growth in the transportation and communications infrastructure linking the region with areas of settlement in the United States, including travel agencies specializing in trips to Central America and courier and transport services facilitating the transfer of letters, remittances, and packages.

The most dramatic manifestation of the importance of Central American immigration for the sending societies has been the growth of remittances and their impact on the economies of their home countries. Despite their generally low wages, a significant proportion of Central Americans send remittances to families in their home countries on a regular or occasional basis. Most of these are used for basic consumption (food, clothing, utilities) or housing, education, or health care, but they also constitute a major source of foreign reserves for the respective countries. By the year 2000, it was estimated that Central Americans were sending approximately $3.5 billion annually to their home countries. Salvadoran family remittances in that year were approximately $1.8 billion; in some years remittances have equaled or surpassed El Salvador's export earnings. Remittances from Guatemalans were approximately $600 million in 2000, and those from Nicaraguans around $800 million, representing 25 percent of that country's GDP (Orozco 2002).

In addition to individual remittances, Central American immigrants from particular towns or communities have formed hometown associations that raise money for specific projects. These association have multiple origins. Some came from mutual support societies (called "*fraternidades*" among Guatemalans), which assist families in the event of the death of a family member, often providing funds to send the body of the deceased back to the home community for burial. The first Salvadoran association in Los Angeles was allegedly formed in 1987, following the devastating 1986 earthquake in El Salvador, by immigrants from Santa Tecla (a suburb of San Salvador) and Ahuachapán (a western province). The amnesty of the 1986 Immigration Reform and Control Act (IRCA) enabled some Central Americans to travel home for the first time; many were shocked at the devastation they found and began to raise funds on their return. In some cases the initiative for the hometown associations came from relatives or community leaders in the home community.

The associations grew rapidly in the 1990s, partly as a result of the peace processes in several countries, which enabled people to travel freely in regions that had been affected by war or political violence. Also, by this time growing numbers of the 1980s cohort had obtained documentation and become more settled, and much of the leadership and active membership were drawn from these more established groups. By the late 1990s there were an estimated fifty-five Salvadoran and thirty-five Guatemalan hometown associations in Los Angeles, although the number has fluctuated as some associations disappear and new ones are formed. In some cases the founding members of the hometown associations had been politically active in the 1980s, but while some have maintained their political orientation, others insist on the political independence of their individual organizations, noting that they have members from different political perspectives.

The hometown associations raise funds through various activities, particularly parties which bring together members of the community from a given

U.S. city or region. Typically, tickets are sold in advance for a raffle; the drawing is held at the party itself, with the winner receiving a prize supplied by a local Central American business, such as a television set or airline tickets to the home country. Funds may go to purchasing vehicles or equipment for the home community (ambulances, medical supplies, school books), building clinics or painting a school, street paving, or developing potable water supplies. One of the most active of the associations is the Salvadoran association of Santa Elena, the Comité de Amigas de Santa Elena, which has branches in San Francisco, where it was initially formed, in Los Angeles, Houston, and Washington, D.C., in addition to the headquarters in Santa Elena itself (Eekhoff 1995).

Indigenous groups generally have their own associations and, in addition to raising funds for projects in their home communities, they are often oriented toward maintaining their cultures and languages. Some Guatemalan Mayan groups (e.g., the Q'anjob'al in Los Angeles) have their own marimba bands, and the annual anniversary of the town's patron saint is often commemorated in parallel festivities in the home community and the particular community of townspeople in the United States.

Aside from the hometown associations, other organizations provide assistance in funds or in kind to their home countries. For example, the Alianza Hondureña de Los Angeles, in addition to its work on immigration issues, has sent toys to children in Honduran hospitals at Christmas time and food to Hondurans affected by the 2001—2002 drought. Casa Nicaragua has sent computers to a Nicaraguan organization that provides training for street children in Managua. U.S.-based Central American organizations raise funds and send aid to home countries affected by natural disasters, such as Hurricane Mitch in November 1998 and the Salvadoran earthquakes of January and February 2001. They also send delegations to Central American countries, while political, labor, and cultural representatives from Central America travel to the United States to meet with constituencies or counterparts from the respective immigrant communities. As noted above, sports teams based in particular communities may travel back and forth to play with their compatriots in the respective Central American or U.S. immigrant communities. Many shops, stores, markets, and restaurants catering to Central American neighborhoods in U.S. cities import some of their products from Central America. Remittances or resources brought by return migrants may form the basis for the establishment or maintenance of business ventures in Central America, in some cases based on the marketing of U.S. products.

Their role as transnational actors is a potential source of political, as well as economic, influence for Central American immigrants in their home communities and national societies. In addition, the growth of the Central American immigrant community in the United States and the significance of remittances have evoked a response from governments and business groups in the home countries, who increasingly recognize their U.S.-based populations as an important resource and potential market and view the organized Central American immigrant groups as a conduit for reaching the populations in the United States. Government officials have established programs to provide legal services to their U.S.-based constituents. Newspapers established by Central Americans in major U.S. immigrant centers emphasize the connections of immigrants to their home communities and carry ads for transport companies, express courier services, and travel agencies. Construction and real estate companies in El Salvador and other countries encourage migrants in the United States to invest in land and housing back in their home countries, and in some cases Central American banks and companies establish branches in U.S. cities, such as the Tapachulteca market of El Salvador, which opened a branch in Pico Union, a major entry area for Central Americans coming to Los Angeles. Government agencies, NGOs, and business groups in both the United States and individual Central American countries have engaged in discussions and undertaken initiatives to channel remittances, hometown-association resources, and other funds to promote development projects in Central American countries.

Through their individual and collective contacts with their families and home communities, Central American migrants have created a dynamic transnational sphere of action with important economic, political, social, and cultural implications for both their countries of origin and their communities in the United States. This sphere of action is continually strengthened and expanded as increasing numbers of migrants and nonmigrants are incorporated and new forms of transnational interaction are introduced.

THE NEXT GENERATION AND THE ISSUE OF IDENTITY

Similar to other immigrant groups, young Central Americans tend to become acculturated into U.S. society more quickly than the older generation. But studies of second-generation immigrants have noted the complexity of the process of accommodation in U.S. society and argue that many of these children and youth may assimilate into an underachieving minority culture rather than mainstream U.S. society.[15] The children of many first-generation Central American immigrants grow up in the impoverished inner cities of Los Angeles, Miami, and other metropolitan areas, exposed to deteriorating housing conditions, inferior schooling, and in some cases drugs and gangs. Inevitably, this environment, combined with the experience of discrimination, limited opportunities, and lack of material resources, affect the values, expectations, and behavior patterns of some members of this generation, who, like many of their peers, are characterized by limited aspirations, low levels of skills, early pregnancies, and in some cases drug or gang activity. For Central Americans who immigrated in the 1970s and 1980s, there was the added factor that many had witnessed violence in their home countries, lost family members or close friends to violence, or even been involved in the government or guerrilla armies.

U.S. gangs become transnationalized as a result of the return of gang members to their home countries, particularly through deportation. This has resulted in the rapid expansion of U.S.-based gangs in some of the major cities, and increasingly in more remote areas, of their home countries. In much of Central America, the lack of economic opportunity and the recent history of violence have been additional factors in the spread of gangs.

Although a cohesive ethnic or immigrant community may reinforce values that offset the negative influences of the immediate surroundings, issues of ethnicity and identity are complicated among those Central American immigrants whose families deliberately downplay their nationality by rarely discussing it at home. Identity for Central American children may be further complicated when they grow up in neighborhoods or enter schools where the dominant ethnic population is Mexican or Cuban or, in the case of the Creole and Garifuna populations, Puerto Rican or Dominican. For a variety of reasons, Central American immigrant children in California have sometimes been encouraged to say they were from Mexico.

Recruitment into an underclass is not inevitable. Several Central American youths who grew up in inner-city neighborhoods in Los Angeles and had friends who were gang members attributed their own resistance to gang culture to their involvement in other activities, such as church-based groups or sports, or to encouragement from particular teachers to pursue their education. Growing numbers of young Salvadorans, Guatemalans, Nicaraguans, and Hondurans, including many raised in inner cities, are completing high school and going on to college and important positions in their communities (Fernández-Kelly and Curran 2001; Hamilton and Chinchilla 2001).

In contrast to those who would downplay their national identity, many first-generation Central American immigrants are determined that their children not lose touch with their cultural and national roots. Some view a reinforcement of their culture and history as a means of insulating their children from the negative influences of deteriorating inner cities. Politically oriented Central Americans—whether Nicaraguans in Miami who opposed the Sandinista government or Salvadorans and Guatemalans in Los Angeles who supported revolutionary movements in their countries—seem to be particularly inclined to impart a strong national or political identity to their children. Another example is provided by those Garifuna who distinguish themselves from African Americans by pointing out their roots and taking pride in the assertion that they were never slaves. As discussed earlier, Mayan and Garifuna immigrants are particularly concerned with preserving their cultures and languages and passing them on to the next generation.

Perceptions of discrimination or efforts to distinguish themselves from other ethnic groups have led some youths to think more systematically about their national origins or cultural roots or to identify more strongly with their, or their parents', country of origin. Interestingly, this national identification may either reinforce an underclass status or be a factor in mobility. Studies of Nicaraguan youth in Miami found that many who feel marginalized by the dominant society emulate the adversarial culture of other marginalized youth and see themselves increasingly as Nicaraguan, in a form of reactive identity. In contrast, those who were adjusting more successfully to U.S. society identified themselves as American or Hispanic/Latino (Fernández-Kelly and Curran 2001).

At the same time, as increasing numbers of Central American youth graduate from high school and go on to college, some become active in groups or organizations that emphasize their ethnic, regional, or national identities. As early as the 1980s, some Central American college students became active in Central American student associations, a process that has continued. California State University at Northridge (CSUN), in the San Fernando valley, a major settlement area for Central Americans in Los Angeles, enrolled a significant number of Central Americans, many of whom became active in CAUSA (Central American United Student Association). Partly at their instigation, sympathetic faculty members, administrators, and community leaders formed the first Central American studies program in the country at CSUN in 1999.

Artistic expression has become a means of expressing or reinforcing identity. Several young Central American poets and writers in California have formed a group, Epicentroamerica, and have written and published poems and essays on a variety of themes ranging from personal to political issues, including domestic violence, imperialism, sexuality, identity, and ethnicity. Central American artists and writers have also set up organizations to sponsor poetry readings, art exhibits, and conferences featuring work by Central Americans in the United States and from Central America.

Art and other forms of self-expression have also been important in initiatives by some community and civic groups to address the needs of gang members and "at-risk" youth. Some analysts of gang culture stress the elimination of violence, rather than the elimination of gangs, arguing that gangs may serve as a surrogate family or community for young people that have had little positive experience of either, and these groups seek to provide opportunities for a different lifestyle. Along with programs to provide educational opportunity and skill training, some programs incorporate poetry, theatre, or art workshops as a means of self-expression as well as a possible source of income. One example is Homies Unidos, initially formed in 1996 by gang members in El Salvador, many of whom had been deported from the United States, and advocates on their behalf. Homies opened a chapter in Los Angeles in 1997, and its projects now include an arts program, tutoring to enable youth to acquire a GED certificate and, in some cases, go on to college, job training, civic and legal education, and training in life skills and leadership development.

CONCLUSION

Central Americans in the United States are distinguished by their diversity and the rapidity of the changes they have experienced in a relatively short period of time. Within less than twenty years, they have evolved from a small, barely recognized population to a significant immigrant sector. In 1990, over a million people claimed Central American ancestry, and in the 2000 census these groups numbered over 1.6 million. Central Americans continue to be concentrated in major receiving cities such as Los Angeles, Miami, and New York, but they are becoming more dispersed as a result of direct or secondary migration to different parts of the country in search of jobs, and Central American and Mexican immigrants are becoming an increasing proportion of the population in some areas where immigrants had previously been unknown.

While sharing many characteristics with other immigrants, Central Americans are distinguished by their national and ethnic diversity and the particular character of their migration during the 1980s. Many Central Americans maintain their particular ethnic or national identity and their contacts with their respective countries of origin, or they have combined incorporation into U.S. society with continued interaction with their own ethnic and national group both in this country and in their home countries. Their presence in the United States is evident in the growing number of restaurants, markets, travel agencies, and other small businesses providing particular food and other services to Central Americans in the community, as well as their special religious, national, or ethnic ceremonies, festivals, music, and dance. In their countries of origin, their remittances have provided an important and in some cases indispensable contribution to the economy, and the rapid growth of hometown associations and other organizations in the United States has provided a significant impetus to civic projects in their home communities.

Today, Central American immigrants in the United States find themselves between two worlds, and for many, neither the United States nor their countries of origin offer prospects for much improvement in the near future. Given the absence of economic opportunity in their home countries, many will continue to struggle with insecure, low-wage jobs, depressed inner cities, and often uncertain legal status in the United States. Increased U.S. security measures following the September 11, 2001, attacks, as well as the economic slowdown, will undoubtedly affect the employment opportunities and legal options for Central American and other immigrants already in the United States whose legal status is uncertain.

But despite the difficulties they encounter, an important number of Central Americans have adjusted rapidly to the United States, becoming at least partially incorporated into the U.S. economy and culture. Although a large number are poorly paid workers, and many live in poverty, Central Americans also include a substantial middle class, and many others have been able to improve their conditions over time. Their remittances and their collective contributions to their home communities have given rise to further examples of transnational interaction as Central American government officials and business groups attempt to tap into the resources of their compatriots in the United States or collaborate with them in developmental projects in their home countries. We can anticipate that over time growing numbers of Central Americans in the United States will rise to leadership positions in the labor movement, community organizations, education, and politics and government in their communities in the United States, and increasingly at the national level, and that their important contributions will enable them to exercise growing economic, social, and political influence in their countries of origin.

NOTES

1. In contrast, approximately two-thirds of the population of Mexican ancestry were born in the United States, and most of the foreign-born came prior to the 1980s.
2. These numbers may not have been comparable, since respondents had the option of listing themselves as Latino or Hispanic or "mixed," without designating a specific category, in the 2000 census.
3. More detailed information on the relation between conditions in Central America and Central American migration can be found in Hamilton and Chinchilla 1991, 2001.
4. On Honduran immigration to the United States, see England and Kroghmal 1997. On the Garifuna specifically, see England 2000, Macklin 1997.
5. For example, many Central American women came to Washington, D.C., as a result of recruitment by employers of U.S. and international agencies to work as domestic or child care workers in the 1960s and 1970s (see Repak 1995).
6. As noted by Stevens-Arroyo in his contribution to this volume, beginning in the 1960s many priests and other religious groups were inspired by the Second Vatican Council of the Catholic Church and the Medellin Conference of Bishops in Latin

America, which advocated an increased emphasis on the needs of impoverished groups and encouraged efforts to relate Christian doctrine to the everyday lives of people. The scarcity of priests in some areas of Latin America resulted in the training of catechists to lead religious discussions and in some cases administer sacraments. Some priests and catechists who saw the structural causes of poverty in the exploitation and repression of large sectors of the population were active in organizing groups to question and resist these conditions.

7. See discussion under "Issues and Initiatives in the 1980s," below.
8. See discussion under "The Next Generation and the Issue of Identity," below.
9. There had been earlier attempts to "gentrify" parts of Westlake in Los Angeles during the 1980s, taking advantage of its proximity to downtown, which was experiencing a business boom at the time. One of the most ambitious plans was a redevelopment project for Central City West, the northeastern part of Westlake, which was slated to replace existing housing with expensive residential and commercial buildings. Pressures from grassroots organizations, with the assistance of sympathetic city officials, resulted in the projected inclusion of low-cost housing, parks, and child-care facilities. This project was halted indefinitely, however, as a result of the recession of the 1990s.
10. Many African Americans as well as Mexican Americans were affected by the loss of well-paying manufacturing jobs beginning in the 1970s. The growth of low-wage industry in areas such as garment manufacturing during this period was dependent on the availability of a low-wage labor force; many garment factories in fact closed down or moved to Mexico when wages increased. In other cases, African Americans were moving out of certain types of low-wage jobs, such as hotel and restaurant work, into other, often white-collar jobs. In the case of the building-cleaning industry, however, companies took advantage of an undocumented immigrant labor force to shift from union to nonunion workers, resulting in a substantial drop in wages and other benefits, particularly in Los Angeles, although in other cities, unions such as the Service Employee International Union (SEIU) succeeded in retaining their previous wages and benefits.
11. For an analysis of the struggles of Salvadorans to obtain legal status, see Coutin 2000. On the issue of asylum for Nicaraguans in Miami, see Portes and Stepick 1993.
12. This did not extend to the Hondurans and Nicaraguans who came after Hurricane Mitch, in some cases with the mistaken impression that they would also be covered.
13. Other factors were also relevant to the decline in wages, including Los Angeles's history as an antiunion city and the dramatic growth in office building, among other construction and real estate ventures, which led to a proliferation of nonunion cleaning companies.
14. Transnationalism has been defined as processes through which migrants forge and sustain social fields linking the societies or origin with areas of settlement (Basch, Glick, Schiller, and Blanc 1994).
15. These studies attribute acculturation to a complex interaction of social processes, parental characteristics, and ethnicity, among other factors (Portes and Rumbaut 2001). For immigrant youth in inner cities, assimilation into U.S. society often means assimilation into an underclass marked by low expectations, underachievement, and, in the worst cases, criminal activity. Parents with relatively high levels

of education and high expectations for their children's achievement may offset negative inner-city environments by influencing their children's future, and a strong immigrant or ethnic community can also reinforce values and behavior patterns counter to those of the immediate social environment.

REFERENCES

Basch, Linda, Nina Glick Schiller, and Christine Szanton Blanc. 1994. *Nations Unbound: Transnational Projects, Postcolonial Predicaments, and Deterritorialized Nation States.* Amsterdam: Gordon and Breach.

Burns, Allen F. 2000. "Indiantown, Florida: The Maya Diaspora and Applied Anthropology." In *The Maya Diaspora: Guatemalan Roots: New American Lives*, ed. James Loucky and Marilyn M. Moors, 152–71. Philadelphia: Temple University Press.

Chinchilla, Norma, and Nora Hamilton. 1999. "Changing Networks and Alliances in a Transnational Context: Salvadoran and Guatemalan Immigrants in Southern California." *Social Justice* 26, no. 3 (fall): 4–26

Córdova, Carlos. 1996. "Central American Migration to San Francisco: One Hundred Years in Building a Community." In *Central Americans in California: Transnational Communities, Economies, and Cultures*, ed. Nora Hamilton and Norma Chinchilla, 15–19. Proceedings of a Conference at the Center for Multiethnic and Transnational Studies, University of Southern California, Los Angeles, 12–13 May 1995.

Coutin, Susan Bibler. 2000. *Legalizing Moves: Salvadoran Immigrants' Struggle for U.S. Residency.* Ann Arbor: The University of Michigan Press.

Eekhoff, Katherine. 1995. "Las asociaciónes salvadoreñas en Los Angeles y su rol para el desarrollo." In *Migración internacional y desarrollo, Tomo II*, ed. Mario Lungo, 9–44. San Salvador: Fundación Nacional para el Desarrollo (FUNDE).

England, Sarah. 2000. "Creating a Global Garifuna Nation? The Transnationalization of Race, Class, and Gender Politics in the Garifuna Diaspora." Ph.D. diss., University of California—Davis.

England, Sarah, and Walter Kroghmal. 1997. "Hondurans." In *American Immigrant Cultures: Builders of a Nation*, vol. 2, ed. David Levinson and Melvin Ember, 394–400. New York: Simon & Schuster/Macmillan.

Fernández-Kelly, Patricia, and Sara Curran. 2001. "Nicaraguans: Voices Lost, Voices Found." In *Ethnicities: Children of Immigrants in America*, ed. Ruben G. Rumbaut and Alejandro Portes, 127–55. Berkeley: University of California Press.

Fink, Leon, and Alvis Dunn. 2000. "The Maya of Morgantown: Exploring Worker Identity Within the Global Marketplace." In *The Maya Diaspora: Guatemalan Roots, New American Lives*, ed. James Loucky and Marilyn M. Moors, 175–96. Philadelphia: Temple University Press.

Hagan, Jacqueline Maria. 1994. *Deciding to Be Legal: A Maya Community in Houston.* Philadelphia: Temple University Press.

Hamilton, Nora, and Norma Chinchilla. 1991. "Central American Migration: A Framework for Analysis." *Latin American Research Review* 26, no. 1: 75–110.

——. 2001. *Seeking Community in a Global City: Guatemalans and Salvadorans in Los Angeles.* Philadelphia: Temple University Press.

Kahn, Robert S. 1996. *Other People's Blood: U.S. Immigration Prisons in the Reagan Decade*, Boulder, Colo.: Westview Press

Landolt, Patricia, Lilian Autler, and Sonia Baires. 1999. "From Hermano Lejano to Hermano Mayor: The Dialectics of Salvadoran Transnationalism." *Ethnic and Racial Studies* 22, no. 2 (March): 290–315.

Loucky, James. 2000. "Maya in a Modern Metropolis: Establishing New Lives and Livelihoods in Los Angeles." In *The Maya Diaspora: Guatemalan Roots: New American Lives*, ed. James Loucky and Marilyn M. Moors, 214–22. Philadelphia: Temple University Press.

Macklin, Catherine L. 1997. "Garifuna." In *American Immigrant Cultures: Builders of a Nation*, vol. 1, ed. David Levinson and Melvin Ember. New York: Simon & Schuster/Macmillan.

Mahler, Sarah J. 1995. *American Dreaming: Immigrant Life on the Margins*. Princeton, N.J.: Princeton University Press.

Menjívar, Cecilia. 2000. *Fragmented Ties: Salvadoran Immigrant Networks in America*. Berkeley: University of California Press.

Orozco, Manuel. 2002. "From Family Ties to Transnational Linkages: The Impact of Family Remittances in Latin America, *Latin American Politics and Society* 44, no. 2 (summer).

Portes, Alejandro, and Ruben G. Rumbaut. 2001. *Legacies: The Story of the Immigrant Second Generation*. Berkeley: University of California Press.

Portes, Alejandro, and Alex Stepick. 1993. *City on the Edge: The Transformation of Miami*. Berkeley: University of California Press.

Ramos, George. 1988. "Stop Threatening Salvadoran Refugees, U.S. Judge Orders INS." *Los Angeles Times*, 6 September, Metro section

Repak, Terry A. 1995. *Waiting on Washington: Central American Workers in the Nation's Capital*. Philadelphia: Temple University Press

Rodríguez, Nestor P. 1993. "Economic Restructuring and Latino Growth in Houston." In *In the Barrios: Latinos and the Underclass Debate*, ed. Joan Moore and Raquel Pinderhughes, 101–27. New York: Russell Sage Foundation.

Rodríguez, Nestor P., and Jacqueline Hagan. 1999. "Central Americans in the United States." In *The Minority Report: An Introduction to Racial, Ethnic, and Gender Relations*, 3rd ed., ed. Anthony Gary Dworkin and Rosalind J. Dworkin, 278–95. Fort Worth, Tex.: Harcourt Brace College Publishers.

FIVE

TRANSNATIONAL TIES AND INCORPORATION: THE CASE OF DOMINICANS IN THE UNITED STATES

PEGGY LEVITT

ALTHOUGH BASKETBALL is not particularly popular in the Dominican Republic, during his 1996 campaign for the presidency, Leonel Fernández appeared in several television campaign ads "shooting hoops." By doing so, he wanted to remind the Dominican public that he had grown up on the Upper West Side of Manhattan, that he admires U.S. culture and practices, and that, if elected, he would put his international experience and style to work. He also wanted to let the immigrant community know that he appreciated their continuing role in Dominican politics and that he hoped they would remain active in the future. "It matters little," said a 1996 article in *The Boston Globe*, "that Fernández picked up so many American habits in New York that his best friends admit the handsome lawyer falls short when it comes to that hallmark of Dominican culture: dancing the merengue" (González 1999). Fernández's strategy seems to have worked—he was sworn into office in August 1996.

President Fernández was not alone in his assessment of migrants' continuing role in Dominican affairs. In fact, more and more Dominicans remain involved in the economic and political life of their homeland as they establish themselves in the United States. The Dominican case provides an excellent lens through which to understand how migrants actually live transnational lives and what the consequences of these activities are. I begin this essay by providing a brief overview of the historical roots of Dominican-U.S. migration. I then profile Dominicans' social and economic experiences in this country. In the third section, I describe the transnational social field spanning the United States and the Dominican Republic and discuss its consequences for civic and political life in both settings. I conclude with some thoughts on how the Dominican experience challenges us to rethink the boundaries of citizenship, inequality, and cultural production.

THE HISTORICAL ROOTS OF MIGRATION

More than 10 percent of all Dominicans are estimated to live outside the Dominican Republic.[1] In 1999, the country ranked twelfth among those sending the largest numbers of immigrants to the U.S. The second largest voting block of Dominicans, after the Dominican capital of Santo Domingo, now resides in New York City.

Though large-scale migration to the United States from the Republic is relatively recent, its causes are deeply rooted in Dominican economic and political development. The United States has strongly influenced Dominican affairs since the late 1800s. As the Dominican state grew more and more indebted to its U.S. creditors during the first half of the 1900s, the U.S. government literally ran the country or managed its affairs from afar. The United State's economic, political, and cultural dominance over the Republic throughout its history and the patterns of land tenure, commercial agriculture, and industrial development that ensued sowed the seeds of large-scale migration long before it began.

When Dominican leaders proclaimed their independence from Haiti on 27 February 1844, the ways in which they countered opposition from their former rulers set the tone for the new Republic. Liberal leaders wanted to go on the offensive against a possible Haitian occupation while conservatives sought a foreign ally, which would help them stave off further invasions. A major rift split the group, and conservatives eventually won. The new Dominican constitution established a democratic government but also allowed its president to "freely organize the army and navy, mobilize the national troops, and consequently be able to give all orders, decisions, and decrees which are fitting, without being subject to any responsibility" (Moya Pons 1995: 163). By so doing, a marriage between partial democracy and authoritarianism was consummated at the Republic's birth that has remained strong throughout its history.

A second key factor defining Dominican nationhood emerges from its originary rebellion against a harsh Haitian occupation; Dominicans were left with an enduring sense of hatred and distrust toward their neighbors. The Dominican national identity that evolved is, in many ways, an anti-identity. It arose in such strong opposition to Haitianness that, even today, many Dominicans continue to define themselves as nonblacks, or what Haitians are not (Cassá et al. 1986, Torres-Saillant and Hernández 1998). Though blacks and mulattos make up nearly 90 percent of the Dominican population, Afro-Dominicans have never used race to organize for economic and political reform.

The new country faced an uphill economic battle and major unrest. Spain stepped in to establish a political and economic protectorate and to help preserve the country's independence. Tensions arose almost immediately following the Spanish annexation in 1861, and the Restoration War of 1863 reestablished Dominican independence. Sovereignty and economic self-sufficiency, as well as political unity, always proved elusive, however. Politics had basically become a contest between two factions. The large landowners who raised cattle and cut wood in the south supported General Buenaventura Báez. The cultivators and merchants in the north, who favored industrial development and trade, supported General Pedro Santana. In 1879, after more than fifty uprisings and twenty changes in government, Báez took power.

The enormous debt Báez faced when he took office immediately crippled his government. To alleviate this, he negotiated with the United States to sell Samaná Bay, located strategically on the country's northern coast. Báez arranged for an interim loan with a European speculator when it became clear that an immediate agreement was unlikely. The high rate of interest he accepted literally mortgaged the country to a British firm. These monies enabled him to run the government while he waited for U.S. Congressional approval of what had now become a plan to annex the entire Republic to the United States.

Both Dominican and U.S. groups opposed this. Though Báez eventually won support from the Dominican people, the U.S. Senate rejected the proposal in 1871. Nevertheless, the country's continued indebtedness, fears for its sovereignty, and dependence on external resources for economic growth set the stage for foreign investors' long-term dominance over Dominican economic affairs (Georges 1990). U.S. investors quickly achieved predominance. By the end of the century, large portions of major economic sectors had been sold or leased to U.S. companies to alleviate the debt. By 1893, the country owed 17 million pesos, several times its national budget. By 1904, the Dominican government was under increasing pressure from European creditors to make debt payments it could not meet. At the same time, U.S. President Theodore Roosevelt wanted to prevent further European expansion in the Latin American and Caribbean region. In September of that year, the U.S. Secretary of State asked the Dominican government to allow the United States to take charge of its customs agency and to assume control of the collection and distribution of all customs receipts. Dominican leaders also agreed not to change their customs duties without U.S. government consent. By sanctioning this arrangement, Dominican leaders granted the United States an unprecedented role in their nation's financial and administrative affairs that only continued to grow. In fact, by 1914, the State Department requested that a U.S.

comptroller be formally appointed to oversee the nation's financial affairs. When the Dominican Congress refused, the United States imposed one by force. In 1916, when domestic opponents threatened to impeach then President Juan Isidro Jiménes, U.S. leaders, who pronounced the opposition a coup d'etat, landed the marines in Santo Domingo and quickly sent troops throughout the country.

The eight-year U.S. occupation that followed irrevocably incorporated the Dominican Republic into a system of global economic relations that later precipitated migration. Land consolidation begun earlier in the century advanced considerably, creating large numbers of landless peasants (Calder 1984, Del Castillo and Cordero 1980). By 1924, sugar companies controlled almost a quarter of the country's agricultural land; 80 percent of these were controlled by U.S. investors (Gleijeses 1978). This accelerated the expansion of a plantation economy and made the country's economy dangerously dependent on the world sugar market. Restrictions imposed on European investment also increased dependence on the United States, which became the principal supplier of industrial and food imports. This hurt local producers who could not compete with products from the United States that were imported into the country virtually duty free. The occupation also marked the rise of U.S. cultural influences. From then on, English words penetrated the language, baseball replaced cockfighting as the national sport, and U.S. music became a sign of good taste among the urban elite.

The Dominican Republic remained a U.S. protectorate even after the U.S. withdrew its forces in 1924. Though Dominican officials regained control of the administration of their own citizens, the United States still reserved the right to control customs and authorize increases in the public debt. In 1930, Rafael Leonidas Trujillo, a young general who had risen to commander-in-chief of the Dominican Army, took control of the Dominican Presidency by force and began an oppressive, dictatorial rule that lasted for the next thirty-one years. Trujillo successfully transformed the Dominican economy from one primarily dependent on subsistence agriculture to one based on industrial growth. He also accumulated tremendous personal wealth in the process.

Trujillo pursued industrialization through import substitution, using indigenous raw materials to produce goods for the domestic market and decrease the country's reliance on imports. To reduce foreign economic domination, he built his own sugar mills and used state and personal funds to buy back most of the foreign mills operating in the country. He also created new industries or wrested control of existing ones. These enterprises flourished because they were protected from foreign competition and labor unrest and because they received special concessions and tax exemptions from the government. Trujillo also instilled a strong sense of national identity and pride among the Dominican people. By standing up to foreign interests and demonstrating that Dominican companies could succeed on their own, he made Dominicans feel that their country could "sit at the table of nations" for the first time (Derby 1994).

The root causes of migration were firmly established during the Trujillo era. According to Grasmuck and Pessar (1991), migration began in response to social and economic changes brought about by the reorganization of the sugar industry under Trujillo. During the U.S. occupation of 1916–1924, the government expropriated considerable tracts of land and devoted them to sugar production. Output increased significantly and was used almost entirely for export. The intensified concentration of land holdings weakened local subsistence agriculture and created a mobile labor force that depended on the sugar *centrales*, or mills, for seasonal income and employment. The government dedicated most of its resources toward modernizing production in its export sectors, while agricultural production in general remained inefficient and undercapitalized.

Trujillo used his position to establish a monopoly on the commercialization of sugar, cacao, and coffee. Though export earnings from these crops increased during the 1940s and 1950s, benefiting an expanding agro-export sector and a rural petty bourgeoisie, the high proportion of rural land devoted to sugar and other export crops negatively affected other kinds of agricultural production (Sharpe 1977), Since the labor required for export crop production was less than that needed to grow ordinary food crops, fewer people found work in agriculture, and the agrarian labor surplus increased.

Furthermore, under Trujillo the Dominican economy evolved from one based primarily on agriculture to one based on low-level industrialization. Because there was little competition, most of the enterprises that developed were monopolistic, backward, and unproductive. Industrialization was also accomplished without the participation of a national middle class. Trujillo applied tariffs, tax exemptions, and government subsidies to the advantage of a select group of friends. The scope of his control was astounding. Dominicans could not obtain food, shoes, clothing, or shelter without in some way benefiting either Trujillo or one of his family members.

By the late 1950s the Dominican economic miracle began to pale. Declining sugar prices hurt the economy, which still revolved around sugar production. Because Trujillo kept wages low, Dominicans had limited disposable incomes. Their weak purchasing power constrained domestic market growth (Cassá et al. 1986). There was also increasing opposition to the almost daily torture and killing of political prisoners. As economic conditions deteriorated and the regime's critics grew more vocal, U.S. leaders feared that another communist takeover, similar to Castro's in Cuba, was likely to occur.

By 1960, when President Kennedy took office, the U.S. government withdrew its support from Trujillo. He was assassinated in 1961.

A period of political turmoil followed. A U.S.-backed provisional government was organized to hold presidential elections. A progressive leader, Prof. Juan Bosch was elected in 1963, and a democratic constitution was ratified. Seven months later, a group of military officers ousted Bosch from office and formed an unstable alliance with large landowners, industrialists, and international trade merchants to replace him. In April 1965, a military faction called the *Constitucionalistas* broke from the alliance and tried to reinstate Bosch. Their rebellion quickly escalated into a popular uprising. Four days later, 40,000 U.S. marines landed in Santo Domingo to prevent an "allegedly imminent" communist revolution.

Prior to the 1960s, few people migrated from the Dominican Republic. Trujillo severely restricted movement out of the country, fearing his opponents would organize against him from abroad. He also sought to restrict the flow of information entering the country from places like Venezuela or Cuba where authoritarian regimes had been deposed (Georges 1990). Those individuals who did migrate tended to be well off and from the Cibao region. During the 1960s, however, migration to the United States increased from a yearly average of almost 1,000 people during the 1950s to nearly 10,000 people per year during the first part of the 1960s (U.S. Immigration and Naturalization Service [INS] 1970). The first emigrants left fearing Pres. Bosch's left-leaning policies, while later emigrants feared the instability plaguing the country after his defeat.

The overthrow of the Bosch government, the civil unrest that followed, and the subsequent U.S intervention created a pool of potentially volatile antigovernment opponents. To prevent these individuals from further increasing instability, the U.S. government raised the number of visas it issued to allow more people to enter the United States. Migration was intended to act as a political safety valve that would weaken opposition and stabilize the Dominican political scene (Castro 1985, Mitchell 1992). Most of these individuals went to New York City. The first significant wave to migrate from the island, then, were political refugees. Once migration began, however, it was encouraged further by two subsequent political regimes which, though different, both failed to modernize agriculture, excluded labor from the benefits of increasing industrialization, and produced a growing but increasingly frustrated middle class (Grasmuck and Pessar 1991). In many ways, migration provided a needed complement to the development model adopted by the Dominican government between 1966 and 1978 because without such large numbers leaving the country, the state would have been unable to feed many of its citizens or to put them to work.

Elections sponsored by the United States in 1966 installed Joaquin Balaguer, Trujillo's former presidential secretary. His rule, lasting from 1966 to 1978, has been called "Trujillismo without Trujillo" because of the strong continuities between the two regimes (Black 1986). Balaguer also enjoyed strong support from the military, the civil bureaucracy, and a small group of emerging industrialists, and he also maintained power through repression and fear. He pursued economic development through an import-substitution model common in Latin America at the time. He introduced protectionist measures, tariffs, and tax exemptions and easily accessible credit to promote industrial development. He also encouraged economic growth by increasing the number of public sector jobs, by launching large public works projects such as highway and public housing construction, and by securing international loans.

At first, high prices for export commodities, strong foreign investment, and increased government spending resulted in high rates of economic growth. The gross domestic product (GDP) grew an average of 11 percent per year between 1969 and 1974 (Guarnizo 1992). These measures, however, did not translate into long-term job creation. Overall efficiency declined between 1970 and 1977 (Vedovato 1986). Most foreign investment went toward industries requiring more capital than labor. Inflation rose while wages remained stagnant. Though nearly half the Dominican labor force still worked in rural areas in 1970, Balaguer pursued policies that favored urban workers. The price controls he imposed on agricultural products and the terms of exchange he established hurt rural producers. Agriculture's contribution to the GDP declined from 26 to 12 percent between 1965 and 1978 (Vicens 1982). The concentration of land ownership also increased. By 1971, 14 percent of the country's landholders owned 79 percent of all lands, while 70 percent of the population occupied 12 percent of the arable land (Boin and Serullé 1980). Since population-growth rates were high, the sons of these small landowners inherited plots of land that were too small to support their families. These factors triggered a rural exodus to the cities. Between 1965 and 1984, the rural population decreased from 65 to 45 percent of the total population (World Bank 1986). Rural employment also decreased from about 46 percent of the population in 1970 to 24 percent by 1981. At the same time, an urban middle class was emerging as a result of increased professionalism and the growth of certain service-sector jobs. These individuals had consumption aspirations and expectations about their future social mobility that social and economic conditions rendered unattainable (Grasmuck and Pessar 1991). Because most of the industrial growth occurred in sectors requiring more capital than labor, there were too few jobs for those who migrated to the city and a mismatch between employment supply and demand ensued. An estimated 20 percent of Santo Domingo's labor force was unemployed in 1973.

Dominican migration to the United States grew steadily during this period. It rose from 9,250 people in 1968 (after an initial high of 16,503 in 1966) to 13,858 in 1973 (INS 1980). This sustained exodus complemented the capital-intensive industrialization strategy pursued by Balaguer by relieving some of the pressure of the large numbers of unemployed workers who would have remained behind (Grasmuck and Pessar 1991). Since much of his electoral support was rural, rapid urbanization threatened to weaken Balaguer's political base. By allowing relatively high rates of migration, particularly from urban areas, the government exported potential sources of political opposition and was able to remain in power for twelve years (Mitchell 1992).

In 1978, tired of Balaguer's repressive policies and their diminishing economic gains, the Dominican public elected the Partido Revolucionario Dominicano (PRD) candidate, Antonio Guzmán, in what was considered the country's first democratic election. During his first two years in office, Guzmán introduced a number of economic and political reforms. He liberalized the political climate, allowing a number of new labor organizations and unions to be established. He raised the minimum salary. He also created numerous public-sector jobs to lower unemployment and stimulate consumption. Between 1979 and 1982 the number of government employees grew by 72,000 (Espinal 1987).

Despite these efforts, the PRD's first term coincided with the Dominican Republic's worst economic crisis in years. By 1982, declining sugar prices and increasing oil prices and interest rates worsened conditions to such an extent that the International Monetary Fund (IMF) imposed an austerity plan as a condition for assisting the country. The structural-adjustment policies put into place were designed to curtail imports and shift the country's economic focus away from traditional exports to export-processing-zone (EPZ) manufacturing and tourism. Like similar efforts throughout the Caribbean and Mexico, EPZs offer potential manufacturers tax breaks and cheap labor as incentives to relocate parts of their production process overseas. These strategies narrowed the range of employment opportunities available to Dominicans even further. The gross domestic product declined an average of 1.6 percent per year between 1980 and 1988. During the PRD's second administration, under President Jorge Blanco, real salaries declined by 22 percent (Inter-American Development Bank [IDB] 1987). Official unemployment rose from 24 percent in 1970 to 30 percent in 1988.

The government's financial policies also stimulated migration. Exchange policies were revised such that while exports continued to be priced according to the dollar, imports were priced according to a "parallel market" which fluctuated and was normally higher. This meant that Dominican real wages declined considerably, particular in relation to the value of the dollar. By 1987, the minimum monthly salary for a full-time job in the United States was six times higher than what one could earn in the Dominican Republic. These wage differentials also provided Dominicans with a powerful incentive to emigrate (Grasmuck and Pessar 1991).

Further frustration and economic strain prompted the Dominican public to reelect Balaguer in 1986. Under his leadership, the government finally moved the economy away from its dependence on traditional exports. During the 1990s, EPZs and tourism became two of its most important sectors. Revenues from tourism increased from $368.2 million in 1985 to over $1 billion in 1992. Between 1980 and 1988, firms in the EPZs drove up the country's exports from $117 to $517 million. These gains were fragile and continued to be driven by forces located outside the Republic. U.S. companies exempt from paying taxes owned 63 percent of the EPZ industries (Betances 1995). In 1993, over 60 percent of Dominican EPZ workers were women who received an average hourly wage of fifty cents. Though export earnings increased, the Dominican economy remained stagnant at an average growth rate of 1.1 percent (Safa 1993).

When President Leonel Fernandez took office in 1996, he introduced a bold reform package aimed at creating a market-oriented economy that could compete internationally. He proposed a devaluation of the peso, income tax cuts, a 50 percent increase in the sales tax, and a reduction in import tariffs. Though many of these reforms stalled in the legislature, the economy grew vigorously between 1997 and 1998. The estimated GDP real growth rate for 1998 was seven percent. The service sector accounted for 56 percent of the GDP (1996 estimates), followed by industry (25 percent), and agriculture (19 percent), although 50 percent of the labor force was still employed in agriculture, followed by 32 percent in services and government, and 18 percent in industry (1991 estimates). Along with tourism, sugar processing, ferronickel and gold mining, textiles, cement, and tobacco constituted the country's strongest industries. Despite these gains, the social networks precipitating Dominican migration were already firmly in place. Migration has become a way of life for many Dominican families. It has thoroughly transformed many aspects of Dominican society.

A PROFILE OF DOMINICAN MIGRATION

Dominican migration began in earnest in the late 1960s, increased steadily during the 1970s and 1980s, and began to decline slightly in the mid-1990s (Castro and Boswell 2002). Between 1988 and 1998, 401,646 Dominicans were admitted to the United States, almost twice the number from any other

Caribbean country and second only to Mexicans as the principal immigrant group entering the United States from within the Western Hemisphere.

Because anthropologists working in rural communities conducted much of the early research on Dominican migration, it was assumed that most migrants were small- to medium-sized landholding peasants or rural proletarians (Sassen-Koob 1979). Ugalde, Bean, and Cárdenas (1979) first challenged this view when their analysis of the 1974 Diagnos National Study revealed that while over 53 percent of the Dominican population resided in rural areas, only 24 percent of international migrants left from rural parts of the country (Georges 1990). Several subsequent studies found that Dominican migration is principally an urban phenomenon.[2] Castro (1985), however, disputed these findings, arguing that although all classes are represented among the ranks of Dominican migrants, they came overwhelmingly from the working class. He showed that between 1968 and 1978, nearly two-thirds of all Dominicans in the United States were classified as laborers, operatives, or service workers for purposes of the U.S. labor market.[3]

Accurate data collection on the size of any immigrant population is notoriously difficult to come by. The Dominican case is no exception. Researchers using 2000 U.S. Census data and data from the Current Population Survey arrive at different figures.[4] According to the Census Bureau, there were 764,495 Dominicans in the country in 2000. They represented 2.2 percent of the total U.S. Hispanic population and were the fourth largest Hispanic group following Mexicans (58.5 percent), Puerto Ricans (9.6 percent), and Cubans (3.5 percent). Analyses of the Current Population Survey (1997–2000) place these numbers somewhat higher. According to Castro and Boswell (2002), there are 1,014,879 Dominicans in the country while Logan (2001) places the number at 1,121,257, thereby increasing the Dominican share of the Hispanic population to 3.2 percent. Because these figures do not adjust for undercounting, they are likely to underrepresent the actual size of the Dominican population.

Castro and Boswell's analyses of the Current Population Survey (1997–2000) produced the following profile of the Dominican immigrant community. Slightly more females (54 percent) than males (46 percent) make up the Dominican population. They are fairly young. Barely 7 percent are over sixty years of age, compared to 23 percent who are under the age of ten and 44 percent who are under the age of twenty. Despite their phenotypical characteristics, most Dominicans classify themselves as white. Most respondents selected the white racial category (80.2 percent) while 18.3 percent said they were black. This reflects the unique character of the social construction of race in the Dominican Republic. Nearly two-thirds (62.5 percent) had been in the United States since 1989, while 37.5 percent entered between 1990 and 2000. Most are foreign-born (57 percent), but there is substantial U.S.-born component (43 percent, including those born in Puerto Rico). Of those who are foreign-born, only 33 percent were naturalized U.S. citizens. When we combine the first and second generation, 61 percent of Dominicans are citizens of the United States. Dominicans continue to be highly concentrated in the New York–New Jersey Metropolitan area (67 percent), but there are also important concentrations in the Miami–Fort Lauderdale area (7.7 percent) and in Massachusetts (4.1 percent).

Dominicans in the United States face significant challenges. In general, most immigrants arrived without the kinds of occupational and language skills demanded by the changing labor market. The majority entered the United States during a period of major economic restructuring. Fewer well-paying, unionized jobs awaited the unskilled, non-English speaker, while the number of menial, insecure, and low-paying jobs in manufacturing, trade, and service sectors grew. Consequently, while 48.6 percent of all Dominicans were employed in manufacturing in 1979, only 26 percent worked in these jobs by 1989 (Castro and Boswell 2002). Furthermore, many high-tech jobs in health and communications require advanced degrees that most Dominicans do not possess.

As a result, Dominicans rank lower than the U.S. population as a whole, and with respect to other Latino groups, in terms of occupation status, education, and income. Fewer than 10 percent are college graduates. While 42 percent of all Dominicans graduated from high school, 48 percent did not complete a high school degree. The majority work in blue-, gray-, and pink-collar jobs in the service sector (33 percent) or as operators, fabricators and handlers (30 percent). Eleven percent classified themselves as managers and professionals, while 25 percent worked in technical, sales, and administrative-support positions. While the 25 percent of all Cuban workers who held professional and managerial positions nearly matched the figures for the nation as a whole (29 percent), only 17 percent of Puerto Ricans and 11 percent of Dominicans held comparable positions. Similarly, the mean personal income for a full-time worker in the United States was $40,645, again nearly equaled by Cubans ($40,056), but not matched by Puerto Rican ($31,851), Dominican ($27,258), and Mexican workers ($23,727). Finally, while one-quarter of the general population and of Cuban immigrants have college degrees or higher, only 13 percent of Puerto Ricans, 10 percent of Dominicans and 6.2 percent of Mexicans have college degrees.

While the immigrant generation is faring poorly, second-generation Dominicans are exhibiting educational and occupational gains, as Castro and Boswell reveal in their 2002 comparison of U.S.-born Dominicans with those who arrived prior to 1990. While females predominate among foreign-born Dominicans, there are slightly more males among the U.S.-born Dominican population. Only 9 percent of U.S.-born Dominicans twenty-five years of age and older did not complete high school, compared to 53 percent of the pre-1990 cohort. In addition, the proportion of second generation Dominicans who completed a college degree (22 percent) is more than three times as high as the pre-1990 immigrant cohort (7 percent). The median income for U.S.-born Dominican full-time workers ($26,125) surpasses the $20,000 earned by comparable workers who arrived prior to 1990. Finally, U.S.-born Dominicans are almost twice as likely to be employed as professionals and managers (18 percent) than their pre-1990 counterparts (10 percent).

Thus far, the analyses I have presented focus on wage earners, but Dominicans are also well represented among the ranks of small business owners. The majority of these businesses are commercial activities such as groceries and restaurants, personal and business services such as beauty parlors and insurance or travel agencies, and finance firms that cash checks or transfer remittances. In fact, one study revealed that 70 percent of all bodega or small grocery store owners in New York City, with estimated annual sales of $1.8 billion, were owned by Dominicans (Portes and Guarnizo 1991). Unlike their Cuban counterparts in Miami, however, Dominican entrepreneurs have not created an ethnic enclave in the United States (Castro and Boswell 2002).

There is some debate about how much entrepreneurship contributes to economic advancement, and for whom. Some argue that self-employment results in significant economic gains, allowing migrants to overcome their disadvantaged position in the labor market. Portes and Guarnizo (1991), for example, found that the ninety-two firms they studied had a net worth of approximately $35.5 million and yielded some $4.4 million for their owners. Other researchers are less sanguine about the benefits of small-business ownership, arguing that the economic rewards are limited and that they accrue only to a small group. Since only 7 percent of the Dominicans in New York City were self-employed in 1990 (U.S. Census 1992), the overall impact of the Dominican business sector on the community's overall welfare is questionable. Torres-Saillant and Hernández (1998: 79) ask, for example, "whether entrepreneurship among Dominicans is likely to lead to effective capital accumulation, diversification, and expansion by surpassing the limitations imposed by the widespread poverty of the community that constitutes its primary clientele." Although small business development creates some employment opportunities, these jobs tend to pay less and provide fewer benefits than those in native-owned firms (Grasmuck and Pessar 1991, Gilbertson and Gurak 1993). Finally, the media has paid a good deal of attention to those Dominicans involved in drug trafficking. While there are clearly some individuals involved in these kinds of activities, they represent only a small fraction of the community. The vast majority of Dominicans are law-abiding citizens whose reputation has been tarnished by a small few.

DOMINICANS AS TRANSNATIONAL ACTORS

Many U.S. citizens expect migrants to sever their ties to their countries of origin as they become integrated into the United States. They assume that residence will eventually equal membership as migrants shift their allegiance from the countries they leave behind to those where they settle. In contrast, the Dominican experience reveals that increasing numbers of migrants remain strongly connected to their homelands even as they become incorporated into the United States. Migrants use a variety of transnational political, religious, and civic arenas to forge social relations, earn their livelihoods, and exercise their rights across borders. The proliferation of these long-term transnational ties among Dominicans and other groups challenges conventional notions about immigrant incorporation and migrants' continued influence on their sending nations. In the following section, I outline a theoretical approach to transnational migration and describe in detail a Dominican example of these kinds of cross-border practices (see also Levitt 2001b).

When the magnitude, duration, and impact of migration is sufficiently strong, transnational social fields or public spheres spanning the sending and receiving countries emerge. Both the migrants and nonmigrants who live within transnational social fields are exposed to a set of social expectations, cultural values, and patterns of human interaction shaped by at least two, if not more, social, economic, and political systems. They have access to social and institutional resources that imbue them with the capacity remain active in two worlds.

Movement is not a prerequisite for transnational activism. There are those who travel regularly to carry out their routine affairs, whom some researchers call transmigrants (England 1999, Guarnizo 1997). There are also individuals whose lives are rooted primarily in a single sending- or receiving-country setting, who move infrequently, but whose experiences integrally involve resources, contacts, and people who are far away and who imagine themselves within a landscape that crosses borders. And there are those who do not move, but who live their lives within a context that has become transnationalized.

Those frequent travelers, periodic movers, and individuals that stay in one place who engage in transnational practices do so in a variety of ways. Portes, Guarnizo, and Landolt (1999) and Guarnizo (2002) define core transnationalism as those activities that form an integral part of the individual's habitual life, are undertaken on a regular basis, and are patterned and therefore somewhat predictable. Expanded transnationalism, in contrast, includes migrants who engage in occasional transnational practices, such as responses to political crises or natural disasters. Itzigsohn et al. (1999) characterize broad transnational practices as those that are not well institutionalized, involve only occasional participation, and require only sporadic movement. He and his colleagues contrast these with narrow transnational practices that are highly institutionalized, constant, and involve regular travel.

These terms help to operationalize variations in the intensity and frequency of transnational practices. But crossborder engagements also vary along other dimensions, such as scope. Even those engaged in core transnational practices may confine their activities to one arena of social action. Or the same person may engage in core transnational activities with respect to one sphere of social life and only expanded transnational activities with respect to another. There are those, for example, whose livelihoods depend upon the frequent, patterned harnessing of resources across borders while their political and religious lives focus on host-country concerns. In contrast, there are those who engage in regular religious and political transnational practices but only occasionally send money back to family members or invest in homeland projects. Individuals whose activities involve many arenas of social life engage in *comprehensive* transnational practices while others engage in transnational practices that are more *selective* in scope.

These variations demonstrate that transnational practices are not fixed packages that remain constant over the lifecycle. Instead, migrants piece together a constellation of strategies at different stages of their lives and combine these with host-country integration strategies. The resulting configurations produce different combinations of upward and downward mobility. Some migrants are upwardly mobile with respect to both their home and host societies. Others advance with respect to one and stagnate or diminish their position with respect to the other. Still others experience downward mobility in both contexts. These outcomes depend largely on class. Professional, well-educated migrants can choose to remain active in both contexts. They may hedge their bets, using the resources and opportunities they command to implement economic and political strategies in their home and host communities to make the most of both situations and to make sure that if circumstances sour in one setting they have a "plan B" in the other. Migrants with less education, lower skills, and more limited language abilities are pushed into transnational lifestyles. Because they have difficulty gaining a secure foothold in either setting, they must participate economically and politically wherever they can.

Clearly, not all migrants are engaged in transnational practices. Most are likely to undergo the typical transformation from immigrants to ethnics. But recent work suggests that a small but significant group are exhibiting a distinct mode of incorporation. Portes and his colleagues (2002) found that slightly more than 5 percent of the Salvadoran, Dominican, and Colombian migrants they studied were transnational entrepreneurs. Guarnizo (2002) reported that nearly 10 percent of the Colombians, Dominicans, and Salvadorans he surveyed were engaged in some form of regular transnational political activity. Their activities included membership in a home-country political party (9.9 percent), membership in a civic hometown association (13.7 percent), or taking part in home-country electoral campaigns and rallies (7.7 percent). Those engaged in periodic transnational nonelectoral political practices, such as belonging to hometown association membership, supporting community improvement projects, and participating in home-country charitable organizations, numbered more than 25 percent.

The kinds of transnational relationships I describe are not new. Southern and Eastern European migrants who came to the United States in the early 1900s also maintained strong ties to their countries of origin (Foner 2000). But despite similarities, there are also clear differences between the experiences of earlier and contemporary transnational migrants. New communication and transportation technologies permit more frequent and intimate connections between those who move and those who remain behind. The airplane and the telephone make it easier and cheaper to stay in touch. Technological advances heighten the immediacy and intensity of contact, allowing migrants to be actively involved in everyday life in fundamentally different ways than before.

The changing nature of the U.S. economy also means that migrants are incorporated into the labor market in different ways than in the past. In the early 1900s, rapidly industrializing U.S. companies needed low-skilled labor for jobs that often did not require that workers speak English. In contrast, today's migrants enter a postindustrial economy that courts high-skilled workers but offers limited opportunities for the unskilled non-English speaker. Many new migrants find work in the service sector, which pays less, offers fewer benefits, and affords more limited opportunities for advancement than the manufacturing sector.[5]

Furthermore, the kinds of homeland connections sustained by migrants today differ from those in the past because they are forged within a cultural context more tolerant of ethnic pluralism. At the turn of the century, and particularly during the period preceding World War I, migrants were under tremendous pressure to naturalize and become "good Americans." In contrast, the United States of the late twentieth century tolerates ethnic diversity more. The pressure to conform to a well-defined, standardized notion of what it means to be "American" has greatly decreased. Contemporary migrants enjoy the protections of new antidiscrimination and affirmative-action legislation. Displays of continued ethnic pride are normal, celebrated parts of daily life. Those wanting to express allegiances face a less hostile environment within which to do so.

Finally, most of the countries sending the largest number of immigrants to the United States today have completed the process of nation building. As a result, the demands they make of their members, their political discourse, and the ways in which they represent themselves culturally mean that they encourage long-distance nationalism and participation rather than linking activism to return (Morawska 2000, Glick Schiller and Fouron 2001). In 2000, at least ten Latin American and ten Caribbean countries allowed some form of dual nationality (Jones-Correa 2002).

Migration between the United States and the Dominican Republic has produced a thick, broad transnational social field inhabited by individual actors, communities, and organizations. Both sending- and receiving-country factors explain its emergence. As I mentioned earlier, migration provides a much needed palliative for an economy that has left large numbers under- or unemployed. Those who live abroad and those who return to live on the island have become a key factor in the Dominican economy. In 1984, Dominican migrants accounted for 60 percent of the total formal housing sales (Guarnizo 1997). The $796 million in remittances migrants sent in 1995 surpassed all other activities, except for tourism, as sources of foreign exchange (Migration News 1998). By November 1999, projections from the Central Bank of the Dominican Republic reported that migrants had remitted nearly $1.4 billion (Rodriguez 1999). According to a Carlos Doré, a close advisor to former President Fernández, migrants "are sine qua non for Dominican macro-economic stability, including monetary exchange rates, the balance of trade, international monetary reserves, and the national balance of payment" (cited in Guarnizo 1997: 285). The country's economic fortunes continue to be strongly influenced by events in the United States. The Dominican state literally cannot afford to let migrants go.

The case of migration between Boston and Miraflores, a small community located outside the city of Baní, brings to light the positive and negative effects of these strong, enduring transnational connections (see also Levitt 2001a). Migration from this area began in the late 1960s, when the commercialization of agriculture and unequal land-tenure patterns made it increasingly difficult for residents to earn a decent living by farming. By 1994, over 65 percent of the 545 households in Miraflores had relatives in the greater Boston metropolitan area, primarily in and around the neighborhood of Jamaica Plain. The social and economic lives of these transnational villagers has been completely transformed by migration. Many families now rely heavily on the economic support they receive from the United States. In 1994, almost 60 percent of the households in Miraflores said they received at least some of their monthly income from those in the U.S. For nearly 40 percent of those households, remittances constituted between 75 and 100 percent of their income.

Fashion, food, forms of speech, as well as appliances and home decorating styles, also attest to these strong connections. In Miraflores, villagers often dress in T-shirts with the names of businesses in Massachusetts printed on them, although they often do not know what these words or logos mean. They proudly serve coffee with Cremora or juice made from Tang to their visitors. The local *colmados* (grocery stores) stock Spaghettios and Frosted Flakes. These dynamics are enacted in the context of striking contrasts. The electricity in Miraflores goes out nearly every night because the government-run electric company is so poorly functioning and a number of the houses in Miraflores still lack indoor plumbing. Many of the benches in the Miraflores park are inscribed with the names of villagers who moved to Boston years ago. And almost everyone, including older community members who can count on their fingers how many times they have visited Santo Domingo, can talk about "La Mozart" or "La Centre," or Mozart Street Park and Centre Street, two focal points of the Miraflores community in Jamaica Plain.

In Boston, Mirafloreños have recreated their premigration lives to the extent allowed by their new physical and cultural environment. Particularly during the early years of settlement, but even today, a large number of migrants live within the same twenty-block radius. There are several streets where people from Miraflores live in almost every triple-decker house.[6] Community members leave their apartment doors open so that the flow between households is as easy and uninhibited as it is in Miraflores. They decorate their refrigerators with the same plastic fruit magnets that they use in Miraflores and they put the same sets of ceramic animal families on the shelves of their living rooms. Women also continue to hang curtains around the doorframes; these provide privacy without keeping in heat in the Dominican Republic but are merely decorative in Boston. Because someone is always traveling between Boston and the island, there is a continuous, circular flow of goods, news, and information. As a result, when a community member becomes ill, cheats on his or her spouse, or is finally granted a visa, the news spreads as quickly on the streets of Miraflores as it does in Jamaica Plain.

During their visits, phone conversations, and through the videotapes they send home, migrants introduce those who remained behind to the ideas and practices they observed in the United States. Nonmigrants gradually began to adopt these behaviors and develop U.S. culture and consumer styles. This steady infusion of social remittances, combined with migrant and nonmigrants' heightened social and economic interdependence, further encourage transnational village formation and perpetuation (Levitt 2001a).[7]

Other transnational villages also span the Dominican Republic and the United States. Migrants from Tenares, who have settled in Lawrence, Massachusetts, also formed similar ties. People from Sabana Iglesias who moved to

Queens, New York, also stay strongly connected to their sending community. Not everyone who is embedded in this transnational social field, however, feels part of a transnational community. Many migrants from Santiago, the

Republic's second largest city, have settled in the Washington Heights neighborhood of New York City, but they do not all feel part of a transnational social group.

Transnational institutions both create and are created in response to individuals' transnational practices. In the Miraflores case, the Miraflores Development Committee (MDC), with chapters in Boston and Miraflores, was created to improve living conditions in the village. Over the past thirty years, this group has built an aqueduct, a funeral home, a park, and a baseball stadium and funded renovations to the school, health clinic, and community center. These kind of sending-community support activities are not unique. Guarnizo (2002) reports that nearly 10 percent of the Dominican migrants in his study claimed that they regularly participated in a hometown association, while 9 percent frequently contributed money to community projects, and 6 percent supported sending-country charitable organizations. Nearly 20 percent reported that they occasionally engaged in these activities.

The Catholic Church, an already well-established transnational institution, has also transformed itself in response to the new crossborders ties forged by the frequent circulation of parishioners, resources, and clergy between Boston and the island. New Dominican immigrants are incorporated into multiethnic congregations using a generic "Latino" worship style that includes some familiar elements while excluding many uniquely Dominican ones. They tell those who remain behind about their changing religious practices and beliefs. Subsequent migrants arrive already presocialized into many elements of U.S. Latino Catholicism. They continue to infuse fresh "Dominicanness" into the church, though it is a "Dominicanness" that is increasingly pan-Latino in tone. Continuous, cyclical transfers ensued which consolidated these panethnic practices while weakening their uniquely Dominican elements. In this way, transnational ties reinforced religious pluralism at the same time that they abbreviated its scope.

Dominican political life has also become transnational. Long before migration became an important social force, Dominican political parties established a tradition of expatriate political organization in the United Stares. Juan Bosch created the Partido Revolucionario Dominicano (PRD) while in exile from Trujillo in Cuba in 1939. Throughout Trujillo's reign, the PRD used its ties with U.S. political leaders to mobilize public opinion against him. They organized public demonstrations, published open letters in the U.S. press, and enlisted the support of U.S. political leaders to protest human-rights abuses on the island. When the PRD gained power in 1978, leaders shifted their attention to formal Dominican partisan politics and to fundraising, sending as much as $40,000 back to Santo Domingo each month.

In the last three decades, the United States, and New York City in particular, have become critical staging grounds for Dominican political battles. Migrants make significant political contributions. An estimated 15—30% of the funding for the 1994 Dominican presidential campaign came from emigrants (Graham 1997). They also exert considerable influence over how their nonemigrant family members vote. Since many support their nonemigrant family members, they convert their economic clout into political clout by telling those who stay behind whom they should support.

In response to migrants' growing role in island politics, each of the principal Dominican political parties created a U.S.-based party structure that mirrors its organization on the island. The Partido Revolucionario Dominicano (PRD) created community-level committees, aggregated into municipal zones, which were then grouped into regional sections in New England, New Jersey, Florida, Puerto Rico, and Washington. In 1992, the party also approved the creation of base-level committees for Dominicans who became naturalized U.S. citizens and for second-generation Dominican-Americans. Four members of the U.S. sections represent the migrant community on the party's National Executive Committee in Santo Domingo. The party also appointed a coordinator for all U.S. party activities whose job is to facilitate cooperation between party members at all levels on the island and in the United States.

The PRD also began articulating a discourse that was more transnational in tone. As the party's financial dependence on migrant contributions increased, and migrant members made clear their conditions for remaining active in the party, leaders proposed new ideas about the party's relationship to its U.S. constituency. They recognized that the PRD needed a dual political agenda which simultaneously addressed the needs of migrants while furthering Dominican national interests. If the party encouraged migrants to integrate politically in the United States, they would be more strongly positioned to advocate for Dominican national concerns. In exchange, the party would support policies such as lowering taxes on the goods migrants brought back into the country, dual citizenship, and the expatriate vote that migrants favored. Several leaders mentioned the example of the Jewish-American community as the model they wished to emulate. Just as the Jewish-American lobby favorably influenced U.S. policies toward Israel, so the Dominican migrant community could generate support for favorable sugar quotas, terms of trade, and development assistance.

The PRD was not the sole voice encouraging dual membership. In fact, in a televised address, then candidate Leonel Fernández encouraged Dominican migrants to naturalize and assured them they would not lose their rights as Dominican citizens if they did so:

> If you, young mother, or you, elderly gentleman, or you, young student, feel the need to adopt the nationality of the United States in order to confront the vicissitudes of that society stemming from the end of the welfare era, do not feel tormented by this. Do it with a peaceful conscience, for you will continue being Dominicans, and we will welcome you as such when you set foot on the soil of our republic
>
> *(cited in Graham 1997).*

Calls for dual citizenship and the expatriate vote grew stronger throughout the 1970s and 1980s due to the efforts of an emerging entrepreneurial class with business interests in the United States and in the Dominican Republic (Guarnizo 1998). Business owners and emigrant civic associations arranged a number of conferences in New York and in the Dominican Republic to advocate, in the interest of national unity and economic growth, for a constitutional amendment that would institute such changes. These calls went largely unheeded until the mid-1990s when several factors converged to facilitate their approval. Previously, Balaguer's Partido Reformista, while publicly supportive of dual citizenship and expatriate voting, actually blocked their implementation fearing emigrants' potential opposition to the government. Balaguer's position weakened considerably, however, when the international community sided against him when he was accused of election tampering in 1994. European and U.S. governments and international observers forced the president to accept The Pact for Democracy and to remain in office for a reduced two-year term. This agreement comprised several reforms, including the approval of dual citizenship. The reformed constitution, approved in 1996, gives full citizenship rights to Dominicans who opt for a second citizenship, though they cannot be elected president or vice president. The new constitution also grants citizenship to those born outside the country to Dominican parents, thus ensuring the formal inclusion of the second generation and beyond (Torres-Saillant and Hernández 1998). In fact, there is some question about whether current President Hipolito Mejia holds dual nationality. In a December 2001 interview with a Miami radio station, he was quoted as saying that he was a dual national. Two days later, however, he recanted his statement and denied his U.S. citizenship (Dominican Republic One 2001)

The 1996 and 2000 Dominican elections, held in a context of greater accountability and political openness, reflected the emigrant community's strong influence. All major political parties had offices in Boston, New York, and other areas with large emigrant communities. Any politician from the island with serious aspirations had to campaign in Dominican neighborhoods in the United States. Guarnizo (2002) found that nearly 13 percent of the Dominicans he surveyed reported that they belonged to a political party in which they participated regularly, while an additional 23 percent belonged to a political group that they participated in occasionally. Though they could not vote as expatriates, many emigrants returned to the island to cast their ballots (Rother 1996a). Thus, in 1996, PRD presidential candidate José Francisco Peña Gómez acknowledged, "The part they [migrants] play is absolutely decisive, especially in terms of campaign finances"; while candidate Leonel Fernández's campaign chief in the United States stated, "The Dominican community in the United States has tremendous economic weight and political prestige, so of course its influence is being felt." (Rother 1996b: 21).

Both second-round presidential candidates in 1996 also supported a bill that would allow Dominican emigrants to vote from abroad rather than having to return to the island. This measure was passed in December 1997 (Electoral Law 275–97), when the Dominican National Congress approved a new electoral code allowing Dominicans permanently residing overseas to vote in the country's presidential elections and to run for office, including those who are naturalized Americans of Dominican descent (Sagás 1999). Dominicans in New York campaigned extensively for these measures, creating a Pro-Vote Movement for Dominicans Living Abroad (Sontag 1997). Once achieved, these electoral reforms effectively cemented the political importance of Dominicans abroad as contributors, as well as voters. Dominicans living abroad will allegedly be allowed to vote in the 2004 presidential election.

The Dominican government's relationship to emigrants has also changed in the last decade. The government made few systematic attempts to maintain contact with expatriates prior to the 1990s. When mass emigration began in the early 1970s, government efforts focused on channeling the money migrants sent back to the island through official, state-controlled channels. In his 1982 inaugural speech, for example, President Salvador Jorge Blanco outlined a plan to increase interest rates on special savings accounts designed to attract remittances (Guarnizo 1998).

When the PLD was elected in 1996, however, the government began systematically reaching out to migrants and, by so doing, extending the borders of the Dominican state. It no longer referred to Dominicans abroad as *migrantes* (migrants) or *Dominicanos Ausentes* but as Dominicans Residing in the Exterior. In 1999, several U.S.-based Dominicans served in the Dominican Congress. The fact that the Partido de la Liberacíon Dominicana (PLD) designated three legislative seats on its ticket to Dominicans living abroad aided their election. Candidates for these seats run from their hometowns because there is no formal mechanism to elect representatives from abroad. Those elected officially represent districts on the island but unofficially represent their constituencies abroad (Itzigsohn et al. 1999).

CONCLUSION

This chapter highlights various factors that have precipitated Dominican migration, profiles the characteristics of those who move, explores the ways in which Dominican migrants continue to be part of their sending communities as they are incorporated into the United States, and brings to light how community development and political and religious life become transnational in the process. It reveals that, by and large, Dominicans have not brought the kinds of language, education, and job skills demanded by current labor market. As a result, they do more poorly than the national average and than certain Latino groups with respect to some socioeconomic indicators. There are indications, however, that the second generation is making progress and performing better with respect to educational, financial, and occupational outcomes.

Pessar (1996) proposed four explanations for this profile. The first is that economic restructuring means there are fewer jobs that Dominicans are qualified for and that most of these jobs pay low wages. The second is that Dominicans' low educational levels exclude them from higher-paying, more secure jobs. The third is that there are many female-headed households in the Dominican community, which is clearly linked to higher poverty rates. In 1990, almost 40 percent of all Dominican households with children under eighteen in New York City were headed by women and 52 percent of these households were living below the poverty line (Hernández, Rivera-Batiz, and Agodini 1995). Dominican women in New York also earn less than their male counterparts. In 1989, they earned $11,371 annually, compared to $15,139 among males. Finally, racial discrimination also seriously inhibits socioeconomic gains. Poverty among darker-skinned Dominicans is strikingly higher than among Dominicans with lighter skin (Grasmuck and Pessar 1998).

This chapter also underscores the high levels of transnational activism among Dominican emigrants. It also speaks to the complex relationship between transnational migration and development. Most Mirafloreños, for example, have more income and enjoy a more comfortable lifestyle since emigration began. They have a better school, health clinic, and water supply. They feel a stronger sense of civic responsibility and a desire to challenge the political status quo. But they have achieved these gains only through the graces of those in Boston. They cannot sustain this higher standard of living on their own. They have lost faith in Dominican values and in their country's ability to solve its own problems. They have become so dependent on the money, ideas, and values imported from Boston that migration has become an integral part of their everyday lives.

Immigrant life also yields ambiguous rewards. Most Mirafloreños work at jobs that pay more than they have ever dreamed of. They are proud of their

English-speaking children when they do well in school. On the weekends, they go to the mall where they can choose from a range of products so vast it is almost unimaginable. But work consumes them. They leave at five o'clock in the morning, return at two o'clock, eat, bathe, and then work again until ten at night. Their jobs give them little besides a paycheck. Many live near the bottom of the socioeconomic ladder. Since they often work alone, they generally learn little English and few new skills, meaning they have few opportunities to get ahead. They feel more capable when they compare themselves to those who remain in Miraflores and less powerful and effective in their dealings with the host society. Those who regret their choices are prevented from turning back because so many family members and friends now depend on their support.

These widespread, enduring ties also challenge conventional understandings of the determinants of inequality, civic engagement, and community development. They urge us to rethink how and where these social dynamics should be evaluated. For some individuals, the measure of success must be taken transnationally. In the Miraflores case, migrants may fare poorly with respect to socioeconomic indicators in the United States while they achieve significant economic gains with respect to their lives in the Dominican Republic. They work at a continuous string of part-time, low-paying jobs and are subject to frequent layoffs, but they are able to build a new home in Miraflores and significantly raise the standard of living of the household members who remain behind. Furthermore, for many individuals the Dominican community continues to be the yardstick against which they evaluate themselves. It is still the reference group which matters most.

The Dominican case also brings to light the ways in which cultural production has become transnational and the ways in which developments in the home and host country mutually influence one another. The social remittances emigrants send back introduce both positive and negative influences. For example, a vice president of the Partido Revolucionario Dominicano (PRD) characterized migrants' political influence as follows:

> There are greater demands for more democracy within the parties, that the justice system should be separate from the executive branch which is so corrupt. . . . Emigration is a factor in the modernization of the political system in favor of a new type of establishment within the society. It is playing a role, since the people who come back come with these ideas. Even though they haven't participated in the political heart of the U.S., they have lived there. They have a notion of the relationship between public and private and that these distinctions are clearer than those in the Dominican Republic. And these things, any person picks up on them because they see it when their kids go to school or when they pay taxes. If people live this in their

> daily lives, it produces a change in mentality. It is not that they have formed a movement in favor of the rights of citizens, but they have friends and neighbors, and they say to their cousins if you have a problem, go to a lawyer. Don't try to work it out through a friend.
>
> *(PRD vice president, interview with author, Santo Domingo, July 1994)*

Social remittances also wield negative influences as Javier, a fifty-six-year-old nonmigrant in Miraflores described:

> Life in the U.S. teaches them many good things but they also learn some bad things as well. People come back more individualistic, more materialistic. They think that "things" are everything rather than service, respect, or duty. They are more committed to themselves than they are to the community. They just don't want to be active in trying to make the community better anymore. Some learned to make it the easy way and they are destroying our traditional values of hard work and respect for the family.
>
> *(Interview with author, Miraflores, January 1993)*

Cultural influence, however, is clearly a two-way street, and Dominican culture is also making inroads into the broader U.S. cultural arena. Dominican baseball players such as Sammy Sosa and Pedro Martínez have become regional, if not national stars. When former President Bill Clinton asked Sammy Sosa to accompany Hillary Rodham Clinton during the 2000 State of Union address he was not just honoring this baseball great, but also paying tribute to the political importance of New York Dominican community in a very visible public arena. In fact, organizations like the Dominican American Roundtable are working actively to consolidate first- and second-generation Dominicans' place at the political table. The popularity of writers like Junot Díaz and Julia Alvarez, as well as fashion designer Oscar de la Renta, also attest to the growing influence of the Dominican community (Castro and Boswell 2002).

NOTES

1. For a more in-depth account of Dominican history see Hoetink 1982, Wiarda and Kryzanek 1982, Black 1986, Betances 1995, Moya Pons 1995, Betances and Spalding 1996, and Torres-Saillant and Hernández 1998.
2. For additional accounts of Dominican migration, see Gonzales 1970, Peña and Parache 1971, Hendricks 1974, Garrison and Weiss 1979, Kayal 1978, Ugalde and Langham 1980, Pérez 1981, Gurak and Kritz 1982, Castro 1985, Báez Evertsz and Ramirez 1986, Bray 1987, Del Castillo and Cordero 1980, Georges, 1990, Grasmuck and Pessar 1991, and Guarnizo 1992.

3. Whether authors use data from the United States or from the Dominican Republic to assess migrants' characteristics contributes to this dispute.
4. For an in-depth discussion of these differences see Logan 2001.
5. It is true that migrants today enjoy certain opportunities that both foreign and native-born minorities lacked one hundred years ago. Earlier in this century, even native-born minority men, including those with Ivy League degrees, were barred from certain jobs in universities, industry, and the public sector. Present-day migrants also benefit from government initiatives like Affirmative Action (Gold 2000).
6. Triple deckers are typical of the housing stock in certain neighborhoods in Boston. They are three-story houses, generally with one apartment on each floor.
7. Social remittances are the ideas, behavior, social capital, and identities that flow from receiving- to sending-country communities. For more detail, see Levitt 2001a.

REFERENCES

Báez Evertsz, Frank, and Frank d'Oleo Ramirez. 1986. *La emigración de Dominicanos a Estados Unidos: Determinantes socio-economicos y consecuencias.* Santo Domingo: Fundación Friedrich Ebert.

Betances, Emilio. 1995. *State and Society in the Dominican Republic.* Boulder, Colo.: Westview Press.

Betances, Emilio, and Hobart Spalding. 1996. *The Dominican Republic Today: Realities and Perspectives.* New York: Graduate School and University Center of the City University of New York.

Black, Jan Knippers. 1986. *The Dominican Republic: Politics and Development in an Unsovereign State.* Winchester, Mass.: Allen and Unwin.

Boin, J., and J. Serullé. 1980. *La Explotación Capitalista en la República Dominicana* Santo Domingo: Ediciónes Gramil.

Bray, David. 1987. "The Dominican Exodus: Origins, Problems, and Solutions." In *Caribbean Exodus,* ed. Barry Levine, 174–205. New York: Praeger.

Calder, B. 1984. *The Impact of Intervention: The Dominican Republic during the U.S. Occupation of 1916–1924.* Austin: University of Texas Press.

Cassá, Roberto, David Ortiz, Roberto González, and Gilberto Rodríguez. 1986. *Actualidad y perspectivas de la cuestión nacional en la República Dominicana.* Santo Domingo: Editora Buho.

Castro, Max. 1985. "Dominican Journey: Patterns, Context, and Consequences of Migration from the Dominican Republic to the United States." Ph.D. diss., University of North Carolina at Chapel Hill.

Castro, Max, and Thomas D. Boswell. 2002. "The Dominican Diaspora Revisted: Dominicans and Dominican-Americans in a New Century." *The North-South Agenda, Paper 53.* Miami: North-South Center, University of Miami.

Del Castillo, Jorge and Walter Cordero. 1980. *La Economia Dominicana Durante El Primer Cuarto del Siglo XX.* Santo Domingo: Fundación García Arévelo, Inc.

Derby, Lauren. 1994. "Between State and Nation: The Dominican Republic and the U.S. World Order." Paper presented at the Latin American Studies Association, March, Atlanta, Georgia.

Dominican Republic One. 5–7 December 2001. http://www.dr1.com. Accessed 15 January 2002.

England, Sarah. 1999. "Negotiating Race and Place in the Garifuna Diaspora: Identity Formation and Transnational Grassroots Politics in New York City and Honduras." *Identities* 6, no. 1: 5–53.

Espinal, Rosario. 1987. "Labor, Politics, and Industrialization in the Dominican Republic." *Industrial Democracy* 8: 183–212.

Foner, Nancy. 2000. *From Ellis Island to JFK: New York's Two Great Waves of Immigration.* New Haven and New York: Yale University Press and the Russell Sage Foundation.

Garrison, Vivian, and Carol I. Weiss. 1979. "Dominican Family Networks and US Immigration Policy: A Case Study." *International Migration Review* 12: 264–83.

Georges, Eugenia. 1990. *The Making of a Transnational Community.* New York: Columbia University Press.

Gilbertson, Greta, and Douglas Gurak. 1993. "Broadening the Enclave Debate: The Labor Market Experiences of Dominicans and Columbian Men in New York City." *Sociological Forum* 8, no. 2: 205–20.

Gleijeses, Piero. 1978. *The Dominican Crisis: The 1965 Constitutionalist Revolt and American Intervention.* Baltimore: Johns Hopkins University Press.

Glick Schiller, Nina, and Georges Fouron. 2001. *Georges Woke Up Laughing.* Durham: Duke University Press.

Gold, Steven. 2000. "Transnational Communities: Examining Migration in a Globally Integrated World." In *Rethinking Globalization(s): From the Corporation Transnationalism to Local Intervention.* Ed. Preet S. Aulakh and Michael G. Schecter, 95–127. London: Macmillan.

Gonzales, Nancie. 1970. "Peasants' Progress: Dominicans in New York." *Caribbean Studies* 10: 154–71.

Gonzales, Carolina. 1999. "Young Dominicans Chart a New Agenda." *New York Daily News*, 27 February.

Graham, Pamela. 1997. "Reimagining the Nation and Defining the District: Dominican Migration and Transnational Politics." In *Caribbean Circuits: New Directions in the Study of Caribbean Migration*, ed. Patricia Pessar. New York: Center for Migration Studies.

Grasmuck, Sherri, and Patricia Pessar. 1998. "First and Second generation Settlement of Dominicans in the United States: 1960–1990." In *Origins and Destinies: Immigration, Race and Ethnicity in America*, ed. Silvia Pedraza and Rubén Rumbaut. Belmont, Calif.: Wadsworth Press.

——1991. *Between Two Islands: Dominican International Migration.* Berkeley: University of California Press.

Guarnizo, Luis. 1992. "One Country in Two: Dominican-Owned Firms in New York and in the Dominican Republic." Ph.D. diss., Johns Hopkins University.

——1997. "The Emergence of a Transnational Social Formation and the Mirage of Return Among Dominican Transmigrants." *Identities* 4, no. 3: 281–322.

——1998. "The Rise of Transnational Social Formations: Mexican and Dominican State Responses to Transnational Migration." *Political Power and Social Theory* 12: 45–94.

—— 2002. "De la asimilación al transnacionalismo: Determinantes de la acción política transnacional entre los migrantes contemporáneos." Paper presented at Migración Transnacional: Sus Efectos y Tendencias en la Cuenca del Caribe. Conference organized by FLACSO, Santo Domingo, 18–19 January.

Gurak, Douglas, and Mary Kritz. 1982. "Dominican and Colombian Women in New York City: Household Structure and Employment Patterns." *Migration Today* 10, nos. 3–4: 14–21.

Hendricks, Glenn. 1974. *The Dominican Diaspora: From the Dominican Republic to New York City. Villagers in Transition*. New York: Teachers College Press.

Hernández, Ramona, Francisco Rivera-Batiz, and Roberto Agodini. 1995. *Dominican New Yorkers: A Socioeconomic Profile, 1990*. New York: Dominican Research Monographs, The CUNY Dominican Studies Institute.

Hoetink, Harry 1982. *The Dominican People, 1850–1900*. Baltimore and London: The Johns Hopkins University Press.

Inter-American Development Bank (IDB). 1987. *Economic and Social Progress in Latin America*. Washington, D.C.: Inter-American Development Bank.

Itzigsohn, José, Carlos Dore Cabral, Esther Hernández Medina, and Obed Vázquez. 1999. "Mapping Dominican Transnationalism: Narrow and Broad Transnational Practices." *Ethnic and Racial Studies* 22, no. 2: 2316–40.

Jones-Correa, Michael. 2001. "Under Two Flags: Dual Nationality in Latin America and Its Consequences for the United States." *International Migration Review* 34, no. 4: 997–1030.

Kayal, Philip. 1978. "The Dominicans in New York: Part 2." *Migration Today* 6: 10–15.

Levitt, Peggy. 2001a. *The Transnational Villagers*. Berkeley and Los Angeles: University of California Press.

——. 2001b. "Transnational Migration: Taking Stock and Future Directions. *Global Networks* 1, no. 3: 195–216.

Logan, John. 2001. "The New Latinos: Who They Are, Where They Are." Lewis Mumford Center for Comparative Urban and Regional Research, Albany: State University of New York. Available at www.albany.edu/mumford.

Migration News: 1998. "Remittances: Dominican Republic." Electronic document available at http://migration.ucdavis.edu/data/remit.on.www.DomRep html. Accessed 20 September 2000.

Mitchell, Christopher. 1992. "U.S. Foreign Policy and Dominican Migration to the United States." In *Western Hemisphere Immigration and United States Foreign Policy*, ed. Christopher Mitchell. University Park: Pennsylvania State University Press.

Morawska, Ewa. 2000. "The New-Old Transmigrants, Their Transnational Lives, and Ethnicization: A Comparison of Nineteenth/Twentieth and Twentieth/Twenty-First Century Situations." In *America Becoming: Becoming American*, ed. Josh DeWind et al. New York: The Russell Sage Foundation/The Social Science Research Council.

Moya Pons, Frank. 1995. *The Dominican Republic Today*. New Rochelle, N.Y.: Hispaniola Books.

Peña, Javier, and Miguel Parache. 1971. "Emigración a New York de Tres Comunidades: Janico, Baitoa, y Sabana Iglesias." Master's thesis, Universidad Católica Madre Y Maestra.

Pérez, G. 1981. "The Legal and Illegal Dominican in New York City." Paper presented to the Conference on Hispanic Migration to New York City: Global Trends and Neighborhood Change. December, New York University, New York.

Pessar, Patricia. 1996. *A Visa for a Dream*. Boston: Allyn and Bacon.

Portes, Alejandro, and Luis Guarnizo. 1991. *Capitalistas del Trópico: La immigración en los Estados Unidos y el desarollo de la pequeña empresa en la República dominicana*. Santo

Domingo: Facultad Latinoamericana de Ciencias Sociales/Proyecto República Dominicana.

Portes, Alejandro, Luis Guarnizo, and Patricia Landolt. 1999. "Introduction: Pitfalls and Promise of an Emergent Research Field." *Ethnic and Racial Studies* 22, no. 2: 217–38.

Portes, Alejandro, William Haller, and Luis Guarnizo. 2002. "Empresarios Transnacionales: Emergencía y determinantes de una forma alternativea de adaptación económica" Paper presented at Migración Transnacional: Sus Efectos y Tendencias en la Cuenca del Caribe. Conference organized by FLACSO, Santo Domingo, 18–19 January 2002.

Rodríguez, Cindy. 1999. "From Island Politics to Local Politics: Dominicans Making Gains in City Offices." *The Boston Globe*, 14 November.

Rother, Larry. 1996a. "New York's Dominicans Taking Big Role in Island Elections." *New York Times*, 26 June.

——. 1996b. "New York Dominicans Strongly Back Candidates on Island." *New York Times*, 29 June.

Safa, Helen. 1993. "Export Manufacturing, State Policy, and Women Workers in the Dominican Republic." Unpublished manuscript.

Sagás, Ernesto. 1999. "From Ausentes to Dual Nationals: The Incorporation of the Diaspora into Dominican Politics." Unpublished manuscript.

Sassen-Koob, Saskia. 1979. "The International Circulation of Resources and Development: The Case of Migrant Labor." *Development and Change* 9: 509–45.

Sharpe, Kenneth. 1977. *Peasant Politics: Struggle in a Dominican Village.* Baltimore: Johns Hopkins University Press.

Sontag, Deborah.1997. "Advocates For Immigrants Exploring Voting Rights for Non-Citizens." *New York Times*, 31 July.

Torres-Saillant, Silvio, and Ramona Hernández. 1998. *The Dominican Americans.* Westport and London: Greenwood Press.

Ugalde, Antonio, Frank Bean, and Gilbert Cárdenas. 1979. "International Migration from the Dominican Republic: Findings from a National Survey." *International Migration Review* 13: 253–54.

Ugalde, Antonio, and T. Langham. 1980. International Return Migration: Socio-Demographic Determinants of Return Migration to the Dominican Republic. Paper prepared for a meeting of the Caribbean Studies Association, San Juan, P.R.

U.S. Bureau of the Census. 1992. *Census of the Population: General Social and Economic Characteristics.* PC(1)–C23.1. Washington, D.C.: U.S. Government Printing Office.

U.S. Immigration and Naturalization Service (INS). 1970. *Immigration Statistics: Fiscal Year 1969.* Washington, D.C.: U.S. Government Printing Office.

U.S. Immigration and Naturalization Service (INS). 1980. *Immigration Statistics: Fiscal Year 1979.* Washington, D.C.: U.S. Government Printing Office.

Vedovato, Claudio. 1986. *Politics, Foreign Trade, and Economic Development: A Study of the Dominican Republic.* London: Croom Helm.

Vicens, L. 1982. *Crisis Económica, 1978 – 1982.* Santo Domingo: Alfa y Omega.

Wiarda, Howard, and Michael Kryzanek. 1982. *The Dominican Republic: A Caribbean Crucible.* Boulder, Colo.: Westview Press.

World Bank. 1986. *World Development Report.* New York: Oxford University Press.

SIX

THE OTHER "OTHER HISPANICS": SOUTH AMERICAN–ORIGIN LATINOS IN THE UNITED STATES

MARILYN ESPITIA

DURING MY elementary school years, my teachers annually took a head count of all the "Spanish" children in my class. Although the purpose of this exercise was unclear to me at the time, I knew to raise my hand to be included for the tally even though my parents were from Colombia and I was born in the United States. Intuitively, I knew that the count consisted of all the Spanish-speaking children regardless of their birthplace. Later, in middle school, I noticed on my standardized test forms that I was no longer classified as Spanish, but, mysteriously, I had somehow become "Hispanic." This new category apparently still included all the Spanish-speaking children regardless of their birthplace, but now, in addition, actual language capabilities in Spanish seemed not to be required. In high school, when I began to use the label Hispanic as a self-referent, my college-educated brother quickly informed me that the politically correct term was now "Latino," even though it appeared to represent the same people previously referred to under the old umbrella term, Hispanic. It wasn't until my undergraduate years, when I began to meet other Colombian-origin Latinos that my specific background came to the forefront for others and myself. Since then, it has remained in the forefront, even in California and Texas, where I have at different times been presumed to be Puerto Rican (because of my New York City origins) or Chicana. With Colombian pop-star crossover sensation Shakira currently recognizable in the U.S. mainstream, I finally see a glimmer of acknowledgement in others when I tell them that I am Colombian American.

Although this brief recounting of my own experiences as a second-generation South American Latina is not in any way meant to imply that it somehow represents that of a "typical South American," it nonetheless helps to illustrate some key and timely questions about the increasingly complicated dynamics involved in the construction of *latinidad* among U.S. Latinos—that is, a sense of themselves as part of a larger historical and cultural Latino community in the United States (Dávila 2001; Laó-Montes and Dávila 2001). It also begins to reveal some of the ways South American Latinos are gradually coming to play a more important role in that process. With Latinos now officially acknowledged as the largest collective minority group (however problematic that appellation may turn out to be as a political or cultural reality in the future), developing some understanding of the significant roles South Americans now play as a component of the pan-Latino population is an important endeavor in fully comprehending this heterogeneous group.

With these issues in mind, the primary goals of this chapter are, therefore: to provide to a brief overview of South American migration patterns and their contribution to the recent explosive growth of the Latino population of the United States; to identify the key factors and characteristics that may be shaping the construction of *latinidad* as a pan-ethnic identity in the U.S. context; and to speculate briefly on the long-term impact South Americans might exert on the future social, cultural, and political evolution of the U.S. Latino population in both national and hemispheric affairs. To this end, I will review the existing data on the demographic and socioeconomic profile of South American Latinos, the context in both sending regions and in the United States of their immigration, and their settlement patterns as they relate to these issues. This chapter is organized into three sections. The first section briefly describes the basic demographic profile of South American Latinos. Following this description, I will then highlight the key factors surrounding the immigration of South Americans to the United States and situate their patterns within the context of Latin American immigration as well as international migration in general. The last section will then address the settlement experiences of South Americans, with an emphasis on the question of how transnational orientations and practices are maintained and how members of the second generation, in particular, may see themselves as part of an emerging pan-Latino ethnic group. By exploring South American immigration and settlement patterns, demographic structure, and the potential for change in South Americans' political and cultural orientations over time, I hope to demonstrate not only how their own diversity may shape the meaning of what—and who—is Latino but also to offer some reflections on how increasing migration from South America is contributing to the ongoing "Latinization" of the United States.

WHO ARE THE "OTHER HISPANICS" FROM SOUTH AMERICA?

The demographic and socioeconomic profiles of South American Latinos provide some important clues about their social and economic integration as Hispanics into the existing U.S. racial and ethnic landscape. Compared to the Mexicans, Puerto Ricans, and Cubans, who together continue to make up more than three quarters of the total U.S. Latino population, the combined South American Latino population is relatively small, only 5.2 percent of the Hispanic origin population in 2000 (Cresce and Ramirez 2003).[1] In addition, this population of almost two million individuals probably tends to get overlooked because it is inherently diverse across a broad range of variables, including nationality, genetic admixture, language, social class and education, and many other factors. In spite of this striking heterogeneity, South American Latinos share two key characteristics that greatly impact their present status in the United States: the large proportion of their number that is foreign-born and their higher socioeconomic standing in relation to other Latino groups.

South American Latinos originate from a total of nine distinct countries: Argentina, Bolivia, Chile, Colombia, Ecuador, Paraguay, Peru, Uruguay, and Venezuela. Table 1 presents the population size of all the U.S. Latino groups in 1990 and 2000, with detailed information listed for the nine countries. The individual representation of South American Latinos from these countries varies widely, with Colombian-origin Latinos ranking the highest, with recent population estimates of 653,029, and Paraguayan Latinos ranking the lowest with an estimated resident population of 12,807. In addition to being the largest South American Latino group in the United States, Colombian-origin Latinos are also the sixth-largest Latino group overall (after Mexicans, Puerto Ricans, Cubans, Dominicans, and Salvadorans). This sizeable presence in the United States has undoubtedly impacted those communities with the highest concentration of Colombian Latinos and it will be important to examine their areas of settlement to understand the full implications of their growing numbers.

Immediately south of Colombia, the bordering nations of Ecuador and Peru provide the points of origin for the second- and third-largest South American groups in the United States, with population sizes of 380,428 and 339,027, respectively. In a distant fourth, over 120,000 Latinos each identify Argentina and Venezuela as their nations of origin. Such population origins also strongly affect what might loosely be termed the "racial" composition of the general flow of South American transmigrants. Although variation exists in all South American national-origin groups, in recent years the influx has deviated from past patterns, when the majority of South American migrants were middle-class *mestizos*, to a situation that is much more diverse today. As

TABLE 1 U.S. Latino Population by National Origin, 1990 and 2000

ORIGIN	1990		2000	
	NUMBER	%	NUMBER	%
TOTAL	21,900,089	100.0	35,238,481	100.0
Mexico	13,393,208	61.2	22,338,311	63.4
Puerto Rico	2,651,815	12.1	3,539,988	10.0
Cuba	1,053,197	4.8	1,312,127	3.7
Dominican Republic	520,151	2.4	999,561	2.8
CENTRAL AMERICA	1,323,830	6.0	2,435,731	6.9
Costa Rica	57,223	0.3	93,583	0.3
Guatemala	268,779	1.2	574,785	1.6
Honduras	131,066	0.6	333,636	0.9
Nicaragua	202,658	0.9	272,655	0.8
Panama	92,013	0.4	126,500	0.4
El Salvador	565,081	2.6	1,010,740	2.9
Other Central America	7,010	0.0	23,832	0.1
SOUTH AMERICA	1,035,602	4.7	1,847,811	5.2
Argentina	100,921	0.5	132,864	0.4
Bolivia	38,073	0.2	65,220	0.2
Chile	68,799	0.3	98,057	0.3
Colombia	378,726	1.7	653,029	1.9
Ecuador	191,198	0.9	380,428	1.1
Paraguay	6,662	0.0	12,806	0.0
Peru	175,035	0.8	339,027	1.0
Uruguay	21,996	0.1	27,401	0.1
Venezuela	47,997	0.2	122,268	0.3
Other South America	6,195	0.0	16,711	0.0
Spain	519,136	2.4	190,656	0.5
Hispanic	390,945	1.8	1,067,782	3.0
Latino	1,577	0.0	93,783	0.3
Spanish	444,896	2.0	523,323	1.5
Other Hispanic	565,732	2.6	889,408	2.5

Source: Cresce and Ramirez 2003, tables 1 and 6.

will be discussed further below, while middle-class *mestizos* continue to make up a significant portion of migrants from South America, in recent years a much broader mix has been evident, which now includes significant numbers of different groups of *mestizos*, increasing numbers of indigenous peoples, and a significant number of individuals of Afro-Latino heritage. Given the composition of recent migration flows—particularly those of the last years of the twentieth century—it is reasonable to expect that South Americans will continue to contribute to the ongoing diversification of the resident pan-Latino population of the United States (Rodriguez 2000; Brea 2003).

The most recent demographic data on South American Latinos as well as other Latinos are presented in table 2. Perhaps the most striking feature of the South American population is the large proportion of foreign-born individuals. Of course, this feature reflects just how recently South Americans have begun to migrate in significant numbers. Unlike the Mexican- and Puerto Rican–origin populations, which obviously have large U.S.-born components, the majority (73.6 percent) of South American Latinos in the United States are foreign-born (Logan 2002). According to his recent study, Logan estimates that out of the three largest South American groups, Ecuadorians have the largest proportion of foreign-born, followed by Peruvians and Colombians. In addition, it is important to note that a significant proportion of the recent migratory flow from South America to the United States has occurred outside of authorized channels and thus has also contributed to the expanding presence of undocumented immigrants in the United States (Kyle 2000; U.S. Immigration and Naturalization Service 2003).

The large foreign-born proportion of the resident South American population clearly helps to shape the experiences of the Latino newcomers, influencing geographical settlement patterns, processes of socioeconomic integration, and propensities to interact with both Latino and non-Latino U.S. natives. The fact that a large proportion of the resident South American population is undocumented also strongly influences these different behaviors. Estimates generated by the former U.S. Immigration and Naturalization Service (which has since been reorganized as part of the Department of Homeland Security) indicate that the proportion of undocumented immigrants ranges, at the low end, from 8 percent of Uruguayan immigrants to at least 36 percent of all Ecuadorians in the country in 2000 (U.S. Immigration and Naturalization Service 2003). Table 3 presents these estimates of unauthorized migrants for Latin America countries. As other contributors to this volume have noted, the lack of proper documentation for a substantial portion of the foreign-born population obviously constrains economic opportunities, influences possibilities for residential mobility, and strongly affects the possibility of maintaining transnational ties with communities of origin, especially given the heightened enforcement of U.S. borders since September 11.

Despite this large undocumented component, the general socioeconomic profile of South American Latinos tends to be significantly higher than that of other Latino subpopulations (see table 2). In contrast to the other Latinos, South American immigrants have the highest average years of education (12.6)

TABLE 2 Social and Economic Characteristics of Hispanics, by National Origin (Pooled Estimates from the Current Population Survey, March 1998 and March 2000)

ORIGIN	% FOREIGN BORN	% RECENT ARRIVALS	YEARS OF EDUCATION	MEAN EARNINGS	% BELOW POVERTY LINE	% UNEMPLOYED
TOTAL	38.5	44.8	10.7	$9,432	25.2	6.8
Mexico	36.5	49.3	10.2	$8,525	23.3	7.0
Puerto Rico	1.3	26.7	11.4	$9,893	30.4	8.3
Cuba	68.0	26.7	11.9	$13,567	18.3	5.8
Dominican Republic	62.7	45.3	10.8	$7,883	36.0	8.6
CENTRAL AMERICA	71.3	48.2	10.3	$9,865	22.3	6.4
Guatemala	74.8	56.1	9.8	$9,204	27.1	7.9
Honduras	69.0	50.2	10.4	$10,244	27.2	10.8
Nicaragua	72.5	42.7	12.0	$10,506	17.4	4.0
El Salvador	69.6	45.9	9.7	$9,631	20.8	5.1
SOUTH AMERICA	73.6	44.4	12.6	$13,911	13.6	4.3
Colombia	71.7	38.4	12.4	$11,579	16.4	4.8
Ecuador	76.0	48.9	11.8	$11,848	19.0	5.8
Peru	73.0	51.5	12.7	$11,996	11.7	3.0

Note: Central and South American groups are listed if they had 200 or more people in the pooled CPS sample.

Source: Logan 2001, table 1.

and mean earnings ($13,911) and consequently are much more favorably situated in the American socioeconomic structure than are other populations. This is reflected in the low percentage of South American Latinos living below the federal poverty line (13.6 percent) and the low proportion (4.6) of unemployed South American Latinos in the late 1990s. Indeed, in aggregate, the socioeconomic profile of South American Latinos surpasses even that of Cubans, who are typically perceived and commonly portrayed as the most economically stable and successful group among Latinos. Examined individually, Colombians, Ecuadorians, and Peruvians also fare better than Cubans in regard to their years of education and the proportion of their populations that are poor and unemployed. However, the mean earnings among these

TABLE 3 Estimates of the Latin American Unauthorized Immigrant Population Residing in the United States, 1990 to 2000 (per 100,000)

ORIGIN	1990			2000		
	ESTIMATED UNAUTHORIZED POPULATION	TOTAL FOREIGN-BORN POPULATION	ESTIMATED PROPORTION OF UNAUTHORIZED	ESTIMATED UNAUTHORIZED POPULATION	TOTAL FOREIGN-BORN POPULATION	ESTIMATED PROPORTION OF UNAUTHORIZED
Mexico	2040	4298	0.47	4808	9177	0.52
Cuba	2	737	0.00	7	873	0.01
Dominican Republic	46	348	0.13	91	688	0.13
CENTRAL AMERICA						
Costa Rica	5	44	0.11	17	72	0.24
Guatemala	118	226	0.52	144	481	0.30
Honduras	42	109	0.39	138	283	0.49
Nicaragua	50	469	0.11	21	220	0.10
Panama	7	86	0.08	11	105	0.10
El Salvador	298	465	0.64	189	817	0.23
SOUTH AMERICA						
Argentina	7	93	0.08	15	125	0.12
Bolivia	8	31	0.26	13	53	0.25
Chile	6	56	0.11	17	81	0.21
Colombia	51	286	0.18	141	510	0.28
Ecuador	37	143	0.26	108	299	0.36
Paraguay	na	na	na	na	na	na
Peru	27	144	0.19	61	278	0.22
Uruguay	2	21	0.10	2	25	0.08
Venezuela	10	42	0.24	34	107	0.32

Source: U.S. Immigration and Naturalization Service 2003, table 2.

three groups does fall below the mean earnings of Cubans and, more importantly, below the mean earnings of South American Latinos as a group. This difference indicates that the higher average earnings found among South American Latinos may be due to the skewing effects of immigrants from more developed countries in this region, especially Argentina and Chile. For example, data from the 1990 U.S. census demonstrate that approximately one-third of Argentine and Chilean Latinos were employed in professional and managerial occupations (where they presumably command significantly higher wages), compared to only 14 percent of Ecuadorians and 17 percent of Colombians (Cordova and Pinderhughes 1999). In other words, although South American Latinos have a comparatively favorable socioeconomic profile, one must keep in mind that a large variation exists between immigrant groups from the different South American countries of origin, with immigrants from the Southern Cone faring much better than those from elsewhere.

SOUTH AMERICAN IMMIGRATION TO THE UNITED STATES

With almost 74 percent of the South American Latino population being foreign-born, particular attention must be paid to the processes that led to their immigration and consequently shaped their settlement patterns. At first glance, the story of South American immigration to the United States appears to be similar in many ways to that of the rest of Latin America. That is, as is true of most other Latin American immigrants, most South Americans have immigrated to the United States to pursue better economic opportunities, to flee precarious and often violent political environments in their communities of origin, and to join family members already in the United States. However, prior to the most recent influx of migrants, migration from South America had been characterized by a disproportionate movement of urban, educated, and upper-middle-class individuals (Cordova and Pinderhughes 1999; Portes and Rumbaut 1996) This particular phenomenon still dominates a significant proportion of the current immigration flow from South America, although it recently has become more heterogeneous, drawing greater numbers from rural, less-educated, and working-class individuals through the establishment of immigrant networks (Kyle 2000; Guarnizo and Diaz 1999; Julca 2001).

Table 4 presents estimates of the South American foreign-born population in the United States from 1960 through the present. A quick examination of the resident population across the forty years reveals that, at least until fairly recently, overall immigration from South America has been slow and steady, with its greatest growth occurring in the last two decades. This pattern is distinctly different from the more sustained growth and the more recent enor-

TABLE 4 Latin American Foreign-Born Populations in the United States, 1960–2000

ORIGIN	1960	1970	1980	1990	2000
Mexico	575,902	759,711	2,199,221	4,298,014	9,177,487
Cuba	79,150	439,048	607,814	736,971	872,716
Dominican Republic	11,883	61,228	169,147	347,858	687,677
CENTRAL AMERICA					
Costa Rica	5,425	16,691	29,639	43,530	71,870
Guatemala	5,381	17,356	63,073	225,739	480,665
Honduras	6,503	19,118	39,154	108,923	282,852
Nicaragua	9,474	16,125	44,166	168,659	220,335
Panama	13,076	20,046	60,740	85,737	105,177
El Salvador	6,310	15,717	94,447	465,433	817,336
SOUTH AMERICA					
Argentina	16,579	44,803	68,887	92,563	125,218
Bolivia	2,168	6,872	14,468	31,303	53,278
Chile	6,259	15,393	35,127	55,681	80,804
Colombia	12,582	63,538	143,508	286,124	509,872
Ecuador	7,670	36,663	86,128	143,314	298,626
Paraguay	595	na	2,858	6,057	na
Peru	7,102	21,663	55,496	144,199	278,186
Uruguay	1,170	5,092	13,278	20,766	na
Venezuela	6,851	11,348	33,281	42,119	107,031
Latin American Total	774,080	1,570,412	3,760,432	7,302,990	14,169,130

Source (1960–1990): Gibson and Lennon 1999, table 3.

Source (2000): U.S. Census Bureau 2000.

mous increases (both in actual size and growth rates) found in the Mexican, Cuban, Salvadoran, and Guatemalan immigrant communities over the past ten years. As a result, where these other national communities were able to form a critical mass almost overnight (or, in the case of Mexicans, renew and greatly augment established communities), South Americans have not been able to do so in the same manner until recently, when their population sizes have become significant. In other words, although some Argentines, Colombians, and Chileans may have slowly formed small communities in certain cities over the years, their smaller numbers did not allow for the same kind of ethnic infrastructural development (for example, businesses, community organizations, or civil- and/or human-rights organizations) that occurred with most of the other larger national communities. Thus, many of the earlier

South American immigrants may have depended on broader Spanish-language institutions and resources rather than country-of-origin-specific ones, creating greater opportunities for interaction between Latino immigrant groups and possibly a future basis for the development of a pan-Latin American identity.

South Americans' generally higher levels of education almost certainly affected their patterns of adaptation and community development. Having, in most cases, entered the country with higher levels of education and other forms of "social capital" than was true of virtually all other groups with the possible exception of Cubans, the earliest South American immigrants probably found it easier to blend into higher strata of the American socioeconomic structure. Indeed, during the so-called brain drain era of migration that occurred in the economically fluid period following the end of World War II, an inordinate number of highly educated and professional individuals, specifically doctors, engineers, scientists, and other skilled South American workers, entered the United States (Reimers 1992). This flow was most prevalent among Colombians and Argentines, as is evident from the size of their U.S. populations by the end of 1960 (as shown in table 3). Primarily, the most skilled and talented individuals (including those who possessed basic English skills) with contacts in the United States initiated the move in order to maximize the economic rewards associated with their already favorable occupational status (Portes 1976). In other words, these professionals were responding to the limited employment opportunities within their domestic markets by pursuing the higher wages and career opportunities found in the United States (Marshall 1988). This brain-drain flow from South America was part of a larger immigration phenomenon that also attracted similarly qualified individuals from Asia and elsewhere in the world (Reimers 1992).

The passage of the Immigration and Nationality Act Amendments of 1965 exerted mixed effects on both the potential and actual northward flow of South American immigrants. On the one hand, the codification of new occupational preferences in the law kept the door open to potential brain-drain South American migrants. As David G. Gutiérrez notes in the introduction to this volume, although the Immigration Act of 1965 is primarily known for the abolition of the national-origins quota system and the strengthening of the family reunification preference, for the first decade following its passage the law actually worked to select immigrants with high-level skills because Congress did not apply the same "first-come, first-served" family preference system to the Western Hemisphere until 1976 (Pastor 1984). Consequently, although immediate relatives of U.S. citizens (i.e., spouses and children) were exempt from the quota, immigration from the Western Hemisphere during this era was largely dominated by a different set of priorities, which required labor certification and other immigration restrictions based on "social capital" issues such as levels of literacy, ability to pay various taxes, and whether a potential immigrant was likely to become a public charge. The 1965 act also marked the first time that Congress established numerical restrictions on visas for the Western Hemisphere (including Latin America). Thus, these otherwise "liberal" changes in U.S. immigration law had the paradoxical effects of maintaining an influx of South American technical elites, increasing the waiting period for other migrants attempting to enter through officially authorized means, and contributing to the rapid increase in the number of undocumented migrants entering the United States from Latin America. Indeed, undocumented migration from Mexico in particular, but also from Latin America generally, began to rise significantly within a decade of the passage of the 1965 act (Reimers 1992).

The exodus of mostly educated, upper- and middle-class immigrants from South America during this time was (and still is) certainly enhanced by the unstable economic structure of many South American countries. Like other regions of Latin America, beginning in the early 1970s South America also experienced significant shifts in its economy and policies that left many rural inhabitants without jobs and urban middle- and working-class individuals with decreasing job opportunities and wages (Skidmore 2001; Brea 2003; Pellegrino 2000; Bonilla et al. 1998). With most of South America's gradual transition from economies based largely on agriculture and extractive industries to systems based on import-substitution policies and, finally, to the current neoliberal trade and free-market economic regimes, the opportunities for individuals to maintain positions that earn sufficient wages or offer the prospect of social mobility have eroded dramatically. Indeed, the recent collapse of free-trade negotiations at Cancún, Mexico, the political disruptions caused by similar, grassroots protests in Venezuela, Bolivia, Ecuador, and elsewhere, and the strong current attempt by Brazil and Argentina to block U.S. efforts to expand coverage of the North American Free Trade Agreement (NAFTA) to South America all provide further evidence of both the increasing social restiveness on the southern continent and the depth of the social and economic restructuring that has taken place there in recent years.[2]

Such strains are perhaps seen most poignantly in the changing circumstances of two comparatively prosperous South American nations, Argentina and Venezuela, which have historically received more immigrants from their South American neighbors than they have sent their own abroad (Brea 2003; Pellegrino 2000; Marshall 1988). Prior to 1999, Argentina was typically hailed as the leading example of the success of neoliberal free-market economic policies (Wucker 2002). However, as has been true most notably in Mexico, toward the end of the twentieth century several signs, including an increasing unemployment rate, rapidly increasing interest rates, and the nation's steadily diminishing ability to pay its rising debt to both the private sector and the International Monetary Fund, pointed to the steady erosion and current fragility of its economy (Wucker 2002). As a result, immigration from Argentina to the United States—particularly of members of its educated and urban elite—has increased significantly in recent years (Brea 2003; Jachimowicz 2003). In Venezuela, on the other hand, the left-wing presidency of Hugo Chávez has created civil unrest and economic recessions (Cameron and Major 2001). In the Andean region, Venezuela has long been the most economically stable nation because of its reserves of petroleum. In the last three to five years, however, the volatility of the oil market and the wide-ranging social dislocations caused by the ongoing restructuring of the regional economy have forced many people into unemployment (or chronic underemployment)—and have stimulated a significant emigration of many educated and middle-class Venezuelans (Brea 2003).

Rising levels of civil unrest, and the state-sponsored violence that often accompanied them, have combined to stimulate rising rates of emigration from several South American nations. For example, the rise of the Pinochet regime in Chile during the early 1970s and the subsequent military coup and violent excesses of the ruling junta in Argentina obviously contributed to the forced emigration and exile of thousands of Chilean and Argentine citizens (Skidmore 2001; Marshall 1988; Cordova and Pinderhughes 1999). Similarly, from its beginning Colombian immigration to the U.S. was greatly stimulated by a political period of the late 1950s known by Colombians as "La Violencia" (Reimers 1992; Cordova and Pinderhughes 1999). More recently, educated middle-class Colombians continue to flee the country in order to avoid the internal fighting by left-wing guerillas and the military, the incessant violence spawned by narcotics trafficking, and the increasing incidence of kidnapping perpetrated by guerillas attempting to extort ransom from individuals, corporations, and government agencies (Marin 2002; Chace 2000). Although Chile and Argentina have recently begun the painful process of healing and have taken the first fitful steps toward a kind of "democratization," deep tensions in these societies, combined with the precariousness of their economic positions, leave the ultimate outcome of these processes in some doubt and thus also raise questions about the potential for more South American emigration in the future.

However much changing economic and political circumstances have stimulated an exodus of South Americans to the United States, the delayed effects of changes in U.S. immigration law and policy should not be underestimated. After an initial period of anxiousness and uncertainty created in Latin America by passage of the 1965 INA Amendments, the subsequent implementation of a stronger family reunification system in 1976 for the Western

Hemisphere finally allowed permanent legal residents from Latin America to petition for other family members such as their spouses and unmarried children to join them in the United States. U.S. citizens of South American origin could also apply for reunification with their adult children (regardless of marital status) and their siblings. Over time, these changes in policy naturally resulted in the expansion of a more diverse immigration pool from Latin America and allowed for the subsequent increases in legal immigration from the South American continent.

Although illegal migration from Latin America has increased slowly but steadily since the 1960s and 1970s, the U.S. government has long considered this phenomenon primarily a Mexican trend and thus focused most of its enforcement resources on the U.S.–Mexico border. However, as has been true of migrants from elsewhere in the world, the increase in the number of business, tourist, and student visas from Latin America and Asia also suggests the increasing pattern of another form of unauthorized migration, where individuals simply remain in the United States after their visiting periods expire (Reimers 1992). The Immigration and Reform and Control Act of 1986 (IRCA), which allowed temporary agricultural workers and undocumented immigrants residing in the U.S. since 1982 to "regularize their status" (to use the bureaucratic language of the INS) also presented an opportunity for a significant number of unauthorized Latin American immigrants to apply for legal residency in the United States and subsequently petition for their family members residing abroad. Although the vast majority of applications for permanent resident status under IRCA's provisions went to Mexicans and Central Americans, approximately 3.2 percent of the 2.7 million successful applicants were of South American origin (U.S. Department of Labor 1986). As previously noted in table 3, the increasing population of unauthorized migrants from South America in the United States adds to the complexity of that issue for the governments of both the United States and the countries of origin.

SETTLEMENT PATTERNS AND THE EMERGENCE OF *LATINIDAD* IN THE SOUTH AMERICAN POPULATION

Although it is too early to venture any definitive conclusions about how the distinctive patterns of initial emigration from South America, the shifting contexts of their reception in the United States, and their subsequent patterns of adjustment and settlement will ultimately affect these immigrants' social, cultural, and political orientations as members of American society, several trends suggest some tentative answers to these complex questions. Specifically, in terms of *latinidad*, it is critical to examine how transnational behaviors by South American Latinos serve as a resource for maintaining country-of-origin affiliations and how local Latino groups may potentially shape the process of creating a pan-ethnic community.

Among South American Latinos, some intriguing preliminary research has been conducted on different kinds of transnational practices among Colombians, Peruvians, and Ecuadorians—not coincidentally the largest three South American groups (Jones-Correa 1998; Kyle 2000; Guarnizo and Díaz 1999). Among all three groups, some of the strongest forms of transnationalism are the existing networks of chain migration that span the United States and the sending countries. One of the most interesting aspects of the emergence of South American immigration networks is how they have developed across long distances to assist in the process of illegal migration, whether by land, sea, air, or a combination of all three. One study, in particular, has documented how networks have been used to allow Ecuadorians from rural areas to immigrate to the United States (Kyle 2000). These networks have allowed for a greater diversification than previous immigration trends because migrants do not have to provide all of the financial resources for the trip. Rather, they can promise to pay off their debt once in the United States. As other contributors to this volume have noted, the establishment of these transnational networks among South American migrants over the past twenty years has been one of the most distinctive features of the population flows between the two continents. These networks, like those binding other immigrant groups, allow for information, labor, and capital to be easily exchanged between two or more nations. For example, part of this established immigrant network also includes a courier service that allows immigrants in the United States to regularly send money and packages to their homeland and receive news and packages from family members still residing abroad. Such practices allow for the maintenance of strong country-of-origin affiliations, especially among members of the immigrant, or "first-generation," cohort.

Among Colombians, these transnational practices have manifested themselves in local organizations in the United States. It is well documented that Colombians often form civic organizations that closely mirror the class system they were part of prior to immigration (Portes and Rumbaut 1996; Jones-Correa 1998). These organizations often sponsor cultural celebrations such as Colombia's Independence Day in July, musical showcases of folkloric dance and music groups, soccer and other organized sports leagues, and activities to mobilize the Colombian community against the continuing violence and other hardships in Colombia (Portes and Rumbaut 1996; Chapárro 2002). Since dual citizenship is extended to Colombian immigrants naturalized in the United States, these organizations are also used to organize campaigns for political candidates in Colombia and to encourage Colombian immigrants to vote at their consulates in the United States (Jones-Correa 2001). These transnational organizations obviously serve as sites where country-of-origin identities and ties are strengthened even among those who have settled permanently in the United States.

How these networks will ultimately affect the emergence of sociocultural and political orientations among South American Latinos in the United States largely remains, however, an open question. Increased security measures along U.S. borders will undoubtedly influence the extent to which South Americans can maintain meaningful transnational ties over time. But despite the obstacles created by these trends, it is clear that at least over the short term thousands of South Americans will continue to maintain such ties through previously established social networks, businesses, and organizations. Of course, the recent moves by Colombia and several South American states to extend dual nationality to their expatriates abroad will probably also contribute to the maintenance of such ties and networks, regardless of U.S. border policy.

The presence of Spanish-language media is also important to both transnational and local U.S. practices of South American immigrants, as it is another critical source of information and consumption. Colombian immigrants of all class backgrounds seem to share, at least initially, tastes in Spanish-language media, which, in turn, seem also to reinforce at least some country-of-origin identifications and ties. For example, the importation of Colombian *telenovelas* (soap operas), radio shows, and television news to the to U.S. Latino consumer markets has certainly strengthened the sense of a Colombian community and has exposed other Latino groups to the distinct issues and cultures presented by Colombians (Davis 2002). The resiliency of such behaviors and tastes over time—as well as the persistence of Spanish-language dominance among this overwhelmingly foreign-born population—remains to be seen, however. While it might be reasonable to expect that if immigration trends remain constant in the future, then language preference and other cultural behaviors will continue to be reproduced in the U.S. context, though if migration flows are constrained by increasing U.S. security measures, the future is more uncertain.

Class divisions and other differences in social capital among South American migrants will also probably play an important role in the ways new immigrants and their children become socialized in the United States. Of course, until recently, the general socioeconomic profile of South American residents of the United States has been more in line with Cubans than with any other Latino group. Thus, just as the Cuban experience had until recently largely been seen as lying outside the "typical" Latino experience in American society, South Americans were largely seen as exceptions to more general social and cultural trends. However, current immigration trends indicate that although a significant proportion of the flow of South American migrants continue to originate in the upper socioeconomic strata of Latin American society, the troubled economies and political situations in many countries are just as obviously increasing the pressure on working-class individuals to consider emigrating, either through legal means or through unauthorized channels (Kyle 2000; Guarnizo and Diaz 1999; Julca 2001). If this pattern continues, it may well contribute to a significant social bifurcation in the United States between better-educated, middle-class, and legal South American immigrants, on one end, and less-educated, working-class, and unauthorized migrants on the other. This trend has already been suggested in research on the growing Colombian and Peruvian populations (Guarnizo and Diaz 1999; Julca 2001).

Equally critical to the process and potential direction of the social integration of South American Latinos in the United States are the specific contexts of reception they face, which, of course, deeply influence the ways they ultimately fit into the communities in which they settle. For example, in the Southwest the Latino experience has long been strongly shaped, if not actually defined by the presence of a well-established—and growing—Mexican-origin population, whereas in the Northeast, Puerto Ricans and, more recently, Dominicans have strongly influenced the character both of local Latino communities and the local variants of *latinidad* that have emerged in those communities. Thus, population densities and ratios and the geographic location of South American settlement can be expected to play key roles in the ways they will relate to other Latino groups and to the modes of cultural identity and expression that emerge as a result.[3]

The settlement and residential patterns among South American Latinos are of significant interest because, unlike the other three Latino groups, they are not geographically concentrated in one particular region or state of the country. Table 5 lists the sixteen states with the largest populations of South American Latinos. As the table indicates, their largest numerical presence is felt in the states of New York, Florida, California, New Jersey, and Texas. This residential pattern demonstrates that South Americans are currently represented in regions where Mexicans, Puerto Ricans, and Cubans traditionally dominate. As a consequence, it is not likely that South Americans will play a key role in the ways local notions and practices of *latinidad* are conceived of and practiced. Indeed, it may well prove the case that in areas where South Americans settle next to existing Latino populations, they will adjust to prevailing Latino patterns of acculturation and social interaction. For example, in Los Angeles, entrepreneurial Colombian immigrants tend to cater their businesses to Mexicans and Central Americans rather than other South Americans (Guarnizo, Sánchez, and Roach 1999).

TABLE 5 Composition of U.S. Latino Population by Country/Region for Top 16 States, 2000

STATE	% S. AMERICAN	% MEXICAN	% PUERTO RICAN	% CUBAN	% DOMINICAN	% C. AMERICAN	% OTHER	TOTAL LATINOS
New York	16.25	9.57	38.63	2.30	22.75	9.32	1.17	2,867,583
Florida	16.67	14.39	19.03	32.60	3.99	11.22	2.10	2,682,715
California	2.73	84.07	1.41	0.72	0.09	9.54	1.44	10,966,556
New Jersey	23.02	9.64	34.47	7.25	12.83	10.39	2.40	1,117,191
Texas	1.61	89.70	1.20	0.44	0.14	4.28	2.63	6,669,666
Virginia	19.56	23.90	13.45	2.71	1.80	35.29	3.29	329,540
Illinois	3.88	79.04	10.89	1.27	0.30	3.93	0.70	1,530,262
Connecticut	13.70	7.64	63.33	2.32	4.16	5.56	3.29	320,323
Massachusetts	10.19	5.52	49.29	2.19	17.18	13.40	2.24	428,729
Maryland	18.82	18.74	12.08	3.17	4.06	39.83	3.29	227,916
Pennsylvania	7.98	14.97	62.56	2.85	5.28	4.33	2.03	394,088
Georgia	6.80	66.46	8.66	3.05	1.14	10.61	3.29	435,227
North Carolina	5.07	68.22	8.66	2.05	1.14	11.57	3.29	378,963
Arizona	1.48	92.67	1.55	0.46	0.16	2.24	1.44	1,295,617
Rhode Island	14.02	6.82	29.35	1.31	27.73	17.48	3.29	90,820
Louisiana	8.38	33.47	7.99	8.82	1.91	36.12	3.29	107,738

Source: Logan 2001, table 4.

However, another important relationship to examine is where South American Latinos constitute the largest share of a local U.S.-Latino population because in such places it is much more likely that the construction of *latinidad* will be substantively different than in a locale like the state of Arizona, for example, where Mexican-origin Latinos obviously dominate the group. Although more research is needed to confirm this, one can already see the emergence of new, hybrid forms of *latinidad*—expressed in language, cuisine, dress, music, dance, art, literature, and in increasing rates of inter-Latino partnering and intermarriage—in the cities of the Northeast and in other urban areas where no single Latino national subpopulation predominates. Indeed, in cities like Washington, D.C., Miami, Houston, and parts of the San Francisco Bay Area, separate nationality-group clusters continue to form loose-knit communities, but they are otherwise drawn together in new, syncretic, Spanish-language-based cultural contexts. Not surprisingly, in such contexts South American Latinos are probably much more likely to be incorporated into a process of adaptation and acculturation that is pan-ethnic in nature, although it must be kept in mind that the maintenance of strong ties with their countries of origin will probably continue to exist simultaneously. In the end, however, the complexity and uncertainty of such dynamic processes must be kept in mind before we attempt to make any hard and fast predictions about the future orientations and behaviors of South American Latinos in the United States. As the political scientist Michael Jones-Correa has noted in his recent study of Latino politics in New York City:

> Ethnic choices are made not only on the basis of the immediate context, but also on the basis of previous contexts which may appear at first glance to be no longer relevant. This is particularly the case with immigrants. Latin American immigrants' ethnic identities are shaped not just by the choices they make in the United States, but also by the weight of identity choices made in the past. Previous constructions of identity have a kind of inertia to them; they become the raw materials for ethnic choices and ethnic politics in the United States. . . . These continuities, however, do not play out in any straightforward fashion: identities submerged in the home countries can resurface, and previous identities can take on a different significance in a new context.
>
> *(Jones-Correa 1998: 122)*

THE SECOND GENERATION

It may well be, however, that the best predictor of the future of South American Latinos in the United States lies with their U.S.-born children. The available statistics show that for South American Latinos, approximately 26 percent are born in the United States (Logan 2002). With the bulk of South American immigration occurring after 1980, children born in the United States to this cohort are most likely to be under the age of eighteen and still living at home with their immigrant parents. Consequently, it is reasonable to expect their socioeconomic integration will be strongly shaped both by their parents' own experience and by the powerful influences of American consumer culture as they grow up as Latinos in the United States. However, several questions arise concerning the potential social trajectories of the so-called second-generation Latinos of South American heritage. On the most fundamental level, a question is raised about whether or not the higher socioeconomic status of many South American immigrants will allow their children to take advantage of their relative "head start" by leveraging their access to higher levels of social capital to achieve higher levels of education and social mobility in U.S. society. Again, given the relatively short time a sizable South American population has been in the United States, it may be too soon to predict answers to this question.[4]

However, the existing literature on other immigrant groups such as Mexicans and black migrants from the Caribbean suggests, contrary to popular myth about the workings of the American "melting pot," that those maintaining stronger ties to their immigrant backgrounds are more likely to experience upward social mobility, whereas those identifying with established ethnic groups (i.e., U.S.-born Chicanos in the case of ethnic Mexicans and African Americans in the case of Caribbean settlers) are more likely to adopt adversarial views of the United States, develop antisocial or oppositional behaviors, and, ultimately, experience downward assimilation (Portes and Rumbaut 2001; Zhou 2001; Waters 1996; Suárez-Orozco and Suárez-Orozco 1995). Indeed, unlike the case of South Americans, who are scattered in communities across the United States, part of the success of the Cuban community has been attributed to its cohesion, even across generations. Thus, if South American Latinos follow the trajectory of other second-generation groups, their socioeconomic outcomes will be highly dependent on how they come to identify and affiliate themselves within their own community and other groups (including both U.S. "minorities" and non-Latino whites).

An examination of intermarriage rates may provide some initial hints about the possible future orientation and self-identification of South American Latinos. Much more research needs to be done in this vital area, but according to one recent study on intermarriage among various Latino subgroups based on New York City, using data in 1991, South American immigrants (who were counted in this study as one group) were shown to have the lowest rates of intermarriage (Gilbertson, Fitzpatrick, and Yang 1996).[5] However, intermarriage rates among second-generation South American Latinos in New York City significantly increased, to the extent that fully 70 percent reported their spouse's background from a different Latino group or as non-Hispanic.

Based on this 1991 study of South American adults, it can be speculated that there are at least two possible trajectories of integration for this group. First, for those high-status South American settlers who can successfully cross lines of "race" and culture through intermarriage and incorporation into mainstream U.S. institutions, the process of integration may well mimic the experience of previous generations of "white" European immigrants. Again, research on this question is thin, but given the substantial intermarriage rates of South American Latinos with non-Hispanics in New York City, there does seem to be some evidence to support this view (Gilbertson, Fitzpatrick, and Yang 1996). On the other hand, given the many cultural, linguistic, and historical commonalities that bind South American Latinos, many may choose to identify themselves as part an emerging pan-ethnic Latino group. However, there are risks associated with this strategy, especially for working-class members of the growing South American Latino population. As noted briefly above, if research findings for other "native" Latino populations can be applied to more recently arrived South American Latinos, their life-chances and patterns of acculturation may be adversely influenced by the socioeconomic status of the Latino group dominant in a particular locale. For example, if the overall low economic status of Puerto Ricans and Dominicans in New York City is considered, South American Latinos who choose to associate and affiliate with such populations may be more likely to experience social pressures that lead to "segmented assimilation" and downward mobility.[6]

There is also recent evidence that second-generation South American Latinos identify with their parents' country of origin. Again, in New York City, where there is a substantial community of Colombians, Ecuadorians, and Peruvians, research shows that these U.S.-born Latinos maintain active ties with their parents' countries of origin via regular trips to these South American nations, personal remittances to family members abroad, and participation in U.S.-based ethnic organizations (Kasinitz et al. 2002). Thus, it may be that in addition to a pan-ethnic identity, ties with their parent's country of origin may also serve to buffer some risks of "downward" assimilation.

CONCLUSION

The diverse experiences of South American Latinos highlight the increasing complexity of the social terrain on which the construction of Latino identities in the United States will occur in the years to come. This brief review of the

South American–origin population's demographic characteristics, socioeconomic profiles, immigration history, and settlement patterns immediately reveals the internal heterogeneity within the category of "South American Latinos." Although the comparatively skewed class background of the extant South American Latino population virtually assures that middle-class individuals will continue to enjoy advantages unavailable to most other U.S. Latinos (with the possible exception of ethnic Cubans), the unsettledness of the South American social, economic, and political environments—and the similarly unsettled nature of U.S. society in the first years of the twenty-first century—also raises significant questions about the future social trajectories of South American Latinos. As the other chapters of this volume indicate, as intriguing as these issues are to observers of the ongoing "Latinization" of the United States, at this point the definitive answers to these questions will become clear only with the passage of time.

NOTES

1. I use the simulated totals calculated by Cresce and Ramírez rather than the official U.S. Census totals because the simulated totals include individuals who self-identified as Hispanic, self-identified into a specific group, and those who reported a place of birth or ancestry of "Hispanic" origin.
2. For insightful journalistic discussion on these increasingly complex and politically charged issues, see, for example, *The Economist*, 18 September 2003, on Cancún; Larry Rohter, "Bolivian Peasants' 'Ideology of Fury' Still Smolders," *New York Times*, 20 October 2003; and Tony Smith, "Argentina and Brazil Align to Fight U.S. Trade Policy," *New York Times*, 21 October 2003.
3. For discussion of this process in a larger context, see Frances R. Aparicio, chapter 9, this volume.
4. For general discussions of the issues associated with the so-called second generation, see Portes 1996; Rumbaut and Portes 2001; and Portes and Rumbaut 2001.
5. Although this rate can be interpreted as evidence that South American immigrants maintain company within their own country-of-origin group, it can also be misleading, given that it is not clear from the statistics if, for example, Colombians are marrying Colombians or Colombians are marrying Peruvians. Nonetheless, it can be safely assumed that there is some cohesion present at the regional level.
6. For discussion of a similar line of argument, see David. G. Gutiérrez, introduction and chapter 1, this volume.

REFERENCES

Brea, Jorge A. 2003. "Population Dynamics in Latin America." *Population Bulletin* 58, no. 1.

Bonilla, Frank, Edwin Meléndez, Rebecca Morales, and María de los Angeles Torres. 1998. *Borderless Borders: US Latinos, Latin Americans, and the Paradox of Interdependence.* Philadelphia: Temple University Press.

Cameron, Maxwell A., and Flavie Major. 2001. "Venezuela's Hugo Chávez: Savior or Threat to Democracy?" *Latin American Research Review* 36, no. 3:255–66.

Chace, James. 2000. "The Next New Threat." *World Policy Journal* 17, no. 1:113–15.

Chaparro, María Alejandra. 2002. "Little Colombia: Teen Immigrants Make New Lives in the United States." *Hemisphere: A Magazine of the Americas* 11, no. 3:8–11.

Cordova, Carlos B., and Raquel Pinderhughes. 1999. "Central and South Americans." In *A Nation of Peoples: A Sourcebook on America's Multicultural Heritage*, ed. Elliott R. Barkan, 103–10. Wesport, Conn.: Greenwood Press.

Cresce, Arthur R., and Roberto R. Ramírez. 2003. "Analysis of General Hispanic Responses in Census 2000." *Population Division Working Paper No. 72.* Washington, D.C.: U.S. Census Bureau. Available at http://www2.census.gov/census_2000/datasets/Sim_Hispanic_Totals/General_Hispanic_Working_Paper_%2372.pdf.

Dávila, Arlene. 2001. *Latinos Inc: The Marketing and Making of a People.* Berkeley: University of California Press.

Davis, Martha Ellen. 2002. "An Antidote to Crisis: Exploring the Colombian Musical Diaspora in Miami." *Hemisphere: A Magazine of the Americas* 11, no. 3:4–7.

Gibson, Campbell J., and Emily Lennon. 1999. "Historical Census Statistics on the Foreign-born Population of the United States: 1850–1990." *Population Division Working Paper No. 29* Washington D.C.: U.S. Census Bureau. Available at http://www.census.gov/population/www/documentation/twps0029/twps0029.html.

Gilbertson, Greta A., Joseph P. Fitzpatrick, and Lijun Yang. 1996. "Hispanic Intermarriage in New York City: New Evidence from 1991." *International Migration Review* 30, no. 2:445–59.

Guarnizo, Luis E., and Luz Marina Díaz. 1999. "Transnational Migration: A View From Colombia." *Ethnic and Racial Studies* 22, no. 2:397–421.

Guarnizo, Luis E., Arturo I. Sánchez, and Elizabeth M. Roach. 1999. "Mistrust, Fragmented Solidarity, and Transnational Migration: Colombians in New York City and Los Angeles." *Ethnic and Racial Studies* 22, no. 2:367–96.

Haslip-Viera, Gabriel, and Sherrie L. Baver. 1996. *Latinos in New York: Communities in Transition.* South Bend, Ind.: University of Notre Dame Press.

Jachimowicz, Maia. 2003. "Argentina's Economic Woes Spur Emigration." *Migration Information Source. Migration Information Source*, 1 July 2003. Available at http://www.migrationinformation.org/Feature/display.cfm?ID=146.

Jones-Correa, Michael. 2001. "Institutional and Contextual Factors in Immigrant Naturalization and Voting." *Citizenship Studies* 5, no. 1:41–56.

——. 1998. *Between Two Nations: The Political Predicament of Latinos in New York City.* Ithaca, N.Y.: Cornell University Press.

Julca, Alex. 2001. "Peruvian Networks for Migration in New York City's Labor Market, 1970–1996." In *Migration, Transnationalization, and Race in a Changing New York*, ed. Héctor R. Cordero-Guzmán, Robert C. Smith, and Ramón Grosfoguel, 239–57. Philadelphia: Temple University Press.

Kasinitz, Philip, Mary C. Waters, John H . Mollenkopf, and Merih Anil. 2002. "Transnationalism and the Children of Immigrants in Contemporary New York." In *The*

Changing Face of Home: The Transnational Lives of the Second Generation, ed. Peggy Levitt and Mary C. Waters, 96–122. New York: Russell Sage Foundation.

Kyle, David. 2000. *Transnational Peasants: Migrations, Networks, and Ethnicity in Andean Ecuador.* Baltimore: John Hopkins University Press.

Laó-Montes, Augustin, and Arlene Dávila. 2001. *Mambo Montage: The Latinization of New York.* New York: Columbia University Press.

Logan, John R. 2002. "Hispanic Populations and Their Residential Patterns in the Metropolis." Albany, N.Y.: The Lewis Mumford Center for Comparative Urban and Regional Research at the University of Albany. Available at http://mumford1.dyndns.org/cen2000/HispanicPop/HspReportNew/page1.html.

——. 2001. "The New Latinos: Who They Are, Where They Are." Albany, N.Y.: The Lewis Mumford Center for Comparative Urban and Regional Research at the University of Albany. Available at http://mumford1.dyndns.org/cen2000/HispanicPop/HspReport/HspReportPage1.html.

Marin, John Marulanda. 2002. "The Urban Battlefield: Will Colombia's Armed Conflict Spread to the Cities?" *Hemisphere: A Magazine of the Americas* 11, no. 3:20–23.

Marshall, Adrianna. 1988. "Emigration of Argentines to the United States." In *When Borders Don't Divide: Labor Migration and Refugee Movements in the Americas*, ed. Patrica R. Pessar. Staten Island, N.Y.: Center for Migration Studies.

Oboler, Suzanne. 1995. *Ethnic Labels: Latino Lives: Identity and the Politics of (Re)Presentation in the United States.* Minneapolis, MN: University of Minnesota Press.

Pastor, Robert. 1984. "U.S. Immigration Policy and Latin America: In Search of the 'Special Relationship.'" *Latin American Research Review* 19, no. 3:35–56.

Pellegrino, Adela. 2000. "Trends in International Migration in Latin America and the Caribbean." *International Social Science Journal* 52, no. 3:395–408.

Portes, Alejandro. 1976. "Determinants of the Brain Drain." *International Migration Review* 10, no. 4:489–508.

——, ed. 1996. *The New Second Generation.* New York: Russell Sage Foundation.

Portes, Alejandro, and Ruben Rumbaut. 1996. *Immigrant America: A Portrait.* Berkeley: University of California Press.

——. 2001. *Legacies: The Story of the Immigrant Second Generation.* Los Angeles: University of California Press; New York: Russell Sage Foundation.

Reimers, David. 1992. *Still the Golden Door: The Third World Comes to America.* New York: Columbia University Press.

Rodríguez, Clara E. 2000. *Changing Race: Latinos, the Census, and the History of Ethnicity in the United States.* New York: New York University Press.

Rosenfeld, Michael J. 2001. "The Salience of Pan-National Hispanic and Asian Identities in U.S. Marriage Markets." *Demography* 38, no. 2:161–75.

Rumbaut, Rubén G., and Alejandro Portes, eds. 2001. *Ethnicities: The Children of Immigrants in America* . Berkeley: University of California Press; New York: Russell Sage Foundation.

Schoultz, Lars. 1998. *Beneath the United States: A History of U.S. Policy Toward Latin America.* Cambridge, Mass.: Harvard University Press.

Skidmore, Thomas. 2001. *Modern Latin America.* New York: Oxford University Press.

Suárez-Orozco, Marcelo, and Carola Suárez-Orozco. 1995. *Transformations: Migration, Family Life, and Achievement Motivation Among Latino Adolescents.* Stanford, Calif.: Stanford University Press.

Suro, Roberto and Jeffrey S. Passel. 2003. "The Rise of the Second Generation: Changing Patterns in Hispanic Population Growth." Washington, D.C.: Pew Hispanic Center. Available at http://www.pewhispanic.org/site/docs/pdf/PHC%20Projections%20final.pdf.

Suro, Roberto. 2002. "Counting the 'Other Hispanics': How Many Colombians, Dominicans, Ecuadorians, Guatemalans, and Salvadorans Are There in the United States?" Washington, D.C.: Pew Hispanic Center. http://www.pewhispanic.org/site/docs/pdf/other_hispanics.pdf.

U.S. Census Bureau. 2000. "Summary File 3: Place of Birth (Matrix PCT19)." Available at http://factfinder.census.gov/servlet/DTTable?_ts=87654049868.

U.S. Department of Labor. 1996. *Characteristics and Labor Market Behavior of the Legalized Population Five Years Following Legalization.* Washington, D.C.: U.S. Government Printing Office.

U.S. Immigration and Naturalization Service. Office of Policy and Planning. 2003. "Estimates of the Unauthorized Immigrant Population Residing in the United States, 1990 to 2000." Available at http://uscis.gov/graphics/shared/aboutus/statistics/Ill_Report_1211.pdf.

Waters, Mary C. 1996. "Ethnic and Racial Identities of Second-Generation Black Immigrants in New York City." In *The New Second Generation*, ed. Alejandro Portes, 171–96. New York: Russell Sage Foundation.

Wucker, Michele. 2002. "Searching for Argentina's Silver Lining." *World Policy Journal* 19, no. 4:49–58.

Zhou, Min. 2001. "Straddling Different Worlds: The Acculturation of Vietnamese Refugee Children." In *Ethnicities: Children of Immigrants in America*, ed. Rubén G. Rumbaut and Alejandro Portes, 187–228. Berkeley: University of California Press; New York: Russell Sage Foundation.

SEVEN

GENDER AND THE LATINO EXPERIENCE IN LATE-TWENTIETH-CENTURY AMERICA

PIERRETTE HONDAGNEU-SOTELO

WHAT TOPIC could be more expansive, slippery, and unwieldy than a discussion of the contours and tenor of gender relations among Latino groups in the United States at the end of the twentieth century? To begin with, the title of this chapter is a misnomer: there is no one, singular Latina or Latino experience in the United States. This has always been the case, but given the diversity of individuals and groups who take shelter under the contemporary Latino umbrella, this is probably truer at this moment than ever before. Similarly, as a result of major advances in the conceptualization and practice of gender studies over roughly the same period, the simplistic binaries that were once used as tools to understand gender—such as "male and female sex roles," "gay and straight," "modern and traditional"—no longer hold up. Although the questioning of old categorical distinctions has been a positive move, advancing our thinking about gender, it has also exposed new ambiguities and raised new questions, which, while they may indeed better reflect how the social world operates, inject new uncertainties.

Taking this ever-shifting terrain into account, this essay is an attempt to provide an overview of the changing dynamics of gender in a Latino population that has undergone tremendous transformation over the past forty years and, in the process, has changed the shape of American society. I argue that gender relations among Latinos now exhibit greater gender egalitarianism than was prevalent several decades ago. This transformation has been propelled by the transition away from traditional systems of gender rooted in rural, agrarian societies to modern ones anchored by urbanization, industrialization, and the expansion of education. The effects of this change are exhibited in the increased participation of Latinas in wage and salaried labor, so that motherhood and breadwinning are now often combined. The trend toward greater equality between Latino women and men is also shaped by general institutional changes in the late-twentieth-century United States. In this context, traditional Latino patriarchal assumptions—that only men can be wage earners, that motherhood negates wage earning, and that Latina women need not pursue education or participate in politics—have been challenged, both in ideology and practice.

This chapter opens with an introductory discussion about gender systems generally and then turns to an analysis of how gender has been constructed as an integral component of Latino cultures. I then briefly consider how the concomitant rise of "second-wave" feminism in the United States (and internationally) interacted with rapid demographic change to provide the foundation for important shifts in the structure of gendered systems among Latino populations in the United States. These shifts are then examined more closely by focusing on the nexus between work and the Latino family, with particular attention given to the larger social implications of changes in gender roles in the growing resident Latino population. The chapter concludes with brief and necessarily tentative speculations about the potential trajectory of gendered systems in the Latino population in the near future.

THINKING ABOUT GENDER

Gender refers to the cultural and social aspects of being a man or a woman in a particular place and time. Gender differences typically reflect unequal power arrangements that tend to valorize men and their contributions and traits, and devalue women and their qualities. The conceptualization of gender has come a long way from the period in which gender roles and larger gendered social systems were seen in terms of strict binaries of essential, inherited male traits on the one hand, and female attributes on the other. Early feminist academic scholarship was strongly guided by social psychology, led by the paradigms of socialization and sex roles. According to this view, children learn their appropriate sex roles through a series of behavioral rewards and punishments. Proponents of socialization argued that relatively static roles and sanctions guide everyday actions and choices, leading women and men to enact behavior which fits the "pink" or "blue" scripts they had been taught as children. This conditioning also lead people to occupy social spheres neatly divided into "the private and the public." The fundamental insight of early feminist scholarship was understanding how these binaries produced differences that were not functional for society—as some had previously claimed (see, for example, Parsons 1954), but which served rather as the basis for inequality and male privilege. This allowed feminists to identify and analyze women's relative powerlessness and to plan strategies for social change.

This was an empowering way for women to see the world, but it also ultimately proved to be a limiting one. It tended to ignore how large-scale social structures and institutions differentially place women and men in society, and it located the origins of gender differences primarily in early socialization and in individual personality. This produced a static picture, suggesting that what happens in one's childhood fixes adult agency. Logically, this led to the conclusion that changing early childhood experiences could eradicate sexism. Sexism was erroneously identified as a primarily individual, rather than as a social and institutional, practice. Another problem with these early approaches is that they tended to reduce gender to a dichotomy consisting of men's privilege and domination versus women's victimization and subordination. "Women" and "men" were polarized as opposite, essentialized categories, each with particular characteristics and experiences.

The last twenty to thirty years of feminist scholarship have complicated these static binaries and disrupted these categories, which were previously assumed to be universal. Gender is now understood as relatively fluid, plastic, and malleable, and it is more widely accepted as a dynamic process unfolding across a broad range of possibilities rather than as an invariant category. As many studies have shown, social scripts inherited from childhood and mainstream cultural ideals about how women should act are often transgressed. As those working from a perspective of symbolic interactionism have suggested, it may be more accurate to analyze how people actually "do gender," as people constantly reconstruct, enact, and perform gender differences and displays (West and Zimmerman 1987). In this view, gender is a routine and recurring accomplishment that is learned, contested, and relearned every day.

Feminist scholars today pay more attention to both differences *and* similarities among women and men—and between them. Driven by heightened awareness of the manner in which race, class, and gender intersect and interact to shape women's and men's social locations, we now see that not all women are similarly subordinated and not all men occupy social positions of power and status. Similarly, there is heightened awareness that men routinely exhibit what were once considered "feminine" traits and that women routinely adopt what were once widely thought to be exclusively "masculine" behaviors, and this obviously has stimulated a profound rethinking about how gender roles are constructed, maintained, and changed over time. Scholarship conducted by "other" women—women of color and lesbians in particular, including many Latina scholars, social critics, and essayists—has helped to remedy earlier essentialized views of gender, and so has the move away from the focus on individuals to a greater recognition of how macrolevel structural forces and social institutions, such as the economy, the class system, colonial legacies, different levels of educational attainment, politics, and religion, and other factors shape and constrain gendered behavior (see, for example, Baca Zinn et al. 1986; Anzaldúa 1987).

It is important to note that not all women are similarly situated at the bottom of social hierarchies, and not all men occupy positions of privilege, authority and status. The intersection and interaction of race, class, and gender are critical to understanding contemporary relations between and among women and men. When focusing on Latinos in the United States, a large proportion of whom are foreign-born, we need to take into consideration the manner in which hierarchies of citizenship and global inequalities also inform gender relations, a topic that is addressed below.

THE LATINO CULTURAL CONTEXT

Gender relations are imbued with, but not dictated by, cultural mandates. This is an important point to emphasize because for many years, Mexican Americans, other Latinos, and Latin Americans generally were conceived of and studied as racial ethnic groups whose behavior was seen as primarily or even solely determined by cultural legacies and mandates. The ideas that Latinos are fatalistic, more collectively and family-oriented than individualistic, and passive rather than active run deep in many texts written before the civil-rights and second-wave feminist movements compelled serious rethinking of such assumptions. In many cases, these putative cultural traits were used to rationalize or explain both the existence of deep levels of social inequality in the Spanish-speaking nations of Latin America and Latino subordination, poverty, and social deviance in the United States.

Many Americans are acquainted with the traditional gender prescriptions of Latino and Latin American culture. Although scholars have conclusively demonstrated that these have always been contested in the ways people live their lives (Baca Zinn 1980; Deutsch 1987; Pescatello 1973; Stevens 1973), movies, television, and other mass media outlets still readily reproduce these caricature-like images in monolithic strokes (Fregoso 1993). Still, as much of these images are based on invidious stereotypes, one can argue that traditional Latin American gendered systems have been characterized by a situation in which women were expected to be subservient and defer to the wishes of men, male children typically occupied positions of relatively higher status within families, and women's sexuality and "honor" were considered areas of family life over which strict control should be maintained. For women and girls, these cultural mandates traditionally have been modeled on the Catholic Virgin. Traditional gender rules emanating from the figure of the Virgin prescribe dependence, subordination, selfless devotion to family, bodily modesty and shame, acceptance of surveillance, restricted spatial mobility, and premarital virginity. The last serves as both a symbol of desirable femininity and the axis on which family honor hinges. For boys and men, ideals of *machismo* call for men to be sexually assertive, independent, and emotionally restrained and to wield authority over wives and children. These cultural mandates derive largely from preindustrial Latin American agrarian societies. Their origins lie in Spanish culture (itself influenced by the Islamic Moors), Catholicism, the conquest of the indigenous peoples of the Americas, and the subsequent society of *mestizos* (people of mixed heritage).

Latino culture is now seen as far more diverse, plastic, and fluid than in these earlier approaches and, for reasons that will be discussed in more detail below, this is particularly true of Latinos in the United States—although gender relations in Latin America have also undergone radical shifts in recent decades. In the United States, it is probably more accurate to talk about Latino cultural traditions as a plurality shaped by distinctive national, regional, and class formations, rather than as a monolithic entity. It is undeniable that cultural mandates have loomed large historically in Latino gender relations and that they require close attention and interrogation in any analysis of contemporary gender systems. Once again, however, it is important to keep in mind that "culture" remains open to change by structural forces and social institutions, and human agency is never dictated. In this regard, it is useful to think of cultural mandates as serving more as socially constructed prescriptions about what *should* be, and less as accurate, objective, or empirical descriptions of social life as it is actually lived by women and men. As normative prescriptions for social behavior, they are sometimes used less as scripts and more as metrics for resistance and transgression. In other words, people may react to, rather than enact, specific cultural dictates. In other instances, as illustrated in the following section, familiar cultural icons and symbols take on new meanings.

For example, in an empirical study of how young Mexican American women in Texas view *La Virgen de Guadalupe* (the patron saint of Mexico and, by extension, of Mexican Americans), theologian Jeanette Rodríguez (1994) found that this important religious figure, which could be interpreted as a representation of traditional cultural mandates of subordination and modesty, is now seen very differently by young women. Unlike their forebears, contemporary women were more likely to embrace and interpret *la Virgen* as a symbol of strength and quiet determination rather than as a symbol of passive subordination. Not all Latinas and Latinos in the contemporary period share and celebrate these views. Deep disagreements about cultural values related to sex and gender remain, and these different positions have provoked contentious battles. When *la Virgen* is promoted as an independent and strong image of Latina indigenous womanhood, that image may threaten elements of the Latino, Catholic, patriarchal status quo. In 2001, when one Chicana feminist artist, Alma López, exhibited a work of art representing *la Virgen* with exposed legs and stomach, also depicting a female angel's bare breasts, religious and community leaders in New Mexico organized a protest to censor and remove this piece of art from a museum. While the artist saw her depiction of *la Virgen* as portraying "beauty and strength," López contends that the male leaders who protested it described it as "blasphemy, sacrilegious, the devil, a tart, a stripper" (A. López 2001: 255). Clearly, cultural and religious mandates regarding gender and sexuality remain deeply contested areas among Latinos in the contemporary period, and bitter battles will almost certainly continue to emerge over attempts to impose one meaning over another.

Still, in other cases people may cling to particular cultural values of gender but find that the social resources for the realization of these values are not accessible. This is illustrated by the case of Latina women who may cling to the belief that a woman's place is in the home but out of necessity may actively engage with public institutions through employment, social services, or other community institutions (Fernández-Kelly and García 1997; Menjívar 2000; Pessar 1995; Prieto 1992). In all of these instances, it is important to keep in mind the power of human agency to challenge and transform culture, and the malleability of cultural values and mandates.

THE IMPORTANCE OF IMMIGRATION AND U.S. FEMINISM FOR THE STRUCTURING OF LATINO GENDER SYSTEMS

The power of human agency in the face of a rapidly changing environment is perhaps most clearly seen in the gendered transitions that have occurred as a result of the interaction of massive population movements from Latin America to the United States and the concomitant demographic revolution that has resulted in what is arguably a significantly more open gendered society in the United States. As I have noted in other work, two of the most radically transformative forces in recasting contemporary life in the United States are feminism and immigration (Hondagneu-Sotelo 2000). After a mid-twentieth-century hiatus in immigration, the last three decades of the twentieth century witnessed a vigorous resurgence of migration to the United States. As many commentators in this volume and elsewhere have observed, new immigrants now mostly hail not from Europe, as they did in the early part of the twentieth century, but from Asian, Latin American, and Caribbean nations. This is a diverse immigration population, not only with respect to ethnic and national origins, but also in terms of socioeconomic class and legal status. Latino immigrants in this period have entered the United States with a diversity of citizenship and legal-status arrangements, with Cubans largely granted and Salvadorans largely denied political refugee status; Puerto Ricans accepted as nominal U.S. citizens due to their nation's colonial status; and Mexicans, who have migrated in the greatest numbers by far, living in the United States both legally and illegally. Unlike their earlier, European-origin predecessors, U.S. immigrants in the late twentieth century include not only poor, manual workers but also substantial segments of entrepreneurs and highly educated urban professionals.

Census figures clearly demonstrate the scope of the changes that have transformed U.S. society over that period. In 1960, the U.S. Census counted a pan-Latino population (that is, both native and foreign-born) of only about 7 million people (Bean and Tienda, 1987: 59). But as David G. Gutiérrez notes in his introduction to this volume, disparities in economic opportunity between the United States and Latin America, political instability in many Latin American nations, and dramatic improvements in communication and transportation technologies laid the foundations for one of the most dramatic epochs of migration in human history. By 1970, the pan-Latino population of the United States grew to 9 million, and by 1980, to 14 million (Delgado and Stefanic 1998: xvii). The pace of migration rapidly accelerated after that. By 1990, the combined foreign-born and native population of Latino origin grew to 22 million. By 2000, after one of the most intense periods of immigration in American history, the Latino population had grown to 35 million, or nearly 13 percent of the total population of the United States—and this number did not include the 3.8 million inhabitants of the American Commonwealth of Puerto Rico (see Gutiérrez, chapter 1, this volume).

The historical tendency of both U.S.-born and immigrant Latinos to settle in urban areas greatly magnified the effects of this massive demographic transformation. Immigrants and their families tend to settle in clusters, and, increasingly, many big cities have become Latino immigrant cities. According to the 2000 census, more than one-fifth of the entire Latino population of the United States live in just four metropolitan areas: Los Angeles County (4.2 million), Miami-Dade County (1.3 million), Harris County, Texas, (1.1 million), and Cook County, Illinois (1.1 million). In eight of the ten largest cities in the United States (New York, Los Angeles, Chicago, Houston, Phoenix, San Diego, Dallas, San Antonio) Latinos now constitute anywhere from a low of 25.4 percent of total populations (in San Diego), to highs of 46.5 percent (Los Angeles) and 58.7 percent (San Antonio) (U.S. Census Bureau 2001: table 36, 39). If one factors in the multiplier effect of the presence and rapid recent expansion of the

Spanish-language print-media, broadcast conglomerates such as Televisa and Univisión, and the number of Spanish-language radio stations that enjoy leading Arbitron ratings, the reach of Latino cultures in the United States is much greater.

Population growth was so great in the 1980s and 1990s that Latinos began to leave saturated labor markets along the U.S.-Mexico border to seek work and upward mobility in new areas of settlement. Thus Latinos, and especially Latino immigrants, are migrating to work and live in all kinds of rural and small-town areas throughout the United States. Pundits and scholars alike now frequently announce the imminent "browning of the Midwest," the "Latinization of the Southeast" and the "Mexicanization of the Northwest." As the last nomenclature suggests, Mexican immigrants appear to be the ones primarily fueling this trend, as they either leave saturated labor markets and big city problems in Los Angeles or forego the Los Angeles step altogether in favor of new jobs in northwestern apple orchards, Midwestern slaughter houses and packing plants, or southeastern poultry farms and carpet factories. Increasingly, Guatemalans and other Latinos, driven in part by the search for safer schools and communities for their children, are going to Utah and Nevada to work in factories, hotels, and restaurants, while Salvadorans, who concentrate in California, Washington, D.C., and Texas, are also found performing low-wage service jobs in suburban Long Island. Similarly, Mexicans, once virtually absent in New York City, have migrated there steadily since the early 1980s, and now constitute a solid occupational niche in New York City flower vending. Throughout the country, industries have restructured in ways that increase their reliance on low-wage immigrant labor from Latin America and the Caribbean. Consequently, gone are the days when textbooks could confidently capture Latino geographical dispersion by announcing that "Mexican Americans live in the Southwest," "Cubans in Miami," and "Puerto Ricans in the northeast." Recent international and internal migration patterns have dramatically challenged these neatly circumscribed intraethnic regional divisions. To be sure, those Latino concentrations continue, but they are now accompanied by geographic diversity.

Although it is impossible to predict precisely how this ongoing process of demographic revolution, urbanization, and geographic dispersal will influence the ways in which gendered relations are forged in the increasingly complex and variegated Latino population, if trends established in the 1980s and 1990s hold into the future, it seems certain that the Latino presence in the United States will now be situated far and wide, in numerous industries, neighborhoods, and institutions in every one of the fifty states. It also seems most likely that the twenty-first century will witness new levels of public participation and achievement by Latinas and fewer restrictions on women and girls in Latino families. The majority of Latinos in the United States are either immigrants or the children of immigrants, and even here, where we might expect to see more traditional patterns among recent arrivals from the Dominican Republic, Mexico, El Salvador, and Puerto Rico, we see increasing women's participation in politics, education, and employment (Goldring 2003; Hardy-Fanta 1993; Hondagneu-Sotelo 1994; Jones-Correa 1998; López 2003; Menjívar 2000). The reasons for these trends are complex. Some of the breakdown of more rigid traditional Latino gender roles and systems can be attributed to the cosmopolitan influences of living in urban areas in a post-feminist environment in which more women routinely work out of the home, regularly contribute to their own and their families' support, and thus develop self-images and expectations that may be dramatically different from those learned in more traditional, rural environments in Latin America. The increasing fluidity of gender roles and systems can also be partially attributed to the socializing effects of American popular culture and American public education, no matter how flawed the public education system otherwise is.

But one could also reasonably argue that it is the legacy of the second-wave feminist movement of the 1960s and 1970s that has most effected change in gendered systems in the United States—and that this sea change has had a strong residual effect of creating opportunities for Latinas in their relations with men, and in the range of possible roles they can now play in society generally. Feminism has provoked far-reaching transformations on the social landscape not only in the United States, but also in Latin America, where many countries had feminist political movements in the early twentieth century.[1] While those who have promoted feminist social movements in recent decades may rightly surmise that the feminist project of transforming society into a more egalitarian one for women and for all people is far from complete, the expansion of opportunities for many women living in the United States has occurred at a staggering pace. Using the mid-twentieth century as a benchmark, it is startling to acknowledge the prevalence, by the late twentieth century, of women, including married women with young children, throughout the paid labor force, and even in the highly coveted professions of law and medicine. While the gendered division of labor at home seems more resistant to change, even on that front there have been important shifts toward greater egalitarianism. And as we shall see, these moves toward greater domestic egalitarianism have occurred even in those families believed by many to be the most culture-bound and impervious to social change, Latino families. The direct consequences of the organized feminist movements include many features of late-twentieth-century life that many in the United States, especially the young, today take for granted. These include the proliferation of shelters for abused women; legislation criminalizing domestic violence and discrimination against women and girls in sports, education, work, and politics; laws against sexual harassment in the work place; and the expansion of reproductive rights.

More circuitous perhaps, but still worth acknowledging, is the role of the Civil Rights Movement in pushing the nation to end all forms of legal discrimination, including racial exclusion provisions in immigration law (see Johnson, this volume). After the enactment of the Civil Rights Act in 1964, dramatic changes came about in immigration law, particularly the termination of the Bracero Program agreements for Mexican contract labor for western agriculture at the end of 1964 and the Immigration and Nationality Act Amendments of 1965. This latter piece of legislation conclusively ended racial exclusionary policies that had previously denied entry to Asian immigrants and codified family reunification as the legal basis for obtaining legal permanent resident-immigrant status in the United States.

While the Immigration Nationality Act amendments particularly opened up the doors that had previously been closed to Asian immigrants, immigrants from Latin America also eventually benefited from new provisions in the law that gave high priority to the principle of family reunification. In the Mexican case, for example, this revision allowed wives to immigrate legally after their husbands had obtained legal permanent residency. Although the 1965 act imposed for the first time an annual quota of 120,000 visas for the Western Hemisphere, it importantly allowed former bracero contract workers who had legalized through employer certification to legally bring their families to the United States. In recent years, many immigration scholars have cautioned that the 1965 law was neither the sole nor decisive factor in promoting this immigration. This is true, as the mass immigration of the late twentieth century has its root causes in structural changes in the global economy and, in particular, in the myriad of economic, military, and political connections established between the United States and those nations which eventually became sources of U.S.-bound migration. The extent to which many foreign-born immigrants could be legally admitted into the country, however, *is* part of the legacy of the Civil Rights Movement—and of the liberalization of immigration law that arguably sprang from it (Bach 1978).

THE WORK/FAMILY NEXUS

In any case, the intersection of a more liberal civil-rights and gender-rights environment with the massive growth of the pan-Latino population of the country laid the foundation for significant changes in the structure and practice of gender relations among Latinos. This is perhaps most easily demonstrated by examining the changing relation between work and family in Latino subcultures. Again, however, in discussing these changes it is important to remember that gender is not a variable like sex (female or male), but rather a relational and constantly contested social system of power. For this reason, I draw on studies based on relatively small samples to illustrate the nuances of Latino gender relations as expressed in families and work. These studies of smaller samples give us a better understanding of the dynamics of gender.

The social construction of gender is fundamentally about power, and, as such, it has important consequences for the distribution of resources and the division of labor. For this reason, the ways in which gender inequalities unfold in families has probably received more attention than any other area in gender scholarship, and this is certainly true of the research on Latinos, a group widely known as being family centered. Studies looking at the relationship between wages and the household division of labor were initially prompted by early debates in second-wave feminism, but these were also fueled by concerns among Latina feminists, especially Chicana feminists working in the Chicano movement. Before visiting the issues and findings that prevail in the research on gender and Latino families and work, let us consider how this research both diverges from and approximates feminist research on white families and work.

A good deal of early-1970s second-wave feminism focused on women's subordination in the home. In *The Feminine Mystique* (1963), Betty Friedan identified confinement in the private, domestic sphere as the source of oppression for women, but she was really addressing the concerns of specific women—middle-class, college-educated, white women. Women's housework and absence from the labor force were seen as the universal source of their subordination. Posed in this fashion, "the problem which had no name" seemed readily resolvable with exhortations for women to participate in the public sphere of employment and politics.

As many commentators have since pointed out, Friedan and other 1970s Anglo-American, middle-class feminists of that ilk had overlooked that many working-class women and women of color were already in the paid labor force. Employment had not spawned liberation in the home for working-class women of color. Rather, occupational exploitation and racism in the public sphere had more often made the family a source of refuge. As Maxine Baca Zinn (1975) argued in an early feminist article, for many Chicanas and other Latinas, Latino families are simultaneous sites of patriarchal dominance and racial and class solidarity.

One of the great and lasting contributions of second-wave feminism is the recognition of unpaid housework and care work as work that benefits society. Yet the ways that women of different class and racial or ethnic groups approach housework was not always specified by early feminist scholarship. Among other things, the literature tended to overlook the fact that some elite women purchase housework services, and other women—poor women of color and, today, immigrant women of color—perform this work for pay in other people's homes and without pay in their own homes.

As already noted, a dominant feminist idea held that public employment would lead to all women's liberation from sexism. This literature overlooked not only the different occupational opportunities available to different groups of women. It also ignored the fact that historically, for some poor and working-class women, remaining outside of the paid labor force and taking care of one's own home and children were seen as achievements and privileges, not as sources of subordination. This has been true for a variety of Latinas in the United States. As one Cuban American woman in Miami explained to researchers after accepting employment in the garment trade only for a temporary period, and then only in order to advance family socioeconomic mobility,

> there's no reason for women not to earn a living when it's necessary; they should have as many opportunities and responsibilities as men. But I also tell my daughter that the strength of a family rests on the intelligence and work of women. It is foolish to give up our place as a mother and a wife only to go take orders from men who aren't even part of your family. What's so liberated about that? It is better to see your husband succeed and to know you have supported one another.
>
> *(Fernández-Kelly and García 1997: 225)*

When women face racial discrimination, sexism, low wages, and exploitative working conditions in the public sphere, staying home sometimes is a welcome respite from those restricted labor-market experiences. One young Mexican immigrant wife and mother of three young sons told me that when her husband requested that she withdraw from paid work in a factory, she responded eagerly. She explained her response not only in terms of her husband's cultural mandates, but also with respect to her very limited job opportunities:

> He is one of them that likes his woman in the house and coming home to find me here. That's what they are accustomed to. . . . It seemed fine to me. I didn't have a job that I liked very much. It wasn't as though I had an important job, then perhaps I would have preferred to stay [employed].
>
> *(Hondagneu-Sotelo 1994: 137).*

Class, occupation, and culture mediate the different meanings women experience from public/private divides. One woman's privilege becomes another's burden.

Latinas' formal labor force participation rates *are* lower than those of women from other racial- and ethnic- group categories. According to the census data for 2000, the percentage of Latina women in the labor force reached 56 (Suárez-Orozco and Páez 2002: 27). This figure represents significant upward movement from 1973, when 40 percent of Latinas were in the labor force (Moreno and Muller 1996: 39), but both figures are probably underestimates of Latinas income-earning activities. Historically, Latinas have worked in jobs rendered "invisible" by the ways in which they are perceived and performed. Throughout the Southwest, a long historical legacy of Mexican American women working as private domestic workers, laundresses, and migrant farm workers and in canneries has been obscured. These sorts of jobs simply do not fit with models of nineteenth- and twentieth-century industrial employment. When women hold paying jobs that are performed on a seasonal schedule, on a part-time basis, or actually in the home, as are contemporary childcare and industrial home work in the garment industry, these jobs also do not seem to "count" as jobs. Similarly, when women work in the informal, unregulated sector of the economy, their income-generating activities are not likely to be counted by the census or other official surveys. Still, it is significant that Latinas continue to have lower rates of labor force participation than do white, black, and Asian American women in the United States.

What informs Latino women's and men's decisions, practices, and ideals about work and family arrangements? What explains the diversity of work and family arrangements, and what explains Latina women's relatively lower labor-force participation rates? Are cultural attitudes the driving force, or is it social structure and its attendant arrays of institutions, resources, and rules, which prove to be the determining factor? Debates over Latinas' approach to work and family negotiations have often been posed this starkly, although the answers are never so simple. On the one hand, a long legacy of Eurocentric social-science scholarship has located explanations for all factors of social life among Latinos in a paradigm of cultural deficiency. Assumptions of traditional values and fatalism have fueled a long legacy of research based on "blame-the-victim" cultural deficiency models. Chicana and other Latina social scientists writing in the late twentieth century have countered this view with one that places strong emphasis on social structure, discrimination, and material resources. Research by feminist Chicana social scientists has consistently countered the cultural explanations with indicators of the structural impediments to full equality for Latina women in the United States (Baca Zinn 1975, 1994; Ybarra 1982; Zavella, 1987).

While it remains true that wives, regardless of employment, class, and racial or ethnic group, still do the majority of household work, change has clearly occurred in recent decades. Still, compared to patterns that prevailed fifty years ago, men in the United States, acting as fathers and husbands, have begun to take on some housework responsibilities. What explains men's willingness to do so?

A large body of research suggests that the amount of money that spouses earn shapes household divisions of labor. This correlation between women's employment and men's increased involvement in household chores holds true in Latino families, although studies disagree on the extent to which these modest changes reach meaningful levels. In a study based on in-depth interviews with twenty middle-income Chicano couples in southern California, for example, sociologists Scott Coltrane and Elsa Valdez (1997) found that relative incomes earned by spouses proved to be a good predictor of spousal participation in household chores. When Chicano men earn substantially more than their wives, they are less likely to perform a substantial amount of housework and child rearing. When Chicano men earn less than their wives and when their careers have been stymied, their wives seem to encourage more successfully their husbands' participation in housework and active child rearing. Consistent with a broad array of other studies, sociologists Coltrane and Valdez found men taking more responsibility in the arena of child rearing and less in the poorly visible and less rewarding work of house cleaning.

However, in another study of Chicano dual-earner families (Pesquera 1993), the researcher found that while the earning gap between husbands and wives shapes household arrangements, it is not the only factor. This study indicates that occupational positions held by the wives also determined the extent to which Chicano men in the research sample performed housework. When this researcher compared housework arrangements among Chicana professionals, clerical workers, and blue-collar workers, she found that the professionals and blue-collar workers had the highest expectations for their husbands' participation in household labor, while women clerical workers clung closely to traditional ideological tenets that allocate housework to women. Accordingly, not only relative earnings, but also ideological stances, occupation, and work schedules influence who does what in the home.

Among a group of undocumented Mexican immigrant families residing in northern California, my own research (Hondagneu-Sotelo 1994) reveals substantial modifications in household gender arrangements, mostly in the direction of greater gender egalitarianism. In general, the Mexican immigrant women seem to make great strides in achieving greater spatial mobility, greater say in family decision-making processes, and, in some important cases, in achieving a more equitable division of household labor. While other studies about gender and Latino immigrants view women's employment and earnings in the United States as the primary catalyst for these changes, I believe that migration processes themselves are also critical to the reconstruction of gender relations in the United States. When husbands and wives are separated for long periods of time during the early stages of immigration, spousal separation mandates that men will have to take some responsibility for their own daily upkeep (cooking, cleaning, laundry) and women will face new obligations previously the domain of their husbands (decision making, budgeting, mediating public encounters). These transformative experiences inform the gendered division of household labor when the family is reunited.

Latinas are not a monolithic group, however, and hence we see tremendous variety in the ways in which work and family issues are negotiated (Baca Zinn 1994). In the last decades of the twentieth century, in an era defined by high rates of middle-class women's labor-force participation, high rates of migration from Latin American and the Caribbean, and increasingly accentuated inequalities of wealth and income, new family and work patterns began emerging among Central American, Caribbean, and Mexican migrant women. This pattern, which I have referred to elsewhere as "transnational motherhood," (Hondagneu-Sotelo 2001; Hondagneu-Sotelo and Avila 1997) involves Latina immigrants' employment and residence in the United States while their children and families remain "back home" in their country of origin. Although not confined to women who work as nannies or housekeepers in the United States, it does appear, for reasons specific to the schedules, pay scales, and structures of that job, to be especially salient among this group. For instance, in a nonrandom survey I conducted among 153 Latina immigrant domestic workers in Los Angeles, fully 40 percent of those who were mothers reported that at least one of their children lived in Mexico or Central America.

Why have thousands of Central American, Caribbean, and, increasingly, Mexican women left their children behind with grandmothers, other female kin, the children's fathers, or paid caregivers while they themselves migrate to work in the United States? They have responded to the exigencies of a new political economy of globalization, one that has extended the market for cleaning and caring services. Now that middle-class mothers are in the workforce, relatively privileged families can outsource the work of cleaning and caring to immigrant women from third world nations. This allows these middle-class women, mostly white mothers and wives, the privilege to opt out of their own gender oppression in the home without exhorting middle-class husbands and fathers to share the burden. This, in turn, creates new family inequalities further down the global class chain, whereby some families are denied face-to-face relations.

These are not altogether new arrangements. In fact, one precursor to these arrangements can be found in the mid-twentieth-century Bracero Program, which in effect legislatively mandated Mexican "absentee fathers" who came to work as contracted agricultural laborers in the United States. This longstanding arrangement still occurs today, although it is no longer legislatively mandated. When these men come north and leave their families in Mexico—as they did during the Bracero Program, and as many continue to do today—they are fulfilling their breadwinning obligations toward their families. When women do so, however, they are embarking not only on an immigrant journey, but on a more radical gender-transformative odyssey. As they initiate separations of space and time from their communities of origin and from their homes, children, and sometimes husbands, they must cope with stigma, guilt, and criticism from others. The ambivalent feelings and new ideological stances that emerge in tandem with these new arrangements are still in formation, but tension is evident. As they wrestle with the contradictions of their lives and beliefs, and as they leave behind their own children to care for the children of strangers in a foreign land, these Latina domestic workers innovate new rhetorical and emotional strategies.

Not all families are torn apart by immigration and transnational processes, and some are even brought closer together through their struggles for economic survival. In the last years of the twentieth century, many Mexican and Central American immigrant families settled into permanent jobs and communities in the United States, and as they did, they helped foment a new wave of community unionism. Contrary to the predictions of anti-immigration groups who long feared that immigrant workers would depress wages and weaken organized labor, this new union movement is largely fueled by the efforts of U.S.-born Latino workers *and* Latino immigrant workers from Mexico, Central America, and the Caribbean. Organizing as hotel and restaurant workers, as janitors, as drywall installers and other construction workers, and as home health aids, in the late 1990s they have created innovative social-movement strategies for winning demands from their employers. Job demands which once centered on wage and hour issues now encompass basic family issues, such as family health insurance and affordable housing.

Economic restructuring, as Cynthia Cranford's (2000) research indicates, provides the backdrop for the emergence of these developments. As the office-janitorial industry was increasingly subcontracted to smaller firms throughout the 1970s and 1980s, small competitive office-cleaning businesses recruited Mexican and Central American immigrant men *and women* as favored employees. The wages were typically lower than those that had been paid to U.S.-born men, the former workers in this occupation. As relatively newly arrived immigrants with dire financial needs, these immigrant workers often had no alternatives but to accept these low-wage, downgraded, dead-end jobs. In the process, the janitorial occupation has undergone a radical transformation, as it is now a job, in Los Angeles at least, which is institutionally occupied by Latino immigrant men *and women*. In recent years, guided by the efforts of some very talented organizers, these workers have struggled to improve the quality of their jobs and pay, and, in the process, both labor organizing and familiar work/family arrangements have changed.

In Los Angeles, the creative, militant efforts of one very successful union, the Service Employees International Union's (SEIU) "Justice for Janitors" campaign organized vociferous street protests in some of the toniest corporate business districts of southern California. Throughout the 1990s, in the shadows of high-rise corporate centers in Century City, Westwood, and in downtown Los Angeles, immigrant Latinos wearing brightly colored union T-shirts, and together with their children, have taken to the streets with demands for workplace fairness and economic justice. These protests culminated in a large general strike during the spring of 2000. In the process, old patterns of work and family relations have fallen by the wayside.

Fieldwork conducted by Cynthia Cranford on the union movement of Justice for Janitors in Los Angeles during the late 1990s chronicles a host of innovative public-protest methods and new work-family-union arrangements. As women have taken to the street to shout out their demands, men have taken on greater responsibilities for children and household. And in the process, all kinds of domestic tasks have moved from the home to the streets. Particularly telling is Cranford's rendition of how the work of caring for small children, generally associated with women and conducted in the private sphere of home, is today extended into the public sphere by striking Latino male workers:

> I noted varying degrees of men's mothering among couples of janitors. For example, at one march a woman was pushing a stroller with a small child in it around the line. After a short while, she rolled the stroller over to a man who was handing out flyers to tenants, who attached his picket sign to the stroller. As the child lay in the stroller, asleep, the man continued to hand out flyers. On a different occasion, a (married) couple of janitors brought three children with them. The woman walked the picket line with two children who looked about 5 and 7. The man looked after an infant in a stroller as he handed out flyers. This man had to engage in more mothering than the one mentioned above. When the baby began to fidget, then cry loudly the man picked her up and . . . continued to hand out flyers with the child in one arm.
>
> *(Cranford, 2000: 35).*

kind of weak sauce.

Street scenes from contemporary Los Angeles suggest a revival of similar transformations, witnessed in the classic 1954 movie *Salt of the Earth*. The fictionalized movie, based on a real labor struggle of Mexican Americans in New Mexico, chronicled a miners' strike that occurred in the early 1950s. A unique product of the mining families and blacklisted Hollywood movie makers, the film still surprises contemporary audiences with its progressive views on how racism, sexism, and class exploitation work together.

In the movie, Mexican American miners initially exclude from their organizing campaign their wives and their wives' demands for better housing, running water, and sanitation. Once it becomes apparent that the labor struggle can only be won with the effort of the women, the women take over the picket lines, and the men are relegated to passively sitting on the sidelines, holding babies. When their wives are then jailed, they shout out and demand from their jailers the basic rights of social reproduction. In one memorable scene, jailed women and children shout out, "We want the [baby] formula," and chant, bang on the jail bars, and raise their voices to demand food, beds, and bathrooms: "*Queremos comida. . . . Queremos camas. . . . Queremos baños.*" After the men are forced to do the housework on their own, their political demands change, and they too demand hot running water and learn to see that unpaid housework is work too. As one husband says to another as they are hanging laundry out to dry when the women are in jail, "There's two kinds of slavery, wage slavery and domestic slavery."

Scenes from contemporary Los Angeles of the striking janitors and from *Salt of the Earth* are certainly not necessarily representative of Latino work and family arrangements, but they do provide striking illustrations of how old patterns of household labor may rupture during moments of accelerated social change. During heightened moments of social- and labor-movement protest, familiar, taken-for-granted, gendered divisions of labor may be deeply contested. Old ideas about who should do what may be contested ideologically or simply by the urgencies of the moment.

Critical to this process may be the erosion of occupational segregation by sex in low-wage jobs. Here again, the janitorial industry serves as an important exemplar. Latina immigrant janitors are working in low-paid, low-status jobs, but these are not stereotypically "female jobs." Unlike clerical jobs in an earlier era, janitorial jobs do not appear to be on the road to becoming "feminized" and deskilled. In fact, workers are organizing to upgrade their jobs and wages and to win basic job benefits. The absence of occupational segregation by sex, the job scheduling, and the relative equality in wages may open the door to more equitable household divisions of labor. While these sorts of patterns may emerge among unionized Latino immigrant workers with stable jobs, or among Mexican American middle-class families, the picture at the bottom of the socioeconomic ladder is less encouraging. The proliferation of female-headed households and endemic poverty among Latino immigrant workers, and among U.S.-born Chicanos and Puerto Ricans unable to get a foothold in the U.S. economy, does not suggest a trend toward great gender egalitarianism, but rather new entrenched patterns of poverty, and of race and gender subordination.

CONCLUSION

This essay has sketched out an overview of some of the ways in which gender informs work and family arrangements among Latinos in the United States, with a focus particularly on the largest and fasting growing segment of the Latino population—the new Latino immigrants from Mexico and Central America. While gender egalitarianism has not been attained among Latinos—or any other racial or ethnic group in the United States—we have seen, in the twentieth century, a definitive movement toward a greater plurality of gender arrangements and a general trend toward greater gender parity in the workplace and in many families. A new plurality of family and work arrangements prevails *even within groups*, defying easy generalizing statements.

How will the complexities of globalization and the United States' position within the larger world economy shape gender and social relations among Latinos in the years that lie ahead? My speculations hinge on the growth of Latinos in the United States, their continuing geographical diversification, and on new patterns of employment prompted by globalization. The Latino population in the United States is now hailed as the United States' largest "minority" group, outnumbering African Americans; most demographers believe the Latino numbers will continue to grow. Accompanying this trend, as we have seen, is increasing Latino geographical diversity and occupational diversity. This last factor, I believe, will prove critical in reconstructing and remaking Latino gender relations.

In this new context of globalization, we can expect to see still more increases in the rates of salaried and wage employment for Latinas. Many Latinas will be working in the lower echelons of our burgeoning service industry, while a few will occupy key positions in the professions and in business. Alongside college-educated, bilingual, and bicultural Latina professionals and managers—some of whom will take key jobs in the command posts of globalization—we will see a much larger cohort of Latinas, many of them new immigrants, toiling in a broad spectrum of service jobs in hotels, restaurants, hospitals, offices, convalescent homes, and private residences. In this regard, as I have noted elsewhere (Hondagneu-Sotelo 2001, 2002), today's gendered demand for immigrant labor is quite different than nineteenth- and earlier-twentieth-century patterns, where Asian, European, and Mexican *male* workers were recruited for manufacturing and primary extractive industries. Globalization has remade the United States so that it cannot function without immigrant labor, and especially without female immigrant labor. *Braceras* in homes and hospitals have replaced the braceros of yesterday. In this context, family and gender relations are being renegotiated in a myriad of ways.

In spite of the tremors of globalization and the diverse family and work arrangements, some very traditional ideals about how Latino women and men should act still echo throughout various institutions. Across socioeconomic groups, generations, and national/ethnic categories of Latinos, however, strong, patriarchal cultural mandates have been at least destabilized, if not dethroned. To the extent that these changes have come about, they have been prompted less by overt feminist exhortations for gender equality and more by structural changes in the economy. Even when ideas that women belong in the home and men in the workplace remain firmly entrenched, dual-worker family arrangements make those ideas hard to put into practice. When culture is trumped by class, gender inequalities do not disappear, but their articulations cannot remain the same.

NOTE

1. The first wave of feminism refers to the suffragist movement of the late 1800s and early 1900s, and the second wave, to the women's liberation movement of the 1960s and 1970s. Most Americans are acquainted with the suffragist movement for women's rights in the United States, led by Susan B. Anthony and Elizabeth Cady Stanton, yet remain unaware that most Latin American nations had similar women's movements in the same historical period. In Puerto Rico, for example, suffragists and working women organized to promote educational and voting rights for women in the early twentieth century (Azize-Vargas 2002), and, in Mexico, advocates for women's rights held major feminist congresses in Mérida, Yucatán, in 1916 and in Mexico City in 1921 (Cotera 2002).

REFERENCES

Anzaldúa, Gloria. 1987. *Borderlands/La Frontera: The New Mestiza*. San Francisco: Spinsters/Aunt Lute.

Azize-Vargas, Yamila. 2002. "The Emergence of Feminism in Puerto Rico, 1870–1930." In *Latino/a Thought: Culture, Politics and Society*, ed. Francisco H. Vazquez and Rudolfo D. Torres, 175–84. Lanham, Md., and Boulder, Colo.: Rowman and Littlefield Publishers.

Baca Zinn, Maxine. 1975. "Political Familism: Toward Sex Role Equality in Chicano Families." *Aztlán* 6, no. 1: 13–26.

——. 1980. "Employment and Education of Mexican American Women: The Interplay of Modernity and Ethnicity in Eight Families." *Harvard Educational Review* 50: 47–62.

——. 1994. "Feminist Rethinking from Racial Ethnic Families." In *Women of Color in U.S. Society*, ed. Maxine Baca Zinn and Bonnie Thornton Dill, 303–14. Philadelphia: Temple University Press.

Baca Zinn, Maxine, Lynn Weber Cannon, Elizabeth Higgenbotham, and Bonnie Thornton Dill. 1986. "The Costs of Exclusionary Practices in Women's Studies." *Signs* 11 (winter): 270–307.

Bach, Robert L. 1978. "Mexican Immigration and U.S. Immigration Reforms in the 1960s." *Kapitalstate* 7: 63–80.

Bean, Frank, and Marta Tienda. 1987. *The Hispanic Population of the United States*. New York: Russell Sage Foundation.

Coltrane, Scott, and Elsa Valdez. 1997. "Reluctant Compliance: Work-Family Role Allocation in Dual-Earner Chicano Families." In *Challenging Fronteras: Structuring Latina and Latino Lives in the U.S.*, ed. Mary Romero, Pierrette Hondagneu-Sotelo, Vilma Ortiz, 229–46. New York: Routledge.

Cotera, Marta. 2002. "Our Feminist Heritage." In *Latino/a Thought: Culture, Politics and Society*, ed. Francisco H. Vazquez and Rudolfo D. Torres, 215–19. Lanham, Md., and Boulder, Colo.: Rowman and Littlefield Publishers.

Cranford, Cynthia. 2000. "We Shall Not be Moved: Gender and Citizenship Claims in the Corporate City." Unpublished manuscript.

Delgado, Richard, and Stefanic, J., eds. 1998. *The Latino/a Condition: A Critical Reader*. New York: Routledge.

Deutsch, Sarah 1987. *No Separate Refuge: Culture, Class, and Gender on an Anglo-Hispanic Frontier in the American Southwest, 1880–1940*. New York and Oxford: Oxford University Press.

Fernández-Kelly, M. Patricia, and Anna M. García. 1997. "Power Surrendered, Power Restored: The Politics of Work and Family Among Hispanic Garment Workers in California and Florida." In *Challenging Fronteras: Structuring Latina and Latino Lives in the U.S.*, ed. Mary Romero, Pierrette Hondagneu-Sotelo, and Vilma Ortiz, 215–28. New York: Routledge.

Fregoso, Rosa Linda. 1993. *The Bronze Screen: Chicana and Chicano Film Culture*. Minneapolis: University of Minnesota Press.

Friedan, Betty. 1963. *The Feminine Mystique*. W. W. Norton.

Goldring, Luin. 2003. "Gender Status and the State: The Gendering of Political Participation and Mexican Hometown Associations." In *Gender and U.S. Immigration: Contemporary Trends*, ed. Pierrette Hondagneu-Sotelo, 341–58. Berkeley and Los Angeles: University of California Press.

Hardy-Fanta, Carol. 1993. *Latina Politics, Latino Politics: Gender, Culture, and Political Participation in Boston*. Philadelphia: Temple University Press.

Hondagneu-Sotelo, Pierrette. 1994. *Gendered Transitions: Mexican Experiences of Immigration*. Berkeley and Los Angeles: University of California Press.

——. 2000. "Feminism and Migration." *The ANNALS of the American Academy of Political and Social Science* 571: 107–20.

——. 2001. *Doméstica: Immigrant Workers Cleaning and Caring in the Shadows of Affluence*. Berkeley and Los Angeles: University of California Press.

——. 2002. "Families on the Frontier: From Braceros in the Fields to Braceras in the Home." In *Latinos: Remaking America*, ed. Marcelo M. Suárez-Orozco and Mariela M. Páez, 259–73. Berkeley and Los Angeles: David Rockefeller Center for Latin American Studies, Harvard University and University of California Press.

Hondagneu-Sotelo, Pierrette, and Ernestine Avila. 1997. "'I'm Here, But I'm There': The Meanings of Latina Transnational Motherhood." *Gender and Society* 11: 548–71.

Jones-Correa, Michael. 1998. *Between Two Nations: The Political Participation of Latinos in New York City*. Ithaca: Cornell University Press.

López, Alma. 2001. "Silencing Our Lady: La respuesta de Alma." *Aztlan: A Journal of Chicano Studies*, 26, no. 2: 249–67.

López, Nancy. 2003. "Disentangling Race-Gender Experiences at Work: Second Generation Caribbean Young Adults in New York City." In *Gender and U.S. Immigration: Contemporary Trends*, ed. Pierrette Hondagneu-Sotelo, 174–93. Berkeley and Los Angeles: University of California Press.

Menjívar, Cecilia. 2000. *Fragmented Ties: Salvadoran Immigrant Networks in America*. Berkeley: University of California Press.

Moreno, Susan E., and Chandra Muller. 1996. "Latinas in the U.S. Labor Force." In *Women and Work*, ed. Paula J. Dubeck and Kathryn Borman, 38–41. New Brunswick, N.J.: Rutgers University Press.

Parsons, Talcott. 1954. "The Kinship System of the Contemporary United States." In *Essays in Sociological Theory*, ed. Talcott Parsons, 189–94. New York: Free Press.

Pescatello, Ann, ed. 1973. *Female and Male in Latin America*. Pittsburgh: University of Pittsburgh Press.

Pesquera, Beatríz. 1993. "'In the Beginning He Wouldn't Lift Even a Spoon': The Division of Household Labor." In *Building with Our Hands: New Directions in Chicana Studies*, ed. Adela de la Torre and Beatríz M. Pesquera, 181–95. Berkeley and Los Angeles: University of California Press.

Pessar, Patricia R. 1995. "On the Homefront and in the Workplace: Integrating Immigrant Women into Feminist Discourse." *Anthropological Quarterly* 68, no. 1: 37–47.

Prieto, Yolanda. 1992. "Cuban Women in New Jersey: Gender Relations and Change." In *Seeking Common Ground: Multidisciplinary Studies of Immigrant Women in the United States*, ed. Donna Gabaccia, 185–201. Westport, Conn.: Greenwood Press.

Rodríguez, Jeannette. 1994. *Our Lady of Guadalupe: Faith and Empowerment Among Mexican-American Women*. Austin: University of Texas Press.

Stevens, Evelyn P. 1973. "Marianismo: The Other Face of Machismo in Latin America." In *Female and Male in Latin America*, ed. Ann Pescatello, 89–101. Pittsburgh: University of Pittsburgh Press.

Suárez-Orozco, Marcelo M., and Mariela M. Páez. 2002. "Introduction: The Research Agenda." In *Latinos: Remaking America*, ed. Marcelo M. Suárez-Orozco and Mariela M. Páez, 1–37. Berkeley and Los Angeles: David Rockefeller Center for Latin American Studies, Harvard University and University of California Press.

U.S. Bureau of the Census. 2001. *Statistical Abstract of the United States: 2001*. Washington, D.C.: U.S. Bureau of the Census.

West, Candace, and Don H. Zimmerman. 1987. "Doing Gender." *Gender and Society* 1, no. 2: 125–51.

Ybarra, Lea. 1982. "When Wives Work: The Impact on the Family." *Journal of Marriage and the Family* 2: 169–77.

Zavella, Patricia. 1987. *Women's Work and Chicano Families: Cannery Workers of the Santa Clara Valley*. Ithaca, N.Y.: Cornell University Press.

EIGHT

FROM BARRIOS TO BARRICADES: RELIGION AND RELIGIOSITY IN LATINO LIFE

ANTHONY M. STEVENS-ARROYO

INTRODUCTION

The recent history of Latinos in the United States is a tale of social movements that are similar to the earlier Civil Rights Movement among African Americans. History has recognized the leadership of the Rev. Martin Luther King Jr. and the central role of the traditional black churches in supplying a forum, eager recruits, and public legitimacy. But while there is recognition of the religious origins of the movement among African Americans, religion is absent from many accounts of contemporary Latino history.[1]

As I will describe, the churches and the peoples' religious convictions in the Latino experiences since 1960 have shaped our communities and their collective cultural consciousness and social advancement. While not casting religion as the only factor in the emergence of a Latino community in the United States during the past forty years, this article will underline the religious dimension in the history examined by other contributors to this volume.

Religion has always been easier to experience than to define. It is a mistake to believe that religion is confined to the four walls of church buildings, the sermons of clergy, or the private feelings of pious individuals. The deepest emotions about birth and death, sacrifice and heroism, loyalty and companionship, commitment and aspiration are wrapped in religious symbolism. This chapter departs from the premise that religion is a shared legacy that identifies a group with particular values about humanity. But if religion is not to be confined to church buildings and clergy, neither is it invisible, mystical, and completely subjective. By nature, religion binds people together in communitarian actions that express social values. What a person believes in faith is summoned by religion to praxis in civic space. Traditional religion has often been more encompassing of value systems, largely because there was less ability in past societies for Latinos to find social institutions that reflected their social cohesion. I would not think it controversial to assert that in the sixteenth century, religion was the major vehicle for collective identity for Aztecs, Mayans, Taínos, and also for the Spaniards who came to the shores of the Americas. Because of these religious origins, Latino cultures today can trace many key elements of traditional expression and social practices to the hybrid Catholicism of the American baroque period (Stevens-Arroyo 1998; Weber 1992: 329 ff.). Sixteenth-century Iberian Christianity was syncretized, at times intentionally and at times unwittingly, with the cosmic mix of races, cultures, and languages in the Americas, so that many European traits of Catholicism were changed and native religious experience of the Americas was recast to embrace the doctrines of Christianity. Describing this process as *mestizaje*, the Mexican American theologian Virgilio Elizondo (1992) concludes that this religious mixing has a result analogous to the mixed-blood offspring (*mestizo*) of an interracial marriage: origins and heritage are shared.

Rather than enter into the philosophical definitions of this religious *mestizaje*, it may be more useful to recognize how few problems Latino people have in experiencing it. The expression of religious belief covers every niche in Latino society, from the churchgoers singing in processions on Good Friday or gathering families for Sunday school to the Latino pugilists who bless themselves with the sign of the cross before a boxing match and the gang members who have religious images tatooed on their arms and chests. Decades ago, the *vellonera* or jukebox at the neighborhood cantina spun out *boleros* and *corridos* in which God, the Virgin, and the saints were frequently mentioned; today, salsa and rap singers continue that tradition. Latino families turn to religion for baptism, marriage, and burial. Our homes have crosses over the bed and altars with candles and holy pictures or *estampillas* are found in ceremonial niches, especially in the poorest homes (Stevens-Arroyo and Díaz-Stevens 1993a). Latinos revere the unadorned elements of nature by placing earth, rocks, and plants within these sacred spaces. Concern for sexuality and success often find expression in rituals derived from African religions or from beliefs in reincarnation and spiritism.

Each of these examples join personal faith with social tradition and aesthetic expression. Moreover, the old-time religion has been invested with new and vital social meanings, for example, in the contemporary emergence of the *Día de los Muertos* in Los Angeles, which began as a protest against police brutality (Medina 2000a), or the *Fiesta de Santiago Apóstol* in New York's Loisaida neighborhood that celebrates an African heritage. Even people long separated from the four walls that house institutionalized religion often profess a need to nurture themselves by contact with Latino spirituality. Incense burners in Aztec motif and santos, the home-carved images of the saints in the Iberian Catholic style, turn up in unlikely places.

Religious behavior, however, cannot be fully understood without reference to faith, churches, dogma, and clergy. Much as workers and management are linked by factors of economic production, popular and institutional religion are joined in a "religious production" (Maduro 1982). The relationships between the "management" and the "laborers" of religion often wax and wane in accordance with social and historical currents. At times antagonistic, at times collaborative, the institutional and the popular in religion are two aspects of a single reality. To grasp how religion has affected Latinos, we need to recognize that religion includes two dimensions: the popular, wherein cultural religion is operative, and the institutional, wherein religious institutions and agencies serving Latinos formulate policies. I offer here an outline of the processes that produce these kinds of changes, attempting to describe how popular and institutional religion have interacted across class boundaries.

An analogy with contemporary marketing practices may explain how Maduro's notion of "religious production" applies to the Latino experience. In the 1970s, the Xerox Corporation's photocopier became so identified with the process that the brand name "xerox" became a word in the English language. Since then, many other firms have improved upon the copy process and ironically the Xerox Corporation faced bankruptcy during the year 2000 because the original invention has been duplicated and surpassed. Despite the sea change in technology and the economy, however, "to xerox a report" still serves as a synonym in everyday conversation for "to photocopy a report." In comparison, many social experiences among Latinos rose from a religious milieu that defined them. A candlelight procession in the barrio to protest gang violence, flowers placed on the spot where a child has been killed by a stray bullet or speeding car, and calls for a "crusade" against drug dealing are all social events that use the symbols and traditions of religion to motivate and mobilize Latinos. Even if today these efforts may be classified as "cultural" or "political," they are linked to religion much as the photocopy business is to the Xerox Corporation.

It would seem best to concede that religion and culture have overlapping categories in a synthesis that might be termed, "cultural religion" (Stevens-Arroyo 1999). This article attempts to avoid a recurrent temptation to melt down syncretic religious expression to its component parts. Syncretism, I would suggest, is best understood when its ambiguities are accepted as dynamically interactive.[2]

The relationships between religious institutions and the people's cultural religion assume various forms. We have myriad examples in the past of church leaders denouncing as "pagan" or "superstitious" the religious practices of Latinos and Latinas acting out their cultural religion. But more recently, institutional religion has shown a progressive stance by encouraging and adopting practices of Latino cultural religion as doctrinally acceptable, particularly in ritual practice (see Elizondo and Matovina 1998). Many of these changes can be measured empirically. For instance, we can count how many church buildings today are meeting places for community organizers, information centers for immigrants, and refuges for victims of domestic violence when compared with previous decades. That calculation tells us whether more or less resources are dedicated to serve Latinos. On such an empirical basis, we can then interpret the degree and effectiveness of the church relationship to Latino social needs.

RELIGION AMONG LATINOS AND LATINO RELIGION

Religion with "Latino" as a modifier may be considered as an empirically verifiable social experience. Much in the way that a cuisine may be "French" or "Italian," the Catholic or Methodist faith is enriched by being "Latino" Catholic or "Latino" Methodist. Latino religion, as distinct from Latin American and Euro-American religion, began with conquest by the United States of Texas in the 1830s and continued with the nineteenth-century wars that produced the annexations of the Southwest, California, and Puerto Rico. In each of these instances, the cultural religion of the people, which had developed under the aegis of Spanish colonial Catholicism, encountered the institutions and agencies of religion from a Protestant and Euro-American United States. It is not within the scope of this chapter to provide a detailed analysis of these annexations, but several consequences are relevant to this review of history since 1960.

Clearly, by identifying acceptance of the Gospel preached in Protestant churches with the values of individualism, capitalism, democracy, and separation of church and state, conversion of Latinos to Protestantism strengthened the process of Americanization. The Spanish state had limited, when it had not prohibited, the establishment of Protestant churches, a legacy which was not much altered even with the rise of anticlerical liberalism in the nineteenth century in Spain and Mexico. Behind the victorious U.S. troops marching into the Latino homelands came the armies of Protestant missionaries, armed with the bible and enjoying the advantages of a Protestant bias in U.S. culture. The annexations of Latino homelands after 1848 and again after 1898 in Puerto Rico launched Protestantism with immediate and often spectacular growth rates that directly parallel the eclipse of Latino cultural traditions and the abolition of Spanish institutions.

We should be cautious, however, about too easily dismissing the potential for Protestantism to address Latino needs (See Silva Gotay 1997: 330–46; 373–75). In the 1930s during the Great Depression and again in the radical 1960s, liberal Protestants questioned the triumphalism of civil religion in the United States. Although these countermovements were uneven and not without contradictions, the logic of education and modernity induced the mainline Protestant churches to adopt progressive stances on civil-rights issues and to open the way for a generation of Latino leaders to receive ministerial training. Thus, the 1960s witnessed the emergence of Latino Protestant spokespeople, many of whom were the children of converts. A generation of Protestant Latino church leaders had been able to acquire the professional qualifications necessary for denominational influence. However, the middle-class status of those in the mainline churches is not always repeated in more conservative Evangelical and Pentecostal denominations. As a result, there are clear class differences among the various Protestant groups, making it difficult to lump them into a single category.

Latino Catholicism took a different route. The nineteenth-century Catholic Church in the United States imposed an "immigrant" paradigm upon the Latino Catholics in the conquered territories of Texas, California, the Southwest, and Puerto Rico. By organizing a parish on the basis of language and offering services in a specific, non-English European tongue, Catholicism had delivered ministry to Germans, Poles, and Italians arriving in the United States. These churches were called "national parishes" and were contrasted with the territorial parish based on geographic boundaries and in which English was used for services and ministry (Vidal 1988). It is understandable, if not excusable, that what had worked to incorporate the Germans, Poles, and Italians into U.S. society was supposed to work as well for Mexicans and Puerto Ricans. National parishes for Latinos were supposed to disappear as soon as the Latinos learned English. There was a clear expectation from Catholic leaders that, with time, the English language and American customs would displace Spanish, just as among European immigrants, the old country's tongue and cultural traditions had surrendered to English and Americanization (Dolan 1992: 176–78; 372–73).

However, the Latino Catholics in Texas, California, and the Southwest were not "immigrants": they were conquered peoples, more like the Irish conquered by the British or the Poles defeated by Prussians than like the Irish Americans in Boston or the Polish immigrants to Chicago. The imposition of an immigrant paradigm rather than an identification with a nascent irridentism of Mexicans and Puerto Ricans constituted U.S. Catholicism's "original sin," and an Americanizing attitude penalized the church's effectiveness in preserving the faith (Stevens-Arroyo 1995). Since there were about as many

Latino Catholics in 1850 as Euro-American Catholics, the decision to subordinate the Latino half of U.S. Catholicism to the Euro-American mode of organization and administration has to be considered a political decision made for the purpose of proving the Americanism of Catholicism rather than for pastoral reasons, which would have sought the best mode of serving the people of God.

In New Mexico and California, where the Spanish-language churches were the oldest Catholic institutions in the territories, the official policy was to build new English-speaking parish complexes for those who spoke English. In practice, that segregated the Spanish-speaking Mexicans. An ecclesiastical form of Jim Crow was repeated in much of California, Texas, and the Southwest until the 1950s: the institutions were separate but not equal (Dolan and Hinojosa 1994: 133–37). Latinos had either to continue a religious production that was officially subordinated to an Americanizing Catholicism or reject Latino Catholicism for the sake of upward mobility. The resistance of Latino Catholic intellectuals to this cruel imposition of a Eurocentric Catholicism at the expense of a Latino Catholicism is outlined elsewhere (Stevens-Arroyo 1980). It appears that most Latinos preferred to remain in the "Mexican" churches, even though that produced the anomaly of converting America's oldest Catholicism into a "foreign" Catholicism that needed missionary attention supported by philanthropy.[3] The process was repeated in its essential details in the takeover of Puerto Rican Catholicism after 1898 (Stevens-Arroyo 1994).

Latinos who clung to their traditions and who preferred to pray in Spanish were shunted to Latino national parishes, much the same as the process for European groups on the way to assimilation. Tomasi's study of Italian national parishes (1975) shows that, from the perspective of the immigrants, the national parish was usually much more than a temporary home until English was learned. Rather, it became a permanent institution that symbolized the preservation of the language and cultural religion of one's ethnic nationality. Even for assimilated, second- and third-generation Poles, Italians, and the like, the national church in the old neighborhood was worthy of pilgrimage during ethnic festivals, family reunions, and political troubles.

In somewhat the same way, Latino Catholicism was able to maintain its identity through religious production within the confines of national parishes. But while this kind of ecclesiastical ghettoization provided a reservoir of Catholic traditions that flowed into Latino identity, it also deepened the separation between Latino popular religion as celebrated in the national parish and an institutionalized Catholic Church that wielded power within U.S. society and politics. The two were often seen as inimical, so that upward mobility in the institutionalized church came at the price of abandoning Latino cultural religion. David F. Gómez describes the hostility he felt as a Latino in a

Catholic seminary, and he found it impossible in the 1960s to be both Catholic and Latino (Gómez 1973: 15–29). "I discovered," he said, that "the seminary had prepared me to be a good Catholic priest but not necessarily a good human being" (20).

The Latino "problem" within the U.S. Catholic Church was similar to the Euro-American Catholic dilemma vis à vis the U.S. public. American public opinion had frequently criticized the split loyalty among Catholics who lived in the U.S. but continued to speak the languages and sponsor the politics of the homeland. To which country were Catholics loyal: America or a foreign homeland? And were not all Catholics obliged under pain of sin to obey the pope rather than secular authorities? This questioning was part of the 1960 election-year debate over the Catholicism of John F. Kennedy. And while the Kennedy electoral victory in 1960 indicated an acceptance of Catholicism as part of U.S. civil religion, that response came only after the official church had spent a century suppressing those expressions of Catholicism that did not depend upon speaking English.

The process is clearest for the Euro-American Catholics. More prosperous second- generation ethnic families had left the national parish for English-speaking parishes. Such social mobility into the territorial parishes was generally encouraged by the bishops. After World War II, this trend was greatly accelerated because of the suburbanization of the children of the European immigrants. Ironically, the movement out of the cities by these Euro-American Catholics created economic opportunities for the Latino Catholics. The urban areas abandoned by the Americanized second- and third-generation immigrant Catholics seeking the suburbs were populated by Latinos who had long been U.S. citizens, but whose rural origins had prevented wholesale Americanization.

THE POST–WORLD WAR II URBAN MIGRATIONS

Between 1945 and 1960, most churches had to rethink their existing ministry programs because of the massive postwar migration of Latinos out of rural Texas, New Mexico, and Puerto Rico toward big cities. The Reverend John MacKay of the Presbyterian Church, Father Leo Mahon in Chicago, Archbishop Robert Lucey in San Antonio, and Msgr. Ivan Illich of the Archdiocese of New York are some of the clergy who were distinguished not only by a ministerial zeal, but also by their ability to explain to their ecclesiastical confreres the consequences of doing nothing to minister to Latinos.

Both mainline Protestantism and Catholicism were rudely awakened to the inadequacy of their approaches to Latinos because of the impressive gains in

Latino membership by Pentecostalism. Newly urbanized Latinos had difficulty finding continuity with the cultural religion of their homelands in the big city. As a result, the Pentecostal churches found new Latino members throughout the 1950s. Some commentators on this process among Puerto Ricans in New York described anomie as the cause for conversion of Puerto Rican Catholics to evangelical and Pentecostal churches (Poblete and O'Dea 1960). In retrospect, this was an oversimplification of religious choice, but, in fact, a principal appeal of Pentecostalism has been its ability to create interpersonal relationships that constitute a fictive family (León 1994). Piri Thomas describes the Pentecostal appeal from his own experience:

> The most beautiful thing about Pentecostals was their ability to pour themselves into the power of the Holy Spirit. They could blend—like nobody's business—into the words of the Holy Scripture and do their best to uphold their conception of Christianity. It was a miracle how they could shut out the hot and cold running cockroaches and king-size rats and all the added horrors of decaying rotten tenement houses and garbage-littered streets, with drugs running through the veins of our ghetto kids. It was a miracle that they could endure the indignities poured upon our Barrios.
>
> *(Piri Thomas, cited in Stevens-Arroyo 1980: 152)*

In a conversation with his aunt, the former convict Piri hears the testimony about faith that it so common among Pentecostals:

> It's what binds much of us poor Puertorriqueños together. It gives us strength to live in these conditions. It's like being part of a familia that is together in Cristo and we help each other with the little materials we may possess.
>
> *(Piri Thomas cited in Stevens-Arroyo 1980: 153)*

As has been pointed out by scholars of the Latino Pentecostal experience, the early history of the church reflected a sense of Latino togetherness, with Mexican preachers converting Puerto Ricans and vice versa (Alvarez 1996). The success in the 1950s on the urban scene was the harvest of solid efforts of an earlier generation in offering Latinos religious experience in their language and focusing on their need for community. Pentecostalism, organized as it is on an congregational level, is not directly affected by many denominational and organizational issues. Seminary training and study are much less complicated among Pentecostals than among Catholics and mainline Protestants. However, although Pentecostal churches addressed the faith needs strongly felt by Latinos, they were not always accepted by their Euro-American counterparts. As late as the 1990s, Pentecostals from Puerto Rico were excluded from the largest of the U.S. Pentecostal associations because of their refusal to preach in English.

Catholicism may have been slower in mobilizing resources for Latinos, but, when action was finally taken, there were major consequences. For instance, when the governing body of the Catholic Church recognized that the postwar demographic movement of Latinos was likely to be a continuing trend, the bishops financed an office to coordinate special attention to these laborers in many different dioceses. The intent was to create an interregional network of churches as services for the seasonal migrants as they left Texas and passed through the Midwest. The Bishops' Committee for the Spanish-Speaking was created in 1945, with Bishop (later Archbishop) Robert Lucey as its driving force (Privett 1988). A decade later, the Archdiocese of New York created a similar regional effort in the northeastern United States to coordinate Catholic programs for the Puerto Rican migrants (Díaz-Stevens 1993b). The exodus of Cubans after the fall of the Batista dictatorship in 1959 was the exception rather than the rule to the urban migration of Latinos because it brought not the rural poor, but a relatively prosperous urban middle-class Cuban cohort to the States. But the model perfected among Mexican Americans and Puerto Ricans for an apostolate of pastoral outreach and organized social concern benefited these Cubans, who settled mostly in south Florida and parts of New Jersey (Prieto 1995). The official church efforts represented generous amounts of funding for all the Latino groups, the dedication of enormous personnel resources, and a continuing effort to review these programs for their efficiency. Along with similar commitments from mainstream Protestant churches, the early 1960s were characterized by church involvement in addressing the material needs of Latinos on a previously unreached scale (Sandoval 1990).

It is important to emphasize that the major migrations to the big cities by Mexican Americans and Puerto Ricans represented the *urbanization of U.S. citizens*. Immigration laws until 1964 did not permit the large-scale entry of people from Latin America, although an exception was made for Cubans who could claim an exile status. It is true that the Puerto Ricans resembled "foreigners" in that they came from an island where Spanish was the spoken language and the conventions of Spanish law and culture were institutionalized. But, since 1917, Puerto Ricans have been U.S. citizens. Similarly, the migration from New Mexico and southwest Texas to California and the Midwest consisted of people who had been U.S. citizens for generations. These relocations of large numbers of people who previously had lived in rural or agricultural settings became the salient demographic event of the decade (Moore 1994). In fact, the urban migration of Latinos born into U.S. citizenship—not to be confused here with Latin Americans—should be historically seen in the mold of other great internal migrations: the "Okies" to California in the lean years described in John Steinbeck's *Grapes of Wrath*, and Southern blacks to northern cities beginning in the twentieth century.

The response of urban Catholicism to the Latino migrations created a new hybridization of the popular religiosity rooted in the Iberian past. The processions, the devotions, and the pious societies that organized religious life for Latino Catholics who had left their homelands for the big city may have seemed to be the same as the earlier traditions, but the conscious effort to replicate the old in a new social context constituted an act of creativity and religious imagination. The white suit or dress for First Communion, the photographs taken at this rite of passage, the positioning of a banner of Our Lady of Guadalupe in the sanctuary of the church, and other such moments constituted the repetition of traditional Latino Catholic culture within the context of U.S. society. Like the Pentecostal experiences described by Piri Thomas, these were Catholic experiences reshaped by migration to big cities of the U.S.

THE STRUCTURES OF CHURCH MINISTRY

By the opening of the 1960s, there had been a qualitative change in the scope of attention and the dedication of resources from the Catholic Church. In New York, for instance, the national parish, with its limited resources and relatively inferior status, was abandoned as the principal dispenser of pastoral care. Instead, the doors of the territorial parishes were opened up to Latinos, and the Euro-American clergy were trained in the Spanish language and Puerto Rican culture. Now a single parish served two groups. And although united under the same roof, services were offered in separate languages, often with the English speakers in the grand setting of the large church, and the Spanish speakers in the "basement church." Even while noting the inherent inequality in this arrangement, Ana María Díaz-Stevens commends the considerable scope of this effort and its impact upon the clergy who were recruited for service to the Puerto Ricans (1993b: 117–45). She argues that the experiences of these middle-class Euro-American priests often gave them a critical perspective on the limitations of their own training and the too comfortable stance of the institutional church towards the material needs of the Puerto Ricans, the major Latino group in New York at that time. We ought to recognize that the importation of a vital Latino popular religion had an impact on non-Latino clergy and the institutional church, preparing the way for a network of allies and supporters when Latino-led movements were launched.

Leadership within the U.S. Catholic Church has tended to be highly clericalized. The financial resources to enter a seminary, the long years of study, and the obligation of celibacy make the road to clerical leadership an especially difficult one. However, as the migration toward urban centers throughout the post–World War II period enlarged the educational aspirations and elevated the economic status of the Latino migrants, it also produced a cohort of Latino priests, seminarians, and religious sisters. Thus, by the 1960s Catholicism had begun to approximate many Protestant denominations in developing ethnic clergy to minister to the needs of Latino believers. But in Catholicism, the hierarchical nature of authority concentrated in the hands of bishops was a much higher barrier than was found in Protestantism. As a result, clericalism, that is, decision making left only to clergy, impeded the development of Latino Catholic lay leaders into Latino community leaders. Felix Padilla assesses why the church-sponsored Caballeros de San Juan, who had been very effective during the 1950s in Chicago, floundered in the 1970s:

> In the final analysis, Puerto Ricans became just another "immigrant group" for the Catholic Church to accommodate, . . . it sought to do charity by trying to alleviate suffering by serving as a buffer without attacking institutional racism.
>
> *(Padilla 1987: 136–137)*

THE CURSILLO: LATINO WITNESS AS RELIGION

The remarkable movement called the Cursillo, or "little course," unlocked the religious potential of Latinos as no clerical program of the 1950s could have done, no matter its good intentions. The Cursillo that was brought to the U.S. in 1957 drew its origins from faraway Mallorca, Spain. In a country recovering from a bitter Civil War that ended in 1939 without fully resolving issues of anticlericalism and ecclesiastical authoritarianism, the clergy had been distanced from the laity. Catholic Action leaders in Mallorca had organized lay people to deliver a series of talks to cover the major points of Catholic belief, knowing that the expression of faith convictions by ordinary believers would contradict the notion that religion was a clerical terrain. The peer approach found success among working-class people in Spain during the 1940s and developed into a movement approved by the Catholic Church.

It takes *cursillistas* to make more *cursillistas*. The movement crossed the Atlantic when two Spanish pilots who had made the Cursillo in Spain were stationed for specialized training at a U.S. airbase in Texas. They formed a team of instructors with Father Gabriel Fernández to present the first American Cursillo in Waco, Texas, in 1957 (Kelley 2000). More *cursillistas* meant more Cursillo teams. By 1960, the Cursillo had moved beyond the wide-open spaces of Texas and spread to the Midwest and the East Coast.

The doctrine taught in the Cursillo was traditional Catholicism. But while the content was conservative, the mode of transmittal proved dramatically effective in moving people away from rote performance of religion toward heartfelt commitment. The Cursillo encouraged personal testimony about a faith experience. It used emotions without confusing these with superficial feelings. The dynamics of instruction during the three-day exercise take place with a strict separation of the sexes and the atmosphere of a monastery, in which there is fasting, silence, spartan living conditions, and a daily prayer regimen. The personal dynamics unfold within the context of familiar cultural values. Gospel values are grafted onto the elements of popular culture. Thus, for instance, the Spanish folk song "De Colores" is given a spiritual meaning, and other familiar tunes are played on a guitar, with new lyrics that recall the spiritual experience. The Cursillo concludes with a public reception for the newly initiated where they are greeted in a festive atmosphere by those who have previously undergone the experience. Each *cursillista* is expected to speak, offering individual testimony as to what has been experienced and what personal lifestyle choices have been made, whereupon the members of the movement pledge assistance to the new recruit in implementing the new resolves. The Cursillo introduced a conversion movement within Catholicism, definable in sociological terms as similar to the "reborn Evangelical." Personalized testimony feeds the movement, motivating its members and attracting new converts.

The decision early in the 1960s to import the Cursillo Movement as a part of the Catholic outreach to Latinos was a key factor in refocusing the church's ministries (Díaz-Stevens 1993b: 109–13). By constitution, the Cursillo is a lay movement: the priest belongs in the background—only one talk during the three-day retreat is specifically assigned to the clergy (Vidal 1988). The lay Latino leadership of the Cursillo, however, produced adaptations that corresponded to the socioeconomic realities of the U.S. For instance, in Spain, only married women were permitted to make the Cursillo, and they had to wait until their spouses became *cursillistas*, whereas in the United States, single women were allowed to participate. The commonsense language of the laity in the Cursillo helped lower the class barriers erected between official religion and believers. Most importantly, each of the local parish groups was linked through a diocese to a national directorate. Puerto Rican *cursillistas* from New York and New Jersey were members in a national organization with Mexican American counterparts from Texas and California. And while the Cursillo did not eliminate clericalism, it did provide a training ground for Catholic lay leadership.

By 1962, only five years after its introduction, the Cursillo Movement was found in fifty dioceses of the United States. (Díaz-Stevens and Stevens-Arroyo 1998: 136). The movement continued to grow and integrate its leadership into local church structures. Twenty years later, 25 percent of Latino Catholic respondents considered the Cursillo the most important factor in the practice of religion, more even than the Second Vatican Council (González and LaVelle, cited in Díaz-Stevens and Stevens-Arroyo 1998: 136). The appeal of the Cursillo is recounted by Chicano militant Armando Rendón, who was forced to abandon his preconception that religion was only for women and children.

> Not only was much revealed to me about the phony guilt lingo of religion which I had grown up believing was the Church, but there was an added and highly significant side effect—cultural shock! I rediscovered my own people, or perhaps they redeemed me. Within the social dimension of the Cursillo, for the first time in many years I became reimmersed in a tough, macho *ambiente*. Only Spanish was spoken. The effect was shattering. It was as if my tongue, after being struck dumb as a child, had been loosened.
>
> Because we were located in cramped quarters, with limited facilities, and the cooks, lecturers, priests and participants were men only, the old sense of *machismo* and *camarada* was revived and given new perspective. I was cast in a spiritual setting which was a perfect background for reviving my Chicano soul. Reborn but imperfectly, I still had a lot to learn about myself and my people. But my understanding deepened and renewed itself as the years went by.
>
> *(Rendón 1971: 323–24)*

Perhaps the most significant aspect of the movement was the way it demanded a new Catholic commitment. Rendón says he was "reborn" after the Cursillo, becoming actively involved in the cause of social justice for Latinos in California. Rendón's experience could be multiplied by more than a hundred thousand. "*Cursillistas* became the prairie grass that caught fire and spread the flame of resurgence from coast to coast" (Díaz-Stevens and Stevens-Arroyo 1998: 137).

LATINOIZATION AND MILITANCY

Although the Civil Rights Movement of the 1950s and 1960s was initially focused on the injustices committed against African Americans, Latinos gradually entered into the movement. Senator Robert Kennedy of New York added to the 1964 Voting Rights Act a clause that required a bilingual ballot in electoral districts with high concentrations of Spanish-speaking people. Along with the War on Poverty, this measure was designed to incorporate Latinos into the U.S. political process. President Lyndon B. Johnson may have had the elimination of poverty as his chief concern, but he also arranged measures to insure that the federal funds pouring into the barrios required the enlistment of African Americans and Latinos into the organizational structure of these neighborhood agencies. This met the partisan objective of recruiting new voters into the Democratic Party to replace the older generations of Euro-Americans who had moved to the suburbs in the 1950s and had begun to vote as Republicans (see DeSipio, chapter 11, this volume).

The empowerment of leaders from the minority groups was canonized in the antipoverty legislation and affected the churches. Monsignor Robert Fox of the Archdiocese of New York, for instance, responded to local conditions by redirecting charitable efforts for Latinos away from clerical paternalism.

> The point . . . is that the question of the liberation of others is the question of the liberation of me. Can I, in my relationship with others, allow them to challenge me? . . . And can I do this in a context with other people in which I allow them to write in my flesh the revelation of who they are, and I write in their flesh a revelation of who I am? . . . Can all of us so radically believe in love, that we will allow ourselves to get into the developing solution which human experience is, and come more and more to be conscious of who we are? This is what it seems liberation is about.
>
> *(Msgr. Robert Fox, cited in Díaz-Stevens 1993b: 169)*

Alfredo López, of the militant Puerto Rican Young Lords in New York, criticized this program from the perspective of secular radicalism. He challenged the church's effort to increase minority participation in the power structure because it was focused on "the fact that Puerto Ricans aren't allowed a piece of the pie. That the pie has rotten apples is not a question" (López 1973: 275). But Lopez's secular skepticism was contradicted by the close cooperation between the Catholic Church and the Young Lords in Philadelphia. Carmen Whalen (1998) describes the mentoring in political strategy that the militants received from the Catholic priest, Thomas Craven. Unlike the cynicism toward Catholicism from Puerto Rican leaders like López in New York, in Philadelphia the young militants drew inspiration from the church. Los Angeles was more like Philadelphia than New York because Latino militancy was fostered by the church. Católicos Por La Raza, an important contributor to the rise of Latino Catholicism, was an organization born on the campus of Loyola Marymount, and it prospered in a Catholic environment.

Certainly, the church's efforts did not accomplish all that secular militants expected, but there were solid achievements. Many church programs begun by non-Latino priests and nuns became essential steps in preparing Latinos to assume leadership roles in the schools and civic organizations, much as the segregated black colleges had provided a generation of educated black leaders for the Civil Rights Movement. By the 1960s, Catholic Latinos were offered leadership opportunities comparable to those that had been provided by Latino Protestantism since the 1930s. The difference was that four out of five Latinos professed to be Catholic, so that there were significantly more people to lead than among Latino Protestants and Pentecostals.

While the clerical character of the Catholic hierarchy meant that only priests or nuns could officially assume charge of certain ministries, many parishes in fact depended upon nonordained Latinos and especially Latinas to perform functions of organizing and educating members of the congregation. A Latino head of the Cursillo, for instance, might have leadership responsibilities—which included preaching—for the 120 *cursillistas* in his parish. The Protestant minister, who was often nonordained, performed similar functions for his congregation of 120 total members.

The most significant change in the role of Latino Catholic leadership was related to the Second Vatican Council. Social change and political involvement figured prominently on the postconciliar agenda. Fox's effort in New York resonated with similar efforts in other large cities. It was a belated use of a Latin American model of Catholic Action instead of an imposition of the immigrant assimilationist paradigm. Rather than trying to protect Catholic interests as defined by a Euro-American institution, the Catholic reformers like Fox "sought to influence and transform all of society" (Díaz-Stevens 1993b: 150). While recognizing that many of these sweeping goals went unrealized while he headed the Office for the Spanish-Speaking Apostolate, Fox insisted that the inclusion of Latinos in new, laic, decision-making church roles prepared these people with the skills to enter politics. In an interview after he had retired from the chancery position, he noted that he had always allowed people to "work at their own pace, and if need be, make mistakes in order to better prepare themselves for future tasks and events" (quoted in Díaz-Stevens 1993b: 171). Fox represented a "type" of non-Latino Catholic clerical activist that profoundly altered the expectations of Latino Catholics vis à vis their church (Díaz-Stevens 1993b: 172ff.).

In 1965, just as the War on Poverty was gathering resources, the racial quotas of the existing Immigration Law were abolished so that the majority of immigrants to the U.S. would no longer reflect the Euro-American dominance in the nation's population. The Dominican Republic and the nations of Central America quickly joined Mexico as major sending societies for Western Hemisphere immigration to the U.S. Significantly, the wave of Latin American immigrants were encountered by new Latino leaders who were not inclined to repeat the century-old doctrine of Americanization by the churches.

With the reforms of the Second Vatican Council (1962–1964) that were mandated for world-wide Catholicism, the U.S. church made a fateful decision about the liturgy. The Council required that the mass be celebrated "in the language of the people," which meant that Latin was to be replaced by the vernacular of each country. But what was "the language of the people" in the United States? Clearly, English was the dominant language of the second generation of Euro-American Catholics: the Irish, Italians, Polish, and the others. But training clergy to speak Spanish in programs such as the Cursillo, which was designed with Spanish-speaking Catholics in mind, had been successful in retaining Latinos within Catholicism. Hence, in 1965, the National Council of Catholic Bishops (NCCB) decided to allow Spanish to be substituted for Latin in parishes serving Latinos. In effect, this decision made a bilingual country out of the Catholic United States, three years before the U.S. government voted in 1967 to create the first federally funded bilingual-education program. Although it came more than a hundred years after the first annexation of Latino homelands, this was the first of many steps that unraveled the policy of treating Latinos as if they were all immigrants like the Euro-Americans. Moreover, the reform movement carried over into many other aspects of social service delivery and community development. The caricature of Catholicism as a reactionary church where clerical powers resist change was now inverted, with many progressive policies mandated from above. When conservative Catholics complained about the conciliar reforms they found that the Vatican and the hierarchy were now enforcing the changes.

The sweeping changes of the Second Vatican Council ought not be underestimated. For those born after 1964, the contrasts between Catholicism before and after the council may not be clearly felt, but the juxtaposition of these ecclesiastical reforms with the sociopolitical upheavals of the late 1960s created an unprecedented opportunity for the transformation of Latino religion. As Garry Wills (1972) has shown, the Catholic Church began to advocate a pace for social change that changed its public image from a quiet supporter of government into a nettlesome agitator. Symbolic of the new spirit was the setting aside of a fund of several million dollars for grants directly to faith-based action groups at the grassroots. Called the "Campaign for Human Development," the NCCB created this social-justice fund at the behest of Bishop Francis Magavero of Brooklyn, New York. Much like the War on Poverty, the Campaign for Human Development required petitioners for its funds to belong to grassroots groups, often led by lay leaders from a minority group. Social issues were to be addressed by direct community involvement, and, because most Latinos profess loyalty to Catholicism, they were the principle beneficiaries of this renewed church, just as African Americans who are largely Protestant had bestirred the mainline churches. A cohort of Latino Catholic leadership was shaped by these events.

RELIGION AS A FACTOR IN LATINO IDENTITY

The Latino movements sailed on the same seas as the Civil Rights Movement among African Americans, following many of these currents, buffeted by similar opposition and dissent, with religious activism and secular militancy competing for dominance. But the Latino movements also had special characteristics. Latino militancy emerged during the anti–Vietnam War protests of the 1960s. The political splits that occurred among the African American community, with the competition for focus between domestic reform and radical war protests, were not as damaging to the Latino movements, which instead were shaped by the convergence of the domestic and international protests (Juan González 2000). The Latino movements not only supplied a critique of unjust U.S. laws, as the early Civil Rights Movement had done, they also targeted the United States' treatment of other nations. The boiling rage among the war protesters against U.S. imperialism in Vietnam was extended retroactively to the nineteenth-century acquisition of the Latino homelands. And just as the college campus was the incubator for the antiwar movement among the Euro-American students, there was considerable agitation in the universities among Chicano and Puerto Rican students. They protested for academic departments that would teach them about these Latino cultures and the history of the homelands. The stirring of a Latino consciousness was endowed with an intellectual pedigree when places as distant as City College in New York and the California State University at Northridge in Los Angeles were marching to the same drummer.

The result was what has been dubbed, "Third Worldism" (Stevens-Arroyo 1994: Díaz-Stevens and Stevens-Arroyo 1998: 137–140). From this perspective, militant Latinos viewed Latino communities not as "territories" or U.S. "possessions" but as "the homeland"—in Spanish "*la patria*"—of peoples who had struggled in the past against the Spanish Empire and were struggling against twentieth-century U.S. imperialism. In Third Worldism, colonialism against Latinos assumed the role that slavery had for African Americans: it was the explanation for poverty and low social achievement.

The Puerto Rican independence movement had long relied on such a conception (see Stevens-Arroyo 1980), and there had always been a thread of internationalism among Mexican Americans in the United States, particularly from visionary labor organizers like Bert Corona (M. García 1994). But Third Worldism among Latinos in the 1960s openly embraced the anti- imperialist premises of socialism, when not also advocating an end to capitalism. In Third Worldism, the heroes from Latin America were also icons for Latinos: Fidel Castro was celebrated for leading a military victory over U.S.-supported counterrevolutionaries; Emiliano Zapata of the Mexican Revolution in 1910 was the paragon for the movement; Pedro Albizu Campos of the Puerto Rican Nationalist Party in the 1950s was a prophet. Third Worldism gathered each of these historical leaders and their causes under its wings. It proclaimed the sovereign rights of peoplehood for Latinos in the United States, popularizing the term "Chicano" to refer to people of Mexican ancestry in Texas, the Southwest, and California in order to show that they were neither Mexican nationals nor hyphenated Americans. The conquered territories were rebaptized as "Aztlán," the original homeland of the Aztecs before they migrated southward to establish an empire over the Mexican peoples (Muñoz 1989).

Perhaps the most enduring of the expressions of Latino Third Worldism of the 1960s was the poem attributed to Rodolfo "Corky" Gonzales (1972). Entitled "Yo Soy Joaquín," this composition applied elements from the Mexican Revolution and a subsequent Cristero Revolt to the Chicano struggle. The mythical voice captured in Gonzales's poetry revisits the historical events of a native of California, Joaquín Murrieta, who took revenge upon Euro-American invaders for their abuse of Murietta, his family and his people. This Joaquín was the primordial Chicano in the sense that he was not an immigrant from Mexico, but a native of California who antedated the 1849 gold miners. The revenge Murrieta accomplished in his time is linked to the power of the Mexican Revolution and is pictured as the framework for a contemporary struggle. Important to Gonzales's description of Latino religion is an identification both with Christ and a deposed Aztec ruler.

> We start to MOVE.
> La Raza!
> Mejicano!
> Español!
> Latino!
> Hispano!
> Chicano!
> or whatever I call myself,
> I look the same
> I feel the same
> I cry
> and
> Sing the same
> I am the masses of my people and
> I refuse to be absorbed.
> I am Joaquín
> The odds are great

but my spirit is strong
My faith unbreakable
My blood is pure
I am Aztec Prince and Christian Christ
I SHALL ENDURE!
I WILL ENDURE!

The fusion of Chicano secular militancy with cultural religion may be explained in part because Corky Gonzales was a youth minister for the Presbyterian Church. But the popularity of the poem as a rallying cry for the Chicano Movement transcended any particularized denominational affiliation.

The mixture of religious symbolism in the movements of the 1960s was not the exclusive property of Latinos. The connection of the Civil Rights Movement with the churches has already been described, but the antiwar movement also was connected to religious pacifist groups such as the American Friends Service Committee and outspoken activist clerics such as the Catholic priests Daniel and Philip Berrigan (Wills 1972: 230–50). The mixture of religion, culture, and politics in "Yo Soy Joaquín" found an echo in the anti–Vietnam War draft protests and the effort to drive the ROTC from the campus of the University of Puerto Rico. Among Chicanos, the militant combination of all three was evident in the effort by Reies López Tíjerina, beginning on 5 June 1967, to assert sovereignty over northern New Mexico by a forcible takeover of the country courthouse in Terra Amarilla, New Mexico. Something of a modern-day Quixote, López Tíjerina appealed to land grants from the days of the Spanish colonial empire as justification for confronting U.S. political power (Busto 1991). His band of militants was willing to defend their moral rights by force, although with no realistic expectation of legal victory. They chose to assault the public conscience.

The recourse to militancy in a religious defense of rights had a counterpart in Latin America. "The Theology of Liberation" was a mobilization of the people that blended religion with direct action in defense of culture and political rights (see Maduro 1982). The connections between the Latin American phenomenon and its Latino counterparts was to be strengthened in coming years, but already in 1967 the pieces were in place for a Latino social movement to arise from among believers.

THE LATINO RELIGIOUS RESURGENCE

Recent studies of social movements have produced agreement on several characteristics that distinguish a movement from other types of organizations:

> Identity (definition of the protest group); opposition (a challenge to the repression of certain ideas or interests); and integrity (actions based on universal values and universal realities). Social movements . . . influence the course of historical development taking a leading role in social change. They perform several functions: they mediate between individuals and structures or social realities; they serve to clarify collective beliefs; and, lastly, they exert pressure on public authorities and the elites in power.
>
> *(Alain Touraine, cited in Díaz-Stevens and Stevens-Arroyo 1998: 130)*

These elements were present in an extraordinary mobilization of religious believers in a period that has been described as "the Latino Religious Resurgence." The reforms of the Second Vatican Council, the liberation theology, the War on Poverty, Third Worldism, new immigration and civil-rights laws, a cohort of Latino university students, the antiwar protests, bilingual education, national networks of public Latino leadership, the emergence of national Latino television networks—all were factors that interacted with the others. It is possible that if any one element had been lacking in the mix, the religious movement either would not have occurred or would have been less effective.

In these extraordinary circumstances, the discovery of common interests among Mexican Americans, Puerto Ricans, and other peoples trying to systematize church reforms to benefit the Spanish-speaking people of faith had the effect of creating a Latino religious movement that transcended the particular goals of any one of the participant groups. The resurgence became a religious equivalent of the coalitions formed by Mexicans and Puerto Ricans in Chicago described by Felix Padilla:

> Latino ethnic identification is not the combination of various group's behavioral patterns, nor does it persist independent of their intergroup social behavior. Rather Latinismo represents a collective-generated behavior which transcends the individual group's national and cultural identities.
>
> *(Padilla 1985: 162)*

Like Padilla's conception of "Latinismo" in American politics, the resurgence permitted national and local religious groups to act cohesively on a national stage.

LA CAUSA

The signal event that marshaled the religious forces was support for the Mexican American farmworkers' strike organized by labor leader César Chávez in

Delano, California. Called, appropriately, "*la causa*," historians sometimes overlook this effort's religious roots. Since the radical 1930s, labor organizations had attempted to weld together Mexican migrant farm workers with limited results. The efforts of Ernesto Galarza and Bert Corona among Mexican Americans (M. García 1994) and Jesús Colón and Bernardo Vega among New York Puerto Ricans (Sánchez Korrol 1993) were community oriented, but shaped by secular ideologies. Chávez was a different kind of labor leader because his ideological commitment to the organizing was accompanied by a *cursillista*'s understanding of Catholicism. His followers among the migrant farm workers were mobilized by both his labor organizing and a fervent evocation of his faith. The black eagle of the nascent farmworkers' association was accompanied by the banner of Our Lady of Guadalupe. Chavez's Cursillo experience is often evident in his speeches. Consider, for instance, the closing words of his presentation at the Mexican-American Conference held in Sacramento, California, 8–10 March 1968, where he scolded the participants for having neglected to invite more church leaders.

> Therefore, I am calling for Mexican American groups to stop ignoring this source of power. It is not just our right to appeal to the Church to use its power effectively for the poor, it is our duty to do so. It should be as natural as appealing to government, and we do that often enough. Furthermore, we should be prepared to come to the defense of that priest, rabbi, minister, or layman of the Church, who out of commitment to truth and justice gets into a tight place with his pastor or bishop. It behooves us to stand with that man and help him see his trial through. It is our duty to see to it that his rights of conscience are respected and that no bishop, pastor or other higher body takes that God-given, human right away. Finally, in a nutshell, what do we want the Church to do? We don't ask for more cathedrals. We don't ask for bigger churches or fine gifts. We ask for its presence with us, beside us, as Christ among us. We ask the Church to sacrifice with the people for social change, for justice, and for love of brother. We don't ask for words. We ask for deeds. We don't ask for paternalism. We ask for servanthood.
>
> *(César Chávez, cited in Stevens-Arroyo 1980: 121)*

Chávez's appeals to the Catholic Church should not overshadow the important role played by liberal Protestants. Protestant ministers had been the first to minister to the farm workers in the fields. After the strike was organized, Protestants were quick to create support networks. The education of ministers about the moral dimensions of the farmworkers' movement led to the founding in 1969 of the Hispanic-American Institute in Austin, Texas, by the

Presbyterian, United Methodists, Episcopalian, and Lutheran churches (Díaz-Stevens and Stevens-Arroyo 1998: 167–69).

The picket lines at Delano were supported by a wide range of church people who saw Chávez as a man of faith: *Time* magazine saw in this Latino Catholic a parallel to the African American Protestant Martin Luther King Jr. (Díaz-Stevens and Stevens-Arroyo 1998: 143–44, citing the article from 4 July 1969). Sensing that public opinion would prove a powerful ally against the growers, Chávez called upon the general U.S. public to boycott the table grapes produced in the Delano fields. It had taken almost two years, but *la causa* became a national issue when public figures such as the Kennedy family supported the grape boycott. The National Council of Catholic Bishops, the World Council of Churches, and a host of other church organizations mobilized their members to join in solidarity with the farm workers. Predictably, the Republican Governor of California, Ronald Reagan, declared the union "communist." Newly elected President Richard Nixon ordered the armed forces to increase their orders of grapes in order to break the strike and weaken the financial impact of the boycott on the growers. It was in this context of struggle that the resurgence took shape.

LATINO CHURCH MILITANCY

In Los Angeles, on the campus of Loyola Marymount University, the Chicano student group Católicos por la Raza (CPLR) was formed to press the church to support Chávez. But the eighty-three-year-old cardinal of Los Angeles, James Francis McIntyre, was a prelate noted as much for his conservative politics as for an authoritarian style of governing. On Christmas Eve 1969, CPLR organized a procession with more than four hundred Mexican American Catholics bearing lighted candles to the steps of St. Basil's Church, a four-million-dollar edifice where the Cardinal was to preside over a televised mass (see Gómez 1973 and discussion in Stevens-Arroyo 1980: 125–33). To demonstrate the exclusion of Spanish speakers from the concerns of the cardinal, a mass in Spanish was celebrated by Euro-American priests, after which CPLR passed out leaflets demanding a release of financial reports on the premise that the Archdiocese of Los Angeles did not devote enough resources to the ministry of Chicanos, who, of course, represented one of the church's largest constituencies. But when about fifty members of CPLR decided to attend the English services as well, they found that the main doors to St. Basil's had been locked. Hundreds of the people still milling about after the Spanish-language mass began shouting and banging on the doors for them to open. When some Mexican Americans finally managed to enter by a side entrance, they were physically pushed out by off-duty policemen. The marchers outside were incensed and began shoving back. Without warning, the Los Angeles Police Department's crack riot squad, wearing helmets, bearing shields, and swinging billy clubs, rushed from out of the cardinal's residence and began assaulting the Mexican Americans on Wilshire Boulevard, carting dozens off to jail. Inside the spacious church, Cardinal McIntyre addressed the public after communion had been distributed. Referring to Católicos Por la Raza, McIntyre said:

> We are ashamed of the participants and we recognize that their conduct was symbolic of the conduct of the rabble as they stood at the foot of the cross, shouting, "Crucify him!"
>
> *(Cardinal McIntyre, cited in Stevens-Arroyo 1980: 129)*

Many of those arrested were charged with a misdemeanor for disrupting a religious service, and the seven who were found guilty were sentenced to ninety days in jail.

The week after Christmas, the Puerto Rican bishop Antulio Parrilla Bonilla was in California visiting prominent activists who had been imprisoned for refusal to answer the Vietnam War draft (Stevens-Arroyo 1980: 90–91). Bishop Parrilla was known in his native Puerto Rico for his support of independence for the island and a critical stance towards American military power that also made him the first U.S. Catholic prelate to denounce the war as immoral. When he heard of the confrontation in Los Angeles, he celebrated mass in Spanish with priests and members of CPLR on an open lot within clear view of St. Basil's. His was an act of symbolic importance that linked Puerto Ricans and Chicanos, the protests against the war and the Chávez-led strike, the prophetic voice of a bishop and the militancy of lay leadership. It was a seed that found fertile ground.

It may be argued that the reaction to the inexcusable behavior of Cardinal McIntyre helped make stronger the militancy of Latino Catholics. As cited above, a social movement is formed around a group identity, opposition to a clearly defined institution, person, or policy, and a call to moral integrity. The rejection of *la causa* by Cardinal McIntyre spurred other Catholics eager to emphasize the teaching of the Second Vatican Council that the church was composed of all the people of God and not merely its hierarchical leaders. Much as the African Americans had appealed to the Declaration of Independence as a document by which to judge the actions of those who opposed the Civil Rights Movement, Latinos emphasized the documents of the Second Vatican Council as the charter of their crusade and the reason that they were right and the church's old guard was wrong about the UFW.

In order to coordinate nationwide support for the boycott, Father Ralph Ruiz had already called for a meeting of Catholic leaders supporting *la causa* scheduled for Tucson, Arizona, in February 1970. Reacting to the rancor generated by the CPLR confrontation and buoyed by the support of progressive clerics, the two dozen Chicano priests decided to form an association along ethnic lines that would support the farm workers. The vision for reform was not limited to the immediate crisis of the UFW. The priest organizers recognized that larger issues of discrimination needed to be challenged. Changes in the Catholic Church were now on the agenda, including the naming of Mexican American priests as bishops so that never again would the hierarchy make decisions without Mexican American input as equals within church leadership. The new group took the title Padres Asociados para Derechos Religiosos, Educacionales y Sociales, or "PADRES" (Stevens-Arroyo 1980: 139–40). In forming this group, full membership was reserved for Chicano priests, relegating Euro-Americans to an associate membership and excluding them from leadership posts. At the time, the advantages of uniting Mexican American priests around a common heritage was valued above the disadvantages of excluding potential allies on the basis of ethnicity. Resurrecting a term used in the Mexican Revolution and invoked in the poem, "Yo Soy Joaquín," the value of PADRES was described as "*carnalismo*," a strong expression of ideological kinship.

Within three months, one member of the new PADRES, Patricio Flores of Houston, was named a bishop, the first Mexican American so designated. In June 1970, the NCCB announced a negotiated settlement with the growers that constituted a victory for the farm workers. Before the year was over, Cardinal McIntyre had retired, and Timothy Manning, a prelate who supported *la causa*, was named as his replacement. By the time PADRES held its first national meeting in Los Angeles in February of 1971, Juan Arzube had been chosen as an auxiliary bishop for the archdiocese where the ugly confrontation had taken place in 1969.

Catholic women in religious life have different networks than the priests, and it is not surprising that some Latina religious sisters sought to form an organization parallel to PADRES. A planning meeting in April 1971 in Houston was convened by Gloria Gallardo, a Sister of the Holy Spirit and by Sister Gregoria Ortega of Victory Knoll. That November in Santa Fe, New Mexico, Las Hermanas was formally organized (Medina 1998). In contrast to its male counterpart, Las Hermanas extended full membership to all Latinas, not just Mexican Americans. Both of these organizations set goals that went well beyond the immediate task of supporting the farm workers. They sought a general reform of the church to make it more responsive to Mexican Americans on two fronts: commitment to issues of social justice and an education in cultural and theological matters in order to sustain that commitment. Importantly, they echoed the secular conviction that institutional aid to Latinos should be organized and led by other Latinos (Medina 2000b).

Although they had been generated in conflict, these efforts by Mexican American priests and sisters were welcomed by progressive elements of the hierarchy of the Catholic Church. Some bishops recognized the value of inviting such energy into the policy-formation process of the church. Episcopal support for a native leadership had its repercussions on the Bishop's Committee for the Spanish-Speaking. The regional office in the Midwest, which had been a sort of social-services agency for farm workers, was transplanted to the headquarters of the United States Catholic Conference in Washington, D.C. The person chosen to administer this recast division for Spanish speakers was Pablo Sedillo, a layman who brought administrative skills appropriate to the task of representing interests wider than just those of Mexican American farm workers.

The agenda of the new Washington office was compatible with the efforts of the incipient movement: in fact, the two strengthened each other. If the movement had consisted only of PADRES and Las Hermanas, the voice of Latinos would have been left outside the church, asking to be invited to internal discussions. But with the inclusion of the office funded by the bishops within the bureaucracy, a special dynamic was quickly achieved. The agenda of the organizations became the plan of action submitted by the office to the bishops. Linkage of the grassroots to a highly visible office in Washington strengthened both ends of the equation. On the one hand, the movement organizers were able to gain an immediate hearing in the halls of power; on the other, the office had foot-soldiers and grassroots supporters directly engaged in ministry.

A vital link in the chain was the foundation of the Mexican American Cultural Center (MACC) in San Antonio, Texas. Similar to the program that had been organized at the Catholic University of Puerto Rico to train priests of the Archdiocese of New York in the language and culture of the Puerto Rican migrants during the 1950s, MACC sprang from a program for seminarians in San Antonio. But the agitation among PADRES and Las Hermanas for education in their own culture and history—a gap in their formal education which was blamed on an overly narrow seminary curriculum—meant that MACC appealed to a wider base than just seminarians in San Antonio. Moreover, the director for MACC was a young and capable priest, Virgilio Elizondo, who possessed great charisma as an organizer and an educator. In a sense, MACC was "adopted" by PADRES and Las Hermanas as their educational center. The triumph of the farm workers in California lent an aura of historical vindication to the efforts of MACC, PADRES, Las Hermanas, and the Division for the Spanish-Speaking in Washington. The desire to reform the church to provide more effective services to Latinos was shared by many in U.S. Catholicism, and each of the organizations encountered wide acceptance within the church.

The awareness that social change could be effected within the church to benefit the Latino poor was the distinguishing mark of a new generation. Thus, in addition to the characteristics of a social movement, the resurgence also exhibited a strong linkage to a young generation of Latino church leaders. The distinguished Mexican American historian Mario García has shown how important generational considerations were to Mexican American civic leaders. Noting that "a political generation is not a biological generation," García cites Karl Mannheim:

> We shall therefore speak of a generation as an actuality only where a concrete bond is created between members of a generation by their being exposed to the social and intellectual symptoms of a process of dynamic destabilization.
>
> *(Karl Mannheim, as cited in M. García 1989: 4 n. 13)*

The generational attraction of PADRES and Las Hermanas made them more than Mexican American organizations. Drawn into the movement were young clergy and religious women from all the Latino nationality groups who had not been directly mobilized by the call to support the strike of the California farm workers. The general goal of reforming the church enabled PADRES and Las Hermanas to embrace young Latino priests and sisters around the country during a period when the Second Vatican Council had created "dynamic destabilization" within Catholicism, preparing the way for a social movement.

THE *ENCUENTRO*

In light of the rapid organization and political energy generated by Mexican Americans within the church supporting the farmworkers' strike, it is ironic that the most significant organizational input for the resurgence came from Puerto Rican–dominated New York and from a non-Latino church bureaucrat, Father Robert L. Stern. A canon lawyer, trained in Rome, from a Jewish-Irish family, Stern was named Director of the New York Archdiocese's Office for the Spanish-Speaking in the fall of 1969. Distant from the *la causa*, he viewed his task not from the picket lines but through the lens of chancery bureaucracy. Stern set about codifying a structure of governance that used the dry language of canon law to secure a seat at the planning table for Latino leaders. Although in a strict sense the Coordinating Committee he created was only an advisory group for the decisions he would make, in fact the committee functioned as a democratic body that formed policy. Stern also invited as collaborators with his office all the priests of Latino heritage he could identify, even if this meant lending them influence and visibility beyond the normal expectations of a church that usually observes strictly the rules of seniority. Ironically, many of the changes demanded in a militant voice by PADRES and Las Hermanas were quietly implemented in the New York Archdiocese through a democratic mechanism for developing policy by consulting lay leaders.

In September of 1971, at the annual meeting of the Catholic Interamerican Cooperation Program (CICOOP), Stern invited Father Edgar Beltrán, a Colombian priest who worked for the Latin American Episcopal Conference (CELAM), to conduct a planning workshop for the Coordinating Committee. Stern intended for Beltrán to help the archdiocese develop a five- year plan of action. But Beltrán's previous position had prepared him for developing such plans for the Catholics of an entire country, not merely a diocese. In October, at a National Congress of Religious Educators meeting in Miami, Florida, Beltrán was instrumental in gaining from the hundred or so Latino participants a formal petition to the NCCB for a greater attention to Latino affairs, including a call for a meeting at a national level to develop a five-year plan for all the Latinos in the United States. Stern and Beltrán linked their proposals and the division led by Pablo Sedillo backed the idea, as did PADRES, Las Hermanas, MACC and Bishop Patricio Flores, auxiliary Bishop of San Antonio, Texas (Stevens-Arroyo 1980: 181–83). With such an array of interest groups united in a single request, the NCCB could hardly refuse to authorize a congress, called "The Hispanic Pastoral Encounter" (or simply the "*encuentro*"). The ecclesiastical approval solidified the legitimacy of all of the Latino groups that had allied themselves under the banner of reform and mobilized greater church resources to benefit Latinos.

Astutely, Stern connected the East and West Coasts by persuading the New York Archbishop, Terrence Cardinal Cooke, to advocate the appointment of a Puerto Rican laywoman, Encarnación Padilla de Armas, to the Washington office. Mrs. Padilla had rich experiences in efforts during the 1950s in the training and educating of clergy for ministry to Latinos. As an administrator in the labyrinthine ways of New York's social-service bureaucracy, she brought an East Coast sophistication to the efforts of the Washington office.

The first *encuentro* was held 19–22 June 1972 at Trinity College in Washington, D.C. The conference was organized around workshops devoted to seven specific issues of church concern. Several general sessions offered the participants a theological and pastoral framework. Plenary sessions considered the documents prepared by each of the workshops that were designed to develop a plan of action around specific goals. The idea of Fr. Stern, the canon lawyer, was to require that each of the dioceses should send representatives chosen in a process approved by their bishop. Consequently, the several hundred participants who gathered in Washington were official delegates of their dioceses.

The *encuentro* spoke the language of the church. For example, Father Elizondo of MACC used theology to describe Latino culture as a "popular religiosity." Cast in that way, what anthropologists often classified as "religious culture" became "cultural religion." By thus bestowing theological significance upon Latino traditions, Elizondo argued that it was a church duty to preserve a culture that had helped preserve the Catholic faith. Bishop Flores's presentation crowned Latino popular religiosity with a historical legitimacy that echoed the Latino history spelled out in the poem "Yo soy Joaquín" and in countless university classrooms of Chicano Studies:

> The church cannot ignore the presence of fifteen million Spanish-speaking persons in the United States. They cannot be put into the same institution without taking into account their own particular background. The Mexican Americans who were here before the coming of the English-speaking, as well as the Spanish-speaking who have migrated here recently, have brought and have their own mentality, their language, their culture, their religion and their own needs. All of these elements are part of a beautiful spiritual heritage which will last in the Spanish-speaking outside of their Motherland. . . . The church cannot insist that in order to be first-class citizens and Christians we must "Americanize ourselves" . . . the mere statement disorients us. If we were born on this continent we are already "Americans." What do we have to be or do in order to "Americanize" ourselves?
>
> *(Patricio Flores, cited in Stevens-Arroyo 1980: 192)*

Bishop Flores detailed ways in which the Catholic Church should empower Latinos to organize their own ministry for themselves rather than pass through the process of slavishly imitating programs run for immigrants by Euro-Americans. The bishop concluded with a veiled warning:

> The bishop who has not wanted to share his authority and responsibility with another Catholic [Latino] bishop has already shared it with Protestant ministers and bishops who have taken away so many of his people.
>
> *(Patricio Flores, cited in Stevens-Arroyo 1980: 194.*

The effect of the 1972 *encuentro* was what journalist Moises Sandoval has aptly characterized as "A People on the Move" (Sandoval 1990). The documents detailing each of the workshop conclusions were submitted to the NCCB for review. While not all of the resolutions were adopted, their general goals were accepted in a response issued by a commission of bishops the following year (Stevens-Arroyo 1980: 201–7). Instead of pacifying the movement, the favorable reception from the bishops engendered a resolve to intensify the pace of reform. Latino leadership believed that since the efforts behind the first *encuentro* had produced positive results, more *encuentros* would produce more concessions from the Roman Catholic hierarchy.

From 1972 until 1977, twenty local *encuentros* were held to examine new issues and evaluate progress on those already proposed. The local *encuentros* generally followed the same processes of delegate selection, democratic participation in developing issues, and consensus on plans for specific action. Ironically, the centuries-old hierarchical discipline of Catholicism had made the democracy of the Latino leaders all the more potent, since the strategy of securing official standing for the delegates gave them clout within Catholicism. By the time the second *encuentro* was assembled in June of 1977 at the same Trinity College in Washington, the movement had penetrated to all levels of church organization throughout the United States, installing the same principles of empowerment and church reform. Importantly, the lay people, such as those in the Cursillo, stood together with the clergy and sisters in pushing for the reforms. The gathering of the Latino delegates even merited a special prerecorded radio message from Pope Paul VI at the Vatican in Rome:

> We wish the best for you, beloved brothers and children. Hence We invite you to conserve and nourish your own heritage, adapting it to local needs without forgetting, among other things, those valid elements of popular religiosity which, when well oriented, can prepare for an authentic encounter with God in Christ.
>
> *(Paul VI cited, in Stevens-Arroyo 1980: 322–23)*

That recorded message put the prestige of the papacy on the side of a movement that insured bilingualism and biculturalism within the church, advocated strong action in defense of social justice, and fostered native Latino leadership at all levels of church decision making. Such achievements in five short years were of historic proportions.

The principal achievements of the Catholic *encuentros* from 1972 until 1985 can be summed up in four basic notions that permeated the theological, political, and organizational goals of the delegates (Díaz-Stevens and Stevens-Arroyo 1998: 155–58). The successes within the churches closely parallel similar victories through the myriad federal programs that improved the educational, health, economic, and social status of most minorities between 1965 and 1980 (Haveman 1997). The *encuentros* argued for representation so that Latinos would be found at every level of church leadership. The *encuentro* documents were premised upon the idea that if all ethnic groups were to be given equal opportunity, they would usually achieve equal success. But it was clear that Latinos were drastically underrepresented in ecclesiastical leadership positions, such as the Catholic episcopacy, when compared with the numbers of Latinos in the church. A goal was set to name Latino bishops and other kinds of leaders in proportion to the numbers of Latinos in a diocese. This represented a considerably large step, considering that Latinos constituted at the time 25 percent of all Catholics and in some dioceses were a majority. Nor were bishops the only leaders subjected to this logic: principals of Catholic schools and directors of finance and religious education were included, thus opening doors for Latina sisters and lay persons to assume functions once reserved to the male clergy. These arguments were the ecclesiastical versions of affirmative action, and they were generally successful.[4]

The movement also advanced the argument that Latinos were the best exponents of their own culture, a principle I have called "cultural idiosyncrasy" (Díaz-Stevens and Stevens-Arroyo 1998: 156, passim). There already had been a commitment to celebrate rituals by using the Spanish language. Some of the non-Latino bishops may have viewed the use of Spanish as a stopgap measure until Latinos learned English. But the *encuentro* documents transformed the linguistic need into an affirmation of cultural difference. Spanish was to be used in order to maintain the Latino cultures. On that basis, the need to have Latino leaders at every level of church activity was now considered a permanent enrichment of U.S. Catholicism. How better to assure the people that their cultural differences would be preserved than to have one of their own placed in charge?

In addition, the new liberation theology from Latin America brought the premise that poverty was a sign of oppression. Latinos argued that the church's commitments to social justice around the world could not exclude their needs within the United States. By pointing to the colonial history of invasion and conquest by U.S. troops of Texas, the Mexican territories, and Puerto Rico, the neocolonialism that framed a Latin American denunciation of the United States was adapted to the Latino experience.

Finally, the *encuentros* appealed to the calls of the Second Vatican Council for a democratization of church leadership. By structuring the workshops so that each of them produced a set of resolutions and a working plan that was voted upon only by diocesan delegates, the *encuentro* had broken new ground for democracy within U.S. Catholicism. Lay leaders, especially women, were able to participate as equals with priests and sisters in the *encuentro* deliberations of the 1970s, just as the Cursillo had empowered the laity in the 1960s. The militancy of the Chicano activists was strengthened by adopting a model of lay participation in policy formulation that closely followed the initiative developed by Fr. Stern in New York.

The key to the movement was education. The most acceptable of the *encuentro*'s recommendations for the bishops had been the call for special courses of empowerment, especially for lay leaders. The Mexican American Cultural Center in San Antonio was held as a model for all dioceses. At MACC throughout the 1970s, the best and the brightest leaders and educators developed the recommendations from each of the five-year plans into a vital theology that was to permanently enrich U.S. Catholicism. The curriculum at MACC was not just history or theology, but praxis—an effective plan for action developed from shared reflection. The emphasis upon what might be called "continuing education" was accompanied by a modest opening of Catholic parochial schools to more Latino students. However, even with youth, the principal tools for education were retreats and training programs (Stevens-Arroyo and Díaz-Stevens 1993b).

THE INTELLECTUAL ROOTS OF THE RESURGENCE

Although this Latino militancy was initially targeted at the Catholic Church, the primary faith institution for Latinos, most of these key notions were to carry over to the other denominations. There was little that was automatic in the adaptation to the theological and organizational premises of the churches. Without a leadership with strong commitments to build and maintain this social movement, the resurgence would not have been successful.

The arguments may have been borrowed from the secular militant groups, but they were adapted to fit a religious context. For instance, the conclusions of the first *encuentro* began with a preamble that used the argument of proportional representation to make diversity, not Americanization, the "true value" to be fostered by the church:

> "E pluribus unum" and "In God we trust" mark the spirit of the people of the United States of America and of the Church of Christ. The strength of the unity of our country and our Church is proportionate to the respect for the individual persons, families and ethnic groups that compose them.
>
> (Encuentro *document, cited in Díaz-Stevens and Stevens-Arroyo 1998: 187)*

The principle of cultural idiosyncrasy was invoked as well:

> Every people has a right to self-determination and . . . the most effective instrumentality of development of a people is an indigenous leadership. . . . In education and formation, a harmonious and organic development of each person demands a respect for, understanding of, and realization of the

> potentialities of the culture and society in which he lives and from which he has sprung.
>
> *(Encuentro document, cited in Díaz-Stevens and Stevens-Arroyo 1998: 185–86)*

The documents employed statistics on poverty and low educational achievement among Latinos to specify what sort of church-based programs were required in the promotion of social justice. Acceptance of the *encuentro* documents by the bishops—which had been ensured by the structure of delegate selection—legitimized the democratization in the formulation of church policies.

Most importantly, these documents became blueprints for action. Unlike some secular manifestos and declarations of the Latino movements whose stipulations went unimplemented, the majority of the reforms outlined by the *encuentro* were incorporated into Catholic Church policies. Moreover, new organizations at the local level were created to implement the changes and to provide a constant monitor on progress, or the lack of it, and report to a recognized authority, the Office for the Spanish-Speaking. After the first *encuentro*, the office was elevated to the rank of a secretariat within the complex USCC. With its new title, the office was no longer limited to social services and was expected to inject the concerns of the movement into all of the agencies of the national organization of the Catholic Church: liturgy, education, political lobbying, and the like. At the same time, local parishes benefited from a more open climate that encouraged grassroots engagement in government programs (I. García 1996).

While many secular counterparts such as La Raza Unida Party, MEChA, and the Young Lords (see Torres and Katsiaficas 1999; Muñoz 1989; and Gutiérrez, chapter 1, this volume) have floundered in the 1990s, Latino church movements have demonstrated more stamina. This pattern reflects a similar trend reported for religiously affiliated organizations of "direct action" that are more stable than secular equivalents (Epstein 1991). The growth of faith-based groups, in contrast to the diminution of the secular militant organizations, has made community organizations more likely to be linked to churches than to political or labor associations (Gittell et al. 1981). I believe the superior effectiveness of the church movements can be explained by their ability to unite different ideologies. This capacity prevented a splintering over internal squabbles. This is not to deny that there were different camps within the resurgence. The principal differences were defined in *Prophets Denied Honor* (Stevens-Arroyo 1980: 175–79; see Díaz-Stevens 1993b: 220–43) as the "pastoralists," who were primarily interested in reforming church institutions and the "liberationists," who sought church resources to address the material needs of the people through social service and community agencies. There was a natural convergence of both groups around common plans of action that required the church to practice internally among Latinos the same concern it professed outwardly in public and political issues of social justice. The usual course was to appoint a Latino leader to an ecclesiastical position as administrator of a program targeted on Latino needs. Thus both the pastoralist and liberationist expectations were met simultaneously.

THE SHORTCOMINGS

Of course, the resurgence was not without its struggles and failures. For instance, the New York Office for the Spanish-speaking Apostolate was dismantled between 1972 and 1975 by a hierarchy frightened by the power of the Latino laity that had been sent as delegates to the first *encuentro* (Díaz Ramírez 1990). Díaz-Stevens views the resurgence in Gramscian terms, as the development of organic intellectuals within the Latino church communities. She compares the achievements of the movement to the definition by Antonio Gramsci of democratic centralism that requires "an organic unity between theory and practice, between intellectual strata and popular masses, between rulers and ruled" (1993b: 213). A similar analysis of PADRES has been supplied by the Chicano scholar Gilbert Cadena (1987). Both scholars point to an inevitable conflict arising when the institution considered its hegemonic control to have shifted towards Latinos. This tail-wagging-the-dog phobia of the bishops is described in detail by Díaz-Stevens in terms of the New York Archdiocese (1993b: 229–43). However, the repressive measures in New York and in some other dioceses could remove the messengers, but not the message. Local dioceses had to participate in all the *encuentros* because refusal to do so would have violated national policy, and harsh policies were often reversed under peer pressure from other bishops. Today, one is more likely to hear complaints from progressive Latinos that the director of the office for Latinos does not do enough instead of encountering the protest from the 1970s that there was no church office for Latinos.

The resurgence of Latino religion has continued to contribute significantly in shaping contemporary Catholicism. For instance, Latinos devised programs to deal with a lack of native clergy, which caused a reliance on lay leadership. Today, those conditions describe all of U.S. Catholicism (Schoenherr and Young 1993), not just the experience of Latinos. The emphasis upon a culturally rich liturgy and the empowerment of the laity are areas where the programs devised for Latinos have been carried over to other Catholic groups. In light of current demographic projections, it is safe to say that U.S. Catholicism in the twenty-first century will greatly resemble the model espoused by Latinos at the third *encuentro*, held in August 1985 with some 1,150 diocesan delegates gathered in Washington, D.C.:

> We also announce a model of Church that is open to the people's need, placing its buildings at the disposal of the people and recognizing the reality of Hispanics as a poor community. We affirm a model of priesthood that is more in contact with the people it serves, dedicated to persons, not material buildings, and exercising leadership in smaller communities.
>
> *(Secretariat for Hispanic Affairs,* Pueblo Hispano—Voz Profetica, *Washington, D.C.: National Catholic Conference, cited in Justo González 1990: 65)*

Without obscuring its considerable successes, the resurgence can be criticized for having emphasized the Mexican American experience at the expense of other national groups. While the successes of the Mexican Americans in Texas and New Mexico were spectacular in institutional terms, the demographic homogeneity and historic roots of Catholicism in these regions were unrepeatable in other settings where Latinos were not as numerous nor as well established. Non–Mexican American leadership in areas such as south Florida, where Cuban Americans were a majority, and in the New York area, where Puerto Ricans and Dominicans predominated, looked to themselves rather than the national office for solutions to their particular problems (Stevens-Arroyo 1994; see also Tweed 1997), thus lessening the movement's national cohesiveness. For example, the struggle related by Goris (1995) about Dominicans seeking church sponsorship for a protest against the execution of a Dominican immigrant in the state of Texas was a cause with national implications that received no support from the national secretariat.

Perhaps the greatest surprise in the resurgence was the church's inability to fully anticipate that the Charismatic movement would replace the Cursillo in importance among Latino Catholics and that Pentecostal and Evangelical congregations would grow at the expense of mainline Protestantism. The Catholic Charismatics and Pentecostals pray alike, rely on healing rituals, and prefer emotionally pitched preaching, although the Catholic Charismatics accept the teachings of the Catholic Church on grace, justification, devotion to Mary, and the papacy. To maintain this distinction, Catholic Charismatics will close their prayer session with a hymn to the Blessed Mother—something totally absent from the Pentecostal tradition. Once the Charismatics made this and other concessions to dogma, the movement gained considerable support from the Catholic hierarchy. In Houston, Texas, there is a downtown church building that coordinates all Charismatic Catholic ministries and provides an official space in which the unique prayer style of the Charismatics has full dominion.

As a movement focuses on the interiority of spiritual renewal, the Charismatics have been generally less likely than the *cursillistas* to incorporate social action as part of their faith commitments, although the *cursillistas*, Charismatics, and Pentecostals all function as a sects within the parish, with close-knit associations and strong bonds of fictive family. But whereas the Cursillo is made only once in a lifetime, the Charismatics and Pentecostals hold their prayer meetings several times a week. Today, Catholic Charismatics have softened the differences between the original Pentecostal religion and Catholicism, making Pentecostalism more a way of praying and less a distinct (and often anti-Catholic) religion.[5]

MAKING THE BARRICADES INTO ORGANIZATIONS

The elections of a new and more conservative pope, John Paul II, in 1979 and the conservative Ronald Reagan as president of the United States the next year began to close opportunities for the expansion of the resurgence goals both on the ecclesiastical front, where more conservative prelates were chosen, and on the political side, where drastic cuts in social programs were dictated from Washington. Moreover, the established principles of the movement were now rebuffed with counterarguments about "reverse discrimination" and the need to "end the welfare mentality." Latino Catholics and mainline Protestants were forced to beat a retreat from the front lines (Díaz-Stevens and Stevens-Arroyo 1998: 180–211). The expansive phase of the resurgence was over.

In the conservative tide of the 1980s, the alliance between the pastoralists and the liberationists wore thin at a national level. Since the pastoralists had always been interested in church organization, they were usually the directors of policy for the institution. As funds contracted and public support for social programs waned, the pastoralists were often forced to choose between dedicating resources to community services or continuing church-based projects. Most often, the church-based projects won out. Liberationists complained that the movement was no longer serving the material needs of the people in combating oppression. Lupe Angiano, then Director of the South West Office for the Spanish-Speaking, articulated the liberationist position:

> I would like to challenge us to depart from traditional church structures—where orders come from the *top down*—or competitive structures that isolate one program or organization from the other. I see little value in Hispanics trying to organize an Apostolic Plan of Action if in fact such a plan is based on repeating or trying to duplicate what already exists. It seems to

me more in keeping with our Christian ideals and cultural values that we organize structures based on a philosophy of broad participation completely given to community, cooperation and service.

(Lupe Anguiano, cited in Stevens-Arroyo 1980: 311)

In contrast, pastoralists viewed the affirmation of culture within religious expression as the first step in liberation. In a minor scale, this was an ecclesiastical repetition of the conflict between Hegelian idealists and Marxist materialists arguing over where the highest priority should be placed. Most pastoralists did not disparage community organizing around material needs: in fact, they anticipated that winning the "cultural war" within the church would make community organizing more effective because the Americanizing tendency of U.S. Catholicism would be replaced. The 1996 visit of Pope John Paul II to the United States crowned the achievement of the pastoralist goals:

> The pope also loves the sons and daughters of the church who speak Spanish. Many of you have been born here or have lived here for a long time. Others are more recent arrivals. But you all bear the mark of your cultural heritage, deeply rooted in Catholic tradition. *Keep alive that faith and culture.*
>
> *(Sermon on the Great Lawn in New York City's Central Park, 1996, cited in Díaz-Stevens and Stevens-Arroyo 1998: 191; emphasis added)*

Significantly, the pope admonished both those recently arrived from Latin America and those who, as Latinos, were born and raised in the United States to avoid Americanization. There are indications in the results offered by the PARAL Study (Stevens-Arroyo et al. 2002) that the pastoralist emphasis on culture is not disconnected from the capacity of a parish or congregation to foster agencies that address material needs along the lines advocated by liberationists. Today, as governments both federal and local, have developed programs throughout the 1990s that fund faith-based community agencies, the churches are well positioned to once again unify the pastoralist and liberationist impulses (Wood 1999; see also Verba, Schlozman, and Brady 1995).

THE ACHIEVEMENTS

Although this analysis has focused upon the Catholic experience of a Latino Resurgence, the four principles at the root of the resurgence ideology were also adapted by Protestants (Justo González 1990). Mainline Protestant denominations, such as Methodists, Presbyterians, and American Baptists, did not have Latino membership that in any way was as large as in Catholicism

(Díaz-Stevens and Stevens-Arroyo 1998: 37), but they did have a rich tradition of service and social outreach to the needy. Utilizing the principles of the movement, the Protestant leadership not only asserted a need for attention to Latino social needs, but they repeated the Catholic message about the representation of indigenous leadership and a new focus upon maintaining cultural diversity (I. García 1996). In not so subtle ways, Latino Protestants definitively cut away the Americanization tendency that had plagued their denominations even more than Catholicism. By repeating the arguments articulated at the Catholic *encuentros*, many denominations secured roles for various caucus and advisory boards that shaped policy for their churches in ways that paralleled the agencies that administered to Latino Catholicism. Interestingly, many Protestant churches now house multiple congregations speaking multiple languages under the same roof, echoing the "basement church" of the Catholic experience. The Methodist theologian Justo González wrote of the fruits of the resurgence in an award-winning 1990 book:

> We find ourselves walking along the same path with Roman Catholics. This new ecumenism has a practical and political side. The civil rights movement has its counterparts in the Hispanic community, and in those counterparts Catholics and Protestants have been drawn together. In these struggles, Protestant and Catholic Hispanics march arm in arm and are thus learning to undo many of the prejudices that have divided them. . . . Furthermore, this new ecumenism is not limited to issues of "life and work." It also includes what have traditionally been called matters of "faith and order." Indeed, it is our contention that there can be no division between life and work on the one hand and faith and order on the other, for as we work and live out the gospel we gain new insights into the meaning of our faith and the proper order for the church.
>
> *(González 1990: 74)*

The PARAL Study (Stevens-Arroyo et al. 2002) confirms that, except for differences resulting from the size of a typical urban community, the mainline Protestant congregations and the Roman Catholic parishes provide virtually the same services to the people and consider cultural expression important in virtually identical ways. Moreover, the ARIS Study found that the percentage of Hispanics identifying with any Protestant denomination has dropped in the past ten years from 26 percent in 1990 to 22 percent in 2001 (Kosmin, Mayer, and Keysar 2001). These results suggest that there is a growing need for a redefinition of Latino Protestantism within the general boundaries of Latino identity.

The slowest of the churches to adopt Latino-movement principles and theology were the Evangelicals, Pentecostals, and the Jehovah's Witnesses, many of which had long-standing theological traditions of avoiding entanglements with politics. These theologies did not lack commitment to the issues that concerned all Latinos, but they did not encourage the churches to create or-

ganizational mechanisms to mobilize collective action around these issues (Pérez y González 1995; Wood 1999). Well ahead of his Evangelical peers, the Reverend Raymond Rivera interpreted the Pentecostal experience as one focused on "the theology of survival," arguing as early as 1976 that this was a form of the theology of liberation cited by the Catholic and mainline Protestant leadership (Stevens-Arroyo 1980: 338–39).

The entry of conservative churches into the political arena came just as the impetus from the Latino religious resurgence among Catholics and mainline Protestants was diminishing. Evangelicals in the United States were mobilized in the 1980s by the Moral Majority of the Rev. Jerry Falwell and the Christian Coalition formed by the televangelist Pat Robertson (Williams 2000). Although these efforts were targeted primarily at English speakers, they had a noticeable impact on Latino Pentecostals and Evangelicals. Thus, for instance, Puerto Rican Pentecostals fostered community organizing in the South Bronx as an antidote to programs led by radicals and liberals. Reaganite politics eventually placed Pentecostal ministers in influential positions. Ironically, once placed in positions of political influence, many Evangelicals pressed for additional funds for federally funded housing programs, food stamps, and other such "liberal" efforts to alleviate poverty.

The theologian Eldin Villafañe adopted a Pentecostal perspective to reflect on the entry of Pentecostals and Evangelicals into politics:

> When justice is understood as "love rationally distributed," in essence one principle, a certain "wholism" is maintained in socio-political affairs. This prevents a dichotomy that can lead to atomistic realms— . . . a negative role for government, and a conservative and status quo political ideology. . . . Actions on behalf of the oppressed in the arena of politics and society at large are actions of love. Love can seek the expansion of the role of government, one that is concerned for social and economic welfare, thus a positive and active role for government. . . . The strategy of the Spirit is to empower its people to incarnate its love in just action in the world.
>
> *(Villafañe 1993: 214–15).*

His theology helps explain why Pentecostals and Evangelicals support an agenda of governmental involvement with faith-based communities that requires significant levels of funding. In sum, Pentecostal and Evangelical leaders have come to find more in common with their activist Catholic and Protestant counterparts than might have been expected on the basis of ideology alone. The needs of the people became a most important factor in bringing together denominations that had carefully avoided cooperation in the past (Villafañe 1993: 84–102). In sum, although Latino Pentecostalism entered politics as an ally of the Republican Party against liberal policies, nearly two decades later, it has changed that orientation. The Republican Party's embrace in 2001 of an expanded social-service funding through churches, called "Charitable Choice," is a reversal of the antigovernment stance of the Reagan years. The PARAL Study (Stevens-Arroyo et al. 2002) found that although Evangelicals and Pentecostals were more likely to classify themselves as "conservative" in politics than Catholics and Protestants, there was not a significant difference between them and all other pastors towards the use of government funds by churches to aid the material needs of the people.

For its part, Latino Catholicism continued to make adaptations in the 1990s, even after many of the more ambitious programs and agencies suffered declines in effectiveness. Catholicism can be credited with reducing the differences between Latinos and Latin Americans. Because of the territorial nature of parish organization, most Catholic churches often have several language and national groups as members. Newly arriving immigrants from Latin America automatically become members of a parish when they move into a neighborhood. Thus, the process that originally forged unity among the different regions, each of which had a different nationality, now seeks the same unity within a single parish unit. The pattern is sometimes repeated in the Protestant and Pentecostal experiences.

The constant influx of Latin American immigrants helps preserve the Spanish language among Latinos who often become bilingual rather than abandon the Spanish language. At the same time, the organizations and agencies headed by Latinos with social and political skills are put at the service of the Latin American immigrants. The analysis provided by Anneris Goris (1995) of a Puerto Rican/Dominican parish, suggests that the newly arrived and already settled meet most effectively in a church setting. In an area that requires more systematic study, it appears that in many instances the contemporary assimilation of Latin American immigrants is to the Latino community and not the Euro-American society of the United States.

THE RESULTS OF THE RESURGENCE IN RELIGION TODAY

The successes of the resurgence can be summarized on several key fronts. First, church resources, both Catholic and Protestant, have been substantially reallocated to serve the varied needs of Latinos. A wide gamut of educational, social, and material issues are addressed by many denominations as part of their ministries. Among faith-based Latino communities, social ministries are often run by the lay people (Coleman 1996). Second, the number and visibility of Latino clergy in policy-making positions has increased, especially at more local levels where Latino leaders exercise considerable influence. Virtually every denomination has its caucus or council that allows Latinos to speak to policy formulation. Third, cultural religion has moved to center stage in the United States. Traditions that were once opposed by Americanizing leadership have been embraced as elements of cultural religion. For instance, the Hispanic Liturgical Commission has fashioned a new ritual—not found among Euro-American Catholics—for a church celebration of the *quinceañera*, wherein a young woman pledges chastity until marriage. The young woman, wearing an elaborate white dress similar to a bridal gown, enters the church with attendants in tuxedos and formal dress. Kneeling before the altar, the young woman makes a solemn promise at the invitation of the priest. The church celebration is crowned with a reception mirroring the social status of the young woman. Some Latino Protestants practice the *quinceañera*, emphasizing its cultural rather than religious importance, thus blurring the distinctions in an already ambiguous mix. In the more ordinary circumstances of weekly rituals, the ecumenical exchanges follow this same pattern. Pentecostals include Latino folk rhythms in the repertoire of worship, enriching services that formerly overrepresented the Euro-American and African American traditions, while Catholics sing the Pentecostal *coritos* with gusto. Both sing from a hymnal that publishes compositions from many traditions. Fourth, the raison d'être of Latino religion has been explained in theological terms, such as Virgil Elizondo's theological *mestizaje* and other notions, such as "local theologies" (Schreiter 1985). Denominations that often preferred citing biblical passages to systematic theological reflection are participating in efforts to ground Latino religious experiences upon a set of core principles that at once are theological and crossdenominational. Fifth, lay people are generally more disposed to cooperation in faith-based community-development organizations that strive to concretize social justice and holistic ministry in specific projects targeted on local needs and led by indigenous leaders. In this way the public realm has acquired a sense of moral responsibility (Stevens-Arroyo 1997). While the social involvement of Latino churches is substantial, I do not wish to suggest that they have ended or will end poverty and discrimination. In fact, the continuing impoverishment of Latinos vis à vis the general U.S. society argues for even more attention from the churches to the needs of the community (Moore and Pinderhughes 1993; Díaz-Stevens and Stevens-Arroyo 1998: 20–34).

Sixth, the feminization of religious leadership was intensified among Latinos. By building on traditions wherein the fostering of religious practice was a role assigned primarily to women, the professionalization of church leadership as an effect of the resurgence meant that Latinas gained enormous influence and prestige within religious institutions. For instance, women are the heads of 19 percent of Latino parishes in the Roman Catholic Church, despite the rules in that denomination that ordain only males (Stevens-Arroyo et al. 2002). Called "the matriarchal core" (Díaz-Stevens 1993a), this trend adds a uniquely Latina dimension to the study of gender roles in contemporary society. Seventh, the Latino experiences have fostered a transnational Latino identity. As many of the contributors to this volume have noted, "transnationalism" refers to the capacity for a person to possess simultaneously different national identities. While it has always been recognized that immigrants to the U.S. reflect cultural, linguistic, and political loyalties to the country they left behind, the assimilationist premise held that incorporation into U.S. society would replace these old loyalties with new ones dictated by life in the States (see Stevens-Arroyo 1994). I view contemporary transnationalism among Latinos as a repudiation of the bias toward only one loyalty and inevitable assimilation into U.S. society. It seems to me that a growing number of Latinos today have multiple identities, some that reflect needs specific to life in the United States, but not exclusive of continuities with the Latin American experience. In the context of a global economy, instant communications, and easy transportation between countries, the old pattern of immigrant nostalgia for the abandoned homeland is no longer as common. Instead, immigrants can alternately choose among the politics, sports, and entertainment of the United States and Latin America, literally by pushing a button on a television remote. The increasing frequency of dual nationality and/or citizenship gives legitimacy to these multiple identities that transcend national boundaries. The new and more complex ties to various homelands discernible in the Latino experiences are also found among other immigrant groups in the United States (see Ebaugh and Chafetz 2000; Warner and Wittner 1998), adding importance to a study of this phenomenon as a new dimension of contemporary U.S. society.

CONTEMPORARY SPIRITUALITY

The general absence of religion as a theme in academic discourse about Latino history and culture has already been lamented (see note 1). But ironically, the sacred has been restored to popular culture (Kavolis 1988), especially since the dissolution of the Soviet Union in 1991. Accordingly, religion has made a comeback among Latino elites, particularly among those producing literary works or commenting on culture from within the academy. The tendency to use culture as ideology has been documented among several groups and is in fact a worldwide trend (Williams 1996). Today, cultural religion and religious culture have been utilized to protect group identity not only for Latinos, but also for African Americans, Filipinos, Vietnamese, and many other national groups (Roof 1998). U.S. Catholicism in particular has witnessed a revival of traditional piety (Johnson 1998) and of ethnic traditions among older immigrant groups, such as the Italians and Irish, manifested by restoration of traditional devotions (Orsi 1996) and Celtic practices (Baumann 2000).

Among Latinos and Latinas, sacred symbols and practices of popular religion are elements of a Latino cultural identity that serve as a critical ideology. Although this issue is addressed in the theological description of *mestizaje*, attachment to these symbols derived from religion does not always equate to religious practice in a worshiping community. In fact, some, like Gloria Anzaldúa (1987), consider religious symbols as their own cultural property and prefer to speak of "spirituality" in order not confuse their embrace of the sacred with practices linked to institutionalized religion (see also Stavans 1995).

There is a sense in which this mode of thinking about religious issues is a nondenominational claim to the popular religiosity described by theologians. Whereas Elizondo and others would see popular religiosity and institutionalized religion as inseparably linked, this nonconfessional view of spirituality sees opposition and resistance to the formal workings of church. Appeal to symbols and traditions is not intended to bring the popular and the preached closer together, but to sever them so that the people no longer need have recourse to organized religion in the practice of a religious spirituality.

There are different degrees in this resistance: some are simply antibureaucratic and secularizing versions of the orthodox theological insistence on the importance of popular religiosity: others are overtly anti-Christian and approximate what is usually called "paganism." In many cases, spirituality without religion makes no moral claims based on God. Spiritual choices are presented as expressions of one's own values, independent of divine commandments.[6] Individuals may discover a preference for certain behavior in their spiritual journey, but sin does not exist as a theological category.[7] Spirituality freed from Christian faith is claimed to be both antithetical and superior to religion (Griffin 2000). Discourse on the body, in great part traceable to Foucault, has been used to assault Christian conceptions of marriage, virginity, and sexual identity (see Gutiérrez 1991). Together with ecology, feminism, astrology, and New Age beliefs, indigenous religious expressions have become a part of contemporary spirituality that does not utilize religious structures or agencies. With the license provided by postmodernism for revisionist versions of history, a new interpretation of Latino history is being composed wherein the sixteenth-century *mestizaje* of civilization and religion can be discounted in favor of a anti-institutional Latino spirituality. Artists and writers, in particular, have incorporated this sentiment into their production, suggesting meanings for the Cross of Christ or Our Lady of Guadalupe that have been interpreted by many as antagonistic to Christian faith.[8]

It is important to include these expressions as part of Latino religion on the premise that wherever there is a "sacred," there is religion. I might be faulted by some for including spirituality in this review of Latino religion and religiosity because these products of literary and artistic elites do not represent the faith of tens of millions of Latino Christians. Nonetheless, my premise has been that religion goes beyond the four walls of religious buildings and permeates much of society. Whether as "religious culture" or as "cultural religion," such expressions are part of the Latino experience. David Carrasco, in a provocative essay about "Jaguar Christians" (1995), paints a scene of Ricoeur's phenomenological distress as the occasion for syncretism, which is rooted in "a much harder, deeper, more complex matter than what is in immediate consciousness" (77–78). Following his lead, I think these religious expressions outside the embrace of organized religion are contributors to a sociohistorical process that is much larger than any one of its interactive parts. These expressions produced by an articulate and talented Latino elite, whether within religious orthodoxy or not, affect the conceptualization (some would say "construction") of Latino culture.

Ricoeur's notion of phenomenological distress ties together these disparate expressions because, in its various manifestations, Latino religion continues to struggle against injustice. Even if the paintings, poetry, and novels of the literary elites neither build buildings nor give food to the hungry, clothe or console the suffering, or organize strikes or marches for social justice, they make a contribution to the ongoing Latino experience of religion. The new religious art and literature develop further symbols of resistance. They cast African and indigenous religious expression as foil to Americanization and Europeanization. Like the spirituality movements in cultural matters, Latino parishes and congregations within Christianity exhibit trends away from a rigid Eurocentric orthodoxy, continuing the process begun during the resurgence.

THE INDIGENOUS REVIVAL IN LATINO RELIGION

Indigenous religious traditions in the Americas have gained a significant influence over Latino religion since 1992. What was conceived as a hemispheric celebration of the transatlantic voyage of Christopher Columbus witnessed instead a revival of a Native American identity. The reaffirmation of pre-Hispanic culture took various forms. There is renewed pride in those sectors of Latin America where the native population survives physically and linguistically in distinct societies, as, for instance, in Chiapas, Mexico, where the revival had important political repercussions. But the indigenous heritage is present in less dramatic ways, such as the seeking of herbal cures, the experience of an initiated healer or *curandera/o*, and the usage of sweat as a form of purification.

The indigenous religious revival at times constitutes a rejection of Christianity for the "old ways": it is now common to see groups practicing Aztec (Mexico) or Taíno (Caribbean) rites at the powwows, or Native American celebrations that are held periodically in the United States. However, the revival is also present among tens of millions of Latino Christians. The celebration of Mass in San Fernando Cathedral in San Antonio features children dressed as Aztecs who dance down the main aisle during the offertory procession (Elizondo and Matovina 1998). The identification of religion with Latino popular culture extends to the civic and social arena for public events. For instance, the celebration of the Mexican Day of the Dead is a sixteenth-century result of the syncretism of Aztec ancestor worship with the Catholic Feast of All Souls (which itself was a syncretization in the sixth century with the Celtic New Year). Intended as a day of prayer for the souls in Purgatory, in Los Angeles *el Día de los Muertos* has been organized as a civic commemoration of victims of police brutality (Medina 2000a). These examples demonstrate that the religious imagination of Latinos continues to be creative, both within and outside church settings.

THE AFRO-CARIBBEAN EXPERIENCES

Among Latinos from the Caribbean, the affirmation of Afro-Caribbean religions runs parallel to the reclaiming of Native American roots elsewhere. Many of these religions originated among slave populations of the islands and have acquired a theology by incorporating heavy doses of Iberian Catholicism and elements of theosophy and spiritualism (Stevens-Arroyo and Pérez y Mena 1995). These Afro-Caribbean religions have functioned ubiquitously, if clandestinely, in all of the island societies from colonial times into the twentieth century. The niche occupied by these religions was hidden within the ample diversity of Catholicism. Believers attended Catholic masses and processions, wore medals and crosses, blessed themselves with holy water, and received communion. But they also practiced specialized rites such as animal sacrifices, sought protection from curses, requested hexes on their enemies, and prayed to the spirits for sexual powers, success in business, and good luck. In the contemporary context of urban centers such as New York, the different strands of traditions from Cuba, Puerto Rico, the Dominican Republic, and Haiti have been woven together (Pérez y Mena 1998).

Different theories have emerged among academics to explain the persistence of these religious beliefs, such as slaves' ignorance of the difference between African and Christian believers or purposeful deception of their masters. Most of these explanations reflect the low tolerance in organized religion for African elements. Church approval has been less forthcoming for the Afro-Caribbean experiences than for Native American religious expressions, probably because the religious legitimacy given to vengeance, animal sacrifice, and sexual power in the Afro-Caribbean religions has made them vulnerable to a Christian denunciation as "devil worship." With a new-found respect for diversity in religious expression, however, it is more common for Christian leaders to search for ways to interpret these Afro-Caribbean traditions within Latino popular religiosity.

Nonetheless, the vitality of Afro-Caribbean religion is outside of Christianity today. Santería is the most widespread of the Afro-Caribbean religions in the United States. Called "Lucumí" in Cuba where it originated as an American expression of Yoruba religion, Santería among Latinos has now absorbed many other elements as well. Santería requires animal sacrifice to obtain a blood offering for the rituals of worship and healing. These sacrifices were targeted by the city of Hialeah in Florida in a series of prohibitions issued in 1987. But after lengthy legal battles, in November 1992 the U.S. Supreme Court upheld a 1989 Florida decision striking down the ordinances of Hialeah against the Lucumí Church of Babalú Ayé (Campo 1995). The effect of the Supreme Court decision has been to augment the tendency to establish Afro-Caribbean worship as a religion among many others in the United States, where all the rituals are constitutionally protected. In the future, Afro-Caribbean religions will increasingly stand alone without the need of a Catholic "disguise." One can expect that new religions will appear among Latinos, probably attracting non-Latino members in the process.

CONCLUSION

Religion among Latinos continues to be the social vehicle that transports the majority of our people through the moments of joy and tragedy that constitute for families and individuals life's rites of passage. But during the period under examination, its institutionalized resources also have assumed a major role in shaping cultural identity, giving impulse to social movements, motivating millions to community action, fostering the feminization of community leadership, and stimulating a greater awareness of a pan-Latino and transnational reality.

In this chapter, particular attention has been given to the Latino religious resurgence that made the greatest of changes in religious expression for a period beginning in 1967 with the strike by the farm workers in California led by César Chávez. The rallying of support for the many phases of *la causa* was quickly turned into a militancy to reform the churches and was led by a generation of Latino clergy and religious women. Considered as a social movement, the Latino religious resurgence mobilized institutional resources through the *encuentros* and a host of church-based educational and community agencies to the benefit of large numbers of Latinos nationwide. In the space of less than twenty years, church people moved from the barrios to the barricades, transforming religious institutions into bulwarks of social change.

Although the original movement and its leaders do not enjoy their former prominence, there is a palpable difference in the scope and style of church organization, resembling what Antonio Gramsci described as "organic leadership." It remains to be seen if the churches will continue to support the advancement of Latinos as African Americans are replaced as the nation's largest "minority." But several measures can be introduced to provide a yardstick with which to measure religious contributions to the social benefit of Latinos. Will the Catholic Church make accessible to Latinos its schools, not only in terms of admitting pupils to the classrooms, but especially in adapting curriculum to reflect Latino identity? Will mainline Protestantism continue to foster the development of Latino leadership, even if that leadership diverges from the traditional class setting of Protestantism in the U.S., wherein one changes denominations along with income? Will Latino Evangelicals and Pentecostals mobilize their followers towards social activism and aggressive pursuit of funding for grassroots agencies that attend to material needs? Will the artistic expression of a religious culture that emanates from a highly talented and influential intellectual elite contribute to the rescue of alienated youth in the barrios where drugs, teenage pregnancies, and gang values threaten the fabric of social cohesion? Each of the components of the Latino religious world faces a challenge in the shaping of a common future. The social role of the churches may change from revolutionary to evolutionary points of people power, but it appears that religion has placed itself irreversibly within the civic space as a voice for Latinos and Latinas.

Nonetheless, there are questions to be asked about the future. Since the Catholic Church continues to hold a policy that refuses baptism for a child unless the parents practice Catholicism by church attendance, there are Latinos who find themselves without a church for their "religious culture." Where will these people go to celebrate life, death, and marriage? This loss is reflected in the drop of the percentage of Latinos calling themselves "Catholic" from 65.8 percent in 1990 to 59 percent in 2001 (Kosmin, Mayer, and Keysar 2001). Lack of affiliation with a particular religion, however, is not the same as becoming an atheist. The ARIS study found that the fastest growing membership category for the U.S. was "no religion," growing for Hispanics from 6 percent in 1990 to 12 percent in 2001. The growth in the number of unaffiliated believers may make nondenominational expressions of spirituality more important for larger numbers of Latinos.

Whatever the results, religion must be judged by religious norms to fully assess its impact. We need to recognize that the utopian dimension of religion always makes its political goals "not of this world." Even as these words are written, a new *causa* has triumphed in the case of massive community resistance to the U.S. Navy bombing of the Puerto Rican island of Vieques (Stevens-Arroyo 2000). In peaceful marches and conscientious civil disobedience, the religious leadership of virtually every denomination in Puerto Rico has begun a movement to force the withdrawal of U.S. militarism in the Caribbean. Despite failures and deceptions through all of human history, religion and religious institutions continue to inspire people in ways that hint at the marvelous.

NOTES

1. Religion is absent from two recent books on Latino social movements, Juan González's *A Harvest of Empire* (2000) and *Latino Social Movements* (1999), edited by Torres and Katsiaficas. A similar absence is evident in Stavans's (1995) review of Latino literature, and neither "religion" nor "church" are in the index of the copious *The Latino/a Condition* (Delgado and Stefancic 1998). While the scholarly effort of the authors in each of these works might be respected, their exclusion of religion results in works of narrow scope. One is left with serious doubt as to the reliability of such studies in describing Latino experiences.
2. For more on this issue, see Díaz-Stevens and Stevens-Arroyo 1998: 48–78. While in the past, the rejection of syncretism as a legitimate process in religion led some to overestimate the importance of orthodoxy from the Iberian Catholic perspective, there is now a similar rereading of syncretism from the viewpoint of indigenous religions. I believe with David Weber (1992: 359) that the attempts to stereotype Iberian Catholicism as a unilaterally imposed hegemonic control of Native American religion is a modern version of the sixteenth-century black legend that unfortunately is more a result of bigotry than of objective analysis. I encourage the reader to adopt a critical stance towards syncretism as an uneven process that combines coercion and free choice, power with powerlessness, faith commitment with self-interest, and the sundry ambiguities of human social behavior.
3. We find, for instance, that the Extension Society of the Catholic Church dedicated many efforts at fund-raising to support Catholic parishes in the Southwest, Texas, and California, just as Protestant Mission Societies provided similar aid for their denominational outreach to Spanish speakers. See Dolan and Hinojosa, 1994: 98.
4. For instance, in 1972 there were only two Latino bishops (not counting Puerto Rico's five bishops). Five years later there were a dozen, and in 2002 there were more than twenty.

5. Pentecostalism may be classified into five categories: 1) classical Pentecostal movements based on the teachings of Charles F. Parham and William J. Seymour; 2) neo-Pentecostalism, increasingly common among mainline Protestant churches since 1960; 3) Catholic Charismatics, founded as a movement in 1967 at Duquesne University and which has approximately ten times as many members as the Assemblies of God, the largest Pentecostal denomination; 4) independent, interdenominational, or unaffiliated churches, which may be the fastest growing category in the Protestant experience; 5) third world indigenous movements, many of which have added indigenous religious beliefs into Pentecostal worship. See Villafañe 1993: 86–87, discussing the study of Vinson Synan.
6. There is a long-standing debate among experts of religion as to whether the "immanent divine," such as that found in many forms of Buddhism, constitutes an equivalent to the "transcendent divine" of Judaism, Christianity, and Islam. Transcendent thought places God as a person distinct from the creature; immanent thought places divine power within the individual, something like a force that can be touched after undergoing intense training. The issue is a theological one beyond the scope of this chapter.
7. However, morality should not be considered the exclusive property of religious persons, because the god of religion is not the only transcendent goal possible to individuals. Patriotism, altruism, and professional integrity are among the other goals that can summon transcendence.
8. The painting *The Piss Christ* by artist David Serrano captures the ambiguity of juxtaposing a traditional religious image in a degrading contemporary setting.

REFERENCES

Alvarez, Carmelo E. 1996. "Panorama Histórico de los Pentecostalismos Latinoamericanos y Caribeños." In *En La Fuerza Del Espíritu: Los Pentecostales en América Latina: Un Desafío a Las Iglesias Históricas*, ed. Benjamin E. Gutiérrez, 35–56. Santiago, Chile: CELEP.

Anzaldúa, Gloria. 1987. *Borderlands/La Frontera: The New Mestiza*. San Francisco: Spinsters/Aunt Late.

Baumann, John. 2000. "Celtic Practices." In *Encyclopedia of Contemporary American Religion*, ed. Wade Clark Roof, 1:102–4. New York: Macmillan.

Busto, Rudy V. 1991. "Like a Mighty Rushing Wind: The Religious Impulse in the Life and Writing of Reies López Tijerina (Chicano Pentecostalism)." Ph.D. diss., University of California, Berkeley.

Cadena, Gilbert R. 1987. "Chicanos and the Catholic Church: Liberation Theology as a Form of Empowerment," Ph.D. diss. University of California, Riverside.

Campo, Orlando do. 1995. "The Supreme Court and the Practice of Santería." In *Enigmatic Powers: Syncretism with African and Indigenous Peoples' Religions Among Latinos*, ed. Anthony M. Stevens-Arroyo and Andrés I. Pérez y Mena, 159–80. The PARAL Series, vol. 3. Bildner Center Books: New York.

Carrasco, David. 1995. "Jaguar Christians in the Contact Zone." In *Enigmatic Powers: Syncretism with African and Indigenous Peoples' Religions Among Latinos*, ed. Anthony

M. Stevens-Arroyo and Andrés Pérez y Mena, 69–80. New York: Bildner Center Books.

Coleman, John A., SJ. 1996. "Under the Cross and the Flag." John Courtney Murray Lecture, Fordham University, New York. *America* 174, no. 16 (11 May): 6–14.

Delgado, Richard, and Jean Stefancic, eds. 1998. *The Latino/a Condition: A Critical Reader*. New York: NYU Press.

Díaz Ramírez, Ana María. 1980. "The Life, Passion, and Death of the Spanish-Speaking Apostolate of the Archdiocese of New York." In *Prophets Denied Honor*, ed. Antonio M. Stevens-Arroyo, 208–13. Maryknoll, N.Y.: Orbis Books.

Díaz-Stevens, Ana María. 1993a. "The Saving Grace: The Matriarchal Core of Latino Catholicism." *Latino Studies Journal* 4, no. 3 (September): 60–78.

——. 1993b. *Oxcart Catholicism on Fifth Avenue*. Notre Dame, Ind.: University of Notre Dame Press.

Díaz-Stevens, Ana María, and Anthony M. Stevens-Arroyo. 1998. *Recognizing the Latino Resurgence in U.S. Religion: The Emmaus Paradigm*. Boulder, Colo.: Westview Press.

Dolan, Jay P. 1992. *The American Catholic Experience*. Notre Dame, Ind.: Notre Dame University Press.

Dolan, Jay P., and Gilberto M. Hinojosa, eds. 1994. *Mexican Americans and the Catholic Church, 1900–1965*. Notre Dame Series on Hispanic Catholics in the U.S., vol. 1. Notre Dame, Ind.: University of Notre Dame Press.

Ebaugh, Helen Rose, and Janet Chafetz, eds. 2000. *Religion and the New Immigrants*. Walnut Creek, Calif.: Altamira Press.

Elizondo, Virgil. 1992. *The Future is Mestizo*. New York: Crossroad Publishing Co.

Elizondo, Virgil, and Timothy Matovina. 1998. *San Fernando Cathedral: Soul of the City*. Maryknoll, N.Y.: Orbis Books.

Epstein, Barbara. 1991. *Political Protest and Cultural Revolution: Nonviolent Direct Action in the 1970s and 1980s*. Berkeley: University of California Press.

García, Ismael. 1996. "A Theological-Ethical Analysis of Hispanic Struggles for Community Building in the United States." In *Hispanic/Latino Theology: Challenge and Promise*, ed. Ada María Isasi-Díaz and Fernando F. Segovia, 289–306. Minneapolis: Fortress Press:

García, Mario T. 1989. *Mexican Americans: Leadership, Ideology, and Identity, 1930–1960*. New Haven, Conn.: Yale University Press.

——. 1994. *Memories of Chicano History: The Life and Narrative of Bert Corona*. Berkeley: University of California Press.

Gittell, Marilyn, Bruce Hoffacker, Eleanor Rollins, Samuel Foster, and Mark Hoffacker. 1981. *Limits to Citizen Participation: The Decline of Community Organizations*. Beverly Hills, Calif.: Sage Publications.

Gómez, David F. 1973. *Somos Chicanos: Strangers in Our Own Land*. Boston: Beacon Press.

González, Juan. 2000. *Harvest of Empire: A History of Latinos in America*. New York: Viking.

González, Justo. 1990. *Mañana: Christian Theology from a Hispanic Perspective*, Nashville, Tenn.: Abingdon.

Gonzales, Rodolfo "Corky." 1972. *I Am Joaquín*. New York: Bantam Books. Poem copyright 1967. Reproduced with permission in *Prophets Denied Honor*, Antonio M. Stevens-Arroyo, 15–20. Maryknoll, N.Y: Orbis, 1980.

Goris, Anneris. 1995. "Rites for a Rising Nationalism: Religious Meaning and Dominican Community Identity in New York City." In *Old Masks, New Faces: Religion and Latino Identities*, ed. Anthony M. Stevens-Arroyo and Gilbert R. Cadena, 117–42. New York: Bildner Center Books.

Griffin, Wendy. 2000. "Spirituality." In *Encyclopedia of Contemporary American Religion*, ed. Wade Clark Roof, 2:698–99. New York: Macmillan.

Gutiérrez, Ramón. 1991. *When Jesus Came, the Corn Flower Mothers Went Away*. Stanford: Stanford University Press.

Haveman, Robert H., ed. 1997. *A Decade of Federal Antipoverty Programs: Achievements, Failures, and Lessons*. New York: Academic Press.

Johnson, Mary, SND de N. 1998. "The Reweaving of Catholic Spiritual and Institutional Life." *The Annals of the American Academy of Political and Social Science* 558 (July): 135–43.

Kavolis, Vytautus. 1988. "Contemporary Moral Cultures and the 'Return of the Sacred'" *Sociological Analysis* 49, no. 3 (fall 1988) 203–16.

Kelley, Dennis. 2000. "Cursillo Movement." In *Encyclopedia of Contemporary American Religion*, ed. Wade Clark Roof, 1:167. New York: Macmillan.

Kosmin, Barry A., Egon Mayer, and Ariela Keysar. 2001. *American Religious Identification Survey (ARIS)*. New York: City University of New York.

León, Luis. 1994. "Somos Un Cuerpo en Cristo: Notes on Power and the Body in an East Los Angeles Chicano/Mexicano Pentecostal Community," *Latino Studies Journal* 5, no. 3 (September): 60–86.

López, Alfredo. 1973. *The Puerto Rican Papers: Notes on the Re-Emergence of a Nation*. Indianapolis: Bobbs-Merrill.

Maduro, Otto A. 1982. *Religion and Social Conflicts*. Maryknoll, N.Y: Orbis Books.

Medina, Lara. 1998. "Las Hermanas: Chicana/Latina Religious-Political Activism, 1971–1997." Ph.D. diss., Claremont Graduate University.

——. 2000a. "Day of the Dead." In *Encyclopedia of Contemporary American Religion*, ed. Wade Clark Roof, 1:176–77. New York: Macmillan.

——. 2000b. "Las Hermanas." In *Encyclopedia of Contemporary American Religion*, ed. Wade Clark Roof, 1:383–84. New York: Macmillan.

Moore, Joan. 1994. "The Social Fabric of the Hispanic Community Since 1965." In *Hispanic Catholic Culture in the U.S.: Issues and Concerns*, ed. Jay Dolan and Allan Figueroa Deck, 6–49. Notre Dame, Ind.: University of Notre Dame Press.

Moore, Joan, and Raquel Pinderhughes. 1993. *In the Barrios: Latinos and the Underclass Debate*. New York: Russell Sage.

Muñoz, Carlos Jr. 1989. *Youth, Identity, Power: The Chicano Movement*. Verso Haymarket Series on North American Politics and Culture, New Left Books: New York.

Orsi, Robert. 1996. *Thank You, St. Jude: Women's Devotion to the Patron Saint of Hopeless Causes*. New Haven, Conn.: Yale University Press.

Padilla, Felix. 1985. *Latino Ethnic Consciousness: The Case of Mexican Americans and Puerto Ricans in Chicago*. Notre Dame, Ind.: University of Notre Dame Press.

——. 1987. *Puerto Rican Chicago*. Notre Dame, Ind.: University of Notre Dame Press.

Pérez y González, María Elizabeth. 2000. "Latinas in the Barrio." In *New York Glory: Religions in the City*, ed. Anna Karpathakis and Tony Carnes, 287–96. New York: NYU Press.

Pérez y Mena, Andrés. I. 1998. "Cuban Santería, Haitian Vodun, Puerto Rican Spiritualism: A Multicultural Inquiry into Syncretism." *Journal for the Scientific Study of Religion* 37, no. 1: 15–27.

Poblete, Renato, and Thomas O'Dea. 1960. "Anomie and the 'Quest for Community': The Formation of Sects Among the Puerto Ricans of New York." *American Catholic Sociological Review* 21 (spring): 18–36.

Prieto, Yolanda. 1995. "Continuity or Change? Two Generations of Cuban American Women" *New Jersey History* 113: 1–2, 47–60.

Privett, Stephen A., SJ. 1988. *The United States Catholic Church and Its Hispanic Members: The Pastoral Vision of Archbishop Robert E. Lucey*. San Antonio: Trinity University Press.

Rendón, Armando. 1971. *Chicano Manifesto*. New York: Collier Books.

Roof, Wade Clark. 1998. "Religious Borderlands: Challenge for Future Study." *Journal for the Scientific Study of Religion* 37, no. 1 (March): 1–14.

Sánchez Korrol, Virginia, ed. 1993. *The Way it Was and Other Writings*. Houston: Arte Público Press.

Sandoval, Moises. 1990. *On the Move*. Maryknoll, N.Y: Orbis Books.

Schoenherr, Richard, and Lawence A. Young. 1993. *Full Pews and Empty Altars: Demographics of Priest Shortage in U.S. Catholic Dioceses*. Madison: University of Wisconsin Press.

Schreiter, Robert J. 1985. *Constructing Local Theologies*. Maryknoll, N.Y.: Orbis Books.

Silva Gotay, Samuel. 1997. *Protestantismo y Política en Puerto Rico, 1898–1930*. San Juan: Editorial de la Universidad de Puerto Rico.

Stavans, Ilan. 1995. *The Hispanic Condition: Reflections on Culture and Identity in America*. New York: HarperCollins.

Stevens-Arroyo, Antonio M. 1980. *Prophets Denied Honor*. Maryknoll, N.Y.: Orbis Books.

——. 1994. "The Emergence of a Social Identity Among Latino Catholics: An Appraisal." In *Hispanic Catholic Culture in the U.S.: Issues and Concerns*, ed. Jay Dolan and Allan Figueroa Deck, 77–130. Notre Dame, Ind.: University of Notre Dame Press.

——. 1995. "Latino Catholicism and the Eye of the Beholder: Notes Towards a New Sociological Paradigm" *Latino Studies Journal* 6, no. 2 (May): 22–55.

——. 1997. "Building a New Public Realm: Moral Responsibility and Religious Commitment in the City." In *The City and the World*, ed. Alberto Vourvoulias-Bush and Margaret Crahan, 147–58. New York: Council on Foreign Relations Press, 1997.

——. 1998. "The Evolution of Marian Devotionalism Within Christianity and the Ibero-Mediterranean Polity" *Journal for the Scientific Study of Religion* 37, no. 1: 50–73.

——. 1999. "Theology and the Secularization of Religious Traditions" Paper read at the Society for the Scientific Study of Religion—Religious Research Association Annual Conference, 6 November, Boston, Massachusetts.

——. 2000. "Catholicism's Emerging Role in Puerto Rico." *America* 182, no. 13 (15 April): 8–11.

Stevens-Arroyo, Anthony M., and Ana María Díaz-Stevens. 1993a. "Religious Faith and Institutions in the Forging of Latino Identities." In *Handbook for Hispanic Cultures in the United States*, ed. Felix Padilla, 257–91. Houston: Arte Publico Press.

——. 1993b. "Latino Church and Schools as Urban Battlegrounds." In *Urban Schooling in America*, ed. Stanley Rothstein, 245–70. Westport, Conn.: Greenwood Press.

Stevens-Arroyo, Anthony M., and Andrés I. Pérez y Mena, eds. 1995. *Enigmatic Powers: Syncretism with African and Indigenous Peoples' Religions Among Latinos*. The PARAL Series, vol. 3. Bildner Center Books: New York.

Stevens-Arroyo, Anthony M., Anneris Goris, Ariela Keysar, and Andras Tapolcai. 2002. *The PARAL Study: A Report on the National Survey of Leadership in Latino Parishes and Congregations*. New York: RISC.

Tomasi, Silvio. 1975. *Piety and Power: The Role of Italian Parishes in the New York Metropolitan Areas, l880–l930*. New York: Center for Migration Studies.

Torres, Rodolfo D., and George Katsiaficas, eds. 1999. *Latino Social Movements: Historical and Theoretical Perspectives*. New York: Routledge.

Tweed, Thomas A. 1997. *Our Lady of the Exile: Diasporic Religion at a Cuban Catholic Shrine in Miami*. New York: Oxford University Press.

Verba, Sidney, Kay Schlozman, and Henry Brady. 1995. *Voice and Equality*. Cambridge, Mass.: Harvard University Press.

Vidal, Jaime R. 1988. "Popular Religion Among the Hispanics in the General Area of the Archdiocese of Newark" Part 4 of *Nueva Presencia*, 235–348. Newark: Archdiocesan Office of Pastoral Planning.

Villafañe, Eldin. 1993. *The Liberating Spirit: Towrd an Hispanic American Pentecostal Social Ethic*. Grand Rapids, Mich: William B. Eerdmans.

Warner, R. Stephen, and Judith G. Wittner, eds. 1998. *Gatherings in Diaspora: Religious Communities and the New Immigration*. Philadelphia: Temple University Press.

Weber, David J. 1992. *The Spanish Frontier in North America*. New Haven, Conn.: Yale University Press.

Whalen, Carmen Theresa. 1998. "Bridging Homeland and Barrio Politics: The Young Lords in Philadelphia." In *The Puerto Rican Movement: Voices from the Diaspora*, ed. Andrés Torres and José E. Velázquez, 107–23. 1998. Philadelphia: Temple University Press.

Williams, Rhys H. 1996. "Religion as Political Resource: Culture or Ideology?" *Journal for the Scientific Study of Religion* 35, no. 4 (December): 368–78.

——. 2000. "Social Movements and Religion in Contemporary American Politics." In *Religion and American Politics: The 2000 Election in Context*, ed. Mark Silk, 52–62. Hartford, Conn.: The Pew Program on Religion and the News Media, Trinity College,

Wills, Garry. 1972. *Bare Ruined Choirs: Doubt, Prophecy, and Radical Religion*. New York: Delta Books.

Wood, Richard L. 1999. "Religious Culture and Political Action" *Sociological Theory* 17, no. 3 (November): 307–22.

NINE

U.S. LATINO EXPRESSIVE CULTURES

FRANCES R. APARICIO

CULTURAL EXPRESSION always involves more than simply artistic creation or entertainment. For politically subordinated groups like Latinos, cultural expressions help them acquire a sense of space and belonging within their local communities and in the larger, dominant society (See Roach 1995). Given the history of migration, displacement, and marginalization that many Latinos have faced in the United States, forms of expressive culture such as popular music, visual arts, performance arts, film, and literature have served as important sites for exploring bicultural identity, debates on representation, and the cultural agency and role in U.S. history of people of Latin American descent.

The historical and colonial relations of power that have characterized U.S.–Latin American relationships need to be considered in understanding the role of expressive cultures among Latinos in the United States. They have been displaced by the historical and economic forces of colonialism, capitalism, industrialization, and, most recently, the globalized economy. This displacement is experienced not only physically and geographically, as in the case of Puerto Rican migration or Mexican and Central American immigration, but also psychologically and culturally, as in the case of native-born Latinos and Latinas. U.S. schools and other dominant social, educational, political, and cultural institutions undermine culturally different behavior and traditions in the name of assimilation and Americanization. Thus, young Latinos have been dispossessed, to varying degrees, from their cultural heritage, be it language, rituals, cultural memories, or other forms through which all people reaffirm their social and cultural selves.

In this context, expressive cultures play multiple roles. The arts are not only entertainment, but also expressions through which U.S. Latinos, both as performers and as audience, can reconnect—either symbolically or through their bodies and senses—to their traditional cultures of origin, to their heritages and languages. Expressive cultures have offered Latinos in the United States a space for collective identification and self-recognition in the larger context of their invisibility within the dominant society.

Expressive cultures also serve to reactivate Latinos' memories of cultural traditions by integrating many of the elements of history, identity, and self that the process of cultural colonization has fragmented. As Juan Gutiérrez, the director of a Puerto Rican folkloric musical group in New York, has stated, the teaching, performance, and recovery of Afro–Puerto Rican folkloric music in New York, among U.S. Puerto Ricans in particular, exemplifies the recuperative role of music for a community whose members have lived under constant symbolic and material attacks as a racial minority (WBGH 1993). Likewise, a Mexican American woman from San Antonio, Texas, who has been an active participant in the tradition of the *pastorelas*, a representation of the Nativity scene, has expressed the central role that local cultural performances play in establishing a collective memory for her community:

> We need our traditions to be noticed here in America and here in our nation. I mean, we can't lose them along the way, you know. Striving to go forward, yes, I mean, technology brings us forward and everything, but we can't lose where we came from, it's very important, and that's why I stay, too. Like I said, it comes from education. We have to preserve what's ours. Yes, go forward and be a united nation, but also don't forget where you came from.
>
> *(quoted in Flores 1997: 124)*

Elsie's words illustrate the strong awareness among Latinos of the importance of reaffirming cultural memory through expressive cultures. For her, the *pastorelas* not only reconnect local Mexican Americans to their past and to Mexican folklore—that is, they create a continuity in memory and serve as an educational tool—but they also serve to diminish the dehumanizing and fragmentary aspects of modern society, particularly the impact of technology. Although Latino cultures are not necessarily antithetical to the technologies of modernity, and indeed many Latino artists and writers have capitalized on new technologies, Elsie's comment illustrates what Stuart Hall has argued is the recuperative mode of producing cultural identity, a process that offers "a way of imposing an imaginary coherence on the experience of dispersal and fragmentation, which is the history of all enforced diasporas" (Hall 1990: 224). Through these "imaginative rediscoveries" of "essential identities" that take place through the recovery and reconstruction of the past, Latinos in the United States strengthen the connections between their own selves and their "expropriated" histories, silenced and taken away from them by dominant institutions.

Indeed, U.S. Latino expressive cultures offer alternative narratives in which the voices and perspectives silenced by dominant histories are foregrounded. For instance, Puerto Rican folkloric and urban working-class music, like *plenas* and salsa, and Mexican American *corridos* (ballads in the oral tradition that tell stories of local heroes and events), often relate stories of immigration, racism in the United States, and the vicissitudes of living subordinated by economic, social, racial, and cultural factors. These oral traditions express the point of view of the working-class and marginalized sectors. Afro-Caribbean and Chicano urban experiences are likewise revealed in the lyrics of rap, a musical form that represents historical continuities with both popular musical and deeply political forms of the Caribbean and African American experience. The Chicano murals in California and the Southwest visually document figures and important historical characters in Mexican and Mexican American history that have been systematically excluded from official U.S. history texts. They give visibility, through forms and figures, to the points of view of the local, disenfranchised communities and to the struggles waged against displacement, racism, and police brutality, on the very same public walls and spaces that witnessed such struggles. In Chicago, for instance, the Puerto Rican and Mexicano communities have produced a variety of murals throughout the city that recognize local and national heroes in their history. From local firemen represented as winged angels, to Chicano, Puerto Rican, and Latin American political figures such as César Chávez, Che Guevara, and Pedro Albizu Campos, these figures in the Chicago murals trigger a process of commemoration for their viewers. In New York City, memorial murals have emerged since the 1980s to remember the many local victims of police brutality and mourn the loss of local heroes.

In the literary realm, the ethnic memoir, the predominant genre in U.S. Latino literature, attempts to reclaim a past and a childhood not because they are "uniquely one's own" (Fox 1996) informed by the individualist ethics of Anglo-America, but instead because they claim a space for the local and collective presence of Latino cultures in the larger narrative of U.S. history. In addition, these autoethnographies—so called because they explore how the individual is continuously formed and informed by the history and political economy of local communities—document the myriad ways in which Latinos negotiate between or among two or more cultures. These narratives foreground not only the participation and contributions of the communities to the making of the United States, but also explore instances of resistance and the reaffirmation of cultural difference. From young, female narrators such as

Sandra Cisneros's Esperanza (1989) and Nicholasa Mohr's Nilda (1973), to the highly male-centered narratives about growing up Latino and male in the barrio—for instance, Piri Thomas (1967) and Luis Rodríguez (1993)—these voices, read together, serve as alternative narratives that demand recognition of the significance of everyday Latino lives in the public sphere of literature.

However, as Latinos become increasingly integrated into U.S. institutions, and as large conglomerates and the mainstream media begin to act as the sole producers of the arts, film, and popular music, the alternative values of these expressive cultures are not as clearly delineated as in the past, when cultural productions remained at the margins of the industry and were still predominantly under the control of individual artists, writers, filmmakers, and local producers. Many cultural expressions have been transformed from local, community rituals to nationally visible expressions or to official folklore for tourist consumption, a process of recontextualization that inevitably alters their original meanings, their ideal audiences, and the social and cultural interpretations made possible by the texts and their contexts.

By the turn of the twenty-first century, the expression of U.S. Latino cultures have shifted, and they represent a much more diverse array of perspectives about what it means to be of Latin American descent within the United States. Factors such as the mainstreaming of expressive cultures, the increasing presence and power of a Latino bourgeois sector within the United States, the diversification of experiences related to social class, immigration, generational differences, race, gender, and sexuality, among other factors, have led to a much more complex repertoire of expressive cultural texts and productions. Thus, while many cultural texts continue to play an important rôle in decolonization, as previously discussed, it is also true that the positions represented in Latino expressive cultures have become much more divergent and heterogeneous as diverse artists, musicians, filmmakers, and writers position themselves individually in their explorations of their bicultural identities.

Historically speaking, Latino arts and cultural texts have shifted because of the different positions from which they have emerged. This essay explores these transformations, as Latino expressive cultures move from the margins of the dominant U.S. society during the 1960s and 1970s into an increasing integration within U.S. industries. A process of co-optation has been evident as oppositional expressions become absorbed by industry or institutions, thus neutralizing their radical content. Yet as co-optation takes place, new forms of resistance emerge from the ground up. If a growing awareness of multiculturalism during the 1980s had a tremendous impact on the increasing acceptability and consumerism of Latino identities and cultures, at the same time it limited the degree and transformed the expressions of political opposition that were present in the 1960s and 1970s. During the 1990s, a globalized music and literary market, for instance, made possible the national and international visibility of a select number of Latino musicians, actors and actresses, and writers. Yet this boom, motivated by an increasing consumer power among U.S. Latinos, has not necessarily translated into social equity and empowerment for the larger Latino population in the country. How, then, do Latino expressive cultures continue to address issues of self-empowerment for their primary audiences while addressing the cultural needs and desires of larger, intercultural, and even non-Latino audiences?

An overview of the various forms of Latino expressive culture, as these have emerged, developed, and been consumed and received by both Latinos and non-Latinos since 1965, will shed light on the complex ways in which these expressive cultures serve as sites from which to explore negotiations about identity, power, and history. They are located in shifting dialectics between resistance and consent, between reaffirming cultural differentiation and the constant pressure for integration into U.S. society. The fact that many of these cultural texts explore Latino hybrid identities suggests that Latino expressive cultures have played a major role in the ways in which Latinos themselves define their identities, and these expressions also provide insight into the processes through which the dominant society has represented Latinos.

THE STRUGGLES OVER REPRESENTATION

When Brazilian actress, dancer, and singer Carmen Miranda came to the United States in the 1930s, her body, her accent, and her fruit basket together became the principal markers of the ways in which Hollywood objectified and made exotic the cultures from "south of the border" (Aparicio and Chávez-Silverman 1997: 1–7). Both Miranda and Desi Arnaz served as "the foundational images" for dominant representations of Latinos in the United States (Sandoval-Sánchez 1999: 21–61). Social critics have argued that these egregious stereotypes represent a continuation of the political conflicts between Spain and England during the sixteenth and seventeenth centuries and of the definitions of Latin America in U.S. expansionist projects, such as Manifest Destiny (Kanellos 1998: 12–142). From Disney's *Three Caballeros* in the 1940s, which articulated the politics of the hemispheric Good Neighbor policy, a precedent to today's globalization, to more recent, still highly egregious yet contradictory examples of Latin stereotypes in media—the scene of Selma Hayek dancing barefoot in the kitchen and sitting in the toilet in *Fools Rush In*, the Taco Bell chihuahua, the prototypes of love and violence in *Desperado*, and the collective gaze and fixation on Jennifer López's butt, recently regendered by Ricky Martin's own pelvic movements—the representations of Latinos both by dominant institutions and, at least in part, by cultural insiders continue to trivialize the contributions of our communities to the United States. If, as Stuart Hall has argued, identity is contingent on representation, then Latino identity in the public space continues to be partly informed by these stereotypical constructions. These images tend to be much more accessible and disseminated throughout the United States and globally than the cultural representations that U.S. Latinos have constructed for themselves. That Latinos, in contrast to Anglos and other European ethnic groups, do not have alternative images to counteract the negative, exoticized, or stereotypical ones, is an essential component of understanding why these images are so highly contested.

For example, a discussion of the representation of Puerto Ricans in the popular TV show *Seinfeld* and the ensuing controversy and responses regarding the 1998 Puerto Rican Day Parade sheds light on the relations between media images and Latino cultural expressions, as well as on the role of expressive cultures in contesting dominant stereotypes. In May 1998, *Seinfeld*'s second-to-last episode depicted Jerry and his friends stuck in a major traffic jam due to the congestion caused by the Puerto Rican Day Parade in New York City. Kramer, at one point, accidentally sets the Puerto Rican flag on fire and, in order to put it out, he stomps on it, angering the Puerto Ricans around him. At one point a crowd of Puerto Ricans, referred to as a "mob," tries to push their car to the side, an act that, as one of the protagonists puts it, "happens everyday in Puerto Rico." In an Internet survey by Latino Link (1998) following the episode, numerous viewers shared their reactions to this media representation of Puerto Ricans and to a statement by William Santiago (1998) asking the networks for a public apology. While the episode evoked public outcries over the disrespect and the caricature-like image with which Puerto Ricans were depicted, the network insisted that they did not feel they had insulted or stereotyped the community.

While some Puerto Ricans felt that the show had been innocuously humorous, most of those surveyed agreed to boycott the program and were able to articulate a historical perspective on the politics of representation for U.S. Puerto Ricans. It is significant that many respondents referred to *West Side Story* as the film that had helped to fix dominant constructions of Puerto Ricans in the United States, a sort of representational watershed from which it has been difficult to disengage. That in 1998, forty years after *West Side Story*, the media would still not recognize the problematic politics behind the *Seinfeld* episode, speaks to the lingering cultural segregation in this society. As Manuel Mirabal, president of the Puerto Rican National Coalition, commented, "Obviously they [the media executives] are on another planet to believe no one would be offended" (Associated Press 1998).

Both William Santiago's statement and Mirabal's response allude to the core of this controversy. Given the invisibility of Puerto Ricans in the dominant media, the representational choice by *Seinfeld*'s writers was extremely significant. As Raúl Yzaguirre, president of the National Council of La Raza, commented at the time, "The image of a mob vandalizing Seinfeld's car may be the only one NBC audiences will have of Puerto Ricans after Thursday night's episode" (Associated Press 1998). Finally, the fact that the *Seinfeld* episode is set during the Puerto Rican Day Parade in New York City trivialized the forty-year tradition of this public event. This event has symbolically and physically allowed Puerto Ricans to appropriate the public space of the city and become its protagonists for one day in a cultural performance and in a performance of culture, one of the most important symbolic achievements for Puerto Ricans in the United States. This annual public display serves as a ritual of renewal and hope for the community, as it has been described:

> It was a joyous occasion and a vibrant parade, with drum majorettes dressed like Middle Americans but moving to syncopated Caribbean rhythms exemplifying the mix of North and Latin American that is today's "Nuyoricans," or New York Ricans. As the marchers made their way up Fifth Avenue past Rockefeller Center, little girls in red, white, and blue waved Puerto Rican flags from their fathers' shoulders in time to the salsa beat. "We are here to show our pride in being Puerto Rican and to celebrate our culture," one man in the crowd explained as others nodded agreement. "We are *both* Americans *and* Puerto Ricans."
>
> *(Winn 1992: 579)*

Seinfeld's episode "wiped that record away in 15 minutes" (Associated Press 1998). For Jerry and his friends, the parade was reduced to another daily urban nuisance, traffic congestion, and one exacerbated by the anger of the passers-by. This discrepancy over the meaning of the parade reveals that there is very little space for intercultural understanding or, at least, tolerance, on the part of television writers. Most revealing, however, is that two years after the episode, Anne Peyton Bryant, a white woman who was one of a number of female victims of sexual assaults by a group of young males in Central Park during the Puerto Rican Day Parade of 2000, invoked the *Seinfeld* episode to refer to the violence that society could expect from this particular event. This statement was made during an interview on the *Geraldo Rivera Show* on 13 June 2000. While the central issue at hand was the sexism, the violence against women, and the indifference of the New York police agents to these attacks, all of which revealed the insensitivity of our society to women's safety, Ms.

Peyton Bryant's comment clearly evinced the long-term impact that the *Seinfeld* show had on Anglo and non-Latino viewers regarding Latinos as criminals and inherently violent. On 16 June, in contesting Ms. Peyton's statements and the criminalizing discourse around Puerto Ricans, the National Congress for Puerto Rican Rights issued a statement denouncing the Central Park attackers, the abuse against women, and the racist assumptions of the news and media accounts that associated these crimes with the Puerto Rican Day Parade (National Congress for Puerto Rican Rights 2000).

The protest over this episode and the ensuing discourse reveals the historical continuity with which dominant media have shaped and controlled images of Latinos and Latin Americans or have outright excluded them from the screen. It also suggests that dominant forms of Latino representation supersede Latino accounts of themselves and their expressive cultures in the formation of the popular imagination in this country. That most Latinos made reference to *West Side Story* on the e-mail responses to the *Seinfeld* episode and did not include, for instance, Latino theater in the 1960s and 1970s as an alternative cultural expression, reveals that both Latino and non-Latino audiences use dominant media, rather than Latino expressive cultures, as their primary agents for cultural referencing. While many U.S. Latino cultural expressions, performances and texts attempt to question dominant notions about Latinos, their existence does not preclude the impact that dominant images continue to have on how Latinos see themselves. Indeed, the impact of dominant images on the ways in which young Latinos define themselves and valued their identity, culture, language, and heritage was a major concern that fueled the oppositional Chicano and Nuyorican poetry of the 1960s and 1970s.

CULTURAL NATIONALISM IN THE EAST AND THE WEST: PERFORMING OPPOSITIONAL IDENTITIES

When the Chicano poet Alurista published *Floricanto en Aztlán* in 1971, he defied the dominant dictates of Anglo publishing houses that had rejected his manuscript because it mixed English and Spanish. This linguistic hybridity, to be sure, was only a euphemism for the rejection of the significantly radical voices that Alurista's performative and political poetry represented. The alternation of English, Spanish, Nahuatl, and black English, the diverse linguistic registers and local dialects in the poems, challenged the monolingual assumptions of U.S. editorial practices at the time, assumptions that, despite the increasing public presence of Spanish in media, advertising, and literary markets twenty years later, still permeate attitudes and policy making in major institutions. That *Floricanto en Aztlán* was ultimately published by the UCLA Chicano

Research Center suggests that the U.S. literary institutions never really opened up to the particular literary production of this politically effervescent period.

Because of its oppositionality and the articulation of an ideology of Chicano cultural nationalism, this particular literary corpus and period remain relatively ignored by the general public. Cultural nationalism for Chicanos in the west and Southwest and for Nuyoricans in the east strongly opposed the racism, the exclusion from power and institutions, and the silencing of the history of Mexican Americans and U.S. Puerto Ricans from official texts. In order to oppose the forces of Americanization, assimilation, and outright racism implemented through education, federal laws, land ownership, the political economy of the barrios, criminal laws, and the justice system, among other sources, members of the Chicano and Nuyorican movements not only denounced the inhumanity of Anglo America, but also reaffirmed, through symbols, language, music, and the arts, the Mexicanness and the Afro–Puerto Rican and indigenous aspects of these two communities in the United States. For example, the concepts of "Aztlán" and "Borinquen"—both references to mythical historical homelands—respectively, reaffirmed the notion of a geocultural territory that marked the origins of Chicano and Puerto Rican history and identity through the recovery or invention of indigenous myths and stories. Cultural nationalism thus became a movement that constructed a particular, essential, and collective identity that activists argued was needed to decolonize and motivate members of the larger community to become more active in fighting the system.

However, as critics have written, this essentialism became one of the major failures of cultural nationalism. On both coasts, the recuperative project of cultural reaffirmation and preservation weakened the potential for social change because cultural nationalism limited its audiences and potential identifications (Klor de Alva 1998: 70). While it is true that cultural essentialism limited the impact of the Chicano and Nuyorican movements because it excluded women, gay and lesbian individuals, and others who may not have identified with the mostly working-class, male, and nationalist perspectives forwarded by this position, it is also true that this literary production did engage in critically questioning official history, as in the case of the colonial relations between the United States and Puerto Rico or the silenced contributions of migrant workers in the labor force of the United States. Some rereadings of this literary corpus suggests that Chicano and Nuyorican artists, writers, and intellectuals at the time were aware of the challenges of addressing multiple, heterogeneous identities and creating potential interracial coalitions, at least in their symbolic language. A clear example of this intercultural dialogue was Carlos Santana's Chicano rock, which was centrally informed by Afro-Caribbean rhythms and musical forms.

It can also be argued that the national myths of origin for Chicanos and Puerto Ricans were necessary first steps in the development of a decolonizing cultural politics. For cultures under attack by the dominant society and systematically invisible in it, the challenge of analyzing internal cultural differences and acknowledging internal hybridity may have been a political risk at a time when members of these movements were being policed and investigated, arrested and killed. It also may have represented a symbolic risk at a time when collective mobilization was essential for attracting the attention of the media and major institutions such as the schools and city and federal governments. While these movements may have relied too heavily on essentialist notions of identity and on mythical versions of history, it is also true that cultural nationalism, especially in its symbolic forms, partly succeeded in empowering subordinated Mexican Americans and U.S. Puerto Ricans by offering a historical corrective to their invisibility in U.S. society. By offering a social vision that relocated their identities and "home" within themselves and the barrio rather than outside of themselves—as dominant society attempts through assimilation—this period of activism and artistic production provided hope and a source of empowerment for the dispossessed. While in the twenty-first century cultural nationalism would fail even to recognize the internal diversity of the U.S. Latino population, the act of reading this literary production still empowers many young Latinos across the country who are striving to identify with what they read. In this sense, it still serves as an educational decolonizing tool.

From the mid-1960s through the 1970s, Chicano literature, music, and arts and Nuyorican poetry, music, and theater, emerged in the specific context of political struggles and mobilization. In the west, César Chávez's activism, the grape boycotts, the Delano March, and the development of the United Farm Workers, the Los Angeles School Blowouts, Reies Tijerina's radical opposition to the appropriation and occupation of Mexicans' lands in New Mexico, and Corky Gonzales's Crusade for Justice in Denver, Colorado, all marked the particular style, language, and ideologies of Chicano literary production (See David Gutiérrez, chapter 1, this volume). Alurista's performative and political poetry was composed for and recited and widely performed during marches, boycotts, and rallies. The Actos by the Teatro Campesino—one-act plays written collectively—emerged as a tool for raising political consciousness among the farm workers. And the pinto poetry—poetry written by Chicano prison inmates such as Raúl Salinas—denounced the injustices of the legal system against the Chicano male. "El Louie," an archetypically ironic and defiant poem by José Montoya, articulated the experiences and cultural contradictions experienced by the pachuco. The pachuco period was informed by an aesthetics of style and surface that allowed these young, urban, zoot-suited

Mexican Americans to redefine and reaffirm their marginalized identities in the urban centers of the west and Southwest (mostly Los Angeles and El Paso). Chicano murals emerged also in the midst of urban struggles, struggles that expressed opposition to the dislocation of Chicano neighborhoods and communities due to highway construction, police brutality, and urban neglect. Numerous didactic murals attempted to create consciousness by depicting the figures of significant historical heroes and mythical figures, from Moctezuma to Zapata, from César Chávez to la Virgen de Guadalupe, and by involving the youth in the collective making of the murals themselves. Agency and dignity were reclaimed in these vivid depictions of Mexican and Mexican American participation in world, Latin American, and U.S. histories while simultaneously appropriating the walls and public spaces within the barrios and cities.

The multilayered conflicts embedded in these murals are revealed in the historical shifts they have undergone. For instance, Willie Herón's *The Wall That Cracked Open*, first painted in 1972 in East Los Angeles, was recently unveiled and reconstructed after it had been whitewashed. In Lansing, Michigan, a mural originally painted in the 1970s by the Centro Renacimiento collective was discovered in 2000 as a restaurant owner demolished a second wall in the process of renovation. That these murals had been physically erased, through whitewashing, by superimposing walls, and even by other Chicano artists as part of city-led efforts at graffiti blasting, exemplifies the struggles over representation and public space that Latinos continue to face. Their survival can also be seen as a sign of Latino strength and persistence in the face of historical and political challenges.

In New York, the Young Lords Party also worked hand in hand with artists, musicians, and poets in the creation of social consciousness to fight racism and colonialism. Salsa music from the early 1970s—such as that of Eddie Palmieri, Willie Colón, and Héctor Lavoe—evinces strong voices and compelling lyrics reaffirming the African heritage of Puerto Rican culture, denouncing U.S. colonialism, and reaffirming the popular image of the Puerto Rican male as the cultural hero of the community in his confrontation with the dominant system. Salsa musicians such as Charlie Palmieri and others were also active in community workshops, educating Puerto Rican youth about their musical heritage as a corrective to the assimilationist educational system. In 1975, Nuyorican poets Miguel Algarín and Miguel Piñero established the Nuyorican Poet's Cafe as an alternative venue for the performance of minority and subordinate cultures. Poems such as Miguel Piñero's "A Lower East Side Poem" (1978) and Pedro Pietri's "Puerto Rican Obituary" (1973) denounced Anglo capitalism and imperialism while reaffirming a new, hybrid cultural identity rooted in the urban plight of the New York barrios. A poetry that was conscientiously articulated in antibourgeois aesthetics—that deployed the imagery of the neglected and deplorable conditions of the neighborhoods, such as cockroaches, tar, lack of heating, blades, and drugs—it claimed a space of its own at a time when there were no poetic voices representing that world.

In "speaking truth to power," this strong denouncement, however, was accompanied by a utopian view that found hope under the bleak living conditions of racism and economic neglect. Encapsulated at the end of Pietri's poem in the phrase "Aquí to be called negrito / means to be called LOVE," this tone also underscored the reaffirmation of the Lower East Side as a new geocultural space where hybrid, Nuyorican identities found a home. The ideal audience for this literary corpus was not the Anglo "other," but the Puerto Rican working poor in New York. Like their Chicano counterparts, these texts—musical, visual, or verbal—were directed primarily to the Latino residents of the barrios, although they mostly circulated among intellectuals. They served to create political and social consciousness and mobilization, although their distribution was limited at the time. In order to achieve this, they constructed a fixed and clear binary between the humanitarian Latino cultures and the dehumanized Anglo capitalist society, as seen in Alurista's *Floricanto en Aztlán.* Yet they powerfully critiqued the colonized minds of our own communities—as in Miguel Algarín's "Mongo Affair" (1978) or Pietri's "Puerto Rican Obituary,"—as both are calls to dismantle the internalized materialist values that capitalism has engendered.

Theater was also an important literary genre on both coasts. Drama and staged performances have been central to Latino expressive cultures since Luis Valdez first worked with the farm workers in developing the Actos—short agitprop dramatic pieces that enacted the conflicts and power dynamics between growers and workers, the oppressors and the oppressed, and explored possibilities for liberation and social change (see Valdez 1990). This theater was fueled by a strong legacy of indigenous rituals; a strong historical tradition of religious dramas, such as the *pastorelas* (shepherd plays); popular theater; and social critique in Mexico and the Southwest. For instance, the Mexican popular traditions of *carpas* and *tandas* served as traveling comedy and entertainment that addressed local and national issues through satire, parody, or humor. These were oppositional performances aimed at the popular masses.

The political aims of the emerging Chicano movement were enhanced and disseminated through staged performances. The Actos, the later work of the Teatro Campesino, student theater groups, and other community-based popular theater (for example, Teatro de la Esperanza and Teatro Libertad) were deployed as didactic tools for creating consciousness and eventual empowerment. Again, the ideal audiences were the local and regional Latino communities who were exhorted into social awareness and political and cultural activism through these texts. As Alberto Sandoval-Sánchez has summarized, "Actos: Inspire the audience to social action. Illuminate specific points about social problems. Satirize the opposition. Show or hint at a solution. Express what people are feeling" (Sandoval-Sánchez 1999: 105).

In New York City, likewise, community-based theater groups emerged during the 1970s. Some, like Pregones, established in 1979 by Rosalba Rolón and other Puerto Rican actors and actresses, have worked with the Puerto Rican and Latino communities in the Bronx, doing presentations for the schools and for local audiences that integrated popular traditions, oral tradition, and working-class expressions. Other theater groups wrote using the social conditions of the community itself as the bases for their scripts. Issues such as migration, the struggles of adapting to the United States, unemployment, linguistic colonialism and the imposition of English, gender and family conflicts, domestic violence, and AIDS and health concerns have all been addressed by these groups in the process of "community empowerment" (Winn 1992: 584). These dramatic traditions, then, should not be considered uniquely entertainment, but rather alternative forms of political, social, and cultural mobilization that were strongly informed by Latin American political theater, the Cuban Revolution, and Brechtian innovations in drama. Given their marginality and limited economic resources, many of these theater groups disappeared, while others have developed into larger companies. However, if, as Alberto Sandoval-Sánchez (1999) reminds us, Latino theater moved "from community-building into entertainment" in the 1980s and 1990s, it is also true that new forms of theatrical performance—for example, the solo performance artist—will emerge and counteract the mainstreaming tendency of the 1980s to, in turn, be co-opted over time.

BETWEEN ABSORPTION AND DIFFERENCE: THE FAILED DECADE OF THE HISPANIC

Chicana scholar Yolanda Broyles-González (1986) writes that the 1980 Teatro Campesino production, *El fin del mundo*, marked their last performance as a collective theater and signaled Luis Valdez's entry into Hollywood and Broadway and the eventual demise of El Teatro Campesino as a collective. This occurrence signals a partial shift from the alternative spaces of community arts to the mainstream, individualist logic of art as a commodity. This shift, in terms of process of production, ideal audiences, and institutional spaces, is indicated by the contrast between the early Actos and the musical entitled *Corridos* (Broyles-Gonzáles 1986: 179). In fact, the collective cultural work of the 1970s subsided into the mainstreaming tendency informed by the political context of the 1980s: the Reagan/Bush years, the wars in Central America, and the self-proclaimed decade of the "Hispanic." Yet while some cultural productions, such as Teatro Campesino and the visual arts, moved toward mainstreaming and dominant audiences, indeed complying with the politics behind the homogenizing, government-imposed term "Hispanic," this does not automatically imply that contestatory ideologies altogether disappeared.

Inserting their work in more mainstream venues—some theater on Broadway, some films in Hollywood, the first Hispanic Arts Exhibit, and *salsa romántica*—meant that many Latino cultural authors had to negotiate in more subtle ways the contradictory needs of ideal Anglo and Latino audiences. These artists also came from different social and class experiences and educational backgrounds, which, in many cases, differed from the marginal identities and self-taught formations of the authors, writers, and artists of the 1960s and 1970s. The local, community-based languages that were used in expressive venues in the 1970s—the Spanglish, colloquialisms, slang, and regionalisms—shifted mainly to English, a change that accommodated a diversity of audiences but also represented the dominant language of the cultural producers of the 1980s, mostly second-generation Latinos who had been the recipients of affirmative action and had been schooled in English. The production of murals in public spaces began to shift to the private realm of museums, where Latino visual arts assumed a new value as an individual, bourgeois commodity rather than as a collective, community-building process. In turn, salsa music was commodified by the Cuban American music industry in Miami. *Salsa romántica* was a nonpolitical, romantic trend in salsa that homogenized the strident sounds of the 1970s and replaced the oppositional lyrics with romantic formulas and individually based love songs that served as background music for dancing and entertainment.

Yet this partial mainstreaming, which represented one strain of cultural production, did not lead exclusively to a systematic shift in ideologies. While the hard-core, masculinist salsa of the barrio was being displaced by the homogenizing, more commercial *salsa romántica* in the 1980s, artists such as Willie Colón—nicknamed El Malo (the bad guy) in the 1970s—and Rubén Blades continued to compose and record songs with relevant and timely lyrics, such as "Tiburón" (The shark) and "Siembra" (Sowing), songs that, respectively, denounced U.S. imperialism in Latin America and proposed utopian forms of social interaction. In view of the co-optation of salsa music by the conglomerates, it is not a coincidence that Latino rap and hip-hop styles became more popularized among the youth, who rejected salsa as the music of their parents.

After emerging in the 1970s as local forms of intercultural and interracial expression among African American, Puerto Rican, and Chicano urban youth, rap, break dancing, and hip-hop eventually also became commodified and produced by the large musical conglomerates. However, the voices of artists such as Mellow Man Ace, Kid Frost, Gerardo, Latin Empire, and others expressed strong critiques of U.S. society and continued to explore, in ways analogous to the interlingual poetry of the 1960s and 1970s, the diverse cultural and racial nature of Latino identity and collective self. In other words, in important ways the oppositionality of Chicano and Nuyorican poetry was continued in the discourse of rap. While certain cultural forms and expressions were being co-opted, other cultural expressions constantly emerged from the communities themselves, which counteracted the homogenizing tendencies of the former. As was true of other immigrant subcultures in the United States, Latino expressive cultures during the 1980s exhibited the effects of the push and pull of the forces of mainstreaming, integration, and institutionalization, on the one hand, and new and continuous oppositional forces, on the other, that explored new forms of identity and urged resistance to assimilation.

Yet Latino cultural productions during the 1980s also revealed a much more sophisticated, intercultural, and heterogeneous definition of collective identity than the cultural nationalism of the 1960s and 1970s had seemingly offered. As more Latinos began to write, perform, compose music, and paint, they began to speak to each other through cultural productions and performances, establishing internal critiques of older paradigms like cultural nationalism, embodying and celebrating the heterogeneity of the Latino community, and redefining identity as a process, a social construction rather than the product of fixed, essential being. First, the strong, radical critiques of Chicano cultural nationalism by Chicana feminists opened up new paths for understanding hybrid, postcolonial identities and questioned the male-centered utopian views of the Chicano cultural renaissance. Secondly, in the 1980s the public voice of a writer like Richard Rodríguez revealed that Latinos could be politically heterogeneous, as conservative, indeed, as their Anglo counterparts, who had been demonized by the cultural expressions of the 1970s. However, his classic *Hunger of Memory* (1982) ironically documents the personal experience of cultural and linguistic dispossession that the Chicano movements had so strongly struggled against.

While Chicano critics largely dismissed Rodríguez's autoethnographic narrative as the act of a *vendido* (sell out) and a problematic story of blind assimilation, in hindsight critics now see that Rodríguez's body, language, and personal choices were themselves products of the internal colonialism experienced by Mexican Americans, particularly during the 1950s before the institutional gains of the Civil Rights Movement. *Hunger of Memory*, then, exemplifies the ambiguities of the 1980s, a period marked by an apparent mainstreaming of many Latino productions, yet whose own internal conflicts and contradictions revealed the continuing colonizing processes that inform the everyday lives of Latinos and, more specifically, the fractured nature of Chicano history since World War II, if not before. The English-only movement—which emerged in Dade County in opposition to the official bilingualism that the Cuban exile community had effected—the emerging attacks against bilingual education exemplified in and mediated by Richard Rodríguez, and the growing anti-immigrant sentiment that led to California Propositions 187 and 209 in the 1990s were all in fact reactions to the demographic growth of Latinos, as much as to their increasing presence in the public spheres.

The 1980s and 1990s witnessed the largest influx of Latin Americans into the United States. This growth, with its concomitant diversification of the population's demographic profile, not only triggered reactionary and nativist attitudes against Latinos, but, most significantly, a growing awareness among Latinos themselves of their internal and growing heterogeneity. In this context, the emergence of a Cuban American literary corpus that expresses and effects a shift from Cuban-exile literature in Spanish to a literary identity more akin to ethnic Americans, particularly among women writers (see Rivero 1989; Torres 1986), exemplifies this tendency. This shift was partially informed by the internal racial and class transformations that the Cuban exiles unwittingly confronted as a result of the Mariel boatlifts. At this time, there is a growing interest among authors, musicians, and performance and visual artists to begin exploring the hybrid spaces of identity suggested by demographic changes, ideological transformations, and new identities in formation. These explorations, however, came to fruition in the early 1990s, particularly in the works of Latino performance artists such as Culture Clash and John Leguízamo, which I will discuss below.

Yet the internal critiques and gender bending of performance art would not have been possible without the pioneering work of Chicana writers and scholars, whose incisive gender critiques of Chicano cultural nationalism constituted the most significant development in literary and critical studies since the early 1980s. Authors such as Gloria Anzaldúa, Cherrie Moraga, and Chela Sandoval were pioneers in proposing new identity paradigms and models of solidarity that would cross racial, gender, class, and geographical boundaries. While the Chicano cultural renaissance and the Nuyorican movement marked a strong opposition to the dominant society in the 1970s, both largely ignored the gender inequities in U.S. society, as well as in their own communities. Cultural nationalism maintained women figures within the patriarchal paradigms inherited from Mexico, the Caribbean, and Latin America at large. Women characters and voices were either absent, secondary, or cast into stereotypes of the saintly mother or the whore. Most of the women who were writing or otherwise producing cultural expressions during the 1960s and 1970s were not recognized or published, although many of these artists actually provided leadership and vision to projects supposedly authored by men.

Chicana feminists such as Elizabeth Martínez, Magdalena Mora, Marta Cotera, and others objected to the masculinist tenets of the early Chicano movement. Criticism extended even to the otherwise venerated El Teatro Campesino, for, as Yolanda Broyles-Gonzalez writes, the tendency in theater history has been to "place individuals, usually male individuals" at the center of cultural productions, thus silencing the contributions of women and other members of these collectives and groups (1986: 163). Broyles-Gonzales argues that scholarship and cultural historiography erased the collective nature of these theater groups and, following the tenets of American individualism and Mexican patriarchy, associated these movements with individual Chicano men. As one of the actresses involved with the theater movement observed, it was El Teatro Campesino who created Luis Valdez, rather than the opposite. Broyles-Gonzales's work on El Teatro Campesino begins to rectify this pattern and reclaims the contributions of the many women who participated in its writing, composition, production, and performances. Her critique is a part of a larger revisionism of late-twentieth-century history. On the one hand, the gender critiques of the Chicano movement and the male-centered Chicano cultural renaissance proposed an epistemological critique that led to a profound revisionary movement among a growing number of Latino studies scholars in the 1980s and 1990s. On the other hand, they led to the leadership of Chicanas in the development of theories about third-world women and women of color in the United States and in the formation of theories about transnational, postcolonial identities and relationships. These critiques proved so powerful that they in turn helped to transform U.S. feminism and Latino studies as fields of inquiry.

During the second half of the 1980s, Chicana writers in particular emerged and gained visibility as cultural producers. Initially published either by their own independent presses, small feminist outlets, or Latino presses in the United States—Arte Público Press, Bilingual Review Press, Third Woman Press—Chicana poets, essayists, and fiction writers began to establish a strong presence in the literary world. The voices of Lorna Dee Cervantes, Bernice Zamora, Sandra Cisneros, Ana Castillo, Helena María Viramontes, Gloria Anzaldúa, Cherrie Moraga, and others have engaged readers in a doubled feminist and cultural critique: they denounced the patriarchy of the Chicano world and the Chicanas' systematic exclusion by Anglo, middle-class, white feminism. By foregrounding the economic, labor, social, cultural, and gendered contributions of mostly working-class Mexican American women to U.S. society and the development of a Chicano "familia" ("familia" as family and as metaphor for the larger cultural entity) and by exploring the multiple forms of oppression—based on class, gender, and sexuality—that they and their mothers and grandmothers experienced, these writers have been responsible for initiating one of the most dynamic and central literary and cultural bodies in Latino letters.

On the East Coast, the contestatory voices of Puerto Rican women writers such as Sandra María Esteves, Luz María Umpierre, Rosario Morales, and Judith Ortiz Cofer also provide a much-needed female alternative to the male-dominated Nuyorican corpus. Esteves has been officially included as one of the few female writers who were part of the Nuyorican movements during the 1970s, and, of those voices, only Esteves has had continued recognition as a published poet. Despite their diverse social experiences, U.S. Puerto Rican women writers have explored how Puerto Rican national identity has been historically represented through female figures and how migration has impacted the identities and social roles of Puerto Rican women. As they write about the many cultural and gender negotiations they have had to engage as first- or second-generation Puerto Ricans in the United States, their works offer feminist alternatives to the male-centered narratives of island-based authors who located the evils of immigration and displacement in the female body (such as René Marqués in *La carreta*) or who created exclusively male, homosocial worlds as their points of reference (Miguel Piñero's work comes to mind here).

Exploring the history and power dynamics of the border and south Texas, as well as the ensuing bicultural identities that emerged out of the U.S./Mexican historical conflict and political struggles, Gloria Anzaldúa's *Borderlands/La Frontera* (1987) represented a foundational text for border theory, hybridity, sexuality, and postcolonial studies. Aurora Levins Morales, her neighbor in Oakland, California, also proposed new paradigms that would transcend national boundaries, patriarchy, and cultural colonialism in the context of U.S. Puerto Ricans. In collaboration with her mother, Rosario Morales, Levins Morales, in *Getting Home Alive* (1986), explores the different historical experiences of mother and daughter, informed by migration, home, gender roles, racism, and social injustice. Both Rosario and Aurora also recognize and reflect on their own social and racial privileges. In the chapter entitled "Child of the Americas," Levins Morales reaffirms the hybrid nature of her multiple racial and cultural identities as a Jewish, North American, Puerto Rican woman. Like Anzaldúa's "new *mestiza*," these complex, multifaceted identities have emerged from the violence of colonial encounters in the contact zones of the Southwest and the colony of Puerto Rico. Morales and Morales also explore the multiple circulation of cultures by reconstructing the history of their Jewish and Puerto Rican ancestors, proposing new models of feminist solidarity that would do away with the masculine paradigms and the machismo embedded in Latin American socialism. Even class identity is relative and shifts from one generation to another, as mother and daughter narrate very different stories about growing up poor and middle-class on the island and on the mainland.

Although certain similarities can be discerned in the work of Chicana and U.S. Puerto Rican women writers, Chicana feminism stands in contrast to what became a largely middle- or upper-class, white, Caribbean Latina literary corpus in the 1990s (Esmeralda Santiago, Judith Ortiz Cofer, Aurora Levins Morales, Julia Alvarez, Cristina García, and Rosario Ferré). Many of these Latina writers represent the lives of middle-class, white Caribbean women in the United States, lives that validate in many ways the American Dream mythology. Chicana writers such as Cisneros (1989) and Castillo (1994), in contrast, propose social critiques of gender and culture that are informed by and deeply rooted in their experiences as working-class women of color. Indeed, Chicana literature differs significantly from the fictions of the authors mentioned above not only because they are rooted in the lives of working-class and working poor women, but because they sharply critique assimilation and the structural forms of racism and oppression as these are imposed on the bodies, psyches, and lives of working-class women of color. The works of Helena María Viramontes, for instance, in *Under the feet of Jesus* (1995) or "Cariboo Cafe" (1985) can only stand in sharp contrast to the world inhabited by Alvarez's García Girls (1991). Although the first two are narratives of immigration and foreground political refugees as protagonists, Alvarez's narrative of an upper-class, white Dominican woman does not even begin to scratch the surface of how class oppression, citizenship, and race are intertwined with the politics of gender.

In fact, the marketing in the 1990s of Caribbean Latina narratives of integration into U.S. society as "bestsellers" by New York literary agents and editors has co-opted the two central elements of oppositionality from Latino literature: gender and sexuality, as well as the form of the ethnic memoir. Marketing decisions, such as the inclusion of Rosario Ferré in the U.S. Latina literary corpus or the publicity built up around Julia Alvarez as "the" voice of Dominicanos in the United States, attest to the power of mainstream institutions in transforming and mediating the U.S. Latino literary canon. Few, if any, of the Chicano and Nuyorican poets of resistance ever signed contracts with the big publishing houses, and when they did they confronted major ideological conflicts regarding the editing, marketing, packaging, and representation of their work, as was the case for Martín Espada—which speaks strongly to the real effects of mainstreaming on the power of Latino cultural and ideological critiques.

The most dynamic illustration of expressive cultures' articulation of a new look at the growing diversity within the U.S. Latino community comes from comedy and performative work, especially that of John Leguízamo, whose scripts rewrite and challenge not only Latino national identities, but also traditional gender roles. Performance artists as diverse as Carmelita Tropicana, Mónica Palacios, Guillermo Gómez-Peña (1993, 1996), Culture Clash, and the Taco Shop Poets have developed a contestatory language about Latino invisibility in the media through performance arts. As diverse as this artistic form is, the solo and the group performances of these individuals reveal the need to move beyond traditional theater and comedy venues in order to create effective, original scripts that address the broad range of contemporary issues affecting U.S. Latinos. For instance, Guillermo Gómez-Peña, Coco Fusco (1995), and Roberto Sifuentes—in performances such as "Border Brujo" (1988–1989)—have explored the border as a concept through which one can examine bicultural identities and the ways in which Anglo society and the U.S. government have subordinated Mexicans through labor practices and public policy on immigration, language, race, and gender politics. Gender roles and sexuality have been equally foregrounded as categories of social and individual identities that need to be explored alongside national, racial, and ethnic identities. The works of queer performance artists, such as Carmelita Tropicana, Marga Gómez, and others, question dominant notions about Latina lesbians and propose new, oppositional views that foreground both the convergences and ruptures between sexuality and cultural identities (Arrizón 1999).

John Leguízamo's *Mambo Mouth*, performed in 1991 and released as a video in 1992, constitutes a radical critique of essentialized, national identities among Latinos, as well as of dominant views about them. Leguízamo has successfully maintained a progressive political stance while also accepting acting roles in Hollywood. *Mambo Mouth*, first aired by HBO in 1992, gave voice to the negative images that have been ascribed to Latinos, such as the prostitute, the Latin lover, and the "illegal" immigrant, thus demythifying and devaluing both the dominant notions of Latinos and the internal racism and hierarchies among Latinos themselves. Leguízamo's political comedy in *Mambo Mouth* stems from the heterogeneous Latino identities that the Colombian American comedian and writer performs. Capitalizing on a uniquely chameleonic talent for performing flowing identities, Leguízamo provocatively explores the diversification of Latinos in the United States and the internal conflicts among them, but he also highlights the collective oppression by racist structures and normative gender roles both "within" and "outside" the Latino sector. In vignettes full of fast-paced monologues, Leguízamo forces audiences to invert and dismantle stereotypes. For instance, the scripts for the Latin lover and for the Latina prostitute constantly remind the audience that their identities are based on exterior definitions rather than individual traits. The impact of language and images on the social attitudes toward these characters is reaffirmed through the self-parodic stance of the scripts and the nonverbal gestures Leguízamo employs, that is, the performative aspects of the body. Leguízamo constantly plays with definitions of cultural identity as fixed, biological essence in order to suggest its basis as a social construction. His vignette on the Latino/Japanese crossover is a complex, fascinating study on how Latinos perceive Asians as much as it is an examination of the nature of culture and of the culture of nature. Leguízamo performs a Latino who passes for Japanese in order to be acceptable to dominant U.S. society. To locate cultural identity as it is revealed on the body of the performer challenges audiences to reflect on the processes by which society subordinates individuals and on how definitions of culture take place on the very bodies of Latinos themselves.

Leguízamo's political oppositionality is most clearly seen in the vignette about the undocumented Latino who is arrested at La Guardia airport. His words address a dominant audience, threatening it with an inversion of the typical dominant/subordinate dyad. In this performance, Leguízamo compels audiences to imagine and engage with a future in which Latinos will be the majority and will push Anglos out of the United States and into Canada, making them "illegal" bodies in a foreign country. He also enumerates the contributions to the labor and economy of the United States that Latinos make, naming jobs that are as invisible as the bodies that perform them. Most interesting about this particular vignette is the denouncement of Latinos who are used as agents of the state, as the undocumented subject addresses the Latino border patrol agent who has imprisoned him. Recognition of diverse political positions within the Latino population became an increasingly important part of Latino cultural texts of the late 1980s, a set of narratives that began to construct a much more multilayered, contradictory, and ideologically heterogeneous profile of Latino identities in the United States. Leguízamo's skit and the larger body of his work speak directly to dominant U.S. institutions and to audiences who are complicit in national efforts to demonize and eject Latinos from the United States. John Leguízamo's exploration of traditional gender roles is as radical as his scathing critiques of the flaws in his own culture.

CROSSING OVER IN THE 1990S: TRANSNATIONAL IDENTITIES AND GLOBALIZATION

According to Alicia Gaspar de Alba (1998), the CARA Exhibit (Chicano Art: Resistance and Affirmation) that began in 1990 and ended in 1993 marked an important point in the cultural politics of Chicano art. First, it was an attempt to present a more politically authentic representation of Chicano art as it has developed since the heyday of the Chicano movement and as it has engaged the local communities from which it emerged, a perspective that was absent from the Hispanic Arts in the United States Exhibit during the 1980s. The 1980 exhibit in Washington, D.C., was based on the "Hispanic" paradigm and diluted the historical specificity of the visual arts of each national group. The CARA exhibit, in contrast, was planned precisely to show that Chicanos could enter the master's house—the spaces of the museum—without compromising the political critique inherent in their arts nor the specific political history that informed their artistic production.

This exhibit also demonstrated that Chicano visual artists themselves had very different views as to the political nature of their collective project. As Gaspar de Alba suggests, the various social and political positions of the artists, academics, and administrators involved in the planning of this event indicated that, by the late 1980s, Chicanos themselves could not be easily located as either inherently "oppositional" or "integrationist," to put it in schematic terms. While the "veteranos stressed an essentialized level" of Chicano identity as determined by "differences without and similarities within its community," the "new kids on the block" (feminists, gays, and lesbians) advocated an "Americanized level of representation in which Chicano/a identity extends outside of its essentialist demarcations and finds affinity with political crosscurrents in mainstream culture, particularly issues of gender, sexuality and artistic license that actually oppose the 'essential' Chicano identity" (Gaspar de Alba 1998: 101). The long discussions and difficult negotiations that took place within and among the various planning committees, between Chicanos and Anglos, and among Chicanos of different generational, gender, and ideological positions, illustrate how heterogeneous Chicano artists had become by the late 1980s and early 1990s. While the CARA Exhibit successfully reclaimed, reaffirmed, and relocated Chicano political and cultural oppositionality in the hallowed spaces of a museum and a dominant society intent on diluting the political effervescence of the past, it was also significantly contained by the very politics of funding, administration, and museum policies, which were fueled by the conservative national politics arrayed against the arts and minorities and informing cultural politics in the United States at the end of the 1980s.

As a cultural event of national magnitude, the CARA exhibit exemplified the dilemmas facing producers of Latino expressive culture in the 1990s. This decade evinced an increasing contradiction and gap between the integration of minority cultures into dominant institutions under the politics of "multiculturalism" and the simultaneous processes of cultural marginalization and subordination of U.S. Latinos in the legal and public-policy realms, which were evident in the campaigns to abolish bilingual education and affirmative action. Internally, the 1990s also posed a challenge to Latinos themselves as they grappled with increasingly complex issues of individual and collective identity. By the 1990s, the three principal groups–Mexican Americans, U.S. Puerto Ricans, and Cuban Americans—faced local, regional, and national demographic diversification as a result of the migratory flux of the 1980s, as well as an increasing class differentiation. As always, U.S.-born Mexican Americans, many of whose families have lived in the Southwest for generations, were being conflated with recent immigrants, undocumented workers, and non–English speakers. In New York City, Puerto Ricans lost their primary place as the largest Latino group and began to confront new social realities as they adjusted to the growing presence of Dominicans, Colombians, other South Americans, and, particularly, indigenous Mexican immigrants from Oaxaca. Cuban Americans in Miami now have to share their public identity and political privileges with Nicaraguans, Salvadorans, and myriad South Americans, not to mention the working-class, poor, and Afro-Cuban refugees who continue to arrive on the coasts of Florida. How then do Latinos now reconcile the history of their own political and social struggles as domestic minorities and the collective memory of the civil-rights struggles with immigrants whose historical memory resides outside the U.S. borders? How can expressive cultures speak to the ongoing colonial politics of the United States without eliding the new realities of the circulation of identities, cultures, peoples, and capital between the United States and their original countries in Latin America? In short, how can Latinos as ethnic minorities speak for other Latinos as immigrants? Can expressive cultures continue to serve as a symbolic space of belonging for such diverse social and historical subjects?

Throughout the first half of the 1990s, the paradigm of multiculturalism impacted all spheres of the arts in the United States, and since then a clear trend emerged in which "Latino culture" enjoyed a new vogue. Mainstream acceptance of all things Latino was manifest in a number of areas: Latino arts and installations in museums; the use of Latin popular music in TV ads; the use of Spanish and Spanglish in the advertising industry; and Latino writers signing major contracts with the New York literary establishment, as each press selected one or two writers as their multicultural icons. In 1988, rewarming an old trope, *Time* proclaimed that Hispanic culture was "break[ing] out of the barrio" and announced the impending, yet already cemented, mainstreaming of U.S. Latinos, from fashion designers to actors and actresses, from musicians such as Celia Cruz to the growing audibility of Spanglish in U.S. cities. This phenomenon preceded and anticipated an even more visible "Latin boom" in the late 1990s (*Time* 1988).

Multicultural practices in education and the arts did more than acknowledge Latinos; they also catered to the aesthetic, cultural, and educational needs of the dominant society. How, then, do Latino artists negotiate the pressure to write and produce for larger mainstream audiences instead of exclusively for an ideal audience of other Latinos, as the writers of the 1970s set out to do within the complex "freedom" of their marginality? How can they develop and maintain their own sense of cultural and political oppositionality and difference when they are inserted in dominant venues and mediated by Anglo agendas? As Chicano artist Malaquías Montoya asked about the CARA artists:

> "What became of those commitments and what caused their modification? Could it be that the same system, which was opening the museum doors and at the same time planning the overthrow of Allende in Chile had changed? Or was it the artists who had started to change? Had Chicano artists really not understood that the system that supported apartheid in South Africa and at the same time provided funds for the advancement of Chicano liberation had something up its sleeve? A system that feeds with one hand and strangles with the other?"
>
> *(quoted in Gaspar de Alba 1998, 99)*

Indeed, Latino identity politics and oppositionality in the 1990s contested the systematic racism and colonization in the legal and political realms, such as anti-immigration policies, anti–affirmative action policies, anti–bilingual education policies, further economic stratification, an increase in drop-out rates due to educational crises in the public school systems, revolving-door policies at the workplace, and antiunion tactics. As Montoya (quoted in Gaspar de Alba 1998) so trenchantly noted, in the midst of deepening systematic inequities in American society, a central issue was how Latinos would react to their perceived mainstreaming in the popular imagination of the United States. The question became one of reconciling growing media visibility and the sexual objectification of pop singers with a continuing and systematic exclusion from television and the body politic. Other pressing questions loom: Where can Latinos locate their agency at this time? Will Latino transnational experiences dilute or revitalize the traditional discourses around Latino cultures and identities?

In an effort to at least speculate about possible answers to these questions, the last section of this essay will examine three case studies of Latino expressive cultures: the musical career of slain Tejana singer Selena and the more general question of the role of Latino singers as cultural heroes for their local and regional communities; the Latin-music boom and the crossover dilemma; and the multimedia project of *Americanos*, led by Mexican American actor and cultural activist Edward James Olmos. Together, these three examples elucidate the processes by which Latino cultural expressions continue to function as sites of resistance, negotiation, and even outright oppositionality at the turn of the new century. In response to the increasing public perception of Latinos as foreigners and "illegal" immigrants, the result of anti-immigration policy and sentiments, the question of belonging in the United States has been a central one. Yet, as most Latino singers and actors evince, integration is neither smooth nor unidirectional; it is a process fraught with contradictions. For instance, the bicultural Tejana identity of Selena, or the ways in which U.S. citizens such as Ricky Martin are labeled as musicians "crossing over," exemplify the ways in which Latino cultural agents negotiate their own sense of belonging with dominant notions about Latinos as cultural others.

CULTURE, AGENCY, AND BELONGING

Killed in 1995 by the president of her fan club, Selena Quintanilla Pérez, known simply as Selena, became an icon of Tex-Mex border culture, Latina sexuality and sensuality, and the promise and possibilities of a Latina artist crossing over to a non-Latino market. While Selena established herself in her lifetime as a central and significant role model for Mexican American youth in Texas and the Southwest, after her death her face and her figure, her music, her fashions, and her life became commodities in high demand, not only in Texas, her home state, but all over the United States. Selena also became a healing and almost sacred figure for the Mexican American community, 30,000 of whom paid their respects to her during her funeral (Patoski 1996). Many of her admirers have subsequently made pilgrimages to her burial place in Corpus Christi. Selena's power and pervasiveness after her death represent a double and antithetical phenomenon, at once characterized by a communal spirituality and by its opposite, an ever-increasing commercialization of her music, her persona, and her fashions.

While it has been said that Selena only became nationally renowned because of her tragic and untimely death, she had already recorded her first English-language album, *Dreaming of You*, before she died. This project indicated the coming direction of her singing career. Beginning as a local and regional star of Tex-Mex music, particularly traditional *cumbias* that her brother and composer, A. B. Quintanilla, transformed into pop songs in the *cumbia* and *ranchera* styles, Selena eventually became a mainstreamed act, singing and recording only in English. In the process, both the Tejano/Latin texture of her music and her audience changed. A particular scene in the movie *Selena* powerfully captures the historical irony of the singer's decision to attract a mainstream audience. While Selena is performing in San Antonio, the producers suggest to Abraham Quintanilla, her father and agent, that Selena is ready for a crossover project. Quintanilla's face, set against the background of the

Alamo, asserts with great certitude that Selena is ready to take over the Anglo market. In this context, the decision to seek a crossover audience suggests a symbolic reconquest of Texas and of the United States by Mexican Americans, represented by the voice, body, and charisma of Selena. Already hailed by critics and journalists as the next Gloria Estefan in the genealogy of Latina superstars, Selena had signed major contracts and agreements with companies such as Coca-Cola and Sony Discos even before recording in English. In early 1990 Capitol-EMI Latin bought Cara Records from Bob Grever, bringing Selena, as well as Tex-Mex musical groups such as La Mafia and Mazz, into major distribution networks and at least potential national visibility (Patoski 1996).

After her death, however, she became an overnight icon of Tejana identity and culture in the United States and in Latin America. Her face appeared in major magazines and print venues such as *Texas Monthly*, and *People* dedicated a whole issue to her life and career. Her music was anthologized, remixed, and remastered. A month after her death, "Selena had five CDs on The Billboard 200 chart, an accomplishment previously only achieved by superstars like Garth Brooks, Elvis Presley, and The Beatles" (Burr 1999: 189). Five years later, an entire cottage industry celebrating her life and music had sprung up. Her father opened the Selena Museum; fans visit El Mirador de la Flor, her memorial site in Corpus Christi; the musical *Selena Forever* has been performed in San Antonio; her fashion styles continue to sell; and Q Productions has issued a number of Selena dolls. In addition, various Web sites pay homage to her music, style, and persona and continue to memorialize her as a cultural and artistic hero who gave Tex-Mex border culture unprecedented visibility.

The cultural irony behind Selena's potential crossover, which truly occurred only after her death, is that Selena was a U.S. citizen, born and raised in Texas, and an English speaker. She learned Spanish in order to sing about her cultural heritage. However, the historical marginalization of the Tejano Mexican community from the mainstream musical market and from dominant institutions limited Selena's visibility until after her death. The commodification of her figure, music, and persona at the hands of the industry and her own father does not erase the hope that she brought to many Tejanos during her career, a hope that has been explained, in part, by her strong charisma, her function as a role model for young Tejanas, and by the spiritual elements accorded to her after her death. The symbolically healing function, combined with her powerful personality on the stage and in everyday life and her accessibility, has allowed subordinate sectors to feel hope about their own lives through her life and music, a hope that has also been attributed to the disappointment of Tejano Mexican constituencies with their elected officials (Limón 1998: 189–91)

If Selena's posthumous success marked her ultimate mainstreaming, Ricky Martin's show-stopping performance at the 1999 Grammy Awards took this phenomenon to another level. Martin's personal success opened the door to a growing number of Latino artists, including rock-and-roll veteran Carlos Santana, who scored with the multiplatinum *Supernatural* (also in 1999), and other Latinos such as Marc Anthony, Jennifer López, Enrique Iglesias, Christina Aguilera, and Shakira.

While the growing success of these artists reflects, on one level, their crossover appeal, their recent successes are also at least partially attributable to the steadily expanding Latino consumer market in the United States and, indeed, in all of greater Latin America. In the United States, Latino buying power has already exceeded an earlier estimate made for the year 2020: 500 billion dollars. Latin music sales were more than $570 million dollars in 1998 (Farley 1999: 77) This suggests that U.S. Latinos are finally being recognized as consumers, although this new status has not totally erased the criminalizing discourses that traditionally surround them. It also suggests that music is a global market and multicultural in terms of its consumers. Diverse audiences attend the concerts of Ricky Martin and other Latino entertainers, and, in this sense, these spectacles themselves lead to potential intercultural interactions and knowledge. Martin's public performances, for example, reveal how elements of resistance and consent are inextricably intertwined and embodied by the same singer. For example, audiences can identify specific forms of Afro–Puerto Rican styles in Martin's bodily movements. The rhythms of the Puerto Rican *bomba*, historically performed on the island by the slaves and later by working-class Afro–Puerto Ricans, are evident, in residual ways, in Martin's pelvic dancing and in his dialogue with his drummers. In addition, many Latinos also know that the title of the song "Living la vida loca" constitutes a more generalized and mainstreamed version of the urban Chicano expression, a reference to gang life. In contrast, in Martin's song "*la vida loca*" refers to parties and feeling good. This example of mainstreaming and rewriting a complex, painful, and marginalized life—*la vida loca*—would suggest that Martin's music represents a co-optation of Latino life in the United States. It is. On the other hand, the position that the Puerto Rican singer took against the presence of the U.S. Navy on the island of Vieques attests to the overt oppositional political roles that Latino public figures such as him can assume.

The dominant discourse that labels these Latino singers a "crossover" phenomenon is evidence that Latinos are still situated outside the U.S. national body, and it is, as many critics would argue, that eroticized difference that makes them so attractive to mainstream U.S. audiences. This also reveals the residues of racism that are still at play in the national embrace of Latino pop music. While it is true, as U.S. Puerto Rican writer Esmeralda Santiago has observed, that many of these Latino singers are white and European looking (a statement that can be equally applied to Latina Caribbean writers) and that racial identities inform the selection of particular individuals as "stars," it is also true that the subordination of Latinos operates in other forms of expression, including the realm of language. While the term "crossover" refers to performers who sing in another language and to other audiences and then shift to a general, mainstream U.S. audience, in the case of the Latin music boom it has served to relocate these singers—who are all U.S. citizens and born in the United States or Puerto Rico—as foreigners, outside of the U.S. national body. If Ricky Martin is a crossover because he sang in Spanish in the past, his U.S. citizenship, accorded by virtue of the Jones Act of 1917 to all Puerto Ricans (at a time when the U.S. needed young men to enter the military), is erased or elided from the question of belonging. This raises the question: Is Martin crossing over to an U.S. audience, or is the U.S. crossing over to Puerto Rican music?

Ricky Martin has not necessarily changed his repertoire. Since he was in the prototypical "boy group" Menudo, his style has continued to be pop rock. In fact, Menudo was as much a mainstream act in the 1980s as Martin is in the 1990s. In 1980, Menudo's arrival in New York City was compared "to the arrival of the Beatles in the same city back in 1964." In 1983, the group broke the record for "the largest audience ever assembled" at Mexico's 150,000-seat Azteca Stadium (Krulik 1999: 18). The difference is temporal; in the late 1990s the U.S. music industry has promoted these singers and opened up the market for their increasing consumer power. While the U.S. audience is now much more ethnically diverse, given the demographic growth of Latinos, the crossover label seems ironic when applied to Latino singers such as Martin and Selena, who have been part of a national pop scene throughout. While Latin music is technically defined by the industry as music that has 51 percent or more Spanish lyrics, then speaking about Ricky Martin as crossover may not be totally incorrect. Yet Latin music in Spanish has had a long history of production, performance, and reception within the domestic borders of the United States (the first *plenas* were recorded in Spanish in New York City in the late 1910s, and Tex-Mex *conjunto* music has been performed in Spanish since the late nineteenth century). Yet, as long as Latino communities, as a subordinate sector, constitute the central consumers of that music, their music will be defined by the industry as a secondary market. Once Anglo listeners buy the music and attend performances, then these performers will more likely be legitimized by the industry. Ricky Martin's high level of popularity and consumption, for instance, is due to the ways in which he deploys Latin rhythms while diluting and masking them through more generic pop and rock song structures. While he capitalizes on the exoticizing erotics of his pelvic movements, his white skin color is also at play with the blackness suggested through his dancing styles, a form of self-blackening that becomes, in fact, the site for intercultural meanings and reception.

Salsa meets pop and hip-hop in the works of Marc Anthony, Jennifer López, Brenda Starr, Corrine, DLG, the Dominican group Proyecto Uno, and other interpreters of the 1990s, giving way to new, hybrid musical hits that combine the traditional salsa sounds of their parents' generation with the new forms of musical expression preferred by urban Latino youth. Just as Selena fused Anglo pop sonorities with the traditional rhythms and genres of Tex-Mex to appeal to the youth market, these musical hybrids attest to the continuing need for re-membering, for collective history and memory, among U.S. Latinos. The ways in which Latino artists rewrite older, extant musical lyrics, structures, melodies, and rhythms into new musical arrangements speak to the constant need of artists—and their audiences—to recognize themselves simultaneously in the traditions of the past with the innovations of the present. Thus, the presence of past musical classics within new, hybrid structures evinces the central role of cultural and historical memory for U.S. Latinos, a memory that, as discussed earlier, has helped Latinos to survive their experiences of displacement and fragmentation. Musical fusions with hip hop, gospel, and r&b, as in La India's recordings and singing styles, establish associations between Latinos and African Americans, cultural affiliations that have persisted historically throughout the diaspora in music and popular culture. The styles and sounds of pop that mediate some salsa music from the East Coast allow this music to be more easily embraced by Anglo-Americans and a larger, less specialized listening audience, particularly the youth sector. While the music, video images, and some singers are still marketed and packaged through the lens of the dominant society, the fact that they are playing on mainstream radio has also opened up the potential for the identification with, and reaffirmation of, Latinidad (a strong sense of Latin American and interlatino cultural affinity and solidarity) among minority and Latino youth, a Latinidad that expresses a higher degree of integration into U.S. society yet does not necessarily index assimilation.

Interlatino musical forms have also become significant at a time when Latino groups have begun to interact and to share more systematically with other Latino national groups in urban centers. For instance, Carlos Santana's music since the 1960s has always been a fusion of Afro-Caribbean rhythms and Mexican and Mexican American themes and melodies, all driven by traditional rock and roll sensibilities. He popularized "Oye como va," a composition by the late Puerto Rican "King of Salsa," Tito Puente. Olga Tanón's recording of Mexican romantic ballads in collaboration with Marco Antonio Solís, and Marc Anthony's version of Juan Gabriel's song, "Hasta que te conocí," foreground the common affiliations among Latino listeners, which romantic ballads, or *boleros* as they are known in Spanish, have established across generations. These incursions into Mexican ballads by Caribbean singers reflect the long historical interactions between Puerto Rico and Mexico through popular music. They could also reflect the recognition on the part of the singers that Mexicans are now New York's new Latino cultural presence.

Latino transnationalism has been most evident in the growing popularity of rock *en español* in California and throughout the United States. That a musical form totally produced and performed in Spanish would experience such high levels of popularity within the United States indicates the increasing power of Latino communities in defining cultural commodities. It has also fueled the increasing presence of Spanish as a public language in the United States, while it continues an oppositional critique that emerged in Latin American expressions of resistance against U.S. imperialism and capitalism. Like hybrid salsa forms from the East Coast, rock *en español* inflects rock rhythms with the diverse repertoire of Latin American rhythms and musical forms, from Aztec and pre-Columbian melodies and instrumentation to the tropical rhythms of mambos and *música tropical* and the urban sounds of hip-hop and rap.

Many traditional *salseros* in New York have denounced these new hybrid forms of salsa and Latino music as evidence of co-optation and mainstreaming. Any contamination with styles and arrangements of pop music is suspect in the eyes of musicians who have struggled to create "authentic" styles that would reaffirm their cultural difference from dominant Anglo society. Yet these hybrid forms and musical fusions have helped to structure new generational identities and interracial styles. Rather than renounce the positions of difference and resistance that their parents articulated in the 1960s and 1970s, these new Latino musicians, interpreters, and artists reconfigure them in new arrangements. Perhaps, as cultural producers, they feel an urgent need not to reaffirm their difference, but rather to appeal to a generational identity and to an urban youth sector whose lives more closely match theirs.

In the context of exploring a Latino sense of belonging and our historical contributions to the making of the United States, the *Americanos* project (2000) exemplifies the most ambitious attempt ever to rewrite stereotypes and extol and celebrate Latino hybrid culture. It shows the dialectics between the integrationist impulse and the reaffirmation of Latino cultural difference and diversity from U.S. mainstream society. Conceptualized by Edward James Olmos, Lea Ybarra, and Manuel Monterrey, this multimedia project has capitalized on new technologies and on the simultaneity of various artistic media in order to saturate U.S. audiences with their cultural corrective. *Americanos* includes a photography book, a traveling exhibit for the next five years, a CD of a variety of Latino musicians (Debrow 2000), a concert, an HBO documentary, and Internet sites that accompany the exhibits from city to city. This project speaks to the potential for intercultural collaboration between Latinos and Anglos and to the tactical value of establishing cosponsorships with major corporations such as Time Warner, U.S. West, and Farmer's Insurance, and with the federal government (the Smithsonian was a key player in this project). Thus, the visibility and social power of a figure such as Edward James Olmos, known for his social activism on behalf of Latino youth, were central in ensuring the commitment of these private and public organizations. The project has only just begun, as the book is now being widely sold nationwide; the HBO documentary received the Sundance Film Festival Award in 2000, and the traveling exhibit has been viewed by thousands in the City Museum of New York and in other urban centers throughout the country.

According to the producers and writers, *Americanos* is an ideal title for this project because it foregrounds the incomplete and ambiguous meanings of labels and terms. Informed by the ways in which Latino poets such as Tato Laviera (1985) have transformed the term "American," the project's creators decided on *Americanos* because it explicitly labels Latinos as an integral part of an America that had heretofore only seen itself as Anglo. It also simultaneously reaffirms Latinos' cultural difference through the use of the Spanish version of "American." The project's creators intended, through the use of this term, to correct the internalized colonialism that underlay Latin Americans' use of "Americanos" to refer only to Anglo-Americans and not to themselves. Thus, once again, this title is recuperative as well as critical, and it is intended to rectify the common misconception of Latinos as outsiders and to exhort audiences to embrace Latinos as part of U.S. society.

All texts in the *Americanos* project, however, foreground the unresolved tensions among Latinos between the integrationist urge and the reaffirmation of difference. The project's goal is twofold: to educate non-Latinos about Latino contributions to the United States and to offer Latinos images and cultural texts with which they can identify and insert themselves into history. As Olmos stated in the project's opening lecture at Chicago's Field Museum on 18 August 2000, this collection of photos is "like a glass of water in the desert." Echoing the concerns raised by Latino leaders regarding the need for more realistic and comprehensive images of Latinos in the media (in the discussion about *Seinfeld*), Olmos's metaphor foregrounds the need for self-produced images that will capture the everyday life and the big and small contributions of this population to the United States.

However, the decolonizing potential of the project is limited by its strong celebratory, unitary, and utopian tones. Because *Americanos* is ultimately about fostering integration and reaffirming Latino dignity, there is little space for honestly exploring either the history of racism or the social injustices, chronic and worsening educational crises, and current structural obstacles that Latinos face in their everyday lives in contemporary American society. For instance, as Jiménez-Muñoz and Santiago-Valles make abundantly clear in chapter 2 of this volume, for many Puerto Ricans even on the mainland, the term "Americanos" is not one with which they can identify given the long history of colonial violence against them and their island. Because *Americanos* intends to insert Latinos into the U.S. social imaginary as agents and contributors to "American" society, it seems to have been wary of producing images of victimization or powerlessness. In this way, then, what is not said is as powerful as what is told or visually represented.

The photography itself, which represents the collective work of thirty prizewinning photographers from across the country, focuses on close-ups of Latino faces, a technique that, throughout the book, creates a visual text and narrative of Latino lives as a human story. Indeed, this technique is central to the book's decolonizing project for Latino viewers. It allows them to envision themselves as part of this visual history, thus providing a partial corrective to their invisibility in the media and in television. This goal is reaffirmed in the open-ended text of the traveling exhibit, in which Latinos can contribute their own photos to the Web sites. The viewers thus function as coauthors of the ongoing history that is being shared. In Chicago, the exhibit included a photo exhibit by Latino youth sponsored by the Yolocalli Youth Program, thus providing marginalized youth the opportunity to be producers of knowledge and art in the public space.

While the collection of photography addresses important sites, such as labor, the family, spirituality and the sacred, gender, social contributions, racial diversity, rituals, sports, and cultures and the arts, the idealistic and generally celebratory tone of the written texts undermines the dramatic ironies of many of these images. For example, the image of a Latina seamstress sewing a U.S. flag is particularly telling. While on the surface it speaks to the contributions of Latino workers to the literal making and material production of America, the Gap sweatshirt that she is wearing could be read to symbolize the labor struggles of Latinas and women who toil in sweatshops contracted by the Gap, Nike, and other American multinational corporations in so-called free processing zones. The sewing machine, then, can be seen as a symbol of the relationship between economic development, female labor, and racism, so clearly delineated in this feminist icon of the Latina worker sewing. Yet viewers may read this photo as an integrationist pose in the absence of the other, alternative discourses of reference about labor, gender, and race. Thus, what *Americanos* lacks is precisely a contextualization of its images within the historical tradition of Latino cultures of resistance.

While the photo book overtly denounces the poverty and invisibility of the migrant worker along the U.S./Mexico border through photos of a woman named Marisol and her family and pictures of migrant workers—and uses for the CD cover and publicity stills the image of Luis Estrada picking tulips in Oregon—images of successful Latinos and Latin Americans are also used to counteract the reality of the working-poor Latino sector. In the documentary, for instance, Cuban American advertising executive Tere Zubizarreta clearly explains that her agenda is to erase stereotypes, yet her work replaces one unidimensional imagery—the poor Latino—with another, that of the executive/professional, white Latino. While the representation of multiple social classes among Latinos is necessary and historically appropriate, it is also important for Latino and non-Latino audiences to understand the historical and political factors that have led to socioeconomic differences.

The documentary speaks much more overtly about the structural, political, educational, and cultural forms of racism that Latinos face within the United States. It features the very heterogeneous identities and racial complexity of Latino communities, as well as the politically contradictory positions among U.S. Latinos, poignantly illustrated in the figure of Glicet Garvey, a second-generation Mexicana who is a Border Patrol agent. What distinguishes this documentary from the photo book, the CD, and the travel exhibit is the structuring and recurring presence of El Vez, the Chicano singer whose performative mimicry of Elvis Presley expresses strong critiques about racism in the United States. This particular device allows audiences to reflect on and critique the diverse Latino voices and what is said about Latinos in the documentary. Traditional symbols of U.S. patriotism and the dominant society, such as the Statue of Liberty, the term "American," the U.S. flag, and the song "America, the Beautiful" (on the CD) are constantly recontextualized through the more radical Latino voices, the hybrid mixing with Latino rhythms and sounds, or their juxtaposition with images and voices that dismantle their very historical power.

Americanos is an open-ended text and a collective process. Despite its ideological limitations, as it continues to travel around the country for the next five years it almost certainly marks a significant intervention in Latinos' long struggles over representation. The power of the project to mobilize Latino audiences is still to be seen. Viewers can become active agents in giving meaning to these texts and in enhancing the awareness of their own lives. *Americanos* capitalizes on this potential and on the possibilities for generating a truly positive intercultural knowledge. I can imagine, for a moment, Lisa Demetriou, a Puerto Rican police officer whose photo and voice were included in the traveling exhibit, running into Jerry Seinfeld at the City Museum of New York, where *Americanos* is featured, and reiterating to him the profound connections between this public ritual and her own identity as a "Nuyorican." The shared, intercultural knowledge made possible by cultural interventions such as the multimedia *Americanos* and the agency of Latino voices telling their stories may well make a difference in interethnic relations in the future. But care must be taken. Instead of a message communicating a facile and harmonious vision of integration, a message that argues that "we are all the same" and erases the history of colonization and the ongoing subordination of the peoples of Latin American descent in the United States, it is imperative that we increase the public knowledge about Latino expressive cultures in a manner that gives voice to Latinos' own collective self-conceptualizations, rather than representations that objectify their lives and silence their voices. In this light, Latino artists, writers, musicians, and intellectuals continue to struggle and strategize over issues of representation, despite our increased participation in the industry and our growing demographics.

REFERENCES

Algarín, Miguel. 1978. *Mongo Affair*. New York: Nuyorican.

Alurista. 1971. *Floricanto en Aztlán*. Los Angeles: Chicano Research Center, University of California, Los Angeles.

Alvarez, Julia. 1991. *How the García Girls Lost their Accents*. Chapel Hill, N.C.: Algonquin Books.

Anzaldúa, Gloria. 1987. *Borderlands/La Frontera: The New Mestiza*. San Francisco: Aunt Lute Books.

Aparicio, Frances R., and Susana Chávez-Silverman. 1997. *Tropicalizations: Transcultural Representations of Latinidad*. Hanover, N.H.: University Press of New England.

Arrizón, Alicia. 1999. *Latina Performance: Traversing the Stage*. Bloomington: Indiana University Press.

Associated Press. 1998. "Hispanic Group Protests 'Seinfeld.'" 8 May. http://www.msnbc.com/news/164409.asp. Accessed 15 May 1998.

Broyles-Gonzales, Yolanda. 1986. "Women in El Teatro Campesino: 'Apoco Estaba molacha La Virgen de Guadalupe?'" In *Chicana Voices: Intersections of Class, Race, and Gender*, ed. Teresa Cordoba et al., 162–87. Austin, Tex.: Center for Mexican American Studies.

Burr, Ramiro. 1999. *The Billboard Guide to Tejano and Regional Mexican Music*. New York: Billboard Books.

Castillo, Ana. 1994. *Massacre of the Dreamers: Essays on Xicanisma*. New York: Plume/Penguin Books.

Cisneros, Sandra. 1989. *The House on Mango Street*. New York: Vintage.

CNN. 1998. "Hispanics protest 'Seinfeld' burning of Puerto Rican flag." 9 May. http://www.cnn.com/SHOWBIZ/9805/09/seinfeld.hispanics.Ap/index.html. Accessed 15 May 1998.

Debrow, Steve. 2000. *Americanos: A Musical Celebration*. Atlantic Records. 83181-2.

Farley, Christopher John. 1999. "Latin Music Pops." *Time*, 24 May, 74–79.

Flores, Richard R. 1997. "Aesthetic Process and Cultural Citizenship: The Membering of a Social Body in San Antonio." In *Latino Cultural Citizenship: Claiming Identity, Space, and Rights*, ed. William V. Flores and Rina Benmayor, 124–51. Boston: Beacon Press.

Fox, Geoffrey. 1996. *Hispanic Nation: Culture, Politics, and the Constructing of Identity*. Tuscon: The University of Arizona Press.

Fusco, Coco. 1995. *English is Broken Here: Notes on Cultural Fusion in the Americas*. New York: The New Press.

Gaspar de Alba, Alicia. 1998. *Chicano Art: Inside/Outside the Master's House*. Austin: The University of Texas Press.

Gómez-Peña, Guillermo. 1993. *Warrior for Gringostroika*. Saint Paul, Minn.: Graywolf Press.

——. 1996. *The New World Border*. San Fransisco: City Lights.

Hall, Stuart. 1990. "Cultural Identity and Diaspora." In *Community, Culture, Difference*, ed. Jonathan Rutherford, 222–37. London: Lawrence and Wishart.

Kanellos, Nicolás. 1998. *Thirty Million Strong: Reclaiming the Hispanic Image in American Culture*. Golden, Colo.: Fulcrum Publishing.

Klor de Alva, J. Jorge. 1998. "Aztlán, Borinquen, and Hispanic Nationalism in the United States." In *The Latino Studies Reader: Culture, Economy, and Society*, ed. Antonia Darder and Rodolfo D. Torres, 63–82. Oxford and Malden, Mass.: Blackwell Publishers.

Krulik, Nancy. 1999. *Ricky Martin: Rockin' the House!* New York: Pocket Books.

Latino Link. 1998. Feedback on Seinfeld. http://www.latinolink.com/feed.html. Accessed 15 May 1998.

Laviera, Tato. 1985 *AmeRícan*. Houston: Arte Público Press.

Leguízamo, John. 1992. *Mambo Mouth*. Polygram Video. Produced by Jeff Ross. Directed by Thomas Schlamme. 60 min. Videocassette.

Limón, José E. 1998. *American Encounters: Greater Mexico, the United States, and the Erotics of Culture*. Boston: Beacon Press.

Marqués, René. 1963. Reprint, 1971. *La carreta*. Río Piedra, P.R.: Editorial Cultural.

Mohr, Nicholasa. 1973. *Nilda*. Houston: Arte Público Press.

Montoya, José. 1970. "El Louie." *Rascatripas* 2. Oakland, Calif. No pagination.

Morales, Aurora Levins, and Rosario Morales. 1986. *Getting Home Alive*. Ithaca, New York: Firebrand Books.

National Congress for Puerto Rican Rights. 2000. "Central Park Attackers Are Enemies of the Community." 16 June. E-mail statement by rperez@boricuanet.org.

Olmos, Edward James, Lea Ybarra, and Manuel Monterrey, eds. 1999. *Americanos: Latino Life in the United States*. Boston: Little, Brown And Company.

Olmos, Edward James and Nick Athas. 2000. *Americanos: Latino Life In the United States*. Television program. HBO.

Patoski, Joe Nick. 1996. *Selena: Como La Flor*. New York: Boulevard Books.

Pietri, Pedro. 1973. *Puerto Rican Obituary*. New York: Monthly Review Press.

Piñero, Miguel. 1980. "A Lower East Side Poem." In *Herejes y mitificadores: Muestra de poesía Puertorriqueña en los Estados Unidos*, ed. Efraín Barradas and Rafael Rodríguez, 96–99. Río Piedras, Puerto Rico: Ediciones Huracán.

Rivero, Eliana. 1989. "From Immigrants to Ethnics: Cuban Women Writers In the United States." In *Breaking Boundaries: Latina Writings and Critical Readings*, ed. Asunción Horno-Delgado, 189–200. Amherst: University of Massachusetts Press.

Roach, Joseph. 1995. "Culture and Performance in the Circum-Atlantic World." In *Performativity and Performance*, ed. Andrew Parker and Eve Kosofsky Sedgwick, 45–63. New York: Routledge.

Rodríguez, Abraham, Jr. 1993. *Spidertown*. New York: Penguin Books.

Rodríguez, Luis J. 1993. *Always Running: La Vida Loca: Gang Days in L.A.* Willimantic, Conn.: Curbstone Press.

Rodríguez, Richard. 1982. *Hunger of Memory: The Education of Richard Rodríguez*. New York: Bantam Books.

Sandoval, Chela. 1991. "U.S. Third World Feminisms: The Theory and Method of Oppositional Consciousness in the Postmodern World." *Genders* 10 (spring): 1–24.

Sandoval-Sánchez, Alberto. 1999. *José, Can You See? Latinos on and off Broadway*. Madison: The University of Wisconsin Press.

Santiago, William. 1998. "Seinfeld does the hack." Latino Link, 11 May. http://www.latinolinkcom/opinion/opinion98/05110sei.htm. Accessed 15 May 1998.

Time. "A Surging New Spirit." 1988. *Time*. 11 July.

Torres, María de los Angeles. 1986. "From Exiles to Minorities: The Politics of the Cuban Community in the United States." Ph.d. diss., University of Michigan.

Thomas, Piri. 1967. *Down These Mean Streets*. New York: A. A. Knopf.

Valdez, Luis. 1990. *Early Works*. Houston: Arte Público Press.

Viramontes, Helena María. 1985. "The Cariboo Cafe." In *The Moths And Other Stories*, 59–75. Houston: Arte Público Press.

——. 1995. *Under the Feet of Jesus*. New York: Dutton.

WBGH-Boston And CPB. 1993. *The Latin and Caribbean Presence in the United States*.

Winn, Peter. 1992. *Americas: The Changing Face of Latin America and the Caribbean*. New York: Pantheon Books.

TEN

THE CONTINUING LATINO QUEST FOR FULL MEMBERSHIP AND EQUAL CITIZENSHIP: LEGAL PROGRESS, SOCIAL SETBACKS, AND POLITICAL PROMISE

KEVIN R. JOHNSON

INTRODUCTION

Latinos historically have had an ambiguous and problematic status in the U.S. system of law and jurisprudence. This tenuous relationship has complex origins. On the most fundamental level, Latinos have been disadvantaged legally as well as socially because they have long been considered racially inferior by many Anglo-Americans. In addition, as "foreigners," Latinos were often viewed as culturally, religiously, and linguistically different and inferior as well.

As was the case for African Americans, the inferiority ascribed to Latinos was legally codified in many ways. Although perhaps not as systematic as the structure of racial repression constructed in the Jim Crow South, Latinos suffered legally enforced discrimination in public education; public accommodations, such as theaters, swimming pools, hotels, and restaurants; access to jobs and economic opportunity generally; and in their ability to serve on juries and be judged by juries of their peers. As was also the case for African Americans, Latinos frequently availed themselves of legal rights and remedies. Indeed, repression often served as the catalyst that led Latinos to protest, form advocacy and civil-rights organizations, and pursue litigation to challenge civil-rights violations. However, until recently, legal rights and remedies available to African Americans often were denied Latinos because they were classified as "white" under the law.

This essay explores three interrelated sets of legal issues that have most influenced the Latino population of the United States since the 1960s. Although other issues also have been important to Latinos over the period, the legal issues surrounding (1) immigration, nationality, and citizenship; (2) civil rights in the U.S. juridical context; and (3) access to public education have been among the most serious and most chronic facing the growing Latino community in the later part of the twentieth century. How the United States addresses these increasingly critical, overlapping concerns in the new millennium will help determine whether Latinos will move toward enjoying equal status with "white" Americans as they steadily grow as a proportion of the U.S. population.

If history serves as any indication, Latinos will face many challenges in vindicating their civil rights in the United States. The past has been marred by legally sanctioned anti-Latino discrimination. At the same time, the law occasionally has served as a powerful tool for guaranteeing Latino rights. It has helped spur activism and political organizing. As a double-edged sword, law will in all likelihood have a continuing relevance to the Latino quest for civil rights.

U.S. IMMIGRATION LAWS AND THEIR ENFORCEMENT: THE LATINO STRUGGLE FOR FULL CITIZENSHIP

Since 1960, immigration and nationality issues in the United States have become increasingly complex and controversial. Two interrelated sets of factors have contributed to the increasing social ferment over immigration. The first and most obvious is the increasing rate of migration from Latin America and Asia. The second has to do with the attendant demographic transformation of American society and the growing realization that the United States is an increasingly multicultural and multiracial nation. These two factors in tandem have generated widespread and growing adverse reaction to the newcomers. This, in turn, has led to a renewed interest in public support for an overhaul of the U.S. immigration laws.

1965: THE END OF FORMAL RACIAL DISCRIMINATION IN IMMIGRANT ADMISSIONS AND THE EMERGENCE OF THE IMMIGRATION "PROBLEM"

As has long been true in U.S. immigration history, much of the modern debate over immigration in fact centers on race. This remains true even after the most overt racist elements of U.S. immigration law and policy were scrapped in the mid-1960s. In 1965, Congress abolished the discriminatory national-origins quota system that had been a cornerstone of U.S. immigration law since 1924. This change in the law dramatically transformed the racial demographics of immigration. Whereas nearly 80 percent of all immigrants to the United States in the 1920s originated in Europe, by the 1990s this trend had been reversed. Since then, only about 11 percent of all immigrants originated in Europe. Most of the rest of the lawful immigrants came from developing nations populated by people of color, especially people from the Spanish-speaking nations of Latin America.[1] In fiscal year 1997, for example, Mexico was the country of origin of 18.4 percent of all lawful immigrants—and a much higher proportion of all immigrants if undocumented entries are considered.[2] Mass migration from the Dominican Republic has changed the flavor of New York,[3] as well as the "all-American" game of baseball.[4] Immigrants from Mexico, Central America, the Dominican Republic, Cuba, and other Latin American nations joined established Latino communities in this country, such as the Cuban community in south Florida and the Mexican American community in the Southwest.

Latin Americans also dominate the immigration that occurs outside of officially sanctioned channels. In 1996, for example, the estimated undocumented Mexican population in the United States was at least 2.7 million persons, or about 54 percent of the estimated U.S. total of 5 million undocumented persons. In addition to Mexico, El Salvador, Guatemala, Honduras, the Dominican Republic, Nicaragua, Colombia, Ecuador, and Peru ranked in the top twenty sending countries of undocumented immigrants.[5]

As has been true historically, most immigrants to the United States come to the country seeking economic opportunity. However, since the 1965 revisions to the Immigration and Nationality Act, a preference system has been established that gives immigration preferences based on the principle of family reunification and, to a lesser extent, to the entry of immigrants with skills deemed necessary to the U.S. economy. In addition, refugee and human rights provisions of U.S. immigration laws also offer relief to aliens fleeing political persecution in their homelands, which has proven to be an important legal avenue for Latin American immigration. From the time that Congress passed the Refugee Act of 1980 and other legislation, tens of thousands of Central Americans have applied for asylum each year.[6] Of course, Cuban refugees have also contributed significant numbers to the growing influx of Latin American immigrants since 1960. They have transformed south Florida, "Latinized" Miami, and deeply affected the national political scene as politicians strive to secure the "Cuban vote."[7] The national furor over the extraordinary custody battle over young Elián González, if nothing else, shows the political importance of the Cuban American community to national politics.[8]

One of the great ironies and largely unintended consequences of the liberalization of U.S. immigration law in 1965 was that the policy change rekindled the same racist attitudes that the reforms sought to remedy. Much of this was due to the rapid increase in undocumented migration from south of the border that occurred after the law passed. Coinciding with the demise of the "Bracero Program"—the massive foreign-labor importation program that Congress ended at the end of 1964—the reform of U.S. immigration law had little effect on the patterns of labor migration from Mexico and other Latin American nations, which had already become a deeply rooted part of the American economy. Indeed, as the Immigration and Naturalization Service (INS) began apprehending and repatriating increasing numbers of Spanish-speaking undocumented workers in the late 1960s and 1970s, immigration officials were replaying a process that had occurred in similar circumstances several times before, most notably in the great repatriation campaigns of the early 1920s, in the 1930s, and again during the INS's infamous "Operation Wetback" in 1954.[9] Although the repatriation of Mexican and other Latin American nationals since then has been much less publicized than the campaigns that occurred during the Great Depression and the 1950s, apprehensions and repatriations (by then called "voluntary departures") reached half a million annually by the early 1970s and have fluctuated between that level and more than one million every year since.

RESPONSE: THE IMMIGRATION REFORM AND CONTROL ACT OF 1986

In the early 1970s, Congress began to explore ways to reassert control over the nation's borders. Most of these legislative efforts were blocked by a strong, if in some ways odd, coalition of Latino civil rights activists and employers' lobbies. However, after years of debate, in 1986 Congress finally passed the so-called Immigration Reform and Control Act (IRCA). IRCA reflected both the punitive mood in Congress and the extent to which Latinos had become a political force to be reckoned with: although the legislation imposed harsh penalties on American employers who "knowingly" hired undocumented workers, Latino activists had also forced Congress to add a provision for the "regularization of status"—popularly known as an amnesty—of undocumented noncitizens who could prove continuous residence in the United States since 1 January 1982. The law also allowed nearly 100,000 entrants from Cuba and Haiti to gain legal U.S. residency. As a result of the "amnesty" provisions of IRCA, by 1991 nearly 2 million former "illegal aliens" were allowed to become legal residents under the law.[10]

However, IRCA ultimately did little to stem the flow of undocumented entries into the United States, and by the late 1980s, the anti-immigrant sentiment that had simmered below the surface of American politics again began to be heard. The strange coalition of corporate interests and Latino political activists was able to fend off moves to impose immigration restrictions for a time, but pressure continued to mount, especially after California voters sent Congress a clear message by passing the anti-immigrant measure, Proposition 187, in 1994. That law, which a court enjoined from going into effect, would have eliminated all public benefits for undocumented immigrants and barred undocumented immigrant children from the public schools. Unmistakably directed at Mexican immigrants, the Proposition 187 campaign played on anti-Mexican themes.[11]

RESPONSE: 1996 IMMIGRATION "REFORM"

After a period of intense debate, in 1996 the U.S. Congress followed California's lead by passing a series of draconian immigration and welfare reform laws designed to facilitate the removal of aliens and to ensure that immigrants who remained did not "abuse" welfare benefits. The new legislation also funded the Border Patrol at its highest levels in U.S. history. The INS instituted new operations along the southern border designed to cut off undocumented immigration from Mexico. This military presence redirected Mexican and other Latin American migrants to more dangerous routes in desperate efforts to make it to the United States, often suffering and dying from inclement conditions and rough terrain, as well as being victimized by crime.[12] Thousands of migrants have died as a direct result. As will be discussed below, Cubans, Central Americans, and other Latino immigrants have experienced the sting of the recent intensification of immigration enforcement as well.

The 1996 immigration reforms, which include such features as mandatory detention, expedited removal, and the extraordinary elimination of judicial review of certain removal orders, have significantly impacted the Latino community in the United States. Namely, immigration "reform" facilitated deportation of long-term Latino residents. In a much-publicized example, the INS initiated removal proceedings under the new law against Jesus Collado, convicted of a single nonviolent crime more than two decades ago as a youth (when it was *not* a deportable offense) and currently a law-abiding family man, to the Dominican Republic.[13] In fiscal year 1999, the INS formally deported a record number of aliens (nearly 179,000) with Mexicans and Latin Americans constituting *more than 92 percent* of those removed from the country.[14] It is important to note that these formal deportations were in addition to the normal number of "voluntary departures" effected by the INS, which continued at a rate of several hundred thousand per year. Not coincidentally, the 1990s saw an increase in hate crimes against Latinos, including some directed at those assumed to be immigrants by private citizens acting as vigilantes claiming to enforce the immigration laws along the U.S. border with Mexico.[15]

THE IMPACT OF IMMIGRATION-REFORM EFFORTS ON LATINOS: DISCRIMINATION IN EMPLOYMENT

Efforts to combat illegal immigration have ripple effects on Latino employment in this country. Because the 1986 reform law subjects employers who employ undocumented persons to sanctions, many businesses engage in discrimination against all "foreigners," including U.S. citizens and lawful immigrants of Latin American ancestry.[16] Lawful and undocumented immigrants have long faced difficulties in organizing unions because of their uncertain immigration status as well as their employment in the unskilled, low-wage labor market.[17] However, despite the crackdown on illegal immigration, undocumented workers readily find jobs in the United States. Employers often claim that undocumented immigrants will do work that ordinary "Americans" will not do, such as farm work, for the wages that employers want to pay.[18] To a large degree, their claims are true, but the massive use of undocumented Latino labor in the United States is also a clear manifestation of the extent to which economic restructuring in the Western Hemisphere has in effect integrated the labor market across borders (for elaboration of this argument see Gutiérrez, chapter 1, and also Jiménez-Muñoz and Santiago-Valles, chapter 2, this volume).

DENIAL OF SOCIAL MEMBERSHIP

The monumental efforts over the course of the 1990s to seal the borders to prevent migration from the south sent an unmistakable message to Latinos in the United States about their place in society. These measures helped cement the notion that they are second-class citizens and fortunate to be in this country at all. Such attitudes have inevitably influenced how the established Latino community has viewed the immigration issue. Indeed, at least part of the established Latino community in the United States shares some of these concerns over immigration.[19] Fault lines have developed between established Latino communities and recent immigrants from Latin America. In the Southwest, for example, Mexican Americans and Mexican immigrants at times have experienced tense relations in places like East Los Angeles and Phoenix, Arizona. Similarly, some established Cuban Americans in south Florida did not welcome the new migrants from Cuba in the "Mariel boatlift" of 1980.[20] As we shall see, however, the nature of immigration enforcement, which is directed at all people of Latin American ancestry, often galvanizes the Latino community against the calls for immigration enforcement.

The diversity of opinion about undocumented immigrants reflects deep ambivalence about the place of undocumented immigrants in U.S. society,[21] an ambivalence that is reinforced by the reluctance of the general public to acknowledge how the United States' pursuit of global free market economic policies virtually ensures the continuous circulation of both sanctioned and unsanctioned immigrant workers into the American labor market. Undocumented immigration continues, and cheap labor remains available for employers. Increased border enforcement creates the illusion of addressing the problem, but the reality is that, in the absence of jobs that pay at least a living wage in the immigrant "sending" nations of Latin America, labor migration will almost certainly continue for the indefinite future.

DEMANDS FOR ASSIMILATION

A kind of social myopia is reflected in the frequently made charge that, unlike past European immigrants, Latin American immigrants fail to assimilate into the mainstream. Arguments to restrict immigration have historically incorporated exaggerated claims that racially different immigrants—such as the Irish in the 1800s, who today appear fully integrated into U.S. society—fail to assimilate.[22] Some, including high profile Latinos like Linda Chávez and Richard Rodríguez, criticize Latin American and Asian immigrants who allegedly maintain a separate ethnic identity and refuse to become a part of the American mainstream.[23] The alleged failure has been cited as an argument to restrict immigration levels and to limit the migration of people from developing nations populated primarily by people of color.[24]

Such assimilationist arguments tend to ignore the effects of globalization in stimulating mass human migrations and the deep racism that exists in U.S. society. While assuming that Latin American immigrants refuse to assimilate, the proassimilationists ignore the fact that enduring racism in the United States makes it more difficult for immigrants of color, particularly those from communities that have suffered long histories of discrimination in this country, to assimilate into the mainstream. The restructuring of the U.S. economy since the 1970s has also militated against the potential assimilation of immigrants. If, as in the past, successful integration into the socioeconomic mainstream of American society is still based at least in part on the access to the kinds of jobs that allowed immigrants and their children to develop an economic stake in that society, then the steady movement of those jobs to cheaper, overseas job markets has undermined the possibility of that kind of integration today. The continuing segregation of Latinos in housing and schools, the emergence of inner-city gangs centered on the drug trade, and the passing on of disadvantaged status from one generation of Latinos to the next all exemplify this point.

Moreover, the continued salience of racial difference is further demonstrated by the fact that society continues to demand and expect "assimilation" from Latinos who are already citizens. For example, Puerto Ricans, who are often perceived by the general public as immigrants even though they (including those born in Puerto Rico) are legally U.S. citizens, have been accused of not assimilating.[25] As systematically demonstrated by Jiménez-Muñoz and Santiago-Valles's contribution to this volume (chapter 2), even though Puerto Ricans have been citizens of the United States for nearly a century, when assessed by any socioeconomic or political measure, it is obvious that the Puerto Rican community remains on the margins of American society. With large numbers mired in poverty on the mainland and those on the island denied direct representation in the United States Congress and the right to the vote for president, Puerto Ricans continue to "enjoy" what is at best a form of second-class citizenship.[26]

In any event, as the evidence demonstrates, Latinos in fact assimilate, learn English and embrace American work and family values.[27] This fact is generally ignored by the advocates of restrictionist measures who level the "failure to assimilate" claim against today's immigrants.

LATINO RESPONSE: NATURALIZATION AND POLITICAL ACTION

The demand for citizenship among Latinos increased in the 1990s as the social costs of noncitizen status rose along with anti-immigrant hysteria, aggressive deportation campaigns, and sharply reduced public benefits for noncitizens.[28] Facilitated in part by the relaxation by many Latin American nations of various legal requirements on dual nationality, the naturalization rates of Latin American immigrants, previously criticized for being relatively low, increased dramatically in the 1990s. However, in an unfortunate replay of previous historical periods of high immigration, increasing requests for naturalization provoked a backlash and claims that "criminal aliens" were unlawfully naturalizing with the help of a presidential administration seeking to increase Democratic voters. Such charges resulted in a congressional investigation.[29] Not coincidentally, INS denials of naturalization petitions during this period rose significantly.[30] Thus, Latin American citizens experienced a classic catch-22: they were criticized for not assimilating if they did not naturalize, but when they tried to change their citizenship status they were accused of abusing the process.

More ominously, the recent increase in rates of immigration helped to reignite a movement to review the fundamental rules of U.S. citizenship, especially the clause of the Fourteenth Amendment that grants birthright citizenship to all persons born in United States territory—including those who are born to undocumented parents.[31] Such a change would constitute a break with over a century of legal precedent.[32] The fact that the proposal would deny citizenship to so many Latinos alone suggests racial motives. Not coincidentally, concerns with naturalization and citizenship have grown at a time that the ranks of Latino citizens are increasing substantially and many observers acknowledge growing Latino political power.

Ultimately, as Louis DeSipio argues in his contribution to this volume (chapter 11), increasing naturalization of U.S. citizens of Latin American ancestry may well translate into Latino voting strength and facilitate Latino efforts to attain full membership and equal citizenship. Successful voting-rights litigation since the 1960s has helped level the playing field in the political arena, although much remains to be done.[33] During the 1990s, Latinos have been elected in increasing numbers to political office.[34] Recent developments also bode well for future political participation and activism. Community activism has fueled change. Organized labor, once a staunch opponent of immigration because of the fear of cheap immigrant labor, now courts undocumented immigrants in its organizing efforts and political activities.[35] On the negative side, the tragic events of September 11, 2001, have spawned a new nativist outburst. The U.S. government has made increased efforts to seal the borders, tighten visa monitoring, and facilitate deportation of noncitizens for relatively minor immigration violations. Anti-immigrant sentiments have influenced the political process and have damaged Latino immigrants through heightened border enforcement and restrictionist laws and policies.[36]

LATINO CIVIL RIGHTS: LEGAL PROGRESS AND SOCIAL SETBACKS

In the American legal system, Latino civil rights have not been traditionally thought of as "civil-rights" concerns at all. U.S. society generally has viewed civil rights as primarily an issue of African American/white relations.[37] The Latino population, however, has a long tradition of civil-rights activism in the United States, and this activism has intensified all the more with the demographic changes brought by immigration and immigration laws since 1965.

The history of Latinos' quest for full membership in U.S. society began almost at the moment of their incorporation. For example, in the case of Mexican Americans, protest against unequal treatment in violation of their rights as citizens began immediately following the end of the Mexican American War in 1848. Although their rights of citizenship were consistently assaulted by practices such as gerrymandering, encroachment on their lands (both communal lands and property held in fee simple), discrimination in public facilities, poll taxes, and prohibition from serving on juries, Mexican Americans fought back either through litigation, or through more direct means up to, and including, acts of violence.[38]

Since the early 1960s, Latinos of all national backgrounds have built on this tradition of activism to press their civil-rights claims. Among the most important of these have been the areas of immigration law and enforcement and language (and, by extension, other "cultural") issues. As argued above, Latinos have long been perceived by white—and black—Americans as "foreign" in the United States, a dubious stereotype that continues to have concrete impacts on modern Latino lives. The presumption of foreignness causes more than simply intangible injury.

IMMIGRATION AND CIVIL RIGHTS

Since the 1970s, Latinos have become increasingly active in protesting and taking legal and political action against what are widely regarded as heavy-handed immigration-law enforcement efforts by the INS. For obvious reasons, much of the activism in this area in the early 1970s emanated from the Mexican American and Mexican immigrant community.[39]

This is clear when we consider recent Latino reactions to the excesses of routine immigration enforcement by the INS and other agencies of the law. For years, people who "look" Latino have been more likely to be stopped and questioned by the Border Patrol at the border, at airports, and in the workplace. Indeed, as noted above, in some instances, U.S. citizens of Latin American ancestry have been unlawfully deported, especially during periods of repression such as the removal campaigns of the Great Depression, the 1950s, and again in the 1970s. In the 1990s, Congress went to great lengths to expedite and increase the removal of Latin Americans from the country.

Today, INS enforcement efforts increasingly occur far from the border, in places such as Georgia, Illinois, and Nebraska. This development results from the fact that Latin American migration is no longer limited to the border region but also is transforming the Midwest, South, and the East Coast. Latinos now work in a broad variety of occupations in virtually every state of the union. Although the highest levels of the U.S. government have condemned racial profiling in criminal law enforcement, the practice remains central to modern immigration enforcement in the United States.[40] As a result, Latinos routinely find themselves questioned about their citizenry and subjected to immigration enforcement procedures.

MEXICAN IMMIGRATION AND THE CIVIL RIGHTS OF PEOPLE OF MEXICAN ANCESTRY

In 1975, the U.S. Supreme Court held that Border Patrol officers on roving patrols may lawfully stop vehicles "only if they are aware of specific articulable facts, together with rational inferences from these facts, that reasonably warrant suspicion that the vehicles contain aliens who may be illegally in the country," not simply because the persons appear to be of Latin American ancestry.[41] However, the Court also noted that "the likelihood that any given person of Mexican ancestry is an alien is high enough to make Mexican appearance *a relevant factor*, but standing alone . . . does not justify stopping all Mexican-Americans to ask if they are aliens" (emphasis added). Racial stereotypes about people of "Mexican appearance" being undocumented immigrants, thus can help justify an immigration stop.

INS enforcement efforts have resulted in many civil-rights lawsuits. For example, in 1992, faculty, students, and staff at Bowie High School in El Paso, Texas, brought a class action claiming a pattern and practice of serious civil-rights deprivations by the Border Patrol.[42] In this case, Border Patrol officers stopped the automobile of local high school football coach Benjamin Murillo, a Mexican American and U.S. citizen whose family has lived in this country for generations, who was wearing a Bowie High School football coach shirt, pointed a gun at his head, and conducted a search of his car without probable cause. Border Patrol officers also stopped David Rentería and Juan Carlos Jacquez while they walked home after a high school graduation rehearsal, questioned them about their citizenship status and, without provocation, beat Rentería. On another occasion, the Border Patrol demanded to know the citizenship status of Nieden Susie Díaz as she walked home from school; one officer "for no apparent reason knocked Nieden down to the ground and kicked her about twenty times." A court entered an injunction prohibiting such lawless conduct. The parties subsequently settled the lawsuit, with the INS agreeing not to violate the constitutional rights of the class in the future and created a complaint procedure to remedy any INS violations of the settlement.

In July 1997 in the city of Chandler, a suburb of Phoenix, Arizona, local police, in cooperation with the Border Patrol, in an action dubbed "Operation Restoration" among law-enforcement officials but known as "Operation Round-Up" in the Mexican American community, stopped cars with occupants who "looked Mexican" at checkpoints to inquire about their immigration status. In a practice that is common in many other locales in the United States, police also stopped patrons at stores allegedly frequented by undocumented persons to inquire about their immigration status. According to the Arizona Attorney General, the police entered the homes of suspected undocumented immigrants without warrants or probable cause and stopped "numerous American citizens and legal residents . . . on multiple occasions . . . for no other reason than their skin color or Mexican appearance or use of the Spanish language."[43]

Allegations like these have been made too frequently over too long a period to be dismissed as mere aberrations.[44] Community activists long have argued that law enforcement officers regularly stop Latinos for nothing other than "driving while brown." In a 1985 case challenging such enforcement efforts, a chief Border Patrol agent testified that "he relied upon a person's appearance to substantiate 'reasonable suspicion' so long as it was 'not strictly Hispanic appearance.'" He said "an officer could rely, along with Hispanic appearance, on a 'hungry look,' or a person's age. . . . [A]gents testified they relied on, in addition to Hispanic appearance, [other factors including] a 'dirty, unkempt appearance,' . . . and the fact that a person wears work clothing."[45] The court enjoined the INS from unlawful stops based on Hispanic appearance.

The civil-rights lawsuits continue. In a typical action brought by Latino plaintiffs, *Hodgers-Durgin v. de la Vina*, a court of appeals in 1999 addressed a case in which the INS stood accused of stopping motorists of Latino descent in the state of Arizona—a state with a large Latino population—without reasonable suspicion.[46] In many cases of challenging Border Patrol stops, the officers admittedly relied upon Hispanic appearance.[47] The government explained its position clearly in one case:

> *The government urges the fact that the driver was Hispanic tends to give the agent reasonable suspicion that the driver was involved in illegal activity.* The government reasons that most illegal immigrants in Texas are Hispanic and . . . that this makes it more likely that this driver was also an illegal immigrant, or was involved in the trafficking of aliens. . . . The government [by pointing out that the officer] noticed that the driver was Hispanic, is trying to demonstrate a direct correlation between the driver being Hispanic and the likelihood that he is an illegal alien or is concealing illegal immigrants. This correlation is not adequate, especially given the percentage of Hispanic people that make up the population of this area.[48]

Cases challenging the use of undocumented immigration profiles are by no way limited to the border region. For example, a court in 2002 addressed a case in which Ohio State Highway Patrol Officers stood accused of stopping, detaining, and interrogating Latinos about their immigration status based on their race. A federal court had addressed a similar claim against Michigan and Illinois law-enforcement officers in the 1970s.[49]

Unlike other areas of law enforcement, immigration enforcement can lawfully be premised on race. Once Border Patrol officers are permitted to consider race, however, there is no realistic check on their discretion—and this obviously opens the door to rampant civil-rights violations of U.S. citizens of Latino ancestry. Proclaiming that race was only one factor for an investigatory stop, they can easily rationalize acting on a racial "hunch."[50] Moreover, as one court observed, "Border Patrol officers may use racial stereotypes as a proxy for illegal conduct without being subjectively aware of doing so."[51] Nor do devices exist that effectively deter Border Patrol abuses. The Supreme Court has held that the exclusionary rule generally does not cover deportation proceedings, so that the fruits of an unlawful stop, including one based exclusively on race, may be admissible. Similarly, internal INS complaint systems have proven to be of marginal utility in deterring unlawful conduct by Border Patrol officers.[52]

Ultimately, the perception among many Latinos is that race is *the* determinative factor to Border Patrol officers investigating alleged violations of the immigration laws. Despite the Supreme Court's directive to the Border Patrol not to consider race as the *exclusive* factor in deciding to investigate a person's immigration status, it is difficult to dispute that

> immigration authorities can still effectively stop and interrogate anyone they meet . . . providing only that the [person] looks foreign. While they cannot in theory question people on the basis of racial or ethnic appearance alone, they in fact do so consistently, and no one familiar with the realities of immigration enforcement would suggest the contrary.[53]

At times, the INS correctly targets undocumented Latin Americans but abuses their civil rights. Abuse of Mexican and Central American immigrants attempting the arduous trek across the southern border has been well documented. For example, in 1996, law-enforcement authorities in Riverside, California, without provocation beat two undocumented Mexican immigrants (Alicia Sotero Vásquez and Enrique Funes Flores) in a horrific event captured on videotape. In an even more tragic case, two Marines in Texas in 1997 shot and killed a Mexican American goat-herder, Esequiel Hernández Jr.—a U.S. citizen with no previous criminal record—while looking for drug traffickers along the increasingly militarized border. New border enforcement operations in high-volume border hubs such as El Paso and San Diego have redirected migrant streams to more dangerous routes, and, as a result, thousands of migrants have died both of exposure and crime.[54]

EFFORTS TO HALT CUBAN MIGRATION

Although the United States welcomed those who fled Cuba after the revolution through the 1970s as part of the international war on communism, the influx of Cuban migrants known as the "Mariel boatlift" in 1980 changed everything (see García, chapter 3, this volume). Concerned with a possible mass migration of the poor, blacks, criminals, homosexuals, and otherwise "undesirable" immigrants, the United States detained many Cuban immigrants who came in 1980.[55] The courts authorized such conduct and even permitted the indefinite detention of people whom the Cuban government refused to allow to return.[56] In the 1990s, fear of another influx of Cubans led the U.S. government to scramble to reach an agreement with the Cuban government to prevent another such mass migration.[57]

In their attempts to keep Cuban migrants on rafts from reaching the United States, the Coast Guard has resorted to questionable tactics, including using pepper spray and physical force.[58] Such conduct is encouraged by the law, which affords Cubans a full panoply of rights (and likely asylum) if they make it to shore, but few (and probable return to Cuba) if apprehended on the high seas.[59] Known by the U.S. Coast Guard as the "feet wet, feet dry" policy, relief is afforded to Cubans who make it to land ("feet dry") and denied to those apprehended on the sea ("feet wet").

EFFORTS TO STOP CENTRAL AMERICAN MIGRATION

As Chinchilla and Hamilton note in their contribution to this volume, Central Americans fleeing the political violence of their homelands have fared no better than other migrants. In the early 1980s, President Reagan's administration began a policy of detaining Central Americans and making affirmative efforts to convince them to "voluntarily" return to their homelands without pursuing their right to apply for asylum. A court in 1990 declared the policy to be unlawful.[60] In 1991, the U.S. government settled a lawsuit in which Guatemalan and Salvadoran asylum applicants alleged foreign-policy bias in the denial of their asylum claims.[61] In this case, the evidence showed that the U.S. government encouraged people fleeing Sandinista-led Nicaragua, a sworn enemy of the Reagan administration, to apply for asylum in the 1980s, although it previously had denied almost all claims of Nicaraguan applicants when an authoritarian ally had led the country.[62] In 1997, political action ultimately helped Central Americans obtain immigration relief through an act of Congress.[63]

THE NEGATIVE IMPACTS ON LATINOS

The concerted efforts to deny entry and deport Latinos cause symbolic and status injuries beyond the immediate harms to the people directly affected. Latin Americans often are presumed as the primary, if not sole subjects of immigration-law enforcement, often regardless of their actual citizenship status or whatever their family and personal history in the United States. This necessarily takes a personal toll on them and certainly affects whether they enjoy the status of full members and equal citizens of U.S. society. The efforts to limit entry of Latin Americans into the United States reveal volumes about Latinos' true status in this country. In too many cases, it confirms their second-class citizenship.

LANGUAGE AS A CIVIL-RIGHTS ISSUE FOR LATINOS

Language proves to be another point of contention in the civil-rights arena between people of Latin American ancestry and members of the "non-Hispanic white" majority in the United States. In 1990, there were more than 17.3 million homes in the United States in which Spanish was the principal non-English language spoken, and this number has obviously increased dramatically since then.[64] As immigrants came to this nation, U.S. society has pressured them to assimilate and become "American," which includes adopting English.[65] Early in the twentieth century, legal excesses in the efforts to enforce language conformity among immigrants resulted in Supreme Court landmarks protecting the rights of linguistic minorities.[66] Assimilationist pressures have generally been one of many factors, including the need for English-language skills for economic survival, which contributed to immigrant minorities' learning English. Assimilationists nonetheless condemn multiculturalism's tolerance of language diversity and claim that it is "splintering" U.S. society.[67]

Latin American immigration has unquestionably fueled the English-only movement in the United States. Cuban migration, for example, spurred English-only legislation in Florida, and many other states have passed either English-only laws or referenda.[68] Latin American immigration has proven especially troublesome to adherents of mandatory English. Spanish obviously is the primary language in most of Latin America, and with millions of Americans now speaking Spanish as their primary or secondary language, the widespread use of Spanish in daily life is guaranteed well into the future. Indeed, unless new draconian immigration laws are passed and even harsher enforcement measures are adopted, Latin American immigrants will continue to come to the United States, thus continuing to bring Spanish with them and thereby ensuring its continued presence in the United States.

The law has played a central role in the attempted implementation of language conformity. In 1991, the U.S. Supreme Court in *Hernández v. New York* held that, despite the obvious racial impacts, Spanish speakers could be stricken from juries when Spanish would be translated at the trial of a Latino criminal defendant.[69] Although ultimately invalidated on First Amendment grounds, a racially divided electorate in Arizona adopted a law prohibiting state employees from communicating in a language other than English in conducting governmental business.[70] A number of states, including California, have passed advisory laws declaring English to be the state's official language. In response to growing numbers of linguistic minorities, employers, with the acquiescence of the courts, have increasingly embraced English-only regulations in the workplace.[71]

It is perhaps too early to tell how the continuing controversy over language issues will play out in the resident Latino population. But it is clear that English-only laws and regulations have provoked controversy and tension because some Latinos view them as demeaning, unfair, and racist. The subtle message is that Spanish is "foreign" and causes problems that would evaporate if the language, and Latinos, would disappear. Such actions effectively tell Latinos that the Spanish language, which is central to their identity, is inappropriate for conducting professional affairs or private conversations in the workplace. Similarly, bilingual education, which Cuban immigrants—often held up as the exemplar of assimilation—initially pressed for in the 1960s, and which later grew in popularity among other Latinos, has become a continuing source of controversy. With the changing immigrant demographics since 1965, it has been increasingly under attack. In 1997, for example, the California voters enacted a law, in the face of heavy Latino opposition, which barred bilingual education in public schools.[72]

In modern times, as has been true historically, language often is employed as a proxy for race. English-only rules and attacks on bilingual education disparately impact the Latino community. Despite the concerns of English-only advocates, the empirical evidence is that Latin American immigrants in fact learn English and that English is embraced by subsequent generations.[73] Nonetheless, language remains a source of racial tension in a fight for status in U.S. society. Mandatory English undercuts Latino claims to full membership and equal citizenship and will almost certainly remain a major bone of contention in American political life for years to come.

EDUCATION: ENSURING EDUCATIONAL EQUALITY FOR LATINOS

The issue of education historically has always been a crucial issue for minority and immigrant mobility in the United States. As the Supreme Court emphasized in the landmark case of *Brown v. Board of Education* in 1954, education "*is the very foundation of good citizenship.*"[74] From 1960 to the present, ensuring access to public education for Latinos—and the full citizenship rights that at least in theory are supposed to come with higher levels of education—has been extremely difficult. Primary and secondary education for Latinos has long been the victim of what can most generously be termed benign neglect drifting toward crisis. And access to institutions of higher education, which increased for a time in the 1970s and 1980s, has since drastically diminished. Such developments promise to have a lasting negative impact on future generations of Latinos. Because Latino educational attainment lags far behind other groups, one blue-ribbon presidential commission proclaimed in 1996 that "educational attainment for most Hispanic Americans is in a state of crisis."[75]

IMPROVING PUBLIC ELEMENTARY AND SECONDARY EDUCATION: SCHOOL-FINANCING LITIGATION

Over the course of the late twentieth century, attempts at intentional de jure segregation of Mexican Americans in the United States in the public school system for the most part failed.[76] Beginning early in the twentieth century, legal cases brought by Latino advocacy groups, such as the League of United Latin American Citizens (LULAC) and, more recently, the Mexican American Legal Defense and Education Fund (MALDEF), slowly but surely chipped away at the structure of segregated public education that had characterized the schooling experience of most Latinos since the mid-nineteenth century. Landmark cases won by Latino plaintiffs, such as *Alvarez v. Owen* (The Lemon Grove School District Case, California, 1931), *Westminster School District v. Méndez* (California, 1947), and *Delgado v. Bastrop Independent School District* (Texas, 1948), all established important legal precedents in the national legal battle to end formal segregation that culminated in the U.S. Supreme Court's landmark decision in *Brown v. Board of Education* in 1954.[77] These cases all secured the rights of Mexican American children from segregation in the public schools.

But as has been true for African Americans in the wake of *Brown v. Board of Education*, Latinos continue to be subjected to de facto segregation in public school districts across the nation. This primarily resulted from housing segregation throughout the United States and the practice of sending children to neighborhood schools. Indeed, school segregation of Latinos has increased in the 1980s and 1990s. According to a 1999 study, "the data shows continuously increasing segregation for Latino students, who are rapidly becoming our largest minority group and *have been more segregated than African Americans for several years.*"[78]

Given the difficulties experienced in attempting to end de facto segregation of the schools and housing, Latinos have redirected focus and pressed for equality in public school financing. Public school funding based on local property taxes has created and maintained inequitable educational systems; poor neighborhoods have fewer resources for schools than more affluent localities. The U.S. Supreme Court in the 1973 decision of *San Antonio Independent School District v. Rodríguez* held that education is not a fundamental interest that subjects school-financing schemes to strict judicial scrutiny.[79] This holding effectively removed educational rights from the purview of the U.S. Constitution. Upholding a claim challenging disparate school funding, the California Supreme Court, however, in the famous decision of *Serrano v. Priest* in 1976, held that education was a fundamental interest under the California Constitution and that remedial action was necessary.[80] Since that decision, however, little has changed. School-finance litigation in several states over a span of three decades has failed to meaningfully improve Latino access to equal educational opportunities.[81] In California, as the percentage of Latino students has increased in the public schools, spending per pupil has declined precipitously.

Latino efforts to achieve educational equity have proven increasingly important as they have grown as a proportion of the students in public schools.[82] In 1996 and 1997, a plurality (nearly 40 percent) of the students in the California and New York City public schools were Latinos. Latinos constituted over 50 percent of the students in public schools in Miami and Houston, 32.1 percent in Chicago, and 12.5 percent in Milwaukee.[83]

Not coincidently, with the increase in Latinos in the public schools, efforts, including California's much publicized Proposition 187, have been made to keep undocumented children out of the classroom. In the 1982 decision of *Plyler v. Doe*, however, the Supreme Court invalidated a Texas law barring undocumented children from public elementary and secondary school education.[84] The Court rejected the creation of a "permanent caste of undocumented [Mexican] resident aliens, encouraged by some to remain here as a source of cheap labor, but nevertheless denied the benefits that our society makes available to citizens and lawful residents." Similarly, bilingual education, once required by the Supreme Court, has come under attack and now is generally banned in the public schools in California, Massachusetts, and other states.[85]

Other problems, such as crime, arise from the limited educational opportunities available to Latinos. Dwindling educational opportunities and high dropout rates no doubt contribute to the relatively high incarceration rates among young Latino males. Moreover, the criminal-justice system targets young Latinos, and to a lesser extent Latinas, in the United States. Puerto Ricans in New York, Cubans in south Florida, and Mexican Americans in the Southwest have experienced the sting of racial profiling in law enforcement. The dogged persistence of the popular stereotype of Latinos as criminals, gang members, and the like, contributes to this dynamic.[86]

THE BATTLE OVER AFFIRMATIVE ACTION IN HIGHER EDUCATION

As the twentieth century came to a close, the burning national debate on affirmative action in higher education deeply affected the Latino community. From the 1960s through the 1980s, affirmative action was in place in almost all institutions of higher education. In 1978, the U.S. Supreme Court, in *Regents of University of California v. Bakke*, endorsed the consideration of race in public-university admissions as a tool to ensure a diverse student body.[87] The 1990s, however, opened an entirely new chapter as attacks on affirmative action increased. Besides the claim that affirmative action deviated from admission based on "merit," the claim also was made—sometimes by those known as progressives—that Latinos illegitimately reaped the benefits of programs designed to remedy discrimination against African Americans.[88]

The evolving law influenced the attacks on affirmative action. Over the course of the 1980s and 1990s, a conservative majority of the Supreme Court moved toward a color blind conception of the Equal Protection Clause of the Fourteenth Amendment and away from the concept that race might legitimately factor into admission and other decisions to remedy past discrimination.[89] This evolving jurisprudence encouraged a federal court of appeals to invalidate the University of Texas law school's affirmative-action plan. It also led rejected white applicants to sue the University of Michigan law school, with the backing of conservative political organizations, for considering race in the admissions process.[90] The political process followed suit. A vanguard in the affirmative-action rollback of the 1990s, the Board of Regents of University of California eliminated race and gender from any consideration in admission to the University of California. The California voters subsequently passed an initiative proclaiming an end to all "racial preferences" in the state.[91] The results of these actions have been devastating. Latino enrollment in institutions of higher learning dropped immediately, and earnest attempts by admissions committees to develop weighted admissions formulae that somehow make up for the loss of Latino students have generally proven futile. Although aggregate numbers of Latino enrollment in institutions of higher education have begun to climb, they continue to be significantly underrepresented as a proportion of the population in colleges and universities.[92]

Latinos did not silently acquiesce to the devastating attacks on affirmative action. In Texas, a concerted political effort by Latino and other minority legislators convinced the state legislature to pass a law that made the top 10 percent of the graduates of every high school in the state, including predominantly minority schools, eligible for admission to the University of Texas. The Regents of the University of California endorsed a watered-down 4 percent version of the Texas plan and more recently have advocated doing away with one of the SAT exams as a requirement for UC admission.[93] The "solution," however, avoids the hard question of how to improve elementary and secondary public schools in poor- and working-class neighborhoods and ensure that high school graduates are adequately prepared for college.

Other measures have been taken in higher education that disparately affect the Latino community. Consistent with political efforts to keep undocumented children out of elementary and secondary schools, efforts have been made to exclude the undocumented from public colleges and universities.[94] Moreover, ethnic-studies programs, including Chicano studies, have been challenged as lacking intellectual rigor. The percentages of Latino faculty on college campuses across the country remain low and promise to become lower as the numbers in colleges and universities dwindle due to the demise of affirmative action.

Assuming that affirmative action remains part of the nation's future, Latinos must face some difficult questions. For example, should students from established Latino families subject to discrimination in this country and recent Latin American immigrants from well-to-do families stand on equal footing? In part this depends on the rationale for affirmative action, that is, whether it is designed to remedy past discrimination or ensure diversity in the student body. Similarly, should only poor, rather than middle-class, Latinos be entitled to affirmative-action benefits?[95] Because Latino students constitute such a large and growing proportion of the United States' school-age population, these nettlesome issues will undoubtedly continue to dominate debates over the direction of U.S. public education in the first years of the new century and beyond.

Ultimately, Latino access to elementary, secondary, and college education is related. Absent improved elementary and secondary education, true access to higher education, with or without affirmative action, appears to be a diminishing dream for many Latino students. Only with a true commitment to an overhaul of the system of public education in this country are educational opportunities for Latinos likely to improve. The law obviously has its limits, and political action holds the true promise for such far-reaching change.

CONCLUSION

As the year 2000 came and went, Latinos faced formidable barriers to their struggle for full membership and equal citizenship in the United States. Although U.S. law often served to thwart the struggle, it sometimes also worked as an avenue for positive social change. As I have argued in this essay, Latinos' relationship to the U.S. legal system will in all likelihood continue to cut both ways; Latinos have been able to secure important civil-rights gains through the legal system. At the same time, however, Latinos have experienced setbacks in their quest to reduce discrimination in immigration law and its enforcement, educational equity, and language rights.

In the end, political solutions may be the most promising for addressing the many legal and policy issues facing the Latino community. Recent activism, and the increasing naturalization rates of Latin American immigration, suggest the positive potential for political action. Legal relief, such as that provided through voting-rights litigation may be a means to facilitate political action. As was the case for African Americans, legal and political efforts in combination appear necessary to achieve lasting social change.

At least for the foreseeable future, the civil-rights concerns of Latinos are unlikely to change substantially from the those that remained at the close of the twentieth century. Immigration and citizenship, civil rights, and education are central to the advancement of Latinos in the United States. Until these foundational issues are addressed satisfactorily, Latinos will experience great difficulties joining the mainstream and becoming full members and equal citizens of the United States. Part of the overall solution will be raising consciousness among lawmakers, policymakers, and the public that civil rights concerns implicate Latinos, Asian Americans, Native Americans, and others, as well as African Americans. This will be no small feat. As the recent national flap over Senator Trent Lott's racially tinged comments at Strom Thurmond's 100th birthday party indicate, despite the explosive growth of the Latino population over the past forty years, black/white relations continue to dominate the national consciousness. Nonetheless, recognition of the civil-rights complexities of a multiracial, multicultural United States is a necessary first step toward addressing the problems faced by Latinos.

NOTES

1. See U.S. Department of Justice, *1997 Statistical Yearbook of the Immigration and Naturalization Service* (Washington, D.C.: U.S. Government Printing Office, 1999), 26, table 2.
2. See U.S. Department of Justice, Immigration and Naturalization Service, Office of Policy and Planning, *Annual Report: Legal Immigration, Fiscal Year 1997*, (Washington, D.C.: Government Printing Office, January 1999), 5.
3. For an analysis of the impact of Dominican, as well as Colombian, immigration on New York City, see Alejandro Portes and Rubén G. Rumbaut, *Immigrant America: A Portrait*, 2d ed. (Berkeley: University of California Press, 1996), 110–12.
4. For the history of Dominican players, as well as Latinos generally, in major league baseball, see Marcos Bretón and José Luis Villegas, *Away Games: The Life and Times of a Latin Baseball Player* (New York: Simon & Schuster, 1999).
5. See U.S. Department of Justice, *1997 Statistical Yearbook*, 200, table N.

6. See ibid., 77, table E. For discussion of Central American migration from 1970 to 1990, see Carlos B. Cordova and Raquel Pinderhughes, "Central and South Americans," in *A Nation of Peoples: A Sourcebook on America's Multicultural Heritage*, ed. Elliott Robert Barkan (Westport, Conn.: Greenwood Press, 1999), 103–10. See generally Susan Bibler Coutin, *Legalizing Moves: Salvadoran Immigrants' Struggle for U.S. Residency* (Ann Arbor: University of Michigan Press, 2000); Cecilia Menjívar, *Fragmented Ties: Salvadoran Immigrant Networks in America* (Berkeley: University of California Press, 2000).
7. See generally María Cristina García, *Havana USA: Cuban Exiles and Cuban Americans in South Florida, 1959–1994* (Berkeley: University of California Press, 1996); Felix Roberto Masud-Piloto, *From Welcomed Exiles to Illegal Immigrants: Cuban Migration to the U.S., 1959–1995* (Lanham, Md.: Rowman & Littlefield, 1996).
8. See *González v. Reno*, 212 F.3d 1338 (11th Cir.), *cert. denied*, 530 U.S. 1270 (2000).
9. See Francisco E. Balderrama and Raymond Rodríguez, *Decade of Betrayal: Mexican Repatriation in the 1930s* (Albuquerque: University of New Mexico Press, 1995); Juan Ramón García, *Operation Wetback: The Mass Deportation of Mexican Undocumented Workers in 1954* (Westport, Conn.: Greenwood Press, 1980); Camille Guerin-Gonzales, *Mexican Workers and American Dreams: Immigration, Repatriation, and California Farm Labor, 1900–1939* (New Brunswick, N.J.: Rutgers University Press, 1994). For an analysis of the legal history of undocumented Mexican migration to United States, see Gerald P. López, "Undocumented Mexican Migration: In Search of a Just Immigration Law and Policy," *UCLA Law Review* 28 (1981): 615.
10. Reed Ueda, *Postwar Immigrant America* (Boston: St. Martin's Press, Bedford Books, 1994), 48–49.
11. See Kevin R. Johnson, "An Essay on Immigration Politics, Popular Democracy, and California's Proposition 187: The Political Relevance and Legal Irrelevance of Race," *Washington Law Review* 70 (1995): 629.
12. See, for example, Illegal Immigration Reform and Immigrant Responsibility Act of 1996, Pub. L. No. 104–208, secs. 501–553, 110 Stat. 3009, 3670–81; Antiterrorism and Effective Death Penalty Act of 1996, Pub. L. No. 104–132, secs. 423, 502, 110 Stat. 2105, 2260–77; Personal Responsibility and Work Opportunity Reconciliation Act of 1996, Pub. L. No. 104–153, 110 Stat. 2260 (1996); also see below for discussions of human rights abuses along border. See generally Peter Andreas, *Border Games: Policing the U.S.-Mexico Divide* (Ithaca, N.Y.: Cornell University Press, 2000); Timothy J. Dunn, *The Militarization of the U.S.-Mexican Border, 1978–92: Low-Intensity Conflict Doctrine Comes Home* (Austin: CMAS Books, University of Texas at Austin, 1996); Douglas S. Massey, Jorge Durand, and Nolan J. Malone, *Beyond Smoke and Mirrors: Mexican Immigration in an Era of Economic Integration* (New York: Russell Sage Foundation, 2002).
13. See Matter of Collado-Muñoz, 21 Immigration and Nationality Decisions 106, Interim Decision No. 3333 (Board of Immigration Appeals, 1998).
14. See U.S. Department of Justice, Immigration and Naturalization Service, "INS Sets New Removals Record" (Washington, D.C.: Government Printing Office, 12 November 1999).
15. See, for example, National Council of La Raza, *The Mainstreaming of Hate: A Report on Latinos and Harassment, Hate Violence, and Law Enforcement Abuse in the*

1990s (Washington: National Council of La Raza, 1999), which documents hate crimes against Latinos; *San Diego Unified Port District v. U.S. Citizens Patrol*, 63 Cal. App. 4th 964, 74 Cal. Rptr. 2d 364 (1998), addressing case in which private citizens known as the "Airport Posse," wearing shirts stating "U.S. Citizen Patrol," searched for undocumented persons at an airport; Michael Janofsky, "Immigrants Flood Border in Arizona, Angering Ranchers," *New York Times*, 18 June 2000, reporting on Arizona ranchers using force and taking undocumented persons into custody along border.

16. See U.S. Commission on Immigration Reform, *U.S. Immigration Policy: Restoring Credibility* (Washington, D.C.: U.S. Government Printing Office, 1994), 78–81, summarizing patterns of discrimination by employers against national origin minorities; U.S. General Accounting Office, *Immigration Reform—Employer Sanctions and the Question of Discrimination: Report to the Congress* (Washington, D.C.: U.S. Government Printing Office, 1990), which found evidence of a pattern of widespread discrimination by employers against national-origin minorities.
17. See, for example, Maria L. Ontiveros, "To Help Those Most in Need: Undocumented Workers' Rights and Remedies under Title VII," *NYU Review of Law and Social Change* 20 (1993–1994): 607. Organization efforts, however, have proven more successful in recent years. See David G. Gutiérrez, "Ethnic Mexicans and the Transformation of 'American' Social Space: Reflections on Recent History," in *Crossings: Mexican Immigration in Interdisciplinary Perspectives*, ed. Marcelo M. Suárez-Orozco, (Cambridge: Harvard University Press ed., 1998), 309, 325–26. See generally Héctor L. Delgado, *New Immigrants, Old Unions: Organizing Undocumented Workers in Los Angeles* (Philadelphia: Temple University Press, 1993).
18. See Wayne A. Cornelius, "The Structural Embeddedness of Demand for Mexican Immigrant Labor: New Evidence from California," in ," in *Crossings: Mexican Immigration in Interdisciplinary Perspectives*, ed. Marcelo M. Suárez-Orozco, (Cambridge: Harvard University Press ed., 1998), 115, which offers empirical evidence of demand for immigrant labor in California. This view feeds on stereotypes about people of Mexican ancestry as less than human. See John O. Calmore, "Exploring Michael Omi's 'Messy' Real World of Race: An Essay for 'Naked' People Longing to Swim Free," *Law and Inequality* 15 (1997): 25, 72, which says that the "'dirty Mexican' image permits the justification for restricting Mexicans to laboring in the agricultural fields—in this context, 'dirty' means 'suited for labor in the fields.'" (footnote omitted); see also Guadalupe T. Luna, "'Agricultural Underdogs' and International Agreements: The Legal Context of Agricultural Workers Within the Rural Economy," *New Mexico Law Review* 26 (1996): 9, for an analysis of the dispossession of persons of Mexican ancestry from agricultural lands in Southwest.
19. See David G. Gutiérrez, *Walls and Mirrors: Mexican Americans, Mexican Immigrants, and the Politics of Ethnicity* (Berkeley: University of California Press, 1995).
20. See Gloria Sandrino-Glasser, "Los Confundidos: De-Conflating Latina/os' Race and Ethnicity," *UCLA Chicano-Latino Law Review* 19 (1998): 69, 89–90, n. 81, which mentions the "intra-Cuban American community conflict" caused by influx of Cuban immigrants in 1980.
21. See Linda S. Bosniak, "Exclusion and Membership: The Dual Identity of the Undocumented Worker Under United States Law," *Wisconsin Law Review* 1988 (1988): 955.

22. See, for example, *The Chinese Exclusion Case* (*Chae Chan Ping v. United States*), 130 U.S. 581, 595 (1889), which upheld the Chinese exclusion law, explaining that "it seemed impossible for [the Chinese] to assimilate with our people or to make any change in their habits or modes of living."
23. See, for example, Linda Chávez, *Out of the Barrio: Toward a New Politics of Hispanic Assimilation* (New York: Basic Books, 1991); Richard Rodríguez, *Hunger of Memory* (Boston: Godine, 1981); see also John J. Miller, *The Unmaking of Americans: How Multiculturalism Has Undermined the Assimilation Ethic* (New York: Free Press, 1998).
24. See, for example, Peter Brimelow, *Alien Nation: Common Sense About America's Immigration Disaster* (New York: Random House, 1995); Richard D. Lamm and Gary Imhoff, *The Immigration Time Bomb: The Fragmenting of America* (New York: Truman Talley Books, 1985); see also George J. Borjas, *Heaven's Door: Immigration Policy and the American Economy* (Princeton, N.J.: Princeton University Press, 1999), which notes that increased emphasis on the skills of immigrants in immigration laws would change the current racial demographics of immigration and contends that certain immigrant groups develop and propagate a culture of public-benefit dependence.
25. See Chávez, *Out of the Barrio*, 139–59.
26. See Carmen Teresa Whalen, "Puerto Ricans," in *A Nation of Peoples: A Sourcebook on America's Multicultural Heritage*, ed. Elliott Robert Barkan (Westport, Conn.: Greenwood Press, 1999), 446, 456–61, for data on the status of Puerto Ricans in contemporary United States. See generally José A. Cabranes, "Citizenship and the American Empire," *University of Pennsylvania Law Review* 127 (1978): 391; Ediberto Román, "The Alien-Citizen Paradox and Other Consequences of U.S. Colonialism," *Florida St. University Law Review* 26 (1998): 1.
27. See generally Pew Hispanic Center and Henry J. Kaiser Family Foundation, *2002 National Survey of Latinos* (Washington, D.C. and Menlo Park, Calif.: Pew Hispanic Center and Henry J. Kaiser Family Foundation, 2002), for survey data reflecting Latino assimilation into U.S. social life.
28. See T. Alexander Aleinikoff, "The Tightening Circle of Membership," *Hastings Constitutional Law Quarterly* 22 (1995): 915.
29. See Linda Kelly, "Defying Membership: The Evolving Role of Immigration Jurisprudence," *University of Cincinnati Law Review* 67 (1998): 185, 197–209. A subsequent Justice Department investigation concluded that, although some naturalization petitions were erroneously approved due to hasty processing, the Clinton Administration had not acted for political ends in the Citizenship USA program. See "IG Report Finds INS's 'Citizenship USA' Program was Flawed, But Not for Political Reasons," *Interpreter Releases* 77 (2000): 1198.
30. See Patrick J. McDonnell, "INS Denials of Citizenship Climb Sharply," *L.A. Times*, 14 June 1999, reporting that denial of naturalization petitions by INS rose by 25 percent during first six months of the 1998–99 fiscal year, including a 1,624 percent increase in Los Angeles.
31. See Peter H. Schuck and Rogers M. Smith, *Citizenship Without Consent: Illegal Aliens in the American Polity* (New Haven, Conn.: Yale University Press, 1985).
32. See *United States v. Wong Kim Ark*, 169 U.S. 649 (1898).

33. See, for example, *Garza v. County of Los Angeles*, 918 F.2d 763 (9th Cir. 1990), *cert. denied*, 498 U.S. 1028 (1991). See generally Rodolfo O. de la Garza and Louis DeSipio, "Save the Baby, Change the Bathwater, and Scrub the Tub: Latino Electoral Participation After Seventeen Years of Voting Rights Act Coverage," *Texas Law Review* 71 (1993): 1479, analyzing the impact of the Voting Rights Act on Latino electoral participation.
34. See Elliot Robert Barkan, *And Still They Come: Immigrants and American Society 1920 to the 1990s* (Wheeling, Ill.: Harlan Davidson, Inc., 1996), 174–75.
35. See, for example, Mary S. Pardo, *Mexican American Women Activists: Identity and Resistance in Two Los Angeles Communities* (Philadelphia: Temple University Press, 1998), for a discussion of resistance and activism by working- and middle-class Chicanas in Los Angeles area; George M. Anderson, "New Tides of Immigration: Immigrants and Labor Unions," *ASAP* 183 (2000): 12, for a discussion of organized labor's changing position on immigration and immigrants; Nancy Cleeland, "Migrant Amnesty Urged; Rally: About 20,000 Rally in Los Angeles to Demand Federal Legislation," *L.A. Times*, 11 June 2000, a report on a rally sponsored by organized labor that attracted 20,000 people clamoring for new amnesty.
36. See Kevin R. Johnson, "September 11 and Mexican Immigrants: Collateral Damage Comes Home," *DePaul Law Review* 52 (forthcoming, 2003).
37. The focus of this essay is on domestic civil-rights law, which is dominated by the anti-discrimination model. International human-rights law, which often seeks to guarantee substantive rights in addition to eliminating invidious discrimination, is beyond the scope of this essay. Elsewhere, I have expressed skepticism about the ability of international law to eliminate racial discrimination in the U.S. immigration laws. See Kevin R. Johnson, "The Moral High Ground? The Relevance of International Law to Remedying Racial Discrimination in the U.S. Immigration Law," in *Moral Imperialism: A Critical Anthology*, ed. Berta Esperanza Truyol-Hernández (New York: New York University Press, 2002), 285.
38. For analyses of early Mexican American civil-rights struggles, see David J. Weber, *Foreigners in the Native Land: Historical Roots of the Mexican Americans* (Albuquerque: University of New Mexico Press, 1973); Robert J. Rosenbaum, *Mexicano Resistance in the Southwest: The Sacred Right of Self-Preservation* (Austin: University of Texas Press, 1981); Juan Gómez-Quiñones, *The Roots of Chicano Politics, 1600–1940* (Albuquerque: University of New Mexico Press, 1994).
39. For discussion of the coalescence of Latino political action on behalf of immigrants in this period, see David G. Gutiérrez, "'Sin Fronteras?': Chicanos, Mexican Americans, and the Emergence of the Contemporary Immigration Debate, 1968–1978," *Journal of American Ethnic History* 10, no. 4 (1991): 5–37. Since then, other Latinos have been integrally involved in the debate over both U.S. immigration policy formulation and immigration-law enforcement.
40. See "Memorandum on Fairness in Law Enforcement," *Weekly Compilations of Presidential Documents* (President Clinton), 35 (9 June 1999): 1067: "no person should be targeted by law enforcement because of the color of his or her skin."
41. *United States v. Brignoni-Ponce*, 422 U.S. 873, 886–87 (1975); see *United States v. Martínez-Fuerte*, 428 U.S. 543 (1976). But see *United States v. Martínez-Fuerte*, 428

U.S. 543, 572 (1976) (Brennan, J., dissenting), contending that permitting the Border Patrol to consider race in stops will "target motorists of Mexican appearance" and will ensure that border enforcement "inescapably discriminate[s] against citizens of Mexican ancestry and Mexican aliens in this country for no other reason than that they unavoidably possess the same 'suspicious' physical and grooming characteristics of illegal Mexican aliens."; *United States v. Montero-Camargo*, 208 F.3d 1122 (9th Cir. 2000) (en banc), disregarding *Brignoni-Ponce* and holding that, because of the dramatic increase in the Hispanic population since 1975, Border Patrol cannot consider "Hispanic appearance" in making immigration stops.

42. *Murillo v. Musegades*, 809 F. Supp. 487 (W.D. Tex. 1992); see Arizona, California, New Mexico, and Texas Advisory Committees to the United States Commission on Civil Rights, *Federal Immigration Law in the Southwest: Civil Rights Impacts on Border Communities* (Los Angeles: U.S. Commission on Civil Rights, 1997), 15–20, describing the litigation and settlement.
43. Office of the Attorney General of Arizona, *Results of the Chandler Survey* (Phoenix: State of Arizona,1997), 31; emphasis added.
44. See, for example, *LaDuke v. Nelson*, 762 F.2d 1318 (9th Cir. 1985), *modified*, 796 F.2d 309 (9th Cir. 1986). See generally Alfredo Mirandé, *Gringo Justice* (Notre Dame, Ind.: University of Notre Dame Press, 1987), documenting the long history of Border Patrol abuse of persons of Mexican ancestry.
45. *Nicacio v. INS*, 797 F.2d 700, 704 (9th Cir. 1985).
46. 199 F.3d 1037 (9th Cir. 1999) (en banc), dismissed the case on technical jurisdictional grounds.
47. See, for example, *United States v. Cruz-Hernández*, 62 F.3d 1353, 1355–56 (11th Cir. 1995); *United States v. Rodríguez*, 976 F.2d 592, 595 (9th Cir. 1992), *amended*, 997 F.2d 1306 (9th Cir. 1993); *United States v. Franco-Muñoz*, 952 F.2d 1055, 1056 (9th Cir. 1991), *cert. denied*, 509 U.S. 911 (1993).
48. *United States v. Rubio-Hernández*, 39 F. Supp. 2d 808, 835–36 (W.D. Tex. 1998), emphasis added; see also *United States v. Jones*, 149 F.3d 364, 369 (5th Cir. 1998).
49. See *Farm Labor Organizing Comm. v. Ohio State Highway Patrol*, 308 F.3d 523 (6th Cir. 2002); see also *Ramírez v. Webb*, 787 F.2d 592 (6th Cir. 1986), enjoining discrimination by INS against Latinos in Michigan; *Illinois Migrant Council v. Pilliod*, 540 F.2d 1062 (7th Cir. 1976), the same ruling in Illinois, *modified*, 548 F.2d 715 (7th Cir. 1977), en banc.
50. See Edwin Harwood, "Arrests Without Warrant: The Legal and Organizational Environment of Immigration Law Enforcement," *UC Davis Law Review* 17 (1984): 505, 531–32, which states, based on fieldwork in border enforcement, that "it is easy to come up with the necessary articulable facts after the fact," which is known among Border Patrol officers as "'canned p.c.' (probable cause)."
51. *González-Rivera v. INS*, 22 F.3d 1441, 1450 (9th Cir. 1994), citing Charles R. Lawrence III, "The Id, The Ego, and Equal Protection: Reckoning With Unconscious Racism," *Stanford Law Review* 39 (1987): 317; see *United States v. García-Camacho*, 53 F.3d 244, 248 n.7 (9th Cir. 1995), quoting *González-Rivera*.
52. See *INS v. López-Mendoza*, 468 U.S. 1032 (1984); Bill Ong Hing, "Border Patrol Abuse: Evaluating Complaint Procedures Available to Victims," *Georgetown Immigration Law Journal* 9 (1995): 757.

53. Elizabeth Hull, *Without Justice for All: The Constitutional Rights of Aliens* (Westport, Conn.: Greenwood Press, 1985), 100.
54. See, for example, Amnesty International, *United States of America: Human Rights Concerns in the Border Region with Mexico* (New York: Amnesty International, 1998), 44–47, describing events surrounding the killing by U.S. Marines patrolling the border of U.S. citizen Esequiel Hernández; American Friends Service Committee, *Human and Civil Rights Violations on the U.S. Mexico Border 1995–97* (San Diego: American Friends Service Committee, 1998), documenting human rights abuses; Karl Eschbach et al., "Death at the Border," *International Migration Review* 33 (1999): 430, documenting deaths caused by border crossings from Mexico to United States; Bill Ong Hing, "The Dark Side of Operation Gatekeeper," *UC Davis Law Review* 7 (2001): 121, documenting the human costs of border-enforcement operation near the U.S./Mexico border in southern California; Kevin R. Johnson, "Some Thoughts on the Future of Latino Legal Scholarship," *Harvard Latino Law* Review 2 (1997): 101, 124–25, analyzing the significance of beating undocumented people on videotape; Jorge A. Vargas, "U.S. Border Patrol Abuses, Undocumented Workers, and International Human Rights," *San Diego International Law Journal* 2 (2001): 1, documenting human-rights abuses of undocumented Mexican immigrants by the Border Patrol; see also *Arizona v. Manypenny*, 451 U.S. 232 (1981), reviewing the criminal prosecution of a Border Patrol officer convicted of the assault with a deadly weapon of a migrant near the U.S./Mexico border. See generally Dunn, *Militarization of the U.S.-Mexico Border*.
55. See Sandrino, "Los Confundidos," 85–90.
56. See, for example, *Barrera-Echavarría v. Rison*, 44 F.3d 1441 (9th Cir. 1995) (en banc). See generally Mark S. Hamm, *The Abandoned Ones: The Imprisonment and Uprising of the Mariel Boat People* (Boston: Northeastern University Press, 1995).
57. See T. Alexander Aleinikoff, David A. Martin, and Hiroshi Motomura, *Immigration and Citizenship: Process and Policy*, 4th ed. (St. Paul, Minn.: West Group, 1998), 1174–75. See generally Joyce A. Hughes, "Flight from Cuba," *California Western Law Review* 36 (1999): 39, summarizing legal responses to Cuban migration to United States since Fidel Castro came to power in 1959.
58. See James Kitfield, "A Fast Boat to Miami," *National Journal* 31 (1999): 765; Rick Bragg, "Cubans Now Choosing Smugglers Over Rafts," *New York Times*, 21 July 1999.
59. The legal justification for this policy was established in *Sale v. Haitian Ctrs. Council, Inc.*, 509 U.S. 155 (1993), in which the Supreme Court held that Haitians interdicted on the high seas had no legal right to apply for relief from return to Haiti, even if they feared political persecution upon return.
60. See *Orantes-Hernández v. Thornburgh*, 919 F.2d 549 (9th Cir. 1990).
61. See *American Baptist Churches v. Thornburgh*, 760 F. Supp. 796 (N.D. Cal. 1991).
62. See Kevin R. Johnson, "A 'Hard Look' at the Executive Branch's Asylum Decisions," *Utah Law Review* (1991): 279, 338–39, 347–48.
63. See Nicaraguan Adjustment and Central American Relief Act, Pub. L. No. 105–100, 111 Stat. 2160 (1997).
64. See Barkan, *And Still They Come*, 152–53, table 8.1.
65. See, for example, Kevin R. Johnson, "'Melting Pot' or 'Ring of Fire'? Assimilation and the Mexican-American Experience," *California Law Review* 85 (1997): 1259;

Sylvia R. Lazos Vargas, "Deconstructing Homo[geneous] Americanus: The White Ethnic Immigrant Narrative and Its Exclusionary Effect," *Tulane Law Review* 72 (1998): 1493; George A. Martínez, "Latinos, Assimilation, and the Law: A Philosophical Perspective," *UCLA Chicano-Latino Law Review* 20 (1999): 1. See generally Kevin R. Johnson, *How Did You Get to Be Mexican? A White/Brown Man's Search for Identity* (Philadelphia: Temple University Press, 1999).

66. See, for example, *Meyer v. Nebraska*, 262 U.S. 390 (1923), invalidating state law prohibiting teaching of any language other than English in schools.

67. See, for example, Arthur M. Schlesinger Jr., *The Disuniting of America* (New York: Norton, 1992).

68. See Sylvia R. Lazos Vargas, "Judicial Review of Initiatives and Referendums in Which Majorities Vote on Minorities' Democratic Citizenship," *Ohio State Law Journal* 60 (1999): 399, 438–47.

69. 500 U.S. 352 (1991). The Supreme Court previously held that Mexican Americans could not be excluded from petit and grand juries. See *Hernández v. Texas*, 347 U.S. 475 (1954); *Castañeda v. Partida*, 430 U.S. 482 (1977).

70. See *Ruiz v. Hull*, 191 Ariz. 441, 957 P.2d 984 (Arizona Supreme Court, 1998), *cert. denied sub nom.*, 525 U.S. 1093 (1999).

71. See Christopher David Ruiz Cameron, "How the García Cousins Lost Their Accents: Understanding the Language of Title VII Decisions Approving English-Only Rules as the Product of Racial Dualism, Latino Invisibility, and Legal Indeterminacy," *California Law Review*, 85 (1998): 1347; Yxta Maya Murray, "The Latino-American Crisis of Citizenship," *UC Davis Law Review* 31 (1998): 503, 546–59; see also Steven W. Bender, "Direct Democracy and Distrust: The Relationship Between Language Law Rhetoric and the Language Vigilantism Experience," *Harvard Latino Law Review* 2 (1997): 145.

72. See California Secretary of State, *California Voter Information Guide Primary Election: June 2, 1998 Ballot Pamphlet* (Sacramento, Calif.: California Secretary of State, 1998), 75–76, reprinting the text of Proposition 227. See generally Kevin R. Johnson and George A. Martínez, "Discrimination by Proxy: The Case of Proposition 227 and the Ban on Bilingual Education," *UC Davis Law Review* 33 (2000): 1227; Rachel F. Moran, "Bilingual Education as Status Conflict," *California Law Review* 75 (1987): 321. For analysis of early bilingual education litigation pursued by Mexican Americans, see George A. Martínez, "Legal Indeterminacy, Judicial Discretion, and the Mexican-American Litigation Experience, 1930–1980," *UC Davis Law Review* 27 (1994): 555, 606–11.

73. See T. Alexander Aleinikoff and Rubén G. Rumbaut, "Terms of Belonging: Are Models of Membership Self-Fulfilling Prophecies?" *Georgetown Immigration Law Journal* 13 (1998):1, 11–14 (1998), reviewing empirical evidence.

74. 347 U.S. 483, 493 (1954); emphasis added.

75. President's Advisory Commission on Educational Excellence for Hispanic Americans, *Our Nation on the Fault Line: Hispanic American Education* (Washington, D.C.: Government Printing Office, 1996), 16; see also, for example, Elias López, Enrique Ramírez, and Refugio I. Rochín, *Latinos and Economic Development in California* (Sacramento: California Research Bureau, 1999).

76. See Martínez, "Legal Indeterminacy," 574–606, documenting litigation to desegregate public schools from 1930 to 1980.
77. See generally Thomas P. Carter, *Mexican Americans in School: A History of Educational Neglect* (New York: College Entrance Examination Board, 1970); Guadalupe San Miguel, *Let All of Them Take Heed: Mexican Americans and the Campaign for Educational Equality in Texas, 1910–1980* (Austin: University of Texas Press, 1987); Rubén Donato, *The Other Struggle for Equal Schools: Mexican Americans During the Civil Rights Era* (Albany: State University of New York Press, 1997); Stanton Wortham, et al., eds., *Education in the New Latino Diaspora* (Westport, Conn.: Ablex Publishers, 2002); Margaret E. Montoya, "A Brief History of Chicana/o School Segregation: One Rationale for Affirmative Action," *La Raza Law Journal* 12 (2001): 159; *Westminister School Dist. v. Méndez*, 161 F.2d 774 (9th Cir. 1947); *Delgado v. Bastrop Independent School District*, Civ. No. 388 (D.C.W.D. Tex. 1948); *Alvarez v. Owen*, No. 66–625 (California Superior Court, San Diego County, filed 17April 1931, The Lemon Grove case.
78. Gary Orfield and John T. Yun, *Resegregation in American Schools*, (Cambridge, Mass.: Harvard University, 1999), 2, emphasis added.
79. 411 U.S. 1 (1973).
80. See *Serrano v. Priest*, 18 Cal. 3d 728, 557 P.2d 929 (1976), *cert. denied sub nom.*, *Clowes v. Serrano*, 432 U.S. 907 (1977); *Serrano v. Priest*, 5 Cal. 3d 584, 487 P.2d 1241 (1971); see, for example, *Edgewood Ind. School Dist. v. Meno*, 893 S.W.2d 450 (Tex. 1995), reviewing the latest efforts of the Texas legislature to ensure compliance after finding that the school financing system violated various provisions of Texas Constitution; see also J. Steven Farr and Mark Trachtenberg, "The *Edgewood* Drama: An Epic Quest for Educational Equity," *Yale Law and Policy Review* 17 (1999): 607, tracing the history of the *Edgewood* litigation and its impact.
81. See Peter Enrich, "Leaving Equality Behind: New Directions in School Finance Reform," *Vanderbilt Law Review* 48 (1995): 101; Note, "Unfulfilled Promises: School Finance Remedies and State Courts," *Harvard Law Review* 104 (1991): 1072; see also James E. Ryan, "Schools, Race, and Money," *Yale Law Journal* 109 (1999): 249, analyzing the relationship between school finance and school desegregation litigation. See generally Martha Minow, "Reforming School Reform," *Fordham Law Review* 68 (1999): 257.
82. See Orfield and Yun, *Resegregation in American Schools*, 7, table 3. presenting statistical data showing nearly that 40 percent of public school students in California were Latino, slightly higher than white students.
83. Ibid., 8, table 4.
84. 457 U.S. 202, 218–19 (1982).
85. See *Lau v. Nichols*, 414 U.S. 563 (1974), holding that the San Francisco School District violated Title VI of Civil Rights Act by failing to provide an appropriate curriculum to non–English speaking children.
86. See Robert García, "Latinos and Criminal Justice," *UCLA Chicano-Latino Law Review* 14 (1994): 6; Cynthia Kwei Yung Lee, "Race and Self-Defense: Toward a Normative Conception of Reasonableness," *Minnesota Law Review* 81 (1996): 367, 442–52: Mary Romero, "State Violence, and the Social and Legal Construction of

Latino Criminality: From El Bandido to Gang Member," *Denver University Law Review* 78 (2001): 1081. See generally Cruz Reynoso, "Hispanics and the Criminal Justice System," in *Hispanics in the United States: An Agenda for the Twenty-First Century*, ed. Pastora San Juan Cafferty and David W. Engstrom (New Brunswick, N.J.: Transaction Publishers, 2000).

87. 438 U.S. 265 (1978).
88. See, for example, Roy Howard Beck, *The Case Against Immigration,* (New York: W. W. Norton & Co., 1991), 191; Michael Lind, *The Next American Nation* (New York: Free Press, 1995), 116, 131.
89. See, for example, *Adarand Constructors, Inc. v. Peña*, 515 U.S. 200 (1995), holding that all racial classifications, including those in federal programs designed to foster minority businesses, are subject to strict scrutiny; and *City of Richmond v. J.A. Croson Co.*, 488 U.S. 469 (1989), holding to similar effect.
90. See *Hopwood v. Texas*, 78 F.3d 932 (5th Cir.), *cert. denied sub nom.*, 518 U.S. 1033 (1996); *Grutter v. Bollinger*, 288 F.3d 732 (6th Cir. 2002); see also *Podberesky v. Kirwan*, 38 F.3d 147 (4th Cir. 1994), which invalidates as unconstitutional a merit scholarship open only to African Americans, *cert. denied*, 514 U.S. 1128 (1995). In December 2002, the Supreme Court agreed to review the constitutionality of the University of Michigan's affirmative action policies. See *Grutter v. Bollinger*, 123 S.Ct. 602 (2002).
91. See *Coalition for Economic Equity v. Wilson*, 122 F.3d 692 (9th Cir.), upholding the initiative in the face of a constitutional challenge, *cert. denied*, 522 U.S. 963 (1997).
92. See Kenneth R. Weiss and Mary Curtius, "Acceptance of Blacks, Latinos to UC Plunge," *Los Angeles Times*, 4 April 1998; Kenneth R. Weiss, "SAT Gap for Latinos and Blacks Grows," *Los Angeles Times*, 8 August 2000; and "For Immigrant Kids, A World of Struggle," *Los Angeles Times*, 29 May 2001.
93. See Tex. Educ. Code sec. 51.803(a) (1998); Kenneth R. Weiss, "UC Regents OK Plan to Admit Top 4%," *L.A. Times*, 20 March 1999. The events culminating in the passage of the Texas law are discussed in David Montejano, "On *Hopwood*: The Continuing Challenge," in *Reflexiones: New Directions in Mexican American Studies*, ed. Neil Foley (Austin, Tex.: CMAS Books, University of Texas at Austin, 1998) , 133.
94. See Michael A. Olivas, "Storytelling Out of School: Undocumented College Residency, Race, and Reaction," *Hastings Constitutional Law Quarterly* 22 (1995): 1019; Victor Romero, "Postsecondary School Education Benefits for Undocumented Immigrants: Promises and Pitfalls," *North Carolina Journal of International Law and Commercial Regulation* 27 (2002): 393.
95. See Kevin R. Johnson, "Immigration and Latino Identity," *UCLA Chicano-Latino Law Review* 19 (1998): 197, 207–8; see also Rachel F. Moran, "Unrepresented," *Representations* 55 (1996): 139.

ELEVEN

THE PRESSURES OF PERPETUAL PROMISE: LATINOS AND POLITICS, 1960–2003

LOUIS DESIPIO

AT THE dawn of the contemporary era of Latino politics, Latinos[1] arguably determined the outcome of a presidential election. In 1960, Mexican Americans in Texas organized to elect John Kennedy through a network of *Viva Kennedy!* clubs and voted at unprecedented levels. Their votes tipped the Texas election to the Democrats. With Texas's Electoral College votes committed to Kennedy, there was little incentive for his opponent, Richard Nixon, to contest Illinois's electoral votes (which included fraudulent votes for both parties). These two states gave Kennedy the victory.

In the forty years since, and despite a vast growth in the Latino population, this accomplishment has not been repeated. On the contrary, and despite a vast expansion in the number of Latinos voting, Latino votes are frequently irrelevant to electoral outcomes. Of perhaps greater concern, it has been rare to see grassroots community organization in Latino communities that compared to what the *Viva Kennedy!* clubs established in 1960. While there have certainly been exceptions, mass mobilization has been the exception in Latino communities. Like the population as a whole, then, Latino politics (whether electoral or community) has become less participatory over time.

This chapter begins by examining the *Viva Kennedy!* campaign to identify why its experience was unique in Latino political history. Using *Viva Kennedy!* as a foundation, the essay then examines the structural limits and

The author would like to express his appreciate to David Gutiérrez for a thoughtful and careful reading of an earlier draft of this essay.

opportunities that Latinos have faced in politics over the last forty years and assesses how they have organized to overcome limits and seize political opportunities. The chapter concludes with an evaluation of Latino participation in electoral and community politics today.

As will be evident, there is no one form of Latino politics. This essay broadly looks at three forms—electoral, organizational, and interest based. Many in the Latino community cannot participate in electoral politics, and many who are eligible do not participate regularly. Electoral politics is, nevertheless, the primary means by which Latinos have sought to organize and make demands on American politics in the years since 1960. Elections are also the primary way in which majority political institutions engage Latinos and Latino interests. A second form of politics that is a focus in this essay is community-organizational politics. Organizations offer a resource for all Latinos to make demands on political institutions. Organizations allow for the articulation of much more focused demands—such as the needs of parents in a specific school or workers in a specific workplace—than do electoral politics. As a result, organizations (and therefore, organizational politics) are somewhat more ephemeral, but they remain an active focus of Latino political activity. Finally, this essay examines Latino political interests. It is these interests that will guide the future of Latino organizing. Equally importantly, these interests indicate that despite the many actual and potential divisions in Latino communities—such as divisions arising from different national origins or ancestry; generational differences; legal or juridical status; and so on—the majority of Latinos can increasingly be understood as having core political issues and concerns in common.

Regardless of the locus of politics, Latino politics between 1960 and the present has been characterized by a recurring pattern—specifically that expectations for Latino political impact precede the ability of Latino communities to deliver on these expectations. These unmet expectations create another barrier that Latinos must overcome to ensure that their interests are met by U.S. political institutions.

VIVA KENNEDY! AND THE FOUNDATIONS OF LATINO ELECTORAL INFLUENCE

In 1960, Latinos—primarily Mexican Americans—organized and voted at unprecedented levels. Polling was in its infancy, and polling of Latinos nonexistent, but it is reasonable to argue that Mexican Americans in Texas provided John Kennedy with the key margin he needed in the Electoral College to win the Presidency (García and de la Garza 1977).[2] While this would be a remarkable achievement today, it was all the more so in 1960. Nationally, the Latino population was small, and in Texas even smaller. In addition, Latinos in Southwestern states including Texas were still limited in how freely they could exercise the franchise. Latinos had organized at the local level since at least the 1880s, but there was only limited contact between Latino community organizations across communities. Nevertheless, the closeness of the election and the unprecedented mobilization of Mexican Americans (and, to a lesser degree, Puerto Ricans) ensured the Kennedy victory. Although this remarkable success has yet to be repeated, the 1960 Latino campaign laid the foundation for the next generation of Latino politics.

The next section of this essay examines the norms of Latino politics in 1960 and beyond. For now, it is important to recognize the accomplishments of *Viva Kennedy!* and the strategies they offer as an important lesson from which today's campaigns could learn (I. García 2000). With organizational and financial support from the national Kennedy campaign, Mexican Americans and Puerto Ricans established community-based *Viva Kennedy!* clubs in heavily Latino areas in the Southwest, upper Midwest, and New York. These organizations built on existing local organizations but added several important dimensions. *Viva Kennedy!* was the first explicitly partisan national Latino organization. The clubs maintained their autonomy from the national campaign and linked the objectives of the national campaign to local needs. They built a membership base and, in many cases, charged dues, but their primary goal was to register voters, pay poll taxes, and turn voters out for the Kennedy-Johnson ticket. Finally, the clubs were loosely linked, not just across the Southwest, but nationwide. The language was not used at the time, but 1960 was the first case of "Latino" electoral politics, in that *Viva Kennedy!* targeted Mexican Americans and Puerto Ricans through the same campaign structure.

Organization of this scale for partisan ends was new in Latino communities, but it alone was not enough to ensure Latino influence on the outcome of the election. Instead, this influence occurred because of three exogenous factors—the closeness of the election, the near equal division of non-Hispanic votes in Texas, and the importance the Kennedy campaign placed on winning Latino votes in Texas. Few presidential elections in U.S. history have proved to be as close as 1960. In the popular election, Kennedy beat Nixon by just 119,000 votes. The Electoral College was similarly close, with the victory coming down to two states—Illinois and Texas. In Texas, the Kennedy victory was a mere 46,000 votes.

Although a number of factors contributed to Kennedy's victory in Texas, the mobilization of Latino voters—many of them for the first time—may well have tipped the balance in JFK's favor. White voters in Texas were nearly evenly divided, and neither candidate was confident of victory. The Kennedy campaign consequently decided to dedicate a significant part of its resources to winning Tejano votes. In addition to the organizing funds dedicated to the *Viva Kennedy!* clubs, the Kennedy campaign also dedicated a national campaign staff member—Carlos McCormick—to coordinate *Viva Kennedy!* efforts. More importantly, John and Jacqueline Kennedy personally campaigned in heavily Mexican American areas. John Kennedy spoke of his immigrant and Catholic roots to establish a bond with Mexican Americans. He also made a specific promise—the appointment of a Mexican American to an ambassadorial post in Latin America. Jacqueline Kennedy spoke Spanish at rallies targeted to Mexican Americans and cut what is probably the first Spanish-language television commercial dedicated to winning Latino votes. None of these outreach strategies had previously been used in a national campaign.

Did this effort make the difference in Texas? Without opinion polling, it is not possible to say conclusively. Estimates from the era, however, indicate that Kennedy won more than 90 percent of the Mexican American vote in Texas and that approximately 200,000 Mexican Americans voted in that state, giving Kennedy a 160,000 vote cushion from Mexican American voters—180,000 Kennedy votes minus 20,000 Nixon votes (García and de la Garza 1977: 101; Gómez-Quiñones 1990: 88–92). White voters gave a 150,000-vote plurality to Nixon. Clearly, Kennedy could not have won without the Mexican American voters. A more interesting question, but one that can never be answered, is whether it was the *newly mobilized* Mexican American voters—those registered or mobilized by *Viva Kennedy!*—who gave Texas and the national election to John Kennedy.

Why was Latino influence not to be felt again for many years in national electoral politics? Perhaps most importantly, no presidential race was as close for another forty years. In 1964, for example, Lyndon Johnson could well have redeployed the *Viva Kennedy!* infrastructure, but he did not need to (Pycior 1997). Johnson's lead was large throughout the race. This pattern repeated itself in all races but 1976 and 2000. In 1960, and for many years beyond, the small size of the Latino electorate meant that races had to be very close and to depend on the electoral votes of one of the states of high Latino residence for Latino influence to be felt. It was only in the 1980s and 1990s that Latinos could realistically be influential in all but the closest elections.

Secondly, Latinos themselves failed to maintain the level of organization that they had achieved in 1960. The *Viva Kennedy!* infrastructure remained for a time after the election and served as the foundation for the Political Association of Spanish-Speaking Organizations (PASSO). Its leaders lost a common focus, though, and the membership bases rapidly disappeared (I. García 2000). It would be at least a decade and a half before there was another "national" Latino political organization, and the organizations that emerged in the mid-

1970s did not make building a mass base one of their priorities. Some *Viva Kennedy!* leaders focused their organizational energies on receiving government jobs (of which few were successful). Others sought election to office or returned to a focus on local politics. Whatever the new direction of these leaders, it is important to note that after 1960, no national Latino coordinating structure existed. It would take at least a decade and a half to reestablish the foundation for coordinating activities nationally or regionally. Finally, the near unanimity of Latino voters in the 1960 race had slowly dissipated over time.

Thus, in the beginning of the contemporary era of Latino politics, Latinos achieved their most electoral influence. The strategies used to win their votes—a targeted ethnic campaign under the direction of a campaign-staff member with group-specific responsibilities—were to reappear in various campaigns that followed, but the circumstances under which their votes proved important—a close race in which their votes were actively sought by one of the candidates—was not to reappear for forty years.

BARRIERS AND OPPORTUNITIES

The Latino influence felt in the 1960 election and the relative lack of political influence in the period since can be explained in large part by the impact of the two political and institutional regimes of Latino community mobilization in this period. The first regime was shaped by the manipulation and selective exclusion of Latino participation that characterized the early years of the contemporary era (roughly from the 1960s through the early 1970s). The regime was in decay by the 1970s but was largely ended through state action—the implementation of the federal Voting Rights Act (VRA) of 1965 and, more specifically, the extension of coverage of the act's provisions to Latinos in 1975. The second regime—in which some Latinos are active and influential politically and others are not—could only appear once the VRA ended machine manipulation and state exclusion of Latino votes.

Today's Latino politics reflect the evolution of this second regime, in which demography largely shapes who participates and who does not. Institutions that have in the past mobilized new residents and nonparticipants are weaker today than they have been in the past. Elections, for example, are frequently noncompetitive. Parties focus their energies on regular voters and expend little effort to make participants of nonparticipants. And community-based organizations in Latino communities are often weak and elite driven. As a result, the majority of Latinos who are eligible do not vote, nor are they active in community-based organizations. An ever-growing share of the Latino population cannot participate in electoral politics, and many do not participate in community politics. These demographic limits and the failure of institutions to engage many Latinos in politics create an " electorate in reserve" that is the source of the perpetual expectations for Latino political influence. The following section addresses each of these issues in turn and argues that while Latinos have not come close to achieving the impact they had on the 1960 presidential election, they should eventually become more politically influential in U.S. national, state, and local politics.

DECAYING MACHINES AND EXCLUSION

Although many have argued that the modern era of Latino politics began with the success of the *Viva Kennedy!* campaign, the extension of the Voting Rights Act (VRA) to Latino and other specified "language-minority" populations in 1975 was probably much more important to the long-run expansion of Latino electoral opportunities and the goal of Latino empowerment. Prior to 1975, Latino politics, as such, did not exist. Mexican Americans faced obstacles to political participation that included political machines, gerrymandering, poll taxes, and, in some areas, the threat of violence comparable to that experienced by African Americans in this era. Puerto Ricans were selectively included and excluded from urban political coalitions in areas where they resided (Jennings and Rivera 1984; Cruz 1998). Cuban American politics was in its infancy, and its focus was primarily on the politics of exile and the destruction of the Cuban Revolution and Fidel Castro (M. C. García 1996; Torres 1999. See also García, chapter 3, this volume). To the extent that these diverse experiences can be homogenized, the Latino politics of this era was made up mostly of U.S.-born Latinos, as new immigration was comparatively low, and focused on demands for civil rights and equal educational opportunity.

The Mexican Americans and Puerto Ricans who composed the Latino electorate in 1960 were largely marginal to national and local politics both before and after 1960. Undeniably, there had been some notable political "firsts" in the 1950s and 1960s, such as the first Latinos elected to the U.S. Congress from Texas, California, and New York in the modern era (Henry B. González from Texas in 1961, Edward R. Roybal from California in 1962, and Herman Badillo from New York in 1969) or the first Latino elected as the mayor of a major American city in the modern era (Raymond Telles elected in El Paso in 1957).[3] But, the more dominant pattern was manipulation and exclusion of Latino votes throughout much of the country.

As was true of other ethnic groups at different points in American history, Mexican Americans and Latino voters were often manipulated, if not actually controlled, by political machines, some of which were Latino controlled. Political machines are groups that control the activities of a political party and trade a combination of rewards (such as jobs, government services, or money) and threats for the support of voters. Machines often rely on a large population of ill-informed voters who trade their loyalty for personalistic connections to the machine's leader, or the "boss," who controls the rewards that the machine offers its supporters. The power of the boss was that he (there were few women bosses) controlled the votes of a high enough share of the electorate to ensure that the machine remained in power.

This machine manipulation of Latino votes in the late nineteenth and first half of the twentieth centuries was more the norm in South Texas, urban Texas, New Mexico, Arizona, New York, and Chicago. As a result, at the dawn of the contemporary era of Latino politics in the 1950s and 1960s, Latino electoral participation was more common than in the African American community, and, because of their involvement with machines, Latinos were often elected to local offices. Despite these opportunities, most Latinos who participated in politics did not do so freely. It is important to keep in mind, however, that the Latino participation machines were not without reward to some Latinos. Throughout the late nineteenth and early twentieth centuries, Latinos were elected to office in the Southwest, particularly in areas of high Latino population densities like New Mexico, certain districts of Arizona, and some communities in Texas along the U.S.-Mexico border. This ongoing experience with electoral politics meant that Latino community organizing in the 1950s and 1960s focused as much on how to use the franchise (and to overcoming the barrier of the poll tax) as to getting it, which was one of the major emphases of African American activism until 1965.

While there are little data on Latino voting before 1960, some data exist from the 1960s and early 1970s. These show the difference between African American and Latino electoral participation in this era. Prior to the VRA, black participation in the South ranged from the low single digits to no more than 20 percent (Davidson and Grofman 1994). In this same period, however, the share of Mexican American adult citizens voting ranged from the high 30s to the low 50s, depending on the survey and the locality (there are no comparable data on Puerto Ricans in this era).

A study of registration and voting in Los Angeles and San Antonio at the time of the 1964 election, for example, showed Mexican American voter-turnout rates of 50 and 38 percent, respectively (Grebler, Moore, and Guzmán 1970: 564). A study of "Mexican American counties" in Texas (primarily rural counties) from the 1960s showed voter turnout of between 30 and 55 percent (McCleskey and Merrill 1973). A third study from the 1960s demonstrated a gap between the eligible Latino electorate (adults who had paid the poll tax) and the actual Latino electorate. Latinos made up 5.6 percent of the former and 3.1 percent of the actual electorate (McCleskey and Nimmo 1968). Only one national study of

Latino voting prior to the 1975 extension of the Voting Right Act exists. According to this study, in the 1972 presidential election, approximately 44 percent of the "Spanish surnamed population" reported that they were registered and 37 percent reported that they voted (U.S. Bureau of the Census 1973).[4]

These voter-turnout rates should not obscure the fact that some Latinos faced intimidation or violence if they tried to exercise the franchise (Navarro 1998). But they should also make clear that Latinos did not face complete exclusion. Instead, machines used Latino votes when they needed them. By the 1960s, when the influence of machines began to weaken nationwide, Latinos were increasingly able to organize and elect candidates of their choice, without machine interference, particularly in urban areas.

This pattern of voter manipulation and selective exclusion might seem to resemble the experiences of European ethnics in the early part of the twentieth century, but it differed in one key respect. The machine domination of Eastern and Midwestern cities generally lasted no more than two generations or, if it did last longer, shifted the manipulation from one ethnic population to another. In the Southwest, on the other hand, manipulation of the Mexican American vote lasted for nearly one hundred years. Machine domination of the Mexican American vote was certainly in decline by the 1960s, and Latinos were organizing and electing candidates independently. But it was the extension of the Voting Rights Act to Latinos in 1975 that ultimately broke the influence of machines and spurred the creation of an independent Mexican American and Latino electorate.

THE VOTING RIGHTS ACT AND MAJORITY-MINORITY DISTRICTS

In many ways, modern black and Latino politics began with the passage of the Voting Rights Act in 1965 and its extension to Latinos in 1975. Initially, the VRA covered only African Americans. The act provided procedural guarantees that ensured that blacks in the South could register and vote without intimidation and that local jurisdictions could not change voting rules or procedures without Justice Department approval (Davidson and Grofman 1994). This nationalization of voter protection ensured a dramatic increase in black voter participation and an increase, albeit slower, in the number of African American elected officials.

In 1975, Congress extended the VRA to Latinos and other "language minorities" (ethnic groups that were determined to have faced multigenerational discrimination in the United States—Latinos, Asian Americans, Native Americans, and Alaskan natives). In addition to the protections guaranteed to African Americans in 1965, Congress added one resource for Latinos and the other language minorities—bilingual election materials.

The initial impact of the VRA for Latinos was nowhere near as dramatic as for African Americans. As indicated, prior to the VRA, Latinos did vote, so the impact was not to be felt in new electoral participation. The VRA did reduce machine control of the Latino vote, but this was already substantially in decline. The bilingual election materials provided a resource for some voters and are certainly of great symbolic importance. These bilingual materials were mandated to remedy the failure of schools in the Southwest to teach English to Mexican Americans. The generation that suffered this educational discrimination has largely aged and developed English competence. To the extent that bilingual election materials are used today, naturalized citizens are their prime users. But studies have demonstrated that they not widely used (de la Garza et al. 1992: 126, table 8.22)

A more significant impact for Latinos as well as African Americans came in 1982 when Congress amended and extended the VRA. The most important amendment was one that required that jurisdictions covered by the act draw districts that would be likely to elect the candidate of their choice, usually a co-ethnic, when the concentration of racial or ethnic minorities allowed it to. This requirement to create so-called majority-minority districts marked a substantial shift in the balance of power between minority communities and the redistricting process. Prior to the amendments, jurisdictions often divided black and Latino population concentrations into multiple districts and therefore limited the impact of new black and Latino votes. After the 1982 Amendments, on the other hand, minority community leaders could use the Justice Department and, ultimately, the federal courts, to overcome local resistance to the creation of districts likely to elect minority officeholders.

Majority-minority districting requirements have had dramatic effects. In 1973, the six states with the largest Latino populations had 1,280 Latino elected officials. By 2000, this number had grown to 3,645 in the same states (Arizona, California, Florida, New Mexico, New York, and Texas), an increase of over 184 percent (Pachon and DeSipio 1992; NALEO Educational Fund 2000). By 2002, this number had risen to 5,537 Latino elected officials.

Whether these rapid gains will continue in future redistrictings is an open question. In the 1990s, the Supreme Court began to question the constitutionality of VRA mandates to create majority-minority districts (*Shaw v. Reno* 1993: 113 S. Ct. 2816; *Bush v. Vera* 1996: 116 S. Ct. 1941), but has yet to rule definitively on the subject. The most recent ruling at this writing (*Hunt v. Cromartie* 2001: 121 S. Ct. 1452) indicates that the swing justice (O'Connor) has come to accept the argument that the odd shape of many majority-minority districts results more from partisanship and incumbency protection than from a disproportionate (and unconstitutional, in her view) attention to race. Regardless of the outcome of this ongoing constitutional debate, the number of districts electing Latinos to office will almost certainly continue to grow because the Latino population is growing so rapidly. The VRA's mandate that local jurisdictions draw districts likely to elect Latino, black, or Asian American officeholders speeds this process because it ensures that local jurisdictions face the potential of costly litigation if they fail to draw districts that reflect the changing demographics of their communities.

LATINO PARTICIPANTS AND NONPARTICIPANTS

The VRA succeeded at ending machine manipulation and expanded the opportunity for Latinos to elect Latinos to office. Other factors, however, continue to limit Latino participation in electoral and community politics. Among the most important of these are four demographic limits—the relative youth of the Latino population; the low levels of formal education in the Latino population; the corresponding concentration of Latinos in the lower strata of the U.S. class system; and, perhaps most crucially, the fact that many Latinos are not U.S. citizens and thus are ineligible to participate in electoral politics. While other ethnic populations have faced similar impediments in the past, none has faced all of them together over such a long period of time.

In the twentieth century, all U.S. electorates have seen increased demographic and class bias in voting and other forms of political participation. These barriers reduce the likelihood that the poor, the less educated, and the young will participate in electoral and community politics. The Latino population has higher concentrations of each of the segments of the population less likely to participate politically and, thus, pays a disproportionate price for the class bias in U.S. electoral politics. In addition to these constraints, as discussed in the next section, Latinos face another barrier to electoral empowerment that is often found among populations with large numbers of recent immigrants: noncitizens cannot vote in most contemporary elections.

The impact of these demographic characteristics on Latino electoral participation is dramatic. Of every 100 Latinos, just 64 are adults (authors' calculations based on U.S. Bureau of the Census 2000a: table 1.1). For the non-Latino population, nearly 75 are adults. Among these adults, Latinos are less likely to be voters. Of the remaining 64 Latino adults in the 100, 17 are voters (in presidential elections), 22 are U.S. citizens who do not regularly vote, and 25 are adults who are not U.S. citizens. For the non-Latino population, 43 of the 75 adults are voters, 29 are U.S. citizen adults who do not vote regularly, and just 3 are not U.S. citizens. Why is this gap between Latinos and the non-Latino population so dramatic?

The impact of the first of these factors—youth—is relatively easily explained. Latino families are larger on average than non-Latino families. As a result, a higher share of the Latino population is under eighteen and cannot vote. Even among adults, however, Latinos are younger on average than non-Latinos by about eight years. The average Latino is twenty-six and the average white non-Hispanic is thirty-four (U.S. Bureau of the Census 2001; see also Gutiérrez, introduction, this volume). Among all populations, the young are less likely to vote. The reasons for this are several and apply equally to Latinos and non-Latinos. The young are less familiar with candidates and voting procedures, and as a result they feel more distant from elections. They are more cynical about the utility of the vote and tend to be more dissatisfied with the options they are presented. Finally, they move more often and, as a result, are less likely to be registered. Thus, the relative youth of the Latino electorate dampens turnout—many are too young to vote, and many adults are relatively less likely to vote than older adults. Both of these characteristics, however, presage at least a potential increase in participation in the future as today's young adults age into the years when voting is more likely. Slightly less than one-quarter of adult U.S. citizen Latinos aged 18 to 20 voted in 1996 compared to over 60 percent of voters aged 65 and older (see table 1).

Voters with lower incomes are also less likely to vote than voters with higher incomes—just as voters with lower education are less likely to vote than voters with higher levels of education. These patterns are true for all populations, but, again, the impact is disproportionately felt among Latinos. Among U.S. citizens twenty-five and older, for example, fewer than 2 percent have less than five years of formal education. In contrast, among Latino U.S. citizens, 9 percent have no more than four years of formal education. At the other extreme, Latinos are less likely to have college degrees or postgraduate education. Only 9 percent of Latino U.S. citizens have earned such degrees compared to 22 percent of U.S. citizens in the population as a whole (U.S. Bureau of the Census 1998). In terms of household income, Latinos also trail the population as a whole. In 1999, households headed by white non-Hispanic U.S. citizens had a median income of $43,287. Latino households headed by a U.S. citizen had median incomes of $29,110 (U.S. Bureau of the Census 2000b: table B). Thus, a higher share of the Latino adult population is found in the education and income cohorts where voting is less likely.

Why do the poor and less educated face greater barriers in registering and voting? Both take time, do not have an immediate reward, and must be done weeks in advance of the election (when interest in the outcome of elections generally is not as high). Knowledge of candidates and issues may be more diffuse, and the procedural requirements, particularly for voter registration, may be unclear, especially for inexperienced potential voters. The poor and the less educated are less likely to be part of networks. For all voters, networks simplify access to information. People with low incomes often work multiple jobs

TABLE 1 Latino Voting, 1996, for Age Cohorts, Years of Formal Education Cohorts, and Household Income Cohorts, for U.S. Citizens.

AGE	LATINO VOTER TURNOUT %
18–20	23.6
21–24	24.4
25–34	37.5
35–44	45.1
45–54	56.6
55–64	59.7
65–74	64.8
75+	60.6
FORMAL EDUCATION	
Less than 5 years	44.9
5–8 years	41.2
9–12 years, no degree	29.7
High school graduate	36.9
Some college	52.8
BA or equivalent	66.9
Advanced degree	80.6
HOUSEHOLD INCOME	
Less than $5,000	30.8
$5,000–$9,999	32.8
$10,000–$14,999	36.5
$15,000–$24,999	38.5
$25,000–$34,999	45.4
$35,000–$49,000	48.9
$50,000–$74,999	59.6
$75,000 or more	64.8
Not reported	41.6

Note: These calculations exclude non-U.S.-citizen Latinos.

Source: Author's calculations based on U.S. Bureau of the Census 1998.

and have less time to acquire information about politics. Finally, the parties and most candidates neglect issues of economic justice and service provision that might prove more engaging to such potential voters.

As with age, the impact of these barriers on the likelihood of voting is dramatic (see table 1). Among adult Latino U.S. citizens, Latinos with some college vote at a rate of 53 percent, and those with a college degree turn out a rate exceeding 66 percent. For Latino U.S. citizens with less than a college degree, turnout rates are lower, with, for example, just 30 percent of Latinos with 9 to 12 years of formal education but no high school degree. Household income has a similar impact. Slightly more than 30 percent of U.S. citizen adults with household incomes of less than $5,000 voted, compared to nearly 65 percent of Latino U.S. citizens with household incomes of $75,000 or more. While there are few Latino households in either of these categories, there are more at the lower end of the income spectrum than the higher end.

Each of these demographic factors reinforces the other to widen the gap between the eligible Latino electorate and the actual electorate. The impact of these demographic characteristics has been much more studied in terms of its impact on voting, but the same patterns appear for other forms of community electoral participation. In other words, Latinos who are younger, have less formal education, or have lower incomes are less likely than more economically or educationally advantaged Latinos to be engaged in community politics. While community groups provide the social networks and sense of efficacy in solving community problems that can overcome the participation-dampening effects of youth, poverty, and low education, the available research evidence finds relatively low rates of membership in Latino community organizations (de la Garza and Lu 1999).

It bears repeating that these patterns of lower than average electoral participation and lower than average engagement in community politics are a function of demographics, not of culturally or ethnic-specific traits.[5] Latinos, however, pay a price for behaving as other populations do because a higher share of the Latino population is young, has low incomes, and/or has low levels of formal education.

NON-U.S. CITIZENSHIP

So far, this discussion of nonvoters has only focused on U.S. citizens who do not go to the polls or are less likely to participate in community organizational politics. A much larger Latino nonvoting population is made up of non-U.S. citizens who cannot vote. Nationally, more than 8 million of the nearly 22 million Latino adults, or approximately 39 percent, are not U.S. citizens (see table 2). To put these 8 million non-U.S.-citizen Latinos in context, their numbers exceeded the number of Latino voters in the 2000 elections by more than 2 million. Noncitizen Latinos are not spread evenly across the nation. In California and Illinois, for example, slightly less than half of Latino adults are not U.S. citizens.

Clearly, it would take much more to move these noncitizens into the electorate and, for many, it is unrealistic to expect this to happen. Latino immigrants without legal status—who number approximately six million—would

TABLE 2 Voting, Nonvoting, and Non-U.S. Citizenship Among Latino Adults, United States and Selected States, 2000

	TOTAL 18+ POPULATION	VOTERS (%)	CITIZEN NONVOTERS (%)	NON–U.S. CITIZENS (%)
United States	21,598,000	5,934,000 (27.5)	7,225,000 (33.5)	8,439,000 (39.1)
Arizona	910,000	247,000 (27.1)	369,000 (40.6)	294,000 (32.3)
California	6,514,000	1,597,000 (24.5)	1,892,000 (29.0)	3,025,000 (46.4)
Colorado	478,000	158,000 (33.1)	191,000 (40.0)	129,000 (27.0)
Florida	2,162,000	678,000 (25.7)	1,065,000 (40.3)	897,000 (34.0)
Illinois	771,000	218,000 (28.3)	182,000 (23.6)	371,000 (48.1)
New Jersey	583,000	179,000 (30.7)	167,000 (28.6)	237,000 (40.7)
New Mexico	484,000	191,000 (39.5)	235,000 (48.6)	58,000 (12.0)
New York	1,706,000	502,000 (29.4)	575,000 (33.7)	629,000 (36.9)
Texas	4,414,000	1,300,000 (29.5)	1,873,000 (42.4)	1,241,000 (28.1)

Source: Author's calculations based on U.S. Bureau of the Census 2002.

have to regularize their status (Bean, Van Hook, and Woodrow-Lafield 2001; Bean et al. 2001). In the present political environment, there appears to be little support among political leaders for an amnesty that would grant widespread legalization, though many undocumented immigrants are able to "become legal" over time through marriage to a U.S. citizen or through the petition of an immediate relative who is a U.S. citizen or a permanent resident. Among those with legal status, immigrants would have to reside in the United States for at least five years and naturalize. Latino permanent residents number approximately three million. Despite the fact that nonnaturalized immigrants cannot participate in electoral politics in most jurisdictions, they are counted for purposes of representation and, probably more importantly, are included in popular discussions of the size of the Latino population that leads to expectations for its influence.

What distinguishes permanent residents (immigrants who reside in the United States legally and may under most circumstances remain in the United States for the rest of their lives) who naturalize from those who do not?

Across all immigrant populations and periods of immigration, immigrants who reside in the United States longer are more likely to naturalize than those with shorter periods of residence (Gavit 1922; U.S. Immigration and Naturalization Service 2002*a*: 222–25, table 55). That said, the speed of naturalization varies by nationality and by region of origin. These variations traditionally showed consistency across regions—with Asian immigrants naturalizing the fastest and immigrants from the Americas naturalizing the slowest—but the patterns are now in flux. Over the past decade, the average immigrant who naturalized from Asia waited approximately seven years after immigrating, the average European immigrant waited nine to ten years, and the average immigrant from Latin America and the Caribbean waited twelve to fourteen years (see U.S. Immigration and Naturalization Service, *Statistical Yearbook of the Immigration and Naturalization Service*, various years). Traditionally, the nationalities with the longest wait between immigration and naturalization are nationals of the two countries that border the United States—Mexico and Canada.

At the individual level, scholars have identified several clusters of factors that explain these diverse rates of naturalization—demographic characteristics, attitudinal and associational variables, immigration and settlement characteristics, and inconsistent bureaucratic treatment. These clusters overlap somewhat. Of these, demographic characteristics of immigrants are the most studied. Income, white-collar employment, professional status, home ownership, years of schooling, and English-language abilities increase the likelihood of naturalization (Barkan and Khokolov 1980; Portes and Mozo 1985; Jasso and Rosenzweig 1990; Yang 1994; DeSipio 1996a). The married are more likely to naturalize than the unmarried, and women are more likely than men. Immigrants who arrived as young children are more likely to naturalize than are those who arrived as teenagers or adults. These demographic characteristics partially explain the more rapid naturalization rates of Asian immigrants and the slower rates of naturalization among Latino immigrants. On average, Asian immigrants are more likely to have the traits that predict speedy naturalization. Latinos, on the other hand, are more likely to have low wages, low levels of formal education, and lower English skills—all factors that discourage naturalization.

In the 1990s, the number of immigrants seeking naturalization surged, with nearly 6 million immigrants naturalizing. The comparable figures for the 1970s and 1980s were 1.5 million and 2.2 million, respectively. The are several clear reasons for this increase in demand for citizenship (DeSipio 1996b). The pool of citizenship-eligible applicants grew dramatically in the early 1990s. The approximately 3 million permanent residents who legalized under the provisions of the 1986 Immigration Reform and Control Act (IRCA) became eligible to naturalize in the early 1990s. The traditional ambivalent attitudes of native U.S. citizens toward immigrants also contributed to this trend. On the one hand, positive national rhetoric about immigrant contributions to U.S. society drove many immigrants to pursue U.S. citizenship. On the other hand, the turn in attitude against immigrants that occurred in many areas of the United States in the mid-1990s had the same effect. California passed Proposition 187 in 1994, which denied state education and social-service benefits to immigrants, and Congress passed the 1996 Welfare Reform bill, which eliminated permanent resident eligibility for federal social-welfare benefits such as Supplemental Security Income and Aid to Families with Dependent Children. Congress also made it easier to deport permanent residents who committed crimes in the United States. Fearing for their children's ability to stay in the United States, these developments drove some parents to pursue naturalization. Administrative changes at the Immigration and Naturalization Service (INS) also encouraged permanent residents to pursue naturalization. Permanent residents with "green cards" (permanent resident visas) more than ten years old had to replace their cards for the first time in the agency's history. The application process for the replacement of a green card was nearly as expensive as applying for U.S. citizenship and also required another renewal of the newly issued greed card after ten years. The INS also repeatedly raised the fee for naturalization in this period.

At the same time, Latino and immigrant organizations increased the resources available to assist immigrants pursue U.S. citizenship. Univisión and other Spanish-language media promoted the importance of naturalization to Latino audiences. In the end, it is not possible to disaggregate the impact of changes on individual Latinos' propensities to naturalize (DeSipio and Pachon 2002), but the cumulative effect was to move the largest number of immigrants in American immigration history to apply for naturalization.

With this surge in naturalization in the late 1990s, the size of the *potential* Latino electorate (U.S.-citizen Latino adults) immediately increased by approximately 2 million (or slightly less than 20 percent). It is not yet clear whether these new Latino citizens will become new Latino voters. If past experience is a guide, however, the majority will not (DeSipio 1996c; Levitt and Olson 1996; Bass and Casper 1999; Minnite, Holdaway, and Hayduk 1999; Ramakrishnan 2000; Mollenkopf, Olson, and Ross 2001). Each of these studies identifies a common pattern in which the naturalized vote at rates comparable to, or lower than, comparably situated U.S.-born citizens. The one exception to this pattern finds the newly naturalized voting at higher levels than U.S.-born Latinos (Pantoja, Ramírez, and Segura 2001). This study looks at Latinos in the 1996 California election, arguably the high point of the anti-immigrant rhetoric that contributed to the factors that drove many immigrants to seek U.S. citizenship.

Skepticism on this point is reinforced by the fact that naturalization of Latino residents has not continued at the record pace of the late 1990s. Approximately 500,000 immigrants applied to become U.S. citizens in 2001, and 700,000 applied in 2002 (DeSipio, Pachon, and Moellmer 2001; U.S. Immigration and Naturalization Service 2002b). Of these, approximately 500,000 are Latino. Historically, this is a high number of applicants, though the numbers applying for naturalization generally remain below the number of immigrants who become eligible to naturalize each year. There is no exact figure for the newly citizenship-eligible each year because there are no official records of permanent residents who emigrate or who die, but it is reasonable to assume that 600,000 to 700,000 immigrants become eligible to naturalize each year.

CONCLUSIONS: AN EVER LARGER ELECTORATE-IN-RESERVE

In the twenty-eight years since the extension of the Voting Rights Act to "language minorities," more Latinos have turned out to vote in each election, and they have made up an increasing share of the national electorate and the electorates of several of the largest states (see table 3). At the same time, the share of adult Latino citizens who turn out to vote has stagnated and, in some cases, declined. In this same period, the number and prominence of Latino community organizations has increased, but there is no evidence to indicate that Latinos are actively engaged in these organizations. Yet, because of the rapid growth in the Latino population, the increasing size of the Latino electorate has masked this stagnation.

What is less commented upon is the even more sizeable growth of nonparticipating Latinos, which include both citizens who do not vote and non-U.S. citizens. These nonparticipants can be understood as an "electorate-in-reserve" who are the victims of a political order in which the more advantaged are more likely to participate. The electorate-in-reserve numbered nearly 16 million in 2000. Of these, 7.2 million were adult U.S. citizen and 8.4 million were adult non-U.S. citizen. Given the proper stimuli, many might choose to participate. Evidence to support this assertion would include the increased Latino demand for naturalization in the 1990s and the surge in Latino voting in California in 1996.

Some of the citizen nonvoters have participated in past elections, and many are registered to vote. Overwhelmingly, when polled, they acknowledge the importance of voting and their desire to vote, but for many reasons, including the demographic ones identified, they do not. Similarly, many permanent residents want to naturalize but have tried and failed to accomplish this goal

TABLE 3 Latino Voters and Share of the National Electorate, 1976–2000.

LATINOS AS A SHARE OF THE NATIONAL ELECTORATE

	TOTAL VOTE	LATINO VOTE	LATINO SHARE %
1976	86,698,000	2,098,000	2.4
1980	93,066,000	2,453,000	2.6
1984	101,878,000	3,092,000	3.0
1988	102,224,000	3,710,000	3.6
1992	113,866,000	4,238,000	3.7
1996	105,017,000	4,928,000	4.7
2000	110,826,000	5,934,000	5.4

LATINO REGISTERED VOTERS AND VOTERS AS A SHARE OF LATINO U.S.-CITIZEN ADULTS, 1980–2000

	LATINO REGISTERED VOTER/ U.S.-CITIZEN LATINOS %	LATINO VOTERS/ U.S.-CITIZEN LATINOS %
1980	53.3	44.1
1984	58.9	48.0
1988	56.6	45.9
1992	58.5	48.3
1996	58.6	44.0
2000	57.3	45.1

Note: These calculations exclude Latinos who are not U.S. citizens.

Sources: 1976–2000 data: U.S. Bureau of the Census. Various Years. Voting and Registration in the Election of November 19XX. Current Population Survey. Washington, D.C.: U.S. Government Printing Office; and 1996 and 2000, on line. These results are summarized in de la Garza and DeSipio (1992, 1996, 1999).

(Pachon and DeSipio 1994; DeSipio, Pachon, and Moellmer 2001). Approximately twice as many Latino immigrants who are eligible for U.S. citizenship have begun to naturalize in some concrete behavioral manner as have completed the process. According to another study, approximately 85 percent of Latino immigrants have either naturalized or want to pursue naturalization (de la Garza et al. 1992: 45, table 2.34). Interestingly, the single most important reason for naturalizing provided by Latino immigrants is to achieve the right to vote (Pachon and DeSipio 1994: 96–97, table 6.11, based on a 1989 survey; DeSipio and Pachon 2002, based on a 2001 survey). Given the right stimuli and community resources, this desire to participate and, among noncitizens, to join the polity, can be tapped, and the reserve can be made part of the electorate (and become active in community organizations), but the resources for mobilization are frequently absent.

In other eras of American political history, community-based organizations served as a resource for political involvement among the politically marginalized. However, contemporary survey data indicate that similar participation patterns exist among those who are active in organizations as among all voters. In any case, as with the propensity to vote, younger, poorer, and less educated Latinos are less likely to participate in community-based organizations and other forms of community politics than are the more economically or socially advantaged (Pachon and DeSipio 1994; DeSipio et al. 1998; de la Garza and Lu 1999). Except for church membership, no community-based organizational activity sees as much participation as does voting. So, at the mass level, community organizations do not overcome the dearth of Latino participation evident in voting (the next section examines how these organizations have shaped Latino political expression in the contemporary period).

The Latino electorate is growing and also making up a steadily greater share of the national electorate, while a minority of the Latino population turns out in each election. The fundamental contradiction is not unique to Latinos, but it appears somewhat more dramatically because Latinos make up a much larger share of adult non-U.S. citizens who are prevented from voting in most U.S. elections and also a larger share of adult U.S. citizens who are less likely to do so. The future engagement or disengagement of the electorate-in-reserve is, in many ways then, the future of Latino politics.

LATINO COMMUNITY ORGANIZING, 1960–2003

Traditionally in the United States and other democracies, ethnic, racial, and other groups of shared interest have overcome barriers by organizing. This is, perhaps, a truism that can be quite difficult to implement, but organization has eventually been rewarded despite the intransigence of the majority population. Perhaps the best example is the African American civil-rights struggle, which required nearly one hundred years of organization to make real the procedural guarantees of the Fourteenth and Fifteenth Amendments. Latino organization dates to the years just after the Treaty of Guadalupe Higaldo and has been an ongoing characteristic of community politics since. *Viva Kennedy!* was successful in part because it was able to build on the organizational infrastructure of an important existing Mexican American civic organization that was established and especially active in Texas—the American G.I. Forum.

Community organizational politics take many forms. They include explicitly political organizations seeking to obtain specific goods and services from the government. They also include less explicitly political religious, civic, cultural, national origin, community, and other organizations that bring people together around a common, often nonpolitical, need. Once this network is in place, however, it creates the opportunity to seek collective solutions to common problems (Rogers 1990; Hardy-Fanta 1993; Ramos 1993; Pardo 1998; Shirley 2002; Warren 2001).

In the years since 1960, organizational efforts and organizational structures in Mexican American and other Latino communities have proliferated. The general trend in organization, however, like the trend in electoral participation, has been the absence of widespread participation and a class bias in who participates.

FROM *VIVA KENNEDY!* TO THE CHICANO MOVEMENT

As argued before, the *Viva Kennedy!* clubs are well remembered in political history for their influence in the outcome of the election of 1960. Arguably, though, their long-term importance is based on quite a different reason. They transformed Latino community mobilization, nationalized it for the first time, and laid the roots for the more aggressive demand making that flowered in the late 1960s and remains a part of the Latino political dialogue today.

Prior to 1960, Latino political mobilization focused primarily on nonpartisan civic organizations, unions, and national origin–based associations that sought to cement the bonds between Latinos in the United States and their countries of origin. The focus of these pre-1960 civic organizations was civil and educational rights, but there was little effort to build a mass movement comparable to the African American civil-rights movement. Unions were something of an exception to this pattern, but the concentration of Latinos in the Southwest—an area of weak unionization—did not work to the advantage of Latino community organization in this era. Most pre-1960 unions focused on specific sectors of the economy, such as mining, agriculture, and, after 1940, defense, metal, and manufacturing industries.

Viva Kennedy! began to change this equation in three ways. After the 1960s, Mexican American and Latino community organizations began to focus more energy on voting and electing Latinos to office. Second, as organizational energies shifted to elections and electing people to office, these organizations expanded their memberships, or, at least, those that they attempted to mobilize. Finally, dissatisfaction with the tokenistic way in which political institutions treated Latinos who were elected to office spurred an increased radicalism in organizational demand making and the creation of new organizations that rejected electoral politics. While these efforts were not universally successful, they did create the foundation for mass movements later in the decade.

The rhetoric of post-1960 Latino community organizations also changed. Civil-rights demands that had long been made became much more strident.

Expectations for government redress increased and government failures were no longer passively tolerated. In addition, for the first time in American political history, Latinos were inside key political institutions and could advocate for Latino civil rights. By the later years of the 1960s, the result was the emergence of a diverse range of community politics and political organizations mobilizing Latinos around a civil-rights agenda. These issues, which were by no means new, included the pressing of land rights claims among descendants of Mexicans who lived in the Southwest in 1848 (the Alianza Federal de Pueblos Libres); exclusion from the agendas of the dominant political parties (La Raza Unida Party and the Young Lords); disaffection among urban Latinos and their exclusion from Anglo political institutions (the Crusade for Justice and the Brown Berets); and exploitation of Latinos in agriculture and their neglect by traditional unions (the United Farm Workers) (Muñoz 1989; I. García 1990; Gutiérrez 1998; Navarro 2000; R. González 2001; López Tijerina 2001). These organizations were, in a real sense, the tip of the iceberg in terms of community mobilization in this era. Latinos also organized at the local level around similar issues. These efforts included high school student walkouts in urban school districts throughout the Southwest and antiwar efforts that culminated in the 1970 Chicano Moratorium in Los Angeles, the largest single Mexican American political demonstration to that point in American history.

This new breed of Latino civil rights organization and activism that emerged in the 1960s differed both in leadership and membership from pre-1960s organizations. The leaders of each of these organizations, and their local equivalents, saw the need to build a political movement. Thus, these organizations sought to incorporate a large membership base in a way that Latino organizations had simply not done prior to this era. Equally importantly, while these organizations had specific foci, they shared a broader interest in ensuring that the United States lived up to its national rhetoric of equality of opportunity. Efforts to unite these various Latino civil rights efforts into a broad national movement ultimately failed, the victim of personality conflicts, ideological divides, and government infiltration (I. García 1990; Navarro 2000). But they transformed Latino political organizing nevertheless. No longer would Latino community mobilizing be primarily a resource for community elites. Equally importantly, the vociferousness of the demand making and the alliances built between these Latino organizations and organizing in other ethnic and racial communities ensured that Latino needs could no longer be simply overlooked or dismissed by national political leaders. The Chicano and Puerto Rican civil-rights movements put Latino needs on the national agenda and laid the foundation for the creation of a pan-ethnic Latino politics that linked local needs and the history of race-based exclusion to a national Latino agenda.

PAN-ETHNIC LATINO ORGANIZATION

With the decline of the activism of the Chicano and Puerto Rican movements in the early 1970s, a new form of Latino organization emerged. These new organizations focused on making a reality of the effort to link the interests of disparate Latino national origin groups into a Latino or Hispanic politics and on influencing public policies affecting Latino communities; thus, mass mobilization generally was not their goal. Some of these new organizations focused on national politics and others on state or local, but they shared a pluralist conception of American politics in which competition between groups with common interests leads to policies that reflect the needs of all the groups that compete. This pluralist approach, and its underlying sense that American politics will reward all citizens as long as they organize and participate, reflected a change from the radicalism of the Chicano and Puerto Rican movements. At the same time, it shifted the focus of community organizing from the mass level to the elite level. Partly as a consequence, this pluralist politics has not proved very effective at regularly mobilizing the electorate-in-reserve. Instead, it makes claims on U.S. society based on the size of the Latino population.

In response to the perceived radicalism of the Chicano movement, national political actors and philanthropies like the Ford and Rockefeller Foundations thought that it was in their interest to invest in building pluralistic national Latino organizations. Consequently, in the late 1960s and early 1970s, the first national Latino organizations were established. These included the Mexican American Legal Defense and Education Fund (MALDEF) and the National Council of La Raza (NCLR). Existing organizations that had tended to be more regionally focused, such as the League of United Latin American Citizens (LULAC), also became national. Each of these organizations had its roots in the Southwest, but the 1970s saw them become pan-ethnic in focus. The inspirations for these new national Latino organizations were often parallel organizations in the African American community. MALDEF, for example, was created to serve as a Mexican American/Latino parallel to the National Association for the Advancement of Colored People Legal Defense Fund.

These organizations reflected a new resource for Latino politics. They sought to link Latino interests nationwide and to speak for all Latinos with a more unified voice. This sometimes has required avoiding divisive issues, such as the explicitly partisan or U.S. relations with the home countries of the various Latino populations. Even with these limits, however, these organizations have identified a broad interest-based agenda that attempts to articulate a united Latino front that transcends individual national origins or ancestries (see further discussion below). They advocate and lobby on specific issues, but more importantly they ensure that Latino needs are always considered in the national policy-making process.

These new Latino advocates from the post–civil rights era represent a resource for identity building and the articulation of a Latino agenda that simply did not exist before 1975. That said, these pluralist Latino organizations are constituted in such a way that they do not help mobilize the electorate-in-reserve. They are top-down organizations that do not rely on a mass base. No contemporary national Latino organization relies on membership contributions to support its operations. Instead, Latino organizations rely on philanthropic, corporate, and government support to sustain them. Their focus on the minutia of policy formulation and intervention and the need to build coalitions with other like-minded groups, further distance these organizations from the mass of the Latino community. The reliance on top-down organization and the elite nature of this form of community organization does not make the Latino community unique, by any means. The cost, however, is somewhat higher for Latinos because larger shares of the Latino population are distant from politics. Mass-based Latino community organizations are the exception, and they rarely survive to sustain a mass-based organizational infrastructure (Padilla 1986; Pardo 1998; Rosales 2000. See also Rogers 1990, as an exception).

IMMIGRANT ACTIVISM

The top-down nature of Latino organizations is continually challenged by the dynamic nature of the Latino population. This pattern of challenge was seen in the 1960s and 1970s in the pressures that led to the new styles of organization and techniques of demand making in the Chicano and Puerto Rican civil-rights movements. The movement organizations supplanted, at least temporarily, the more established community and civic organizations in Mexican American and Puerto Rican communities and replaced forever their accommodationist approach to Latino politics. Today, the most significant challenge to the existing structure of Latino community-based organizations is coming from Latinos whose interests are not immediately served by the civil rights–focused, pan-ethnic Latino organizations that have emerged since the early 1970s.

The surge in immigration over the past thirty-five years is perhaps the most dramatic example of Latinos excluded from contemporary political institutions. The impact of these new Latino migrants appears in three newly emerging forms of Latino community activism (each of which harkens back to earlier periods of Latino-immigrant community organization): mutual aid and cultural maintenance; a transnational politics that exists simultaneously in both the United States and in the country of the migrant's origin; and labor organizing in Latino communities (and the concomitant rebirth of U.S. unions in certain sectors of the labor market).

It is a truism that immigrants organize to meet common needs and to preserve cultural ties to their communities of origin. This pattern continues today and is aided by new forms of communication and transportation that allow ongoing contact with communities of origin. Immigrant communities overflow with clubs, sports leagues, festivals, and cultural celebrations that link migrants, their home communities, and others from the same area in the United States (Levitt 2001; see also Levitt, chapter 5, this volume). These are not inherently political, though they have the potential to become so when the group faces a challenge (either in the United States or in the home community). They can also quickly reform as mutual-aid societies when migrants (or the home community) face need.

These ongoing contacts with the migrant's home community (and home country) have the potential to create a U.S. immigrant politics focused on immigrant-sending countries (Gutiérrez 1999; de la Garza and Pachon 2000; Guarnizo 2001). Initially, many immigrants report that it is the sending countries where their primary political attachments lie. These efforts to create a transnational politics do not greatly distinguish today's Latino immigrants from immigrants from other parts of the world or immigrants from earlier eras.[6] Two aspects, however, are new. Some of these transnational political activities among immigrants are being encouraged by the migrant-sending nations, and some migrants are able to sustain political engagement both in the United States and in their sending countries to an extent that perhaps was not true in the past.

There is no single way in which this transnational politics manifests itself (Smith and Guarnizo 1998). Groups of migrants living in the same community in the United States organize to provide goods or services, such as sponsoring a festival or purchasing a fire engine or ambulance, for the home communities. Evidence exists of migrants returning to the home country or home community to vote or to participate in a community decision (Guarnizo, Sánchez, and Roach 1999; Rivera-Salgado 1999). Immigrants contribute to parties or political candidates from their home countries, and candidates frequently travel to the U.S. to visit with émigrés during the campaign. Finally, some Latin American immigrant-sending countries allow voting from abroad.

Just as immigrant participation in these transnational political activities is on the increase, so are sending-country efforts to solidify the link to their émigrés. Most notably, Mexico, which has long disdained its émigrés, has offered dual nationality and the promise a rapid renaturalization to Mexicans who naturalize as U.S. citizens (González-Gutiérrez 1999). This offer is tempered in that out-naturalized émigrés and their children are offered Mexican nationality, but not full citizenship. This offer of Mexican nationality, nevertheless, reflects a dramatic change in Mexico's historical treatment of its emigrants. Other Latin American nations have gone even further. Colombia allows voting by it nationals abroad, as will the Dominican Republic in its next presidential election. Colombia considered but rejected a proposal to provide representation for Colombians abroad in the national parliament. And all Latin American nations with sizeable émigré populations in the United States now have senior government ministries with responsibility for maintaining ties with émigré organizations (de la Garza and Pachon 2000). This top-down transnational politics is perhaps less new than the grassroots version (González 1999).

There are no reliable data on the frequency of transnational political behaviors among Latino immigrants. The research that does exist indicates that transnational political behaviors decline relatively rapidly as the migrants' social and family networks become more focused on the United States (DeSipio 2000, 2002).

But even if only a small share of Latino immigrants engages in a transnational politics and those that do only do so for a few years after migration, this new emergence of a Latino transnational politics is an important resource for reducing the size of the electorate-in-reserve. Transnational politics offers immigrants a political tool not offered by the pluralist, pan-ethnic organizations that dominate the community politics of U.S.-born Latinos. When issues emerge that affect immigrants, these networks can be mobilized to shape the politics not just of the home country, but also of the United States (Portes and Stepik 1994; Gutiérrez 1999). Transnational politics also offers the opportunity for recent migrants (those most disengaged from U.S. politics) to develop political skills and become part of political networks. It is these skills and networks that can overcome the demographic barriers that many Latinos face when trying to become politically involved. Finally, the issues that transnational politics puts on the table have the potential to broaden the Latino agenda into foreign policy in a way that it has not in the past. A more broadly based transnational politics does run some risks for Latino politics nationally. If the majority population comes to believe that Latino immigrants are more engaged in the politics of their sending countries and that those interests run counter to U.S. interests, transnationalism could spur a new wave of anti-immigrant sentiment. As Latino transnational politics operates today, however, this risk seems low.

The impact of immigrants on Latino community mobilization is not felt just in terms of a nascent transnational politics. Immigrants are shaping domestic politics as well. Perhaps the most dramatic impact has been seen in the revitalization of labor unions in the economic sectors where immigrants are most commonly found (Delgado 1993; Milkman 2000; Parker 2001). In the 1990s, service-sector unions and some skilled-trade unions saw dramatic gains in membership and clout because of a growing membership base among immigrants, particularly undocumented immigrants. Unions, such as the Service Employees International Union, New York's Health and Hospital Workers Union, and Los Angeles's hotel employee unions, are the brightest areas of growth for U.S. trade unions, and these are all immigrant-driven unions. Linda Chávez-Thompson was elected Vice President of the AFL-CIO, arguably partly in recognition of the union's desire to expand their base.

This new spurt in unionization driven by Latino immigrants is important politically for more than just Latino organization. American unionism has been changed. Throughout its history, most mainstream unions have advocated limited migration and opposed any legalization program for undocumented workers. The narrow position of unions toward immigrants has divided liberal coalitions. This has largely changed. Unions, seeing that their future depends on organizing immigrants and, in many cases, undocumented immigrants, have become advocates both of the rights of the undocumented and of legalization.

The impact on domestic politics of immigrants is not simply the result of their seeking to influence their home country's politics or their presence in trade unions. It is immigrant numbers that make the Latino community so appealing a target for parties and candidates. Even though many immigrants cannot participate in electoral politics today, parties and forward-looking candidates recognize that many will someday be participants not just in organizational politics, but also electoral politics. As a result, neglect of the Latino community or Latino needs involves an increasingly greater risk today than it has in the past. Certainly, efforts by the Bush administration to become more sensitive to Latino concerns and issues can only be understood in this light.

LATINO COMMUNITY MOBILIZATION TODAY

In the forty years since *Viva Kennedy!* shifted Latino community organizing from civic (and mostly elite) organizing to partisan and more broadly based community mobilization, Latinos have vastly enriched their resources for nonelectoral politics. The infrastructure of national, state, and local Latino organizations is diverse and offers civic, issue-based, community-based, and partisan organizations to advance Latino (as well as Latino national-origin group) interests. Unlike the situation in 1960, these organizations are players in the allocation of government resources and ensure that Latino demands are heard.

Despite this rich palate of organizations, however, the general direction of Latino community and organizational politics has followed the patterns of

Latino electoral participation, in that it rewards the educated and the socially and economically advantaged. Since the demise of the Chicano and Puerto Rican movement organizations, there has not been a national or even large, regional mass-based Latino organization. Survey data show that few Latinos report membership in national, state, or local Latino organizations (de la Garza et al. 1992: 115, table 8.2; de la Garza and Lu 1999). Again, in this pattern, Latinos follow the general direction of organizational involvement of the population as a whole (Putnam 2000).

The growth of Latino immigrant populations and the nascent efforts among Latino immigrants to shape a politics both in their countries of origin and in their communities in the United States present a fundamental challenge to the pattern that has emerged over the past forty years. This challenge is twofold. The issues of concern to immigrants present a challenge to the agenda of the organizations that have been primarily focused on civil rights (DeSipio and de la Garza In press). Second, immigrants seek an institutional base for demand making. As today's immigrants move toward incorporation into U.S. society and politics, they may well follow the pattern of previous generations of immigrants and see dampened levels of participation. Their large numbers and the multiple foci of their political energies, however, create the possibility that they will invigorate the mass dimension of Latino community and organizational politics in a way not seen since the 1960s (Davis 2000).

LATINOS AND ELECTORAL POLITICS IN THE NEW MILLENNIUM

The discussion so far has evaluated the opportunities and barriers faced by Latinos in seeking to influence U.S. politics over the past forty years and how they have tapped institutional structures to achieve their goals. Despite the relatively low levels of electoral participation and community organization, Latinos are in a much stronger position to influence outcomes at the beginning of the new millennium than they were at any previous time. The number of Latino voters is increasing (though not at as rapid a rate as the Latino population as a whole); the number of Latino elected officials and other leaders has increased dramatically. These elected officials have moved into new positions of prominence, and Latinos of different national origins are increasingly coming into contact with each other and organizing to meet public policy needs that they share. Thus, at the beginning of the new millennium, it is accurate to speak of *a* Latino politics and of *Latino* influence on electoral and policy outcomes. This section evaluates three dimensions of this Latino politics: Latino partisanship, Latino issue preferences, and Latino influence in national (or presidential) politics.

PARTISANSHIP

Latinos are strong partisans. This generalization is true of both U.S. citizens who can participate and noncitizens who cannot. Mexican Americans and Puerto Ricans report strong adherence to the Democratic Party and Cuban Americans to the Republican Party (de la Garza et. al. 1992; *San Jose Mercury News* 2000; Pew Hispanic Center/Kaiser Family Foundation 2002). In most elections, Democratic candidates will receive well more than 65 percent of the Mexican American and Puerto Rican vote and Republican candidates more than 65 percent of the Cuban American vote. Less is known about the partisanship of newer Latino communities, such as Dominicans or Salvadorans, but what is known indicates that they are following the Democratic party loyalty of Mexican Americans and Puerto Ricans, though at slightly lower levels (DeSipio et al. 1998). For each national-origin group, there is also a small but reliable vote for the "minority" party, in other words the Republicans for Mexican Americans and Puerto Ricans and the Democrats for Cuban Americans. This support for the less favored party usually taps 20 percent of each community's vote. These rates of partisanship showed some decline for the Democrats in the 1960s and 1970s (as the Latino vote diversified and polling became more accurate), but they have remained largely constant in the contemporary era (see table 4). Third-party candidates have rarely reached out to Latinos, and Latinos have supported these candidates at lower rates than non-Hispanic whites.

The meaning of partisanship is less clear for noncitizens. They generally follow the partisan leanings of their co-ethnics. Noncitizens are somewhat more likely to report no partisan leanings, but the numbers who report affiliation with neither of the parties generally make up no more than one-third of Latino immigrants. Perhaps the best indication of the partisanship of noncitizens is the partisanship of the newly naturalized. Data exist only for two states. In California, naturalized Latinos register as Democrats at rates higher than the U.S.-born (Arteaga 2000). In Florida, the same pattern appears, though with the opposite partisan outcome: the naturalized are more likely than the U.S.-born to be Republicans (Cuba Research Institute 2000). The highest rate of Republican partisanship is found among émigrés who arrived in the 1960s (see also, García, chapter 3, this volume).

Pundits often like to speak of Latinos as a "swing vote," in other words, as a vote that can convert its preferences in response to specific candidate entreaties and who are, consequently, more appealing to candidates. But this

TABLE 4 National Latino Voting Patterns, 1960–2000.

YEAR/LATINO ELECTORATE	DEMOCRATIC VOTE %	REPUBLICAN VOTE %	OTHER VOTE %
1960			
Mexican Americans	85	15	–
1964			
Mexican Americans	90	10	–
1968			
Mexican Americans	87	10	3
1972			
Mexican Americans[1]	64	36	–
Mexican Americans[2]	85	15	–
1976			
Mexican Americans	92	8	–
Latinos	82	18	–
1980			
Latinos	56	37	7
1984			
Latinos (CBS)	66	34	–
Latinos (NBC)	68	32	–
Latinos (ABC)	56	44	–
1988			
Latinos (CBS and ABC)	70	30	–
Latinos (NBC)	69	31	–
Latinos (*LA Times*)	62	38	–
1992			
Latinos (VRS)	62	24	14
Latinos (*LA Times*)	53	31	16
1996			
Latinos	72	21	6
2000			
Latinos	62	35	3

1. García and de la Garza 1977: 103.

2. Gann and Duignan 1986: 210.

Source: Adapted from de la Garza and DeSipio (1999): table 1.1, with data on 2000 election added.

perception is wrong (de la Garza 1996). The importance of the Latino vote is in its reliable support for one of the parties (the Democrats, except in Florida) at rates far exceeding the non-Latino vote. Latinos are an obvious target for a Democrat in a close race in California, New York, Texas, Illinois, New Mexico, Arizona, or Colorado. Republicans in Florida can similarly rely on Florida Cuban Americans in close races.

Were state-level races to be routinely close, Latinos would be in an enviable position (with the concentration in a few states and high levels of partisanship). In practice, however, the victory margins in many state-level races are quite large, sufficiently large that Latinos cannot be said to have had influence. In California, for example, of the nine general-election races in the 1990s (two presidential, three gubernatorial, and four senatorial), only one would have seen a different outcome if Latinos had not voted (Fraga and Ramírez 2000). Without Latino votes, Diane Feinstein would not have defeated Michael Huffington in California's 1994 Senate race.

That said, it would be inaccurate to undervalue the reliable support that Latinos offer to the Democrats in all states but Florida. California, for example, is now generally a Democratic state in statewide elections because the Democrats can routinely count on 1.25 million Latino votes. Like California, New York statewide races would be more competitive without the 500,000 Latino votes the Democrats can count on. Though routinely Republican in the 1990s, Texas may soon again see greater partisan competitiveness. If Texas does see more partisan competitiveness in the near future, it will be because of the steady growth of the Latino vote, which goes to Texas Democrats by a margin to seven to three.

Republican strategies (outside of Florida) are often pitched as "winning" the Latino vote, but in practice are aimed at reducing this Democratic advantage. For example, if George Bush can push the Republican share of the Latino vote to 40 percent in 2004 from the 35 percent that he earned in 2000, the Republican ticket would earn at least an additional 300,000 votes from Latinos who voted Democratic in 2000. A gain of this number of votes (and the comparable loss to the Democrats) would erase Bush's margin of defeat in the 2000 popular vote (approximately 540,000 votes).[7] If such a switch in Latino balance between the parties were to occur without any change in non-Latino voting, New Mexico would join the Republican vote in the electoral college.

Clearly, the Cuban American case is something of an exception. Cuban Americans, particularly Cuban Americans in Florida, are reliable Republicans, though they use their votes (and their campaign contributions) more tactically than do other Latinos. Cuban Americans in Florida have supported Democrats who take strong anti-Castro positions on U.S. relations with Cuba (Moreno and Warren 2000). Why are Cuban Americans the exception? As they became socialized to U.S. politics, the issue of greatest salience was Cuba. Here, the Republicans had an advantage—they took a harder line against communism in general, and the Democrats paid a price for perceived failures by the Kennedy administration to support Cuban insurgents at the Bay of Pigs and for the resolution of the Cuban Missile Crisis, which, among other things, amounted to a tacit acceptance of Castro's rule in Cuba. In the late 1990s, Cuban Americans demonstrated a new openness to the Democrats, creating the foundation for a higher share of support for the Democrats among Cuban Americans. This opening quickly closed when the Clinton administration pursued its policy of returning Elián González to his father in Cuba (Cuba Research Institute 2000).

Cuban American support for the Republican Party, however, also grew from opportunity. As Cuban Americans began to shift their focus from exile to immigrant politics, they were able to move into elective office in Florida more rapidly through Republican Party channels than Democratic ones (Portes and Stepik 1994). There was only a weak Republican Party infrastructure in south Florida, so winning office did not require both primary- and general-election victories. This focused Republican strategy has been very successful over the past twenty years. Cuban Americans now control most offices in South Florida in areas of their population concentration.

What does the future hold in terms of Latino partisanship? Data from new registrants indicate that Latinos will continue to be strong partisans in the coming years. Voting patterns demonstrate that Republican outreach to Latinos has not seen a higher share of the Latino vote going to the GOP Interestingly, there may be a change among Cuban Americans. Over the past two elections, a higher share of the Cuban vote has gone to the Democratic presidential candidate. These two elections alone may not reflect long-term change. When leadership change comes in Cuba, however, the domestic-issue agenda of Cuban Americans will bring them closer to the Democratic Party, a circumstance that has come to pass several times in the Florida legislature.

ISSUE PREFERENCES

Latino partisanship has historical roots, but more importantly, it is issue driven. The issues that are salient in Latino communities link Latinos to the Democratic Party. This is not to say that there is a perfect match, but the issues that are most important to the majority of Latinos are closer to the Democrats than the Republicans.

Opinion polling from the 1980s and 1990s show a remarkably consistent pattern (de la Garza et al. 1992; DeSipio 1996a; DeSipio et al. 1998; *San Jose Mercury News* 2000; *Washington Post*/Kaiser Family Foundation 2000; Pew

Hispanic Center/Kaiser Family Foundation 2002). The issue agenda of Latinos nationwide is a domestic-policy agenda focused broadly on issues that assist the incorporation of new members and those who have faced past exclusion. Thus, education tops any list of the most important issue facing Latino communities. It is crucial to note, however, that education as it is mentioned by Latinos is the not the education reform that candidates demanded in the 2000 election, for example, student testing, teacher competency, and accountability. Instead, Latinos call for increased funding for education, reduced class sizes, access to higher education, and culturally sensitive curriculums. There have been some exceptions, but Latinos overwhelming support bilingual education as a tool to assist children to learn English (de al Garza et al. 1992: 99, table 7.19). Depending on the survey and the way the question is asked, other issues that shape the Latino policy agenda include public safety, housing, health care, job training, public transportation, and access to economic opportunities.

Ethnic-specific issues are somewhat more likely to appear when Latinos are asked about local issues facing their families or their communities. For the most part, however, the Latino issue agenda is not that distinct from that of the population as a whole. What does distinguish them, however, and places them more centrally in Democratic partisanship, is an expectation that the responsibility for providing these services rests with government. Unlike the majority population, Latinos are willing to pay extra taxes for a richer palette of governmental services. This combination of an agenda built around a domestic social welfare agenda and a call for a larger and more activist government ensures Latino loyalty to the Democratic Party for the foreseeable future.

Republicans, however, can certainly find reasons to hope for a shift in partisan loyalty among some current Latino Democrats. Republicans note, and perhaps overvalue, the strong patriotism voiced by many Latinos, as well as their conservatism on social issues, such as abortion and the death penalty. They also note strong religiosity among many Latinos. They see each of these as opportunities to make inroads among Democratic Latinos. To date, these efforts have not been particularly successful. Latinos are somewhat more socially conservative and traditionally patriotic than other Democrats, but, for most part, these issues do not dominate their agendas.

Non-Cuban Latinos will vote for Republican candidates in some elections, but the circumstances under which they will are rare. First, some Latino Democrats (though not a majority) will support Republican Latino candidates. To date, the Republican Party has nominated few Latinos, and these candidates have not been particularly strong. The second circumstance in which traditionally Democratic Latinos will vote for Republicans is when the Republican is a well-known incumbent and faces a poorly funded Anglo Democrat who does not invest in outreach to Latinos. Texas Senator Kay Bailey Hutchinson (R), for example, won a slight majority of Latino votes in 2000 against a poorly funded Democrat who barely campaigned.

It is also important to observe two issues that are *not* central to the Latino issue agenda. The first of these is foreign-policy issues relating to Latin America. Latinos are interested in Latin America (or, more accurately, their countries of origin or ancestry), but these foreign policy issues do not dominate their agenda. More importantly, their concern with foreign policy generally has more to do with the situation of family members and communities of origin abroad (de la Garza and Pachon 2000; de la Garza and Lowell 2002). Second, immigration does not dominate the agenda, though the rights of immigrants are of significant concern (de la Garza and DeSipio 1998). Latinos, like the population as a whole, would prefer that the number of immigrants to the United States be reduced, but the volume of immigration is not a highly salient issue. They become engaged in immigration as a policy issue when the rights of immigrants are challenged, such as when California considered Proposition 187 (Gutiérrez 1999) and when Latinos are singled out in immigration debates. The primordial tie to the immigration experience can be reinvigorated when the rights of immigrants are challenged. The policy agenda of nonnaturalized Latino immigrants, particularly recent immigrants, is somewhat more focused on home communities (the transnational politics discussed earlier) and on local social-service needs (DeSipio et al. 1998).

Thus, while the priorities of the Latino community may differ somewhat from the population as a whole, the specific issues of concern are very much the same. Generally, Latinos are closer to the Democratic Party nationally, and this issue congruence ensures that they will not soon become a swing vote.

PRESIDENTIAL POLITICS

Between 1960 and 2000, the United States conducted eleven national elections. Only at the end of this period, in the 1990s, have campaigns achieved again what was first accomplished by Latino activists in 1960. The 1990s, for the first time since 1960, saw presidential campaigns dedicate resources to organizing a Latino campaign to parallel *Viva Kennedy!* While Latinos have not since proved as central to the outcome of a presidential election as they did in 1960, they are increasingly likely to be important as their numbers grow, particularly if a higher share of U.S. citizens can be encouraged to go to the polls.

In these eleven elections, three models of Latino participation have appeared—organizational strength and electoral importance, electoral marginality, and organizational strength that did not result in significant electoral influence. The most common of these models is electoral marginality. Arguably, all elections between 1964 and 1984 saw this pattern.[8] Beginning with 1988, it is possible to discern organization within the Latino community to influence outcomes and efforts by campaigns to mobilize Latinos as a cohesive vote. Of the four elections since 1988, Latinos had virtually no influence in the first, and shaped the results of some state elections in each of the other three. Their impact was greatest in 1992 when, arguably, six statewide results (and the accompanying Electoral College votes) would have been different had *no* Latino voted (although the outcome of the race would have remained the same). In 1996 and 2000, two statewide votes would have changed with no Latino voters. This standard—no Latino voting—is, of course, silly. Latinos are a permanent and growing element of the electorate. In only one of the statewide elections over the four most recent presidential elections in which there were organized efforts to win Latino votes was a statewide result changed by *change* in the Latino vote, a combination of a surge in Latino voting and a change in partisanship (in this case an intensification of Democratic partisanship). This occurred in Arizona in 1996. With all the rhetoric about the surge in Latino voting, why is their influence felt so rarely?

The answer has dimensions both internal and external to the Latino community itself and suggests why the growth of Latino influence is incremental in an electoral system like that of the United States (Guerra and Fraga 1996). U.S. presidential elections (the only national election) are organized around states. Most states award Electoral College votes on a winner-take-all basis. So the size of the Latino vote is not as important as its concentration in the states and the division of non-Latino votes in those states. Latinos will be influential when the states they reside in are competitive (in other words, when the non-Latino vote is relatively evenly divided) and when the states where Latinos can influence the outcome are needed by one candidate or the other to build the winning coalition of 270 electoral votes.

These limits serve to reduce the regularity of Latino influence. Over the four elections since 1988, for example, Latinos in New York and Illinois have had little opportunity to use their votes to shape outcomes. Non-Latinos, like Latinos, in these states overwhelmingly voted Democratic. Latino votes are lost in this type of election. Latinos in Arizona and Texas, on the other hand, usually see their votes lost because of the states' strong Republican partisanship (1996 was the exception in Arizona). Thus, close elections work to magnify the impact of the strong partisanship of Latino voters. Texas in 1960 was the perfect example of this. The Tejano vote in 1960 was much smaller than Texas Latino votes today, but the 1960 vote shifted the state from a Nixon to a Kennedy plurality.

By this logic, the 2000 race, which was as close as any U.S. presidential election since 1960, should have worked to Latinos' advantage. With two exceptions, however, the states that were competitive were not states with significant Latino concentrations. The two remaining states—Florida and New Mexico—undeniably saw Latino influence by the lower standard of "had no Latino voted." Had no Latino voted in these two states in 2000, Bush would have won New Mexico and Gore would have won Florida and the presidency. It is hard to argue, however, that Florida or New Mexico Latinos gave the presidency to George Bush. In the 2000 election, the Republican share of the Florida Latino vote declined from the levels of the 1980s and early 1990s. Thus, the increase in Florida's Latino vote arguably weakened the (victorious) Republican ticket. In New Mexico, the Latino vote declined between 1996 and 2000. So Latinos gave a comparable share of their votes to the Democratic candidate as in previous elections, but that meant fewer Democratic votes because of a decline in Latino turnout.

Clearly, numbers alone do not guarantee Latino electoral influence. The institutional arrangements of elections shape the importance of their votes. These examples apply to presidential races, but similar institutional structures shape the opportunities for Latino influence in state and local elections. As the Latino electorate grows, it will be able to influence elections in which there is less of an equal division in the non-Latino electorate (as has been the case in New Mexico for some time). This pattern has increasingly appeared in states like California and Texas, but change comes slowly. Unless there is a sudden surge in Latino electoral participation, however, the growth in Latino influence will be incremental (see table 5).

TABLE 5 Latino Share of the Vote in States with Sizable Latino Populations, 1988–2000.

	1988 %	1992 %	1996 %	2000 %
Arizona	8.9	9.0	11.0	15.0
California	7.9	9.6	11.7	13.9
Colorado	8.9	8.1	7.6	9.7
Florida	7.0	7.1	9.2	11.3
Illinois	3.0	3.0	2.7	4.3
New Jersey	NA	4.8	7.6	5.3
New Mexico	28.4	25.5	32.9	29.5
New York	5.7	5.0	7.5	7.2
Texas	13.8	13.6	17.1	18.6

Sources: U.S. Bureau of the Census. Various Years. *Voting and Registration in the Election of November 19XX.* Current Population Survey. Washington, D.C.: U.S. Government Printing Office. These results are summarized in de la Garza and DeSipio (1992, 1996, 1999).

Organization, either from within the Latino community or without, can jump-start Latino influence. Electoral mobilization comparable to what was seen in 1960 has not been absent from Latino communities, but it has often been misdirected and shortsighted. The most common form of Latino electoral mobilization is voter registration. Beginning in the 1960s, and particularly after the passage of the VRA, Latino organizations have invested extensively in registering Latinos to vote. In this goal, they have succeeded. Because of these efforts, however, Latinos have much higher rates of registered voters who do not go to the polls than do either whites or African Americans (U.S. Bureau of the Census 2002). More labor-intensive voter mobilization efforts, such as personal-candidate or campaign contacts with registered voters, have been demonstrated to be much more effective at getting Latinos to the polls (Shaw, de la Garza, and Lee 2000). Today's campaigns, however, often pass by Latino communities and neglect the personal politics that can be effective in speeding the growth of the Latino electorate (de la Garza, Menchaca, and DeSipio 1994). The 1996 Clinton presidential campaign offers an example of the absence of the personal. In what was otherwise an unprecedented effort to win Latino votes, the campaign focused on an "air war," not a "ground war;" in other words, it was a media campaign, and not a door-to-door campaign. In this, the Clinton campaign implemented a strategy to win Latino votes similar to the one it used to win white non-Hispanic votes (DeSipio, de la Garza, and Setzler 1999).

Campaigns, of course, need to win elections, and an air war gets regular voters to the polls to support the candidate of their choice. As shown, however, Latinos have a much higher share of the adult citizen population who need the initial mobilization to participate and, often, some cues about how to participate (how and where to register, how to negotiate the ballot, and who to vote for when there is not the indicator of "D" or "R" by the candidate's name). So campaigns are necessarily shortsighted. Latino leaders have not developed a parallel set of institutions to promote electoral participation (other than around voter registration). Until these institutions appear or until a new mobilizing issue appears, Latino electoral participation will only grow slowly. Even with continued incremental growth in the Latino vote, however, this is an increasingly risky strategy for candidates and parties. In states and localities with close elections (and close presidential elections that might turn on Latino-concentration states), candidates will increasingly turn to Latinos as a voting resource that can be mobilized. Latinos will respond to issues and mobilization and the electorate-in-reserve will increasingly be a ripe resource for candidates (primarily Democratic candidates) in close races.

CONCLUSIONS: LATINO EMPOWERMENT AT THE DAWN OF THE NEW MILLENNIUM

Throughout the past forty years, the rhetoric of growing Latino political influence has repeatedly preceded true influence. In this sense, Latinos have faced an unusual burden in American politics—the burden of perpetual, though only partially realized, promise. Latinos have undeniably overcome many barriers in the past forty-three years. The legacies of discrimination and exclusion on political behavior have largely been eliminated. What were distinct national-origin groups with some common cultural identifiers in the 1960s now have a common policy agenda and an increasingly intermingled population that frequently identifies as such. Organizational Latino politics ensures that Latinos have the evidence, the technical skills, and are at the table when resources are allocated. Despite the weakness of their top-down organizational style, the national Latino organizational infrastructure was unimaginable in the 1960s. And Latinos make up a steadily greater share of the national electorate and the electorate in several major states. This means that they can increasingly elect the candidate of their choice and are actively sought after as coalition partners in multiethnic local politics. Yet the core dilemma of Latino politics that existed in 1960 remains today. The majority of Latinos are nonparticipants in the community's electoral and community-organizational politics. Few exclude themselves, and most report that they want to participate in elements of the community's politics. But many are excluded in practice because of their immigrant status or demographic profile.

The reasons, then, for the gap between potentially politically active Latino adults and those who actually participate were dramatically different in 1960 than they are today. The manipulation of and general disregard for Latino civil rights in the 1960s has given way to a more passive though no less insidious neglect that characterizes today's politics. Today's "electorate-in-reserve" may make up no greater a proportional share of the Latino population than it did in the past, but with the huge growth in Latino numbers of the past forty years, it is now much larger in real terms.

As a result, the costs to U.S. society of this neglect are greater than they have been at any point in the past. And, more probable nonparticipants join the polity each year. Immigration is at a historic high and shows no signs of abating. In addition, community demographics continue to be weighted toward younger citizens with low levels of formal education and low incomes. The number of these politically marginalized Latinos far exceeds the entire U.S. Latino population in 1960. Unless this disfranchised component of the population is brought into politics (whether electoral or community), there is a strong risk that both they and, perhaps, their U.S.-born children will be lost to the nation and to the Latino community, guaranteeing a longer period of search for the perpetual promise of Latino empowerment.

The rise of Latino politics over the past forty years can be characterized by this notion of perpetual, if only partially realized, promise. This creates a burden for the next era of Latino political development. It will have to balance a continued assertion of political influence based on raw numbers with organization and mobilization to ensure that another generation is not left behind. The organizational politics that was created in response to the civil-rights politics of the 1960s and 1970s alone will not be able socialize this new population to participation. Instead, Latinos must tap new resources and organizational structures to capture the energy and hope that immigrants bring with them to the United States and channel this drive into politics (as immigrants themselves report that they want to). The nascent institutions of transnational politics and union mobilization in the United States—that admittedly engage only a minority of Latino immigrants today—offer the best hope for the foundations of this new generation of Latino mobilization. Only with this incorporation of the vast immigrant electorate-in-reserve and the continued mobilization of the U.S.-born will Latinos close the political gap between inflated expectations and perpetual promise.

NOTES

1. Latino and Hispanic are used interchangeably to identify U.S. residents who trace their origin or ancestry to the Spanish-speaking countries of Latin America or the Caribbean. When possible, this essay disaggregates the experiences of Latino national-origin groups, e.g., Mexican Americans, Puerto Ricans, etc.
2. Two competitive states—Illinois and Texas—gave their Electoral College votes to Kennedy and with them went the presidency. Illinois's election was subject to intense media scrutiny and probable fraud. Had Texas's Electoral College votes gone to Nixon, his campaign would have been able to win with Illinois's votes and would have been much more likely to contest the outcome. Interestingly, Texas's vote was equally subject to machine manipulation, and Mexican Americans were at core of the Texas machine's power, but this "normal" manipulation was subject to much less public concern than was that of Illinois.
3. The first Cuban American was not elected to Congress until 1989 when Illeana Ros-Lehtinen was elected from Florida.
4. These, and all other, Current Population Survey (CPS) data reported in this paper probably *over*estimate actual levels of Latino voting and registration. The CPS asks its respondents to report on whether they were registered and voted in the national election. This survey is done in the weeks just after the election. All populations overreport at rates between 10 and 20 percent, and one study indicates that Latinos

overreport at even higher rates (Shaw, de la Garza, and Lee 2000). Despite this weakness, the CPS voting data are the only national sources of Latino registration and voting that can be compared across elections.

5. There has been some research that indicates that the generation of immigrants has an independent impact above and beyond the impact of demographics on the likelihood of Latino electoral participation and on Latino participation on community and organizational politics (DeSipio 1999). These results are at best preliminary, but they suggest that, relative to naturalized members of the immigrant generation, the third-generation population (the grandchildren of immigrants) are more likely to be members of organizations, to register to vote, and to vote than are the second-generation population (the children of immigrants). Immigrants, regardless of naturalization status, are less likely than the second generation to participate in one or more of seven nonelectoral political activities (signing a petition, writing to the press, attending a public meeting, wearing a campaign button, attending a political rally, volunteering for a political party, or making a campaign contribution).
6. The historical record certainly documents earlier efforts of Latin American immigrants to influence their home country politics—revolutions in Cuba from the late nineteenth century on tapped troops and money from exiles in the United States, and Puerto Rico's transition from Spanish colony to U.S. Commonwealth mobilized migrants in the U.S. to an even more widespread degree than today's controversies over Vieques or the island's status. What distinguishes today's immigrant effort to shape Latin American politics is the degree to which Latin American governments solicit the involvement of their émigrés abroad.
7. This estimate has a large margin of error, due to the weaknesses of exit polling in Latino communities. More importantly, it does not take into account the votes of *new* Latino voters who, even under this rosy scenario for the Republicans, would still give the Democrats a 60 percent to 40 percent advantage.
8. The possible exception is 1976. Because of a close national election, a small shift in the Electoral College would have given the presidency to Gerald Ford. For Latinos to have caused this shift would have been unlikely, however. Ford was the Republican, and Carter took 82 percent of the Latino vote (see table 4). More importantly, there is no evidence of a comprehensive effort to mobilize Latinos by either candidate.

REFERENCES

Arteaga, Luis. 2000. *The Latino Vote in 2000: Are Latinos Pro-Democrat or Anti-Republican?* San Francisco: Latino Issues Forum. October. http://www.lif.org/civic/vote_2000.html. Accessed 27 August 2002.

Barkan, E. R., and N. Khokolov. 1980. "Socioeconomic Data as Indices of Naturalization Patterns in the United States: A Theory Revisited." *Ethnicity* 7: 159–90.

Bass, Loretta E., and Lynne M. Casper. 1999. "Are There Differences in Registration and Voting Behavior Between Naturalized and Native-Born Americans?" U.S. Census Bureau, Population Division Working Paper #28. http://www.census.gov/population/www/documentation/twps0028/twps0028.html. Accessed 16 May 2003.

Bean, Frank, Rodolfo Corona, Rodolfo Tuiran, Karen Woodrow-Lafield, and Jennifer Van Hook. 2001. "Circular, Invisible, and Ambiguous Migrants: Components of Difference in Estimates of the Number of Unauthorized Mexican Migrants in the United States." *Demography* 38, no. 3 (August): 411–22.

Bean, Frank, Jennifer Van Hook, and Karen Woodrow-Lafield. 2001. "Estimates of Unauthorized Migrants Residing in the United States: The Total, Mexican, and Non-Mexican Central American Unauthorized Populations in Mid-2001. Washington, D.C.: Pew Hispanic Center. http://www.pewhispanic.org/site/docs/pdf/study_-_frank_bean.pdf. Accessed 21 August 2002.

Cuba Research Institute. 2000. "Preliminary Results, FIU Cuba Poll." http://www.fiu.edu/orgs/ipor/cuba2000/index.html. Accessed 27 August 2002.

Cruz, José E. 1998. *Identity and Power: Puerto Rican Politics and the Challenge of Ethnicity.* Philadelphia: Temple University Press.

Davidson, Chandler, and Bernard Grofman. 1994. *Quiet Revolution in the South: The Impact of the Voting Rights Act, 1965–1990.* Princeton, N.J.: Princeton University Press.

Davis, Mike. 2000. *Magical Urbanism: Latinos Reinvent the U.S. Big City.* New York: Verso Books.

de la Garza, Rodolfo O. 1996. "El Cuento de los Números and Other Latino Political Myths." In *Su Voto es Su Voz: Latino Politics in California*, ed. Aníbal Yáñez-Chávez, 11–32. San Diego, Calif.: Center for U.S.-Mexican Studies.

de la Garza, Rodolfo O., and Louis DeSipio, eds. 1992. *From Rhetoric to Reality: Latino Politics in the 1988 Elections.* Boulder, Colo.: Westview Press.

——, eds. 1996. *Ethnic Ironies: Latino Politics in the 1992 Elections.* Boulder, Colo.: Westview Press.

——. 1998. "Interests not Passions: Mexican American Attitudes toward Mexico, Immigration from Mexico, and Issues Shaping U.S.-Mexico Relations." *International Migration Review* 32, no. 2 (Summer): 401–22.

——, eds. 1999. *Awash in the Mainstream: Latino Politics in the 1996 Elections.* Boulder, Colo.: Westview Press.

de la Garza, Rodolfo O., Louis DeSipio, F. Chris García, John A. García, and Angelo Falcón. 1992. *Latino Voices: Mexican, Puerto Rican, and Cuban Perspectives on American Politics.* Boulder, Colo.: Westview Press.

de la Garza, Rodolfo O., and B. Lindsay Lowell. 2002. *Sending Money Home: Hispanic Remittances and Community Development.* Lanham, Md.: Rowman and Littlefield.

de la Garza, Rodolfo O., and Fujia Lu. 1999. "Explorations into Latino Voluntarism." In *Nuevos Senderos: Reflections on Hispanics and Philanthropy*, ed. Diana Campoamor, William A. Díaz, and Henry A. J. Ramos, 55–78. Houston, Tex: Arte Público Press.

de la Garza, Rodolfo O., Martha Menchaca, and Louis DeSipio, eds. 1994. *Barrio Ballots: Latino Politics in the 1990 Election.* Boulder, Colo.: Westview Press.

de la Garza, Rodolfo O., and Harry P. Pachon, eds. 2000. *Latinos and U.S. Foreign Policy: Representing the "Homeland"?* Lanham, Md: Rowman and Littlefield Publishers.

Delgado, Hector. 1993. *New Immigrants, Old Unions: Organizing Undocumented Workers in Los Angeles.* Philadelphia: Temple University Press.

DeSipio, Louis. 1996a. *Counting on the Latino Vote: Latinos as a New Electorate.* Charlottesville, Va.: The University Press of Virginia.

——. 1996b. "After Proposition 187 the Deluge: Reforming Naturalization Administration while Making Good Citizens." *Harvard Journal of Hispanic Policy* 9: 7–24.

——. 1996c. "Making Citizens or Good Citizens? Naturalization as a Predictor of Organizational and Electoral Behavior Among Latino Immigrants." *Hispanic Journal of Behavioral Sciences* 18, no. 2 (May): 194–213.

——. 1999. "The Second Generation: Political Behaviors of Adult Children of Immigrants in the United States." Paper prepared for presentation at the annual meetings of the American Political Science Association, Atlanta.

——. 2000. "Adaptation or a New Immigrant Reality? An Agnostic View of 'Transnationalism' Among Latin American Immigrants." Paper prepared for presentation at the meetings of the Latin American Studies Association. Miami. 16–18 March.

——. 2001. "Building America, One Person at a Time: Naturalization and Political Behavior of the Naturalized in Contemporary U.S. Politics." In *E Pluribus Unum? Immigrant, Civic Life and Political Incorporation*, ed. John Mollenkopf and Gary Gerstle, 67–106. New York: Russell Sage Foundation Press.

——. 2002. "Sending Money Home . . . For Now: Remittances and Immigrant Adaptation in the United States." In *Sending Money Home: Hispanic Remittances and Community Development*, ed. Rodolfo O. de la Garza and Briant Lindsay Lowell, 157–87. Lanham, Md.: Rowman and Littlefield.

DeSipio, Louis, and Rodolfo O. de la Garza. In press. "Beyond Civil Rights? Immigration and the Shifting Foundation of Latino Politics." In *Geographies of Latinidad: Mapping Latina/o Studies for the Twenty-First Century*, ed. Matt García and Angharad Valdivia. Durham, N.C.: Duke University Press.

DeSipio, Louis, Rodolfo O. de la Garza, and Mark Setzler. 1999. "Awash in the Mainstream: Latinos and the 1996 Elections." In *Awash in the Mainstream: Latino Politics in the 1996 Elections*, ed. Rodolfo O. de la Garza and Louis DeSipio, 3–46. Boulder, Colo.: Westview Press.

——. 2002. "Are Naturalized Citizens Leading Latinos to Electoral Empowerment? Voting Among Naturalized Latinos Registered to Vote in the 2000 Election" Paper prepared for presentation at the Annual Meetings of the American Political Science Association, Boston, August. http://apsaproceedings.cup.org/Site/papers/032/032004DeSipioLou.pdf. Accessed 26 August 2002.

DeSipio, Louis, Harry Pachon, Rosalind Gold, and Arturo Vargas. 1998. *America's Newest Voices: Colombians, Dominicans, Guatemalans, and Salvadorans in the United States Examine Their Public Policy Needs.* Los Angles and Claremont, Calif.: NALEO Educational Fund and the Tomás Rivera Policy Institute.

DeSipio, Louis, Harry Pachon, and W. Andrew Moellmer. 2001. *Reinventing the Naturalization Process at INS: For Better or Worse.* Claremont, Calif.: The Tomás Rivera Policy Institute.

Fraga, Luis, and Ricardo Ramírez. 2000. "Support for Candidates by Race." Unpublished manuscript. Department of Political Science, Stanford University.

Gann, Louis H., and Peter Duignan. 1986. *The Hispanics in the United States: A History.* Boulder, Colo.: Westview Press.

García, F. Chris, and Rudolph O. de la Garza. 1977. *The Chicano Political Experience: Three Perspectives.* North Scituate, Mass.: Duxbury Press.

García, Ignacio. 1990. *United We Win: The Rise and Fall of La Raza Unida Party*. Tucson: University of Arizona Press.

——. 2000. *Viva Kennedy: Mexican Americans in Search of Camelot*. College Station, Tex.: Texas A&M University Press.

García, María Cristina. 1996. *Havana USA: Cuban Exiles and Cuban Americans in South Florida, 1959–1994*. Berkeley: University of California Press.

Gavit, John Palmer. 1922. *Americans by Choice*. New York: Harper Brothers.

Grebler, Leo, Joan Moore, and Ralph Guzman. 1970. *The Mexican American People: The Nation's Second Largest Minority*. New York: The Free Press.

Gómez-Quiñones, Juan. 1990. *Chicano Politics: Reality and Promise, 1940–1990*. Albuquerque: University of New Mexico Press.

Gonzales, Rodolfo "Corky." 2001. *Message to Aztlán: Selected Writings*. Houston: Arte Público Press.

González, Gilbert. 1999. *Mexican Consuls and Labor Organizing: Imperial Politics in the American Southwest*. Austin: University of Texas Press.

González-Gutiérrez, Carlos. 1999. "Fostering Identities: Mexico's Relations with Its Diaspora." *The Journal of American History* 86, no. 2 (September): 545–67.

Guarnizo, Luis Eduardo. 2001. "On the Political Participation of Transnational Migrants: Old Practices and New Trends." In *E Pluribus Unum? Immigrant, Civic Life and Political Incorporation*, ed. John Mollenkopf and Gary Gerstle, 213–63. New York: Russell Sage Foundation.

Guarnizo, Luis Eduardo, Arturo Ignacio Sánchez, and Elizabeth M. Roach. 1999. "Mistrust, Fragmented Solidarity, and Transnational Migration: Colombians in New York City and Los Angeles. *Ethnic and Racial Studies* 22, no. 2 (March): 367–96.

Guerra, Fernando, and Luis Ricardo Fraga. 1996. "Theory, Reality, and Perpetual Potential: Latinos in the 1992 California Elections." In *Ethnic Ironies: Latino Politics in the 1992 Elections*, ed. Rodolfo O. de la Garza, and Louis DeSipio, 131–45. Boulder, Colo.: Westview Press.

Gutiérrez, David. 1999. "Migration, Emergent Ethnicity, and the 'Third Space': The Shifting Politics of Nationalism in Greater Mexico." *The Journal of American History* 86, no. 2 (September): 481–517.

Gutiérrez, José Angél. 1998. *The Making of a Chicano Militant: Lessons from Cristál*. Madison: University of Wisconsin Press.

Hardy-Fanta, Carol. 1993. *Latina Politics Latino Politics: Gender, Culture, and Political Participation in Boston*. Philadelphia: Temple University Press.

Jasso, Guillermina, and Mark R. Rosenzweig. 1990. *The New Chosen People: Immigrants in the United States*. New York: Russell Sage Foundation.

Jennings, James, and Monte Rivera, eds. 1984. *Puerto Rican Politics in Urban America*. Westport, Conn.: Greenwood Press.

López Tijerina, Reies. 2001. *They Called Me 'King Tiger': My Struggle for the Land and Our Rights*. Houston: Arte Público Press.

Levitt, Melissa, and David Olson. 1996. "Immigration and Political Incorporation: But Do They Vote?" Paper prepared for presentation at the 1996 Northeastern Political Science Association Meeting. Boston. 14–16 November.

Levitt, Peggy. 2001. *The Transnational Villagers*. Berkeley: University of California Press.

McCleskey, Clifton, and Bruce Merrill. 1973. "Mexican American Political Behavior in Texas." *Social Science Quarterly* 53, no. 4 (March): 785–98.

McCleskey, Clifton, and Dan Nimmo. 1968. "Differences Between Potential, Registered, and Actual Voters: The Houston Metropolitan Area in 1964." *Social Science Quarterly* 49, no. 1: 103–14.

Milkman, Ruth, ed. 2000. *Organizing Immigrants: The Challenge for Unions in Contemporary California.* Ithaca, N.Y.: Cornell University Press.

Minnite, Lorraine C., Jennifer Holdaway, and Ronald Hayduk. 1999. "Political Incorporation of Immigrants in New York." Paper prepared for delivery at the 1999 Annual Meeting of the American Political Science Association, Atlanta, Ga. 2–5 September.

Mollenkopf, John, David Olson, and Tim Ross. 2001. "Immigrant Political Participation in New York and Los Angeles." In *Governing Cities: Inter-Ethnic Coalitions, Competition, and Conflict*, ed. Michael Jones-Correa, 17–70. New York: The Russell Sage Foundation.

Moreno, Dario, and Christopher Warren. 2000. "Pragmatism and Strategic Realignment in the 1996 Election: Florida's Cuban Americans." In *Awash in the Mainstream: Latino Politics in the 1996 Elections*, ed. Rodolfo O. de la Garza and Louis DeSipio, 211–37. Boulder, Colo.: Westview Press.

Muñoz, Carlos., Jr. 1989. *Youth, Identity, and Power: The Chicano Movement.* New York: Verso.

NALEO Educational Fund. 2000. *2000 National Directory of Latino Elected Officials.* Los Angeles: NALEO Education Fund.

Navarro, Armando. 1998. *The Cristál Experiment: A Chicano Struggle for Community Control.* Madison: University of Wisconsin Press.

——. 2000. *La Raza Unida Party: A Chicano Challenge to the U.S. Two-Party Dictatorship.* Philadelphia: Temple University Press.

Pachon, Harry, and Louis DeSipio. 1992. "Latino Elected Officials in the 1990s," *PS: Political Science and Politics* (June): 212–19.

——. 1994. *New Americans by Choice: Political Perspectives of Latino Immigrants.* Boulder, Colo.: Westview Press.

Padilla, Felix. 1986. *Latino Ethnic Consciousness: The Case of Mexican Americans and Puerto Ricans in Chicago.* Notre Dame, Ind.: University of Notre Dame Press.

Pantoja, Adrian, Ricardo Ramírez, and Gary M. Segura. 2001. "Citizens by Choice, Voters by Necessity: Patterns in Political Mobilization by Naturalized Latinos." *Political Research Quarterly* 54, no. 4 (December): 729–50.

Pardo, Mary. 1998. *Mexican American Women Activists: Identity and Resistance in Two Los Angeles Neighborhoods.* Philadelphia: Temple University Press.

Parker, Laura. 2001. "Hispanic Immigrants Put Muscle Back Into Unions: Meatpacker Vote Key Test for Labor." *USA Today*, 15 August 15.

Pew Hispanic Center/Kaiser Family Foundation. 2002. *National Survey of Latinos: The Latino Electorate.* Summary and Chartpack. Washington, D.C.: The Pew Hispanic Center. Typescript.

Portes, Alejandro, and Rafael Mozo. 1985. "Naturalization, Registration, and Voting Patterns of Cubans and Other Ethnic Minorities: A Preliminary Analysis." In *Proceedings of the First National Conference on Citizenship and the Hispanic Community*, ed. the NALEO Educational Fund. Washington, D.C.: The NALEO Educational Fund.

Portes, Alejandro, and Alex Stepik. 1994. *City on the Edge: The Transformation of Miami.* Berkeley: University of California Press.

Putnam, Robert. 2000. *Bowling Alone: The Collapse and Revival of American Community.* New York: Simon and Schuster.

Pycior, Julie Leininger. 1997. *LBJ and Mexican Americans: The Paradox of Power.* Austin, TX: University of Texas Press.

Ramakrishnan, S. Karthick. 2000. "Generation Gaps: Race, Immigrant Incorporation, and Voting Participation." Paper prepared for presentation at the annual meetings of the American Political Science Association. Washington, D.C. 31 August–3 September.

Ramos, Henry A. J. 1998. *The American G.I. Forum: In Pursuit of the Dream, 1948–1983.* Houston: Arte Público Press.

Rivera-Salgado, Gaspar. 1999. "Mixtec Activism in Oaxacacalifornia: Transborder Grassroots Political Strategies." *American Behavioral Scientist* 42, no. 9 (June/July): 1439–58.

Rogers, Mary Beth. 1990. *Cold Anger: A Story of Faith and Power Politics.* Denton, Tex.: University of North Texas Press.

Rosales, Rodolfo. 2000. *The Illusion of Inclusion: The Untold Political Story of San Antonio.* Austin: University of Texas Press.

San Jose Mercury News. 2000. "Special Report: A Mercury News Poll of Latinos." http://www.mercurycenter.com/local/center/polldata.htm. Accessed 17 August 2001.

Shaw, Daron, Rodolfo O. de la Garza, and Jongho Lee. 2000. "Examining Latino Turnout in 1996: A Three States, Validated Survey Approach." *American Journal of Political Science* 44, no. 2 (April): 338–46.

Shirley, Dennis. 2002. *Valley Interfaith and School Reform: Organizing for Power in South Texas.* Austin: University of Texas Press.

Smith, Michael Peter, and Luis Eduardo Guarnizo, eds. 1998. *Transnationalism from Below.* Somerset, N.J.: Transaction Publishers.

Torres, María de los Angeles. 1999. *In the Land of Mirrors: Cuban Exile Politics in the United States.* Ann Arbor: University of Michigan Press.

U.S. Bureau of the Census. 1973. *Voting and Registration in the Election of November 1972.* Current Population Reports, Population Characteristics. Series P-20 #253. Washington, D.C.: U.S. Government Printing Office.

——. 1998. *Voting and Registration in the Election of November 1996.* Series P20 #504. Detailed tables. http://www.census.gov/prod/3/98pubs/p20–504u.pdf. Accessed 17 August 2001.

——. 2000a. *Hispanic Population of the United States—March 1999.* http://www.census.gov/population/www/socdemo/hispanic/ho99dtabs.html. Accessed 17 August 2001.

——. 2000b. *Money Income in the United States.* Current Population Reports, Consumer Income, Series P60–209. Washington, D.C.: U.S. Government Printing Office.

——. 2001. *Hispanic Population of the United States Current Population Survey—March 2000.* Detailed Tables. http://www.census.gov/population/www/socdemo/hispanic/hooodtabs.html. Accessed 17 August 2001.

——. 2002. *Voting and Registration in the Election of November 2002.* Series P-20 #542. Detailed tables. http://www.census.gov/population/www/socdemo/voting/p20–542.html. Accessed 20 August 2002.

U.S. Immigration and Naturalization Service. 2002a. *2000 Statistical Yearbook of the Immigration and Naturalization Service.* Springfield, Va.: National Technical Information Service.

——. 2002b. *Fiscal Year 2002, Monthly Statistical Report.* Washington, D.C.: U.S. Immigration and Naturalization Service. October. http://www.ins.usdoj.gov/graphics/aboutins/statistics/msrsep02/index.htm. Accessed 11 December 2002.

Warren, Mark R. 2001. *Dry Bones Rattling: Community Building to Revitalize American Democracy.* Princeton, N.J.: Princeton University Press.

Washington Post/Kaiser Family Foundation. 2000. *National Survey of Latinos in America.* Menlo Park, Calif.: The Henry J. Kaiser Family Foundation. http://www.kff.org/content/2000/3023/. Accessed 16 August 2001.

Yang, Philip Q. 1994. "Explaining Immigrant Naturalization." *International Migration Review* 28, no. 3: 449–77.

21 Feb Class Notes

"Historical Amnesia" → Mexican lynching.
lynching usually seen as black/white issue.
mexicans recorded as "white or Indian"
1848–1928; atleast 597 mexicans
↑ U.S. Mexico war ends ↑ mexican revolution ends?

mexicans justas prone to lynching
but fought back
"Social bandits"
· Jaoquín Murietta
· Tiburcio Vásquez
· Juan Cortina

Plan of San Diego — minorities fight back, "against white arrogance" slaughter — died.

Agrupación, Ligas de protección

CONTRIBUTORS

FRANCES R. APARICIO is professor and director of Latin American and Latino studies at the University of Illinois at Chicago. In addition to producing numerous articles and books chapters on various aspects of Latino popular culture and cultural production, she is the author of *Listening to Salsa: Gender, Latin Popular Music, and Puerto Rican Cultures* (1998); and is co-editor, with Suzanne Chávez-Silverman, of *Troplicalizations: Transcultural Representations of Latinidad* (1997), and,with Candida Jaquez, of *Musical Migrations: Transnationalism and Cultural Hybridity in Latin/o America* (2003). She is also a consulting editor to the journal *Latino Studies.*

NORMA STOLTZ CHINCHILLA received her Ph.D. in sociology from the University of Wisconsin, Madison. She is currently professor of sociology and women's studies at California State University, Long Beach, where she also teaches classes in international studies and directs the Latin American Studies Certification Program. She has published numerous articles on Latin American feminism and on social and economic change in Guatemala, and is co-author,with Nora Hamilton, of *Seeking Community in a Global City: Guatemalans and Salvadorans in Los Angeles* (2001).

LOUIS DESIPIO is associate professor in political science and Chicano/Latino studies at the University of California, Irvine. Prior to joining the faculty at UC Irvine, DeSipio was on the faculty of the University of Illinois at Urbana-Champaign, where he served as a member of the political science department and interim director of the Latina/Latino studies program. He has published widely in the field of Latino politics and is the author of *Counting on the Latino Vote: Latinos as a New Electorate* (1996), and co-author, with Rodolfo O. de la Garza, of *Making Americans/Remaking America: Immigration and Immigrant Policy* (1998). He is also author and editor of a six-volume series on Latino political values, attitudes, and behaviors. The seventh volume in the series, on Latino politics in the 2000 election, will be published in 2004. DeSipio's research focuses on Latino politics, the process of political incorporation of new and formerly excluded populations into U.S. politics, and public policies involving immigration, immigrant settlement, naturalization, and voting rights.

MARILYN ESPITIA is an assistant professor in the Department of Sociology and a research associate of the Center for Immigration Research (CIR) at the University of

Houston. She received her Ph.D. from the University of Texas, Austin, where she specialized in demography and immigration. Her current research examines the ways the naturalization experiences of contemporary Latin American immigrants in the United States challenge the assimilation narrative of citizenship acquisition and how the formation of transnational social spaces shifts the meaning of national belonging.

MARÍA CRISTINA GARCÍA is associate professor of history and director of the Latino Studies program at Cornell University. She is the author of *Havana USA: Cuban Exiles and Cuban Americans in South Florida, 1959–1994* (1996), as well as numerous articles on immigration and the Latino populations in the United States. She is presently completing a book-length study on Central American migration to Mexico, the United States, and Canada.

DAVID G. GUTIÉRREZ is a member of the faculty in history at the University of California, San Diego, where he teaches courses on Mexican American history, comparative immigration and ethnic history, and the recent political history of the United States. Previous publications include *Walls and Mirrors: Mexican Americans, Mexican Immigrants, and the Politics of Ethnicity* (1995); and (as compiler and editor) *Between Two Worlds: Mexican Immigrants in the United States* (1996). He is currently completing a book-length study on the debate over citizenship in twentieth-century U.S. history, tentatively entitled *Ethnic Minorities and the 'Nation': Ethnic Minorities and the Debate over Citizenship*. Gutiérrez received an undergraduate degree in history at the University of California, Santa Barbara, and earned his master's and Ph.D. in American history at Stanford University. He has taught at the University of Utah, Stanford University, and the California Institute of Technology.

NORA HAMILTON is professor of political science at the University of Southern California. A specialist in Latin American politics with an emphasis on migration, political economy, and the politics of Mexico and Central America, she is the author of *The Limits of State Autonomy: Post-Revolutionary Mexico* (1982), and the co-author, with Norma Chinchilla, of *Seeking Community in a Global City: Guatemalans and Salvadorans in Los Angeles* (2001). She is the author of numerous articles and book chapters and is co-editor of *Global Productions: The Garment Industry in the Pacific Rim* (1994) and *Crisis in Central America: Regional Dynamics and U.S. Policy in the 1990s* (1988). Her current research interests include international migration, particularly Central American migration, and the evolution of the Salvadoran and Guatemalan communities of Los Angeles.

PIERRETTE HONDAGNEU-SOTELO is professor of sociology at the University of Southern California. She is the author of *Gendered Transitions: Mexican Experiences of Immigration* (1994) and editor of *Gender and U.S. Immigration: Contemporary Trends* (2003). Her book *Doméstica: Immigrant Workers Cleaning and Caring in the Shadow of Affluence* (2001) won the C. Wright Mills Award from the Society for the Study of Social Problems, three awards from the American Sociological Association, and the 2002 Distinguished Scholarship Award from the Pacific Sociological Association. Her current research examines faith-based mobilizations for immigrant rights in the United States.

GLADYS M. JIMÉNEZ-MUÑOZ is associate professor in the School of Education and Human Development at Binghamton University—State University of New York. She was a Gaius Charles Bolin Fellow in History at Williams College (1992) and a Ford Foundation Post-Doctoral Fellow (1998). She has published numerous articles on race, class, gender, sexuality, nationality, multicultural education, Latinas, cultural studies, AIDS, women's suffrage, and critiques of coloniality. She is currently working on two book-length studies: *"A Storm Dressed in Skirts": Colonial Ambivalence and Puerto Rican Women's Suffrage* and the tentatively titled *Women and Race in Puerto Rico in the Interwar Period.*

KEVIN R. JOHNSON is associate dean for academic affairs and professor of law and Chicana/o studies at the University of California at Davis. Johnson has published extensively on international migration, immigration law and policy, and civil rights, with a particular focus on Latinos. His books include *Mixed Race Americans and the Law: A Reader* (2002); *Reader on Race, Civil Rights, and the Law: A Multiracial Approach* (2001); and *How Did You Get to Be Mexican? A White/Brown Man's Search for Identity* (1999), which was nominated for the 2000 Robert F. Kennedy Book Award. A graduate of Harvard Law School, where he served as an editor of the *Harvard Law Review*, Johnson earned his undergraduate degree in economics from UC Berkeley.

PEGGY LEVITT is associate professor of sociology at Wellesley College and a research fellow at the Hauser Center for Nonprofit Organizations and the Weatherhead Center for International Affairs at Harvard University. Her book, *The Transnational Villagers*, was published in 2001. Another volume, *The Changing Face of Home: The Transnational Lives of the Second Generation*, which she compiled and edited with Mary Waters, was published in 2002. Her current research explores the nexus between transnational religion and politics and the relationship between varied forms of transnationalism in different parts of the world.

KELVIN SANTIAGO-VALLES is associate professor of sociology at the State University of New York, Binghamton, and author of *"Subject People" and Colonial Discourses: Economic Transformation and Social Disorder in Puerto Rico, 1898–1947* (1994). He is currently finishing a book tentatively entitled *Atlantic Racial Regimes in World-Historical Perspective: Coloniality, Class Composition, and the Linking of Puerto Rico and the United States, 1765–2000.* His research and teaching focus is on the Americas and the broader Caribbean with emphasis on the Hispanic Antilles and their populations in the United States. He has also taught courses and published extensively on the African diaspora, cultural and political-economy analyses, and critical theories of "race" and "gender," covering slavery and other forms of racialized labor, social transformations and inequalities brought about by Western culture and global capitalism, and resistances to this way of conceiving and organizing the world.

ANTHONY M. STEVENS-ARROYO is professor of Puerto Rican and Latino studies at Brooklyn College, a Distinguished Scholar of the City University of New York, and director of the Research Center for Religion in Society and Culture (RISC). Widely published in English and Spanish, he has written more than forty scholarly articles and has also authored nine books, including the four-volume PARAL series on religion among Latinos. His 1980 book, *Prophets Denied Honor: An Anthology on the Hispano Church of the United States* (1980) is considered a "landmark of Catholic literature." With his spouse, Ana María Díaz-Stevens, he authored *Recognizing the Latino Religious Resurgence: The Emmaus Paradigm*, which was named an Outstanding Academic Book for 1998 by *Choice Magazine.* A spokesperson for civil and human rights, he has testified before the United States Congress and the United Nations and was named by President Jimmy Carter to the Advisory Board of the United States Commission of Civil Rights, where he served for two terms.

INDEX